Diversity and Social Justice in College Sports:

Sport Management and the Student Athlete

Diversity and Social Justice in College Sports:

Sport Management and the Student Athlete

DIVERSITY AND SOCIAL JUSTICE IN COLLEGE SPORTS: SPORT MANAGEMENT AND THE STUDENT ATHLETE

Dana D. Brooks, Ed.D
WEST VIRGINIA UNIVERSITY

Ronald C. Althouse, Ph.D.
WEST VIRGINIA UNIVERSITY

EDITORS

Fitness Information Technology
a Division of the International Center
for Performance Excellence
262 Coliseum, WVU-PE, PO Box 6116
Morgantown, WV 26506-6116

© Copyright 2007, West Virginia University

Library of Congress Card Catalog Number: 2007930277

ISBN: 978-1-885693-77-8

Production Editor: Val Gittings
Cover Design: Bellerophon Productions
Typesetter: Bellerophon Productions
Copyeditor: Anita Stanley
Proofreader: Val Gittings
Indexer: Val Gittings
Printed by: Sheridan Books
Cover Photos: iStockphoto

10 9 8 7 6 5 4 3 2 1

Fitness Information Technology
A Division of the International Center for Performance Excellence
West Virginia University
262 Coliseum, WVU-PE
PO Box 6116
Morgantown, WV 26506-6116
800.477.4348 (toll free)
304.293.6888 (phone)
304.293.6658 (fax)
Email: icpe@mail.wvu.edu
Website: www.fitinfotech.com

▲ *Contents* ▼

Preface. ix
Dana D. Brooks ▲ Ronald C. Althouse

Prologue xi
Charlotte Westerhaus

Introduction 1
George H. Sage

Section One: Historical Analysis

Chapter 1

Climbing the Racial Mountain:
A History of the African American Experience in Sport. 21

David K. Wiggins

Section Two: Social Justice and Cultural Concerns

Chapter 2

African American Women in Intercollegiate Coaching
and Athletic Administration: Unequal Access 51

Robertha Abney

Chapter 3

The Academic Experiences of African American Collegiate Athletes:
Implications for Policy and Practice 77

Audwin Anderson
Donald South

Chapter 4

From Glory to Glory: The Transition of African American
Athletes from College Sports into Athletic Retirement. 95

Billy J. Hawkins
Brianne Milan-Williams
Akilah Carter

**Section Three: African American Coaching
and Other Leadership Opportunities**

Chapter 5

African American Coaching Mobility Models
and the "Global Market Place" 117

> Dana D. Brooks
> Ronald C. Althouse
> Delano Tucker

Chapter 6

Ethnic Minority Opportunities in College
and Professional Sports: A Business Imperative. 139

> Fritz G. Polite

Chapter 7

An Examination of Athletic Directors'
Perception of Barriers to Employment Opportunities 159

> Doris R. Corbett
> Miguel J. Tabron

Section Four: Media, Media Images, and Stereotyping

Chapter 8

African Americans and the Media: Roles and Opportunities
to Be Broadcasters, Journalists, Reporters, and Announcers 179

> Doris R. Corbett
> Aaron B. Stills

Chapter 9

Mainstreaming and Integrating the Spectacle and Substance
of Scholar-Baller: A New Blueprint for Higher Education,
the NCAA, and Society 201

> C. Keith Harrison
> Jean Boyd

Chapter 10

Taboo's Explanation of Black Athletic Dominance:
More Fiction than Fact 233

> Othello Harris

Chapter 11

Who Am I? Racial Identity, Athletic Identity,
and the African American Athlete 245

> Louis Harrison, Jr.
> Leonard N. Moore

Section Five: Intersection of Race, Sport, and Law

Chapter 12

The Persistence of Unconscious Racism in College Sport 263

Timothy Davis

Chapter 13

Academic Inequity and the Impact of NCAA Rules 281

Timothy Davis

Chapter 14

The Dilemmas and Contradictions of "Gettin' Paid" 295

Scott N. Brooks
Linda J. Kim

Section Six: Sport Administration/Management: Intersection of Race, Class, and Gender

Chapter 15

Beyond Tokenism to Empowerment:
The Black Women in Sport Foundation 313

Linda Sheryl Greene
Tina Sloan Green

Chapter 16

The Globalization of Sport: A Bridge to Advancing Cultures 333

Fritz G. Polite

Chapter 17

African Americans' Consumption of Sport: Race Matters! 357

Ketra L. Armstrong

Epilogue: Looking Toward the Future—Developing a Shared Community

*African American Community: The Dynamics of Race, Class,
Gender, and Community Sports* 379

Earl Smith
Angela J. Hattery

Summary 407

Dana D. Brooks
Ronald C. Althouse

Index 417

About the Editors 424

About the Authors 425

▲ *Preface* ▼

The two highly refereed textbooks, *Racism in College Athletics: The African American Athlete's Experience* (1993) and its second edition (2000), provided a critical critique of the status of race relations in college athletics. Building on the success and popularity of these two books, *Diversity and Social Justice in College Sports: Sport Management and the Student Athlete* represents a groundbreaking analysis of the many diversity issues existing in the sport industry.

Clearly, the sport marketplace is not immune from the various forms of social injustices (i.e., salary inequities, stereotyping, sexism) found in American society and throughout the world. The text is arranged in the following six sections, addressing topics that have been referred to consistently in the sport management/administration literature: One—Historical Analysis; Two—Social Justice and Cultural Concerns; Three—African American Coaching and Other Leadership Opportunities; Four—Media, Media Images, and Stereotyping; Five—Intersection of Race, Sport, and Law; and Six—Sport Administration/Management: Intersection of Race, Class, and Gender.

Target Audiences

Sport management faculty, college administrators, and students enrolled in sport management upper-division courses, sport sociology courses, and African American studies courses will find the text to be an excellent addition to their class reading list and library.

The co-editors express appreciation to Dr. Andrew Ostrow, Director of Fitness Information Technology, a division of the International Center for Performance Excellence, West Virginia University, for his support, patience, and encouragement. We would also like to thank Ms. Linda Hetrick and Ms. Joanne Pollitt for their secretarial and management contributions.

Finally, the quality and educational impact of this text reside with the contributing authors!

Dana D. Brooks
Ronald C. Althouse
Co-editors

Prologue

Charlotte Westerhaus

Diversity and inclusion have been constant, challenging themes in the American experience because we have long been a diverse nation. Within the realm of higher education, the foremost goal of this nation's colleges and universities is to provide the best possible learning environment for all students. The vast diversity of college students and their inclusion within the hallowed walls of academe are particularly compelling. Institutions of higher education must recognize the inherent worth and dignity of every person and seek to promote an understanding of human diversity in all its dimensions.

In 2006, the National Collegiate Athletic Association (NCAA) celebrated one hundred years of creating opportunities for student athletes to realize their dreams in the classrooms and on the playing fields. This year also marks the celebration of 25 years of women's athletics in the NCAA. As the NCAA celebrates its centennial, it has taken an opportunity to reflect on the many achievements and noteworthy moments in the Association's history. The Association, however, is also careful to measure where progress has been made and where deficiencies may continue to exist.

At its most fundamental level, inclusion means having access to opportunities. Equitable participation is the goal, for society generally and for intercollegiate athletics in particular. The NCAA has a responsibility to ensure that student athletes, coaches, and athletic administrators who compete on and work in diverse teams, athletics departments, conference offices, and related organizations experience the same benefits. The NCAA Constitution vests in each institution the responsibility to establish and maintain an environment that values cultural diversity and gender equity among its student athletes and intercollegiate athletics department staff. Likewise, the NCAA's Strategic Plan sets forth a belief and commitment to "an inclusive culture that fosters equitable participation for student athletes and career opportunities for coaches and administrators from diverse backgrounds."

In the late 1980s, former NCAA Executive Director Walter Byers formed two standing committees: the Minority Opportunities and Interests Committee (MOIC) and the Committee on Women's Athletics (CWA). Subsequently, despite the committees' conscientious efforts and sustained advocacy, the 2005 MOIC Biennial Study of the Race and Gender Demographics of Member Institutions' Athletics Personnel reported minimal gains in administrative and coaching positions for racial and/or ethnic minorities.

The 2005 MOIC Study indicates that the percentage of African American senior level administrators has remained virtually unchanged since 1995 with minimal increases among African American women, primarily as senior woman administrators or academic advisors. The largest increases for African American men were less than 3% and were also entry or mid-level positions. (e.g., intern, ticket manager, equipment manager.) The largest increases for African American women were equally small, below 2.5% and also primarily represent entry or mid-level positions (e.g., intern, academic advisor.) The most frequent positions for African American men and women were all entry or mid-level positions. African American men were most frequently hired as academic advisors (11.8%); life skills coordinators (8.8%); strength coaches (8.5%); and equipment managers (7.3%). For African American women, the positions with the highest frequency include life skills coordinator (8.8%); academic advisor (8.2%); and intern (4%)

African American students now represent more than 50% of all student athletes in revenue sports. However, African American representation in athletics administration and coaching, particularly in the highly visible sport of football, continues to lag. According to a 2004 study conducted by the Black Coaches Association (BCA), a total of 18 African American men have occupied the head coaching position in Division IA football since 1979. The BCA Hiring Report Score Card also notes that there are only two Hispanic head coaches in Division IA football and no representation from the Asian American or Samoan American communities.

These low numbers reflect a serious and frustrating problem, and one that NCAA President Myles Brand has addressed repeatedly. The NCAA has developed initiatives such as the Advanced and Expert Coaches Academies to specifically address the critical under-representation of African American head football coaches. Two recent graduates of those academies, Ron Prince and Norries Wilson, were recently hired as the head coaches at Kansas State University and Columbia University. This modest beginning speaks to the outstanding caliber and untapped talent of qualified minority candidates.

The NCAA also established the Office of Diversity and Inclusion in August 2005 and hired me to head the office and address various diversity issues. One of my office's first efforts was a strategic planning initiative to identify strategies and recommendations for moving minorities and women into full representation in both coaching and administrative ranks. These are important steps, but the role of the NCAA's national office is limited. The NCAA is a membership organization, consisting of more than 1200 universities, colleges and related associations. It is the members, represented ultimately by university and college presidents, who decide on future courses of action.

While we recognize that final authority resides with our members, the NCAA—including my office—has a leadership role to play. We can continue to draw attention to important and relevant issues related to diversity and inclusion. In addition, the NCAA can and should engage its membership in developing approaches and undertaking actions that advocate and support its core values. And let me be clear—diversity and inclusion are NCAA core values.

The crucial and salient bottom line is this: The process to ensure equitable and diverse hiring is broken. The NCAA membership must become committed and act.

Hiring is done on campus and not at the NCAA headquarters. Thus, university leadership within the administration, faculty, and the student body—all must focus attention on fixing inequitable hiring practices. It is ironic that some of the most effective hiring practices are already presently being used on university campuses and can be found in the hiring university and college presidents, provosts, deans, directors and faculty. Virtually every viable candidate being considered for university president is evaluated on his or her demonstrative and successful experience with diversity and inclusion. Likewise, searches for athletic administrators and coaches should also be conducted in thoughtful manner with the involvement of the entire campus.

High-performance teams most often include diversity of social and life experiences, educational paths, and cultural backgrounds. Moreover, highly diverse and inclusive organizations perform better and excel at higher levels than those that are not. In fact, research shows that diversity can enhance productivity by as much as 30 to 40%.

A diverse and inclusive culture will not only result in retaining a high-performing workforce, boost productivity, and reduce attrition; it also will translate into an increased pool of applicants vying for athletics administration and coaching positions and attract more suppliers and sponsors interested in associating with intercollegiate athletics.

Managing diversity and inclusion goes beyond merely increasing representation. Intercollegiate athletics is an integral part of higher education and student athletes are students first. That is why the overriding purpose of the NCAA is to integrate intercollegiate athletics into higher education so that the student athletes' educational experience is paramount.

Moreover, the NCAA has a responsibility to provide an environment in which all student athletes learn from one another. The connection between diversity and inclusion and the enhanced learning of college students is clear. Research studies have shown that when college students socialize with college students of a different racial group, the interactions positively contribute to the students' academic development, satisfaction with college, level of cultural awareness, and commitment to promoting racial understanding. Students educated in diverse settings are more motivated and better able to deal with conflicts, as well as appreciate both similarities and differences among their peers.

A recent joint report from the American Council on Education and the American Association of University Professors noted that diversity within education "extends the meaning of personal, social, and moral growth and improves the capacity of college and universities to achieve their missions." Two in three Americans say it is very important that colleges and universities prepare people to function in a diverse society. Fifty-five percent say that every college student should have to study different cultures in order to graduate. By a margin of more than three to one, those who have an opinion say that diversity programs in colleges and universities raise rather than lower academic standards.

Within the NCAA, diversity can be found from institution to institution, team to team, and among each student athlete, coach, administrator, and official.

In sum, diversity and inclusion are core values. Within the realm of intercollegiate athletics, athletics provides unique opportunities for young women and men to internalize the values of hard work, fair competition, and cooperation toward a common goal. Intercollegiate athletics develops the virtues of loyalty, fairness, self-respect, and respect for others and a quest for excellence. Undertaken in the right spirit, college sports promote a sense of community and good citizenship. Thus, the NCAA will remain committed in supporting and promoting a culture in which each person is seen as unique and every individual feels like he or she is a viable and valued part within approximately 1,200 member colleges and universities, conferences, and organizations.

▲ *Introduction* ▼

GEORGE H. SAGE

This volume makes a valuable contribution to the literature on American sports, primarily because there is no other book that focuses on diversity and social justice in intercollegiate sports. Furthermore, each of the book's chapters makes a specific contribution to understanding the structure of intercollegiate athletics and the complex role of African American student athletes, coaches, and administrators in that enterprise. Of course, college athletics is only one form of sports in which African Americans are involved; some 3 million are involved in youth sports and another 700,000 participate in high schools athletics. There are an estimated 72,000 African American college athletes, and several thousand more are professional athletes, coaches, and administrators. Some of the same issues, problems, and challenges that African American's encounter in college sports are also experienced at the other levels of organized sports, and these are also addressed in some of the chapters in this book.

The widespread interest in the study of race relations in college athletics generated by two editions of *Racism in College Sports* edited by Dana Brooks and Ronald Althouse provided a stimulus for this volume. The growing research and publication on this topic, as well as the changing conditions involving African Americans in intercollegiate sports, led Brooks and Althouse to realize a new volume was needed. They have secured essays with a concentration on issues and problems concerning diversity and an attention to their applications for sport management professionals and scholars.

Sport as a Cultural Practice in American Society

To understand the history and dynamics of diversity and race and gender relations in American sport, it is important to recognize that sport is a dominating cultural practice in American social life. Indeed, Charles Prebish (1993), a professor of religious studies at Pennsylvania State University, goes so far as to claim, "Sport is religion for growing numbers of Americans and this is no product of simply facile reasoning or wishful thinking" (p. 62). In spite of the popularity of sport, and the time Americans devote to active participation, reading, TV viewing, and spectating while following their favorite teams and athletes, sport is typically treated by both participants and fans as ahistorical and apolitical in nature. Rarely are sports practices and organizations critically examined for their prevalent attitudes, values, myths, and folklore.

There is little analysis integrating broader social, political, economic, and cultural problems and issues as they relate to sports. This is largely the case because sport and society have traditionally been portrayed as discrete social phenomena, with sports often regarded as a pristine and isolated cultural practice that is untainted by problems and issues of the general society. Americans tend to cherish the illusion that sports are just "fun and games," and those who have held the power and influence in sports have vigorously fought any attempt to change this image. So the American public is fed a diet of traditional slogans, clichés, and ritualized trivia about sports. While these can be comforting to the devoted athlete, coach, sport administrator, and fan, they do not come to grips with the social reality of contemporary sport.

Serious analysis of sport as a cultural practice begins with a realization that this cultural practice cannot be explored as something isolated from the social, economic, political, and cultural context in which it is situated. As a collection of social practices and relations that are deeply rooted in the society of which it is a part, analytical accounts of sport must be grounded in a historical and socially critical examination of the larger political, economic, social, and ideological configurations within society. Thus, the essence of understanding the social relevance of sport is found in its relationship to those broader societal forces of which it is a part. American Studies scholars Gorn and Oriard (1995) declared that "the study of sport can take us to the very heart of critical issues in the study of culture and society" (p. A52). Relevant issues involve sport's relationship to social class, race, gender, and the control, production, and distribution of political, economic, and cultural power. The critical issue that is the central focus of this volume is the race relations in American intercollegiate athletics and the applications for sports management professionals.

Race Relations in American Society

By the time they reach adolescence most Americans understand that institutional racism has been a pervasive part of the American experience since its beginnings. However, because African American athletes are so prominent in the major intercollegiate sports, few in the current under-30-years-of-age generation know that racism has been a salient part of college sports throughout its history. Thus, in a book about race relations in intercollegiate sport it is important to historically situate and culturally locate racism in American society because to really understand the role of race in college athletics, it must be seen from the larger cultural context in which it is situated.

Since its founding as a nation, the United States has been a nation of immigrants. At first most immigrants came from the British Isles, but over the past 200 years there has been an expanding and broadening ethic and racial composition. Today, many racial and ethnic minorities make up the population of the United States. Currently, Hispanics and African Americans are the two largest minority groups with 14% and 13% of the total U. S. population.

Racial discrimination is deeply rooted in America's society. African Americans are the only racial group that has been subjected to an extended period of slavery, and they are the only racial group to have segregation laws passed against them that were supported and fully sanctioned by the Supreme Court (Schneider & Schneider, 2000). Of course, African Americans are not the only minority group in America that has had to struggle for basic civil rights (e.g., Native Americans), but theirs has been a unique and insidious legacy of racial discrimination.

In 1619, twelve years after the establishment of the first English settlement at Jamestown, black Africans were first brought to colonial America. Within 30 years a slave system among colonial plantation owners was thriving, and by the beginning of the 18th century black Africans had become a major source of slave labor and a fundamental element of colonial agricultural and commercial production. By the latter 18th century the ties that bound Great Britain and the American colonies became strained to the breaking point, and the colonists challenged British rule and established independence. This did nothing to alter the system of slavery. The Declaration of Independence and the U.S. Constitution codified racial subordination and discrimination against African Americans. Slavery was sanctioned and African Americans were denied all of the rights of citizenship (Schneider & Schneider, 2000).

It took a civil war and the passage of the 13th, 14th, and 15th Amendments to the U.S. Constitution in the years immediately after the Civil War to officially end the slavery system, confer full citizen rights, and grant the right of suffrage to African Americans. Schneider and Schneider (2000) recounted the wretched aftermath of the laws supposedly won for African Americans through those amendments: "Enforcement of any law, of course, depends in large part on the will of the populace. For a century after the end of the Civil War, the rights of blacks these amendments meant to guarantee were flagrantly violated. . . ." (p. 328). Indeed, by the latter decades of the 19th century many states passed "Jim Crow" laws mandating racial segregation in almost all areas of public life. In effect, then, Jim Crow laws legalized white domination and thus left racism essentially intact. A "separate but equal" system replaced slavery and became an even more efficient instrument of domination and subordination than slavery had been.

It was not until 1954, when the U.S. Supreme Court, in the *Brown v. Board of Education of Topeka* decision, ruled that separate schools are inherently unequal, that the "separate but equal" doctrine was successfully challenged. *Brown* set the stage for desegregation of American schools and, subsequently, the desegregation of other social institutions in the United States. It also set in motion a series of challenges to discrimination against African Americans that culminated in sweeping civil rights legislation in the mid-1960s. So it has only been in the past 40 years that the civil rights of black citizens have been protected by law (Altman, 2004; Katznelson, 2005; McWhorter, 2004).

Although laws protecting the civil rights of African Americans now exist and provide improved conditions in some private and public sectors, domination and subordination of African Americans is still institutionally systemic in American society. Race is still a fundamental determinant of people's position in the social structure. African Americans are still defined as racially different by the white majority and singled out for a broad range of individual and institutionalized discrimination (Brown, Carnoy, Currie, Duster, Oppenheimer, Schultz, & Wellman, 2005; Bonilla-Silva, 2004)

Although that last statement may seem to overstate current conditions, it actually does not. The U.S. Department of Justice reported that 61% of hate crime incidents were motivated by race (Strom, 2001). According to an FBI report titled, "Hate Crime Statistics 2003," hate crimes against African Americans were nearly twice that of all other race groups combined. Nearly 2,548 total hate crimes were motivated by anti-black sentiments, which resulted in 3,150 victims (Malik, 2005). There are typically racial incidents on more than 50 college campuses each year.

There are widespread perceptions that things are getting better for African Americans, but in fact the economic gap between whites and blacks has actually been widening in recent years. African American families have actually lost ground economically to whites over the past 20 years. The Economic Policy Institute's report "The State of Working America 2006/2007" states that in 2004, a black family's median income was 62% of the earnings of their white counterparts (Bullock, 2006). According to the U.S. Bureau of the Census, black households had the lowest median income in 2004 among race groups. The poverty rate among the nation's African Americans in 2004 was 24.7% compared with 8.6% for whites. African American household incomes fell by more than $2,000 between 2001 and 2006. The jobless rate for African Americans has consistently been over twice that of whites. Not only are African Americans twice as likely to be unemployed, but those who are employed are overrepresented in jobs for which pay, power, and prestige are low (Lui, Robles, & Leondar-Wright, 2006; Shapiro, 2005).

Overt discrimination has been largely banished from public places, and polls indicate that whites harbor fewer prejudices than they used to. The United States has made significant steps toward diversity, fairness, and equality of opportunity in hiring and promotion. Some companies have even done remarkably well in promoting African Americans to top positions. But problems and prejudice persist. Token integration in the workplace is more prevalent than demographic balance, even among occupations that are integrated. Also, although there has been some reduction of white advantages in the workplace over the last two decades, they remain substantial. Only a smattering of African American managers has moved beyond middle levels of authority and control in the private sector of American business. In 2005 there were only six African American CEOs in the *Fortune* 500 and one African American CEO in the *Fortune* 1000 (501–1000). Of the approximately 24.8 million non-farm businesses in the United States, only 5.2% were owned by African Americans in 2005, according to the United States Small Business Administration (Oliver & Shapiro, 2006; Shapiro, 2005).

African Americans have largely been excluded from American politics. In the slave society prior to the Civil War, African Americans had no voting rights at all. The purpose behind the 15th Amendment was to grant the right to vote to all citizens, including African Americans. But the extension of the franchise to black citizens was strongly resisted, and over the ensuing 100 years states throughout the nation used a variety of ways to exclude or limit the voting right to blacks. Finally, in 1965 President Lyndon Johnson signed the Voting Rights Act into law. It followed the language of the 15th Amendment and applied a nationwide prohibition against the denial or abridgment of the right to vote on a nationwide basis. It is generally considered the most successful piece of civil rights legislation. While African American voting rights have been secured, they have had little success in being elected to political office in numbers proportional to their percentage of the population. In 2007, the United States Senate was one percent African American and the House of Representatives was roughly nine percent African American.

Educational opportunity has always been a deep-seated value among Americans. Education has served as the most important avenue for success in the world of adult occupational achievement. But the institution of education has had an embarrassing record in dealing with African Americans. The abolishment of slavery seemed to promise that black Americans would share the educational opportunities of whites. But that was not to be. From the latter 19th century to the mid-1950s black students throughout the Southern states were segregated and attended schools with only black classmates. In the rest of the country, since blacks tended to be geographically segregated into ghettos, they attended schools with mostly black students. And they still do. Clayborne Carson (2004) noted that 50 years after *Brown* abolished segregated schools, "most black American school children still attend predominantly black public schools that offer fewer opportunities for advancement than typical predominantly white public schools" (p. 30).

So, although some African Americans have made gains economically, politically, and in educational achievements, many barriers remain to social equality. These barriers are rooted in institutional patterns and practices of racial discrimination that are deeply ingrained in the structure of American society. They demonstrate that America has not yet conquered its heritage of racial inequality. The basic fact is that much inequality and discrimination against African Americans continues, regardless of whether one uses income, employment rates, educational attainment, or political office holding as measures. Martin Luther King's dream that "one day racism would end in America" has not been fulfilled.

Race Relations in Sport

Diversity in American sport—especially racial, ethnic, and gender—has been a persistent issue. On the one hand, conventional wisdom emphasizes that sport is a competitive activity and anyone who demonstrates the desire and skill can be involved. The reality, however, is that various social, structural, and cultural values and practices form barriers to sport involvement for certain categories of people.

Sport is arguably the most ubiquitous among the cultural practices in American society, and it is closely linked to other spheres of social life. It has often been called a microcosm of society. Individual attitudes, values, and beliefs in the broader society become an integral part of sporting practices. Thus, dominant ideas and practices about race relations have been mirrored in American sport. Pervasive and systematic discrimination against African Americans throughout their history in North America has played a continuing and significant role in every era of American sport history, as David Wiggins (chapter 1) eloquently documents in his chapter.

Sports relations between whites and African Americans during the slavery era (1619 to 1865) centered around two sports: boxing and horseracing. Plantation owners frequently selected—and sometimes even trained—one or more of their male slaves and entered them in boxing matches held in conjunction with festive occasions. Under such conditions, black boxers were merely used to entertain their white "masters" and their friends. Horseracing was also a popular colonial sporting event. Horses were, of course, owned by whites, and when training occurred much of it was done by whites, but African Americans were used as jockeys. There was little status for jockeying, and no significant material rewards for it, since slave labor of any kind was free and unpaid. It was viewed as basically a mechanical task, so blacks could be trusted with a task that whites did not care to do anyway. Social relations, then, can be seen as distant, with whites in control and African Americans in subordinate roles, pleasing the dominant white groups (Wiggins, 1997).

As Wiggins notes, after the Civil War African Americans made significant contributions to the rise of spectator sport as boxers and jockeys. Few realize that some sports were even dominated by blacks, such as horserace jockeying (Hotaling,

1999). However, sport remained racially segregated by custom and in some places by law. Freedom had little overall effect on the social relations between blacks and whites in sports in the latter 19ᵗʰ and early 20ᵗʰ centuries. Although a number of African Americans played on professional baseball teams in the early years of the National League, Jim Crowism gradually raised its ugly head. White players threatened to quit rather than share the diamond with black men. Finally, by 1888 major league club owners made a "gentleman's agreement" not to sign any more African American players. This unwritten law against hiring black players was not violated until 1945 when Branch Rickey, general manager of the Brooklyn Dodgers, signed Jackie Robinson to a contract (Peterson, 1992).

As other professional sports emerged, they too barred African Americans from participation. Among a number of the consequences of excluding African Americans from professional sports, one was that it perpetuated privileges for whites because white athletes did not have to compete with an entire segment of the population for sports jobs.

When African Americans were barred from professional baseball, football, and basketball in the late 19ᵗʰ and early 20ᵗʰ centuries, they formed all-black teams and leagues (Hogan, 2006; Lanctot, 2004). The Harlem Globetrotters and the famous players of the black baseball leagues, such as Satchel Paige and Josh Gibson, emerged from this segregated situation. When Jackie Robinson broke the color barrier, first in 1946 in the minor leagues and then in 1947 in the majors, he received much verbal and physical abuse from players and fans who resented a black playing on an equal level with whites. The great major league player Rogers Hornsby uttered a common white attitude at the time: "They've been getting along all right playing together and should stay where they belong in their league" (quoted in Chalk, 1975, p. 78; see also Cahn, 2004; Tygiel, 2004).

Obstacles to African American participation in sport have fallen in almost every sport and in most sport organizations over the past 50 years. African American presence in sport far exceeds what anyone would have predicted in the early decades of the 20ᵗʰ century. Indeed, African American athletes now dominate several sports at the high school, intercollegiate, and professional levels. Some of the most renowned current athletes are African American; they are heroes to millions of Americans—black, white, Hispanic, and all other minorities.

African Americans' astounding success in a variety of sports has led to speculation about the reason for this phenomenon. Throughout American history, African Americans have been subjected to various myths and stereotypes whose purpose was to intimidate and subordinate them, while at the same time providing justifications for racial attitudes and discrimination. In sport various theories and myths were advanced, at first to explain why blacks "couldn't" compete with white athletes, and more recently to explain why they are such a dominating presence in the most popular American sports.

Some analysts of this topic claim that African Americans possess biological characteristics that are advantageous for sport performance. A recent argument for that view is found in a book titled *Taboo: Why Black Athletes Dominate Sports and Why We Are Afraid to Talk About It* (Entine, 2000). Othello Harris's chapter 10 provides an extended critique of the thesis that African Americans possess a racially linked genetic advantage over whites that is manifested in superior sports achievements (see also Miller, 2004).

Most social scientists who have addressed this issue tend to argue that socio-cultural conditions are important contributory factors for African American athletes' rise to eminence. Fundamental to this view is a recognition that many African American athletes have come from low socioeconomic backgrounds, where recreational outlets for the young blacks are mainly sports. Consequently, according to this view, the result has been many hours spent playing in the streets, recreation centers, and playgrounds. A related socio-cultural notion is that excellence in sports has provided one of the few opportunities for African Americans to escape from the slums and ghettos in which many of them live. Thus, hours devoted to honing sports skills, combined with a desire to escape from one's childhood environment, so the argument goes, has caused many African American youth to approach sport with greater motivation to excel than is found with young whites (Edwards, 2004; Hoberman, 1997).

Louis Harrison, Jr., and Leonard N. Moore (chapter 11) take up the differences between racial identity and athletic identity of white (what they term European American) and African American athletes. They describe a theoretical socialization process called *Nigrescence*, which is a black identity development model, a psychology of becoming black, that changes the perception and evaluation of African Americans' racial identity from Eurocentric to Afrocentric. According to this model, this developmental process centers the individual's identity in African American culture (see Cross, 1995 for more details). The five stages of the model are explained by the authors. According to Harrison and Moore, African American males adopt more prominent athletic identities than European American males.

Sport has been the site of enormous injustices and thus a source of frustration, disappointment, and misery for African Americans as they have struggled against the discrimination that has historically been embedded in the American sport culture. But over the past century, sport has also been a place of opportunity for African American athletes, coaches, and athletic administrators. Gradually, they have been given the chance to play, coach, and administer sports at all levels. Opportunities continue to open up, creating hope that the injustices of the past will disappear in the future.

Intercollegiate Sport: The Beginnings

The United States intercollegiate sports system is unique. In most countries of the world sport plays a minor role in institutions of higher education. In the U.S. during the first half of the 19th century, games and sports became a diversion for college students from the boredom of classroom work and limited social outlets. They played a variety of sports, first as unorganized and impromptu games and later as organized intramural and interclass activities. As the number of colleges increased and their geographic proximity to each other decreased, the students at one college began challenging students at nearby schools to sports contests.

The first officially recorded intercollegiate sports event was a rowing race between Harvard and Yale in 1852. At the beginning, intercollegiate sports were organized by the students, usually over faculty objection. In time, with increased organization and the proliferation of sports teams, faculties assumed administrative control over sports.

Over the past century and a half, African Americans have experienced exclusion, segregation, tokenism, and, finally widespread inclusion and opportunity in intercollegiate sports. They were largely absent from intercollegiate sports for most of the 19th century, as college sports mirrored the social norms and patterns of the larger American society. During the late 19th and early 20th centuries college sports were dominated by white, upper-class, Protestant males. A few African American athletes competed for Ivy League and other eastern schools, but they were exceptions. This was an era of Jim Crowism and segregation, and collegiate sports remained segregated, except for isolated instances, until after World War II. At the University of Michigan, for example, from 1882 to 1945 there were only four African American lettermen in football and none in basketball. In 1948 only 10% of college basketball teams had one or more African Americans on their rosters. This proportion increased to 45% of the teams in 1962 and 92% by 1975. The transition from a segregated program to an integrated one is perhaps best illustrated by the University of Alabama: in 1968 there were no African Americans on any of its teams, but its 1975 basketball team had an all-African American starting line-up (Eitzen & Sage, 2003; Martin, 2004).

Until the mid-1960s, most African American college athletes played at historically black colleges in black leagues (they were known as Negro colleges and Negro leagues). Of course, the only reason that all-black colleges existed at all was racial prejudice and discrimination. Nevertheless, the black colleges fielded teams in all of the popular sports, and they played a leading role in women's sports, especially in track and field—Tuskegee with Wilma Rudolph and the Tigerbelles of Tennessee State are prominent examples (see also Liberti, 2004).

Although the system was segregated, black colleges provided an avenue to athletic prominence for many African American athletes—male and female—and they developed more outstanding African American athletes than any other agency of higher education, though many of the athletes were never known outside the African American press and African American community.

Expanding Opportunities for African Americans in College Sports

The impact of World War II, the Supreme Court's 1954 *Brown v. Board of Education* decision striking down separate educational facilities, the massive commercialization of collegiate sports, and the desire by universities to benefit from talented African American athletes in building commercialized athletic programs resulted in more and more universities searching for talented African Americans to bolster their teams. Consequently, black colleges lost their monopoly on African American athletic talent. The best African American athletes found it advantageous to play at predominantly white schools because of the greater media visibility, especially television. This visibility meant a better chance to sign a professional contract at the conclusion of their collegiate eligibility. The result was that athletic programs at black colleges were depleted of the best athletes, forcing several of them to drastically modify their athletic programs and some black leagues to disband.

The growing number of African Americans receiving athletic scholarships in the past three decades at predominantly white universities has been a mixed blessing. On the one hand, athletically talented African Americans have been given the opportunity to attend and graduate from universities that would otherwise have been inaccessible to them. This has allowed some to achieve social mobility and monetary success. On the other hand, the evidence is clear and abundant that many African American college athletes have been exploited in various ways by their institutions. They have been recruited lacking the academic background to succeed in higher education and they have been advised into courses that keep them eligible but are dead-ends for acquiring a college diploma. They have been "stacked" into specific positions in the sport they play, limiting the numbers that are on the starting team. When the athletes' eligibility has been used up, or they have become academically ineligible to compete for the team, they have been discarded and ignored by the coaches who recruited them.

There is little doubt that many opportunities are available today in intercollegiate sport for African American athletes that were not available a generation ago, but racism in college sport has not been eliminated. Many college sports teams still have very few African Americans as participants and coaches, and even fewer in administrative positions. The college sports with few participants and coaches tend to be linked to upper-class patronage, but class linkage is not the entire explanation for African American under-representation in these sports.

Powerful political and economic interests have the wherewithal to insulate themselves against those with whom they do not wish to associate. Laws that prevent African Americans from being kept out do not assure that they will get in. There is compelling evidence demonstrating that those who control intercollegiate athletic programs have created barriers to African American participation and to administrative positions in a number of sports and universities, thus reproducing some of the more odious features of racism.

Although racial discrimination has always been incompatible with the ideals of American sports, widespread intercollegiate sports opportunities for African Americans emerged only when discrimination became incompatible with good financial policy. In those team sports in which "revenue producing" has come to dominate, the contribution of outstanding African American athletes to winning championships and holding public interest has opened up opportunities to African Americans in college sports. Sports more closely linked to upper-class patronage and with less spectator interest have been slow to attract and integrate blacks.

Academic-Athletic Conflicts and African American Athletes

Accompanying the trend toward a form of commercial entertainment sponsored by colleges and universities has been a tension between the integrity of higher education and the economic interests and values of big-time sports. For many who view the mission of higher education as the promotion of scholarship and academic training for careers, there is more than just a tension; there is an inherent incompatibility between an economically driven activity that uses college students as a labor force, which big-time college sport does, and the mission of higher education in promoting scholarship and academic achievement. Audwin Anderson and Don South (chapter 3) locate their essay within this academic-athletic conflict, with a specific focus on recruiting, retention, and graduation rates of African American male athletes. They cast their analysis of the issues and problems within the current situation where nearly twice the percentage of white athletes graduate compared to African American athletes. In an attempt to bring some meaning to the statistical data on graduation rates, Anderson and South focus on forces such as the social meaning of African American maleness, recruitment practices, Propositions 48 and 16, recent reforms adopted by the NCAA, and the economic and academic exploitative nature of big-time college sport, as they relate to graduation rates. Finally, they make a critical appraisal of the use of graduation rates.

A recent NCAA reform policy addresses eligibility, matriculation, and graduation of student athletes, and is called the Academic Reform Movement (ARM). Keith Harrison and Jean Boyd (chapter 9) describe the purpose of ARM, which emphasizes monitoring universities and their retention and graduation success of student-athletes. They then give the details of what is called the "Scholar-Baller Paradigm," the purpose of which is to defeat the stereotyping that limits and obstructs the personal, social, cultural, and educational development of African American student athletes.

Limited Opportunities in Leadership in Sport for African Americans

Access to intercollegiate sport for African American athletes has expanded greatly in the past quarter century, but opportunities in the upper levels of the sport hierarchy have been much more restricted. The higher levels in organizations of all kinds, where the greatest power, prestige, and material rewards reside, are more insulated from direct scrutiny, so those who control access to the higher levels tend to employ subtle strategies of maintaining discriminatory practices. Thus, the oppressed group typically has a difficult time penetrating into the higher paying and prestigious positions. Efforts to eliminate discrimination through the legislative and judicial system tend to produce immediate results, but the results are most noticeable at the lower levels of the social formation.

In the case of intercollegiate athletics, coaching and management jobs are under the control of those who presently have the power for determining who gets selected to these leadership positions. The chapter authored by Dana Brooks, Ronald Althouse, and Delano Tucker (chapter 5) emphasizes the limited mobility for African Americans into coaching and administration positions in intercollegiate athletics. They point out that those African Americans who have overcome the barriers and acquired college coaching and athletic administration positions are overwhelmingly stacked as assistant coaches, and many coaching staffs have only one African American. The authors document that the percentage of African Americans is highest at the entry level in university athletic departments and lowest at the athletic director position.

Brooks, Althouse, and Tucker describe the role the Black Coaches Association and the NCAA have played in developing proactive programs aimed at increasing diversity in college coaching and athletic administration. In the last part of the chapter the authors move to a global perspective, and they examine issues of diversity, race, and gender discrimination in the increasingly global world of coaching and sport administration.

Hiring practices in intercollegiate athletics and professional sports are also analyzed by Fritz Polite (chapter 6). He cites recent statistics to show the appalling lack of people of color and women in the NCAA Division I-A, beginning with the NCAA Executive Director, and proceeding through university presidents, athletic directors and coaches in several different sports. Worse, according to Polite, there is little in the way of initiatives for the development of necessary skill and experience at the universities for the preparation of minorities in any of these positions.

Polite pleads for sport management programs to emphasize the importance of a multicultural perspective, and for these programs to be a vehicle for social change in intercollegiate sports hiring practices. The last third of this chapter is composed of brief biographies of African American men and women pioneers in sport leadership who blazed the trail for current African Americans and other minorities through dedication and professional achievements.

The literature dealing with employment barriers that limit the opportunities in coaching for African Americans is the subject of Doris R. Corbett's and Miguel J. Tabron's essay (chapter 7). First, they review the legislation and judicial rulings that are relevant to employment opportunities for minorities. Next, they identify the various kinds of barriers that confront African Americans who attempt to obtain athletic coaching positions. Last, they describe and discuss initiatives in four major and 10 sub-areas that were identified by the Minorities Opportunity Interest Committee (MOIC) that they claim will be a positive influence on promoting and increasing diversity in coaching.

Minority under representation in sports is not limited to leadership in coaching and sport administration positions. It also extends into the sports media. Allan Wolper (2005), a professor of journalism at Rutgers/Newark University and the ethics columnist for *Editor & Publisher Magazine*, said this about the paucity of African Americans in the newspaper industry: "They are a minority with a miniscule membership—the black sports editors at America's 1,456 daily newspapers. And the journalists who want to join that tiny club remain victims of a mindset that once kept African Americans from becoming quarterbacks in the National Football League" (p. 1).

Opportunities, and the lack of them, are the subject of chapter 8 by Doris R. Corbett and Aaron B. Stills. The media roles on which they focus are broadcasters, journalists, reporters, and announcers. In the first part of their chapter the authors identify eight African Americans that they classify as early leaders and contributors to sport journalism and the broadcast industry. For each early leader they provide a brief biographical sketch of his/her personal background and sport media accomplishments. They then turn to an examination of the modes of diversity, sexism, gender, and racial discrimination that have been a persistent pattern in the mass media industry for decades. The final section of their chapter is devoted to a review of theoretical perspectives that have been employed to explain and understand the discriminatory practices of the mass media organizations.

The Legal System and African American College Athletes

Social theorist Antonio Gramsci (1971) argued that the state "tends to create and maintain a certain type of civilization and citizen . . . and to eliminate certain customs and attitudes and to disseminate others," and the law is "its instrument for this purpose" (p. 246). Certainly, the law has been an instrument for the intercollegiate athletic establishment throughout its history. In the process, African American college athletes have been the victims. The intersection of race and law in college sports is the focus of Timothy Davis (chapter 12). He explains the persistence of unconscious racism in intercollegiate athletics, and argues that traditional civil rights laws have been largely ineffective for protecting the interests of African American college athletes. Davis also examines the implications of the constraints of traditional civil rights laws and the increasing judicial hostility to affirmative action for African American college athletes, coaches, and administrators. In closing, Davis proposes legal and non-legal strategies for eliminating racism in college sport.

In a second chapter (13), Timothy Davis examines the limited litigation strategies that are available to deal with the impact of NCAA rules on academic inequality as it applies to African American college student athletes. The role of law is emphasized by Davis in showing the adverse impact of NCAA rules and policies on African American college athletes. Judicial intervention has served as an external accountability mechanism on the NCAA, causing that organization to improve eligibility policies.

Virtually everyone agrees that big-time intercollegiate athletics is a big business, a business in which all of those who are involved in it receive either a wage or a salary for their work except the athletes who, in effect, are the major labor force in it. Thus, there has been a continuing debate about whether or not big-time college athletes, especially those who play the major revenue sports, football and basketball, should be paid. Scott Brooks and Linda Kim (chapter 14) take up this controversy about compensation for student athletes and center their chapter on African American college athletes at major universities, especially in football and basketball, because African American athletes now dominate those college sports. They discuss the various arguments for and against directly paying the athletes, and the possible consequences if athletes were paid. They conclude that compensation would be appropriate as principles of reciprocity and fairness to the athletes, as well as for its potential to improve the quality of college life, especially for black athletes from poor socioeconomic backgrounds.

African American Women and Intercollegiate Sport

An observation that is frequently made about African American women is that they suffer "double jeopardy," meaning that they are subject to both sexism *and* racism. The two chapters by Robertha Abney (chapter 2) and Linda Sheryl Greene and Tina Sloan-Green (chapter 15) amply confirm this observation.

The focus of Abney's chapter is on the socio-cultural and structural barriers that deny access and opportunities to African American women who aspire to positions as head coaches, college athletic administrators, and administrators in collegiate governing organizations. The forms and features of formal information structural barriers that limit African American women in intercollegiate sports are examined by Abney. She concludes by making 10 recommendation and strategies for change that could be used by various groups in formulating new policies and procedures for redressing the inequalities that now exist for African American women in sport (see also Bruening, 2005).

Greene and Sloan-Green recount their struggle, along with a network of friends they accumulated over the past 30 years, on behalf of African American women in sport. Their mission has been to overcome the myths and limited knowledge about race and gender discrimination, while advancing the visibility, status, and opportunities for black females in sport. The culmination of the collective efforts of this group of African American women was the founding of The Black Women in Sport Foundation (BWSF) in 1992. The purpose of the BWSF is to facilitate and advance the number of black women in every aspect of sport, including, of course, intercollegiate sports.

Intercollegiate sports have broadened and expanded over the past 20 years to give greater access to female athletes, but African American female athletes have benefited only marginally at this point, mainly due to social and gender-related barriers. Many of these barriers will likely be overcome in the future. Still, careers in sports for African American women—whether as athletes, coaches, administrators, sportscasters, etc.—will likely be extremely limited and difficult to attain.

College Athletics and Life after College

In recent years the NCAA has produced television commercial spots featuring college student athletes that emphasize that most of the 360,000 student athletes who participate in college sports annually will be entering non-sport careers upon their graduation from college. The purposes of these TV spots are to dispel the myth that most college athletes transition from college sports into a career in professional sports and to stress that the main objective of a college education is to prepare students for careers outside sport.

Billy Hawkins, Brianne Milan-Williams, and Akilah Carter (chapter 4) examine the transition of African Americans from intercollegiate athlete to a non-athlete post-college career. They describe the NCAA's policies dealing with athletes' post-college careers, using NCAA annual manuals, which articulate the NCAA's goals, missions, and intentions. Next, they review the models and theories that have been employed by researchers in attempting to explain the transition process from college athlete to careers as non-athlete. Finally, the authors describe a survey research project they undertook with former African American college athletes to ascertain the process, problems, issues, satisfactions, and dissatisfactions the former student athletes experienced while making the transition from college athlete to non-athletic careers. Their survey supported other athletic retirement research in that the reality of athletic retirement for African American former college athletes does not conform to the popular notion that college athletes, because of their collegiate sporting experiences, make an easy transition to athletic retirement.

Other scholars who have investigated African American student athletes' post-college lives have found that whether they were provided sound educational opportunities or whether they were merely exploited by the college made a big difference in the athletes' successful or unsuccessful transition to a non-athlete career.

African Americans as Sport Consumers

The enormous increase in youth, high school, and intercollegiate athletics and the massive growth of professional sports have been accompanied by expanded mass media coverage of sports events, especially on television. This industry has generated a huge consumer base of sports fans, and sports spectatorship is arguably the most multicultural practice in American society. Each week, untold millions of spectators consume sport directly through personal attendance at sporting events. But sports fans consume sport to a far greater extent indirectly through mass media outlets—newspaper, magazine, radio, television—than through actually attending sports events.

Ketra L. Armstrong's chapter (17) reviews African Americans' sport consumption patterns and tendencies. She then explores the economic and sociological forces as they relate to African American sports consumers. Last, she summarizes three race-based themes that are significant to African Americans' consumption of sport.

What about the Future?

One can only speculate about the future, but there is general agreement that the expansion of what is now called the global economy will continue. Indeed, in his State of the Union address in January 2000, President Bill Clinton declared that "globalization is the central reality of our time." Contemporary sports are bound up in the globalization process. The creation and expansion of international sport organizations, the codification of international rules for the various sports, the proliferation of global sporting events, such as the Olympic Games and World Cup, and the growing list of internationally renowned sports celebrities, such as Michael Jordan, Mia Hamm, and Yao Ming, are some examples of how sport is becoming more globalized.

Fritz Polite (chapter 16) appraises the trends and strategies of global marketing and global sports marketing, emphasizing the dynamic character of these efforts. For global sports marketing Polite describes the globalization process as it is being played out in sporting events sponsored by several international sport organizations. As a capstone to this discuss, he uses NFL International as an example of a sport organization attempting to market professional American football throughout the world.

The final essay (Epilogue) is authored by Earl Smith, a past president of the North American Society for the Sociology of Sport, and his colleague Angela Hattery. It is a thoughtful, broad-ranging treatise scrutinizing race relations in American society and big-time intercollegiate athletics. A fundamental theme of Smith's and Hattery's essay is that one of the consequences of the pervasive social stereotyping that African Americans have historically experienced has been in stifling their potential in all spheres of American life, including sports. They illustrate the many ways African Americans have been, and continue to be, disadvantaged. They accurately describe the contradictions of SportsWorld, focusing especially on big-time intercollegiate sports, where on the one hand African Americans are provided opportunities to be successful athletes while on the other hand they are stereotypically treated as though they are incapable of academic achievement, or have no interest in academic pursuits.

Within the scope of their main theme, Smith and Hattery address various other topics, such as: African Americans' lives after their careers as college athletes, the "big" business aspects of sports as they impact African Americans, role modeling of African American male athletes, the role of sport in creating identity for African American athletes while social and economic problems escalate for

African Americans in Civil Society, and, finally, the proposes and outcomes of Midnight Basketball and And1 programs for African Americans.

As globalization matures and people throughout the world have more frequent and permanent interaction and relationships, white Americans will by necessity end the denial, disregard, and resistance they have historically used to maintain and sustain racist attitudes and behavior, particularly in sports. White Americans have the power to make a difference in ethnic and racial matters, and they must acknowledge and accept responsibility for the unconscionable white domination that has prevailed in the centuries before the 21st century. For sports, it must begin by confronting the reluctance of the white sports establishment to acknowledge and confront racism. For too long this has been the tactic for refusing to seriously address the widespread racism in sports. In order to enhance a future committed to the acceptance and advancement of diversity, everyone needs to commit some of their professional work to anti-racist activity.

▲▼ Suggested Readings ▲▼

Altman, L. J. (2004). *The American civil rights movement: The African-American struggle for equality.* Berkeley Heights, NJ: Enslow Publishers.

Ashe, A. (1988). *A hard road to glory: A history of the African-American athlete, 1919–1945.* New York: Warner Books.

Bass, A. (Ed.). (2005). *In the game: Race, identity, and sports in the twentieth century.* New York: Palgrave.

Carson, C., Evers-Williams, M., Bauerlein, M., & Burroughs, T. S. (2003). *Civil rights chronicle: The African-American struggle for freedom.* Lincolnwood, IL: Legacy.

Doane, A. W., & Bonilla-Silva, E. (Eds.). (2003). *White out: The continuing significance of racism.* New York: Rutledge.

Lapchick, R. (2001). *Smashing barriers: Race and sport in the new millennium* (Updated ed.). New York: Madison Books.

Miller, P. B., & Wiggins, D. K. (Eds.). (2004). *Sport and the color line: Black athletes and race relations in twentieth-century America.* New York: Routledge.

Wigginton, R. T. (2006). *The strange career of the black athlete: African-Americans and sports.* Westport CT: Praeger Publishers.

▲▼ Study Questions ▲▼

1. Understanding the role of racism in college athletics requires an understanding of racism in the larger American cultural context in which it is situated. Drawing on the description of racism in American society in this chapter, and the knowledge you have acquired about this topic from other sources, historically situate and culturally locate racism in American society.

2. Throughout their history in North America, African Americans have played a continuing and significant role in every era of American sport history. Describe and discuss African American involvement in American sport: (1) before the Civil War; (2) immediately following the Civil War; (3) the last

two decades of the 19th century and up until World War II; (4) after World War II.

3. Over the course of the history of intercollegiate sports in the United States, African American athletes have experienced exclusion, segregation, and tokenism. Discuss the time frames when each of these were occurring and give examples of how these were manifested.

4. Focusing specifically on African American involvement in intercollegiate sports, describe and discuss the involvement of African Americans in intercollegiate sport from the latter 19th century to the present.

5. African Americans' remarkable success in a variety of sports has led to speculation about the reasons for this incredible phenomenon. Identify and discuss the credibility of the ideas and theories that have been advanced to account for this.

6. While African American student athletes now dominate the main revenue-producing college sports, discuss their status with regard to their presence or absence from sport leadership positions in intercollegiate sports.

7. Discuss the experiences of African American college athletes' careers during their post-college lives. Do they differ from white college athletes? If so, in what way?

8. What about the future for African American college athletes, coaches, and sport administrators? Describe the future scenario as you view it for the next 20 years.

References

Altman, L. J. (2004). *The American civil rights movement: The African-American struggle for equality*. Berkeley Heights, NJ: Enslow Publishers.

Bonilla-Silva, E. (2004). *Racism without racists: Color-blind racism and the persistence of racial inequality in the United States*. Lanham, MD: Rowman & Littlefield.

Brown, M. K., Carnoy, M., Currie, E., Duster, T., Oppenheimer, D. B., Schultz, M. M., & Wellman, D., (2005). *Whitewashing race: The myth of a color-blind society*. Berkeley: University of California Press.

Bruening, J. E. (2005). Gender and racial analysis in sport: Are all the women white and all the blacks men? *Quest, 57*, 330–349.

Bullock, L. (2006, July 18). Economic gaps widens between blacks and whites, *New American Media*, News Report, National Newspaper Publishers Association. Retrieved from http://news.newamericamedia.org/news/view_article.htm?article_id=b462dde8f3ffdad09fbd22f0c1a77bf4

Cahn, S. (2004). Cinderellas of sport: Black women in track and field. In P. B. Miller & D. K. Wiggins (Eds.). *Sport and the color line: Black athletes and race relations in twentieth-century America* (pp. 211–232). New York: Routledge.

Carson, C. (2004). Two cheers for Brown v. Board of Education. *The Journal of American History, 91*(1), 26–31.

Chalk, O. (1975). *Pioneers of black sport*. New York: Dodd, Mead.

Cross, W. E. (1995). The psychology of Nigrescence: Revising the Cross model. In J. G. Ponterotto, J. M. Casas, L. A. Suzuki, & C. M. Alexander, (Eds.), *Handbook of multicultural counseling* (pp. 93–122). Thousand Oaks, CA: Sage

Edwards, H. (2004). Crisis of black athletes on the eve of the twenty-first century. In P B. Miller & D. K. Wiggins (Eds.), *Sport and the color line: Black athletes and race relations in twentieth-century America* (pp. 345–350). New York: Routledge.

Eitzen, D. S., & Sage, G. H. (2003). *Sociology of North American sport* (7th ed.) New York: McGraw-Hill.

Entine, J. (2001). *Taboo: Why black athletes dominate sports and why we're afraid to talk about it*. New York: Public Affairs.

Gorn, E. J., & Oriard, M. (1995, March 24). Taking sports seriously, *The Chronicle of Higher Education*, p. A52.

Gramsci, A. (1971). *Selections from the prison notebooks* (Q. Hoare & G. N. Smith, Eds.). New York: International Publishers.

Hoberman, J. (1997). *Darwin's athletes: How sport has damaged black America and preserved the myth of race*. Boston: Mariner Books.

Hogan, L. D. (2006). *Shades of glory: The Negro leagues and the story of African-American baseball*. Washington, D.C.: National Geographic.

Hotaling, E. (1999). *The great Black jockeys*. Rocklin, CA: Forum.

Katznelson, I. (2005). *When affirmative action was white: An untold history of racial inequality in twentieth-century America*. New York: W. W. Norton.

Lanctot, N. (2004). *Negro League baseball: The rise and ruin of a black institution*. Philadelphia: University of Pennsylvania Press.

Liberti, R. (2004). "We were ladies, we just played like boys": African-American womanhood and competitive basketball at Bennett College, 1928–1942. In P. B. Miller & D. K. Wiggins (Eds.). *Sport and the color line: Black athletes and race relations in twentieth-century America* (pp. 83–99). New York: Routledge.

Lui, M., Robles, B., & Leondar-Wright, B. (2006). *The color of wealth: The story behind the U. S. racial wealth divide*. New York: New Press.

Malik, R. (2005, January/February). FBI reports increase in hate crimes against African Americans. *The Crisis*, 9.

Martin, C. H. (2004). Jim Crow in the gymnasium: The integration of college basketball in the American South. In P. B. Miller & D. K. Wiggins (Eds.), *Sport and the color line: Black athletes and race relations in twentieth-century America* (pp. 233–250). New York: Routledge.

McWhorter, D. (2004). *A dream of freedom: The Civil Rights movement from 1954 to 1968*. New York: Scholastic.

Miller, P. B. (2004). The anatomy of scientific racism: Racialist responses to black athletic achievement. In P. B. Miller & D. K. Wiggins (Eds.), *Sport and the color line: Black athletes and race relations in twentieth-century America* (pp. 327–344). New York: Routledge.

Oliver, M., & Shapiro, T. (Eds.). (2006). *Black wealth/white wealth: A new perspective on racial inequality*. New York: Routledge.

Peterson, R. (1992). *Only the ball was white: History of legendary black players and all black professional teams*. New York: Oxford University Press.

Prebish, C. S. comp. (1993). *Religion and sport: The meeting of sacred and profane*. Westport, CT: Greenwood, pp. 62, 74.

Schneider, D., & Schneider, C. J. (2000). *Slavery in America: From Colonial times to the Civil War*. New York: Facts on File.

Shapiro, T. M. (2005). *The hidden cost of being African American: How wealth perpetuates inequality*. New York: Oxford University Press.

Strom, K. (2001). *Hate crimes reported in NIBRS, 1997–1999*. Washington, DC: Bureau of Justice Statistics.

Tygiel, J. 2004). Jackie Robinson: A lone Negro in Major League Baseball. In P. B. Miller & D. K. Wiggins (Eds.), *Sport and the color line: Black athletes and race relations in twentieth-century America* (pp. 167–189). New York: Routledge.

Wiggins, D. K. (1997). *Glory bound: Black athletes in a white America*. Syracuse, NY: Syracuse University Press.

Wolper, A., (2005, November 13). Black sports editors: One black list that shouldn't be short. *Black Athlete Sports Network*. Retrieved from http://www.blackathlete.net/artman/publish/article_01254.shtml

SECTION ONE
Historical Analysis

This book is about the place sport holds in America's cultural values and the institutional racism that has been a part of the sports experience since the founding of the nation. It proposes that an understanding of the social relevance of sport is realized through a study of sport's relationship to social class, race, gender and mechanisms of political and economic domination. In essence, the book's central focus is diversity and social justice in American intercollegiate athletics.

In the first chapter, "Climbing the Racial Mountain: A History of the African American Experience in Sport," David Wiggins shows that even as *overt* racial discrimination against African American athletes on the playing fields has been overcome, parity in sport, especially at the intercollegiate level of participation, remains as elusive as ever. (He notes that the opportunity to gain complete access is denied, erecting barriers to mobility, institutionalizing academic-athletic conflicts, and fostering personal dilemmas in adjusting when athletes are faced with termination of careers.) People continue to hold onto stereotypes that portray African Americans as if predisposed to or biologically programmed for success in sport even when contradicted by a historic record of racial domination—from slavery to present day exploitation of urban, African America student athletes. It is also reasonable to regard the history of race relations in sport as a chronicle of the consequences of pervasive social stereotyping and a direct result of segregation in other social institutions (education, law, politics, medicine, business). Sport was often viewed by minorities, especially African Americans, as a possible route to upward social mobility. As David Wiggins illustrates, the historic forces and experiences of African American athletes took place as often off the playing field as they did on the fields of play: the Civil Rights movement, black athletic revolts, academic performance and graduation rates of Black athletes, as well as the current legitimacy crisis of African American sports agents.

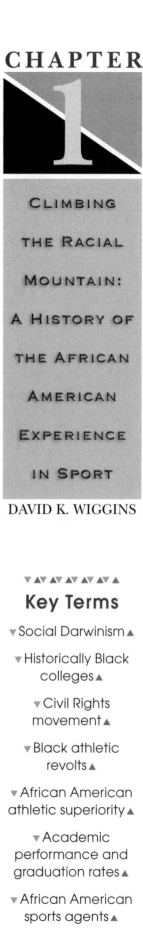

CHAPTER 1

CLIMBING THE RACIAL MOUNTAIN: A HISTORY OF THE AFRICAN AMERICAN EXPERIENCE IN SPORT

DAVID K. WIGGINS

Key Terms

▾Social Darwinism▴

▾Historically Black colleges▴

▾Civil Rights movement▴

▾Black athletic revolts▴

▾African American athletic superiority▴

▾Academic performance and graduation rates▴

▾African American sports agents▴

Abstract ▾ This essay examines the involvement of African Americans in sport from the latter half of the 19th century to the present. Particular attention is paid to the critical events that influenced the status of African American athletes at both amateur and professional levels of sport. A number of outstanding African American athletes distinguished themselves in a variety of different sports during the latter half of the 19th century. Hardening racial policies, combined with a number of other societal factors in the late 19th century, forced African Americans to form their own teams and leagues in a number of different sports. Although a few African American athletes were able to overcome racial barriers and compete in predominantly white organized sport, the large majority participated in sport behind segregated walls throughout the first half of the 20th century. The signing of Jackie Robinson by the Brooklyn Dodgers paved the way for African American athletes to reenter predominantly white organized sport in increasing numbers. African American athletes shed their traditional conservative approach to racial matters and became involved in the Civil Rights movement during the latter part of the 1960s and the early 1970s. African American athletes eventually received a great deal of attention from academicians and became the source of much debate as they realized increasing success as participants, yet continued to endure frustrations wrought by racial discrimination.

Introduction

The history of the African American athletes' involvement in sport has been marked by a number of major successes interspersed with bitter disappointments. Initially exposed to different sports on southern plantations or in larger cities in the eastern half of the United States, a number of outstanding African American athletes distinguished themselves in highly organized sport at both the amateur and professional levels of competition in the years immediately following the Civil War (Ashe, 1988; Betts, 1974; Henderson, 1939, 1972; Lucas & Smith, 1978; Malloy, 1995; Rader, 1983; Ritchie, 1988; Rhoden, 2006; Somers, 1972; D. K. Wiggins, 1979, 1985, 2006; Zang, 1995). By the latter years of the 19th century, the large majority of African American athletes were, for various reasons and under different circumstances, excluded from participating in most highly organized sport and forced to establish their own teams and leagues operated without white interference. With the notable exceptions of boxing and international athletic contests, African Americans established their own organizations behind segregated walls in such sports as football, basketball, and baseball. These separate institutions were a source of great pride to the African American community and served as visible examples of black organizational skill and entrepreneurship during the oppressive years of the first half of the 20th century (Ashe, 1988; Betts, 1974; Grundy, 2001; Henderson, 1939, 1972; Lanctot, 1994, 2004; Liberti, 2004; Lomax, 1998; Lucas & Smith, 1978; Malloy, 1995; P. B. Miller, 1995; Rader, 1983; Rayl, 1996; Rhoden, 2006; Rogosin, 1983; Ruck, 1986; Somers, 1972). The historic signing of Jackie Robinson by the Brooklyn Dodgers in 1945 was the beginning of the end for separate sporting organizations, but it also helped usher in the reintegration of sport in this country. Robinson's signing with the Dodgers, combined with the integrationist policies in the post-World War II era, triggered the reentry and gradual acceptance of African American athletes into various sports. The following two decades witnessed unprecedented growth in the number of African American athletes participating in sport, a growth that proceeded at an uneven rate depending on the particular sport and location (Grundman, 1979; Lowenfish, 1978; Spivey, 1983; Tygiel, 1983; D. K. Wiggins, 1983, 1989, 2006).

Toward the latter part of the 1960s, African American athletes became involved in the Civil Rights movement by actively protesting racial discrimination in sport and the larger society. The two major forums for protest were the Olympic Games and predominantly white university campuses, where African American athletes staged boycotts and spoke out against the racial discrimination experienced by them and other members of the African American community. Although their personal involvement in civil rights issues slowly abated under the weight of the women's rights movement and issues associated with inflation and unemployment, the role of African American athletes in organized sport continued to be of great interest to both academicians and lay people alike. In recent years, African American athletes have garnered front-page headlines, particularly in regard to their exploitation by educational institutions, inability to assume managerial and upper-level administrative positions in sport, and restriction to particular playing positions as well as sports (Coakley, 1990; Edwards, 1973 a, b; Leonard, 1993; Rhoden, 2006; Spivey, 1985; D. K. Wiggins, 1988).

A Taste of Success in Late 19th-Century Sport

The African American athlete's first real taste of highly competitive sport took place in the years immediately following the Civil War. Although some African American athletes had achieved fame prior to the great war between the states, it was not until the bloody conflict ended that large numbers of them would realize national and even international acclaim in a wide range of sports. The newly found freedom following the war and the lasting sporting traditions established during slavery created an atmosphere in which African Americans were more readily accepted into horse racing, baseball, and other sports popular during the period. For example, Peter Jackson, the great boxer from the Virgin Islands by way of Australia, continued the tradition of outstanding black fighters and became a household name among pugilistic fans through his well-known ring battles with such men as James J. Corbett, George Godfrey, and Frank Slavin (Ashe, 1988; Betts, 1974; D. K. Wiggins, 1985). Isaac Murphy and a number of other diminutive African Americans dominated the jockey profession, capturing the Kentucky Derby and many of horse racing's other prestigious events (Ashe, 1988; Betts, 1974; Hotaling, 1995, 2005; Somers 1972; D. K. Wiggins, 1979, 2006). Marshall "Major" Taylor, the great bicyclist from Indianapolis, seized the imagination of racing fans on both sides of the Atlantic with his amazing feats of speed on the oval track (Ashe, 1988; Betts, 1974; Ritchie, 1988; Taylor, 1928; D. K. Wiggins, 2006). Moses "Fleetwood" Walker and his brother Weldy became Major League Baseball's first African American players when they signed contracts with the Toledo Mudhens of the American Association in the mid-1880s (Malloy, 1995; McKinney, 1976; Peterson, 1970; Zang, 1995).

By the latter years of the 19th century African American athletes were being excluded from highly organized sport. Even those African American athletes who had achieved great success were either eliminated or pressured to drop out of their respective sports. The reasons for their elimination from highly organized sport were many and varied, including the dominant culture's belief in black inferiority, general deterioration of black rights, and eventual separation of the races in late 19th-century America. (Davis, 1966; Lucas & Smith, 1978; Rader, 1983; Somers, 1972). The southern black codes, established shortly after the Civil War to insure legal restrictions against the newly freed slaves, became easier to implement toward the end of the century as northern Republicans abandoned their previous commitment to black rights. Further deterioration of black rights resulted from decommitment by the United States Supreme Court toward the latter part of the 19th century. In 1883, the Supreme Court affirmed legislation overturning the 14th Amendment, citing that prevention of discrimination against individuals by states did not prohibit discrimination by individual citizens. In 1896, the famous *Plessy v. Ferguson* case legally sanctioned separation of schools by race and upheld "separate-but-equal" accommodations on railroads. In 1898, the Supreme Court kept many African Americans out of politics by upholding poll-tax qualifications and literary tests for voting (Logan, 1965; Meier & Rudwick, 1963; Woodward, 1966).

The Supreme Court decisions took place in an increasingly more hostile environment where African Americans were being "proven" inferior to whites. The exclusion of African Americans from sport, like the exclusion of African Americans from all walks of life, was given a philosophical rationale based on a combination of social Darwinism, the rise of imperialism around the world, and the spread of pseudoscientific writings by academicians and others. Such well-known thinkers as Herbert Spencer and William Graham Sumner gave support to the belief that African Americans were on the lowest rung of the evolutionary ladder, incapable of surviving in a competitive society due to their intellectual and emotional inferiority (Cochran & Miller, 1961; Logan, 1957; Meier & Rudwick, 1963; Woodward, 1966). Social Darwinism was supported in principle by various members of the dominant culture who believed "nonwhite" people of the new territories annexed during imperialist expansion were merely savages in need of education and cultural enlightenment. The belief in African American inferiority was further "substantiated" by a number of racist treatises and academic studies completed during the period. Prejudiced whites received all the support they needed from academicians in such divergent fields as history, psychology, sociology, biology, and anthropology, who were busily trying to prove African American inferiority through their various writings (Cochran & Miller, 1961; Logan, 1957; Meier & Rudwick, 1963; Woodward, 1966).

Striving for an Equal Share in the American Dream

The segregation of highly organized sport did not stop a select number of African American athletes from continuing to achieve success in certain sports at different levels of competition. Throughout the first half of the 20th century, a number of outstanding African American athletes gained prominence in professional boxing, in college sport on predominantly white university campuses, and in Olympic competition (Ashe, 1988; Betts, 1974; Chalk, 1976; Davis, 1966; Fleischer, 1938; Young, 1963).

Involvement of African Americans in boxing had a long tradition, extending back to the early years of the 19th century when Tom Molineaux, with assistance from Bill Richmond, another famous African American pugilist and trainer of boxers, fought for the heavyweight championship against the Englishman Tom Crib (Brailsford, 1988; Cone, 1982; Frazer, 1999; Goodman, 1980; Gorn, 1994;

Kaye, 2004; J. W. Rudolph, 1979; Shropshire, 2007). A sport that fit nicely into the dominant culture's stereotypical notions of African Americans and legendary traditions of gladiatorial combat, boxing provided a better life for some African Americans while at once helping delimit the conditions of African American identity within American culture and reflecting the racial realities of society in general. African Americans withstood the segregationist policies of the late 19th century and continued to engage in matches, drawing worldwide attention from audiences especially interested in bouts where at least one of the fighters was black (Early, 1989; Kaye, 2004; Sammons, 1988; Shropshire, 2007).

The two most prominent African American fighters of the first half of the 20th century were the similarly legendary, yet decidedly different, Jack Johnson and Joe Louis. Johnson, the powerfully built boxer from Galveston, Texas, became the first African American to capture the world's heavyweight championship, holding on to the title for some seven years before losing to the Pottawatomie giant, Jess Willard, in 1915. As great as Johnson's exploits were in boxing, it was outside the squared circle that Johnson gained the most attention and caused the greatest controversy. He has often been referred to as a "Bad Nigger," a man who played on the worst fears of the dominant culture by marrying three white women and having illicit affairs with a number of others, often prostitutes whom he treated with an odd mixture of affection and disdain. He was absolutely fearless and attracted to dangerous escapades that challenged white conventions and mores. Although a hero to many members of his race, Johnson drew the wrath of segments of both the African American and white communities because of his unwillingness to assume a subservient position and play the role of the grateful black. He was eventually convicted of violating the Mann Act for transporting a white woman across state lines for illicit purposes and was forced to leave the country for a short time before returning home to serve a jail sentence at the federal prison in Leavenworth, Kansas (Farr, 1964; Gilmore, 1975; Hietala, 2002; Kaye, 2004; Roberts, 1983; Shropshire, 2007; Ward, 2004; D. K. Wiggins, 2006; W. H. Wiggins, 1971).

The bitter aftertaste from Johnson's career, combined with continuing racial discrimination in American society, made it virtually impossible for African American boxers to secure championship fights over the next two decades. That all changed in 1937, however, when Joe Louis, the superbly talented boxer from Detroit, became the second African American heavyweight champion by defeating James Braddock. Louis was a decidedly different champion than Johnson. Possessing enormous strength and boxing skills, Louis was a quiet, dignified man who assumed the more subservient role whites expected from members of his race. He became a hero of almost mythical proportions in this country's African American community by demolishing white fighters with remarkable regularity and serving as a symbol of possibility for those subjugated by continuing racial discrimination (Capeci & Wilkerson, 1983; Demas, 2004; Edmonds, 1973; Erenberg, 2006; Hietala, 2002; Kaye, 2004; Margolick, 2005; McRae, 2002; Mead, 1985; Shropshire, 2007; D. K. Wiggins, 2006).

Whereas Louis and Johnson gained fame as possibly America's finest pugilists, a select number of outstanding African American athletes outside the South found success in integrated high school sport and then continued that success in some of the most prestigious predominantly white colleges in the country. Some of these athletes would even realize international acclaim for their great athletic performances. John Baxter Taylor, the great track star, was one such athlete. He attended racially mixed Central High School and Brown Preparatory before enrolling in the University of Pennsylvania. Winner of the 440-yard dash in the 1904, 1907, and 1908 championships of the Intercollegiate Amateur Athletic Association, Taylor was a member of the gold-medal-winning 400-meter relay team in the 1908 Olympic Games in London. Paul Robeson, the great singer, actor, athlete, and civil rights activist, was one of three African Americans among the 250 students at New Jersey's Somerville High School where he starred in football, basketball, baseball, and track and field. After Somerville, Robeson enrolled at Rutgers University where he was selected Phi Beta Kappa and a two-time member of Walter Camp's All-American football team in 1917 and 1918. Fritz Pollard starred in several sports at integrated Lane Technical High School in Chicago before becoming a student at Brown University where he was selected to Walter Camp's All-American football team in 1916. He would eventually become a player with the Akron Pros in a league that evolved into the NFL and later achieved distinction as the first African American head coach in a major team sport when he was hired to lead the Pros in 1921. Jesse Owens, the hero of the 1936 Olympic Games in Berlin, starred at racially mixed East Technical High School in Cleveland before taking his talents to Ohio State University. Woody Strode and Kenny Washington, the UCLA stars who integrated the NFL with the Los Angeles Rams in 1946, both attended racially mixed high schools in Los Angeles; Strode attending Jefferson High School and Washington Lincoln High School. Jackie Robinson starred in several sports at Pasadena's racially mixed John Muir Technical High School in the mid-1930s before moving on to UCLA (Ashe, 1988; Baker, 1986; Behee, 1974; Carroll, 1992, 2004; Chalk, 1976; T. G. Rampersad, 1997; Smith, 1988; Spivey, 1988; Strode & Young, 1990; D. K. Wiggins, 1991, 2006).

The great success of these athletes did not guarantee them equitable treatment or shield them from the hideous race relations of Jim Crow America. In fact, their accomplishments were sometimes overshadowed by the insensitivity and various forms of discrimination they experienced on their individual campuses and outside the halls of academe. African American athletes at predominantly white schools invariably experienced the loneliness and sense of isolation that come with being members of a small minority in a largely white setting. A large number of African American athletes found white campuses and their environs insensitive to their needs, not always providing satisfying social and cultural activities and educational support services necessary for academic success (T. Davis, 1995; L. Miller, 1927; Spivey & Jones, 1975; D. K. Wiggins, 1991; Wolters, 1975).

Perhaps most traumatic for African American athletes were the racially discriminatory acts committed against them by white opponents from other institutions. The most noteworthy of these involved the refusal of white institutions to compete against schools that had African American athletes on their teams. It was especially hurtful to African American athletes when one of their own teammates or coaches were complicit in these blatant forms of racial discrimination. For example, Fritz Pollard recalled with much pain how his own coach at Lane Technological High School in Chicago, R. F. Webster, kept him out of a football game in 1910 versus St. John's Military Academy in Wisconsin because of that school's refusal to play against an African American. An even uglier event occurred when coach Webster intentionally gave Pollard the wrong departure time and left him at the train station rather than telling him directly that the school in southern Illinois scheduled to play Lane Tech was opposed to competing against him because of his color (Carroll, 1994). In 1916 Washington and Lee College of Virginia threatened to withdraw from a football game against Rutgers because Paul Robeson was on the Rutgers team. Rutgers coach George Sanford eventually acceded to Washington and Lee's request, and Robeson was forced to sit out the game, apparently without any protest from the Rutgers community (Fishman, 1969; Gilliam, 1976; D. K. Wiggins, 1991). Approximately 13 years after the Robeson incident, coach Chuck Meehan of New York University acceded to the demands of the University of Georgia by withholding his star halfback, Dave Myers, from a football game between the two institutions. This incident resulted in much debate and protest, including protracted negotiations between the National Association for the Advancement of Colored People (NAACP) and university officials (Spivey, 1988; D. K. Wiggins, 1991; Wolters, 1975). In 1941, New York University complied with the wishes of Catholic University of America by withholding its three African American athletes from a track meet in Washington, DC. In the same year, Harvard University's outstanding African American lacrosse player, Lucian Alexis, Jr., was withheld from a match against the Naval Academy because of that institution's refusal to compete against African American players (P. B. Miller, 1991). The Alexis decision caused a great deal of protest on Harvard's campus and ultimately resulted in the university's announcing that it would never again "countenance racial discrimination" (Brower, 1941, p. 261).

Sport Behind Segregated Walls

As a select group of African American athletes struggled to realize a measure of success in predominantly white organized sport, the African American community established its own separate sporting organizations behind segregated walls and out of view of most members of the dominant culture. Although remarkably similar to white-controlled institutions, these sporting organizations reflected special African American cultural patterns, attesting to the strength and vibrancy of the African American community during the oppressive years of the early 20th century (Ashe, 1988; Gems, 1995; George, 1992; Gould, 2003; Grundy 2001; Henderson, 1939; Lanctot, 1994, 2004; Liberti, 1999, 2004; Lomax, 1998; P. B. Miller, 1995; Peterson, 1970, 1990; Rayl, 1996; Rogosin, 1983; Ruck, 1987).

Prime examples of African American sporting organizations were the athletic programs established at black high schools. Many of the leading black high schools in this country fielded athletic teams, including M Street School in Washington, D.C., arguably the finest high school in America during the early 20th century. There were also separate sports leagues and organizations established in the African American community patterned after those interscholastic sports leagues and organizations established in the white community. In 1906, Edwin Bancroft Henderson, the great physical educator, historian of the black athlete, and athletic administrator, joined forces with five other notable black educators in Washington, D.C., to organize the Interscholastic Athletic Association (ISAA). Made up of schools from Washington, D.C., Indianapolis, Wilmington, Delaware, and Baltimore, the ISAA organized athletic contests in football, baseball, basketball, and track and field. In 1910 Henderson, at the request of Roscoe Bruce, head of

Washington, D.C.'s black public school system, organized the Public Schools Athletic League (PSAL). Modeled after the white public schools athletic leagues located in eighteen cities across the United States, Washington, D.C.'s black PSAL sponsored a vast array of sports for children of various skill levels at both the grammar school and high school levels. The PSAL organized, among other things, a grammar school baseball tournament, intercity soccer league, high school cross country meets, and Saturday night basketball games and dances during the winter months at the city's famous True Reformer's Hall (Henderson & Henderson, 1985; Kuska, 2004; D. K. Wiggins, 1997, 1999).

The ISAA and PSAL in Washington, D.C., would eventually be followed by other high school sports organizations in other African American communities across America. In 1924 fourteen schools formed the West Virginia Athletic Union, a significant event in that it was the first African American statewide athletic association in the South. By 1930 other black state high school athletic associations had been organized in Virginia, North Carolina, Kansas, Missouri, Illinois, Indiana, and Florida. Slower to establish black high school athletic associations were many of those states in the Deep South. Mississippi did not have one until 1940, Arkansas waited until 1942 to create a separate organization, and Alabama finally established a black high school athletic association in 1948 (George, 1992).

Perhaps the most popular sport of these athletic associations was basketball. Although they would sponsor a variety of competitions in different sports, the black state high school athletic associations were seemingly most interested in basketball and showcased it in year-end tournaments. Certainly one of the most important of these tournaments was sponsored by the West Virginia Athletic Union (WVAU). Held for the first time in 1925 at West Virginia State College, the WVAU basketball tournament evolved into an extremely significant sporting event that provided an opportunity for African Americans from every part of West Virginia to come together and share a degree of racial pride and communal spirit (Barnett, 1983). During the early years of the tournament, schools from the southern portion of the state, including Kimball, Gary District, Genoa (Beckley) and Excelsior (War) dominated because of the relatively larger number of African Americans. Between 1934 and 1945, the tournament was dominated by Clarksburg Kelly Miller High School. Coached by the famous Mark Cardwell, Kelly Miller won the state tournament in 1935, 1936, 1942, 1943, and 1944. Between 1946 and 1957, the last year of the tournament, Charleston Garnet and Huntington Douglass would dominate play, partially a result of the transformation of basketball into a more urban or city game (Barnett, 1983).

The WVAU tournament and those sponsored by other black state high school athletic associations would be complemented by a national interscholastic basketball tournament involving outstanding black high school teams from across the country. The National Interscholastic Basketball Tournament was first held in 1930 at Hampton Institute in Virginia. Organized by Charles H. Williams, a noted physical educator and coach from Hampton Institute who had been very instrumental in the creation of the Colored Intercollegiate Athletic Association (now Central Intercollegiate Athletic Association) in 1912, the tournament enjoyed some initial success attracting such perennial powerhouses as Washington, D.C.'s Armstrong Technical High School, Chicago's Wendell Phillips, and Gary, Indiana's

Roosevelt High School. In 1933, however, Hampton Institute ended its sponsorship of the tournament, citing the exorbitant costs associated with running such an event as the reason for its decision. The tournament was held in Gary, Indiana, in 1934 and 1935, at Roanoke, Virginia,'s Lucy Addison High School in 1936, and then back to Gary, Indiana, in 1937, and 1938. The four tournaments in Gary, Indiana, were highly successful, in spite of the fact that it faced stiff competition from the recently organized Southern Interscholastic Basketball (SIB) tournament founded by Cleve Abbott at Tuskegee Institute. Run by Roosevelt's High School's John Smith, perhaps the country's most well-known black schoolboy coach who formed the all-black National Interscholastic Athletic Association (NIAA), the tournament in Gary typically realized attendance each year of some 10,000 and was marked by the outstanding play of some of the best teams in America. Beginning in 1939 the tournament shifted to various sites, including Roanoke, Virginia, and both Durham and Fayetteville, North Carolina, until World War II put a temporary halt to the event in 1942 (George, 1992).

In 1945 the tournament was revived by Tennessee A & I president Walter Davis and the school's athletic director Henry Arthur Keane. Held first in Nashville and then later at Alabama State under the auspices of the newly formed organization titled the National High School Athletic Association, the tournament was highly successful and continued to exist in one form or another until 1964. It was apparent long before 1964, however, that times were changing. Gary, Indiana,'s Roosevelt High School and Indianapolis' Crispus Attucks High School, two of the most famous and powerful black high school basketball programs in the country, did not even play in the tournament since they began participating in 1943 in the recently desegregated Indiana High School Athletic Association championships. The reason for the tournament's change in location from Tennessee A & I to Alabama State resulted from the move toward integration on the part of the Tennessee National High School Athletic Association in 1954 (George, 1992; Paino, 2001; Pierce, 2000).

Complementing the athletic programs at segregated high schools were those established at historically black colleges. Originally organized during the late 19th century, athletic programs at historically black colleges were similar to those at predominantly white institutions in that they began as informal, student-run activities and evolved into highly structured and institutionally controlled phenomena. They were also much like intercollegiate athletic programs on white campuses in that they included a wide variety of sports, were eventually controlled by elaborate bureaucratic organizations, and were rationalized along both educational and social lines. Most historically black colleges competed in all the major team sports, including football, which was one of the most popular sports in the African American community. The annual Thanksgiving Day football games between various schools, including the classic match between Howard and Lincoln (PA), drew thousands of spectators from around the country, contributed to a sense of institutional pride and national reputation, and stimulated school spirit by bringing students, faculty, and alumni together to share in the excitement of common pursuits. Organizational structure was first brought to black college sport in 1912, when the Colored (later Central) Intercollegiate Athletic Association (CIAA) was formed among such well-known institutions as Howard, Lincoln (PA), and Hampton Institute. Shortly after the creation of the CIAA, similar athletic associations were organized, which led to the further legitimacy of black college sport (Ashe, 1988; Captain, 1991; Chalk, 1976; George, 1992; Henderson, 1939; P. B. Miller, 1995).

Differences between athletic programs at historically black colleges and predominantly white institutions were almost as great as their similarities. In contrast to their white counterparts, black colleges lacked the funds necessary to hire large coaching staffs, purchase the latest equipment, and build elaborate athletic facilities. The financial circumstances of most black colleges made it impossible for them to outfit well-equipped teams like those at predominantly white institutions. Sport at historically black schools was also different from athletic programs at predominantly white institutions in that the exploits of many outstanding black college athletes never became known to a larger American audience. Although many of them became household names in the African American community, black college athletes were forced to perform behind segregated walls, which obscured their many exploits from public view and usually minimized the attention they received from the powerful white press (Ashe, 1988; Captain, 1991; Chalk, 1976; George, 1992; Henderson, 1939; Liberti, 1999, 2004; P. B. Miller, 1995; Rhoden, 2006; D. K. Wiggins, 2006).

The last major difference between the two forms of intercollegiate sport had to do with gender and participation in the Olympic Games. Few, if any, male athletes from black colleges participated in the Olympics. Male athletes from black colleges were left at home whereas John Taylor, John Woodruff, and other great performers from predominantly white universities traveled the world competing in the most famous of all athletic festivals. Why there were no male Olympians from black colleges is open to speculation, but it partly stemmed from the fact that predominantly white institutions recruited the best of the elite African American athletes (Ashe, 1988; Chalk, 1976; Henderson, 1939).

Ironically, African American female athletes who participated in the Olympic Games often came from black colleges rather than predominantly white universities. The first wave of African American women Olympians, including high jumper Alice Coachman, the first African American woman to capture an Olympic gold medal, had been members at various times of Cleveland Abbott's great track teams at Tuskegee Institute. The next outstanding group of African American women Olympians, including such great athletes as Wilma Rudolph, Barbara Jones, Martha Hudson, and Lucinda Williams, were products of Edward Temple's famous Tigerbelles track teams from Tennessee State University (Cahn, 1994; Gissendanner, 1994, 1996; W. Rudolph, 1977; Thaxton, 1970; D. K. Wiggins, 2006). The large number of women Olympians from historically black colleges perhaps resulted, as Susan Cahn has suggested, from the fact that African American women athletes were seemingly more accepted in their community than white women athletes were in their own. Although "middle-class white women" avoided track and field because of its reputation as a "masculine endeavor," African American women athletes were training and honing their talents under the watchful eyes of African American male coaches like Abbott and Temple (Cahn, 1994, p. 112). Unfortunately, the acceptance of African American women in a sport such as track and field "also reinforced disparaging stereotypes of black women as less womanly or feminine than white women" (Cahn, 1994, p. 112).

Holding out as much interest to the African American community as college sports were the all-black professional teams and leagues that were organized in early 20th-century America. A legacy from the late 19th century, a number of all-black teams and leagues were established in the three major sports of football, basketball, and baseball. Of these three, baseball was the most highly organized and popular among members of the African American community. The sport enthralled thousands of fans, who found the game a meaningful experience and pleasurable counterpoint to the drudgery of everyday life (Bruce, 1985; George, 1992; Holway, 1988; Lanctot, 1994, 2004; Lomax, 1998; Peterson, 1970, 1990; Rogosin, 1983; Ruck, 1987; White, 1996).

Black baseball's first successful league was formed in 1920 by Rube Foster, the once-great pitcher and manager of the Chicago American Giants. Foster organized the National Negro Baseball League (NNL), an organization patterned along the lines of Major League Baseball and composed of teams from Chicago, Detroit, St. Louis, Kansas City, and Indianapolis. The NNL collapsed under the weight of financial instability and a host of other problems in 1931, just three years after the rival Eastern Negro League (ENL) ceased operation. In 1933, a second NNL was organized and four years later was in competition with the newly created Negro American League (NAL) (Bruce, 1985; Holway, 1988; Lanctot, 1994, 2004; Lomax, 1998; Peterson, 1970; Rogosin, 1983; White, 1996).

These two leagues were the cornerstone of black baseball over the next two decades, representing at once some of the worst features of American racism and the best creative energy of the African American community. The NNL and NAL, although quite stable through much of the 1930s and 1940s, were never able to realize their financial potential, because clubs lacked ownership of baseball parks and were forced to engage in bidding wars for the services of outstanding players. Clark Griffith and other moguls in Major League Baseball never allowed black teams to establish significant profit margins because of the high rent they charged for the use of their ballparks. This situation caused a myriad of other problems, including inadequate working and living conditions for the league's African American players, who already suffered the indignities associated with being members of one of this country's least esteemed minority groups. The players were forced to make long, confined road trips in buses and beat-up old cars, stay in segregated and sometimes dilapidated hotels, and survive on limited meal money. They also had to cope

National Baseball Hall of Fame Library, Cooperstown, NY

Andrew "Rube" Foster, former pitcher and manager of the Chicago American Giants, formed the National Negro Baseball League (NNL) in 1920.

with the frustrations that resulted from being denied service at restaurants, hotels, and other public accomodations (Bruce, 1985; Holway, 1988; Lanctot, 1994, 2004; Peterson, 1970; Rogosin, 1983; White, 1996; D. K. Wiggins, 2006).

African American baseball players, however, overcame the numerous limitations of their separate leagues to carve out meaningful professional careers and more rewarding ways of life. Relative to many other members of the African American community, players in black baseball often enjoyed satisfying lives characterized by adulation and pleasurable experiences. The players who participated in black baseball were like most athletes in that they enjoyed the camaraderie of their teammates, the competition against other talented performers, and travel to different parts of the country. The more talented African American players participated in the greatest spectacle in black baseball, the annual East-West All-Star Game. Founded by Pittsburgh numbers king Gus Greenlee in 1933, the All-Star Game pitted the finest players in black baseball against each other, allowing Josh Gibson, Cool Papa Bell, Judy Johnson, Buck Leonard, Satchel Paige, and other legendary performers to showcase their talents to thousands of fans. Played in Chicago's Comiskey Park, the East-West All-Star Game was a grand social event in the African American community that drew literally thousands of fans each year from all across the country. The large attendance for the East-West All-Star Game, with estimates as high as 50,000 spectators for some of the contests, resulted in much needed profits for Greenlee and other entrepreneurs in black baseball. By 1935 half of the profits were placed into an emergency fund that would assist players who were not paid by financially strapped owners while at the same time protecting owners against extended rainouts (Brashler, 1978; Bruce, 1985; Holway, 1975, 1988; Peterson, 1970; Rogosin, 1983; White, 1996; D. K. Wiggins, 2006).

Campaigns to Reintegrate Lily-White Sport

Coinciding with the creation of all-black sporting organizations were bitter campaigns waged by various individuals and groups against the color line in white organized sport. Of all the groups that hammered away at organized sport for its exclusionary policies, perhaps none were more significant than sportswriters from such well-known African American weeklies as the *Baltimore Afro-American, Chicago Defender, New York Amsterdam News*, and *Pittsburgh Courier*. Clamoring loudly for an end to discrimination in baseball that symbolically, and in actual practice, was most important to the African American community, they led the battle against racism in white organized sport (Brower, 1940; Dorinson & Warmund, 1998; Reisler, 1994; Simons, 1985; Tygiel, 1983; D. K. Wiggins, 1983).

In the late 1930s, for example, the *Pittsburgh Courier's* Wendell Smith began a fervent campaign to eliminate the color barrier in Major League Baseball. From the moment he wrote his first article on baseball's color ban in 1938 to the ultimate integration of the sport some nine years later, Smith waged a fierce battle against the bureaucrats in the national game for their exclusion of African American players. Like other members of his race, Smith abhorred the discrimination in Major League Baseball, believing it symbolized the degraded status of African Americans in this country. He pointed out, through various means, that African Americans could not be considered true American citizens until they gained entry into organized baseball. Although realizing that participation in the national game would

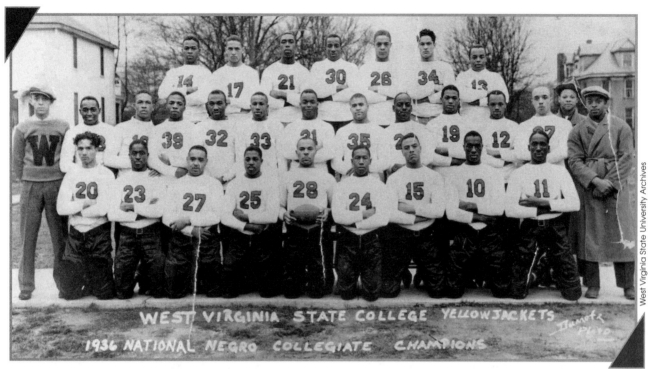

Wendell Smith (far left, in letterman's sweater) played baseball at West Virginia State College, where he was also the sports editor for the school newspaper. He went on to play an important role in the campaign to desegregate Major League Basesball.

not necessarily eradicate political and economic inequality, Smith believed that the desegregation of baseball would help give African Americans the sense of dignity and self-esteem essential for the ultimate elimination of racial discrimination in this country (Dorinson & Warmund, 1998; D. K. Wiggins, 1983).

Smith's campaign to desegregate organized baseball was remarkably aggressive and took many forms. He was suggesting by the beginning of 1939 that African Americans form a National Association for the Advancement of Colored People (NAACP) on behalf of African American players and attack the color line as vigorously as possible. Shortly after announcing his plans to organize an NAACP on behalf of African American players, Smith conducted an exclusive interview with the president of the National League, Ford Frick. The interview with Frick, which was characterized by the typical rhetoric voiced for years by leaders in Major League Baseball, provoked Smith into conducting a series of interviews with eight managers and 40 players in the National League to determine their views on African American players. Culminating in a series of articles in the *Courier* entitled "What Big Leaguers Think of Negro Baseball Players," the interviews were illuminating in that the only person who believed African Americans should be barred from organized baseball was Bill Terry, manager of the New York Giants (Dorinson & Warmund, 1998; D. K. Wiggins, 1983).

In the years immediately following the interviews with National League managers and players, Smith became even bolder in his campaign efforts. He admonished Clark Griffith, owner of the Washington Senators, for his blatantly racist view of African American ballplayers; called upon President Roosevelt to adopt a "fair employment policy" in baseball just as he had done in war industries and governmental agencies; helped arrange a meeting between the baseball commissioner,

Judge Kenesaw Mountain Landis, and the Black Newspaper Publishers' Association; assisted in arranging a tryout for three African American players with the Boston Red Sox; and suggested to Branch Rickey that Jackie Robinson would be the ideal player to integrate the national game (Dorinson & Warmund, 1998; D. K. Wiggins, 1983).

The Walls Come Tumbling Down

The efforts of Smith, as well as those of others involved in their own campaigns to integrate organized baseball, finally paid off in 1945 when Rickey signed Robinson to a contract with the Brooklyn Dodgers. The signing of Robinson was received with unabated enthusiasm by the African American community and immediately catapulted the former UCLA and Kansas City Monarch baseball star into the national limelight. Like Jesse Owens and Joe Louis before him, Robinson became a much needed example of achievement and symbol of possibility for African Americans. He had an uplifting effect on other members of his race by becoming a participant in the sport considered the great leveler in society and America's national pastime (Dorinson & Warmund, 1998; Falkner, 1995; Frommer, 1982; Polner, 1982; Rampersad, 1997; Robinson, 1972; Tygiel, 1983).

Another important outcome of Robinson's signing was that it paved the way for further desegregation of white organized sport at various levels of competition, a process that would not be completed until the latter half of the 1970s. Five months after obtaining the rights to Robinson, Rickey signed two more African American players, Roy Campanella and Don Newcombe, to contracts with the Dodgers. About a year later, Bill Veeck began integration of his Cleveland Indians organization by signing Larry Doby. Other major league teams were slow to follow the examples set by Rickey and Veeck, and integration in organized baseball proceeded at an uneven pace. During the latter part of the 1940s, absence of financial incentives, coupled with the racism and conservatism of baseball executives, limited the number of teams that were willing to take chances on African American players. By 1951, however, the pace of integration quickened as more teams were stimulated to seek African American talent due to the impressive performances of Robinson, Campanella, and others. Three years later, 12 of the 16 teams in Major League Baseball had African American players on their rosters. In 1959, the curtain finally dropped on baseball's color line for good when the Boston Red Sox promoted the talented African American infielder, Pumpsie Green, from their minor league affiliate in Minneapolis (Dorinson & Warmund, 1998; Moore, 1988; Tygiel, 1983).

National Baseball Hall of Fame Library, Cooperstown, NY

In 1945, Jackie Robinson signed a contract with the Brooklyn Dodgers, paving the way for further desegregation of organized sport.

The desegregation of Major League Baseball would be duplicated in other professional and amateur sports over the next two decades. For example, the year after the signing of Robinson by the Brooklyn Dodgers, the color line was broken in professional football. The Los Angeles Rams of the National Football League, under pressure to field African American players and fearful of losing its lease of the Los Angeles Coliseum, signed Kenny Washington and Woody Strode. The two African American stars were, ironically enough, former teammates of Robinson's at the University of California at Los Angeles. In the same year the NFL was integrated, the Cleveland Browns of the newly organized All-American Football Conference signed two African American stars, fullback Marion Motley of the University of Nevada at Reno and lineman Bill Willis of Ohio State University (Gems, 1988; Ross, 1999; T.G. Smith, 1988; Strode & Young, 1990). The American Bowling Congress allowed African Americans to use its lanes for the first time in 1949 (Lucas & Smith, 1978). A year later, Althea Gibson became the first African American to participate at Forest Hills in the United States Tennis Championships, and the color line was broken in the National Basketball Association when the Harlem Globetrotters' Nat "Sweetwater" Clifton signed with the New York Knicks and Chuck Cooper of Duquesne University inked a contract with the Boston Celtics (George, 1992; Gibson, 1958; Lucas & Smith, 1978; Salzberg, 1987). Art Dorrington became organized hockey's first black player in America when he signed with the Pennsylvania Johnstown Jets in 1952. Some 22 years after Dorrington took to the ice with the Johnstown Jets, Lee Elder became the first African American golfer to participate in the prestigious Masters Tournament in Augusta, Georgia (Dawkins & Kinloch, 2000; Lucas & Smith, 1978; McDaniel, 2000; Sinnette, 1998).

Perhaps the most significant battles against white organized sport took place in high school and intercollegiate athletics in the southern part of the United States. The famous 1954 *Brown vs. Board of Education* decision set in motion both individual and collective challenges to racial segregation in interscholastic sport. These challenges would ultimately result in the desegregation of various sports in high schools throughout the South. The first public school system in the South to integrate its athletic program following the *Brown vs. Board of Education* decision was the same public school system to establish the first separate athletic programs in the early years of the 20th century. Almost immediately after the decision, the District of Columbia announced that it had abolished its segregated physical education and athletic programs and merged them into two departments that included both black and white high schools. It also established an athletic conference made up of two seven-school leagues divided by geographical location rather than by the racial composition of the schools (Parris, 1955). The integration of high school athletics in the District of Columbia was duplicated in Baltimore and a few other selected areas, but it would be several years before a large number of other public high schools in the South took similar steps. The reason for the delay resulted from the mass resistance in much of the South to the *Brown vs. Board of Education* decision as evidenced by the creation of citizen's councils, passage of pro-segregation legislation, the substituting of private education for public schools, and an assortment of less obvious measures. Finally, however, as a consequence of further civil rights legislation, continuing struggle over equality of opportunity, and burgeoning black power movement during the 1960s, African American athletes were among the increasing number of African American students who found their way onto the campuses of predominantly white public schools in the South. Not surprisingly, it was in the border states that African American athletes seemingly found their first opportunities to play with and against white athletes. The state of Virginia, which gave us Jefferson, Hamilton, Madison, and other famous promoters of democratic principles, is a good case in point. As early as 1963, only a year after John F. Kennedy sent federal troops to ensure the entry of James Meredith into the University of Mississippi, African American football players Eric Burden and Victor Hundley integrated the predominantly white Newport News and Ferguson High Schools in the Hampton Roads area of Virginia (Johnson, 2004). The most famous instance of racial integration in Virginia high school athletics took place in 1971 at T. C. Williams High School in the City of Alexandria. Largely a result that year of the *Swann vs. Charlotte-Mecklenburg Board of Education* Supreme Court decision, which permitted busing of students to achieve racial integration and put teeth into the mandates of *Brown vs. Board of Education*, all students in Alexandria, both black and white, were placed in T. C. Williams High School. Immortalized in the 2000 movie *Remember the Titans*, the newly constituted school's football team would go undefeated and capture the Virginia State Championship. The most significant aspect of this story is that the head coach of the team was Herman Boone, an African American played so ably in the movie by Denzel Washington, who happened to be born the year of the *Brown vs. Board of Education* case (Bos, 1999).

Integration in high school athletics in the South would be duplicated in that region at the intercollegiate level of competition. For years, African Americans who participated in intercollegiate sport competed for either historically black colleges in the South or predominantly white universities in the North. The chance to compete in intercollegiate athletics for one of the schools in the prestigious Atlantic Coast (ACC), Southwestern (SWC), and Southeastern (SEC) conferences was out of the question for African Americans, who found themselves thwarted by southern racial policies and segregation (Ashe, 1988; Chalk, 1976; Henderson, 1939; Martin, 1993, 1996; D. K. Wiggins, 1991).

By the early 1960s, however, integration slowly began to take place in southern athletic conferences (Martin, 1993, 1996; Paul, McGhee, & Fant, 1984; Spivey, 1983; D. K. Wiggins, 1991). The *Brown v. Board of Education* decision in 1954, combined with the fledgling Civil Rights movement and the desire of educational institutions to achieve prominence in sport, resulted in the gradual integration of athletic programs at schools that had historically refused even to compete against African American athletes. In 1963, the color line was broken in the ACC by football player Darryl Hill of the University of Maryland (Spivey, 1983; D. K. Wiggins, 1991). Two years later, Texas Christian basketball player James Cash became the first African American athlete in the SWC (Martin, 1993; Pennington, 1987; Spivey, 1983; D. K. Wiggins, 1991).

The last major conference to integrate its sports programs was the SEC, a traditional stronghold of both athletic excellence and racial prejudice. Conference schools had received much notoriety for their athletic achievements through the years, but were equally famous for racial intolerance and acts of discrimination committed against African American athletes from northern institutions. Perhaps nowhere was the color line drawn tighter than in athletic programs of SEC schools, which operated against a backdrop of burning crosses and robed Klansmen as well as large stadiums intended for white players only. In spite of these circumstances, segregation in the SEC slowly toppled under the weight of the Civil Rights struggle just as it had in the ACC and SWC. The University of Kentucky, the northernmost school in the conference, led the fight against segregation when football coach Charlie Bradshaw signed African American high school stars Nat Northington and Greg Page in 1966. Over the next few years, African American athletes began to appear in different sports at other SEC schools, with Vanderbilt basketball coach C. M. Newton being the first person to recruit African Americans in significant numbers and the University of Mississippi, in 1971, being the last member of the conference to integrate (Martin, 1993, 1996; Paul et al., 1984).

African American Athletes and the Civil Rights Movement

Integration of southern athletic conferences shared the spotlight with black athletic disturbances that took place on predominantly white university campuses across the country. By the latter part of the 1960s, African American athletes were creating chaos on college campuses by becoming active participants in the Civil Rights movement and protesting racial discrimination in sport and society at large. Inspired by the examples set by such outspoken individuals as Jim Brown, Bill Russell, and Muhammad Ali, African American college athletes shed their traditional conservative approach to racial matters and vehemently protested everything from the lack of African American studies in the curriculum to the dearth of African American coaches and athletic administrators (Brown, 1964; Gorn, 1995; Russell, 1966; Smith, 2007). This path was sometimes paved with dire consequences, many African American athletes enduring the wrath of university administrations and jeopardizing their careers for speaking out on behalf of themselves and other members of their race. The protests also defied easy classification, as they took place on different-sized campuses, in both urban and rural settings, and from one end of the country to the other. Black athletic rebellions occurred, for example, on the campuses of Syracuse University; Oregon State University; Michigan State University; San Francisco State University; University of Washington; University of California, Berkeley; University of Kansas; University of Wyoming; University of Texas at El Paso; University of Arizona; and Oklahoma City University (Edwards, 1969, 1970; Hartmann, 2003; Scott, 1971; D. K. Wiggins, 1988, 1991, 1992).

Rebellious African American athletes sometimes took their protests off campus and into larger settings where they could better publicize their fight for racial equality. Certainly the most celebrated protest of this type was the proposed boycott of the 1968 Olympic Games in Mexico City. In the fall of 1967, Harry Edwards, then an instructor at San Jose State College, assembled a group of outstanding African American athletes who threatened to withdraw from the Games in Mexico City unless certain demands were met. The demands included the removal of Avery Brundage as president of the International Olympic Committee, restoration of Muhammad Ali's heavyweight boxing title, exclusion of Rhodesia and South Africa from Olympic competition, appointment of at least two African Americans to the United States Olympic Committee, complete desegregation of the New York Athletic Club (NYAC), and addition of at least two African American coaches to the men's Olympic track and field team (Bass, 2002; Edwards, 1969, 1980; Hartmann, 2003; Lomax, 2002; Sendler, 1969; Smith, 2007; Spivey, 1985; D. K. Wiggins, 1992).

Edwards and his band of African American athletes, who termed their movement the Olympic Project for Human Rights (OPHR), got their protest off to a
fast start by successfully organizing a boycott of the New York Athletic Club's 100th
Anniversary Track Meet in February, 1968. It became increasingly apparent following the NYAC boycott, however, that there would be no agreement among the
disgruntled African American athletes as to whether to boycott the Mexico City
games. As serious as they were about making a contribution to the Civil Rights movement and protesting racial discrimination, African American athletes found it impossible to forgo Olympic competition and not represent themselves and their
country against the best athletes in the world. For most of the African American athletes, the Olympic games were the ultimate in athletic competition, representing
years of preparation and bringing them potential glory and worldwide acclaim.
To sacrifice the potential acclaim was extremely difficult, even for the most racially
conscious African American athletes (Bass, 2002; Edwards, 1969, 1980; Hartmann,
2003; Johnson, 1972; Lomax, 2002; Smith, 2007; Spivey, 1985; D. K. Wiggins, 1992).

Academicians, Sports Performances, and Continued Evidence of Discrimination

The protests of African American athletes declined in number by the early 1970s.
Desegregation resulting from civil rights legislation of the 1960s, coupled with the
fledgling women's rights movement and problems associated with inflation and
unemployment, took some steam out of the black athletic revolt just as it had the
larger Black Power movement (Rader, 1983; Roberts & Olson, 1989). African American athletes continued to fight racial discrimination, but they increasingly became the topic of discussion among people of both races who had become sensi-
tized to racial issues emanating from the athletic protests of the previous decade.
One of the legacies of the athletic protest movement of the 1960s was that the
problems of African American athletes were made more visible to the American
public. The result was an outpouring of research studies and more popular essays
dealing with the various forms of discrimination committed against African American athletes rather than any substantive changes made in sport itself (Johnson &
Marple, 1973; Loy & McElvogue, 1970; Pascal & Rapping, 1970; Skully, 1974; Yetman
& Eitzen, 1972). Topics receiving a great deal of attention from academicians and
others interested in African American athletes were the phenomenon known as
stacking, unequal opportunities and inadequate reward structures in sport, and
differences in academic and sport performances between African American and
white athletes (Ashmore, 1982; Coakley, 1990; L. P. Davis, 1990; Edwards, 1972,
1973 A, B; Entine, 2000; Hoberman, 1997; Leonard, 1993; P. B. Miller, 1998; Price,
1997; Sailes, 1991; Smith, 1995; D. K. Wiggins, 1989).

A counterpart to this research were a number of efforts by various individuals and groups to insure the fair treatment of African American athletes and
eliminate the last vestiges of racial discrimination in sport. These efforts included
attempts to improve the academic preparation of African American college athletes and increase the number of African Americans in coaching and high-level
administrative positions within sport. In 1983, the National Collegiate Athletic Association (NCAA) attempted to remedy the poor academic performance and low
graduation rates of college athletes by passing a rule known as Proposition 48

(Coakley, 1990; Figler & Whitaker, 1991; Leonard, 1993). Implemented for the first time in 1986, Proposition 48 declared that all freshman athletes would be ineligible to participate on varsity sports teams if they had not achieved a score of 15 on the American College Test (ACT) or 700 on the Scholastic Aptitude Test (SAT). This rule allowed athletes who satisfied just one of these requirements to be accepted into college and be given athletic aid, but they were not allowed to practice with their team as freshmen and forfeited a year of athletic eligibility. In 1989, the NCAA toughened its standards even more by passing Proposition 42, which prohibited universities from providing athletic aid to athletes who did not meet both the GPA and test-score requirements (Coakley, 1990; Figler & Whitaker, 1991; Leonard, 1993).

Propositions 48 and 42 were ultimately designed to encourage high school athletes to commit themselves to academics as well as sports and to insure that universities recruited athletes who were prepared to do the work expected of all students in institutions of higher learning. The two propositions have seemingly had a positive effect at the high school level, where they have encouraged young athletes to take academics more seriously and fostered the development of academic support programs by coaches and sports administrators. Both propositions have been heavily criticized, however, for being unfair to African American athletes. (Coakley, 1990; Figler & Whitaker, 1991; Leonard, 1993). The passing of Proposition 48 had no sooner taken place than many African American educators and civil rights activists began lashing out at the rule for its discriminatory nature. The National Alliance of Black School Educators, the National Association for Equality of Opportunity in Higher Education, and such well-known African American leaders as Jesse Jackson, Benjamin Hooks, and Joseph Lowery were critical of the rule because they believed it was formulated without African American input. They also claimed that the ACT and SAT tests were culturally biased in favor of whites. It was their belief that the scores required for both tests were unfair to African American athletes because nearly 75% of African American students score below 15 on the ACT and more than 50% score below 700 on the SAT (Coakley, 1990; Figler & Whitaker, 1991; Leonard, 1993).

These charges, however, were countered by an equally sincere cadre of African Americans who argued that the propositions were not racially discriminatory and were a step in the right direction (Edwards, 1985; Hackley, 1983). Harry Edwards was a very outspoken advocate of the rule changes, and a substantial number of other African American academicians also supported the tougher academic requirements for student athletes. For instance, Lloyd V. Hackley (1983), chancellor of the University of Arkansas at Pine Bluff, had difficulty understanding how people could link Proposition 48 to racism. He implied that critics of the new rule were unintentionally "retarding the progress of deprived peoples" by claiming racism and arguing against higher academic standards (Hackley, 1983, p. 37). He believed that the only way to improve the academic performance of African American athletes was to support the tougher eligibility requirements included in Proposition 48 rather than decry the unfairness of testing procedures. Anything else was exploitation and nothing less (Hackley, 1983).

The African American community's concern about the academic preparation of African American athletes has been matched by its continuing frustration over the lack of African Americans in coaching and administrative positions within sport. Serious concern over the limited number of African Americans in coaching and administrative positions has been regularly expressed by African Americans since at least the latter half of the 1960s, but has become a cause celebre during the last few years. In 1987, Al Campanis, a top executive with the Los Angeles Dodgers, brought national attention to the topic when he suggested to Ted Koppel on the *Nightline* television program that the scarcity of African Americans in baseball management positions resulted from their lack of abilities: "I truly believe they may not have the necessities to be, let's say, a field manager or perhaps a general manager" (quoted in Chass, 1987, p. B 14). The public outcry following the interview was so great that Campanis was fired by the Dodgers, and Baseball Commissioner Peter Ueberoth hired Harry Edwards to study the problem of racism in Major League Baseball and increase the number of African Americans in management positions (Figler & Whitaker, 1991; Hoose, 1989).

The Campanis interview also helped spark formation of the now well-known Black Coaches Association (BCA). In 1988, two separate groups of socially conscious African American football and basketball coaches merged to form the BCA (Lederman, 1988). Since its inception, the BCA, under the leadership of Executive Director Rudy Washington, has addressed racial inequities in sport and fought to secure coaching and administrative positions for minorities at the high school, college, and professional levels of participation. The BCA has focused much of its attention on the NCAA and mounted an aggressive campaign against the organization in 1993 by boycotting a meeting of the National Association of Basketball Coaches and voicing its concerns about racial inequities in sport with the congressional Black Caucus. More recently, the BCA charged that researchers hired by the NCAA are racially biased, called for a reexamination of the previously mentioned academic standards established by the NCAA, and threatened another boycott in protest of the NCAA's refusal to restore to 14 the number of scholarships for teams in Division I basketball (Blum, 1993, 1994a,b; T. Davis, 1995).

One of the most intriguing concerns emanating from some African Americans, in addition to the questions about the dearth of African Americans in coaching and managerial positions, involves the negative portrayal of African American sports agents and their relationship to African American athletes. Kenneth L. Shropshire, in his *In Black and White: Race and Sports in America* (1996), argued persuasively that African American sports agents have suffered from criticism leveled against them by white sports agents and refusal of African American athletes to utilize their services. Although they have started to recruit more clients, African American sports agents have been slow to realize success because of what Shropshire terms the "negative race consciousness" historically prevalent in the African American community and the socialization process of African American athletes (p. 130). Like other African American businessmen of the past, says Shropshire, African American sports agents have lost African American clients because of the African American community's belief that members of their own race are less competent than whites "in positions requiring good faith and expertise" (p. 129). In addition, African American athletes have likely not sought the services of African American sports agents because of the controlling nature of their mostly white coaches and the "typical media portrayal" of sports agents as competent white males (p. 135).

Shropshire's analysis, which he provides in a wonderfully titled chapter, "The White Man's Ice Is Colder, His Sugar Sweeter, His Water Wetter, His Medicine

Better: Sports Agents," seems correct from a historical standpoint. Examples from the past would confirm the African American community's apparent lack of trust in their own professionals, both within and outside the world of sport. For instance, Edwin Bancroft Henderson lamented in the early part of the 20th century the fact that members of his own race preferred white officials in athletic contests between black schools (D. K. Wiggins, 1997). Henderson argued that the preference for white officials resulted from the African American community's belief that African American officials lacked the competence, trustworthiness, and ability to cope with the intense confrontations that invariably occurred in athletic contests.

> How it happens that our pigmy-minded, victory-at-any cost, blinded race people imagine the work of white officials superior to that done by Savoy, Gibson, Westmoreland, Washington, Abbott, Robinson, Pinder-hughes, Wright, Morrison, Trigg, Coppage, and Douglas, and many others is a puzzle to me.
>
> The only advantage arriving from the use of white officials is from the fact of the peculiar psychology that presents itself when white officials work which causes the poor driven cattle to become blinded to the same errors of commission and omission that would not have escaped had the officials been of the colored race. (Henderson, 1927, p. 20)

The link between Henderson and Shropshire is important because it makes clear that in regards to race, the more things change, the more they stay the same. Although more overt forms of discrimination against African American athletes have decreased over the last few decades, it is apparent that many people still hold to their racist beliefs and deep-seated stereotypical notions about African Americans in both sport and the larger society. More African Americans have assumed coaching positions and even find themselves in some upper-level management positions, and athletes such as Tiger Woods, Michael Jordan, and Venus and Serena Williams have realized enormous success in sport and parlayed that success into millions of dollars in endorsement money and become the darlings of corporate America. The same racialist thinking that resulted in years of segregation in sport, however, is still evident today. The belief that the success of African American athletes results from innate physical skills rather than dedication and hard work has been slow to die out in this country (Chass, 1987; L. P. Davis, 1990; Entine, 2000; Hoberman, 1997; P. B. Miller, 1998; Sailes, 1991; Shropshire & Smith, 1998; E. Smith, 1995; D. K. Wiggins, 1989). So has the notion that African American athletes, like other members of the African American community, are docile, savage, deceptive, childlike, or oversexed, or a combination of all the above. The simple truth is that people, both African American and white, continue to insist on differentiating between human beings based on race (L. P. Davis, 1990; Early, 1980; Entine, 2000; Herrnstein & Murray, 1994; P .B. Miller, 1998; Sailes, 1991; Shropshire & Smith, 1998; E. Smith, 1995; D. K. Wiggins, 1989). Although the scientific literature does not support such claims, people are still convinced that a person's color defines his or her very being and separates the person from others both emotionally and physically. This is what accounts for the attraction of interracial athletic contests, but also explains the racially insensitive remarks uttered by well-known sports prognosticators and top-level baseball executives (Early, 1989).

Based on the historical experiences of African American athletes, only time will tell when the insensitive remarks will finally cease and the last vestiges of racism will be eliminated from sport in this country. The involvement of African Americans in sport has been a turbulent one at best, characterized by major successes as well as a host of problems stemming from continual prejudices and unfounded beliefs in the inequality of the races. As has been shown, African American athletes during the second half of the 19th century realized many triumphs on the athletic field only to have the door of opportunity closed on them by believers in Jim Crow and white supremacy. This process was repeated in one form or another throughout much of the first half of this century and beyond. Although great sums of money and adulation were realized by a select number of African American athletes, the large majority of them were forced either to endure the racial discrimination evident in white-controlled sport or to retreat into all-black sporting organizations where they could realize success among their own group. This was unfortunate because African American athletes, like their white counterparts, merely wanted the opportunity to compete against the best athletes regardless of color and realize the numerous benefits resulting from successful participation in sport. In many regards, the critical events for African American athletes often took place off the field, where their physical abilities were unable to shield them from the racial discrimination in American society. Perhaps the best that can be hoped for at this point in time is that African Americans and whites continue to work together so that the racial mountain can finally be scaled in sport and the larger American society (Hoberman, 1997).

▲▼ Suggested Readings ▲▼

Bass, A. (2002). *Not the triumph but the struggle: The 1968 Olympics and the making of the Black athlete.* Minneapolis: University of Minnesota Press.

Hartmann, D. (2003). *Race, culture, and the revolt of the Black athlete: The 1968 Olympic protests and their aftermath.* Chicago: The University of Chicago Press.

Hoberman, J. (1997). *Darwin's athletes: How sport has damaged Black America and preserved the myth of race.* Boston: Houghton Mifflin.

Miller, P. B. & Wiggins, D. K. (Eds.) (2004). *Sport and the color line: Black athletes and race relations in twentieth-century America.* NY: Routledge.

Rhoden, W. C. (2006). *Forty million dollar slaves: The rise, fall, and redemption of the Black athlete.* NY: Crown Publishers.

Ross, C. K. (ed.) (2004). *Race and sport: The struggle for equality on and off the field.* Jackson: University Press of Mississippi.

Shropshire, K. L. (1996). *In black and white: Race and sports in America.* NY: New York University Press.

Wiggins, D. K. (Ed.) *Out of the shadows: A biographical history of African American athletes.* Fayetteville: The University of Arkansas Press, 2006.

Wiggins, D. K., & Miller, P. B. (2003). *The unlevel playing field: A documentary history of the African American experience in sport.* Urbana: University of Illinois Press.

▲▼ Study Questions ▲▼

1. What societal factors contributed to the elimination of African Americans from sport during the latter stages of the 19th century?

2. Why were a select number of African American athletes allowed to continue participating in professional boxing, predominantly white intercollegiate sport, and the Olympic Games during the first half of the 20th century?

3. Why did the first African American female Olympians come from historically black colleges? Why did the first African American male Olympians come from predominantly white universities?

4. What were the differences and similarities between sport in historically black colleges and sport in predominantly white universities during the first half of the 20th century?

5. Why was the integration of organized baseball so important to the African American community and society at large?

6. Why did Harry Edwards and African American athletes propose a boycott of the 1968 Olympic Games in Mexico City?

7. Why, according to some scholars, have African American athletes been reluctant to employ African American sports agents?

References

Ashe, A. (1988). *A hard road to glory: A history of the African American athlete, 1619 to present* (3 Vols.). New York: Warner Books.

Baker, W. J. (1986). *Jesse Owens: An American life.* New York: The Free Press.

Barnett, C. R. (1983). The finals: West Virginia's Black Basketball Tournament, 1925–1957. *Goldenseal, 9:* 30–39.

Bass, A. (2002). *Not the triumph but the struggle: The 1968 Olympics and the making of the Black athlete.* Minneapolis: University of Minnesota Press.

Behee, J. (1974). *Hail to the victors! Black athletes at the University of Michigan.* Ann Arbor, MI: Swink Tuttle Press.

Betts, J. R. (1974). *America's sporting heritage, 1850–1950.* Boston, MA: Addison Wesley.

Blum, D. E. (1993, October 27). Black coaches head to Congress to press charge of bias in college sport. *The Chronicle of Higher Education,* p. A36.

Blum, D. E. (1994a, January 26). Battle over an additional scholarship symbolizes a much larger struggle. *The Chronicle of Higher Education,* pp. A39–A40.

Blum, D. E. (1994b, March 30). Black coaches and NCAA agree to discuss disputed rules. *The Chronicle of Higher Education,* p. A38.

Bos, C. D. (1999). *Remember the Titans: A story of school integration.* Retrieved October 15, 2005, from http://www.lawbuzz.com/movies/remember_the_titans/remember_the_titans.htm

Brailsford, D. (1988). *Bareknuckles: A social history of prize fighting.* Cambridge: LutterworthPress.

Brashler, W. (1978). *Josh Gibson: A life in the Negro leagues.* New York: Harper & Row.

Brower, W. A. (1940). Has professional football closed the door? *Opportunity, 18,* 375–377.

Brower, W. A. (1941). Prejudice in sports. *Opportunity, 19,* 260–263.

Brown, J. (1964). *Off my chest.* New York: Doubleday and Company.

Bruce, J. (1985). *The Kansas City Monarchs: Champions of Black baseball.* Lawrence: University Press of Kansas.

Cahn, S. K. (1994). *Coming on strong: Gender and sexuality in twentieth-century women's sport.* Cambridge, MA: Harvard University Press.

Capeci, D. J., & Wilkerson, M. (1983). Multifarious hero: Joe Louis, American society and race relations during world crisis, 1935–45. *Journal of Sport History, 10,* 525.

Captain, G. (1991). Enter ladies and gentlemen of color: Gender, sport and the ideal of African American manhood and womanhood during the late nineteenth and early twentieth centuries. *Journal of Sport History, 18,* 81–102.

Carroll, J. M. (1992). *Fritz Pollard: Pioneer in racial advancement.* Urbana: University of Illinois Press.

Carroll, J. M. (2004). Fritz Pollard and integration in early professional football. In C. K. Ross (Ed.). *Race and sport: The struggle for equality on and off the field* (pp. 3–25). Jackson: University Press of Mississippi.

Cashmore, E. (1982). *Black sportsmen.* London: Routledge & Kegan Paul.

Chalk, O. (1976). *Black college sport.* New York: Dodd Mead.

Chass, M. (1987, April 9). Campanis is out: Racial remarks cited by Dodgers. *New York Times,* B13–B14.

Coakley, J. (1990). *Sport in society: Issues and controversies* (4th ed.). St. Louis, MO: Times Mirror/Mosby.

Cochran, T. C., & Miller, W. (1961). *The age of enterprise.* New York: Harper & Row.

Cone, C. B. (1982). The Molineaux Cribb fight, 1918: "Wuz

Tom Molineaux robbed?" *Journal of Sport History, 9,* 83–91.

Davis, J. P. (1966). The Negro in American sports. In J. P. Davis (Ed.), *The American Negro reference book* (pp. 775–825). Upper Saddle River, NJ: Prentice Hall.

Davis, L. P. (1990). The articulation of difference: White preoccupation with the question of racially linked genetic differences among athletes. *Sociology of Sport Journal, 7,* 179–187.

Davis, T. (1995). The myth of the superspade: The persistence of racism in college athletics. *Fordham Urban Law Journal, 22,* 615–698.

Dawkins, M. P., & Kinloch, G. C. (2000). *African American golfers during the Jim Crow era.* Westport, CT: Praeger.

Demas, L. (2004). The Brown Bomber's dark day: Louis-Schmeling I and America's Black hero. *Journal of Sport History, 31,* 253–271.

Dorinson, J., & Warmund, J. (Eds.). (1998). *Jackie Robinson: Race, sports, and the American Dream.* New York: M. E. Sharpe.

Early, G. (1989). *Tuxedo junction: Essays on American culture.* New York: The Ecco Press.

Edmonds, A. O. (1973). The second Louis-Schmeling fight: Sport, symbol and culture. *Journal of Popular Culture, 7,* 42–50.

Edwards, H. (1969). *The revolt of the Black athlete.* New York: The Free Press.

Edwards, H. (1970). *Black students.* New York: The Free Press.

Edwards, H. (1972). The myth of the racially superior athlete. *Intellectual Digest, 2,* 8–60.

Edwards, H. (1973a). The sources of the Black athlete's superiority. *The Black Scholar, 3,* 2–41.

Edwards, H. (1973b, November). 20th-century gladiators for white America. *Psychology Today, 7,* 43–52.

Edwards, H. (1980). *The struggle that must be: An autobiography.* New York: MacMillan.

Edwards, H. (1985). Educating Black athletes. In D. Chu, J. O. Segrave, & B. J. Becker (Eds.), *Sport and Higher Education* (pp. 373–384). Champaign, IL: Human Kinetics Publishers. (Reprinted from *The Atlantic Monthly, 252,* 31–38.)

Entine, J. (2000). *Taboo: Why Black athletes dominate sports and why we are afraid to talk about it.* New York: Public Affairs Press.

Erenberg, L. (2006). *The greatest fight of our generation: Louis vs. Schmeling.* New York: Oxford University Press.

Falkner, D. (1995). *Great time coming: The life of Jackie Robinson from baseball to Birmingham.* New York: Simon & Schuster.

Farr, F. (1964). *Black champion: The life and times of Jack Johnson.* New York: Charles Scribner's Sons.

Figler, S. K., & Whitaker, G. (1991). *Sport & play in American life: A textbook in the sociology of sport* (2nd ed.). Dubuque, IA: Wm. C. Brown.

Fishman, G. (1969). Paul Robeson's student days and the fight against racism at Rutgers. *Freedomways, 9,* 211–229.

Fleischer, N. S. (1938). *The story of the Negro in the prize ring from 1782 to 1938* (3 Vols.). New York: The Ring Book Shop.

Frazer, George MacDonald (1999). *Black Ajax.* New York: Carroll & Graf Publishers.

Frommer, H. (1982). *Rickey and Robinson: The men who broke baseball's color barrier.* New York: MacMillan.

Gems, G. R. (1988). Shooting stars: The rise and fall of Blacks in professional football. *Professional Football Research Association Annual Bulletin,* pp. 1–18.

Gems, G. R. (1995). Blocked shot: The development of basketball in the African American community of Chicago. *Journal of Sport History, 22,* 135–148.

George, N. (1992). *Elevating the game: The history & aesthetics of Black men in basketball.* New York: Simon & Schuster.

Gibson, A. (1958). *I always wanted to be somebody.* New York: Harper and Brothers.

Gilliam, D. B. (1976). *Paul Robeson: All-American.* Washington, DC: New Republic Book Company.

Gilmore, A. T. (1975). *Bad nigger! The national impact of Jack Johnson.* Port Washington, NY: Kennikat.

Gissendanner, C. H. (1994). African American women and competitive sport, 1920–1960. In S. Birrell & C. Cole (Eds.), *Women, sport, and culture* (pp. 81–92). Champaign, IL: Human Kinetics Publishers.

Gissendanner, C. H. (1996). African American women Olympians: The impact of race, gender, and class ideologies, 1932–1968. *Research Quarterly for Exercise and Sport, 67,* 172–182.

Goodman, M. H. (1980). The Moor vs. Black Diamond. *Virginia Cavalcade, 29,* 164–173.

Gorn, E. J. (1994). *The manly art: Bareknuckle prizefighting in America.* Ithaca, NY: Cornell University Press.

Gorn, E. J. (Ed.). (1995). *Muhammad Ali: The people's champ.* Urbana: University of Illinois Press.

Gould, T. (2003). *For Gold and glory: Charlie Wiggins and the African-American racing car circuit.* Bloomington: Indiana University Press.

Grundman, A. H. (1979). Image of intercollegiate sports and the Civil Rights movement: A historian's view. *Arena Review, 3,* 17–24.

Grundy, P. (2001). *Learning to win: Sports, education, and social change in twentieth-century North Carolina.* Chapel Hill: University of North Carolina Press.

Hackley, L. V. (1983). We need to educate our athletes! *The Black Collegian, 13,* 35–37.

Hartmann, D. (2003). *Race, culture, and the revolt of the Black athlete: The 1968 Olympic protests and their aftermath.* Chicago, IL: The University of Chicago Press.

Henderson, E. B. (1927, January). Sports. *The Messenger, 9,* 20.

Henderson, J. H. M., & Henderson, B. F. (1985). *Molder of men: Portrait of a grand old man-Edwin Bancroft Henderson.* Washington, D.C.: Vantage.

Herrnstein, R., & Murray, C. (1994). *The bell curve: Intelligence and class structure in American life.* New York: Basic Books.

Hietala, T. R. (2002). *The Fight of the Century: Jack Johnson, Joe Louis, and the struggle for racial equality.* New York: M. E. Sharpe.

Hoberman, J. (1997). *Darwin's athletes: How sport has dam-*

aged Black America and preserved the myth of race. Boston: Houghton Mifflin.

Holway, J. B. (1975). *Voices from the great Black baseball leagues.* New York: Harper and Row.

Holway, J. B. (1988). *Blackball stars: Negro league pioneers.* Westport, CT: Meckler Books.

Hoose, P. (1989). *Necessities: Racial barriers in American sports.* New York: Random House.

Hotaling, E. (1995). *They're off: Horse racing at Saratoga.* Syracuse, NY: Syracuse University Press.

Hotaling, E. (2005). *Wink: The incredible life and epic journey of Jimmy Winkfield.* New York: McGraw-Hill.

Johnson, D. (2004, May 23). From courts to courts. *Daily Press.* Retrieved October 15, 2005, from http://www.daily press.com/news/dp-brown23,0,2789860.story

Johnson, N. R., & Marple, D. P. (1973). Racial discrimination in professional basketball. *Sociological Focus, 6,* 6–18.

Johnson, W. O. (1972). *All that glitters is not gold: The Olympic game.* New York: Putnam.

Kane, M. (1971, January 18). An assessment of Black is best. *Sports Illustrated, 34,* 783.

Kaye, A. M. (2004). *The pussycat of prizefighting: Tiger Flowers and the politics of Black celebrity.* Athens: The University of Georgia Press.

Lanctot, N. (1994). *Fair dealing and clean playing: The Hilldale Club and the development of Black professional baseball, 1910–1932.* Jefferson, NC: McFarland.

Lanctot, N. (2004). *Negro League Baseball: The rise and ruin of a Black Institution.* Philadelphia: University of Pennsylvania Press.

Lederman, D. (1988, April 13). Black coaches' movement gains momentum: First annual meeting attracts 300. *The Chronicle of Higher Education,* pp. 43–44.

Leonard, W. (1993). *A sociological perspective of sport.* New York: Macmillan.

Liberti, R. (1999). We were ladies, we just played basketball like boys: African American womanhood and competitive basketball at Bennett College, 1928–1942. *Journal of Sport History, 26,* 567–584.

Liberti, R. (2004). Fostering community consciousness: The role of women's basketball at Black colleges and universities, 1900–1950. In C. K. Ross (Ed.), *Race and sport: The struggle for equality on and off the field* (pp. 40–58). Jackson: University Press of Mississippi.

Logan, R. W. (1957). *The Negro in the United States.* Princeton: D. Van Nostrand.

Logan, R. W. (1965). *The betrayal of the Negro from Rutherford B. Hayes to Woodrow Wilson.* New York: Collier Books.

Lomax, M. (1998). Black entrepreneurship in the national pastime: The rise of semiprofessional baseball in Black Chicago, 1890–1915. *Journal of Sport History, 25,* 43–64.

Lomax, M. E. (2002). Revisiting the revolt of the Black athlete: Harry Edwards and the making of the new African-American sport studies. *Journal of Sport History, 29,* 469–479.

Lowenfish, L. (1978). Sport, race, and the baseball business: The Jackie Robinson story revisited. *Arena Review, 2,* 216.

Loy, J. W., & McElvogue, J. F. (1970). Racial segregation in American sport. *International Review of Sport Sociology, 5,* 523.

Lucas, J. A., & Smith, R. A. (1978). *Saga of American sport.* Philadelphia: Lea & Febiger.

Malloy, J. (1995). *Sol White's history of colored baseball with other documents on the early Black game, 1886–1936.* Lincoln: University of Nebraska Press.

Margolick, D. (2005). *Beyond glory: Joe Louis vs. Max Schmeling, and a world on the brink.* New York: Alfred A. Knopf.

Martin, C. H. (1993). Jim Crow in the gymnasium: The integration of college basketball in the American south. *The International Journal of the History of Sport, 10,* 68–86.

Martin, C. H. (1996). Racial change and bigtime college football in Georgia: The age of segregation, 1892–1957. *The Georgia Historical Quarterly, 80,* 532–562.

McDaniel, P. (2000). *Uneven lies: The heroic story of African Americans in golf.* Greenwich, CT: The American Golfer.

McKinney, G. B. (1976). Negro professional baseball players in the upper south in the gilded age. *Journal of Sport History, 3,* 273–280.

McRae, D. (2002). *Heroes without a country: America's betrayal of Joe Louis and Jesse Owens.* New York: Ecco.

Mead, C. (1985). *Champion Joe Louis: Black hero in white America.* New York: Charles Scribner's Sons.

Meier, A., & Rudwick, E. M. (1963). *From plantation to ghetto.* New York: Hill and Wang.

Miller, L. (1927). The unrest among college students: Kansas University. *Crisis, 34,* 187–188.

Miller, P. B. (1991). Harvard and the color line: The case of Lucien Alexis. In R. Story (Ed.), *Sports in Massachusetts: Historical essays* (pp. 137–158). Westfield, MA.

Miller, P. B. (1995). To bring the race along rapidly: Sport, student culture, and educational mission at historically Black colleges during the interwar years. *History of Education Quarterly, 35,* 111–133.

Miller, P. B. (1998). The anatomy of scientific racism: Racialist responses to Black athletic achievement. *Journal of Sport History, 15,* 119–151.

Miller, P. B., & Wiggins, D. K. (Eds.) (2004). *Sport and the color line: Black athletes and race relations in twentieth-century America.* New York: Routledge.

Moore, J. T. (1988). *Pride against prejudice: The biography of Larry Doby.* New York: Praeger.

Paino, D. (2001). Hoosiers in a different light: Forces of change v. the power of nostalgia. *Journal of Sport History, 28,* 63–80.

Parris, W. A. (1955). Integration of athletics in the District of Columbia public high schools. *The Negro History Bulletin, 19,* 14–15.

Pascal, A. H., & Rapping, L. A. (1972). *Racial discrimination in organized baseball.* Santa Monica, CA: Rand Corporation.

Paul, J., McGhee, R. V., & Fant, H. (1984). The arrival and ascendance of Black athletes in the Southeastern Conference, 1966–1980. *Phylon, 45,* 284–297.

Pennington, R. (1987). *Breaking the ice: The racial integration of Southwest Conference football.* Jefferson, NC: McFarland.

Peterson, R. W. (1970). *Only the ball was white.* Englewood Cliffs, NJ: Prentice Hall.

Peterson, R. W. (1990). *Cages to jumpshots: Pro basketball's early years*. New York: Oxford University Press.

Pierce, R. B. (2000). More than a game: The political meaning of high school basketball in Indianapolis. *Journal of Urban History, 27*, 3–23.

Polner, M. (1982). *Branch Rickey: A biography*. New York: Atheneum Publishing Company.

Price, S. L. (1997a, December 8). Is it in the genes? *Sports Illustrated, 87*, 53–55.

Price, S. L. (1997b). Whatever happened to the white athlete? *Sports Illustrated, 87*, 31–52.

Rader, B. (1983). *American sports: From the age of folk games to the age of spectators*. Englewood Cliffs, NJ: Prentice Hall.

Rampersad, A. (1997). *Jackie Robinson: A biography*. New York: Alfred A. Knopf.

Rayl, S. (1996). *The New York renaissance professional Black basketball team, 1923–1950*. Unpublished doctoral dissertation, Pennsylvania State University, State College, PA.

Reisler, J. (1994). *Black writers/Black baseball: An anthology of articles from Black sportswriters who covered the Negro leagues*. Jefferson, NC: McFarland.

Rhoden, William C. (2006). *Forty million dollar slaves: The rise, fall, and redemption of the Black athlete*. New York: Crown Publishers.

Ritchie, A. (1988). *Major Taylor: The extraordinary career of a champion bicycle racer*. San Francisco, CA: Bicycle Books.

Roberts, R. (1983). *Papa Jack: Jack Johnson and the era of white hopes*. New York: The Free Press.

Roberts, R., & Olson, J. (1989). *Winning is the only thing: Sports in America since 1945*. Baltimore: The Johns Hopkins University Press.

Robinson, J. (1972). *I never had it made*. New York: G. P. Putnam.

Rogosin, D. (1983). *Invisible men: Life in baseball's Negro leagues*. New York: Atheneum Publishers.

Ross, C. K. (1999). *Outside the lines: African Americans and the integration of the National Football League*. New York: New York University Press.

Rowe, J. (1988, April). The Greek chorus: Jimmy the Greek got it wrong but so did his critics. *The Washington Monthly, 20*, 31–34.

Ruck, R. (1987) *Sandlot seasons: Sport in Black Pittsburgh*. Urbana: University of Illinois Press.

Rudolph, J. W. (1979). Tom Molineaux: America's "almost" champion. *American History Illustrated, 14*, 8–14.

Rudolph, W. (1977). *Wilma*. New York: New American Library.

Russell, B. (1966). *Go up for glory*. New York: Coward-McCann.

Sailes, G. (1991). The myth of Black sports supremacy. *Journal of Black Studies, 21*, 480–487.

Salzberg, C. (1987). *From set shot to slam dunk*. New York: E. P. Dutton.

Sammons, J. T. (1988). *Beyond the ring: The role of boxing in American society*. Urbana: University of Illinois Press.

Scott, J. (1971). *The athletic revolution*. New York: The Free Press.

Sendler, D. (1969). The Black athlete—1968. In P. W. Romero (Ed.), *In Black America, 1968, The year of awakening* (pp. 325–338). New York: Publishers Company.

Shropshire, K. L. (1996). *In Black and white: Race and sports in America*. New York: New York University Press.

Shropshire, K. L. (2007). *Being Sugar Ray: The life of Sugar Ray Robinson, America's greatest boxer and first celebrity athlete*. New York: Basic Civitas Books.

Simons, W. (1985). Jackie Robinson and the American mind: Journalistic perceptions of the reintegration of baseball. *Journal of Sport History, 12*, 39–64.

Skully, G. W. (1974). Discrimination: The case of baseball. In R. G. Noll (Ed.), *Government and the sport business* (pp. 221–247). Washington, DC: The Brookings Institute.

Smith, E. (1995). The self-fulfilling prophecy: Genetically superior African American athletes. *Humboldt Journal of Social Relations, 21*, 139–163.

Smith, T. G. (1988). Outside the pale: The exclusion of Blacks from the National Football League. *Journal of Sport History, 15*, 255–281.

Smith, T., & Steele, D. (2007). *Silent gesture: The autobiography of Tommie Smith*. Philadelphia: Temple University Press.

Somers, D. A. (1972). *The rise of sport in New Orleans, 1850–1900*. Baton Rouge: Louisiana State University Press.

Spivey, D. (1983). The Black athlete in big-time intercollegiate sports, *1941–1968. Phylon, 44*, 116–125.

Spivey, D. (1985). Black consciousness and Olympic protest movement, 1964–1980. In D. Spivey (Ed.), *Sport in America: New historical perspectives* (pp. 239–262). Westport, CT: Greenwood Press.

Spivey, D. (1988). End Jim Crow in sports: The protest at New York University, 1940–1941. *Journal of Sport History, 15*, 282–303.

Spivey, D., & Jones, T. (1975). Intercollegiate athletic servitude: A case study of the Black Illinois student-athletes, 1931–1967. *Social Science Quarterly, 55*, 939–947.

Strode, W., & Young, S. (1990). *Goal dust*. Lanham, MD: Madison Books.

Taylor, M. M. (1928). *The fastest bicycle rider in the world*. Worcester, MA: Wormley Publishing Company.

Thaxton, N. (1970). *A documentary analysis of competitive track and field for women at Tuskegee Institute and Tennessee State University*. Unpublished doctoral dissertation, Springfield College, Springfield, MO.

Tygiel, J. (1983). *Baseball's great experiment: Jackie Robinson and his legacy*. New York: Oxford University Press.

Ward, G. C. (2004). *Unforgivable Blackness: The rise and fall of Jack Johnson*. New York: Alfred A. Knopf.

Wiggins, D. K. (1983). Wendell Smith, the *Pittsburgh Courier Journal* and the campaign to include Blacks in organized baseball, 1933–1945. *Journal of Sport History, 10*, 5–29.

Wiggins, D. K. (1985). Peter Jackson and the elusive heavyweight championship: A Black athlete's struggle against the late nineteenth century color-line. *Journal of Sport History, 12*, 143–168.

Wiggins, D. K. (1988). The future of college athletics is at stake: Black athletes and racial turmoil on three predominantly white university campuses, 1968–1972. *Journal of Sport History, 15*, 304–333.

Wiggins, D. K. (1989). Great speed but little stamina: The

historical debate over Black athletic superiority. *Journal of Sport History, 16,* 158–185.

Wiggins, D. K. (1991). Prized performers, but frequently overlooked students: The involvement of Black athletes in intercollegiate sports on predominantly white university campuses, 1890–1972. *Research Quarterly for Exercise and Sport, 62,* 164–177.

Wiggins, D. K. (1992). The year of awakening: Black athletes, racial unrest, and the Civil Rights movement of 1968. *The International Journal of the History of Sport, 9,* 188–208.

Wiggins, D. K. (1997). Edwin Bancroft Henderson, African American athletes, and the writing of sport history. In D. K. Wiggins, *Glory bound: Black athletes in a white America* (pp. 221–240). NY: Syracuse University Press.

Wiggins, D. K. (1999). Edwin Bancroft Henderson: Physical educator, civil rights activist, and chronicler of African American athletes. *Research Quarterly for Exercise and Sport, 70,* 91–112.

Wiggins, David K. (2006). *Out of the shadows: A biographical history of African American athletes.* Fayetteville: The University of Arkansas Press.

Wiggins, D. K., & Miller, P. B. (2003). *The unlevel playing field: A documentary history of the African American experience in sport.* Urbana: University of Illinois Press.

Wiggins, W. H. (1971). Jack Johnson as bad nigger: The folklore of his life. *Black Scholar, 2,* 4–19.

Wolters, R. (1975). *The new Negro on campus: Black college rebellions of the 1920s.* Princeton: Princeton University Press.

Woodward, C. V. (1966). *The strange career of Jim Crow.* New York: Oxford University Press.

Yetman, N., & Eitzen, J. D. (1972). Black Americans in sport: Unequal opportunity for equal ability. *Civil Rights Digest, 5,* 20–34.

Young, A. S. (1963). *Negro firsts in sports.* Chicago: Johnson Publishing.

Zang, D. W. (1995). *Fleet Walker's divided heart: The life of baseball's first Black major leaguer.* Lincoln: University of Nebraska Press.

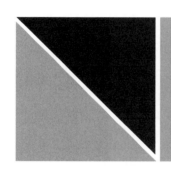

SECTION TWO
Social Justice and Cultural Concerns

E ach of the contributors of the three chapters in Section 2 can say, "Been there, done that!" when it comes to issues and concerns dealing with social justice for African American college athletes. Roberta Abney's thoughtful essay, "African American Women in Intercollegiate Coaching and Athletic Administration: Unequal Access," reminds us that the literature dealing with African American women athletes repeatedly shows that "racist, sexist, and political roadblocks" will be encountered by those in pursuit of careers as coaches or athletic administrators. Abney cannot promise very much. Without a staunch commitment to advancement by academic leadership (university presidents and athletic directors) at an institutional or league level, largely redoubling current effort toward increasing the proportion of qualified minority and female administrators and coaches, gains are apt to remain limited. And even those gains will be realized mostly in dead-end positions, clustered into staffing assignments and in invisible, smaller programs.

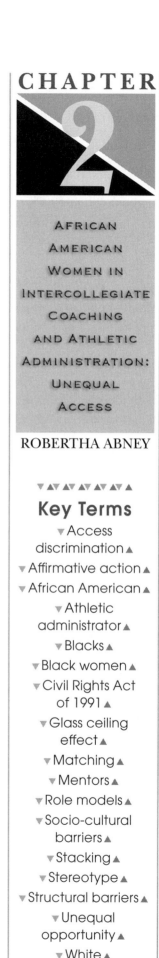

CHAPTER 2

AFRICAN AMERICAN WOMEN IN INTERCOLLEGIATE COACHING AND ATHLETIC ADMINISTRATION: UNEQUAL ACCESS

ROBERTHA ABNEY

▼▲▼ ▲▼ ▲▼ ▲▼ ▲▼ ▲

Key Terms

▼ Access discrimination ▲
▼ Affirmative action ▲
▼ African American ▲
▼ Athletic administrator ▲
▼ Blacks ▲
▼ Black women ▲
▼ Civil Rights Act of 1991 ▲
▼ Glass ceiling effect ▲
▼ Matching ▲
▼ Mentors ▲
▼ Role models ▲
▼ Socio-cultural barriers ▲
▼ Stacking ▲
▼ Stereotype ▲
▼ Structural barriers ▲
▼ Unequal opportunity ▲
▼ White ▲

Abstract ▼ Is access to opportunities as head coach and top-level administrative positions in intercollegiate athletics disparate for African American women? With the increase of African American sport participants in intercollegiate athletics, the use of affirmative action guidelines, and the adoption of the Civil Rights Act of 1991 and Title IX, one would anticipate an increase in the status of African American females as top-level administrators and head coaches in national sport associations and organizations, conference offices, and intercollegiate athletic departments. Unfortunately, that has not occurred. African American male and female coaches and administrators have not attained parity and remain underrepresented in college athletics (Brooks & Althouse, 1993).

Introduction

The paucity of African American women in high positions from head coaches to athletics directors has been described as simply appalling (Lapchick, 2005). In 2001–2002, African American women represented fewer than 2% of coaches and fewer than 1% of athletic director and associate athletic director positions (NCAA, 2001–02). In January 2005, National Collegiate Athletic Association (NCAA) President Myles Brand addressed the lack of representation for women and people of color as athletic directors and head coaches (Lapchick, 2005). Brand (2005) described the situation as bad, stating that the search process used to identify individuals for upper-level positions is not universally open and fair (NCAA News, 2005).

Lapchick's 2004 Racial and Gender Report Card for College Sport revealed several interesting facts about the hiring of women and minorities in intercollegiate athletics positions:

▼ The greatest prospects of professional opportunities in sport for women and people of color exist in college sport, more so than in all of the professional sports combined.

▼ College sport received a B– for race and a B+ for gender.

▼ NCAA member institutions improved their record for gender hiring practices but lost ground on hiring practices by race.

The purpose of this chapter is to examine the socio-cultural and structural barriers that effectively deny access and opportunities for African American women to advance up the career ladder as head coaches and top-level athletic administrators within collegiate national governing associations, sport organizations, conference offices, and intercollegiate athletics departments. Suggestions, strategies, and recommendations for change will be provided.

Historically, there have been socio-cultural and structural barriers that have been identified as hindrances to career advancement for African American women as head coaches and top-level athletic administrators in sport: such as: (a) attitude of society toward minorities and women, (b) poor media images, (c) racism, (d) sexism, (e) lack of role models, (f) lack of mentors, (g) lack of support systems, (h) dead-end positions, (i) politics, (j) glass ceiling effect, (k) stereotypes, (l) stacking/position clustering, (m) lack of access to career resources; (n) lack of access to networks, (o) constant questioning of abilities, (p) people who resented women being in key positions, (q) lack of respect from the administration; and (r) lack of support from bosses, coworkers, and the administration (Abney, 1988). These barriers often deny African American women access to opportunities in head coach and top-level administrative positions.

Socio-Cultural Barriers

Societal Attitude

Socio-cultural barriers involve a combination of both social and cultural factors (Merriam-Webster, 2005). African American women are constantly fighting stereotypical images that impede their chances to obtain more control and influence in the world of sport. African American women face a double barrier—racism and sexism—in sport and society. Hart (1980) suggested that within the black culture, sport involvement provides women of color status and prestige. Coakley (1982) has supported the notion that the African American community places few constraints on the black sportswoman. According to Corbett (2000), oftentimes white America holds a different interpretation of the role and function of sport in the black community, and as a consequence ideological generalizations, stereotypes, discrepancies, and contradictions are promoted in society. African American women have a common value of high achievement and the desire to pursue a coaching and/or administrative position in institutions of higher education (Stratta, 1995, p. 50). However, there are societal and institutional barriers that are hindrances, and thus, many black women are denied the opportunity of achieving such positions. African American women have shown courage and determination in sport and have been instrumental in playing an important role in breaking down color and gender barriers and stereotypes in society (Corbett, 2000). They have emerged from a tradition of invisibility and exclusion from certain sectors of society and have managed to make significant contributions in the sport mainstream culture.

Stereotypes

Overcoming historical suppression has been and continues to be an act of debunking myths and stereotypes. The reinforcement of stereotypes has helped to serve and maintain a system of oppression. "The perpetuation of fatalistic stereotypes coupled with contradictions in the literature concerning the images of African American women have had a profound effect on personal relationships and professional opportunities for African American women in a society that has helped to nurture this oppressive system" (Strata, 1995, p. 50).

Implanted firmly in the minds of many Americans was the image of black women performing low-paying, dead-end jobs. This was due largely to the historical status of black women's work. Therefore, the natural order for many was challenged with the presence of black women in positions of leadership. A black woman's very presence in such a role distorted the perceptions of her place in the labor hierarchy, regardless of her arena of leadership (Benton, 1999).

Sociologist Jewell (1993) related the ways in which the historical and contemporary media portrayed black women as "possessing certain values, belief systems and lifestyles that do not entitle them to receive societal resources, but account for their marginal status in salient societal institutions" (p. x). The "societal resources" Jewell referred to included equal access to education and jobs, not to so-called "entitlements." Jewell contended that the negative images that symbolized black womanhood were not new, but have persisted since slavery, especially those images of the black woman being "a mule of the world," whose backbreaking labor was assumed as a part of the natural order of things, and of the immoral "bad black girl," seen as a willing sexual object. Jewell described three particularly persistent images of black womanhood. The first was "Mammy," who stereotypically was "distinguished by her occupation, emotional qualities, physical make-up and behavior" (p. 38). Portrayed as submissive to her slave owner, and in a later era to her white domestic employer, ever smiling, devoted, and content with her lot in life, she was assumed to have no identity or self, beyond the laboring self. A second image, Aunt Jemima, was much like that of "Mammy" in terms of appearance. She usually was shown as a cook and again was portrayed as "extremely jolly." A third persistent image of black womanhood was that of Sapphire, the sharp-tongued, verbally emasculating "bitch," whose sharp words especially targeted black men (Benton, 1999).

These and other images were perpetuated in the print media, on television situation comedies, and in the treatment of black women in the public arena.

Poor Media Images

African American women are constantly fighting stereotypical images that impede their chances to obtain more control and influence in the world of sport (Lapchick, 2000). According to Schell (2001), more female athletes and women's sports have been in the international and national spotlights through television, newspapers, and magazines. However, minority women are practically non-existent in sports coverage. In the U.S. sports media, minority women receive considerably less coverage than their white female counterparts and are often depicted in a racially stereotypical manner. For example, of the 151 magazine covers published between 1975 and 1989, only 12 pictured minority women, all black women, and only 8% of the featured articles were written about black women with nearly 79% of these articles focused on track athletes or basketball players (Leath & Lumpkin, 1992). Stereotypes, social, and cultural barriers are not the only barriers encountered by African American women. Racism, sexism and structural barriers make it very difficult to gain access to high-quality programs (Eitzen & Sage, 1989).

Racism and Sexism

Both sexual and racial discrimination are burdens that African American women bear in the university setting and in American society. This "double jeopardy" adds to the difficulty of African American women who are seeking career advancement. Alexander (1978) described the double jeopardy as "preventing black women from formal networks such as higher educational training, and informal networks in which social relationships could possibly generate career benefits" (Alexander, 1978).

Richey (1981) identified another form of sexism encountered by minority women in the professions of sport administration and coaching as *womanism* (women who hinder the success of other women).

African American women are isolated and excluded from sport systems and the mainstream culture within sport organizations.

Structural Barriers

As athletes and in the black culture, many black women have a common value of high achievement and the desire to pursue a coaching and/or administrative position in institutions of higher education. However, there are societal and institutional barriers that are hindrances, and thus many black women are denied the opportunity of achieving such positions. African American women must be prepared for racist, sexist, and political roadblocks as they pursue careers as coaches and athletic administrators (Sloan, 2000). College athletic programs are highly structured organizations. According to Knoppers (1992), we must not overlook the structural causes of inequity and the institutionalization of sexism in sport. Structural barriers are formal and informal rules that regulate an entire system of interaction (Quellet, 2005).

According to Ouellet (2005), the combination of formal and informal rules defines not only what is acceptable, but also what is conceivable. On a daily basis minority women are confronted with the reality that white males control the operations of most franchises, college and high school athletics departments, and youth sport programs (Lapchick, 2000). Data continue to suggest that opportunities for women to gain upward mobility to coaching, officiating, and administration remain limited, especially for African American women. According to Acosta and Carpenter (2004), in the past six years, there has been a loss in the presence of a female voice in the athletic directors' offices of NCAA schools. They reported the following results after a 27-year longitudinal, national study of women in intercollegiate sport in 2004:

▼ When Title IX was enacted in 1972, more than 90% of women's teams were coached by women, and 90% of the women's programs were directed by female head administrators. Today, only 18.5% are head administrators and 44.1% are head coaches.

▼ The 18.5% of women's programs directed by females represents an increase from 17.9% in 2002. In 2000, the figure was 17.8%, and in 1998 the figure was 19.4%.

▼ No female at all, at any level, is found in the administrative structure of 17.8% women's athletic programs.

▼ Division I contains the fewest programs lacking a female in the administrative structure (6.3%) with Division II at 30.2% and Division III at 18.8%. Division I averages 5.11 administrators and thus there are more jobs with which to include females. The disparity in the inclusion of females from Division II to III cannot be due to the size of the administrative staff because both divisions are quite similar in size (Division II = 2.46 administrators, Division III = 2.44 administrators).

▼ The average NCAA athletics program employs 3.32 administrators, of whom 1.15 are female (Acosta & Carpenter, 2004).

In athletic administrative roles, black representation has had only a minimal increase from 1995. In 1995–1996, black women held 0.2% of the director of athletics, 1.2% of the associate director of athletics, and 1.4% of the assistant director of athletics positions (refer to Table 1). In 2001–2002, black women held 0.4% of the director of athletics, 1.4% of the associate director of athletics, and 1.9%

Table 1. Athletics Administrative Staff—1995-1996—Overall Percentages

Historically Black Institutions Excluded

		White		Black		Other Minority		Total	
	n	Men	Women	Men	Women	Men	Women	Men	Women
Director of Athletics	884	80.2	15.8	2.5	0.2	0.8	0.5	83.5	16.5
Associate Director of Athletics	593	57.7	34.9	4.7	1.2	1.3	0.2	63.7	36.3
Assistant Director of Athletics	864	62.2	29.9	5.3	1.4	0.9	0.3	68.4	31.6
Senior Woman Administrator	521	3.3	92.7	0.0	3.3	0.0	0.8	3.3	96.7
Administrative Assistant	695	14.2	71.9	3.2	5.8	0.6	4.3	18.0	82.0
Academic Advisor/ Counselor	633	35.5	43.8	12.2	5.8	1.1	1.6	48.8	51.2
Business Manager	363	51.0	41.0	1.9	2.5	1.7	1.9	54.5	45.5

Table 1. (continued)

	n	White		Black		Other Minority		Total	
		Men	Women	Men	Women	Men	Women	Men	Women
Compliance Coordinator/Officer	469	48.8	44.6	3.2	2.3	0.9	0.2	52.9	47.1
Equipment Manager	744	74.7	13.3	5.0	0.8	5.4	0.8	85.1	14.9
Fund Raiser/Development Manager	335	74.9	22.1	1.8	0.3	0.3	0.6	77.0	23.0
Facility Manager	493	73.6	14.8	6.9	0.6	3.9	0.2	84.4	15.6
Faculty Athletics Representative	774	79.3	17.8	1.3	0.4	0.8	0.4	81.4	18.6
Promotions/Marketing Manager	311	69.8	26.0	1.3	0.3	1.9	0.6	73.0	27.0
Sports Information Director	814	84.9	12.9	1.0	0.0	1.0	0.2	86.9	13.1
Asst. or Assoc. Director of Sports Information	461	64.4	32.5	0.7	1.1	0.9	0.4	65.9	34.1
Strength Coaches	502	77.9	9.2	7.8	0.8	4.4	0.0	90.0	10.0
Ticket Manager	333	47.7	47.1	0.9	1.8	0.9	1.5	49.5	50.5
Head Athletic Trainer	886	71.2	26.0	0.2	0.6	1.6	0.5	73.0	27.0
Assistant or Associate Athletic Trainer	872	45.3	50.7	1.0	0.6	1.6	0.8	47.9	52.1
Graduate Assistant	1,014	56.4	34.6	4.2	1.6	2.3	0.9	62.9	37.1
Intern	429	57.8	33.6	3.3	3.0	1.2	1.2	62.2	37.8
Other	440	49.3	32.7	8.0	4.3	3.4	2.3	60.7	39.3
Totals	13,430	59.2	33.2	3.5	1.7	1.7	0.9	64.3	35.7

of the assistant director of athletics positions (refer to Table 2). Although the percentage of black women in senior woman administrator (SWA) positions increased by 1.6% from 1995, there is a lack of uniformity in the titles and responsibilities of the SWA (Tiell, 2004). According to Tiell, over 50% of SWAs did not report a primary title such as associate or assistant athletic director that indicates a formal position on the senior management team.

In (2000), Lapchick reported that, although there are more than 1,000 NCAA schools, only five have minority women as athletics directors. Only 1.5% of all the senior athletics administrators holding the titles of associate and assistant ADs were minority women. In Divisions II and III, 2.8% and 1.8%, respectively, were minority women. Overall, women have made strides in intercollegiate athletics and the number of women in coaching and administrative positions within intercollegiate athletics departments has increased; however, there are very few African American women in the top- and middle-level administrative positions. Most African American women are concentrated in lower-level, dead-end positions

Table 2. Athletics Administrative Staff—2001–2002—Overall Percentages

Historically Black Institutions Excluded

	White		Black		Other Minority		Total	
	Men	Women	Men	Women	Men	Women	Men	Women
Director of Athletics	78.8	15.6	3.3	0.4	1.2	0.7	83.3	16.7
Associate Director of Athletics	56.3	35.4	4.7	1.4	1.4	0.8	62.4	37.6
Assistant Director of Athletics	63.3	27.6	4.8	1.9	1.6	0.8	68.7	30.3
Senior Woman Administrator	0.8	91.6	0.3	4.9	0.1	2.3	1.2	98.8
Administrative Assistant	12.4	71.4	2.6	7.7	0.9	5.1	15.8	84.2
Academic Advisor/Counselor	32.6	43.6	12.1	8.4	1.7	1.7	46.3	53.7
Business Manager	42.3	48.9	1.0	2.6	1.6	3.6	44.9	55.1
Compliance Coordinator/Officer	44.9	43.6	4.2	3.4	1.8	2.2	50.8	49.2
Equipment Manager	73.6	13.1	6.8	0.7	4.7	1.1	85.1	14.9
Fund Raiser/Development Manager	71.3	21.3	4.5	0.5	1.5	1.0	77.3	22.7
Facility Manager	70.1	14.8	8.8	0.5	4.8	1.0	83.6	16.4
Faculty Athletics Representative	71.8	22.1	3.2	0.7	1.8	0.4	76.8	23.2
Promotions/Marketing Manager	62.5	27.9	3.9	2.4	2.0	1.3	68.4	31.6
Sports Information Director	84.9	11.1	1.2	0.5	1.6	0.6	87.8	12.2
Asst. or Assoc. Director of Sports Information	68.5	27.0	1.2	0.7	1.8	0.8	71.5	28.5
Strength Coaches	75.8	12.0	8.6	0.4	2.8	0.5	87.2	12.8
Ticket Manager	45.7	44.8	3.1	0.9	2.0	3.5	50.8	49.2
Head Athletic Trainer	71.2	25.4	0.7	0.2	1.6	0.8	73.5	26.5
Assistant or Associate Athletic Trainer	46.0	46.9	1.5	1.3	2.8	1.5	50.3	49.7
Graduate Assistant	48.6	39.2	5.0	3.3	2.1	1.8	55.7	44.3
Intern	46.3	38.6	5.1	3.7	3.0	2.3	55.4	44.6
Other	39.2	42.8	6.6	5.1	4.9	1.5	50.6	49.4
Totals	53.4	35.9	4.3	2.6	2.1	1.6	59.9	40.1

Dead-end Positions and the Glass Ceiling Effect

African Americans are restricted to certain roles in college sport. In the 2002 NCAA race and demographics study of NCAA institutions' athletic personnel, the percentage of black administrators has increased overall, but the increases are not a result of more blacks in decision-making positions such as athletics director and associate or assistant directors. Most African American women are concentrated in lower-level positions such as other (5.1%), intern (3.7%), senior woman administrator (4.9%), administrative assistant (7.7%), and academic advisor/counselor (8.4%) (refer to Table 2). Ambiguous positions and titles can trap one psychologically and professionally. The glass ceiling effect is composed of organizational, attitudinal, and social barriers that effectively keep women and minorities from advancing up the career ladder (Morrison, White, Velsor, & The Center for Creative Leadership, 1987). Some African American women may never receive job assignments with higher duties than what they were given at the beginning of their employment. This factor could be due to low expectations by supervisors and/or others. Although their job descriptions may allow them to do other types of work, they may not be given the chance. As a result, some women may develop feelings of powerlessness, insecurity, unworthiness, and doubt as to their competence. Political constraints in sport organizations also hinder the opportunities and/or advancement of African American women in intercollegiate athletics.

Politics

Although laws have opened the doors of opportunity for African Americans in intercollegiate athletics, stereotypes, ignorance, societal attitudes towards differences, discriminatory institutional practices, and political roadblocks have limited employment in athletic leadership positions such as athletic administrators, coaches, officials, commentators, athletic trainers, and sports information directors. Laws do not prevent discrimination in employment or participation opportunities—people do. Laws cannot prevent unethical behavior. Laws cannot remove sex discrimination from our society. There is almost always a way to find a way around the letter of the law. Over the past 20 years, it appears that anti-discrimination laws have driven discriminatory treatment, policies, and practices underground as opposed to eliminating such conduct (Women's Sports Foundation, 2001, p. 3). Employment practices and discriminatory treatment have become more artful, more deceiving, and more difficult to uncover and combat (Women's Sports Foundation, 2001, p. 3). When attempting to recruit minority staff or student athletes or to "sell" diversity within the athletic department, administrations ensure African Americans are accessible and used as a means to an end. Lack of familiarity with the formal and informal codes of traditional hierarchies can make the professional experience for talented minority women very challenging. It results in feelings of being overworked, under-appreciated, underpaid, and irate about their profession. According to Sloan-Green (2000), eventually, the few African American females who are currently athletic directors or associate athletic directors will be replaced by men or by white women. Efforts to mentor, embrace, and provide access to resources is available to white females and males to ensure success and mobility in their career development. It is essential that African American women recognize and understand these new, subtle forms of discrimination. They must identify adequate career resources and networks to develop, sustain, and accommodate limited skill development opportunities.

Career Resources and Networks

Abney (1988) surveyed and interviewed African American female administrators and coaches at both black and white institutions and recorded the social and institutional barriers that affect their career mobility. The women constantly had to deal with challenges to their competence and with peer disrespect. Many, especially those employed at white institutions, expressed a feeling of isolation and loneliness because of the lack of cultural and social activities. Being black presented another barrier for African American women at white institutions where they were expected to be the black experts on all African American issues. Employer discrimination in the promotion practices was another cited barrier. Low expectations by administrators and others were mentioned. African American women were given titles without significant or challenging responsibility. African American women are excluded from participating in events, from leadership positions, and from membership on key committees. Individuals usually seek other individuals of the same group for support because of the commonality of their circumstances. Researchers at Texas A&M University found that African Americans do not have the same job prospects as their white counterparts when it comes to being hired as a head coach. Their survey showed that minorities may well face job discrimination issues when applying for coaching positions.

Cunningham (2005) explained that the most obvious type of discrimination is called "access discrimination." "This means you're not given a very good chance to enter the profession. It can come in the form of short coaching searches, no searches at all, no job postings of good jobs and other forms." Discriminatory treatment usually occurs because people are not educated in the importance of ethnic, cultural, and gender diversity and simply do the easiest and most comfortable thing—hire people they know and associate with people just like themselves. We cannot underestimate the impact of discrimination gone underground (WSF, 2001, p. 4). Most women, specifically minority women, do not have access to major sponsors, contributors, and supporters—power connections that can help remedy discrimination simply by their ability to influence those in control of athletics programs. With few if any career, financial, and human resources, it is very difficult for African American women to be successful coaches and athletic administrators. The lack of support systems, networks, and cultural and social outlets in the community often result in feelings of isolation and/or loneliness. Acosta and Carpenter (1994) reported that the decline of female leadership in athletics is a result of (a) the success of the old-boy network, (b) the weakness of the old-girl network, and (c) the lack of support systems for females. Friendship networks, professional contacts, and acquaintances are important influences on the upward mobility of African American coaches (Brooks et al., 1989). Brooks et al. (1989) found that network ties tend to hasten career development, and recommendation by network contacts often takes precedence over the candidate's experience in the field. Abney (1988) revealed that African American women lacked support groups.

Although the Black Coaches Association (BCA), Black Women in Sport Foundation (BWSF), the National Collegiate Athletic Association (NCAA), the National Intercollegiate Athletic Association (NAIA), and the Women's Sports Foundation (WSF) have made efforts to provide support and address the issues and concerns of women and minorities in intercollegiate athletics, issues specifically related to minority women are often deeply submerged within women's and minority men's issues or excluded entirely. The BCA, a voluntary, nonprofit organization, was primarily created to deal directly with minority issues in sports. Issues include the stereotyping of minority coaches and administrators and the lack of minorities opportunities in college athletics (Brooks & Althouse, 2000). The Black Women in Sport Foundation (BWSF), founded in 1992, is dedicated to facilitating the involvement of black women in every aspect of sport in the United States and around the world through the "hands-on" development and management of grassroots-level outreach programs. The BWSF focus is the grassroots approach. They have chosen this approach because it is unique in its ability to address the needs and wishes of young black women and girls and to define the best ways to guide and support them in their paths to life-long achievement.

Coaches and administrators need to establish new networks for minority and female recruiting because existing networks are predominately white male (WSF, 2001, p. 7). Other valuable resources and networks are career role models and mentors.

Role Models and Mentors

Career role models and mentors are of special value to African American women during their career development process. According to Smith (1991), planned interventions with adult role models and mentors do appear to have a positive effect on the career behavior and aspirations of African American youth. Unfortunately, a small number of women are in positions in athletic departments to provide the type of mentoring desired. African American women are rarely hired in high-level coaching and/or athletic administrative positions in colleges and universities. Consequently, there are fewer African American women role models and mentors. In most traditionally white institutions, the African American woman athlete lacks African American women administrators and coaches with whom she can identify. In most traditionally black institutions, African American males occupy a large percentage of the positions in sport. As a result, professional occupations in sport are not perceived as "visible" goals for the African American woman; therefore, she may not desire to pursue them.

The overall percentage of black women in decision-making positions, such as director of athletics or associate or assistant director of athletics, is minute. Overall, 1% of the directors of athletics and 9.4% of the senior woman administrators (SWA) are African American women. Of the 1% (directors of athletics) and 9.4% (SWAs), 0.6% and 4.5%, respectively, of the African American women are employed at HBCUs. Overall, most African American women are stacked within administrative assistant (10%) or academic advisor/counselor (10%) positions in intercollegiate athletic departments. In 2001–2002, the grand total of athletics personnel in NCAA member institutions was **20,065**, and the total number of black women employed in those positions was **725**. Therefore, **3.6%** of all the athletics administrative staff was composed of black women (NCAA, 2003). However, when historically black colleges and universities are excluded from the overall figures, the grand total of athletics administrative personnel in NCAA member institutions was **19,352**, and black women represent only **2.6%** of the athletic administrative staff (see Table 3).

Stacking

According to Lumpkin (2003), stacking is the disproportional allocation of persons to central and non-central athletic positions on the basis of race or ethnicity. Evidence of unequal access can be traced back to the experience of the team positions held by African American women as student athletes. Sport sociologists have presented the theory that African American athletes are stacked in positions that do not require them to become leaders of their teams and are scarce in positions that are more central to the team's operations. Many educators will attest that the sports experience prepares the student athlete for career and life experiences. According to Malveaux (1993), "The teamwork needed to participate in sports

Table 3. Athletics Administrative Staff—2001–2002—Black Women—Overall Percentages

	Black Women HBCU & Majority		Black Women Majority		Black Women HBCU	
	%	N	%	N	%	N
Director of Athletics	1.0	(9)	0.4	(3)	0.6	(6)
Associate Director of Athletics	2.2	(22)	1.4	(14)	0.8	(8)
Assistant Director of Athletics	2.5	(32)	1.9	(23)	0.6	(9)
Senior Woman Administrator	9.4	74)	4.9	(37)	4.5	(37)
Administrative Assistant	10.0	(144)	7.7	(107)	2.3	(37)
Academic Advisor/Counselor	10.0	(105)	8.4	(86)	1.6	(19)
Business Manager	4.1	(22)	2.6	(13)	1.5	(9)
Compliance Coordinator/Officer	4.8	(39)	3.4	(26)	1.4	(13)
Equipment Manager	0.7	(6)	0.7	(6)	0.0	(0)
Fund Raiser/Development Manager	1.1	(7)	0.5	(3)	0.6	(4)
Facility Manager	0.9	(7)	0.5	(4)	0.4	(3)
Faculty Athletics Representative	1.4	(12)	0.7	(6)	0.7	(6)
Promotions/Marketing Manager	3.2	(18)	2.4	(13)	0.8	(5)
Sports Information Director	1.3	(11)	0.5	(4)	0.8	(7)
Asst. or Assoc. Director of Sports Information	1.6	(12)	0.7	(5)	0.9	(7)
Strength Coaches	0.3	(3)	0.4	(3)	0.1	(0)
Ticket Manager	4.9	(24)	0.9	(4)	4.0	(20)
Head Athletic Trainer	0.7	(6)	0.2	(2)	0.5	(4)
Assistant or Associate Athletic Trainer	1.8	(28)	1.3	(20)	0.5	(8)
Graduate Assistant	4.0	(72)	3.3	(57)	0.7	(15)
Intern	3.7	(31)	3.7	(31)	0.0	(0)
Other	7.1	(41)	5.1	(28)	2.0	(13)
Totals	3.6	(725)	2.6	(495)	1.0	(230)

teaches students life lessons about cooperation, human relations, dignity and poise" (p. 54). The role that the student athlete plays on a team can serve as the basis for career preparation. Eitzen and Furst (1989) investigated the relationship between stacking and racism among women. They studied the extent to which stacking was evident in women's collegiate volleyball. White females were found to dominate the setter position whereas African American females were occupying the hitter and blocker positions. The setter position requires leadership and a high degree of interaction, whereas the hitter and blocker are positions requiring quickness, agility, and jumping ability. This finding suggests there may be less opportunity for African American females to gain access to coaching and other managerial positions in volleyball and, by extension, in other sports. Fuller stated,

"Even in sports in which African American women are represented in significant numbers, basketball and track, they are often not in decision making, or what she called 'control' positions" (quoted in Blum, 1993, p. 40). She further stated, "Look at the point guards on many of the teams. The African American women are out there in the scoring positions and making big contributions, but they are not directing traffic" (quoted in Blum, 1993, p. 40). Nearly 73% of the few minority women holding college head coaching jobs are in basketball and track and field. Look in the other sports and we would find what they call in softball a "shut out" (Lapchick, 2000). According to the Women's Sport Foundation (2002), there is a pattern of racial inequality in most NCAA sports. This pattern of racial clustering appears to be related to continuing racism and the disparate impacts of economic inequality on populations of color. Clustering refers to a situation in which student athletes of color have very high participation rates in some sports but very low participation rates in others (e.g., African American minority women are very high in basketball but very low in field hockey). The analysis uncovered an overall pattern of under-representation of females of color in 20 of the 25 intercollegiate sports in which the NCAA maintains participation statistics in 2001 (WSF, 2003, p. 2). According to a 2001 General Accounting Office (GAO) report on intercollegiate athletics, 77% of the NAIA and NCAA women's teams added between 1981 and 1998 were in sports in which female athletes of color are moderately or severely under-represented (see Table 4).

If African American student athletes have a quality intercollegiate athletic experience, an experience in which they believe that they are being provided a legitimate opportunity to succeed and prosper, they will be more inclined to invest in a career in intercollegiate athletics. If more African American student athletes graduate, the pool of those individuals able to consider a career in college athletics will expand (Vance, 1984). A better sporting experience means more interested and qualified candidates for positions as coaches and athletic administrators. African American student athletes must be provided leadership and graduate school opportunities after their playing days are over. Although progress has been made in creating new internships and postgraduate scholarship opportunities at the institutional, conference, and national levels, these opportunities must be expanded (Gerdy, 1994). Our current African American student athletes should be our future coaches, athletic administrators, and conference commissioners. Unfortunately, stacking or position clustering impacts the availability of minorities for upper-level positions in intercollegiate athletic departments.

Position Clustering

The clustering effect has not only affected student athletes, but also impacted African American women in athletic-related careers. African Americans are restricted to certain roles and/or positions in college sport. African American women tend to be under-represented in roles associated with leadership and decision making (Abney, 1988). They are "assistant to"; that is, they serve as coordinators or assistants to a major decision maker. Most African American women are clustered in lower-level positions such as secretary, graduate assistant, assistant coach, administrative assistant, compliance officer, assistant athletic director, athletic academic advisor/coordinator or associate athletic director (Abney, 1988).

Table 4. Sport Participation Percentages of 2000–2001 NCAA Female Athletes of Color Rank Ordered by Sports with Highest Participation Percentages

Rank Order of Sport by Percent Athlete of Color Participation	Percent Participation	Total Female Athletes of Color	Total All Female Athletes	Rank Order by Number of Female Participants
1. Bowling	80%	158	197	22
2. Badminton	33%	11	33	25
3. Basketball	29%	4,141	14,438	5
4. Track-Outdoor	24%	4,466	18,338	2
5. Track-Indoor	23%	3,725	15,961	3
6. Fencing	17%	116	670	18
7. Archery	15%	7	46	24
8. Cross Country	15%	1,803	11,721	7
9. Volleyball	15%	1,926	12,978	6
10. Tennis	14%	1,113	8,230	9
11. Rifle	13%	32	248	21
12. Softball	12%	1,787	15,041	4
13. Gymnastics	9%	123	1,398	14
14. Water Polo	9%	84	954	17
15. Golf	8%	265	3,257	13
16. Rowing	7%	439	6,111	10
17. Soccer	7%	1,348	18,548	1
18. Squash	7%	27	361	20
19. Lacrosse	5%	231	5,069	12
20. Synchro Swim	5%	6	116	23
21. Swim/Dive	5%	470	10.108	8
22. Field Hockey	4%	188	5,126	11
23. Skiing	2%	8	526	19
24. Ice Hockey	2%	28	1,320	15
25. Equestrian	2%	24	1,048	16

As long as racist and sexist practices influence hiring practices, the numbers of African American women in high authority sport positions will not increase. Hiring and promotion decisions can be subjective, and universities use different criteria in making decisions to hire and promote.

Collegiate National Governing Association

National Collegiate Athletic Association (NCAA) Headquarters

According to Lapchick, after several years of progress, opportunities for people of color and women in the highest professional positions at NCAA Headquarters declined. At the vice-president/chief of staff level, African Americans occupied 12.5% (2) of the positions. During the time of the data collection for the report, there were no African American women on staff at the vice-president/chief of staff level. However, in May 2005, the NCAA hired a vice president for Diversity and Inclusion to lead the new NCAA Office for Diversity and Inclusion. The hire of Charlotte Westerhaus gave the NCAA Headquarters three African-American vice presidents and four women. Currently, an African American woman is on staff as a vice president. This recent hire brings the NCAA back to the same numbers as in the last Report Card. At the chief aides/director level, African Americans held 12.5% (5) of the positions. At the administrative level, African-Americans continued to hold 22.2% (37) of the positions and 12.3% (13) of the support staff positions (Lapchick, 2005).

The NCAA claims to be taking positive steps to identify and establish policy and guidelines to deal with the under-representation of African Americans in NCAA coaching and managerial positions (Brooks & Althouse, 2000). NCAA President Myles Brand established the Office of Diversity and Inclusion to bolster the Association's ongoing diversity-awareness campaign and to provide leadership, as well as some measure of accountability, regarding how the national office and NCAA institutions make decisions that reflect an inclusive approach (NCAA News, 2005). However, the inclusive approach is not evident within conference offices. The level of representation of minorities in positions within conference offices is rather alarming. Equal access for African American women to conference commissioner within conference offices has moved slowly.

In 2001–02, the NCAA Minority Opportunities and Interest Committee released the findings of a two-year study on race demographics of NCAA member institutions' athletic personnel. In general, the data revealed that there have been few significant changes in diversity hiring of ethnic minority administrators and coaches over a six-year period in the athletic departments at NCAA member institutions.

The report revealed, overall in athletic administrative roles, that African American representation has had only a minimal increase from 1995.

▼ The percentage of African American administrators has increased overall, but the increases are not a result of more African Americans in decision-making positions such as athletics director and associate or assistant director.

▼ Only in Division III did the percentage of African American athletics directors increase.

Head coach data indicated that, overall, African American representation in both men's and women's teams have increased slightly.

▼ Overall the percentage of African American coaches of both men's and women's teams were up from 1995.

▼ In the divisional breakdown, Division I percentages saw the greatest increase in the number of black coaches of both men's and women's teams.

▼ African American coaches of Division I men's teams overall increased 3% from 1995.

▼ Division II percentages decreased for all teams with African American coaches. (NCAA, 2001–02).

Richard E. Lapchick released *The 2004 Racial and Gender Report Card*, a report on the hiring practices by professional sports teams and college athletics. The report revealed the following findings pertaining to African American women as collegiate athletic directors and head coaches:

[a] None of the athletic directors at Division I institutions, 0.9% of the athletic directors at Division II, and 0.0% of the athletic directors at Division III were African American women.

[a] Of the head coaches at Division I institutions, 1.6% were African American women. 0.7% of the head coaches at Division II and 1.0 percent of the head coaches at Division III were African American women (Lapchick, 2005).

Another step utilized by the NCAA to address the under-representation of women in NCAA managerial positions was to implement the senior woman administrator (SWA) designation.

Senior Woman Administrator (SWA)

The senior woman administrator (SWA) designation is one way to ensure that women stay involved in the NCAA governance structure. According to Sweet (2002), the SWA ought to be fully integrated into the school's athletics programs and contribute as a high-level administrator. That also lets the SWA serve as a role model to the female student athletes and younger staff members, who see a woman as a natural part of the administrative structure. In 1981, the NCAA membership established the senior woman administrator (SWA) designation. First called primary woman administrator (PWA), the title was updated to senior woman administrator in 1990. The SWA is "a female professional athletics administrator who is a member of the institution's senior athletics management team" (NCAA Division II Manual, 2005–06, p. 28). The SWA designation is not a position with SWA responsibilities solely, but is rather a role undertaken by somebody who is part of the administrative structure already (NCAA News, 2002). The SWA should be the senior-most female in that structure and she may have additional responsibilities because of that. The designation of SWA isn't a job. "It indicates the senior-ranking female in the administrative structure, and she has departmental responsibilities similar to others—for example, associate ADs in the athletics department. The SWA holds a meaningful administrative position that calls for her seat at the table and as such she is the SWA" (NCAA News, 2002, p. 4). The purpose of appointing a senior woman administrator is to involve female administrators in a meaningful way in the decision-making process in intercollegiate athletics. The position is intended to ensure representation of women's interests at the campus, conference, and national levels (NCAA, Senior Woman Administrator brochure).

In 2002, the NCAA established the SWA role in the national office. The SWA is charged with overseeing, consulting, and advocating issues related to women in intercollegiate athletics and also women in the national office.

In intercollegiate athletics, women held 99.6%, 100%, and 98.8% of the senior woman administrators in Divisions I, II, and III respectively. White women dominate as senior woman administrators at Division I, II, and III institutions. Of the SWAs at Division I (88.5%) institutions, 8.3% were African American women; 4.6% of the SWAs at Division II (92.6%) and 2.4% of the SWAs at Division III (95.4%) were African American women (Lapchick, 2005). According to Tiell

(2004), Dr. Claire VanUmmerson, Vice President and Director of the Office of Women in Higher Education at the American Council of Education, addressed the issue of the SWA during the Women's Leadership Symposium for Intercollegiate Athletics in May, 2003.

She stated:

> The creation of the SWA was heralded as a breakthrough for women in athletics. However, the intent was to have a real position with real responsibilities. In practice the most senior woman in the athletic department was simply designated as the SWA regardless of her current position. These individuals have fulltime jobs and the designation as SWA. The concept of the SWA was good but it is doing nothing more than giving someone an extra title with no real job description. There is no uniformity in training. It is supposed to be a career ladder move but it is a career path into the middle of nowhere. It is not helping women advance. If women want to advance, they will need experience with budgets and supervising men's teams. (VanUmmersen, 2003)

The NCAA should be credited for taking positive steps to reduce disparities in recruitment and to correct inequalities found in NCAA staff, conference offices, and athletic administrative and coaching positions within the Association's membership.

Conferences

A conference is a group of colleges or universities that governs the conduct of its member institutions' athletic programs. In 2004–05, the NCAA collected data on

Table 5. 1998–1999 Overall Percentages

Historically Black Institutions Excluded

Position	White		Black		Other Minority		Total	
	Men	Women	Men	Women	Men	Women	Men	Women
Commissioner	90.0	7.8	2.2	0.0	0.0	0.0	92.2	7.8
Associate Commissioner	64.4	25.4	5.1	1.7	1.7	1.7	71.2	28.8
Assistant Commissioner	53.4	34.2	5.5	5.5	1.4	0.0	60.3	39.7
Director	37.7	45.3	7.5	3.8	3.8	1.9	49.1	50.9
Associate Director	N/A	N/A	N/A	N/A	N/A	N/A	N/A	N/A
Assistant Director	40.0	40.0	2.9	11.4	5.7	0.0	48.6	51.4
Supervisor/Coordinator of Officials	67.3	26.7	5.0	0.0	0.0	1.0	72.3	27.7
Administrative Assistant (Part-time)	36.4	45.5	0.0	0.0	0.0	18.2	36.4	63.6
Intern	N/A	N/A	N/A	N/A	N/A	N/A	N/A	N/A
Student Assistant (Part-time)	43.8	18.8	6.3	18.8	6.3	6.3	56.3	43.8
Other	60.6	29.5	1.2	5.0	2.1	1.7	63.9	36.1
Totals	61.4	28.1	3.4	3.8	1.8	1.5	66.6	33.4

the racial and gender breakdown of personnel at NCAA member conference offices. Overall, from 1998–99 to 2004–05, the percentage of female conference commissioners increased 5.6% (from 7.4 to 13.0) (refer to Tables 5 and 6). Looking divisionally at the percent of female conference commissioners from 1998–99 to 2004–05, there was a 7.4% increase (from 5.7 to 13.2) in Division I, no change in Division II (no female conference commissioners in either year), and a 7.4% increase (from 13.2 to 20.6) in Division III (NCAA, 2005). The percentage of black women increased 0.5% (from 3.8 to 4.3). However, the percentage of black women as conference commissioners remained the same, 0.0%, from 1998–99 to 2004–05 (refer to Tables 5 and 6). The conference administrator job category with the highest percentage of black women holding that position in 2004–05 was the administrative assistant (10.8%), followed closely by the intern position (10.4%). However, the conference position with the largest decrease in the percent of females holding that title was in the student assistant category, in which, from 1998–99 to 2004–05, there was a decrease of 18.8% (from 18.8% to 0.0%), followed closely by the assistant director position (from 11.4% to 8.2%).

Lapchick's 2004 Racial and Gender Report Card for College Sport revealed several interesting facts:

Commissioner

[a] All (100%) of the 11 Division IA conference commissioners were white males.

[a] In Division I, excluding the historically black conferences, all 31 (100%) of Division I conference commissioners were white, with three (9.1%) being female.

Table 6. 2004–2005 Overall Percentages

Historically Black Institutions Excluded

Position	White		Black		Other Minority		Total	
	Men	Women	Men	Women	Men	Women	Men	Women
Commissioner	84.1	13.6	0.0	0.0	2.3	0.0	86.4	13.6
Associate Commissioner	59.5	29.1	7.6	2.5	0.0	1.3	67.1	32.9
Assistant Commissioner	50.0	31.3	5.6	6.7	1.1	5.6	56.7	43.3
Director	44.0	37.3	4.0	8.0	4.0	2.7	52.0	48.0
Associate Director	30.8	53.8	7.7	0.0	7.7	0.0	46.2	53.8
Assistant Director	44.9	34.7	6.1	8.2	4.1	2.0	55.1	44.9
Supervisor/Coordinator of Officials	69.6	24.0	1.8	0.0	3.7	0.9	75.1	24.9
Administrative Assistant	1.5	83.1	0.0	10.8	0.0	4.6	1.5	98.5
Intern	32.5	46.8	7.8	10.4	1.3	1.3	41.6	58.4
Student Assistant	63.6	18.2	0.0	0.0	9.1	9.1	72.7	27.3
Other	46.4	42.9	7.1	3.6	0.0	0.0	53.6	46.4
Totals	53.3	34.2	3.8	4.3	2.4	2.0	59.5	40.5

Associate Commissioner

ᵃ Five (12.5%) of the 40 listed Division IA associate commissioners were African-Americans males.

ᵃ White women held 11 (27.5%) of the Division IA associate commissioner positions.

ᵃ Out of 73 listed associate posts in Division I, 9.6% were African Americans.

The paucity of African American women as conference or associate commissioners is also prevalent in intercollegiate athletic departments.

Intercollegiate Athletic Departments

Current discussion of affirmative action and equal opportunity might lead a person to believe that a gender and racial balance has been achieved in intercollegiate athletics administration (Abney & Staurowsky, 2003). Recent studies of NCAA member institutions, though, have shown a marked lack of diversity in athletics administrative personnel. For example, 92% of the 200 ADs in Fitzgerald and colleagues' 1993 study were white, and 71.5% of them were men.

Parks, Russell, and Wood (1993) found a similar racial and gender imbalance among 402 NCAA Division IA top-level, middle-level, and first-line administrators, where 92% of the respondents were white and 83% were male.

Abney (1997) investigated the positions held by African American women in intercollegiate athletic departments of member institutions within the NCAA, the National Association for Intercollegiate Athletics (NAIA), and the National Junior College Athletic Association (NJCAA). The results were that a total of 1,912 African American men and women were identified as holding athletic administrative and coaching positions, with 475 or 25% identified as African American women athletic administrators and coaches (see Table 7).

Of the 475, 304, or 64% were coaches. Of the 304 coaches, 12 were identified as graduate assistants, interns, or volunteers, and 26 of the women held another position; that is, coached another sport or were administrators. One hundred seventy-one, or 36%, were athletic administrators. Of the 171, 6 were identified as interns or graduate assistants, and 7 held another position. These percentages are much smaller when compared to the overall number of positions, male and female, within intercollegiate athletic departments. The top five administrative positions held by African American women in intercollegiate athletic departments were secretary/receptionist, academic counselor/student services, athletic trainer, administrative assistant, and business manager/account executive (see Table 8).

Abney (1997) identified 0.44%, or three, African American women as athletic directors. All three women were employed at NCAA member institutions. One was employed at a Division I white institution, whereas the other two were employed at Division II, historically black institutions.

The top five head coaching positions held by African American women in intercollegiate athletics departments were basketball, volleyball, track and field, cheerleading, and softball.

A 1986–87 study reported that the total number of African Americans holding athletic administrative positions was .156 per school, for a total of about 123 in

Table 7.

	NCAA	NAIA	NJCAA	Total
Total number of African American names submitted	0.90% (1736)	0.01% (12)	0.09% (164)	100% (1912)
Total number of African American women	0.94% (449)	0.01% (4)	0.05% (22)	100% (475)
Total number of African American men	0.89% (1287)	0.01% (8)	10% (142)	100% (1437)

Table 8.

	NCAA	NAIA	NJCAA	Total
Secretary/Receptionist	7.8% (42)	0.0% (0)	0.0% (0)	6.2% (42)
Academic Counselor/ Student Services				
Director	2.4% (13)	0.0% (0)	0.0% (0)	1.9% (13)
Assistant	0.93 (5)	0.0% (0)	0.0% 0.0%	0.73% (5)
Athletic Trainer				
Head	0.75% (4)	0.0% (0)	0.0% (0)	0.59% (4)
*Assistant**	2.2% (12)	0.0% (0)	0.0% (0)	1.7% (12)
Administrative Assistant	2.8% (15)	0.0% (0)	0.0% (0)	2.2% (15)
Business Manager/ Account Executive				
Director	1.5% (8)	0.0% (0)	0.78% (1)	1.3% (9)
Assistant	0.56% (3)	0.0% (0)	0.0% (0)	0.44% (3)

*Note: six (6) of the assistant trainers were employed at one institution.

National Collegiate Athletic Association (NCAA) schools. Thus, it was concluded that there is a minority group member in only one out of five of the athletic administrative structures found in NCAA member colleges and universities. The total number of head coaches was .494 per school, for a total of about 387 in NCAA schools. There is no minority group member serving as head coach in either the men's or women's programs in one out of three colleges and universities. Assistant coaches were 1.350 per school, for a total of about 1,065 in NCAA schools (Acosta & Carpenter, 1987).

It was concluded that the number of representatives of minority groups who hold a position as administrator, coach, or assistant coach in all of NCAA sports is about 1,979; in other words, about 2.5 per school, from a pool of all levels of administrators, coaches for all teams in women's programs and men's programs, as well as assistant coaches in these programs (Acosta & Carpenter, 1987).

Although the overall number of women and minorities within intercollegiate athletics departments has increased, the number of African American women as athletic directors and head coaches has not increased significantly and continues to be disappointing.

The 27-year Update by Acosta and Carpenter (2004) reported that 3,356 administrative jobs existed in 2004 for NCAA programs offering women's athletics, an increase of 3,210 jobs from 2002. Women held 41% of all administrative jobs in women's programs but only 18.5% of athletic director jobs. The 18.5% of women programs directed by a female represents an increase from 17.9% in 2002. Division I includes the smallest percentage of programs with a female athletic director (8.7%). Division II includes 16.9%, and Division III includes 27.5%. There are more female college presidents of Division IA schools than there are female athletic directors in Division IA programs. It was concluded that on an average, there is one female involved in athletic administration per school.

In 2004, there were 8,402 head coaching jobs of women's NCAA teams. Women held 3,704 of those jobs, an increase of 127 jobs held by females in 2002; 44.1% of the coaches of women's teams were females, up very slightly from 44.0% in 2002 (Acosta & Carpenter, 2004).

The 27-year Update by Acosta and Carpenter (2004) revealed several interesting facts:

▼ The average size of the administrative staff has grown by 40% in the last 16 years.

▼ The absolute number of females within the administrative structure has grown 160% in the last 16 years.

▼ The average representation of females among the ranks of athletics directors has declined by half of one percent in the last six years.

▼ Female representation is growing in the under ranks of administration but not in the top jobs.

▼ Division I provides the greatest chance to have a female voice in the administration.

▼ Division I provides the smallest chance to have a female head athletic director.

▼ Division III provides the greatest chance to have a female head athletic director.

▼ Division I has the greatest average number of administrators.

▼ Division III has the smallest average number of administrators.

▼ The gender of the athletic director has an impact on the percentage of female coaches hired.

▼ No woman's voice is heard anywhere in the administration of almost 1 out of 5 women's programs.

▼ About 4 out of 5 women's athletics programs are administered by a male.

▼ In all three Divisions, when the athletic director is a male, the percentage of female coaches is lower than when the athletic director is a female.

▼ In all three Divisions, when the athletic director is a male, no female voice is found anywhere in the administrative structure; the percentage of female coaches is also lower than when the athletic director is a female.

(Acosta & Carpenter, 2004)

Suggestions for Change

Change has to occur at the top of an organization in order to impact the entire organization. Until diversification occurs within the offices of national organizations, conference offices, and administrative and athletic departments on college campuses, unequal access will remain a reality for African American women coaches and athletic administrators.

African American women who aspire to obtain and advance in positions within intercollegiate athletics departments are faced with a shatterproof ceiling. The positions are available, but significant numbers of African American women are not being hired in decision-making positions within intercollegiate athletics departments; those who have been hired are in dead-end positions. If hired in the middle-or low-level positions, they are not rapidly advancing up the career ladder to head coach or athletic director positions. The realities of clustering must be addressed if minorities are going to reap the same athletic and educational benefits as their white counterparts (WSF, 2003).

African American women must develop strategies to obtain upper-level positions within intercollegiate athletics. Changes in the following areas would increase the number of African American women in athletics: society's attitude toward African American women; affirmative hiring procedures; elimination of sexism and racism; access to career mentors, role models, networks, and opportunities. African American women should make themselves more visible and qualified, and design or develop programs to help prepare African American women for careers in intercollegiate athletics. With degrees and higher-level athletic experiences, at least minority women will not give employers in the business of sports any excuses about lacking qualifications (Lapchick, 2000).

We must be sure that every coaches association and sport organization has a standing committee or interest group to create the agendas for change (WSF, 2003). The convention program should have a session on recognizing subtle discrimination and the behaviors and responses that keep women (African American, Asian, Hispanic, Native American, and white) out of the coaching and athletic administration professions. These are the groups that can gather data and keep report cards (WSF, 2003). In the 21st century, athletic administrators will be increasingly sensitive to the effects of gender and race on an individual's career aspirations. Abney and Richey (1992) summed it up when they stated, "For minority women to enjoy the benefits of Title IX, there must be individuals in positions that are knowledgeable, committed, and sensitive to the differences and the hiring of minority women. Until this occurs, opportunities will remain limited" (p. 58).

The following are recommendations and strategies for change:

1. Organizations must expand their traditional recruitment networks and seek candidates with non-customary backgrounds and experiences.

2. The top leadership of colleges and universities must demonstrate its commitment to the recruitment and advancement of African Americans by removing obstacles embedded in personnel practices.

3. Formal mentoring and career development programs can help stop minorities from being channeled into staff positions that provide little access to the decision-making positions.

4. Efforts to achieve diversity within athletic departments should be an integral part of strategic plans, and the administration must be held accountable for progress toward breaking the glass ceiling.

5. African American women must receive challenging job assignments and the necessary training to advance.

6. Organizations must establish ongoing training and educational programs on race relations for all organizational members. Such training can help to eliminate many of the barriers of the African American experience of racism and prejudice.

7. African American women must become qualified and compete for leadership roles at all levels in sport and become actively involved in sport associations, organizations, committees, and/or governing bodies.

8. Insist on search and employment committees of diverse composition for every leadership position in sport (WSF, 2001).

9. Insist that the NCAA and other organizations who give grants refuse to fund any organization that does not have a program in place to address the issue of racism in sport (WSF, 2001).

10. Utilize public service announcements, posters, and television to combat the invisibility of African American women in sport. We must celebrate her image (WSF, 2003).

The Black Coaches Association continues to gather data to show the need to hire more African American women head coaches and make institutions aware that blacks are more than just performers on the field, that they have head coaching ability (Brooks & Althouse, 2000). The NCAA Minority Opportunities and Interest Committee (MOIC) monitor the demographics of minorities and women in intercollegiate athletics. The NCAA membership is working to increase the proportion of minority and female administrators and coaches. The Leadership Institute for Ethnic Minority Males, NACWAA/HERS Institute, Coaches Institute, and Coaches Enhancement Grant, as well as the Division II and III Strategic Alliance Matching Grant Programs, are examples of the Association's efforts to enhance the pool of qualified minorities and women in the field of intercollegiate athletics. The Association's membership is hopeful that these programs will have a profound impact on the number of women and minorities in intercollegiate athletics in future years.

▲▼ Suggested Readings ▲▼

Abney, R. (1997, April). *The impact of gender equity on the status of African American women as athletic administrators and coaches in sport.* Paper presented at the meeting of the American Alliance for Health, Physical Education, Recreation and Dance, St. Louis, MO.

Acosta, R. V., & Carpenter, L. J. (2004). *Women in intercollegiate sport: A longitudinal study: Twenty-seven year update 1977–2004.* Unpublished manuscript, Brooklyn College, New York.

Lapchick, R. (2005). The 2004 racial and gender equity report card. University of Central Florida, Institute for Diversity and Ethics in Sport.

National Collegiate Athletic Association. (2003). 2001–02 race demographics of NCAA member institutions' athletics personnel: The NCAA minority opportunities and interests committee's two-year study. Indianapolis, IN: Author.

Women's Sport Foundation. (2001). *Gender equity and the black female in sport.* Retrieved August 14, 2005, from https://www.womensportsfoundation.org/cgi-in/iowa/issues/disc/article.html?record=869.

Women's Sport Foundation. (2003, June). *The Women's Sports Foundation Report: Title IX and Race in Intercollegiate Sport.* Retrieved August 14, 2005, from https://www.womensportsfoundation.org/cgi-in/iowa/issues/disc/article.html?record=955.

▲▼ Study Questions ▲▼

1. Is access to opportunities as head coach and top-level administrative positions in intercollegiate athletics disparate for African American women?

2. List three socio-cultural barriers that have been identified as hindrances to career advancement for African American women as head coaches and top-level athletic administrators.

3. List and explain five structural barriers that have been identified as hindrances to career advancement for African American women as head coaches and top-level athletic administrators.

4. What is the glass ceiling effect?

5. What is clustering?

6. List three strategies implemented by the NCAA to reduce disparities in recruitment and to correct inequalities found in NCAA staff and coaching and athletic administrative positions within the Association's membership.

7. What did Lapchick's 2004 Racial and Gender Report Card conclude about the representation of conference commissioners, associate commissioners, athletic directors, and head coaches?

8. What is the purpose of the senior woman administrator?

9. What was the representation of African American women as senior woman administrators at Division I, II, and III in 2002?

10. Discuss several changes that must occur to diversify national organizations, conference offices, and administrative and athletic departments.

11. List several strategies that African American women must develop to obtain upper-level positions within intercollegiate athletics.

References

Abney, R. (1988). *The effects of role models and mentors on the careers of Black women athletic administrators and coaches in higher education.* Unpublished doctoral dissertation, University of Iowa, Iowa City.

Abney, R. (1997, April). *The impact of gender equity on the status of African American women as athletic administrators and coaches in sport.* Unpublished manuscript. Paper presented at the meeting of the American Alliance for Health, Physical Education, Recreation and Dance, St. Louis, MO.

Abney, R., & Richey, D. L. (1992). Opportunities for minorities. *Journal of Physical Education, Recreation and Dance, 63*(3), 56–59.

Abney, R., & Staurowsky, E. (2003). Intercollegiate athletics. In J. B. Parks & J. Quarterman (Eds.), *Contemporary sport management* (pp. 271–296. Champaign, IL: Human Kinetics.

Acosta, R. V., & Carpenter, L. J. (1987). *Minority group members in athletic leadership.* Unpublished manuscript, Brooklyn College, New York.

Acosta, R. V., & Carpenter, L. J. (1994). The status of women in intercollegiate athletics. In S. Birrell & C. Cole (Eds.), *Women, sport and culture* (pp.111–118). University of Illinois at Urbana-Champaign: Human Kinetics.

Acosta, R. V., & Carpenter, L. J. (2004). *Women in intercollegiate sport: A longitudinal study. Twenty-seven year update 1977–2004.* Unpublished manuscript, Brooklyn College, New York.

Alexander, A. (1978). *Status of minority women in the AIAW.* Unpublished master's thesis, Temple University, Philadelphia.

Benton, S. I. (1999). A descriptive study of four Black women in collegiate athletic leadership roles. Gainesville: The Florida State University.

Black Women in Sport Foundation. (1992). History. Retrieved February 27, 2006, from http://www.blackwomenin sport.org/.

Blum, D. E. (1993). Forum examines discrimination against Black women in college sports. *The Chronicle of Higher Education,* A39–A40.

Brooks, D. D., & Althouse, R. C. (1993). Racial imbalance in coaching and managerial positions. In D. D. Brooks & R. C. Althouse (Eds.), *Racism in college athletics: The African American athlete's experience* (pp. 101–142). Morgantown, WV: Fitness Information Technology.

Brooks, D. D., & Althouse, R. C. (2000). African American head coaches and administrators: Progress But. . . .? In D. D. Brooks & R. C. Althouse (Eds.), *Racism in college athletics: The African-American athlete's experience* (pp. 85–117). Morgantown, WV: Fitness Information Technology.

Brooks, D., Althouse, R., King, V., & Brown, R. (1989). Opportunities for coaching achievement and the Black experience: Have we put marginality into the system? *Proceedings of the 32nd Annual ICHPERD Conference,* 246–254.

Coakley, J. (1982). *Sport in society: Issues and controversies.* St. Louis, MO: C.V. Mosby.

Corbett, D., & William, J. (2000). The African American female in collegiate sport: Sexism and racism. In D. D. Brooks & R. C. Althouse (Eds.), *Racism in college athletics: The African-American athlete's experience* (pp. 199–225). Morgantown, WV: Fitness Information Technology.

Cunningham, G., & Sagas, M. (2005). Texas A&M University, Texas: Laboratory for Diversity in Sport.

Eitzen, D. S., & Furst, D. (1989). Racial bias in women's collegiate volleyball. *Journal of Sport and Social Issues, 13*(1), 46–51.

Eitzen, D. S., & Sage, G. H. (1989). *Sociology of North American sport* (4th ed.). Iowa: Wm. C. Brown.

Gerdy, J. R. (1994). You reap what you sow. *Black Issues in Higher Education, 1,* 30–31.

Hart, M. M. (1980). Sport: Women sit in the back of the bus. In D. F. Sabo, Jr., & R. Runfola (Eds.), *Jock: Sports and male identity* (pp. 205–211). Englewood Cliffs, NJ: Prentice Hall.

Jewell, K. (1993). From Mammy to Miss America and beyond: Cultural images and the shaping of US social policy. New York & London: Routledge.

Knoppers, A. (1992, August). Exploiting male dominance and sex segregation in coaching: Three approaches. *Quest, 44*(22), 210–227.

Lapchick, R. (2000). Women of color in sports: Double jeopardy. Retrieved August 14, 2005, from http://www.sport insociety.org.

Lapchick, R. (2005). The 2004 racial and gender equity report card. Institute for Diversity and Ethics in Sport: University of Central Florida.

Leath, V. M., & Lumpkin, A. (1992). An analysis of sportswomen on the covers and in the feature articles of women's sports and fitness magazine, 1975–1989. *Journal of Sport and Social Issues, 16,* 121–126.

Lumpkin, A., Stoll, S. K., & Beller, J. M. (2003). *Sport ethics: Applications for fair play.* Boston, MA: McGraw-Hill.

Malveaux, J. (1993). Sports scholars aren't the only outstanding students. *Black Issues in Higher Education, 10,* 54.

Merriam Webster (2005). Merriam-Webster online dictionary. Retrieved December 19, 2005 from http://www.m-w. com/cgi-bin/dictionary?va=sociocultural.html.

Morrison, S., White, R. P., Velsor, E. V., & The Center for Creative Leadership (1987). *Breaking the glass ceiling.* Reading, MA: Addison Wesley Publishing Company.

National Collegiate Athletic Association (2002, January 7). Sweet role: NCAA senior woman administrator builds a new position. NCAA News, Retrieved August 14, 2005, from http://www.ncaa.org/news/2002/20020107/active/3901n02.html

National Collegiate Athletic Association (2003). 2001–02 race demographics of NCAA member institutions' athletics personnel: The NCAA minority opportunities and interests committee's two-year study. Indianapolis, IN: Author.

National Collegiate Athletic Association. (2003–04). Senior woman administrator [Brochure]. Indianapolis, IN: Author.

National Collegiate Athletic Association. (2003–04). NCAA Division II manual, Indianapolis, IN: Author.

National Collegiate Athletic Association (2005). 2004–05 race and gender demographics of NCAA member conferences' personnel report. Indianapolis, IN: Author.

National Collegiate Athletic Association. (2005–06). NCAA Division II manual, Indianapolis, IN: National Collegiate Athletic Association.

National Collegiate Athletic Association (2005, January 8). *NCAA president calls for value-based budgeting for intercollegiate athletics programs.* NCAA News, Retrieved December 19, 2005, from http://www.ncaa.org/wps/contentviewer? IFRAME_EMBEDDED =true&CONTENT_URL= ...html

National Collegiate Athletic Association (2005, August 1). *Championing inclusion.* NCAA News, p. 7.

Ouellet, J., (2005). Structural barriers to agreement. Retrieved July 11, 2006, from http://www.beyondintractability.org/essay/structural_barriers.html

Parks, J. B., Russell, R. L., & Wood, P. H. (1993). Marital and other primary dyadic relationships of intercollegiate athletics administrators. *Journal of Sport Management, 7,* 151–158.

Richey, D. (1981). Barriers minority women face in obtaining and remaining in leadership positions. Paper presented at the American Alliance for Health, Physical Education, Recreation, and Dance National Convention, Boston, MA.

Schell, L. A. (2001). (Dis) Empowering images? Media representations of women in sport. Women's Sports Foundation: New York.

Sloan Green, T. (2000). The future of African American female athletes. In D. D. Brooks & R. C. Althouse (Eds.), *Racism in college athletics: The African-American athlete's experience* (pp. 227–242). Morgantown, WV: Fitness Information Technology.

Smith, Y. R. (1991). Issues and strategies for working with multicultural athletes. *Journal of Physical Education, Recreation, and Dance, 62,* 39–44.

Stratta, T. M. (1995). *An ethnography of the sport experience of African American female athletes.* Unpublished doctoral dissertation, Southern Illinois University, Carbondale.

Tiell, B. (2004). Supporting an NCAA amendment to require all intercollegiate athletic departments sponsoring women's athletics to have a female serve on the senior management team. Retrieved August 14, 2005, from http://tuintranet.tiffin.edu/btiell/WLS/SWA%20Research/SWA%20Editorial.htm

Vance, N. S. (1984, April 25). Football study links race, player positions: Reasons aren't clear, three researchers caution. *The Chronicle of Higher Education,* pp. 21, 24.

Women's Sport Foundation. (2003, June). *The Women's Sports Foundation Report: Title IX and Race in Intercollegiate Sport.* Retrieved August 14, 2005, from https://www.womensportsfoundation.org/cgi-in/iowa/issues/disc/article.html?record=955.

Women's Sport Foundation. (2001). *Gender equity and the black female in sport.* Retrieved August 14, 2005, from https://www.womensportsfoundation.org/cgi-in/iowa/issues/disc/article.html?record=869.

Women's Sport Foundation. (2001). *Recruiting, retention and advancement of women in athletics.* Retrieved August 14, 2005, from file://C:\DOCUME~1\LOCALS~1Temp\GJJ4WTNO.htm.

CHAPTER 3

THE ACADEMIC
EXPERIENCES
OF AFRICAN
AMERICAN
COLLEGIATE
ATHLETES:
IMPLICATIONS
FOR POLICY
AND PRACTICE

AUDWIN
ANDERSON
AND
DONALD SOUTH

▼ ▲▼ ▲▼ ▲▼ ▲▼ ▲▼ ▲

Key Terms

▼ Intercollegiate
sports ▲

▼ College athletics
and race ▲

▼ African American
males ▲

▼ NCAA reforms ▲

▼ Graduation rates ▲

▼ Major clustering ▲

▼ Retention of African
American athletes ▲

Next, the book turns to Anderson and South's research about "The Academic Experiences of African American Collegiate Athletes," which confronts questions about the *racial gap* in educational outcomes (e.g., academic majors, graduates rates) for college athletes. With some considerable caution, Anderson and South review the presumed "egalitarian principles" (Knight Foundation, 1991) used to address the academic credentials of student athletes and, next, weigh consequences of these interests for African American athletes. Their analysis opens by looking at the "social meaning of African American maleness," that is, breaking away from a cultural stereotype of low expectation. This is followed by consideration of recent NCAA academic reform practices. In the current context of large-scale, commercialized college athletic programs, Anderson and South are cautious of various academic benchmarks to handle the relationship between education and athletics, asking whether and to what extent exploitation appears in the guise of "athletic eligibility." Their mission is to arrive at a critical appraisal of the issues and practices of the "uses of graduation rates." Their question "what does a low graduation rate mean?" prompts serious recommendations.

Abstract ▼ Among the rationales for intercollegiate sports is the belief that participation will provide individuals with educational and status enhancement opportunities. For many athletes, and African American athletes in particular, this is not necessarily the case. Over the past 20 years, sociology and sport literature has documented racial differences in educational outcomes for college athletes. In fact, recent disclosures of graduation rates by the NCAA revealed that a higher percentage of white athletes graduated from college as compared to African American athletes. This work focuses on some of the circumstances that have not been favorable for the purpose of education for African American athletes. Our analysis starts by looking at the social meaning of African American maleness followed by a section on recent NCAA academic reforms. Final discussion addresses academic experiences of African American athletes and the issue of graduation rates.

Introduction

To appreciate the experiences of African Americans in big-time collegiate athletics, both athletics and academics must be addressed. A basic tension between big-time athletic values and goals and those of higher education has been widely recognized (Asher, 1986; Chu, 1989; Lawry, 1991; Hawkins, 2001; Benson 2000; Eitzen & Sage 2003). Among the traditional goals of higher education are the promotion of academic achievement and academic integrity. The overriding goal of big-time sports is to win—which translates into high-level entertainment and big revenues. It has been the task of the National Collegiate Athletic Association (NCAA) to promote and enhance the marketability of collegiate sports and simultaneously to maintain the sense of amateurism and academic integrity. The more successful the NCAA is in achieving one of these goals, the more difficult it becomes to achieve the other.

The trend among NCAA member institutions has been toward promoting entertainment. As a result, such a vast array of rules has been promulgated to regulate collegiate sports recruiting, and participation, those athletic programs and individual athletes are in constant peril of infractions. This context is applicable for athletes in general but it is experienced variously by different categories. Sociological analysis often focuses on differences among various social categories within a population. The act of using categories as a basis for analysis does not assume that such categories are necessarily different because of inherent biological or intellectual traits. Rather, the causal emphasis focuses on differential experiences by given categories. Among the more consistently important categorical differences are those of race, sex, class, and age.

Persons forming major social categories are likely to develop different world views and to experience different opportunities. In addition, individuals will be accorded different identities and statuses and will exhibit different behaviors. In short, the authors acknowledge that race categories are not discrete biological entities. Yet, social notions of race categories do have meaning and consequences for those who are assigned to these categories by themselves or others. This essay will focus on the collegiate sports experiences of African American males. More specifically, it will investigate racial differences in graduation rates and the academic experience of college.

If there is a position that we take in this work it is one of pro-education. Our wish is that this work will become part of the debate and dialogue of college athletes, coaches, academic advisors, athletic directors, and college administrators. Our goal is to help facilitate changes that will make circumstances favorable for the purpose of education for the African American athlete.

The Problem

Sport participation in American society has long been viewed as a vehicle for the assimilation of newcomers. As a conduit into mainstream American life, sport has been viewed as teaching the values of hard work, teamwork, and discipline. Proponents of sports developed a number of rationales for sport in society, its inclusion in higher education, and in the character development of individual participants (Schendel, 1965; Webb, 1969). Detractors have pointed to excesses, dysfunctions, and conflicts of interest in sport (Edwards, 1969; Eitzen, 1989). Among the rationales for intercollegiate sports is the belief that participation in intercollegiate sports will provide the athlete with educational opportunities (Naison & Mangum, 1983). For many athletes, and African American athletes in particular, this is not necessarily the case. Over the past 15 years, sociology and sport literature has documented racial differences in educational outcomes for college athletes (Naison and Mangum, 1983; Raney, Knapp & Small, 1986; Spivey & Jones, 1975; Warfield,

1986; Lapchick, 2003). In fact, as recently as the 1990–91 academic year disclosures by the NCAA of graduation rates revealed that nearly twice the percentage of white athletes graduated from college compared to African American athletes—26.6% for African Americans compared to 52.2% for whites. That gap has closed considerably. Disclosure of the graduation rates for the 2002–03 academic shows a rate of 48% for African Americans and 59% for whites. A discussion and analysis of graduation rates appears later in this chapter.

African Americans were absent from big-time college sport for most of the 20th century. In the first half of this century, African American college students attended historically black colleges and universities (Willie & Cunnigen, 1981). This trend began to reverse itself in the years following World War II. At the beginning of World War II, of the approximately 45,000 African American students enrolled in higher education, only about 10% were enrolled in predominately white colleges or universities (Mingle, 1981). Presently, most African American college students attend predominately white institutions. Approximately 1 in 10 African American males currently in Division I universities is an athlete (Coakley, 2004).

Several conditions were responsible for the abovementioned trend, not the least of which was the 1954 Brown decision of the U.S. Supreme Court, which outlawed separate educational facilities. Another important factor was the establishment of federal financial-aid programs for students and institutions. In the 1950s, the National Scholarship Service and Fund for Negro Students (NSSFNS) was established (Mingle, 1981). Legal and economic factors provided the foundation leading to the migration of African American students to predominantly white universities. This migration pattern also included African American student athletes.[1]

Harry Edwards has been an important voice in bringing the unique social and political situation of the African American athlete to the forefront (Edwards, 1969). According to Edwards, the manpower vacuum created by World War II, the 1954 Supreme Court decision, and the urge by whites to further exploit African Americans economically resulted in African Americans being allowed to venture into big-time college athletics (Edwards, 1969). African American athletes also found it to their advantage to play for predominantly white schools (Edwards, 1969; Eitzen, 1989).

College Athletics and Issues of Race

In *The Souls of Black Folk* (1969), renowned scholar W. E. B. Du Bois proclaimed that the prevailing issue of 20th-century Americans would be the problem of the "color line" (p.xi) Conservative thought in the latter years of the 20th century and the early years of the 21st century presents us with an interesting version of "colorblindness." The suggestion is made that our society does not have a race problem because we judge people on the basis of character and merit, not skin color. Though disputed (Marger, 1985; Takaki, 1987), this view was held to be true especially in the area of sports. There is much evidence that in reality, skin color continues to have a dramatic impact on one's life chances and opportunities for

1. Our discussion will be concerned primarily with the African American male athlete. This is in no way meant to disparage the experience of the African American female athlete. There are two fine chapters on African American female athletes in this volume that do more justice to that experience than space permits here.

improved mobility and success. To say that our society is colorblind at this moment in history amounts to aversion to, and neglect of, real problems and issues.

If our society is ever going to "solve" problems of race (assuming it is not an insurmountable problem), it must face, in an honest and humane manner, the issues and implications of race. Likewise, if big-time college athletics is going to solve its much publicized problems and dilemmas, it also must face honestly the issues and implications of race and race relations.

In the spring of 1991, the Knight Foundation's Commission on Intercollegiate Athletics released a report on abuses in college athletics.[2] The Commission expressed concern that "abuses in athletics had reached proportions threatening the very integrity of higher education" (Knight Foundation, 1991, p. 1). The report highlighted some of the problems of college athletics and proposed some change and remedies. Yet the report (about 40 pages) made only four indirect references to the issue of race in college athletics. In the first chapter of the report appears the statement, "Sports have helped break down bigotry and prejudice in American life" (p. 3). A section entitled "Focus on Students" includes this statement: "Intercollegiate athletics exist first and foremost for the student athletes who participate whether male or female, majority or minority . . ." (p. 8). Later, the report recommended that grants-in-aid for low income athletes be expanded to the "full cost of attendance; including personal and miscellaneous expenses" (p. 19). And finally the Statement of Principles notes: "Every student athlete—male and female, majority and minority, in all sports—will receive equitable and fair treatment" (p. 31).

The egalitarian principles put forth by the Commission are to be commended, and there is no intention here to question the sincerity of their effort. Yet, the issue of race and the educational condition of the African American athlete were not directly addressed.

In June 2001, the Knight Foundation issued another report titled *A Call to Action*. The emphasis of this report was on the degenerative effect of commercialism on college sport. The report uses very strong and unequivocal language in denouncing the growing impact of commercialism in undermining the academic mission and integrity of institutions of higher learning. For example, "Big-time athletics departments seem to operate with little interest in scholastic matters beyond the narrow issue of individual eligibility. They act as though the athletes' academic performance is of little moment" (Knight Foundation, 2001, p.14). Further, "Athletes are often admitted to institutions where they do not have a reasonable chance to graduate. They are athlete-students, brought into the collegiate mix more as performers than aspiring undergraduates. Their ambiguous academic credentials lead to chronic classroom failures or chronic cover-ups of their academic deficiencies" (p.16). Finally and succinctly, "Big-time college football and basketball have been thoroughly professionalized and commercialized" (p.23). Commendable for its forthrightness on the tension between commercialism and academics, yet, with the exception of a mention on page 15 on the racial difference in graduation rates among Division I football players, the report ignores the difficult, complex issue of race in college sport. Perhaps our society is at a point in

---

2. It should be noted that the Knight Commission is an independent organization and is not a part of the NCAA.

time when we should expect no tackling of race in such a report. We are in an era in which race is not supposed to matter because we have gotten past race. An era in which ignoring race is equated with virtue—a sense of being on higher moral ground. An era when the mentioning of race in any discourse on societal issues may be met with the accusation of *playing the race card*—the suggestion being that it is inappropriate to speak of race or racial consequences. Given this, along with the increasing commercialism in college sport, chances that the institutional and cultural view of the African American athlete will change may seem remote. Yet, our contention is that perceptions can and must be addressed and remedied.

We also take the position that there is a considerable amount of exploitation or victimization of student athletes in big-time collegiate sports. Further, we contend that African American youth are especially vulnerable. We are aware of inherent difficulties in making the case for exploitation. Exploitation involves both an objective condition and subjective evaluations. Some, in observing a situation will emphasize the former, others the latter. We will argue that a number of structural and cultural conditions are favorable for outcomes that lend themselves to interpretations of exploitation.

Through socialization, by emulation of esteemed role models and as a consequence of subcultural values, African American youth are highly oriented to the goal of a sports career (Rudman, 1986; Anderson et al., 1990). Interacting with this condition is the fact of relatively few career options. The colleges need African American youth to help provide high level entertainment to match large scale revenue opportunities. There is virtually no avenue to professional sport careers, especially football and basketball, except through college participation.[3] Colleges are faced with a paradox of maintaining academic integrity while providing entertainment with youth who are often academically ill-prepared. The athletes may not be particularly devoted to scholastic pursuit but have few options for gaining social mobility in American society.

The differential in power for these two interests is immense. Colleges can dictate that youth must be capable of generating big-time entertainment to generate big dollars in exchange for rather small amounts of compensation and the hope of securing a professional sports position. Intense competition results because the number of positions is small and the players, numerous. To gain one of the scarce positions athletes, especially those with less talent, must single-mindedly pursue that goal to the exclusion of academic interests. Therefore, the end result for many is little monetary reward, little education, and an accumulation of debilitating injuries.

It seems that the issue which most needs to be addressed is the educational experiences of African American athletics in revenue-producing sports (e.g. football and basketball) at our nation's universities. We currently are witnessing declining university enrollment rates for African American students, especially African American males (Marden, 1992). This is occurring at a time when we are also witnessing conflicts over multiculturalism in university curricula, a backlash against affirmative action policy, cutbacks in student financial aid, "race" politics, political correctness, and questions about the appropriateness of quotas in hiring.

---

3. The authors are well aware that in recent years there have been a small number of elite high school basketball players who have bypassed college and gone directly into the National Basketball Association.

In light of this, an argument can be made that the recruitment by universities of African American athletes provides these athletes with an increasingly unique opportunity for an education. We wish to bring particular attention to the word *opportunity*. Webster's New World Dictionary (1998) defines opportunity as "a combination of circumstances favorable for the purpose" (p. 950).

For the remainder of this work we will focus on some of the circumstances that have not been favorable for the purpose of education for African American athletes. We will start by looking at the social meaning of African American maleness, followed by a section on academic reforms by the NCAA. We will then speak to issues of the academic experiences of African American, including graduation rates.

Social Meaning of African American Maleness

In a very important piece of work by Fordham and Ogbu (1986), it was found that many inner-city African American youth define academic success as "acting white." The implication of this position is that academic success is the domain of whites. This perception leads Fordham and Ogbu to suggest that many African Americans discourage their peers, perhaps unconsciously, from emulating white academic striving and achievement. As a result, African American students who are academically able do not put forth the necessary effort in schoolwork and, consequently, perform poorly in educational settings. To the extent that this is true, what does it mean, to use the opposite term, to "act black"?

In recent history, we have witnessed the label used to describe persons of African descent change from Negro to black to Afro American to African American. What do these changes connote? Does each label connote a different set of behaviors, attitudes, dispositions, and lifestyles that define and delineate? The view held here is that the changes connote an ongoing search for identity, a search for a home on America's cultural landscape, a quest for a self-generated definition of what it means to be of African descent and a native-born American.

Sports have been held up in our society as an arena in which African Americans, particularly males, could compete and achieve without the bane of discrimination, an activity where merit was rewarded and achievement was unambiguous and evident to all. For the African American male, sport has provided an activity in which to forge an identity. But, one must ask, what of this identity? Where did it come from? Is it self-generated? Why does it involve such physicality? Why was this identity not forged through medicine or law?

It seems plausible to argue that the aforementioned labels connote a different way of interpreting experiences during this ongoing quest for identity. Certainly the "angry black man" of the 1960s interpreted his experiences differently than the "docile Negro" of previous times. In this vein the label African American has the potential for eliciting a new interpretation, a broader and fuller interpretation of maleness than is proffered by the American stereotype.

Karenga (1980) took a particular view of the African American male. He contended that the major problem in the African American community is the lack of a cultural base or cultural identity. He also contended that the media's influence on African Americans, in particular males, has been maximized in the absence of a strong cultural base and identity. Karenga maintained that African Americans possess a "popular culture" rather than a "national culture." Popular culture is defined as the "societal perception and stereotypes of your group" (p.18), whereas national culture is more of a self-generated (group-based) definition. The first is externally generated and imposed; the latter is a self-definition by the subject group.

Marable (1986) presented a similar position by suggesting that the essential tragedy of being African American and male is the inability of African American men to define themselves apart from the stereotypes that the larger society imposes on them. Marable contended that through various institutional means these stereotypes are perpetuated and that they permeate our entire culture. Marable's position is that not only have the stereotypes informed the larger cultural image of the African American male, but have also had a long-standing influence on how the African American male develops a definition of self.

The historical stereotypes of the African American male have been very narrow and usually physical. The image has been of a laborer, or super athlete, or sexual stud. The more menacing part of the stereotype has the African American male as a predator or criminal. These views have been coupled with the stereotype that African American males are unintelligent and incapable of learning. The major point to be made here is that these are not self-generated definitions, even though they may be in part accepted by African American males.

If the label African American does have the potential for eliciting a new interpretation of identity, it must allow for a more multidimensional identity. Certainly it must include an educational dimension. For African American athletes, particularly those in football and basketball programs on predominately white campuses, there must be a consciousness that their academic lives are being constructed in part by people who question their ability to learn. They cannot lose sight of the fact that the perception of others toward them has a history and the outcome of their academic careers is being shaped by those perceptions. Race still matters, and an active battle needs to be waged against the assumptions of others as well as against the culture of low expectations to which they themselves have acquiesced. A view of themselves as complete men—spiritual, intellectual, and physical men—will not come from those who do not know them and their experiences. It must come from their collective selves.

NCAA Academic Reforms

> "For fifteen years we have had a race problem. We have raped a generation and a half of young black athletes. We have taken kids and sold them on bouncing a ball and running with a football and that being able to do things athletically was going to be an end in itself." (Joe Paterno, cited in Coakley, 1986, p.143)

The above remark by Pennsylvania State University head football coach Joe Paterno, spoken from the floor of the 1983 NCAA Convention, is said to have provided the emphasis that led to passage of Proposition 48 [By-law 5-l (J)]. This proposition was proposed by the American Council on Education and implemented for the 1986–87 academic year. The by-law established the academic requirements that high school seniors must meet in order to be eligible for participation as freshmen in NCAA sanctioned Division I sports. The requirements were:

1. High school seniors must maintain a 2.0 grade point average in a curriculum that contains at least three English credits, two math, two natural or physical science and two social science courses. At least 11 academic courses in high school must have been taken by a prospective athlete.

2. High school seniors must achieve a combined score of 700 on the Scholastic Aptitude Test (out of 1600), or a score of 15 on the American College Testing Exam (out of 36).

More stringent revisions of these standards, called Proposition 16, were passed by the NCAA in 1992 and went into effect for athletes entering college in August 1995. The number of "core" courses increased to 13 from the previous 11. With a high school grade point average of 2.00 (C), the student now needs a minimum score of either 1010 on the Scholastic Aptitude Test (SAT) or a combined score of 86 on the American College Test (ACT) to gain full admission status. With higher grade point averages, a decreasing scale of SAT or ACT scores are required (www.ncaa.org).

From their inceptions, Propositions 48 and 16 have been met with controversy (Picou, 1986; Eitizen and Sage, 2003). According to Sage (1989), Proposition 48 is a classic example of "blaming the victim." Sage contends that NCAA places the blame on the student athlete for being academically ill prepared for college level work. Yet, the cause of the problem is that university officials have been willing to admit academically ill-prepared students for reasons of competitive sports success. Sage (1989) sees the NCAA's call for higher academic standards as a "charade" that has moved attention away from the "commercialized structure of major college athletic programs and focused it on the athlete" (p. 169).

Sage's points are well taken. Clearly one of the major antecedents of the conditions that led to Proposition 48 was the recruitment of academically marginal students and the employment of various methods to keep them eligible. Also, the admission of academically marginal students is primarily a problem of revenue sports (football and basketball).

One of the fallouts or latent functions of the by-law is that it created a situation whereby the nation's junior colleges, which are not governed by the by-law, act as a kind of "feeder" to Division I schools. Division I schools are in some cases accountable for the education of the student athlete for only two years, and in some cases even a shorter period of time. It is likely that in some colleges and universities the junior college transfer in football could exhaust athletic eligibility by maintaining academic eligibility for only two semesters. This situation does not facilitate education and creates a structural situation that lends itself to exploitation.

Indeed, over the past several years some African American youth have been following a course of attending community colleges with the expectation that they will be "taken care of" academically—that they will automatically qualify for admission to Division I programs or that academic counselors in athletic programs will "arrange" matters to make them eligible. Such practices have led to allegations of questionable or fraudulent course credits (Chronicle of Higher Education, August 16, 1996, p. A37). According to recent reports form the NCAA, African American junior college transfers have graduation rates 15–20% lower than their white counterparts. Further, in Division I-A football, African American junior college transfers graduate at a rate 15% lower than African Americans who enter four-year schools as freshmen. Similarly, in Division I-A basketball, African American junior college transfers have graduation rates 6% lower than African-Americans who enter four-year schools as freshmen (www.ncaa.org, 2006).

The major fallout of the by-law has been its racial consequences. Reports show that 85% of those losing eligibility under Proposition 48 have been African American (Cross and Koball, 1991; Johnson, 1988). In addition, Proposition 48 disqualified a sizeable percentage of African American athletes who might have graduated. According to Grambling State University president Dr. Joseph Johnson (1988) 40% of the athletes that have graduated in the past would be ineligible under present rules. Chu (1989) gives figures which show that if Proposition 48 standards had been applied in the years 1977–1980 they would have disqualified 69% of the African American and 54% of the white athletes who went on to graduate.

Proposition 48 was also met by direct charges of racism by presidents of the nation's historically black colleges. Joseph Johnson, who was Chairman of the National Association of Equal Opportunity in Higher Education Athletic Committee at the time Proposition 48 was passed, speaking on behalf of 114 black institutions, stated:

> It was our collective view that Proposition 48 was a very poorly thought out proposal. We were concerned because we knew that the rule would impact most severely on black athletes. It was thrust upon us; none of us were included in any of the debates about the proposition. That was the thing. We thought it was unfair because we are members of the NCAA, and the Proposition was brought to the floor by the American Council on Education without our input. (Johnson, 1988, p.4)

Proposition 48 has a particularly negative effect on historically black institutions, which have a long tradition of remediating the academic shortcomings of African American students. It has exacerbated the financial difficulties faced by athletic programs at these institutions (Edwards, 1989). As pointed out by Johnson, traditionally black institutions do not have the economic resources to finance the education of students made ineligible by Proposition 48 until they are eligible. Some black college presidents have even proposed that black institutions be exempt from Proposition 48 standards or be allowed to establish their own standards (Edwards, 1989).

Harry Edwards is the most visible and well known spokesperson on the plight of the African American athlete in American sports. His activist position on improving the academic condition and image of the African American athlete is well documented. His work in the area is so important and persuasive that one cannot speak to the social condition of the African American athlete without recognizing the contributions of Edwards. He has taken a position (see Edwards 1984, 1985) that is at odds with many African American educators and coaches. Edwards sees the establishment of Proposition 48 as a method of stemming the exploitation of African American athletes in the collegiate setting. Edwards even goes as far as to argue that the cutoffs for ACT and SAT scores should be higher, which would result in less exploitation. He feels that lowering the standard would send the message to African American athletes that they are not intellectually capable of achieving these standards. Edwards also contends (as do these authors) that African American athletes themselves must take a stand against their own exploitation. They must have an interest in getting an education.

The idea of a universal academic standard appears to us to be a bit problematic. It seems to ignore the fact that some universities are more academically challenging and rigorous than others. A counterproposal that has some potential for remediating the problem of admissions and low graduation rates would hold universities responsible for not recruiting athletes who do not have a reasonable chance of performing up to that university's standards, whatever those standards may be.

We should mention two other issues currently being pursued that might present uncertain hope of circumventing eligibility guidelines. One of these is the possibility of invoking "learning disabilities" as a basis for academically qualifying with less than standard scores (Chronicle of Higher Education, January 5, 1996, p. A47).

The other item is the growing number of so-called "prep schools." A recent online editorial by *The New York Times* characterizes these schools as places where bogus grades are given to barely literate athletes who often take no real courses. Their investigation found schools without classrooms where the only teachers were the coaches (NYTimes.com, March 2, 2006)

African American youth are ill-served by such schemes to circumvent academic eligibility guidelines. Their interest would appear to be better served by pursuing opportunities offered by The Princeton Review Foundation and promoted by the National Alliance of African American Athletes to enhance test scores (*USA Today*, October, 30, 1996). The thrust of this new effort is not to "fight" standards of eligibility—though they may sometimes appear unfair—but to promote SAT workshops that provide practice and analysis designed to produce better test results.

The most recent reforms passed by the NCAA came in January, 2005. Raising the six-year graduation rates of athletes to above 50% is the primary goal of the new reforms (Sperber, 2005). The new reforms will prescribe escalating penalties for schools that don't graduate players (Griffin, 2005). Starting in December, 2005 the NCAA issued an annual Academic Progress Rate (APR) to its member schools. The APR will be used to determine if member schools are in compliance with academic progress standards (progress toward degree, improvement in grade point average, 50% graduation rate over a five-year span). For the first year the APR will only serve as a warning. Failure to meet compliance standards in subsequent years could result in loss of scholarships, lost of post-season play, and the possible loss of regular-season play (Griffin, 2005).

Academics

Our previously stated goal in this work was to help facilitate changes that will make circumstances favorable for the purpose of education for the African American athlete. African American athletes at predominantly white institutions continue to be faced with a particular set of problems. One of these problems is overcoming the stereotype of being intellectually inferior while possessing innate athletic superiority. Often the message given to African American athletes is, "You are inferior intellectually. We do not expect you to achieve academically. You are here because of your athletic ability."

In a study by Kiger and Lorentzen (1987) it was found that type of sport and race were negatively related to university academic performance for males. Minority male athletes and revenue-producing sport athletes tend to do less well. Adler and Adler (1989) found that student athletes enter college with high expectations, then over the course of their college careers make a pragmatic adjustment and resign themselves to inferior academic performance. This adjustment on the part of the students was due to time demands of sport and the coaches' steering them to manageable athletic-related majors such as physical education and recreation. The athletes received greater reinforcement for athletics than for academics.

More recently Benson (2000) found that the marginal academic performance of a small sample of Division I African American football players was due to the interrelated practices of peers, teachers, coaches, advisors, and the athletes themselves that established and reinforced limited academic expectations. From the beginning of their college careers, starting with recruitment, they "perceived implicit and/or explicit messages that school was not important, that they were not considered intellectually capable students, were not expected to do well in school, and were not cared about as individual student learners" (Benson, 2000, p. 229). They were spoken to by their peers about the minimum they had to do academically, advisors chose courses for them without their input, efforts to communicate academic interest to advisors were ignored, and coaches gave lip service to the issue of academics (Benson, 2000).

The above-mentioned studies point to some very serious problems for the educational experiences of athletes. In order to improve the situation we feel the following issues must become part of discourse on college athletes and education. These issues address problems faced by all student athletes. However, in the context of this essay, it is important to note that African American athletes are more vulnerable to these conditions.

1. Except under unusual circumstances the athlete's academic schedule should not be made out by the athletic department with little or no student participation. The responsibility for academic careers must be, in part, the responsibility of the individual athlete, and the individual athlete must claim ownership of this responsibility. To not do so retards the opportunity for intellectual development. If the experience of attending college is to provide preparation for life, the athlete's dependency on the athletic department to "take care of things" retards maturation and provides no preparation.

2. Along the same lines, academic advisors for student athletes should report to an academic Dean or the Office of the Provost. Individuals who hold academic advising positions in athletic departments are not faculty. They need to be accountable to the academic arm of the university.

3. The notion that sports is a fertile avenue of upward mobility for African American males must be dispelled. Educational attainment provides far more upward social mobility for African American males than does sport. The emphasis should therefore be on education as the most fertile avenue of upward social mobility.

4. The one-year renewable grant-in-aid sends out an anti-educational message. It says that you are an athlete first, and your opportunity to get an

education is dependent on your athletic achievements. The grant-in-aid should be renewed for up to five years and should be terminated only for academic reasons. Consistent with the best practices as proposed by the Coalition on Intercollegiate Athletics (2005), we recommend that the authority for revoking a scholarship rest with the chief academic officer.

5. Given the time demands of collegiate football and basketball it is difficult to stay on schedule for graduation. Some of the revenue generated by intercollegiate sport could be put into a fund that would provide financial resources for the completion of education once a player's eligibility ends.

6. The playing of NCAA Division I football games on Wednesdays and Thursdays should be eliminated. Given travel time, too much time is missed from classes.

Graduation Rates

The issue of graduation rates among college athletes has been given much scholarly as well as popular attention in recent times (Suggs, 1999; Suggs, 2002; Suggs, 2003a). It has also resulted in federal legislation (HR1454) better known as the Student-Athlete Right-to-Know Act. This act requires federally funded colleges and universities to report annually the graduation rates of student athletes by sport, race, and sex. These data are to be supplied to high school officials and made available to families so that more informed decisions might be made in choosing among college options. This proposal has spurred action by the NCAA to collect data from its member institutions beginning October, 1991 to implement the intent of the Act. Findings from 2003 graduation rates preliminary survey data are given in Table 1.

In evaluating graduation rates for athletes, several considerations are in order:

1. How do athlete graduation rates compare with non-athlete rates?

2. How do categories of athletes compare with similar categories of non-athletes, *viz.* African American male athletes with African American male non-athletes?

3. Should graduation rates be accepted uncritically as a measure of institutional responsibility?

4. Do graduation rates reveal much, if anything, about academic counseling programs? Do the high graduation rates at Duke and Georgetown, for example, mean they have superior academic supports for their athletes in comparison with schools having lesser rates?

5. It is not purely a matter of whether a degree is obtained, but also a matter of what type degree.

6. Issues of uniformity in how graduation rates are compiled and defined must be addressed and solved.

Table 1. Graduation Rates of Division I Male Athletes Entering College, 1996–97 and Graduating Within Six Years by Race and Selective Sport

Graduation Rates	Percentage
All male students	56%
White	59%
Black	35%
All male athletes	55%
White	59%
Black	48%
All football athletes	54%
White	61%
Black	48%
All male basketball athletes	44%
White	52%
Black	41%

Source: 2003 NCAA Graduation Rates Report. www.ncaa.org

Collectively, the research on student athlete graduation rates has reached the following conclusions among many.

1. The graduation rates of all male college athletes (55%) are about the same as the graduation rates of all male non-athletes (56%) six years after entering college. However, there are great variations by school, race, and type of sport.

2. African American male athletes graduated at slightly higher rates (48%) than did their non-athlete counterparts (35%).

3. Generally, but with a few exceptions, the most competitive basketball program schools have graduation rates lower than those schools that do not make it to the NCAA tournaments.

4. African American male student athletes in basketball had the lowest graduation rates of any category (41%).

Critical Appraisal of Use of Graduation Rates

There are a few important issues that deserve consideration in making appraisals of graduation rates. First, how do the graduation rates of top-performing programs in football and basketball compare to other schools.

Overall graduation rates for college athletes have increased over the years (46% for class entering in 1984 compared to 62% for class entering in 1996). How do the graduation rates for the top-performing programs in football and basketball compare? *The 2005 Racial and Gender Report Card* provides data on the graduation rates for college football bowl teams and college basketball men's Sweet 16 teams for 2004–05 (Lapchick, 2005). The report shows that for the 56 schools that participated in post-season bowl games, 27 (48%) graduated less than 50% of their players, while 39 (70%) graduated less than 50% of their African American players. In addition, 30 schools (55%) had graduation rates for African American players at least 20% lower than the rate for white players. On the other hand, some schools have impressive graduation rates for student athletes overall as well as for African American student athletes. Table 2 below shows the 2004–05 college football bowl teams with the highest student athlete graduation rates.

Table 2. Top Graduation Rates for College Football Bowl Teams, 2004–05 in Percentages

School	Football Athlete	African Amer. Athlete	White Athlete	Overall Students
Notre Dame	77	76	76	94
Boston College	78	74	82	87
Syracuse	78	69	91	77
Virginia	75	63	93	92
So. Mississippi	66	67	64	53
Purdue	63	59	65	64

Source: 2005 Racial and Gender Report Card: College Sports.

Lapchick (2004) provides similar data for college basketball's Sweet 16 for 2004. He notes that only four of the schools would have been eligible to play if they had been required to have graduation rates of at least 50%. Only 11 of the 16 schools reported their graduation rates. It was found that 4 (36%) of the 11 schools had graduation rates for their basketball players 30 to 39 percentage points lower than the overall rate for athletes.

A second issue that might confound graduation rates is the phenomenon of clustering. Clustering occurs when athletes in certain sports are overrepresented in certain courses and majors. According to Coakley (2004) we tend to see the phenomenon in sports and teams that place eligibility over academics and intellectual growth. A study by Upthegrove, Roscigno, and Charles (1999) found a concentration of African Americans in sports where the athletic-academic tension is greatest, revenue-generating and commercialized programs—namely football and basketball. The available data on clustering is almost exclusively in regards to football programs. A recent article looked at the choice of academic majors for football players on teams involved in college bowl games during the 2002 season (Suggs, 2003b) and concluded that there were clusters of athletes in particular majors in all cases. The author of the piece contended that academic advisors steer athletes into degree programs that make it easier to meet NCAA academic standards, particularly in men's football and basketball, where institutions admit based on athletic ability rather than academic potential. This trend is said to be likely to increase as NCAA has phased in tougher academic standards.

Some athletic directors defend such steering on grounds that it is professors and administrators who approve majors and not the athletic department (Suggs, 2003b). John Anderson, associate athletic director for academic services at Texas Tech, opposes clustering and points out those athletes are majoring in legitimate academic programs that meet academic needs (*Dallas Morning News*, February 19, 2005). It has also been pointed out that some schools may discourage athletes from declaring a major in their first year and place them in generic programs like general studies or interdisciplinary studies. This practice allows them to take core courses early in their careers (Miller, 2005). Some have called for the disclosure of athletes' majors. William Dowling, an English professor at Rutgers and the head of a faculty watchdog group called the Drake Group, contends that colleges should disclose information about what athletes major in as well the aggregate GPA's of the students in those majors. Similarly, Andy Geiger, athletic director at Ohio State, has suggested a system for reporting to the NCAA what athletes major in and why (Lederman, 2003).

It is acknowledged that systematic attention to graduation rates may function to sensitize universities and some prospective students to the degree to which universities are adhering to academic goals, yet, it would be a mistake to accept uncritically the position that such emphases are all positive.

A labeling theory perspective would project some unwanted or unintended consequences of the Student Athlete Right-to-Know Act. Schools labeled as nonacademic through this procedure would likely be avoided by academically interested students and/or parents. Those students wishing a nonacademic athletic experience would have an officially recognized list of schools that would offer a nonacademic athletic experience. Thus, the effect would be to continue or even exacerbate the problem of low graduation rates for some schools.

Meaning of Graduation Rates

What does a low graduation rate mean? As some wags have indicated it could mean that while we have lowered standards to let some athletes in we have not yet gone the next step of according unearned degrees. It might mean that schools with the highest graduation rates are expending the most effort on behalf of the athletes that they admit. Rather, it is much more likely that high graduation rates reflect selectivity in admissions. There are a finite number of blue chip athletes who are also blue chip scholars. Some programs are able to recruit these few. If other programs are to compete athletically they must accept good athletes with lesser degrees of scholastic potential. Finally, there are programs that will have to settle for athletes with still greater scholastic deficits. It seems unreasonable to expect similar admission standards and graduation rates in each of these situations.

Rather than promoting a national standard for admissions and graduation rates, perhaps it would be more reasonable to assess these measures against the mission of the school, its own admission standards and graduation rates. Perhaps it would be more meaningful to try to evaluate what a school does to advance the scope and skills of those athletes that they do admit. A case study approach might yield some remarkable incidents of "scholastic progress" on the part of students who could never enter one of the more traditional programs.

Summary and Recommendations

The marriage between education and athletics is likely to endure for the foreseeable future. There will be occasional spats, mediated by the NCAA and the Council of Presidents, but academic interests have become so interwoven with those of sport entertainment that dissolution is unlikely. Indeed, without well-planned policies it is likely that the economic potential of big-time sports will result in the sports partner dominating the union.

African Americans, particularly inner-city African Americans, have been socialized to expect professional sports careers all out of proportion to reality (Edwards, 1973). Given this condition, coupled with the relative lack of alternative occupational opportunities and virtually no other avenues to the pro game, African Americans are particularly vulnerable to exploitation. The colleges need manpower to produce an exciting spectacle in order to enhance revenue. African Americans want the experience and exposure necessary to get to the pros.

These basic facts are unlikely to change to any considerable degree, thus they must be taken as a given in proposing any solutions.

1. If more effective "minor league" or other preparatory arrangements were provided by the system, then there would be fewer athletes in academia who do not want to be there. In no other industrialized world power is the college expected to be a training ground for professional sports. Two new basketball leagues for teenagers now are being planned (Chronicle of Higher Education, May 10, 1996, p. A48) to provide developmental opportunities for youth who do not enroll in college. The Teenage Professional Basketball League is scheduled to begin play in the summer of 1997.

2. We should continue or develop policies which assure that the athlete can participate in a meaningful educational experience, after admission.

3. When in the collegiate setting, the athlete should be paid in a manner somewhat more commensurate with his or her economic productivity.

4. The income from collegiate sports should be distributed among colleges more equitably than currently, thus removing some of the emphasis on winning at all costs.

5. The tenure of coaches should be determined in part by considerations other than winning, thus allowing them to be more responsive to academic and character-building concerns.

6. Universities should be prepared to spend some of the money generated by sports in assuring counseling, tutoring, and related services to those athletes in need because of time and energy expenditure on behalf of the school.

The issues that we raise and our proposals for solution certainly do not exhaust the possibilities. Some of our proposals would no doubt raise additional issues and problems of their own. Our views are shaped by the nature of our discipline and a combined experience of some 40 years of working with athletes in the academic setting. It is our sincere hope that the promise of higher education and status attainment will become a more universal reality for the African American student athlete. We pledge our efforts to that end and trust that student athletes will assume their individual responsibilities in this collective endeavor.

▲▼ Suggested Readings ▲▼

Davis, T. (1995). The myth of the superspade: The persistence of racism in college athletics. *Fordham Urban Law Journal* 22(2), 615–698.

Eitzen, S. D. (2005). *Sport in contemporary society: An anthology* (7th ed.). Paradigm Publishers.

Hoberman, J. (1997). *Darwin's athletes: How sport has damaged black America and preserved the myth of race.* Boston: Houghton Mifflin.

King, C. R., & Springwood, C. F. (Eds.) (2001). *Beyond the cheers: Race as a spectacle in college sport.* Albany: State University of New York Press.

Shulman, J. L., & Bowen, W. G. (2001). *The game of life: College sports and educational values.* Princeton, NJ: Princeton University Press.

Sperber, M. (2000). *Beer and circus: How big-time college sports is crippling undergraduate education.* New York: Henry Holt and Company.

▲▼ Study Questions ▲▼

1. What were the conditions that led African American students to start attending predominately white colleges and universities following WWII.

2. Why are the authors critical of the two Knight Commission Reports? Why do the authors feel the issue of race was avoided in these reports?

3. In what ways do the authors suggest we be critical about graduation rates?

References

Adler, P., & Adler, P. A. (1989). From idealism to pragmatic detachment: The academic performance of college athletes. In D. S. Eitzen (Ed.), *Sport in contemporary society: An anthology* (pp. 142–157). New York: St. Martin's Press.

Anderson, A., Warfield, J., Picou, J. S., & Gill, D. A. (1990). Race and the educational orientations of college athletes: Implications for career counseling. *Applied Research in Coaching and Athletics Annual,* 27–40.

Asher, M. (1986). Abuses in college athletics. In R. Lapchick (Ed.), *Fractured focus* (pp. 5–20). Lexington, MA: D. C. Heath and Company.

Benson, K. F. (2000). Constructing academic inadequacy: African American athletes' stories of schooling. *The Journal of Higher Education, 17*(2), 223–246.

Chu, D. (1989). *The character of American higher education and intercollegiate sport.* New York: State University of New York Press.

Coakley, J. (1986) *Sport in society: Issues and controversies* (3rd ed.). St. Louis: Times Mirror/Mosby.

Coakley, J. (2004). *Sport in society: Issues and controversies* (8th ed.). Boston: McGraw Hill.

Coalition on Intercollegiate Athletics (2005). Academic integrity in intercollegiate athletics: Principles, rules, and best practices. www.ncaa.org

Cross, L. H., and Koball, E. G. (1991). Public opinion and the NCAA Proposal 42. *Journal of Negro Education, 60,* 181–194.

Davis, T.(1996) African American student athletes: Marginalizing the NCAA regulatory structure? *Marquette Sports Law Journal 6* (2), 199–228.

Dubois, W. E. B. (1969). *The souls of black folk.* New York: Signet.

Edwards, H. (1969). *The revolt of the black athlete.* New York: The Free Press.

Edwards, H. (1984). The collegiate athletic arms race: Origins and implications of the "Rule 48" controversy. *Journal of Sport and Social Issues, 8,* 4–22.

Edwards, H. (1985). Beyond symptoms: Unethical behavior in American collegiate sport and the problem of the color line. *Journal of Sport and Social Issues, 9,* 3–13.

Edwards, H. (1989). The black "dumb jock": An American sports tragedy. In D. S. Eitzen (Ed.), *Sport in contemporary society: An anthology* (3rd ed., pp. 158–166). New York: St. Martin's Press.

Eitzen, D. S. (1989). Ethical dilemmas in sport. In D. S. Eitzen (Ed.), *Sport in contemporary society: An anthology* (3rd ed., pp. 300–312). New York: St. Martin's Press.

Eitzen, D. S., & Sage, G. H. (2003). *Sociology of North American sport* (7th ed.). Boston: McGraw Hill.

Fordham, C., & Ogbu, J. (1986). Black student's school success: Coping with the burden of "acting white." *The Urban Review, 18,* 176–206.

Griffin, T. (2005, February 27). NCAA academic reforms: If few pass, fewer will play. *San Antonio Express News.* Section C.

Hawkins, B. (2001). *The new plantation: Internal colonization of black student-athletes.* Winterville, Georgia: Sadiki Press.

Johnson, J. (1988). Personal interview. *New Perspectives, 19*(4), 10–12.

Karenga, M. (1980). *Kawaida theory: An introductory outline.* Inglewood, CA: Kawaida.

Kiger, G., & Lorentzen, D. (1987). Gender, academic performance and university athletics. *Sociological Spectrum, 7,* 209–222.

Knight Foundation Commission on Intercollegiate Athletics (1991). *Keeping faith with the student-athlete: A new model for intercollegiate athletics.*

Knight Foundation Commission on Intercollegiate Athletics (2001). *A call to action: Reconnecting college sports and higher education.*

Lapchick, R. (2004). *2004 racial and gender report card.* The Institute for Diversity and Ethics in Sport: University of Central Florida.

Lapchick, R. (2005). *2005 racial and gender report card.* The Institute for Diversity and Ethics in Sport: University of Central Florida.

Lawry, E. G. (1991, May 1). Conflicting interests make reform of college sports impossible. *The Chronicle of Higher Education,* A44.

Lederman, D. (1991, March 27). College athletes graduate at higher rate than other students, but men's basketball players lag far behind, a survey finds. *The Chronicle of Higher Education,* Volume XXXVII, A1.

Lederman, D. (1991, July 10). Black athletes who entered colleges in mid-80's had much weaker records than whites, study finds. *The Chronicle of Higher Education,* Volume XXXVII, A31.

Lederman, D. (2003, November 19). Major issue: Athletes' studies. *USA Today.* www.USAToday.com

Marden, C. F. (1992). *Minorities in American society* (6th ed.). New York: Harper Collins.

Marable, M. (1986). The black male: Searching beyond stereotypes. In R. Staples (Ed.), *The black family: Essays and studies* (pp. 64–68). California: Wadsworth.

Marger, M. N. (1985). *Race and ethnic relations: American and global perspectives.* California: Wadsworth.

Miller, J. (2005, February 19). One major issue: Do athletes get easy ride? *Dallas Morning News.* www.dallasnews.com

Mingle, J. (1981). The opening of white colleges and universities to black students. In G. Thomas (Ed.), *Black students in higher education* (pp. 18–29). Westport, CT: Greenwood Press.

Naison, M., & Mangum, C. (1983). Protecting the educational opportunities of black college athletics: A case study based on experiences of Fordam University. *Journal of Ethnic Studies,* 119–125.

National Collegiate Athletic Association (2003). NCAA graduation rates report. www.ncaa.org

National Collegiate Athletic Association (2006). Impact of proposed academic reform initiatives on junior college students. www.ncaa.org

New York Times (2006). Betraying student athletes. March 2. www.NYTimes.com

Picou, J. S. (1986). Propositions 48, 49-B and 56: Implications for student-athletes, coaches and universities. *The Journal of Applied Research in Coaching and Athletics, 1,* 135–147.

Raney, J., Knapp, T., & Small, M. (1986). Pass one for the Gipper: Student athletes and university coursework. In R. Lapchick (Ed.), *Fractured focus* (pp. 53–60). Lexington, KY: D.C. Heath and Company.

Rudman, W. J. (1986). The sport mystique in black culture. *Sociology of Sport Journal, 3*(4), 305–319.

Sage, G. H. (1989). Blaming the victim: NCAA responses to calls for reform in major college sports. In D. S. Eitzen (Ed.), *Sport in contemporary society: An anthology* (3rd ed.). New York: St. Martin's Press.

Schendel, J. (1965). Psychological differences between athletes and non-participants in athletics at three educational levels. *Research Quarterly, 36*, 52–67.

Sperber, M. (2005). When "academic progress" isn't. *The Chronicle of Higher Education, 51*(32), B14.

Spivey, D., & Jones, T.A. (1975). Intercollegiate athletic servitude: A case study of the black ethnic student athlete, 1931–1967. *Social Science Quarterly, 55*, 939–947.

Suggs, W. (1999). Graduation rates hit lowest level in 7 years for athletes in football and basketball. *Chronicle of Higher Education, 46*(3), A58.

Suggs, W. (2002). Athlete's graduation rates hit all-time high. *Chronicle of Higher Education, 49*(6), A47.

Suggs, W. (2003a). Athlete's graduation rates set a record. *Chronicle of Higher Education, 50*(3), 35.

Suggs, W. (2003b). Jock majors. *Chronicle of Higher Education, 49*(19), A33.

Takaki, R. (1987). *From different shores: Perspectives on race and ethnicity in America.* New York: Oxford University Press.

Upthegrove, T. R., Roscigno, V. J., & Charles, C. Z. (1999). Big money collegiate sports: Racial concentration, contradictory pressures, and academic performance. *Social Science Quarterly, 80*(4), 718–737.

Warfield, J. (1986). *Corporate collegiate sport and the rule of race issues for counseling: Debate and understanding* (pp. 30–36). Boston: Boston University Press.

Webb, H. (1969). Professionalization of attitudes toward play among adolescents. In G. S. Kenyon, (Ed.), *Aspects of contemporary sport sociology.* Chicago: The Athletic Institute.

Webster's New World dictionary of American English (3rd college ed.), (1988). New York: Simon and Schuster.

Willie, C., & Cunnigen, D. (1981). Black students in higher education. *Annual Review of Sociology*, 177–198.

An emerging concern in the broader context of social justice is "life after the game." *From Glory to Glory: The Transition of African American Athletes from College Sports into Athletic Retirement* opens a new avenue of understanding about career mobility as the black athlete transitions into a non-athlete, post-college career. Anchored by an overview of NCAA policies on post-college careers, Billy Hawkins, Brianne Milan-Williams, and Akilah Carter explore models of post-career transition, the nature of adaptation and adjustment, the ease and dysfunction encountered in such mobilities. Folded into their assessment, the authors report on their research among former African American college athletes, describing problems, issues, processes, and dissatisfactions experienced during their transition to non-athletic careers. All in all, survey findings suggest that African American collegians do not make an easy transition to athletic retirement, and that negotiating the transition may rest, indeed, on opportunity and support to acquire meaningful educational competencies.

CHAPTER
4

FROM GLORY
TO GLORY:
THE
TRANSITION
OF AFRICAN
AMERICAN
ATHLETES
FROM
COLLEGE
SPORTS INTO
ATHLETIC
RETIREMENT

BILLY J. HAWKINS,
BRIANNE
MILAN-WILLIAMS,
AND
AKILAH CARTER

Key Terms

▾Athletic retirement▴
▾Transition▴
▾Intercollegiate
athletics▴
▾NCAA CHAMP/Life
Skills Program▴

Abstract ▾ This paper will focus on the transition of African American athletes from intercollegiate athletic competition to a career. It will provide an overview that will include the National Collegiate Athletic Association (NCAA) stance on the welfare of student athletes, a literature review of models and theories that have detailed athletic transition, the unique experiences of African American athletes striving for social mobility in an environment of perceived limited opportunities, and an analysis of data collected on former African American athletes who have made a transition from athletic competition to a career, or who are continuing their education. Examining these issues could be helpful to sport management practitioners, athletic academic counselors, coaches, parents, and African American student athletes. There are too many accounts of athletes having tremendous success in competing and increasing the economic gains of athletic departments, yet they have been less successful in athletic retirement, unfortunately, with many succumbing to depression or a small percentage conforming to the pressures that foster criminal behaviors. These occurrences can be reduced with the right initiatives and the critical mass of people willing to make a difference.

Introduction

Athletic administrators, counselors, agents, coaches, sport psychologists, and the athletes themselves all have a vested interest in doing all they can to smooth the transition from what clearly is a brief career as an athlete to the more long-term endeavor of a contributing human being.
—LeUnes and Nation (1996, pp. 554–555)

The period of transition from intercollegiate athletics into a career can be a challenging experience for many intercollegiate athletes, especially for African American athletes. Athletic retirement, whether through selection process, age, or injury, has been an important area of inquiry. For example, researchers have engaged this topic from the point of surveying athletes' levels of satisfaction at the end of their intercollegiate athletic careers. A study of 1123 student athletes (426 male and 697 female athletes) found that 89% of the females and 90% of the males looked forward to the expiration of their intercollegiate athletic participation (Greendorfer & Blinde, 1985a). Furthermore in another example, Perna, Ahlgren, and Zaichowsky (1999) examined athletic retirement induced by injury and found that there was reduced life satisfaction among a sample of Division I athletes. This study found the reduction in life satisfaction was greater for African American athletes than whites.

Athletic retirement is a topic of significance for sport management practitioners for several different reasons. One reason is because the continuity of maintaining a competitive and entertaining event can be disrupted when athletes transition from one level to the next or into another career. With the tenure of blue chip athletes in certain revenue-generating sports decreasing with early entry into the draft, Division I athletic departments are challenged with maintaining a competitive balance to ensure minimum economic loss. Another scenario that poses a challenge to sport management practioners is when a star player suffers a career-ending injury. The aspect of athletic retirement or transition that impacts sport management practitioners is being able to consistently market and promote a product (athletic performance) that is inconsistent and has a transient nature, as well as to entertain a demanding student fan base that changes from year to year. For example, what challenges do sport management practitioners face when a star athlete leads a team to a national championship and then decides to enter the draft early? What happens when a student athlete meets the National Basketball Association's (NBA) age requirement, as when Carmelo Anthony left Syracuse University, after leading the team to the NCAA men's basketball championship, to enter the NBA draft a few months later?

Athletic retirement is also a topic of significance for sport management practitioners because millions of youth pursue sport as a means of social mobility. This provides athletic departments, in general, with a consistent pool of talent to select from and create successful programs. Ultimately, these youth dream of one day becoming professional athletes. Unfortunately, the popular press and research literature is quite explicit in denoting the chances of achieving direct social mobility from intercollegiate sports into professional sports. Of the major three professional sports, the following are the probabilities of making it into professional sports from college: 1.3% (1 in 75) of senior male basketball players will get drafted by a NBA team, 2% (1 in 50) of senior male football players will get drafted by a National Football League (NFL) team, 10.5% (less than 11 in 100) senior male baseball players will get drafted by a Major League Baseball (MLB) team.[1] This data clearly illustrates the limited possibility that an athlete will expe-

---

1. For estimated probability of competing in athletics beyond college, see the following website: http://www.ncaa.org/research/prob_of_competing. For information on how the NCAA determine these probabilities, visit the following website: http://www.ncaa.org/research/prob_of_competing /probability_of_competing2.html#methodology.

rience direct social mobility into professional sport. It also illustrates the need for sport management practitioners to take a more active role in preparing student athletes for careers outside of becoming professional athletes.

Even when there are no opportunities to compete at the professional level, the benefits of intercollegiate athletic participation are not without merit. The NCAA overall graduation rates have increased to 62%, and athletes are graduating at a faster rate than the regular student body (NCAA Division I Graduation Rates, 2003). The graduation rate for African American males athletes still lag significantly at 43%, while the African American female athlete graduation rates is at 60%.[2] Although the rates for African American males are low, they have increased in the past ten years. A worthy note of caution regarding the increased graduation rates among African American male athletes involves the degrees that these athletes are earning from their respective institutions. A case study of academic clustering among major college football players showed that African American males are graduating with degrees that earn considerably less than their white male teammates (Thornton & Hawkins, 2006). For example, 62% of the black athletes who graduated during the last year studied graduated with degrees with an average income range of $20,000 to $24,999, while 53% of the white athletes graduated with degrees with a average income range of $25,000 to $29,999. This is significant when you factor in the fact that 61% of the team were African American and 82% of the starters were African American (100% of the defense are African American and 64% of the offense are African American) (Carter, Thornton, & Hawkins, article in review). Increased rates of graduation are great; however, making sure students are graduating with degrees that will allow them to transition into a job market with marketable and employable skills is also important.

Despite the odds of making it into professional sports, many young athletes try to defy the odds and achieve the dream of becoming professional athletes. Although the opportunities have increased with the expansion of leagues and addition of "minor" leagues (e.g., Arena Football League or NBA Developmental League), the number and level of talent and skill of athletes competing for these positions are increasing, especially with the import of international talent in certain major league sports (e.g., basketball and baseball). These professional sports leagues in the U.S. provide much more lucrative opportunities for players migrating from their respective countries. This migration will undoubtedly increase the level of competition and the number of players competing for a limited number of positions; potentially a better product, but fewer opportunities.

The allure of fame and fortune has been a deception to many athletes, yet there are other opportunities available for those who will not make it as professional athletes but will graduate with a college degree. Many who start out with dreams of becoming professional athletes will more than likely experience indirect social mobility after their intercollegiate athletic careers have ended. Indirect social mobility can be defined as transitioning into a career path other than becoming a professional athlete. The most obvious form of indirect social mobility is when an athlete obtains a college degree and is able to transition into a career or labor force as a gainful employee. During the 2005 NCAA Men's Basketball Final

2. For a detailed breakdown of graduation and explanation of computation, see the following website: HYPERLINK "http://www.ncaa.org/grad_rates/2003/d1/index.html" http://www.ncaa.org/grad_rates/2003/d1/index.html.

Four, the NCAA aired a series of public service announcements (PSA's) that emphasized the fact that each year over 360,000 NCAA student athletes will be competing in careers other than sports.[3] These commercials illustrated the reality of indirect social mobility: the fact that many intercollegiate athletes will not become professional athletes but will transition into other careers. Furthermore, it is classified as indirect social mobility because there is clear evidence that an individual with a bachelor's degree will earn nearly twice as much as an individual with a high school diploma. For example, in 2003, African Americans with college degrees earned 60% more than African Americans with high school diplomas, and whites with college degrees earned 49% more than whites with high school diplomas (see Wirt, et al, 2005). Thus, for sport management practitioners, especially those working in intercollegiate administration, assisting athletes in preparing for careers outside of being professional athletes is paramount.

Because athletic retirement will be the road most traveled by the majority of athletes after their intercollegiate athletic careers, this chapter will focus on the transition from intercollegiate athletic competition to a career, among African Americans athletes. It will provide an overview that will include the National Collegiate Athletic Association (NCAA) stance on the welfare of student athletes, a literature review of models and theories that have detailed athletic transition, the unique experiences of African American athletes striving for social mobility in an environment of perceived limited opportunities, and finally an analysis of data collected on former African American athletes who have made a transition from athletic competition to a career or continuing education.

NCAA and Athletic Retirement

The National Collegiate Athletic Association (NCAA) is the governing body of the most visible and lucrative intercollegiate athletic divisions, and it often sets the standard that other intercollegiate governing bodies follow. Since it governs one of the most visible and lucrative intercollegiate athletic divisions, the way in which the NCAA approaches athletic retirement is worthy of examination.

The athlete is the major commodity in intercollegiate athletics; therefore, athletes' welfare during and after their eligibility ends should be the primary concern of the National Collegiate Athletic Association (NCAA) and its member institutions, not just in theory but also in practice.[4] The NCAA publishes manuals each year that state all of the Association's goals, missions, and intentions. Included in these manuals for Divisions I, II, and III is a section 2.2 entitled "The Principles of Student Athlete Welfare." Athletic retirement should fall under the umbrella of the NCAA's Principles of Student Athlete Welfare. This portion is divided into six subsections, four of which are of particular relevance to athletic retirement.

This portion of the *NCAA Manual* (2003a-c) lays out the Association's intentions to "protect and enhance the . . . welfare of student athletes" (p. 3). Athletic retirement and post-career depression should be points of concern when it comes

---

3. To see the PSA's go to http://www2.ncaa.org/index_sports.php; accessed on July 30, 2005.
4. Athletes are a major commodity in the sense of their use value in marketing and selling sporting goods and sport paraphernalia (e.g., jerseys, etc.). They are also the critical mass of the labor force for corporate athleticism. Although a variety of staff members contribute to the promotion and planning of the sporting event, the performance and performers make the spectacle, thus creating the product.

to a college athlete's welfare, as these topics relate specifically to bylaws 2.2.1, 2.2.3, 2.2.5, and 2.2.6. These areas clearly fall under section 2.2 and athlete welfare that the NCAA so vehemently professes to safeguard.

Section 2.2.1 maintains that the activities and requirements of NCAA athletes should be in harmony with the enhancement of their overall educational experience. Part of this enhancement should include increasing the awareness of the potential difficulty athletic retirement poses and implementing pre-retirement planning as part of the college experience. Some coaches, athletes, and administrators may argue that discussing the issue of retirement is counter-productive or defeating for those who wish to pursue a professional career in their chosen sport (Crook & Robertson, 1991). According to the Knight Commission (2001):

> Sadly though, it comes as a rude surprise to many athletes yearning for a professional sports career to learn that the odds against success are astronomically high. Approximately 1 percent of NCAA men's basketball players and 2 percent of NCAA football players are drafted by NBA or NFL teams—and just being drafted is not assurance of a successful professional career. "Student athletes" whose sole and now failed objective was to make the pros suddenly find themselves in a world that demands skills their universities did not require them to learn. (p. 16)

Not only are these former athletes lacking the preparation and coping skills necessary to ease the transition out of athletics, they now must rely on the scholastic education received while at their institution of higher learning. The Knight Commission (2001) delivered appalling results from its investigation into the state of college athletics. According to the published findings:

> Big-time athletics departments seem to operate with little interest in scholastic matters beyond the narrow issue of individual eligibility. They act as though the athletes' academic performance is of little moment. The historic and vital link between playing field and classroom is all but severed at many institutions. (pp. 14–15)

Although athletic departments are known to provide tutors and study hall for athletes, there is often a hidden agenda behind these services, because "the academic support and tutoring athletes receive is too often designed solely to keep them eligible, rather than guide them toward a degree" (Knight Commission, 2001, p. 16).

Section 2.2.5 specifically gives each member institution the responsibility of ensuring that their coaches and administrators are held accountable for being fair, open, and honest with their athletes. While the section is vague in how these three things relate to athlete welfare, one could argue that intentionally not discussing athletic retirement with athletes is a violation because the coaches and administrators are ignoring an issue that is clearly important to the athletes' welfare. Coaches in particular have the opportunity to breach the topic of athletic retirement due to the amount of time they spend with their athletes. In addition, coaches have the privilege and ability to use the NCAA's compulsory maximum of 20 hours per week in any way they see fit—which can include requiring their players to attend certain talks, programs, or functions. As a general rule, "Coaches are closest to the athletes and have the most influence on the quality of their collegiate experience" (Knight, 2001, p. 25).

Finally, bylaw 2.2.6 points again to each institution and stresses the responsibility of ensuring that athletes are involved "in matters that affect their lives" (NCAA, 2003, p. 3). Athletic retirement is undoubtedly a serious matter that affects all intercollegiate athletes. The NCAA is trying to meet this challenge by developing programs to assist student athletes in matters affecting their lives, on and off the field.

In 1994, the NCAA instituted the CHAMPS/Life Skills Program (Challenging Athletes' Minds for Personal Success). This program is committed to academic and athletic excellence, personal and career development, and service. Preparation for athletic retirement falls nicely under the CHAMPS/Life Skills commitment to personal development that specifically pledges, "To support the development of a well-balanced lifestyle for student athletes, encouraging emotional well-being, personal growth and decision-making skills" (NCAA, CHAMPS/Life Skills Program Commitment Statements section, 2004, p. 3). This program provides a forum for important issues to be addressed within the athletic and university settings. While pertinent topics such as sexual assault and eating disorders—two areas commonly addressed—are important and should not be devalued, there are few matters that will inevitably affect every single athlete like athletic retirement. Since athletic retirement is vaguely addressed in the NCAA's approach to the welfare of athletes, this chapter will examine several models and theories associated with athletic retirement and provide some insight into athletic retirement among former collegiate African American athletes.

This following section reviews models and theories concerning athletic retirement, including factors such as playing a significant role in how an athlete adapts to this life change, reactions to retirement, and possible interventions to ease the transition into athletic retirement. A discussion regarding implications of the literature findings is also included.

Models and Theories on Transition from Athletic Competition

At some point in our lives, the majority of us will experience a retirement from our current occupation. For most, this will occur later in life as we reach senior status and ages in the 60s or 70s. This is a fairly normal and expected event that one plans for well in advance. However, certain populations experience this retirement earlier in life and either do not expect it or are not prepared for the implications of such an event. Professional and elite amateur athletes fall under this category.

Literature regarding athletic retirement has emerged slowly over the past 35 years. The first definitive study was done by Mihovilovic (1968) entitled, "The Status of Former Sportsmen," and relatively few have followed his lead in recognizing athletic retirement and the adjustment of the athlete following retirement as an area worthy of study. Coakley (1983) is perhaps the most commonly cited study subsequent to Mihovilovic (1968). According to Coakley (1983), "Some ex-athletes have made a successful transition from active involvement in competitive sport to other satisfying activities, but others cling to their trophies, sport identities, and memories in ways that seem to impede their development" (p. 3).

A discrepancy exists in the reactions of athletes to the end of their sporting careers. Why do some athletes transition out of sports and into a second career without much difficulty while others fall victim to depression and other traumatic responses? Ogilvie and Taylor (1993) reason, "The often single-minded pursuit of excellence that accompanies elite sports participation has potential psychological and social dangers. . . . The personal investment in and the pursuit of elite athletic success, though a worthy goal, may lead to a restricted development" (p. 770). The sport sub-culture often fosters behaviors that are overdeveloped regarding physical skills and abilities, yet limited in nurturing other skills that are required to function effectively outside of the sporting environment.

A review of athletic retirement literature revealed that a number of models and theories from a variety of disciplines, including social gerontology and thanatology, have been developed to explain the unique experience of an individual's transition from competitive athlete to non-athlete post-career (Crook & Robertson, 1991; Ogilvie, 1987; Ogilvie & Taylor, 1993; Rosenberg, 1993; Wolff and Lester, 1989). Social gerontology denotes the life satisfaction in relation to aging. As it relates to sport retirement, four of the concepts presented in the social gerontology theory were found to be most applicable to individual perceptions: activity, continuity, disengagement, and social breakdown theory (Greendorfer & Blinde, 1985b). Thanatology, or the study of death and dying, explores sport retirement in terms of being isolated socially. Both social gerontology and thanatology are "criticized for their narrowness of approach, and analysis suggests that neither may be applicable to the athlete who voluntarily or involuntarily leaves sport" (Greendorfer & Blinde, 1985b, p. 87).

Five models and theories in particular have detailed the concept of athletic retirement. First and foremost is the Human Grieving Model, authored by psychologist Elisabeth Kübler-Ross. According to Kübler-Ross (1969), when an individual finds out that he is terminally ill, he often goes through distinct grieving stages of denial and isolation, anger, bargaining, depression, and finally acceptance. It is important to note that one can slip back and forth between stages while grieving and that not everyone will reach the final stage of acceptance. In addition, there is no definitive event marking the transition between stages because it is a gradual process (Kübler-Ross, 1969). Kübler-Ross's model is significant in the arena of athletic retirement because the five stages are cited to mirror the retired athlete's grieving process as career termination is often described as a type of death and dying (Baillie, 1993; Blinde & Stratta, 1992; Grove, Lavellee, Gordon, & Harvey, 1998; Ogilvie, 1987; Ogilvie & Taylor, 1993; Rosenberg, 1993; Wolff & Lester, 1989).

A second model is a modification of Ebaugh's Role Exit Theory. Ebaugh's theory focuses on mid-life transitions that apply to centrally important roles, such as sport to an athlete (Drahota & Eitzen, 1998). The Account-Making Model provides a third illustration of how an athlete might come to terms with retirement. In this model, Grove, Lavellee, Gordon, and Harvey (1998) argue that construction of a story of a traumatic event is central to working through and coping with the event.

The fourth model is Taylor and Ogilvie's (1994) conceptual model of athletes' adaptation to retirement. This model specifically takes into account factors related to the athlete's adjustment to retirement, resources available to the athlete, crises experienced during the retirement process, and interventions to ease the transition. Athletes experience dramatic changes when their competitive careers are over, but the way in which they address these changes and the resources they use will, in part, determine how well they transition into retirement (Taylor & Ogilvie, 1994).

A fifth model by Schlossberg (1981) is a prediction model used to determine which athletes would have difficulties in the transition process. Six personality categories were identified 1) athletes who based their identity on athletic performance; 2) athletes who have a large gap between their level of ability and their ability of aspiration; 3) athletes who have few to no experiences with similar transitions; 4) athletes who have emotional and behavioral deficits limiting their ability to cope with change; 5) athletic isolation limiting contact to and ability to maintain supportive relationships; and 6) athletes who lack the resources to cope with the public transition.

To summarize, the five models presented have brought to light the process of athletic retirement. Unfortunately, these models fail to effectively factor the perceptions based on race, class, and gender. However, the models have identified concepts, or factors that affect the rate and ease of transition for the athlete as it relates to sport.

Contributing Factors

A number of factors have been identified that influence or effect an individual's transition from athlete to non-athlete. Seven factors in particular, however, were found to be more prevalent and thus will be discussed further. These factors include the athlete's reason for retirement, level of competition, pre-retirement planning, social support, post-retirement involvement in sport, career satisfaction, and individual characteristics.

Reason for Retirement. Though retirement is inevitable, athletes deal with leaving their sport in a wide variety of ways. The most crucial factor in how an athlete handles the transition from competitive athlete to retired sportsperson is the reason for the retirement. Athletic retirement, in general, is fueled by one of four scenarios: age, deselection, injury, or free choice (Ogilvie & Taylor, 1993).

Age can be viewed in two dimensions, both physiological and psychological. As one ages, it becomes increasingly difficult to maintain strength, endurance, coordination, flexibility, and fine motor skills. Psychologically, the aging athlete may also begin losing both the motivation and incentive to train at the intensity necessary to continually compete at the professional or elite level (Ogilvie & Taylor, 1993).

Deselection may be the most common reason for athletic retirement. As the level of competition increases, fewer and fewer athletes can advance and be successful in their sport. The selection process occurs from Little League to high school to college and on to elite amateur and professional competition. In this process only the best advance, and even they do not remain at the top very for long (Ogilvie & Taylor, 1993).

A third and familiar end to an athletic career is injury. Ogilvie and Taylor (1993) found that:

> Elite athletes perform at such a high level that even a small reduction in physical capabilities may be sufficient to make them no longer competitive at that level. As a consequence, injury need not be serious to have dramatic impact on athletes' performances and, in turn, their careers. (p. 766)

In the case of injury, athletes who are success-oriented have the drive and tenacity to do whatever it takes to return to their sport. This attitude can be both helpful and harmful, as the athlete can be irrational in denying the medical diagnosis and therefore resisting the appropriate treatment, dismissing it as too cautious or conservative. Because of this drive, often athletes do not realize for some time that they are now in athletic retirement. At this point, a career-ending injury may result in serious distress that can manifest itself in substance abuse, depression, and loss of self-esteem (Ogilvie & Taylor, 1993).

A fourth and relatively uncommon cause of retirement is that of free choice. This is obviously the most desirable cause of termination because it generally leads to the most positive transition. The decision by an athlete to retire can be based on a number of personal, social, or sport-related factors, but the voluntary aspect of it often minimizes the difficulty.

Level of Competition. Coakley (1983) states that men and women whose highest level of sport competition is high school or college athletics tend to experience successful adjustment out of sport. The greater ease with which these athletes handle the transition is likely due to the thought that they "would be less likely to have their status and their relationships directly linked to their sports involvement" (Coakley, 1983, p. 3) than professional or elite amateur athletes.

Pre-retirement Planning. Pre-retirement planning plays a crucial role in the transition to retired athlete. The first step is recognizing the inevitability of a sports retirement and thus preparing for that eventuality (Pearson & Petitpas, 1990; Werthner & Orlick, 1986). Such training includes effective money management and long-term financial planning, education and career training, and engaging in other leisure activities (Ogilvie & Taylor, 1993; Pearson & Petitpas, 1990; Crook & Robertson, 1991). In other words, creating a balanced life that does not solely revolve around participation and excellence in one's particular sport will ease the transition.

While leading a balanced life may not sound like a difficult task, many elite athletes find it challenging to look beyond the athletic arena. Ogilvie and Taylor (1993) inform us that, "Many of these athletes may experience a false sense of security that makes career planning a low priority for them" (p. 763). In fact, athletes may fail to prepare because they are reluctant to discuss their retirement while still competing as retirement thoughts may be looked upon as self-defeating (Crook & Robertson, 1991). Realistically, however, the unique schedule of the professional and elite amateur athlete makes it very difficult to pursue and develop interests outside of sport. Practice times, travel schedule, and discouragement by the management and/or coaches make this type of preparation nearly impossible (McPherson, 1993). The Knight Commission (2001) reinforced this concept, specifically in relation to collegiate athletes:

> As soon as they arrive on campus, they are immersed in the demands of their sports. Flagrant violation of the NCAA's rule restricting the time athletes must spend on their sport to 20 hours a week is openly acknowledged. The loophole most used is that of so-called "voluntary" workouts that don't count toward the time limit. In light of these circumstances, academic failure, far from being a surprise, is almost inevitable. (p. 16)

Again, time constraints such as these leave little or no time to cultivate relationships and interests outside of one's sporting culture. Thus, preparing for a career academically and creating the desired balanced life becomes nearly impossible.

Social Support. Social support also factors in to how athletic retirement is handled. Family and friends are critical for a smooth transition because athletes generally have a small support system due to their heavy involvement in sport and lack of time spent outside of the sporting arena. Management, coaches, and teammates who once provided support often avoid or ignore the athlete in retirement (Crook & Robertson, 1991).

Post-retirement Involvement and Career Satisfaction. A study conducted by Werthner and Orlick (1986) found that athletes who did not report difficulty following retirement continued their involvement in sport in some capacity. These data suggest that a decrease in the kind of competitive involvement, but not a complete break away from the sport, may ease the transition. In addition, the majority of athletes who indicated moderate to extreme turmoil revealed dissatisfaction with aspects of their career such as personal performance or their coaches and sporting organizations.

Individual Characteristics. Lastly, individual factors contribute greatly to the athlete's reaction to career termination. Often the degree to which one defines his self-worth in terms of participation and achievement in sport dictates his adaptation to retirement (Werthner & Orlick, 1986). This dependence on sport for identity and self-esteem can make the athlete vulnerable to an identity crisis at the completion of athletic competition (Crook & Robertson, 1991; McPherson, 1993; Werthner & Orlick, 1986). Athletic identity is often a result of:

> . . . intense ego commitment to athletic achievement that is found so consistently in the athletes who are most vulnerable to career-ending emotional traumas. Those athletes who have gained a positive identity and feelings of self-worth primarily through the expression of their motor skills are at greatest risk. (Ogilvie, 1987, p. 219)

Additionally,

> By the nature of their personal sacrifice of time, energy, and interest, allows their sport to become the total focus of their lives. Attaining the desired level of competence and being able to express such in the competitive arena takes precedence over any other form of human expression. (Ogilvie, 1987, p. 213)

Reactions to Retirement

A number of negative reactions can come from athletic retirement. Even if athletes have engaged in pre-retirement planning, they can still fall victim to a variety of unfavorable reactions. Eric Nesterenko, a retired hockey player, gives voice to the troubles that many athletes experience following retirement:

> But the game—the game doesn't prepare you for anything else. And although you knew it mentally, you could say I never absorbed it emotionally. All it leaves you with, when you reduce it, is this memory of an incredible high, an extraordinary alertness. Either you try to re-create that focus or you give it up . . . At my age (46) I'm casting about for something to do. (McPherson, 1993, p. 593)

As the above excerpt illustrates, the retired athlete is forced to find ways to cope with the residual effects of retirement.

According to a study by Curtis and Ennis (1993), of the 109 retired elite level male hockey players surveyed, 75% reported feeling a loss after leaving competitive sport. Of those 82 athletes, 14.6% said they experienced "quite a feeling of loss." This feeling of loss is likened to the grief experienced when a loved one dies and the individual feels powerless to do anything about it. This supports Kübler-Ross's Human Grieving Model, and the five stages of coping with loss come into play, where denial, anger, bargaining, depression, and acceptance can be observed in athletes who feel that they have lost something critical to their existence.

For professionals and elite amateurs, sport often gives meaning and purpose to their lives. Commonly, as young adults, athletes must begin to search for and engage in something that will promote a sense of personal satisfaction in the same way that sport once did. This is often a source of great stress for the athlete who is unprepared for this lifestyle change (Ogilvie, 1987).

Athletes can also experience a loss of status and social identity following retirement (Wolff & Lester, 1989). The effects of this loss can result in decreased life satisfaction, depression, loss of self-esteem, inability to succeed at a second career, and even pathological behavior such as substance abuse, criminal behavior, and suicide. Sinclair and Orlick (1993) found that the most prominent difficulties encountered during the transition were missing social aspects of sport, job and school pressures, and finances. They also found that the most common coping strategies for these athletes were to find another area of interest to focus on, simply to keep busy. Werthner and Orlick (1986) make it clear that though trends exist regarding the retirement of athletes, reactions and perceptions about the retirement remain very individual.

Interventions

Though the majority of athletes make the transition to retirement fairly successfully, clearly there is a significant portion of this population who experience difficulty. This then raises the question: Who should be responsible for preparing athletes for career termination? Ogilvie (1987) suggests that because of coaches' and sport-governing bodies' power to end an athlete's career or determine performance criteria, they should harbor the responsibility of preparing the athletes for their impending retirement. Some athletes actually feel that these individuals and/or organizations owe it to them after the years of time and effort the athletes put forth.

Some organizations have taken on the task of assisting athletes in preparing for athletic retirement. For example, The Unites States Olympic Committee (USOC) has realized the importance of assisting athletes with career termination issues and thus created Career Assessment Program for Athletes (CAPA) in 1980 with services for Olympic or Pan-American Games athletes. In 1989, the USOC developed a manual with the objective of guiding these elite athletes in preparing for life after competition. The U.S. Olympic Committee also provided national athletes the opportunity to attend career counseling training seminars (Ogilvie & Taylor, 1993). In fact, special counseling, psychotherapy, and career planning services have been available since 1981 to any former professional athlete upon request (Ogilvie, 1987).

According to Taylor and Ogilvie (1994), pre-retirement planning seems to have the broadest influence on the quality of adaptation to athletic retirement. "By more clearly identifying factors related to successful retirement, pre-retirement counseling programs could be designated to prevent or alleviate problems" (Crook & Robertson, 1991, p. 123). Such intervention programs emphasize the importance of broadening one's self-identity, enhancing perceptions of control, diversifying social identity, and using the resources available to the individual. Pre-retirement planning must also emphasize the brevity of most sport careers as athletes commonly resist looking ahead to life post-retirement. Lastly, an intervention is most effective when it occurs pre-retirement because it promotes the opportunities of retirement as well as identifying at-risk individuals who are likely to experience future difficulties (Baillie, 1993; Baillie & Danish, 1992; Pearson & Petitpas, 1990; Werthner & Orlick, 1986).

Though pre-retirement planning should be the primary intervention, post-retirement planning is also available and often necessary. Sport psychologists are specifically trained to assist athletes therapeutically in dealing with any emotional distress that may arise. The retired athlete can be expected to experience some form of frustration, doubt, self-identity and self-worth issues, and/or grief, and the sport psychologist can aid in addressing these affective concerns with individual counseling or group therapy (Baillie, 1993; Ogilvie & Taylor, 1993).

Organizations ranging from the U.S. Olympic Committee to the NBA and NFL to collegiate institutions are now realizing that career retirement among athletes can be a difficult adjustment and have begun to develop programs to help athletes make a smooth transition. With the development of these programs and services that treat retirement as a means to an end and not the end, retirement from athletic competition can be a smooth transition into additional career achievements.

African American Intercollegiate Athletes' Experiences with Athletic Retirement

The experiences of African American intercollegiate athletes have been well documented. A significant portion of the literature has highlighted challenges African Americans face as athletes at NCAA colleges and universities. Several researchers have focused on issues concerning recruiting, living conditions, predominance, retention, and graduation rates of African American athletes (see Anderson & South, 1993; Harris, 1993; Lederman, 1991 & 1992; Sellers et al., 1991; Sellers, 1992 & 1993; Spivey & Jones, 1975; Miller, 1927). These studies have examined how African American athletes are highly recruited for their athletic talents and have high attrition rates, but low graduation rates. Other studies have addressed discrimination practices in sports (see Davis, 1990; Berghorn, Yetman & Hanna, 1988; Hawkins, 2001; Koch & Hill, 1988; Leonard, 1987; McPherson, 1976; Clement, 1954). These studies have focused on discrimination, positional segregation, and representation at the collegiate level. Also, in the mainstream media, movies such as, *He Got Game, Love and Basketball, The Program, Blue Chips,* etc., have also documented the experiences of African American intercollegiate athletes. This popular mass media venue has captured varying realities of the experiences of African American intercollegiate athletes and presented alternative, although glamorized and dramatic, perspectives to this social phenomenon.

African American youth, and more specifically males, as opposed to their white peers, are more likely to see sport as their ticket to social mobility. This is captured in the lyrics of one of hip-hop culture's fallen heroes, Biggie Smalls. He proclaimed that there are "two ways out the hood. Have a wicked jump shot or slinging crack rock."[5] Apparently, according to this hip-hop prophet, the avenues for success afforded to many African American youth are either as a drug dealer or as an athlete. This limited perception of opportunities is unfortunately the reality for millions of African American youth. Thus, being narrowly focused on achieving social mobility through sports often leaves many ill-prepared to transition into other careers once their hopes of becoming professional athletes are diminished. This places a premium on the need to examine the experiences of athletic retirement among African American athletes. Athletic retirement should also be examined among African American athletes because of their unique experiences as class fractions of the athletic labor force (see e.g. Hawkins, 2001).[6]

This section will examine the factors associated with athletic retirement among African American who competed in intercollegiate sports. Twenty-one African American former intercollegiate athletes provided us with insight into athletic retirement. Each was given a questionnaire consisting of open-ended and Likert-scale type questions to complete at their leisure and return to the researchers. The questionnaire was designed to access seven factors contributing to athletic retirement discussed previously. In order to gain insight into athletic retirement among African American student athletes, the findings from their responses will be highlighted. The goal was to examine how African American student athletes have fared in making a transition from intercollegiate athletics to a career. Therefore, the following areas were surveyed: level of competition, reason for retirement, pre-retirement planning, social support, individual characteristics (athletic identity and reactions to retirement), and finally, post-retirement involvement and career satisfaction.

Insight on Athletic Retirement among Former African American Athletes

Fifteen males and six females provided insight on the seven factors contributing to athletic retirement. Fifteen (71%) of the participants had graduated with a bachelor's degree or higher, and six (29%) were in the process of completing their degree. The sports the participants competed in were as follow: seven competed in football, six competed in basketball, seven competed in track and field, and one participant competed in volleyball. Fifteen of the participants were scholarship athletes, while six were walk-ons—non-scholarship athletes. Years last competed ranged from 5 to 23 years ago (average = 14.5 years). Therefore, participants were both pre- (62%) and post- (38%) CHAMPS/Life Skills Program (Challenging Athletes' Minds for Personal Success, see page 70).

Level of Competition

Seventy-one percent of the participants competed at the Division I (D-I) level, while the remaining participants competed at either Division II (D-II) or Division

---

5. Lyrics selected from Biggie Smalls' *Things Don't Change*, on his *Ready to Die* album. http://rap.abo ut.com/gi/dynamic/offsite.htm?site=http://ohhla.com/YFA%5Fbig.html
6. Because they migrate to campuses from different social and cultural environments and make up a small percentage of the overall student body, their experiences are uniquely different from that of their white teammates, who can blend into these predominantly white settings and benefit from white privilege, especially when their playing days are done.

III (D-III) levels (4 at D-II and 4 at D-III). Sixty two percent of the participants competed four years, 24% competed for 3 years, 10% competed for two years, and 4% competed only one year.

Reason for Retirement

Nineteen of the participants (90%) responded that the reason for athletic retirement was that they were at the end of their eligibility, while two participants (10%) experienced a career-ending injury that caused their retirement. Sixty-two percent of the participants (9 males and 4 females) believed they could have competed at the professional level, while 38% responded that they had very little chance of making it to the professional level.

Pre-retirement Planning

Seventy-five percent of the participants never talked about athletic retirement, while the remaining 25% talked with either coaches or athletic support staff. Furthermore, the majority of the participants stated that they never had a career-planning class or attended a workshop or lecture that involved athletic retirement. The few participants receiving information about athletic retirement explained that they received information from a position coach, head coach, or counselors. One participant stated:

> Retirement was implied and quietly talked about via the question, "So, what are you going to do next year?" (after graduation or after the season); during senior year—maybe even junior year if your playing time was obviously minimal.

Social Support

Fifty percent of the participants reported having friends outside of sport and 50% did not have friends outside of their teammates. All of the participants reported that their families played an important role as a support system after athletic retirement. Regarding the athletic department staff being a good source of support after athletic retirement, 48% reported that the athletic department staff was not a source of support, while 52% of the participants reported that it was a source of support. Although only 43% were involved in activities and clubs outside of their respective sports, 90% reported having something to identify with after athletic retirement.

Individual Characteristics

The majority of the participants (52%) did not look forward to the end of their intercollegiate athletic competition, and 48% felt prepared for life after intercollegiate competition. Sixty-six percent of the participants felt a void after athletic retirement, and 71% reported being lonely after their intercollegiate career was complete. However, the majority of the participants (81%) reported that the transition into athletic retirement was easy. Some of the comments explaining the ease of the transition were:

▼ "[I was] ready to do something different";

▼ "Love[d] hoops, but was prepared to move on to other responsibilities";

▼ "I was prepared to be a teacher";

▼ "After suffering major knee injury, decided NFL was not in future plans. Started preparing to work even harder to receive college degree"; and

▼ "[I] moved to another phase of playing career, so [it was] natural progression."

Some of the comments explaining the difficulty of the transition were:

▼ "I think it was tough because I came from a poor high school"; and

▼ "I was not ready to stop playing, and I was unprepared for life after collegiate sports."

Although the majority reported ease with this transition, 62% of the participants reported that it took at least a year to feel comfortable. We finally asked participants to best describe their feelings during their last competitive event using the following emotions: happiness, sadness, relief, and despair. Participants' responses to this question are as follows: 28% reported feelings of happiness, 48% reported feelings of sadness, and 24% reported feelings of relief after their last competitive event.

Post-retirement Involvement and Career Satisfaction

The majority of the participants reported that their involvement included coaching (66%), playing at the recreational level (66%), and as a spectator of their respective sport (71%). Therefore, the majority of the participants remain connected to sport in some capacity.

Regarding satisfaction with their competitive careers and athletic retirement, 95% of the participants reported satisfaction with their competitive careers, while 90% reported satisfaction with athletic retirement.

Summary and Recommendations

The purpose of this chapter was to examine transition from intercollegiate athletic competition to a career or the labor force among African American athletes in order to assist sport management practitioners in providing services to make this transition successful, as well as to provide them with insight on the challenges African American athletes face in making this transition. This chapter examined how African American student athletes have fared in making a transition from intercollegiate athletics to a career to gain insight into the seven factors contributing to their athletic retirement.

Twenty-one African American former intercollegiate athletes volunteered to provide us with insight into athletic retirement in the following areas: level of competition, reason for retirement, pre-retirement planning, social support, individual characteristics (athletic identity and reactions to retirement), and finally, post-retirement involvement and career satisfaction. Of the twenty-one participants, fifteen were male (71%) and 6 were female (29%). Fifteen (71%) of the participants had graduated with a bachelor's degree or higher, and six (29%) were in the process of completing their degree. The sports the participants competed in were: seven competed in football, six competed in basketball, seven competed in track and field, and one participant competed in volleyball. Fifteen of the participants were scholarship athletes, while six were walk-ons—non-scholarship athletes.

A summary of the data revealed that the majority of the participants competed at the Division I level. The literature is clear in presenting a multitude of reasons for athletic retirement. However, 90% of the participants reported that the reason for athletic retirement was that their eligibility ended. Two of the participants had a career-ending injury that forced them into athletic retirement.

The majority of the participants reported never having a conversation about athletic retirement with coaching or athletic department staff. The majority of participants also reported never attending a workshop or lecture on athletic retirement. The goal was to see if participants received pre-retirement planning information from coaching staff, athletic academic support staff, or university career centers in the form of workshops, seminars, etc. This is significant because pre-retirement planning benefits in the transition of athletes into other careers.

Regarding social support after athletic retirement, family members were reported to be the most important source of support. This data supports previous findings that family and friends are critical for a smooth transition because athletes generally have a small support system due to their heavy involvement in sport and lack of time spent outside of the sporting arena.

The majority of the participants did not want their intercollegiate athletic careers to end and felt a void after they ended. This coincides with previous finding that highlight the fact that, when athletes have devoted the majority of their early years competing and their self-worth is interwoven in the fabric of their athletic achievement, ending athletic careers is difficult (Crook & Robertson, 1991; McPherson, 1993; Ogilvie, 1987; Werthner & Orlick, 1986). Despite this finding, 81% of the participants reported ease in transitioning into athletic retirement.

Finally, the majority of the participants were satisfied with the intercollegiate athletic careers and athletic retirement, and all of the participants reported having some type of contact with sport. A study by Werthner and Orlick (1986) reported that athletes who continued their involvement in sport in some capacity did not report difficulty following retirement. Thus, having some connection to sport after athletic retirement could explain why 80% of the participants experienced ease in transition and the majority of them were satisfied with the athletic retirement.

Because of the small sample size surveyed, broad generalizations cannot be made. However, the participants' responses provide some interesting insight into African American experiences with athletic retirement. Some of the participants' responses proved consistent with the literature. For example, the majority of the participants who reported being satisfied with their intercollegiate athletic careers were also satisfied with athletic retirement. There was only one participant who reported dissatisfaction with intercollegiate career but satisfaction with athletic retirement. Therefore, the need for creating a positive sporting and education experience is within the control of intercollegiate sport administrators. Because the athletes' experiences in revenue- and non-revenue-generating sports are unique starting with recruitment, then time demands and constraints, local and national media exposure, and performance demands, it is important that programming is developed to meet their needs and insure a quality educational (foremost) and an athletic experience regardless of their wins/losses.

The majority of the participants were performing before the CHAMPS/Life Skills Program was implemented; this could be why a high percentage reported not having any information on athletic retirement. Unfortunately, asking athletes what their plans were after graduation does not warrant a legitimate plan or strategy for athletes preparing for athletic retirement. It is interesting to note that the post-CHAMPS/Life Skills Program also reported not receiving any information about athletic retirement. Athletic pre-retirement planning is a topic that athletic administrators must incorporate into the CHAMPS/Life Skills Program, with mandatory workshops, seminars, and/or classes. Based on several of the participants' responses, after their eligibility ended they were left to fend for themselves, with family as their main source of support. Since family members make up the main source of support in helping athletes cope with retirement, it would be beneficial for athletic administrators to provide family members with literature about athletic retirement to better assist in this pre-retirement planning.

Another recommendation would be for athletic administrators to develop mentoring programs in which former athletes, who have transitioned into other careers, can mentor current athletes about challenges they might potentially encounter. The former athletes can provide insight and assist in developing a plan that increases the chances of a successful transition into other careers.

Athletic retirement is undoubtedly an area where the NCAA and its member institutions can improve in and invest more into the lives of its main commodity—the athletes. Adopting intervention practices similar to the USOC could be beneficial in aiding athletes into transitioning into other careers.

Consequently, despite the controversy this provokes, every athlete participating in revenue-generating sport in Division I athletics (specifically football and basketball), regardless whether the overall athletic department is breaking even, should have a compensation package available upon their graduation to assist them in continuing their education or transitioning into a career. In the average major college athletic program, these two sports generate the most revenue for their respective programs. These sports also contribute the most to the existence of other non-revenue-generating sports, and they attract product endorsement, sponsorship packages, and broadcasting (radio and TV) monies. Therefore, a compensation package for these athletes should go beyond resume development, interviewing techniques, and the few post-graduate scholarships they offer, but include additional training in job skills specific to the students' career objectives.

Based on annual unemployment rates, African Americans still have a disadvantage in the job market, with or without a college degree. Therefore, African American athletes who have competed for four years at the Division I level and have been encouraged to focus on athletics and major in eligibility, instead of attending job fairs, networking with companies officials, etc., are placed at a disadvantage with their peers.

Athletic administrators can better utilize their alumni, athletic donors, and companies in a more "official" capacity by soliciting them to aid in the athletic retirement of junior and senior student athletes, instead of mainly fueling the athletic gluttony to build bigger facilities and give bigger salaries. Bigger is not always better, especially when the commodity is being abused and discarded. This compensation package could include a paid internship for athletes seeking employment upon their graduation. It could be with alumni or donors who own businesses or with some of the many companies that donate to the athletic department or sponsor sporting events. There are a variety of creative opportunities that can emerge in developing this compensation package.

The majority of the participants surveyed reported that it took one to two years to adjust to athletic retirement, which demonstrates a need for better planning. This adjustment period could be reduced drastically with pre-retirement planning, proper preparation, and assistance.

Finally, athletic retirement must also be a priority for African American intercollegiate athletes. Despite the premium many African American athletes place on making it into the pros, the reality is their chances are limited and diminishing, especially with the several professional leagues importing talent from an expanding crop in the global market. African American athletes must take the initiative in pre-retirement planning. They should also demand that their institutions provide them with necessary counseling and assistance to make this transition into athletic retirement. African American athletes must be proactive in shedding the shackles of learned helplessness that is often fostered in athletic cultures of paternalism. Making the assumption that they will be "taken care of" by the benefactors of their athletic talent is false hope. The athletes' ability to become active agents in preparing for their future and careers is critical to their success in transitioning from a glorious athletic career into a glorious profession.

In conclusion, it is important to note that the majority of the participants surveyed have benefited from their educational and athletic experiences. This is hardly the case for many African American intercollegiate athletes. There are too many accounts of athletes having tremendous success in competing and increasing the economic gains of athletic departments, yet they have been less successful in athletic retirement, unfortunately, with many succumbing to depression or a small percentage conforming to the pressures that foster criminal behaviors. These occurrences can be reduced with the right initiatives and the critical mass of people willing to make a difference and insure that this transition will be an experience from glory to glory.

▲▼ Suggested Readings ▲▼

Brooks, D. & Althouse, R. (2000). *Racism in college athletics: The African American athlete's experience* (Eds). Morgantown, WV: Fitness Information Technology.

Brown, S. D., & Heath, L. (1984). Coping with critical life events: An integrative cognitive behavioral model for research and practice. *Handbook of Counseling Psychology.* New York: Wiley.

Chartrand, J. M., & Lent, R. W. (1987). Sport counseling: Enhancing the development of the student athlete. *Journal of Counseling and Development, 6,* 164–167.

Grove, J. R., Lavallee, D., Gordon, S., & Harvey, J. H. (1998). Account-making: A model for understanding and resolving distressful reactions to retirement from sport. *The Sports Psychologist, 12,* 52–67.

Hardy, L., Jones, J. G., & Gould, D. (1996). *Understanding psychological preparation for sport: Theory and practice of elite performers.* New York: John Wiley & Sons, Ltd.

Hawkins, B. J. (2001). *New plantation: The internal colonization of Black student-athletes.* Winterville, Georgia: Sadiki Press.

Sailes, G. A. (1998). *African Americans in sport: Contemporary themes.* New Brunswick, NJ: Transaction Publishers.

Schlossberg, N. K. (1981). A model for analyzing human adaptation to transition. *The Counseling Psychologist, 9*(2), 2–18.

Stankovich, C., Meeker, D., & Henderson, J. (2001). The positive transitions model for sport retirement. *Journal of College Counseling, 4,* 81–84.

Tate, G. (1993). *The effects of the transformation in the Olympic games on the athletic retirement transition process [microform]: American Olympians and retired National Football League athletes.* Philadelphia: Temple University.

Taylor, J. & Ogilvie, B. (1994). A conceptual model of adaptation to retirement among athlete. *Journal of Applied Sport Psychology, 6,* 1–20.

▲▼ Study Questions ▲▼

1. Discuss the NCAA stance on the welfare of student athletes and its purpose for instituting the CHAMP/Life Skills programs.

2. Define and discuss models and theories associated with retirement in general and athletic retirement specifically.

3. List and discuss the factors that influence or affect an individual's transition from athlete to non-athlete.

4. What were some of the measures of intervention suggested by the authors in this chapter?

5. Discuss the significance of athletic retirement to sport management practitioners and the implications it has on their profession.

References

Anderson, A., & South, D. (1993). Racial differences in collegiate recruiting, retention, and graduation rates. In D. Brooks & R. Althouse (Eds.), *Racism in college athletics: The African-American experience* (pp. 79–100). Morgantown, WV: Fitness Information Technology, Inc.

Baillie, P. H. F., (1993). Understanding retirement from sports: Therapeutic ideas for helping athletes in transition. *The Counseling Psychologist, 21*(3), 399–410.

Baillie, P. H. F., & Danish, S. J. (1992). Understanding the career transition of athletes. *The Sport Psychologist, 6,* 77–98.

Berghorn, F. J., Yetman, N. R., & Hanna, W. E. (1988). Racial participation and integration in men's and women's intercollegiate basketball: Continuity and change, 1959–1985. *Sociology of Sport Journal, 5*(2), 87–106.

Blinde, E. M., & Stratta, T. M. (1992). The 'sport career death' of college athletes: Involuntary and unanticipated sport exits. *Journal of Sport Behavior, 15*(1), 3–20.

Carter, A., & Thornton, K. J., & Hawkins, B. J. (in review). Intercollegiate athletics, race, academic reform, and academic achievement: A case study of academic clustering in intercollegiate athletics.

Clement, R. (1954). Racial integration in the field of sports. *Journal of Negro Education, 23,* 222–230.

Coakley, J. J. (1983). Leaving competitive sport: Retirement or rebirth? *Quest, 35,* 1–11.

Crook, J. M., & Robertson, S. E. (1991). Transitions out of elite sport. *International Journal of Sport Psychology, 22,* 115–127.

Curtis, J., & Ennis, R. (1993). Negative consequences of leaving competitive sport? Comparative findings for former elite-level hockey players. In A. Yiannakis, M. J. Melnick, and T. D. McIntyre (Eds.), *Sport sociology: Contemporary themes* (4th ed., pp. 609–622). Dubuque, IA: Kendall/Hunt Publishing Company.

Davis, L. (1990). The articulation of difference: White preoccupation with the question of racially linked genetic differences among athletes. *Sociology of Sport Journal, 7*(2), 179–187.

Drahota, J. A. T., & Eitzen, D. S. (1998). The role exit of professional athletes. *Sociology of Sport Journal, 15,* 263–278.

Greendorfer, S. L., & Blinde, E. M. (1985a). A reconceptualization of the process of leaving the role of competitive athlete. *International Review for the Sociology of Sport, 20*(1/2), 87–94

Greendorfer, S. L., & Blinde, E. M. (1985b). Retirement from intercollegiate sport: Theoretical and empirical considerations. *Sociology of Sport Journal, 2,* 101–110.

Grove, J. R., Lavellee, D., Gordon, S., & Harvey, J. H. (1998). Account-making: A model for understanding and resolving distressful reactions to retirement from sport. *The Sport Psychologist, 12,* 52–67.

Harris, O. (1993). African-American predominance in collegiate sport. In R. C. Althouse and D. D. Brooks (Eds.), *Racism in collegiate athletics,* (pp. 51–74). Morgantown, WV: Fitness Information Technology, Inc.

Hawkins, B. J. (2001). *The new plantation: The internal colo-*

nization of Black sudents athletes. Winterville, GA: Sadiki Publishing.

Knight Foundation Commission on Intercollegiate Athletics (2001). *A call to action: Reconnecting college sports and higher education*. Retrieved from http://www.ncaa.org/databases/knight_commission/2001_report/

Koch, J. V., & Hill, W. V. (1988). Is there discrimination in the "Black man's game"? *Social Science Quarterly, 69*(1), 83–94.

Kübler-Ross, E. (1969). *On Death and Dying*. New York: Touchstone.

Lederman, D. (1991, July 10). Black athletes who entered colleges in mid-80's had much weaker records than Whites, study finds. *The Chronicle of Higher Education*, p. A31.

Lederman, D. (1992, June 17). Blacks make up large proportion of scholarship athletes, yet their overall enrollment lags at Division I colleges. *The Chronicle of Higher Education*, pp. 30–34.

Leonard, W. M. (1987). Stacking in college basketball: A neglected analysis. *Sociology of Sport Journal, 4*(4), 403–409.

LeUnes, A., & Nation, J. R. (1996). *Sport psychology* (2nd ed.). Chicago, IL: Nelson-Hall Publishers.

McPherson, B. D. (1993). Retirement from professional sport: The process and problems of occupational and psychological adjustment. In A. Yiannakis, M. J. Melnick, & T. D. McIntyre (Eds.), *Sport sociology: Contemporary themes* (4th ed., pp. 590–599). Dubuque, IA: Kendall/Hunt Publishing Company.

McPherson, B. D. (1976). Minority group involvement in sport: The Black athlete. In A. Yiannakis, T. D. McIntyre, M. J. Melnick, & D. P. Hart (Ed.), *Sport sociology* (pp. 153–166). Dubuque, IA: Kendall/Hunt.

Mihovilovic, M. A. (1968). The status of former sportsmen. *International Review of Sport Sociology, 3*, 73–96.

Miller, L. (1927). The unrest among college students: Kansas University. *Crisis, 34*, 187–188.

NCAA (2003a). *2003–2004 NCAA Division I Manual: Constitution, operating bylaws, administrative bylaws*. Indianapolis, IN: NCAA.

NCAA (2003b). *2003–2004 NCAA Division II Manual: Constitution, operating bylaws, administrative bylaws*. Indianapolis, IN: NCAA.

NCAA (2003c). *2003–2004 NCAA Division III Manual: Constitution, operating bylaws, administrative bylaws*. Indianapolis, IN: NCAA.

NCAA CHAMPS/Life Skills: Program. Retrieved June 10, 2004, from http://www1.ncaa.org/eprise/main/membership/ed_outreach/champs-life_skills/program.html.

NCAA Division I Graduation Rates Rise to 62 Percent: Increase Attributed to Increased Eligibility Standards. Retrieved September 2, 2003 from http://www.ncaa.org/releases/research/2003090201re.htm.

Ogilvie, B. C. (1987). Counseling for sports career termination. In J. R. May & M. J. Asken (Eds.), *Sport psychology: The psychological health of the athlete* (pp. 213–230). New York: PMA Publishing Corp.

Ogilvie, B. & Taylor, J. (1993). Career termination issues among elite athletes. In R. N. Singer, M. Murphey, & L. K. Tennant (Eds.) *Handbook of research on Sport Psychology* (pp. 761–775). New York: Macmillan Publishing Company.

Pearson, R. E. & Petitpas, A. J. (1990). Transitions of athletes: Developmental and preventive perspectives. *Journal of Counseling & Development, 69*, 7–10.

Perna, F. M., Ahlgren, R. L., & Zaichkowsky, L. (1999). The influence of career planning, race, and athletic injury on life satisfaction among recently retired collegiate male athletes. *The Sport Psychologist, 13*, 144–56.

Rosenberg, E. (1993). Athletic retirement as social death: Concepts and perspectives. In A. Yiannakis, M. J. Melnick, & T. D. McIntyre (Eds.), *Sport Sociology: Contemporary Themes* (4th ed., pp. 601–607). Dubuque, IA: Kendall/Hunt Publishing Company.

Sellers, R. M. (1992). Racial differences in the predictors of academic achievement of Division I student athletes. *Sociology of Sport Journal, 9*, 48–59.

Sellers, R. M. (1993). Black student-athletes: Reaping the benefits or recovering from the exploitation. In D. Brooks & R. Althouse (Eds.), *Racism in College Athletics: The African-American Athlete's Experience*. (pp. 143–174). Morgantown, WV: Fitness Information Technology, Inc.

Sellers, R. M., Kuperminc, G. P., & Waddell, A. S. (1991, Fall). Life experiences of black student-athletes in revenue producing sports: A descriptive empirical analysis. *Academic Athletic Journal*, 21–38.

Spivey, D., & Jones, T. A. (1975). Intercollegiate athletic servitude: A case study of the Black Illini student-athletes, 1931–1967. *Social Science Quarterly, 55*(4), 939–947.

Taylor, J., & Oglivie, B. C. (1994). A conceptual model of adaptation to retirement among athletes. *Journal of Applied Sport Psychology, 6*, 1–20.

Werthner, P., & Orlick, T. (1986). Retirement experiences of successful Olympic athletes. *International Journal of Sport Psychology, 17*, 337–363.

Wirt, J., Choy, S., Rooney, P., Hussar, W., Provasnik, S., Hampden-Thompson, G., Kridl, B., & Livingston, A. *The Condition of Education 2005* (Washington, D.C.: National Center for Education Statistics, 2000), 45, Retrieved July 31, 2005 from http://nces.ed.gov/pubs2005/2005094.pdf.

Wolff, R., & Lester, D. (1989). A theoretical basis for counseling the retired professional athlete. *Psychological Reports, 64*, 1043–1046.

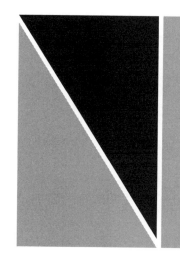

SECTION THREE
African American Coaching and Other Leadership Opportunities

"African American Coaching Mobility Models and the Global Market Place," written by Dana Brooks, Ronald Althouse, and Delano Tucker, characterizes the limited mobility opportunities for African Americans into coaching and higher administrative positions in intercollegiate athletics. The record shows that although talent, hard work, and sacrifice are lauded as conditions for success in sports, positions of leadership in coaching and sports administration are overwhelmingly stacked toward entry positions and into middle level administration. Although the NCAA has made claims of commitment to promoting diversity, the essay discusses the NCAA Self Study (1999) and identifies responsibility of top university officials to address deficiencies at the level of the institution itself. Brooks, Althouse, and Tucker describe the recent programs proposed by the Black Coaches Association and the NCAA (lauded as new departures in Charlotte Westerhaus's *Prologue* to this book) that are aimed at creating diversity and inclusion in collegiate sports. The last part of the essay explores issues of diversity, race, and gender discrimination in coaching and sport in a context of increasing globalization of the sports entertainment business.

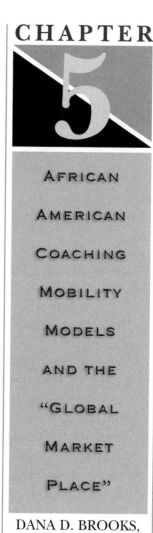

CHAPTER 5

AFRICAN AMERICAN COACHING MOBILITY MODELS AND THE "GLOBAL MARKET PLACE"

DANA D. BROOKS,
RONALD C. ALTHOUSE,
AND
DELANO TUCKER

Key Terms

▼Coaching mobility▲

▼Diversity▲

▼Globalization▲

▼Racism▲

▼Social justice▲

Abstract ▼ During the past two decades, sport management, sport sociology, and legal scholars have critiqued African American coaching and managerial opportunities available at the NCAA Division I level. With the exception of men's college basketball, there is a dearth of African Americans and other ethnic minority head coaches and administrators employed by NCAA member institutions. This chapter identifies employment barriers that ethnic minorities encounter as they seek coaching and administrative parity with their white counterparts. New models attempt to describe the hiring and promoting of ethnic minority coaches at the national and global level of sport organizations.

▲▽▲▽▲▽

Sports, as a cultural expression, has historically been viewed as an area in which talent is valued, and social mobility is the product of hard work, sacrifice, and contribution to the organization. Gifted African American coaches at the national and international level (e.g., Olympics) are becoming more visible and name recognizable as a result of media exposure, athletic program, and coaching success. Over the past sixty years, the names of prominent African American head (male and female) college coaches include: Ed Temple (Tennessee State University—track and field); John B.

McLendon, Jr. (North Carolina College, Hampton Institute, Tennessee State, Kentucky State, and Cleveland State—basketball); John Chaney (Temple—basketball); John Thompson (Georgetown—basketball); Nolan Richardson (Arkansas—basketball); Vivian Stringer (Iowa—women's basketball); Dennis Green (Stanford and Northwestern—football); and Tyrone Willingham (Stanford, Notre Dame, and Washington—football). These coaches are internationally recognized for their coaching prowess, leadership skills, and commitment to the coaching profession.

The May 5, 2003, issue of *Sports Illustrated* listed the 101 most influential minorities in sports. The following African American college coaches and athletic directors' names appeared: Tyrone Willingham (#6), football coach, Notre Dame; Craig Littlepage (#46), athletic director, Virginia; Gene Smith (#47), athletic director, Arizona State; Mike Garrett (#49), athletic director, USC; Tubby Smith (#51), basketball coach, Kentucky; Herman Frazie (#59), athletic director, Hawaii; Kelvin Sampson (#61), basketball coach, Oklahoma; John Chaney (#68), basketball coach, Temple; Doug Williams (#85), football coach, Grambling State; Rob Evans (#89), basketball coach, Arizona State; Teresa Phillips (#91), athletic director, Tennessee State; C. Vivian Stringer (#98), women's basketball coach, Rutgers; Damon Evans (#100) senior associate athletic director, Georgia.

The article stated, "These men and women are reshaping the sports industry and opening doors through which others will follow" (p. 32). This statement may be somewhat misleading and not truly reflect the status of African American men and women coaches and administrative diversity within the NCAA member institution and the sport global market place. Unfortunately, NCAA head coaching and administrative positions today are held primarily by white males. As early as 1993, Anderson began to systematically investigate the lack of cultural diversity among the NCAA-IA coaching ranks. The researcher said the positions of athletic director and head coach were the most visible and prestigious positions. Yet, few African Americans occupy these positions. King and Springwood (2001) noted, "Race continues to imprint intercollegiate athletics, as well as the idioms, identities, and imaginaries animated by it. In fact, as we argue throughout, sport has become an increasingly important space in which individuals and institutions struggle over the significance of race" (p. 8).

In 2000, Brooks and Althouse also concluded that race matters and documented that African American males and females have been underemployed and underrepresented in college athletic leadership positions (e.g., coaches and athletic directors). Supporting this position, the *NCAA News* article (May 22, 2000) "NCAA race report indicates little change in diversity hiring" revealed a marginal change in the make-up of African American administrators and coaches across the various NCAA divisions.

This is a very important finding since the *NCAA News* (September 16, 2002) found an increase in diversity among student athletes (blacks, 2000–2001, was about 27%). Similarly, the 2003–04 *NCAA Race and Gender Report* found that 48% of the student athletes were African Americans. Yet, the hiring of ethnic minorities and female coaches continued to lag (The Diversity Hiring Failure, 2002). King and Springwood (2001) concluded, "Beyond the numbers, race matters because of popular conceptions of the difference it makes" (p. 10). That is, coaches hold physiological and intellectual perceptions about various student athletes and their cognitive and athletic prowess.

Brooks and Althouse (1996) provided an extensive review of the college sport literature and African American sport experiences that permitted the authors to reach the following conclusion: "The recurring theme found throughout the literature was the lack of African American men and women occupying sport leadership positions: coaches, athletic directors, sport officials, athletic trainers, and sport information directors" (p. 29). In summary, the literature tended to cluster around hiring practices and career mobility opportunities for African American males and females (Anderson, 1992; Anderson, 1993; Banks, 1979; Latimer & Mathes, 1985; Massengale & Tarrington, 1977) and arguments put forth to explain why so few African Americans occupy head coaching positions (Abney & Rickey, 1991; Lyons, 1992; Slow going. . . . , 1991).

Legal scholar Kenneth Shropshire (1996) wrote, "In the harshest of terms, the sport industry resembles a black-bottomed pyramid: large numbers of African American athlete-participants, but few African Americans in non-playing positions at the highest levels" (p. 456–457). Shropshire (1996) concluded that the disparities in African American representatives in coaching and managerial positions may be due in part to racism at the institution and unconscious or "old boy"-sponsored mobility philosophy at the next level of excluding ethnic minorities from leadership positions in sport.

May 17, 2004, represented the fiftieth anniversary of the *Brown vs. Board of Education—Topeka* landmark court decision. Unfortunately, the impact of the Brown case has not been fully realized in America. Although African American students and other ethnic minorities gained some measure of access to public education and higher education, they have not realized equal outcomes relative to employment opportunities in the private business sector or within the sport industry. Social justice advocates and scholars are interested in understanding the hiring and promoting process of ethnic minority coaches and administrators (nationally and internationally).

Hiring and Dismissal Process: Playing the Race Card

Sport sociologist George Sage (1975) noted that the hiring and recruitment of a college coach is a complex process. He wrote, "The process by which a person selects an occupational career and prepares for it is a complex mixture of personal characteristics, social background, selective procedures of the occupational gatekeepers, chance, and the actual acquisition of skills and narrative orientations of the occupation. The process is by no means the same for any two persons" (p. 430). Coaching and administrative careers appear to be individualized and vary by gender, race, ethnicity, and type of sport.

Mixon and Trevino (2004) joined a long list of scholars who have attempted to explain the dearth of African American NCAA I-A coaches, especially head football coaches. Unique in the literature, Mixon and Trevino investigated the extent to which the economics of discrimination plays a significant role in the fields of labor economics and college sports. The scholars (Caudill, et al., 1995) applied a lottery-adoption decision-making model in college football coaching. The authors modeled the extent to which racial discrimination was a factor in the dismissal decision in NCAA football between 1990 and 2000. Eighty-one universities were identified in the study. Surprisingly, the authors concluded that race has an impact and role in the process of coaching. Black head coaches were the recipients of favorable treatment relative to non-black coaches by university administrators. The authors noted such factors as gender equality, institutional support, and/or social justice concerns may have an impact on dismissal decision-making. In contrast to this finding, Brooks and Althouse (1999) concluded head coaching and administrative career paths of African Americans (men and women) differ from white coaches and administrators. The researchers found factors such as "old boy networks," "isolation on campus," "stereotyping," "racism," and "tokenism" have an impact on hiring and termination decisions.

No one factor or theory can fully explain the lack of African Americans (men and women) head coaches or administrators. In summary, researchers are unable to fully account for the relatively low upward mobility of African Americans (males and females) promoted to leadership positions (coaches and administrators).

Suggs (2005) concluded, "If an athlete decides to go into sports management, or a coach makes the jump from the side line to the front office, typical entry level positions are marketing, fund raising, business officers, rules compliance, academic advising, or life skills counseling. The first three teach the glad handing, money raising, negotiating, and administrative skills required of modern athletic directors. The second three are peripheral jobs; people may become assistant or associate athletic directors in charge of academic or compliance, but making the jump to the executive box is very difficult" (p. A 34).

Suggs (2005) reviewed NCAA data and found that white men tend to be hired in the first three areas, whereas African Americans and women were hired for the second three. Suggs (2005) concluded that African Americans and women are marginalized and represent an occupation that offered limited access to executive positions within NCAA institutions.

Table 1. Career-Track Jobs for Athletic Directors (2003–04)

	White Men	African Americans	All Women
Fund Raiser/Development Manager	67%	28%	4%
Promotions/Marketing Manager	66%	30%	4%
Business Manager	44%	50%	4%
Assistant Athletic Directors	64%	29%	8%
Associate Athletic Directors	61%	31%	8%
Athletic Directors	89%	7%	3%

(Suggs, 2005)

Suggs (2005) also noted that African Americans disproportionately held the position of administrative assistant (86%) as compared to white males (9%) holding the same position.

Nonetheless, social justice proactive organizations, such as the Black Coaches Association and the Rainbow Coalition, remain advocates for employment equality and diversity within American colleges and professional sports arenas.

Coaching and Administrative Diversity Strategies: From Affirmative Action and Equal Opportunity to Shared Community

As early as 1986, the Black Coaches Association (BCA) began to collect African American employment data at the college level. One year later, the NCAA formed the Minority Opportunities and Interest Committee to review minority hiring practices with NCAA institutions. As a result of this initiative, the NCAA established several programs in an effort to diversify coaching and administrative positions.

In 1994, the Rainbow Coalition developed a five-year affirmative action strategy to help NCAA member institutions diversify their coaching and administrative ranks. Specific recommendations included:

1. Fair employment practices with the focus being on the inclusion of women and minorities in coaching, athletic administration, sports information, and radio/television announcer rates.

2. Recruiting plans targeting minority athletes to revenue and non-revenue funds.

3. Guidelines to encourage a fair percentage of all external purchases of goods and services to minority and women vendors.

4. Plans to include more minorities and women in manufacturing, marketing, and merchandising of school licensure products.

5. College proactive selection, placing at least two qualified candidates on a short list of administrative and coaching assignments.

6. Player training programs in the areas of self-help, lifestyle, career, and personal development.

7. Diversity and humanities training within athletic departments (Rainbow Coalition Develop Diversity Plan for Institutions, 1994). Legal scholar Ken Shropshire (1996) also advocated the implementation of the following affirmative action strategies addressing hiring concerns:

   a. Make a focused effort to recruit members of underrepresented groups.

   b. Utilize diversity and sensitivity training programs.

   c. If necessary, modify employment practices that may tend to underutilize minority members.

   d. Move toward preferential hiring and promotion of members of underrepresented groups.

Hiring Report Card: Black Coaches Association (BCA) Call to Action

The literature suggested some progress has been made over the past two decades in the hiring of African American male head and assistant NCAA basketball coaches. However, African American female head basketball coaches (NCAA I) remain underutilized. In March 2005, there were only three African American female head college basketball coaches: (1) Dawn Staley; Temple, (2) Vivian Stringer; Rutgers, and (3) Pokey Chatman; LSU. Chatman was named the 2004–05 Coach of the Year by the Black Coaches Association, Women's Basketball Coaches Association, and the U.S. Basketball Association.

A more complete analysis of employment data was presented in the *2003–04 Race and Gender Study Report.* The Report compared 1995–96 race and gender NCAA employment data with 2003–04 data across three categories: athletic administrators, head coaches, and assistant coaches. Overall, there has been only a modest increase in the number of African American administrators. "Black men saw the largest increase in the positions of equipment manager, ticket manager, and intern. Black women saw the largest increase in the positions of senior woman administrator, academic adviser, promotions/marketing graduate assistant, and intern" (2003–04 Race and Gender Demographics, p. 8). The administrative positions identified in this report appeared to be marginal and to lack a clear upward mobility path to higher administrative levels of employment.

NCAA head coaching data suggested the largest percentage of African American male head coaches were found in basketball (23%), indoor track (15%), and outdoor track (15%). African American female coaches tend to coach basketball (8%), indoor track (8%), and outdoor track (7%). Asians (n = 12) coached fencing, golf, rifle, soccer, swimming, indoor and outdoor track, and volleyball.

Hispanic males (n = 33) tended to coach cross country, soccer, and tennis. There were only two Native American head coaches (2003–04 Race and Gender Demographics). In 2005, there were only three NCAA African American head football coaches.

The 2003–04 race and gender employment data for African Americans and other ethnic minorities (Division II and III) raises additional concern about the underemployment of female coaches and lack of ethnic diversity within NCAA institutions.

During 2003–04 there were only five (male and female) African American athletic directors in Division II sports, excluding historically black colleges and universities. Most of the African American males and females in this division (n = 15) occupied the positions of equipment managers and academic adviser/counselor (n = 17). Looking at the Division III Level, the majority of African American males held the position of equipment manager (n = 17), facility manager (n = 17), and director of athletics (n = 12). African American females occupied the position of administrative assistant (n = 12). In summary, 2003–04 race and gender data echoes a continued theme: little or no increase in minority representation in coaching and other NCAA leadership positions. It appears student diversity on predominantly white college campuses can be attributed to the significant increase in ethnic minority representation in sports participation, especially in basketball and football. Public outcry, voiced particularly by African American coaches, led to the creation of ethnic minority hiring monitoring systems within the NCAA institutions and professional sport levels.

In October, 2003, the Black Coaches Association announced the establishment of a "hiring report card" to evaluate ethnic minority hiring practices in college football. The report card provided a letter grade (A, B, C, D, F) in the following search and screen criteria: (1) contact with the Executive Director of the BCA and/or Chair of the Minority Opportunity Interest Committee during the hiring process; (2) efforts to interview candidates of color; (3) number of minorities on the search/hiring committee; (4) number of minorities who received on-campus interviews; (5) length of time to hire a candidate; and (6) documented adherence of institutional affirmative action policies. Dr. Keith Harrison, founder of the Paul Robeson Research Center for Academic and Athletic Prowess was given the responsibility to produce the report annually. During the 2003–2004 academic year, there were 28 coaching vacancies (NCAA I-A and I-AA football coaches) (Harrison, 2004). The 2003–04 Report Card for football coaching hiring indicated that 60% (17) of the schools had a final grade of A or B. Dr. Harrison's report noted, "Cornell University was the only university to earn an A in every category. Other institutions receiving a grade of A were: Eastern Michigan University, Mississippi State, University of Cincinnati, University of Akron, University of Arizona, University of Texas-El Paso, Cornell University, and College of the Holy Cross" (Harrison, 2004).

Based on the data obtained in the initial Report Card, Harrison (2004) offered the following recommendations:

1   The NCAA adopts a policy of mandatory cooperation for all member institutions to participate in the annual hiring report card by providing the information and documentation so subsequent reports can be published in a complete and timely manner.

2. A norm is broadly agreed to as to the best ratio for representing campus diversity on all institutional search/hiring committees, including for head football coach.

3. The NCAA adopts an incentive/disincentive formula for equity and diversity hiring practices that parallels recent NCAA academic reform policies.

4. Specific awards for those institutions that comply with diversity.

5. Schools that have open hiring processes receive public recognition not only to give them credit but to encourage other institutions to do the same in the future (p. 17).

It is important to note that during this time period (2004–2005) Sylvester Croom (Mississippi State) became the Southeastern Conference's first African American head coach.

Brooks and Althouse (2000) concluded that the establishment of university affirmative action policies and procedures has not been effective in changing the hiring practices of NCAA institutions. Hiring practices such as selecting candidates who offer the "best fit," unclear job qualifications, institutional waivers of the search and screen process, and lack of commitment to the "spirit" of affirmative action and equal opportunity continue to exist on campuses.

On a positive note, the NCAA has established several proactive "affirmative action" programs in an attempt to increase diversity (gender and ethnic) within coaching and other administrative positions. A list of NCAA Diversity Programs is as follows:

1. Gender Equity/Title IX

2. Leadership Institutes for Ethnic Minority Males

3. Fellows Leadership Development Program

4. NCAA Men's Coaches Academy

5. NCAA Women's Coaches Academy

6. Division II Strategic Alliance Matching Grant Enhancement Program

7. Division III Strategic Alliance Matching Grant Enhancement Program

8. Division III Initiative Grants

9. Diversity Training Workshops

10. Women's Minority Coaches Modeling Grant Program

The NCAA Fellows Leadership Development Program was established in 1994 to assist ethnic minorities and women in gaining access to senior management leadership positions. This is a very important initiative since very few ethnic minorities or women currently hold senior (i.e., Athletic Director) positions within NCAA member institutions.

The Ethnic Minority Enhancement Postgraduate Scholarship for Careers in Athletics Program awards scholarships to ethnic minority students who plan to attend sports-related graduate school programs. This program tries to increase the number of potential ethnic minority applications seeking careers in administration, coaching, and officiating. The NCAA internship program for women and ethnic minorities has been somewhat successful. Between 1989 and 2002, 119 women and other ethnic minorities have served as interns at the NCAA headquarters in Indiana. The program received some level of success, and many of the graduates were hired in the sport industry.

At the academic level, Larsen (2002) reminds us that graduate programs in Sport Management and Sport Administration have an obligation to increase ethnic diversity within their programs. Notable program initiatives can be found at Northeastern University, University of Oregon, and Arizona State University (Larsen, 2002). Drawing on the concept of "supply and demand," these college programs have a common message: increase the pool of women and ethnic minorities who have the skills, desire, and knowledge to enter the sport industry. Sport management/administration faculty should evaluate their student selection criteria to ensure that quality ethnic minorities are selected and graduate from the various graduate and undergraduate programs.

As noted earlier in this chapter, the lack of African American head NCAA football coaches and the lack of African American female head coaches, in general, continue to remain unresolved issues. Old strategies to diversify NCAA coaching and administrative positions have not been successful.

New strategies such as the NCAA's Men's Coaches Academy were established specifically to address the lack of ethnic minority head football coaches. Two of the Academy's six stated objectives are as follows: (1) to introduce ethnic minority coaches to senior level coaches and administrators through a mentoring program, and (2) to raise public awareness of the existing talent pool of ethnic assistants and others. Academy workshops are held prior to the American Football Coaches Association Convention. In 2005, the NCAA Minority Opportunities and Interest Committee began to discuss the narrow focus (lack of minority head football coaches) and expressed concern that the mission of the Academy should expand to include the lack of minority coaches in Divisions I-AA, I-AAA, II, and III. Today, workshop participants attend sessions on public speaking, interviewing skills, fiscal responsibilities, building successful programs and building relationships with alumni and the community, ethical considerations, and issues focusing on academic support. It appears that this program is based on a "deficit skill" model and assumes potential African American head coaches (men and women) lack the essential skills necessary to be employed as a head coach or athletic administrator.

Similarly, it is important to note that legal scholars and social scientists concluded that opportunities for women to gain upward mobility to the coaching ranks and other leadership positions within sports are very limited (Acosta & Carpenter, 1990; Brooks & Althouse, 1993; Eitzen & Sage, 1989). In 2003 the Women's Basketball Coaches Association and the National Federation of State High School Association established a grant program targeting female minority basketball players who have a desire to become coaches at various levels (Grassroots programs, 2005). In a manner similar to other program initiatives, participants learn skill development and the existence of job placement opportunities.

The NCAA publicly stated its commitment to promoting diversity within the workplace. In January 2005, the NCAA Minority Opportunities and Interest Committee developed new strategies in an effort to increase the number of ethnic minorities in NCAA positions. Robert Vowels, Jr., chair of the committee, said, "At the heart of the discussion is whether the committee should be working to increase the number of ethnic minority candidates for athletic director and head coaching positions or focusing on increasing the number of ethnic minorities being hired." He further noted, "The committee can't control how our member institutions and conferences hire, but we can prepare competitive talent for future opportunities and offer guidance on formulating effective strategies for selecting the best candidate for the job" (McKindia, 2005, p. 1).

NCAA Self-Study—Minority Issues

The NCAA Athletic Certification Process, encouraged by the Knight Foundation, was approved for Division I institutions in 1993 (1990–00 NCAA Division I Athletic Certification Handbook). The stated purpose of the certification process was to ensure NCAA member institutions' commitment to integrity in college sports. A team of external peer review evaluators were charged with verifying the institutions' self-study data and operating principles.

Expanding on the information reviewed during the first review cycle, the Second Round of the *NCAA Self-Study Report* (1999–2000) requested information in the four general categories of Governance and Commitment to Rules Compliance, Academic Integrity, Fiscal Integrity, and Equality, Welfare, and Sportsmanship. For the purpose of this chapter the authors will focus discussion on equality, welfare, and sportsmanship, specifically, Operating Principle 4.7, Minority Issue. Each participating NCAA Institution was requested to answer the following Self-Study Evaluation Questions:

   4.2.1 Explain how the institution is organized to further its efforts related to minority issues for both staff and students and provide evidence that matters concerning minority issues are monitored, evaluated, and addressed on a continuing basis.

   4.2.2 For the three most recent academic years, provide the racial or ethnic composition for all full-time senior administrative athletic department staff members, other full- and part-time professional athletic department staff members; full- and part-time head coaches; full- and part-time assistant coaches; faculty-based athletic board or committee member.

4.2.4 For the three most recent academic years, provide the racial or ethnic composition of student athletes who received athletic aid by the eight sports groups listed in the graduation rates disclosure form. Also, for those sports not at the varsity level for three years, indicate the year in which the sport was organized by the institution as a varsity sport.

4.2.5 Report on the institution's implementation of its plan to address minority issues from its previous certification self-study. Specifically include:

a. The Original Plan

b. The Action(s) Taken by the Institution

c. Action(s) Not Taken or Not Completed

d. Explanation(s) for Partial Completion

The NCAA Self-Study Evaluation attempts to hold member institutions accountable for the hiring and promoting of ethnic minorities within the organization. Member colleges are expected to develop action plans to address any deficiencies outlined in the self-study, especially as they relate to minority issues. This is a very good first step. However, college presidents and athletic directors must be held responsible for bringing about employment changes ensuring diversity within their respective institutions.

Diversity and Sport Participation

It is a long-held belief that having a diverse workplace adds value to the organization. IBM identified diversity as a strategic goal and in 1995 the company established a task force (consisting of senior managers) to address diversity as strategy (Thomas, 2004). The task force was divided into the following constituencies: Asians, blacks, people with disabilities, white men, women, gays/lesbians/ bisexuals/transgender individuals, Hispanics, and Native Americans.

After much discussion and analysis of the data, the task force recommended the following strategies to bring about change: demonstrate leadership support (CEO commitment for the activity); engage employees as partners (cultural shift—empower employees in the process); integrate diversity with management practices (diversity training for all new managers); and link diversity goals to business goals (good business). In summary, the process permitted IBM to get closer to its market and focused on the hiring and retention of employees.

Diversity issues (e.g., race, gender) remain an important topic of debate among administrators, managers, and social scientists. Recently, scholars began to investigate diversity research in a sport environment. Cunningham and Sagas (2004) studied how racial dissimilarity from other coaches influenced coach's organizational commitment. Questions were distributed to 600 assistant men's basketball coaches (NCAA I). Data suggested that being different from others in the group does impact the coaches' organizational commitment. It was surprising to note that African American coaches who were in groups with an even mix of whites and racial minorities were the least committed to the organization. Further, African American coaches reported poor work experiences. At the institutional level, in November, 2004, Myles Brand (NCAA President) established the Office for Diversity and Inclusion (Brown, 2004). A vice president, reporting to the president, would be hired to oversee the operations of the office. Bernard Franklin (NCAA Senior Vice President for Governance and Marketing Services) was very optimistic about the new position and stated, "We expect this position to be staffed with a person who can collect and share best practices relating to diversity and inclusion, someone who will bring a national voice. I'm hoping the role will be viewed as an active one, one that member institutions can assess at the front end of issues instead of responding in a crisis mode" (Brown, 2004, p. 3).

On May 23, 2005, Charlotte Westerhaus was hired as Vice President for Diversity and Inclusion. Westerhaus has a wealth of experience in the areas of affirmative action, diversity, leadership, and administration. She also holds a law degree from Indiana University.

Our discussion thus far has focused on the African American coaching and administrative experiences at the American national level. Historically, research focused primarily on the African American athlete's experience and the lack of coaching and other leadership opportunities for African American males and females (Abney & Richey, 1991; Anderson, 1993; Banks, 1979; Brooks & Althouse, 1993; Brooks, Althouse & Tucker, 1997; Tucker, 2000). Issues of racism, diversity, and lack of access to sport management/ administrative positions were discussed at the national level. Proactive NCAA programs and various affirmative action policies were established to enhance the pool of minority applicants. It appears the various NCAA diversity programs were built on a perceived deficit model. That is, there was the perception that ethnic minorities and women lacked the necessary skills to be viable candidates for coaching and other leadership positions. Armed with these new skills, women and ethnic minorities will have a competitive advantage. The various NCAA models assumed that equality of opportunity exists in the sport arena, supporting Blalock's talent model of social mobility.

Retrospectively, the "talent model" is less convincing today because it is largely devoid of the social and historical complexity of sport and race relations in America, or at least about what it can tell us about the role of sport in the culture of race relations. Hartman's work (2003) draws attention to how, during the 1980s, the American sports regime was instrumental in a reconstruction of America's perception of racial inequality and injustice, inside and outside of sport. Hartman, et al. (2003) illustrated how issues of race were buried beneath labels of "community relations" or "human resources," while African American and other minority athletes appear and are represented *without* specific textual reference to race, as if it is only their individual effort and identity that matter. Redefining racial resistance and protest under neutralizing labels of "community relations" and "human resources" required that the sports industry, particularly the NCAA and collegiate facilitators of "equal opportunity and affirmative action," become involved in learning how to avoid social resistance and unrest by incorporating moderate but symbolically powerful racial actors (Jackie Robinson, Michael Jordan, and Walter Payton) into its practice and official policy. Big-time collegiate sport also gained an enormous sponsorship from media moguls and market executives engaged in globalizing their products.

To date, we do not fully understand the impact of globalization of sport on the employment opportunities of males, females, and ethnic minorities. What social and economic factors influence the establishment of sports at the global level? How do race, gender, and ethnicity transcend sport at the international level? How is the coaching community established and maintained at the global level?

Globalization: Redefining Community

Robertson (1992) wrote, "Globalization as a concept refers both to the compression of the world and the intensification of consciousness of the world as a whole" (p. 8). According to Robertson (1992), globalization, which is a complex sociocultural process, has been in existence for centuries.

In an effort to describe the globalization process, Robertson (1992) referred to "voluntaristic" theory and some of its main points:

1. Global "systems" are not reduced to merely societies.

2. Global field is a sociocultural system.

3. Individuals within the globalization process identify themselves as actors.

Robertson (1992) argued that the study of the globalization process should go beyond analysis of world politics and socioeconomic factors.

Similarly, Blanchflower (2000) noted, "Globalization has arisen both through an increased trade in goods plus easier movement of factors of production. Capital and labor across national boundaries" (p. 1–2). Blanchflower (2000) provided an outstanding critique of the impact of globalization on the American labor market. Since 1970, several conditions influenced the labor market: technological change, immigration, declining unions, declining levels of minimum wage, and reduction in the support of college-educated workers.

Globalization and Racism

Writing in *Beyond the Cheers: Race as Spectacle in College Sport*, King and Springwood (2001) noted, "Race continues to imprint intercollegiate athletics, as well as the idioms, identities, and imaginaries animated by it" (p. 8). African American athletes were represented as somehow having overcome problems of race that plagued others like them.

Sport, so it seems, was a model the rest of "Americans" could aspire to as a symbol for dominant liberal individualist ideas about color blindness, racial integration, and cultural assimilation.

Set against the backdrop of the perceived breakdown of the African American family, Cole and her colleagues (1998) argued that the sporting industry adopted new practices for containment and control of black male athletes, thus ensuring that they serve to maintain rather than disrupt established racial images, ideologies, and hierarchies. Sport is offered up, you see, as a socially desirable set of behaviors for young African American men and, alternatively, black urban gangs are deviant and dysfunctional. African American women, too, can be "all they can be," with the diversity angle built into it. Hence, the general recognition of the domestication and assimilation of not only racial difference but of racial deviance and defiance through sport, where athletes are closely watched for signs of racial conduct.

At the global level, issues and definitions of race and racism take on new meaning. Today, we do not fully comprehend the extent to which race has made an imprint on global sport. With some degree of certainty, social scientists found the globalization process has widened the economic divide between the rich and poor and fostered elements of discrimination and racism.

"Those marginalized from the global economy in the United States are disproportionately people of color, and whites experiencing the disruptive effects of globalization often use racism as a way to buffer themselves from downward mobility. The analysis of globalization's impact on the United States, then, must explore the dynamics of race in American society. This is a difficult challenge, as societal racism today is quite different from that of even a generation ago" (Barlow, 2003, p. 3). Barlow (2003) concluded globalization has created a growing social crisis and has permitted whites to gain additional white privileges (some middle class). Social crises, according to Barlow, are manifested in a new division of social inequality.

In a very ominous tone Barlow wrote, "The principal social response to globalization in the United States has not been to embrace global relationships or understanding; however, instead, we live in an era in which public-spirited universalism—the concern for the well-being of the people as a whole—is a decreasing priority. In its place, a new focus on individual responsibility has arisen" (p. 109).

We must begin to address the challenges imposed by globalization on social injustice issues in America and, specifically, within the sports industry. Sport-centered struggles gain an unusual public prominence via widespread media attention, government reforms, regulation of student athletes, and selection of athletic coaches. By and large, the American sports industry approached the 21st century dedicated to a perspective that racial problems in and around sport have been overcome; race in sports is either an illusion or an aberrant actor, or a mistake. In contemporary garb, this stance is culturally consistent with the long-held and deeply felt color-blind, individualist, and integrationist ideals that are embedded in the structure of race and sport relations in American society. As Hartman (2003) notes, diversity is the new "trump card" because such race-neutral discourse tends to overlap and support ideals about racial justice and social harmony.

Globalization, Sport, and the Coaching Opportunities

Harvey, Rail, and Thibault (1996) were some of the first scholars to develop a conceptual and theoretical model to investigate sport at the global level. The authors raised three questions that became the basis for their theoretical model: How is sport being transformed by globalization? How is sport contributing to globalization? How does the globalization of sport affect sport at the national/state level? The authors developed a conceptual model outlining a web of issues that included global and national levels of analysis. National and global level issues such as political, economic, cultural, and social dimensions influence sport participation rates, social mobility, and marketing. Based on the literature, it was concluded that globalization is transforming sport. That is to say, economic, political, and cultural actors are influencing Western sports. It was further concluded that sport does contribute (via mass media and marketing) to the globalization process.

Discrimination within the Coaching Ranks?

Racism and discrimination and other forms of social injustices in American sports and athletics have manifested themselves in the form of "stacking" (the disproportional allocation of persons to control [leadership] and non-control [non-leadership] positions on the basis of race ethnicity) (Jones, Leonard, Schmitt, Smith & Tolane, 1987), few head coaching and administrative roles available to ethnic minority males and females, social isolation, salary differences, and sexism. Today, we do not know the magnitude of the extent to which social injustice conditions (i.e., "stacking," lack of access to decision-making positions, racism) exist at the international sport levels.

Coaching Opportunities at the Global Level: Equal Access or "Black-Bottomed" Pyramid Revisited?

In addition to the questions raised by Harvey, Rail, and Thibault (1996), the authors of this chapter wanted to critique the perceived impact of sport globalization and coaching opportunities for ethnic minority coaches (male and female) at the international (Olympic) and global (elite sports clubs, professional teams) level, and the extent to which racism, sexism, cultural differences, social economic class, and coaching sub-culture expectations influence the hiring and firing of ethnic diverse coaches.

Data suggests that the number of African American male and female athletes playing professional sport in Europe, Australia, and South American continues to increase. Yet, researchers have not systematically investigated social mobility patterns of African Americans and other ethnic minority coaches at the international and global levels. The concepts of racism, exploitation, and diversity may need to be redefined at the global level of analysis.

The authors of this chapter limited their discussion to two widely recognized sports, soccer and professional football (NFL Europe and CFL).

Soccer

Soccer is regarded by many observers as one of the world's most popular sports. In fact, soccer is played in every country in the world. The prevalence of soccer led some observers to conclude that at the "international" and "global" levels this sport is immune to racism and discrimination at all levels of the organization.

Jarvie's (1991) critique of sport, racism, and ethnicity remarked, "In May 1990, a British television documentary indicated that at least 50 percent of Britain's athletic squad and 50 percent of current British boxing champions were black. Second, such a disproportionately high level of athletic participation by various ethnic minority cultures has often been used by liberal-minded sports enthusiasts and certain academics to argue that sport itself is relatively free from racism and that sport, more than any other sphere of society, enjoys a certain degree of democratization and equality" (p. 1). Jarvie (1991) extends the discussion of race, racism, and sport participation away from the traditional line of inquiry focusing on the African American athlete's experience.

Dixon (2005) noted the dearth of black head soccer coaches throughout Europe and South America. Frank Rijkaard, a highly regarded and talented former world class soccer player, is an exception. Coach Rijkaard is the former head soccer coach for Holland. Rijkaard was eventually hired to coach the FC Barcelona Soccer team of the Spanish League.

The globalization of soccer has led to an increased diversity on the field, and a broader spectrum of factors contributing to racism and violence. "Football racism," that is, racist and ethnic-related attacks or discrimination, has occurred in most European countries—Spain, Italy, and Eastern Europe are singled out as the worst bastions of racist crowd behavior—but also in Asian and South American countries, notably Brazil and Argentina. Although attacks are usually aimed at denigrating players, coaches of color and even referees are frequently the target of racism. Finally, *internationally* soccer is gender segregated within the sports establishment. Played by men, it's a people's game forged within complex national identities widely expressed by divisions among social classes. The sports establishment typically handles women's soccer as more or less profitable sports spectacles.

Coaches of color are often plagued by taunts from fans and by media headlines that charge them with race-based ineptitude and low success, creating a milieu of the risk of failure without reprieve, without second chance; once hired, anything short of club success, or a league championship, is perceived as failure. Spain's national coach used racial slurs and epithets during a World Cup qualifier against Belgium, and Dutch fans mocked referee Rene Temmick with anti-Semitic chants leading to the cancellation of a game in progress.

As the 2006 Soccer World Cup approached, the NAACP urged international soccer authorities to eliminate threats and race-based assaults during the World Cup games that were to be held in 12 different German cities. Monkey-like chanting, derisive singing and banners displaying neo-fascist beliefs, spitting, and jeering have been observed to be aimed at players of color. NAACP President Bruce Gordon said these "actions are throwbacks to a disturbing history that should be just that, history." Gordon called for enforceable discipline of any athlete or official participating in racist actions, whether "hooliganism" or more subtle derision from officials.

Boorish behavior by hooligans has long been a problem in European soccer, but anti-discrimination advocates say racial slurs and racially charged incidents are on the rise because of a confluence of factors. Among them: the increasing racial diversity of former all-white clubs, a growing resistance to immigration from African and Arab nations in several European countries, the tendency for race-related conflicts to grab headlines, and greater scrutiny of such incidents. In some areas, including rural eastern Germany, racial tension also appears to be fueled by a lack of economic opportunities for whites.

Specific sanctions that are supposed to be imposed by FIFA (the Federation Internationale de Football Association) on football clubs if players or supporters become involved in racism during matches include: deduction of points, disqualification of a team from competition, fines against individual players, exclusion of fans from stadiums, and powers for referees to blow the final whistle on a match when a racist incident occurs.

Zirin and Cox (2006) expose the relationship between the sports establishment and global power. They are riveted on the possibility of open, violent racism, in relation to the rising number of attacks on non-whites in Germany, since the World Cup provides "an international platform for Neo-Nazi swill" (pp. 1, 2). Combined with the numbers of attacks on non-whites, a spate of racist sloganeering and taunting of black soccer players throughout Europe has set the stage for a display of racism on a global scale. Indeed, Zirin and Cox endorse Shaun Harkin's insightful idea that "football racism" has been aggravated by the rise of anti-immigrant sentiment in Europe.

Shaun Harkin, who played for Coleraine FC in the Northern Irish League and captained the Brown University soccer squad into the NCAA quarterfinals, now works as an immigrant rights specialist in Chicago. He is quoted as saying, "The racist abuse players have faced across Europe is an aspect of a growing backlash against immigrants. Immigration from former European colonies has grown. As in the United States, immigration has been necessary for many European economies and a source of cheap labor—but immigrant communities have also been a convenient political scapegoat in a continent riddled with unemployment and increasingly anxious conditions for workers dealing with the repercussions of deepening neo-liberal policies" (Zirin & Cox, p. 2). In other words, according to Zirn and Cox, "the German government wants to have it both ways: it's proper to foment anti-Muslim bigotry, tighten immigration restrictions and attack asylum seekers, but anti-black racism shouldn't be allowed to sully" national reputations or diminish highly profitable spectacles (p. 2).

Football

It appears American style football has gained popularity and sponsorship throughout Canada and Europe. The international football leagues provided additional playing opportunities for African American athletes and provided a venue of possi-

Photo courtesy of the Toronto Argonauts Football Club.

Michael Clemons began his career with the Canadian Football League's Toronto Argonauts in 1989 after a brief stint in the National Football League. After accumulating 12 all-time team records, he retired from play in 2000 and moved directly into the position of head coach.

ble head coaching jobs. In 2005, nine Canadian football teams consisted of BC Lions, Edmonton Eskimo Football Club, Calgary Stampders, Saskatchewan Roughriders, Winnipeg Bluebombers, Hamilton Tigercats, Toronto Argonauts, Ottawa Renegades, and Montreal Alouettes. During the same time period, the following NFL Europe teams competed: Amsterdam Admirals, Berlin Thunder, Cologne Centurions, Hamburg Sea Devils, Rhein Fire, and Frankfurt Galaxy.

CFL: Canadian Football League—New Opportunities or Dead-End? In 2005, three African American coaches in the Canadian Football League held the title head coach. The majority of the African American coaches in the Canadian Football League (N = 11) were assigned coaching duties as defensive assistant, assistant head coach and defensive coordinator, receivers coach, quarterback coach, special teams coordinator, backs coach/co-defensive coordinator, line coach, quality control coach, and offensive line coach.

Anderson (1993) analyzed career options of selected NCAA Division I-A football coaches. The author tried to determine the relationship, if any, between race and positions occupied within the football coaching organization (e.g., director, head coach, offensive coordinator, defensive coordinator, assistant coach). Anderson (1993) concluded a linear coaching career pattern did exist in college football. Anderson's (1993) research focusing on the African American football coaching experience suggested that African American black assistant coaches tend to coach wide receivers and running backs. Counterbalanced to these findings, African American coaches located within the Canadian football organization are afforded the opportunity to coach across a variety of football playing positions. Hopefully, these coaching experiences will result in possible upward mobility to the head coaching ranks.

NFL Europe: In 2005, Mike Jones (Frankfurt Galaxy) was the only head football coach in NFL Europe. Twenty-three African Americans held the following assistant head coaching positions: offensive coordinator, defensive coordinator, offensive assistant, offensive line, defensive assistant, linebackers, special teams, wide receivers, and running backs.

The increased number of African American assistant NFL Europe coaches may be a result of the initiative between NFL's development programs and NFL Europe to provide athletes an avenue to gain access to the head coaching ranks. NFL Europe African American coaching career mobility paths consisted of previous college playing experience, previous college coaching experience, previous playing experience within the NFL, assistant head coaching experience in the NFL and, in some cases, previous playing experience in NFL Europe.

On January 30, 2004, Luke Jones was appointed head coach of Frankfurt Galaxy. Coach Jones previously coached wide receivers at Liberty University and served as assistant coach, Orlando Rage of the XFL. He also served as an offensive assistant coach for the Rhein Fire (Europe NFL). The Fire team won World Bowl titles in 1998 and 2000.

Today, researchers are trying to better understand the coaching and management career mobility patterns of people of color (males and females) and other ethnic minorities at the international and global level. Coaching and administrative career paths may vary by type of sport, country, level of organization (i.e., clubs, professional ties), and gender. Thus, coaching career patterns at the global level may be individualistic and tied to micro level variables.

To some extent, data of African American coaches employed by the Canadian Football League and NFL Europe tends to mirror NCAA-IA coaching hiring practices. Coaches were hired initially as assistants. The extent to which assistant coaches become head coaches is not completely understood at the global level of sport organization.

Olympic Games: African American Head Coaching Marathon

Writing in *The African American Coaching Experience: A Case of Social Injustice?* Brooks and Althouse (1999) stated: "Historically, African American coaches gained recognition from the international community through the Olympics and service as coaches at historically black colleges and universities. For example, the United States Olympic Track and Field inducted three African Americans into the National Track and Field Hall of Fame: Edward Hurt (1975), Morgan State University; Ed Temple (1989), Tennessee State University; and Leroy Walker (1983), North Carolina Central University (Ashe, 1993)" (p. 2).

The Olympic Games (revived in 1896) provided African American athletes opportunities to participate in sport at the international level, especially in the sport of track and field. Historically, records indicate African American George Coleman Poage won a bronze medal (200 meters) at the 1904 Olympic Games.

Notable former African American Olympic Gold Medal track and field winners include: Alice Coachman, Ralph Boston, Wilma Rudolph, Edwin Moses, Wyomia Tyus, Rafer Johnson, Jesse Owens, Bob Beaman, and Carl Lewis. Since 1932, African American men and women established a long and proud Olympic sport heritage. Unfortunately, few African American men or women held the title head Olympic coach for a specific sport activity.

It is not surprising that George Williams (African American male) from St. Augustine College was selected a head U.S. Olympic track and field coach during the 2004 Games held in Athens, Greece. Unfortunately, Olympic head coaching opportunities have been limited for African American men and women. Pioneer African American Olympic coaches include: Lenny Wilkins (former NBA coach), who coached a 1996 Olympic Gold Medal Team, and Marian Washington (University of Kansas, Basketball), who coached a 1996 Olympic Gold Medal Team.

Administrative opportunities for African Americans within the American Olympic community have been limited. Dr. Leroy Walker, former North Carolina University track coach and organizer of the Pan-African Games in 1971, became the first and only African American president of the United States Olympic Committee (1992–96) (Ashe, 1988; Swanson, 2004).

Thomas and Chaplip (1996) stated, "The selection of coaches for national teams is never an easy task. Some countries try to limit the number of candidates

Photo courtesy of USOC.

Brooks Johnson was assistant women's coach at the 1976 Olympic Games, the 1984 Olympic Team women's head coach in Los Angeles, and the relay coach in 2004. He was inducted into the United States Track Coaches Hall of Fame in 1997 and in 2004 won the Giegengack Award for his outstanding contribution to the development and success of USA Track and Field and the larger community of the sport.

Photo courtesy of the Amateur Athletic Foundation.

Anita DeFrantz earned an Olympic bronze medal as captain of the U.S. rowing team in Montreal in 1976. She served as vice president of the 1984 Los Angeles Games Organizing Committee and was appointed to lifetime membership in the IOC in 1986. She is the first American woman and the first African American to serve on the IOC. She currently serves as president of the Amateur Athletic Foundation, a non-profit organization dedicated to the development of youth sport, which is endowed with surplus funds from the 1984 Olympic Games.

by assuring minimum coaching competencies through certification programs. In other instances, a national federation may have a coaching certification program (p. 136). The authors identified three methods by which national track coaches were identified:

1. Special assignment coaches: Coaches named by national federation.

2. Full-time coach: Coaches are appointed to coach nationally.

3. Personal coach: Coaches are selected based on the unique skills of the athletes (i.e., track and field and gymnastics).

Summary

The year 2004 marked the fiftieth anniversary of the *Brown vs. the Topeka Board of Education* landmark court case. Yet, today, African Americans and other ethnic minorities have not fully enjoyed the status of "equal" partners within the NCAA workplace. The literature clearly outlines the case that ethnic minorities continue to be marginalized in intercollegiate sports and have not gained parity as head coaches and administrators. The NCAA has been somewhat receptive to employ proactive initiatives in an attempt to add diversity in the work place. For all of its good intentions, however, NCAA coaching and administrative positions still remain primarily male and Caucasian.

The literature suggests that coaching careers and administrator's mobility patterns of college coaches and athletic directors are truly unique and often follow an uneven path. There is no one career model that can adequately explain coaching career mobility. Yet, it is unlikely that we should expect to witness a significant increase in the number of ethnic minority (male and female) head coaches and administrators across the various NCAA sport structures over the next ten years.

Globalization has transformed the nature of sport. Similarly, the expansion of national and international sports provides additional employment opportunities as coaches and sport administrators. Unfortunately, few scholars have systematically investigated the impact of race, racism, and coaching/administrator mobility at the international sports level.

▲▼ Suggested Readings ▲▼

Brooks, D., Althouse, R., & Tucker, D. (1997). African American male head coaches: In the "red zone," but can they score? *Journal of African Americans, 2(213),* 91–112.

Brooks, D. & Althouse, R. (1999). The African American coaching experience: A case of social injustice? *Shades of Diversity: Issues and Strategies 1,* 1–12.

Brown, G. T. (2002, October 28). Diversity grid lock: Black coaches aim to shed hiring block. *NCAA News, 39*(22) 1: 16–18.

Cunningham, G. B., & Sagas, M. (2005, May). Access discrimination in intercollegiate athletics. *Journal of Sport and Social Issues, 29*(2), 148–163.

Cunningham, G. B., & Sagas, M. (2004). The effect of group diversity on organizational commitment. *International Sports Journal, 8*(1), 124–131.

Doherty, A. J., & Chelladurai, P. (1996). Managing cultural diversity in sport organizations: A theoretical perspective. *Journal of Sport Management, 13*(4), 280–297.

Friend, J., & LeUnes, A. (1989, July). Overcoming discrimination in sport management: A systematic approach to affirmative action. *Journal of Sport Management, 3*(2), 151–157.

Harvey, J., Rail, G., & Thiboult, L. (1996, August). Globalization and sport: Sketching a theoretical model for empirical analysis. *Journal of Sport and Social Issues, 2,* 58–277.

New world order: After years of battle for fair opportunities, people of color are finally running the show (in some places) and driving the economics in sports. (The 101 most influential minorities in sport). (2003, May 5). *Sports Illustrated, 98*(18), 38–42; 44–46.

Report indicates few gains for blacks at top administrative level. (2002, October 14). *NCAA News, 39*(21), 1–19.

Sagas, M., & Cunningham, G. B. (2004). Treatment discrimination in college coaching: Its prevalence and impact on career success of assistant basketball coaches. *International Sports Journal, 8*(1), 76–88.

▲▼ Study Questions ▲▼

1. Discuss the factors or theories that attempt to explain the lack of ethnic minority NCAA head coaches and administrators.

2. Identify the various NCAA affirmative action and equal opportunity initiatives to increase the number of potential ethnic minority applicants.

3. What has been the impact of globalization on the transformation of sport?

4. Discuss the availability of head coaching and administrative positions for African Americans and other ethnic minorities seeking employment by Olympic teams, NFL Europe, and in the Canadian Football League.

5. Discuss Kenneth Shropshire's model of the "black-bottomed pyramid" and apply this concept to NCAA coaching and administrative hiring practices.

6. Discuss the Rainbow Coalition strategies to enhance diversity among member institutions.

7. What factor led to the Black Coaches Association to establish a "hiring report card"?

8. List and discuss at least three NCAA diversity programs established to assist ethnic minorities and women to gain access to leadership positions.

9. What is the purpose of the NCAA Self-study Program?

10. What is the relationship between sport globalization, racism, and coaching and administrator hiring opportunities?

References

Abney, R., & Richey, D. (1991). Barriers encountered by black female athletes, administrators and coaches. *Journal of Physical Education, Recreation and Dance, 62*(6), 19–21.

Acosta, R. V., & Carpenter, L. J. (1990). Perceived courses of the declining representation of women leaders in intercollegiate sport—1988 Update. (ERIC) Document Reproduction Service, No. ED 314381.

Anderson, D. (1993). Cultural diversity on campus: A look at intercollegiate football coaches. *Journal of Sport and Social Issues, 17*(1), 61–66.

Anderson, K. (1992, September 28). No room at the top. *Sports Illustrated, 77*(10), 62.

Ashe, A. (1988). *A hard road to glory: A history of the African American athlete.* New York: Warner Books.

Banks, O. (1979). How black coaches view entering the job market at major colleges. *Journal of Physical Education and Recreation, 50,* 62.

Barlow, A. (2003). *Between fear and hope: Globalization and race in the United States.* New York: Rowman & Letterfield Publishing, Inc.

Blanchflower, D. G. (2000). *Globalization and the labor market.* Washington, DC: Trade Deficit Review Commission.

Brooks, D. D., & Althouse, R. C. (1993). Racial imbalance in coaching and managerial positions. In D. D. Brooks & R. C. Althouse (Ed.). *Racism in college athletics: The African American athlete's experience* (pp 101–142). Morgantown, WV: Fitness Information Technology, Inc.

Brooks, D. D., and Althouse, R. C. (1999). The African American coaching experience: A case of social injustice? *Shades of Diversity Issues and Strategies, a Monograph Series, 1,* 1–12). Reston, VA: AAHPERD.

Brooks, D., Althouse, R., & Tucker, D. (1997). African American male head coaches: In the "red zone," but can they score? *Journal of African American Men, 2*(213), 93–112.

Caudill, J., Ford, M., Mixon, F., & Peng, T. C. (1995, June). A discrete-time hazard model of lottery adoption. *Applied Economics 27,* 555–561.

Cole, C. L. (1994). Resisting the canon: Feminist cultural studies, sport, and technologies of the body. In S. Birrell and C. Cole (Eds.), *Women, sport, and culture* (pp. 5–30). Champaign, IL: Human Kinetics.

Cole, C. L., & King, S. (1998). Representing Black masculinity and urban possibilities: Racism, realism, and hoop dreams. In G. Rai (Ed.), *Sport and postmodern times* (pp. 49–86). SUNY Press: Albany.

Cunningham, G. B., & Sagas, M. (2005, May). Access discrimination in intercollegiate athletics. *Journal of Sport and Social Issues, 29*(2), 148–163.

Eitzen, D. S., & Sage, G. H. (1989). Racial bias in women's collegiate volleyball. *Journal of Sport and Social Issues, 13*(1): 46–51.

Grass-roots programs advance women, minority coaches. (2005, January 3). The NCAA online.

Harrison, K. C. (2004). The score: A hiring card for NCAA Division IA and IAA football coaching positions. Report submitted to the Black Coaches Association, Indianapolis, Indiana.

Hartman, D. (2003). *Race, culture, and the revolt of the Black athlete: The 1968 Olympic protests and their aftermath* (pp. 251–271). Chicago: University of Chicago Press.

Harvey, J., Rail, G., & Thibault, L. (1996, August). Globalization and sport: Sketching a theoretical model for empirical analyses. *Journal of Sport and Social Issues,* 258–277.

Jarvie, G. (1991). *Sport, racism and ethnicity.* New York: Falmer Press.

Johnson, R. (2003, May 5). Changing the game. *Sports Illustrated, 99*(18), 32–46.

Jones, G. A., Leonard, W. M., Schmitt, R. L., Smith, D. R., & Tolone, W. L. (1987). Racial discrimination in college football. *Social Science Quarterly, 68*(1), 783.

King, C. R., & Springwood, C. F. (2001). *Beyond the cheers: Race as spectacle in college sport.* Albany: State University of New York Press.

Larsen, P. (2002, November 11–12). Diversifying classroom a first step. *Street and Smith's Sports Business Journal,* 19–20.

Latimer, S. & Mathes, S. (1985). Black college football coaches' social, educational, athletic and career pattern characteristics. *Journal of Sport Behavior, 8*(3), 149–162.

Lyons, D. C. (1992, August). Why black coaches and executives are still second-class citizens. *Ebony, 47,* 116–118.

Massengale, J., & Farrington, F. (1922). The influence of playing positive centrality in the careers of college football coaches. *Review of Sport and Leisure, 2*(1), 107–115.

McKendra, J. (2005, February 14). Minority committee says hiring practices need work. *The NCAA News, 42*(4), 6.

NCAA. *1999–2000 NCAA Division1 athletics certification handbook.* Overland Park, Kansas: NCAA Member Survey.

NCAA (2000, May 22). Race report indicates little change in diversity hiring. *The NCAA News, 37*(11), 1–20.

NCAA (2002, September 16). The diversity hiring failure. *The NCAA News.* Retrieved from http:/lwww.ncaa.orgl news/2002/200209 161

New world order: After years of battle for fair opportunities, people of color are finally running the show (in some places) and driving the economics in sports. (The 101 most influential minorities in sport). (2003, May 5). *Sports Illustrated, 98*(18), 38–42; 44–46.

Rainbow Coalition develops diversity plan for institutions. (1994, April 13). *The NCAA News, 31*(15), 5.

Robertson, R. (1992). *Globalization social theory and global culture.* London: Sage Publications.

Sage, G. H. (1975). An occupational analysis of the college coach. In D. Ball & J. Loy, *Sport and social order: Contributions to the sociology of sport* (pp. 391–455). Reading, Massachusetts: Addison-Wesley Publishing Company.

Shropshire, K. L. (1996, January). Merit, ol' boy networks, and the black-bottomed pyramid. *Hastings Law Journal,* 455–472.

Slow going: Black coaches decry a dearth of opportunities. (1991, June 10). *Sports Illustrated, 74*(22), 13.

Suggs, W. (2005). Faces in a mostly white, male crowd. *The Chronicle of Higher Education, 51*(31), A34.

Swanson, R. A. (2004). Leroy Walker. In D. K. Wiggins (Ed.), *African Americans in Sports* (Vol. 2, pp. 385–386).

Armonk, NY: Sharpe Reference.

Thomas, D. A. (2004, September). Diversity as strategy. *Harvard Business Review*, 98–108.

Tucker, D. (2000, November). Black executives in sport: The African American head coach in Division IA football, 2000. Unpublished paper. North American Society for the Sociology of Sport Annual Conference, Colorado Springs, Colorado.

Zirin, D., & Cox, J., (n.d).The 2006 World Cup: Will racism come home to roost? ZNet/Activism; accessed 2006. pp. 1–2.

CHAPTER 6

ETHNIC MINORITY OPPORTUNITIES IN COLLEGE AND PROFESSIONAL SPORTS: A BUSINESS IMPERATIVE

FRITZ G. POLITE

Fritz Polite's chapter on "Ethnic Minority Opportunities in College and Professional Sports: A Business Imperative" weighs the current hiring practices in intercollegiate athletics and professional sports against the notion that a diverse minority workforce makes good business sense. Statistics show that diversity hiring opportunities for people of color and for women in intercollegiate sports are severely under-represented by any measure used. Polite argues that there is limited support and intermittent opportunity for the development of skills or competencies, few internships, and rare experiences in collegiate circles explicitly geared to prepare minorities for any leadership positions. It is his judgment that sports management programs need to arm themselves to ensure a multi-cultural perspective to meet challenges of global diversity.

The problem with the Twentieth Century is a problem of the color-line.

—W.E.B. Du Bois, 1903

Key Terms

▼Diversity▲
▼Equal access▲
▼Access discrimination▲
▼Race/gender▲
▼Ethnicity▲
▼Business imperative▲

Abstract ▼ Race, ethnicity, gender, and career opportunities are hot topics in the sporting world. When discussing the role of sport in our society there appear to be several discourses. Although sport is sometimes viewed as a microcosm or mirror of our society, Brooks and Althouse (1993) contended that sports do not mirror society and its larger social issues. They further stated that due to their entertainment value, society considers sports ahistorical, apolitical, and asocial (Brooks & Althouse, 1993). Many of the same issues pertaining to hiring practices, race, ethnicity, and opportunities that exist in corporate America are also witnessed within the spectrum of sports. This can be specifically pinpointed to the minimal representation of people of color and women in key leadership positions. Many times the discussion of race and sport business opportunities creates an uncomfortable forum for majority members. By focusing on shared concerns, our society will be better able to cope with and understand the historical significance of the impact of racism and discrimination and the virulent undercurrent it has had on our society. A closer examination of sport can assist our society in confronting broader societal problems. The implications associated with the sociological and economic fallout of racism and discrimination have further highlighted the need for continued research and analysis concerning hiring practices and/or opportunities in sport and academia. The notion of diversity as a business imperative in the hiring process in sport have been limited as a general topic of research. Diversity in sport, especially in relation to those who hold positions of power in interscholastic, intercollegiate, and professional sport, seems to be an oxymoron (Fink & Pastore, 1999). Throughout this chapter, the author will identify and highlight statistical data reflecting the demographic make up of the NCAA member institutions. The author will attempt to clearly transcribe, highlight, and analyze records of hiring practices. The author embellishes the notion that in order to increase the number of under-represented groups in collegiate athletics, there must be a concerted effort between the leadership and those groups.

Introduction

Our nation recently recognized the 50th anniversary of the Supreme Court ruling in the *Brown v. Board of Education* case (1954), along with the 40th anniversary of several significant 1964 Civil Rights legislative acts. We are at a critical point in terms of our progress in addressing the issues of race, opportunity, ethnicity, and diversity in our society. As history has unfolded, several significant firsts have taken place during this century. On July 26, 1948 President Harry S. Truman signed *Executive Order 9981*, which established equality of treatment and opportunity in the Armed Forces ("Colin Powell," n.d.). Truman declared that "there shall be equality of treatment and opportunity for all persons in the armed services without regard to race, color, religion, or national origin." This act established the grounds for challenging segregation and making the U.S. military one of the first institutions in America to integrate. On April 15, 1947, Jackie Robinson (Brooklyn Dodgers) became the first African American to break the color barrier in Major League Baseball. More recently, Damon Evans became the first African American athletic director in the history of the Southeastern Conference (SEC) (2003). Another momentous act was the hiring of Sylvester Croom as the first African American head football coach (Mississippi State University) in the SEC (2003).

This chapter will explore the role and scope of leadership opportunities, or lack thereof, for minorities as well as the lack of exigencies of most sport organizations and institutions. Discussions of African American and ethnic minority sport leaders, as well as trail blazers and pioneers will also be addressed. Pioneers who provided the platform for current progress such as Dr. Leroy T. Walker, Ed Temple, Cleveland Abbott, Marian Washington, Eddie Robinson, and Fritz Pollard, along with their significant contributions, will be highlighted. Current professional leadership opportunities in top positions regarding people of color and women will also be analyzed. The chronological and historical hiring process of minorities in the arena of sport and the impact of past and present socio-cultural aspects in job opportunities are critical in providing positive direction for change. Harry Edwards (1985), one of the foremost scholars and pioneers in focusing on the African American athlete in sociology and its implications in sport, stated, "I think that the problems I discussed twenty years ago are now evident to everyone. In twenty years we've moved from a discussion of whether or not there is a problem, to a discussion of how to solve the problem." Investigations into the historical precedence of race and ethnicity in relationship to career opportunities illuminate unique circumstances associated with gender; racial discourses and hiring practices are identified and probed. The area of concentration will be in hiring practices of leadership positions, ethnicity as a business imperative, roles of leadership in the decision-making process, conditions contributing to the changing demographics, as well as prescriptions and solutions for future discussions. Within the intercollegiate realm as well as the professional arena, the issue of *firsts* must take place in order for us to move positively to the next step in aggrandizing the progress of women along with *all* people of color while creating a true egalitarian system. We as a society must move positively forward in providing an even platform in which the notion of firsts no longer exists. Exploring the developmental experiences of coaches, women, athletes, and administrators of color by giving voice to their concerns about their interests, leadership opportunities, and relationships with other student athletes, coaches, and administrators can be undertaken to both acknowledge existence and bring voice to experiences (Bruening, 2005).

This chapter will examine key leadership positions within the collegiate and professional ranks. There are several frontiers within collegiate athletics that still remain predominately white. Racism is still deeply woven into the basic fabric of sport and our society. The issue of race in relationship to hiring practices should be a topic of discussion at all levels of sport whether it is on the amateur, professional, or collegiate level. The subject of race is prevalent within our culture and permeates all facets of our society. Leaders of various organizations are faced with complex issues pertaining to race, gender, diversity, value, equity, and hiring practices. Although significant progress has been made in distinct areas of sport, there has been a void of positive hiring practices in prominent leadership positions at most levels of sport. The lack of diversity in key decision-making positions has further heightened the need for open discussion, dialogue, and research into society's efforts to solve and provide valid answers, prescriptions, or solutions to the issue of race and opportunities for under-represented groups.

The parallels of the historical precedence of slavery, civil rights, gender inequities, and racial policies lead to further inference to the current lack of minority leadership in prominent positions within sport. The lingering effects of racism are prevalent but sometimes subliminal in their mode of operating. This chapter will attempt to analyze hiring practices within college athletics and professional sports as well as develop a platform for discussion of possible social change.

Defining Diversity and Opportunity

Many people view the United States as the ultimate destination for opportunity. These opportunities may exist in various areas to include: real estate, finance, entrepreneurship, and sports. Is access to these areas based on an equitable and fair system? Do race, ethnicity, and gender factor into these opportunities for access? The notion of race and ethnicity, or the creation of a minority or majority status in sport, has created unique circumstances as well as conditions. Cultural groups often refer to an affiliation of people who collectively share certain norms, values, or traditions that are different from those of other groups (Cox, 1994). Cultural diversity is the representation of one social system, of people with distinctly different group affiliations of cultural significance. There are strong indications that the world in which we are living, working, and participating is drastically changing. Past literature indicates a significant increase in cultural diversity that constitutes people with distinctly different group affiliations of cultural significance (Census, 2000). In many circumstances these groups are also referred to as minorities. Minority status has impeded the liberty of millions as ignorance, prejudice, and discrimination often lock the doors of progress for those with differences due to race, sex, age, sexual orientation, disability, or religion (Guttman, 1993;

Weatherspoon, 1988). As these designators of minority status are assigned, there are indications that diversity is increasing in the general workforce, based on personal characteristics such as age, gender, race, ethnic background, religion, sexual orientation, physical ability, and marital and parental status (Wright, Ferris, & Hiller, 1995). The workforce in many nations of the world is becoming increasingly more diverse along such dimensions as gender, race, and nationality (Fullerton, 2000). What does the present landscape look like for minorities in search of access and opportunities within the collegiate and professional ranks?

Diversity is a term that has evolved from various other progressions stemming from the Civil Rights era. Terms such as *multiculturalism*, *race relations*, and *diversity* were buzz words in the late '60s and '70s. The ending of segregation and a strong push of feminism, coupled with the rise of immigrants into the United States work force, caused alarm within organizations and incorporated a new set of concepts, terms, and language. Reluctant business leaders were introduced to new markets, communities, and ethnicities. From a business imperative, the benefits of targeting multiple demographic groups proved challenging as well as profitable for many organizations. Organizations were looking to address the issue of diversity not only as a moral directive, but also as a business imperative.

There are several perspectives regarding the definition of diversity. Joplin and Daus (1997) defined diversity as "any characteristic used to differentiate one person from another." Traditionally organizations have preferred to work, associate, and socialize with persons with whom they could most easily assimilate. This may have caused employers within organizations to tend toward creating a language and culture relevant to the business. Most did not account for those groups that did not look, speak, or adapt to this self-defined culture. Companies were happy and even preferred to have individuals as well as groups that thought and looked like they (i.e., leadership) did. Doherty and Chelladurai (1999) contended that the benefits derived from the successful management of diversity hinges on the existence or development of an organizational culture that values diversity.

Sport Management and Diversity

The basic concept of equality should be a central point in sport management theory and practice. Equal access and opportunity are topics of discussion with multiple discourses. The general principle often focuses on equality and notions of equal access. With a major shift in the globalization of sport management, it is clear that curriculum must reflect this new global concept. Our world is rapidly changing. The world is shifting from relative self-containment to multiple interdependent global societies. Sport management programs must be at the forefront in providing cutting-edge research, practical applications, and progressive leadership in order to be effective in transitioning into this changing global system. The concept of a more integrated and interdependent global economy must be instituted with the framework of our current sport management curriculum. The infusion of diversity, culture, race, gender, sexual preference, and physical disabilities must be a priority in preparing students to meet the challenges of the new millennium. Sport management curriculum must address the ever-changing global aspect of our society. By focusing on our future leaders and the infusion of teaching skills that value diversity in the workplace, our institutions will be better suited to manage within a global society. Effective diversity management within the realm of sport management should be a business imperative that presents a strong return on investment.

Managing Cultural Diversity in Sport

One of the driving factors behind most business organizations is the competitive nature of operating in a profitable state. This creates tensions when sound financial business aspects of collegiate sport are applied to the true challenges of providing a quality academic experience to the student athlete. As the fields, courts, and arenas are changing, the ethnicities of the participants are evolving and creating a chameleon effect. The National Basketball Association is a great example of this. The league is rich in its cultural make up and brings a global spectrum to its presence.

Table 1. NBA Players (2005)
▼ 18 international players (Drafted 2005)
▼ 81 players from 35 countries/territories (Active Rosters)
▼ 1st player picked—Andrew Bogut (Australia)
▼ 11th player picked—Fran Vasquez (Spain)

Table 2. 2005 NBA All-Star Game: Diversity
▼ Broadcast in 214 countries
▼ 97 international telecasters
▼ 45 different languages
▼ Ballots printed in 19 different languages
▼ nba.com—51% of Internet traffic from outside U.S.
(King 2005)

Although the major focus of this chapter is the collegiate arena, it is clear that sport is being played on a global level by international participants. Are these multi-cultured players being managed by a diverse group? Is the leadership well versed on the intricacies of this new and ethnically diverse population?

Progress in Professional Sports

One of the more progressive organizations in addressing issues of participation, diversity, and hiring practices is the National Basketball Association. In the NBA's 2003–2004 season, 76% of the participants were African Americans; 22% were white (Lapchick, 2004). This actually was a decrease in participation of African American players. There has been an influx of international players in the league. Seventeen percent of the players in the NBA were international, and most were from Europe.

Although there have been notable improvements in hiring practices of women and ethnic minorities in professional sports, there still exists considerable room for continued equity and opportunities. Society continues to struggle with issues of race, gender, homophobia, and hiring practices within as well as outside of the world of sport.

NBA League Office

A commitment to the values and true principles of equal access and opportunity are best exemplified by actions rather than by words. Analysis of the hiring practices of the NBA shows that there has been progress, but there is still room for continued progress. Only 29% of all NBA league office professional positions were held by people of color. African Americans constituted 18% of this total, 6% were Latino, and 5% were Asian. Women made up 43% of the league office employees. Within the league office, 71% of the professional positions were occupied by whites. There were 13 people of color in vice president positions in the 2004 season.

Access Denied

Currently the majority of those in leadership positions within the NCAA are white males. The representation of minorities within prominent leadership positions is sparse and progress has been slow. Sagas and Cunningham (2005) examined the variables associated with issues of access discrimination in intercollegiate athletics. One highlighted case study was that of The University of Alabama football program. The candidates were Mike Shula and Sylvester Croom. In terms of experience and past accomplishments, Croom seemed the likely candidate. His resume indicated more experience in both the professional and collegiate ranks. Mike Shula had not coached at the collegiate level; Croom had served in multiple positions at the collegiate and professional level. It raised eyebrows within as well as outside of the industry when Shula was awarded the position as the head coach at the University of Alabama.

How do we attempt to dissect the extraneous variables associated with subjective criteria for opportunities or lack thereof for minorities within collegiate athletics? Greenhaus, Parasuraman, and Worley (1990) identified two types of discrimination: access and treatment. Treatment discrimination "occurs when subgroup members receive fewer rewards, resources, or opportunities on the job than they legitimately deserve on the basis of job related criteria." Access discrimination is when the limitations are not related to actual or potential performance (Ilgen & Youtz, 1986). Cunningham and Sagas (2005) further examined the issues of racism and access discrimination as being particularly salient in the context of higher education. They surveyed a total of 300 Division 1 basketball programs and found that white assistants were more likely to be hired than black assistants if the head coach was white (2005). In addition to NCAA basketball, where 28% of head coaches are black, Division 1 football has a similar issue. Out of the 117 schools that have a football program, only three have black head coaches (Cunningham & Sagas, 2005).

Table 3. NCAA Demographics

POSITION	TOTAL
Commissioners (D1-A)	
White Male	100%
Presidents (D1-A)	
White Male	94.9%
Black	3.4%
Hispanic	2.0%
Women	11.0%
Athletic Directors (D-1)	
Men	
White	88.5% (232)
Black	3.4% (9)
Asian American	0.0% (0)
Latino Hispanic	1.2% (3)
Native American	0.0% (0)
Women	
White	6.5% (17)
Black	0.0% (0)
Asian American	0.4% (1)
Latina Hispanic	0.0% (0)
Native American	0.4% (1)
Coaches (D1) Men's Sports	
Football	
White	96%
Black	2.9%
Other	1.1%
Basketball	
White	76.4%
Black	23.2%
Other	0.4%
Baseball	
White	96.4%
Black	0.9%
Other	2.7%
Coaches (D1) Women's Sports	
Men	
White	52%
Black	3.4%
Asian American	0.9%
Latino Hispanic	1.3%
Native American	0.0%
Other	0.6%

(RGRPC, 2004)

NCAA Member Institutions

There are approximately 1,028 active NCAA member institutions, including 117 schools in Division IA, 118 in Division IAA, and 91 in Division IAAA. Division II has 281 active member institutions and Division III has 421, respectively (Lapchick, 2005). Although these numbers may tend to indicate that there are a vast amount of professional opportunities available within the NCAA organization, further investigation will reveal a significant lapse in leadership/managerial positions. Utilizing data from the 2003–2004 academic year, this chapter includes an analysis of the racial and gender breakdown of specific areas within the NCAA. The data was compiled from the Race & Gender Report Card (2004), NCAA Student-Athlete Ethnicity Report, and the NCAA's study, Race and Gender Demographics of NCAA Member Institutions Athletic Personnel. The author also used data and information from previous studies from the University of Central Florida's Institute for Diversity and Ethics in Sport, Texas A&M's Laboratory for Diversity in Sport, various articles, and prior conducted research. This data reflects the ever-changing fundamental demographic shift taking place on a global scale.

U.S. Census Bureau

In analyzing the demographic make up of sport organizations it is imperative that discussions regarding the drastically changing ethnic infusion of multiple cultures take place. This conglomeration of diversity is changing the landscape of our world as we currently know it. The U.S. Census (2000) was the largest census in the history of the United States, counting 281 million people. The growth rate during the '90s (13%) was more than the rate in the '80s (10%). According to *The Buying Power of Black America* (2005), black households had $650 billion in earned income, an increase of 3.9% over the $631 million earned in 2002. This report has become a very useful tool for corporations that attempt to utilize new and innovative marketing techniques to attract minority consumers.

The Census report also estimates by age, race, and ethnicity that Hispanics and Asians are growing more than 10 times the pace of whites who are not Hispanic (2004). This influx is causing a rapid change in the demographic make-up of the "average" consumer. Divisions of several dimensions are prevalent and cause concern for traditionally white marketers. The white-dominated society is changing dramatically, and it would be prudent to recognize these changes in all aspects of our society. Hispanics constitute 12.5 % of the total population and are now the largest minority group. This growing multicultural population is creating a shift in retailers, marketers, companies, and corporations. Although this data has not reflected significantly in the percentages regarding intercollegiate athletic participation of Hispanics, it is clear that the world as we have known it is changing at a rapid pace. Our society must recognize our world as a global phenomenon, multicultural in its dimensions and expanding rapidly.

NCAA Overview

The following section represents an overview of NCAA Coaching and Administrative Opportunities. Data are as follows:

- ▼ 14,469 head coaches

- ▼ 24,229 assistant coaches

- ▼ 918 athletics directors

- ▼ 2,390 associate and assistant athletics directors

- ▼ 836 senior women's administrators

- ▼ 4,838 academic advisors, compliance coordinators and managers for business development, fund-raising, facilities, marketing, ticket sales and media relations

- ▼ Support staff

(RGRPC, 2004).

In reviewing past and current opportunities in college sports it is important to focus on positions of leadership along with support activities. Those persons in positions to make pivotal decisions should be at the apex of our discussions. Although university presidents as well as athletic directors are working closely with boosters and powerful supporters, they still have significant input into the overall hiring process. During NCAA President Myles Brand's State of the NCAA address in January 2005, he called the lack of opportunity for people of color in football head coaching positions "appalling." He also said the situation was bad for women and people of color as athletic directors and for women as head coaches (Lapchick 2005). The data presented tended to indicate a decline in access for most categories pertaining to women and minorities

At the director level, whites occupied 81.3 % of those positions while African Americans held 12.5% of all director positions, Latinos held 2%, and Asian Americans occupied 4% of all director level positions. These director positions are of significant importance due to the level of influence on decision-making power within the administration.

University Presidents and Vice Presidents in Division IA

One of the most powerful as well as influential positions within all of the institutions of higher learning is that of university/college president. This person is normally charged with the day-to-day operating decisions of the respective institutions. All persons employed by the university fall under the leadership of these presidents. It is critical that these areas of leadership be the central driving point in addressing the issues of opportunities for under-represented people in collegiate athletics.

Table 4. NCAA Presidents

The four African-American presidents:

- ▼ Sidney A. Ribeau, Bowling Green State University
- ▼ Adam W. Herbert, Indiana University, Bloomington
- ▼ Sidney McPhee, Middle Tennessee State University
- ▼ Roderick McDavis, Ohio University

The two Latino presidents:

- ▼ Luis Proenza, University of Akron
- ▼ Louis Caldera, University of New Mexico

The 13 women presidents:

- ▼ Carol Garrison, University of Alabama at Birmingham
- ▼ Jo Ann M. Gora, Ball State University
- ▼ Nancy L. Zimpher, University of Cincinnati
- ▼ Carol A. Cartwright, Kent State University
- ▼ Shirley Raines, University of Memphis
- ▼ Donna E. Shalala, University of Miami (Florida)
- ▼ Mary Sue Coleman, University of Michigan
- ▼ Carol C. Harter, University of Nevada, Las Vegas
- ▼ Nancy Cantor, Syracuse University
- ▼ Diana S. Natalicio, University of Texas at El Paso
- ▼ Judith Bailey, Western Michigan University
- ▼ Judy Genshaft, University of South Florida
- ▼ Karen Holbook, The Ohio State University

(RGRPC, 2004)

Table 5. NCAA Vice Presidents

The African American (male) vice presidents are:

- ▼ Bernard Franklin, vice president for Governance & Membership
- ▼ Ronald Stratten, vice president for Education Services

The four women vice presidents are:

- ▼ Charlotte Westerhaus
- ▼ Judith Sweet, vice president for Championships
- ▼ Elsa Cole, chief legal counsel
- ▼ Sue Donohoe, vice president of Women's Division I Basketball

(RGRPC, 2004)

Table 6. NCAA-IA African American Athletic Directors

There are nine African American athletic directors at Division IA institutions:

- ▼ Eugene Smith, The Ohio State University
- ▼ Damon Evans, University of Georgia
- ▼ Herman R. Frazier, University of Hawaii, Manoa
- ▼ Daryl Gross, Syracuse University
- ▼ Michael Garrett, University of Southern California
- ▼ David Williams II, Vanderbilt University
- ▼ Craig Littlepaige, University of Virginia
- ▼ Kevin Anderson, West Point
- ▼ McKinley Boston, New Mexico State

There are three Latino Division IA athletics directors:

- ▼ Daniel G. Guerrero, University of California, Los Angeles
- ▼ Rudy Davalos, University of New Mexico
- ▼ Barry Alvarez, University of Wisconsin, Madison
- ▼ There are nine women Division IA athletics directors:
- ▼ Anne "Sandy" Barbour, University of California, Berkeley
- ▼ Kathy Beauregard, Western Michigan University
- ▼ Joan C. Cronan, University of Tennessee, Knoxville*
- ▼ Cary Groth, Northern Illinois University
- ▼ Beverly R. Lewis, University of Arkansas, Fayetteville*
- ▼ Lisa Love, Arizona State University
- ▼ Judy MacLeod, University of Tulsa
- ▼ Christine Plonsky, University of Texas, Austin*
- ▼ Deborah A. Yow, University of Maryland, College Park

*Headed separate women's athletics departments ▼ (RGRPC, 2004)

In reviewing the statistical make up of these key power positions, a consistent pattern emerges. The vast majority of these positions are occupied by white males. In Division IA, 94.9% of all university presidents were white, 3.4% were African American men, and 2% were Latino. In Division IA there were no Asian or Native American university presidents. There were 13 females in these positions (11.1%).

College Athletics Directors

The second most important position to discuss, particularly in analyzing opportunities of under-represented people, would be the position of athletic director. This position wields significant decision-making powers. Several important major events have transpired over the past several years. Damon Evans became the first African American athletic director in the South Eastern Conference (SEC). Another significant hiring was Daryl Gross, who became the first African American athletic director in the Big East Conference. There currently are 12 (10.3%) athletic directors who are people of color. Although these appointments indicate significant firsts, they do not rectify the abysmal lack of ethnicity in key leadership positions within collegiate athletics. People of color and women continued to constitute a minimal number of leadership positions. In Division I, whites held 95% of all athletic director positions. White males held a significant percentage of these (88.5%) positions, and white women held 6.5% of these leadership positions. African American men held 3.4%, and Latino men held 1.2%. No Native Americans or Asians held athletic directors positions.

These findings indicate that whites hold 95% of all athletic director positions in Division I. The position of athletic director is one that reflects the vast majority of positions in college athletics that are held by white males. This position also wields tremendous power in terms of hiring practices, administration, boosters/supporters, and general day-to-day operations. Whites held 95% of the athletics director jobs in Division I, 94.1% in Division II, and 95.5% in Division III. This again indicates a significant lack of ethnicity and diversity within key athletic leadership positions in collegiate athletics.

Associate and Assistant Athletic Directors

Within most organizations, it is important for leaders to surround themselves with technically proficient and capable support systems. In college athletics these positions consist of various senior administrative positions. The associate and assistant athletic director positions are instrumental to a successful program. Associate athletic directors function in senior leadership positions. Many times they are acting directors in the absence of the athletic director. These positions may often be directly associated with fundraising and capital campaigns. These are cornerstones for most athletic programs and are commonly referred to as extremely influential positions. They are also the stepping stones to higher administrative positions. In Division I, whites held 89.9% of these positions, 89.2% in Division II, and 94.4% in Division III. African Americans held 7.9% of Division I positions. While white women constituted 27.3% of the positions, African American women held 1.9% of these pipeline positions. These positions provide the basic springboard for progress within the field of collegiate athletics. The data indicate not only limited diversity in key leadership positions, but there seems to be no positive indication of the preparation for future leaders from under-represented groups.

Professional Administration

Collegiate programs also have multiple positions that assist in the overall proficiency and operation of the athletic department. These categories include compliance, business, operations, marketing, ticket sales, media and sports, development, and athletic training. These positions provide unique opportunities for individuals to hone their skills as well as develop the necessary skills and experience to progress professionally and personally.

Whites constituted 87.9% of the positions in Division I. African Americans held 8.2%, Latinos 1.9%, and Asians 0.9%. White men held 60.4%; white women held 27.5%, and African American women held 2.3% of these positions. Although white women constitute a larger percentage of positions at this level than in previous positions, African American women constitute an extremely small statistical percentage.

Coaching

In analyzing the opportunities or lack thereof within the collegiate coaching profession, several factors surface. In Division I basketball coaching positions, 23.2% of all head coaches were African American. This is a positive statistic when compared with the status of African American head football coaches at the Division IA level. At the beginning of the 2004 season, African Americans held 4.2% of all head football coaching positions at the Division IA level. The numbers are bleak when discussing college baseball. There are two African American Division I baseball coaches, which constitute 0.9%, and Latinos held 2.7% of head coaching positions

Table 7. Historical Listing of African American and Latino Division IA Head Football Coaches

Willie Jeffries	Wichita State	5	21-32-0
Dennis Green	Northwestern	5	10-45-0
	Stanford	3	16-18-0
Cleve Bryant	Ohio University	5	9-44-2
Wayne Nunnely	Las Vegas	4	19-25-0
Francis Peay	Northwestern	6	13-51-1
Willie Brown	Long Beach State	1	2-8-2
James Caldwell	Wake Forest	8	14-41-5
Ron Cooper	Eastern Michigan	2	9-13-0
	Louisville	3	13-20-0
Matt Simon	University of North Texas	4	18-26-1
Bob Simmons	Oklahoma State	6	29-37-1
John Blake	Oklahoma	3	11-21-0
Tony Samuel	New Mexico State	4	19-37-0
Jerry Baldwin	Louisiana Lafayette	3	6-27-0
Bobby Williams	Michigan State	2	12-11-0
Ron Dickerson	Temple	5	8-47
Fitzgerald Hill	San Jose State	4	14-32-0
Tyrone Willingham	Stanford	7	44-36-1
	Notre Dame	2	21-15-0
	Washington	0	First season
Karl Dorrell	UCLA	2	12-12
Sylvester Croom	Mississippi State	1	3-8
Barry Alvarez	Wisconsin	14	99-67-4

(RGRPC, 2004)

at this level. Whites held 86% of all the combined divisions head coaching positions in basketball, 97.7% in combined football, and 96.2% in combined baseball.

Division IA college football continues to grow and is a permanent fixture on most university campuses. In Division IA football, the percentage of African American head coaches increased to 4.2% for the 2004 season. Mississippi State hired Sylvester Croom, making him the 19th African American head coach in the history of Division IA football.

The African American football head coaches at the start of the 2004 season were:

▼ Fitz Hill, San Jose State*

▼ Tony Samuel, New Mexico State**

▼ Tyrone Willingham, Notre Dame***

▼ Karl Dorrell, UCLA

▼ Sylvester Croom, Mississippi State

* = Resigned
** = Fired
*** = Fired, now coaching at the University of Washington

Barry Alvarez at the University of Wisconsin—Madison was the only Latino head coach in Division IA football. He also holds the title of Athletic Director.

Representation in Sport Management Programs

This chapter has focused on key leadership positions in intercollegiate sport. It is also important to discuss current demographic make-up of the leadership and faculty of various sport management programs. Over the past century sport has exploded and has become a multi-billion dollar business. To meet this vast expansion, universities and colleges have created a host of sport management programs. Although sport management is indeed a relatively new concept in academe, its acceptance as a legitimate area of study is well documented. The present landscape of these sport management programs, in terms of the cultural diversity make-up, is important for scholars and prospective students. Cultural diversity reflects the unique sets of values, beliefs, attitudes, and expectations, as well as language, symbols, customs, and behaviors that individuals possess by virtue of sharing some common characteristic with others (Adler, 1991; DeSensi, 1994). The forecast for sport management programs must focus on continued growth in the research and study of a multicultural perspective in order to meet the challenges of an ever-changing global world. The education, training, and mentoring of tomorrow's leaders must be a major area of concern for today's institutions.

The final section of this chapter will discuss the notable coaching and administrative achievements of: Eddie Robinson, Frederick D. Pollard, Cheryl Miller, Vivian Stringer, Leroy Walker, Cleveland Abbott, and Ed Temple.

Eddie Robinson

Eddie Gay Robinson was born in Jackson, Louisiana (1919) to parents who were sharecroppers and domestic workers; he was raised during the period of segregation and Jim Crow. He graduated from McKinley High School, and later from Leland College. He married Doris Mott, his childhood sweetheart, in June, 1941. Coach Robinson was appointed head football coach of the Louisiana Negro Normal and Industrial Institute in 1941. The institution renamed itself Grambling State University (Tigers) and he served Grambling in this capacity for 56 years (1941–1997). His tenure lasted through eleven presidents and four major American wars; when he retired, he had won more games than any coach in the history of college football, with a record of 408 wins, 165 losses, and 15 ties. That mark bettered the winning records of such coaching greats as Amos Alonzo Stagg, Pop Warner, and Alabama's legendary Paul "Bear" Bryant. During Robinson's tenure, The Grambling Tigers won eight national black college titles and seventeen conference championships. In 1942, his second season, Robinson fielded a team that went undefeated and was not scored against, a feat that is truly remarkable and extremely rare.

Under Robinson's leadership, Grambling became one of professional football's most productive training grounds. All told, he sent more than 200 Grambling players to the National Football League, including Pro Football Hall of Fame inductees Willie Davis, Junius "Buck" Buchanan, and Willie Brown. The first African American drafted (1949) from a historically black college (Tank Younger) was a product of Coach Robinson's tutelage. The first African American selected in the first round was Buchanan (1963). Another Grambling great who played under Robinson was James Harris. He was signed by the LA Rams (1969) and became one of the first modern-era black starting quarterbacks. Doug Williams became the first black quarterback to start and win a Super Bowl (XXII). He was also selected MVP of the game. Robinson was instrumental in creating and promoting a series of national games (Classics) against other historically black colleges and universities. The most significant is the annual Bayou Classic between Grambling and Southern University. This event has attracted over 70,000 spectators annually. Following the assassination of Dr. Martin Luther King Jr. in 1968, Robinson also established the Urban League Classic. The game was later renamed the Whitney Young Classic, after the death of the National Urban League's former executive director Whitney Young.

Robinson's 56-year tenure at the same institution may never be repeated, and he has observed the social transformation of America through sports over six decades. He may go down in history as one of the most influential figures in sport. His contributions to sport as well as to the development of student athletes as productive citizens in our society are not to be minimized or overlooked. He is a true pioneer and legend.

Fredrick Douglass Pollard

A pioneer in both professional football and racial matters, Frederick Douglass Pollard is an often overlooked figure in the history of professional sports. While the general public is familiar with names like Jackie Robinson and Jesse Owens, the accomplishments of Fritz Pollard have gone largely unnoticed by everyday sports fans.

Born in Chicago in 1894, Pollard lived in a time filled with political turmoil and civil unrest for many ethnic immigrants and especially for African Americans. A versatile athlete, he excelled at football, baseball, and track during his career in high school. He entered Brown University in the fall of 1915, where he led the varsity football team to the Rose Bowl in his first season. In doing so, he became the first black athlete to play in the Rose Bowl. The following year, Pollard became the first African American backfield player to be named to the All-America team.

After serving in the military during World War I, Pollard returned to football in 1919. He joined the Akron Pros of the newly formed American Professional Football Association. One of only two African Americans in the league, Pollard led the Pros to an undefeated record of 8-0-3, and a championship in the league's inaugural season. During that season in 1920, he became the first African American to play quarterback in professional football. The following year, in just its second season, the league that would later become the National Football League produced one of the most notable moments in the annals of the game: Fritz Pollard became the first African American head coach in the history of the NFL.

After a professional career that spanned seven years and included four teams, Pollard made strides to combat the color barrier that the NFL had unofficially imposed on African American athletes. He recruited players from black colleges and in 1928 formed the Chicago Black Hawks, an all-black professional football team. Pollard founded the team with the intention of proving that blacks and whites could compete on the gridiron without incident. The Black Hawks initially played in the Chicago area, scheduling games against white professional and semi-professional teams. Later they traveled to California, and competed against white all-star teams until the team disbanded in 1932. Members of his teams were victims of racial slurs and physical abuse, were denied proper dressing quarters and access to restaurants, and faced other extreme levels of discrimination.

While Pollard's early career focused on football, his later endeavors were of a much broader scope. He was a business man in the truest sense. He established an all-black investment securities company and ran the first all-black tabloid in New York City. He founded Suntan Studios, which trained young black artists for careers in entertainment. For decades, he produced all-black films. Pollard's contributions to society went far beyond the realm of athletics. His role as a pioneer has gone unheralded for so long, yet it remains that the career of Fritz Pollard was nothing short of amazing.

Frederick Douglass Pollard died in 1986, at the age of ninety-two. Almost twenty years after his death, he was finally afforded some of the recognition he deserved. On August 7, 2005, he was inducted into the Pro Football Hall of Fame in Canton, Ohio. Perhaps his election into the Hall of Fame will bring to light the importance of his accomplishments, both on and off the field. His legacy continues with the Fritz Pollard Affinity Group, established by concerned NFL players, coaches, and administrators to address equal opportunity and access for underrepresented players and administrators.

Cheryl Miller

A pioneer in women's basketball was born on January 3, 1964. Cheryl Miller was born in Riverside, California, and went on to have an illustrious career in women's basketball. The road to greatness started early with Cheryl. She was the first player, male or female, ever to win *Parade Magazine's* All-American honor four straight years. She once scored 105 points in a single high school game. During her high school basketball career she lost a total of only four basketball games.

Cheryl went on to attend the University of Southern California from 1982 through 1986. Her accomplishments while attending USC are impressive. She holds nearly every major statistical record at the University of Southern California. Cheryl led USC to back-to-back national titles in 1983 and 1984. In 1983, she was the NCAA All-Tournament MVP. Her many honors included being named Naismith Player of the Year, three time All-American, and three time NCAA All-Tournament team. Her number 31 jersey is retired at USC, making her the first USC athlete to receive that honor. She was also named the WBCA player of the year.

Perhaps Cheryl's biggest accomplishments have come on an international level. She represented the United States in the 1983 and 1986 Pan American Games, the 1984 Olympic Games, and 1986 Goodwill Games. Cheryl won gold medals in the 1983 Pan American games, 1984 Olympics, and 1986 Goodwill Games.

After her playing days were over, Cheryl turned to coaching. She began her coaching career at USC in 1993. She stayed two seasons with the Trojans and compiled a respectable 44-14 record, making the NCAA tournament both seasons. After a short break, she jumped back into coaching with the inception of the WNBA in 1997. She coached the Phoenix Mercury from 1997 through 2000.

Cheryl has devoted her attention to sports commentating. She has appeared on ABC, ESPN, TNT, and TBS as a commentator. Cheryl is the brother of former NBA star Reggie Miller.

Cheryl's legacy includes feats both on and off the basketball court. She was a pioneer in getting women's basketball recognition. She proved that women could play basketball at a competitive level. In fact, *Sports Illustrated* called her the best basketball player in the nation in 1986. She brought attention to the sport not only in the United States, but also on a global and international level.

As Title IX continues to be debated, it is the accomplishments of people like Cheryl Miller that provide the platform for the continued struggle. Her perseverance has opened many opportunities for female athletes around the world, particularly in the United States. Cheryl's accomplishments have served as a model for all athletes. She has been instrumental in showing the sports world that women can be successful on and off the court. She is a true sports icon.

Marian Washington

It is rare that one person is seen as a pioneer to many different groups of people, but Marion Washington is seen as a pioneer in myriad areas. She is a pioneer in the sport of basketball not only for women but for the sports world. At a time when opportunities for African American women were rare, Washington became the exception. Her accomplishments exceeded the boundaries of the basketball court. Marion was more than a basketball coach. She was a teacher, mentor, and legend.

For example, in 1974 Washington began her career as the head women's basketball coach at Kansas University. That same year she founded Kansas' women's track and field team. Just a year later she earned a master's degree in biomechanics and administration. Her mission in life was to be more than just a basketball coach.

In 1984, she was named to the Olympics selection committee. In 1993, she served as the president for the Black Coaches Association, the first woman to serve in that capacity. In 1994, she made history again by becoming the first person to serve two consecutive terms as President of the BCA. In 1995, she was awarded the Giant Steps Award from The Center for the Study of Sport in Society at Northeastern University and the National Consortium for Academics and Sports. In 1997, she won the William I. Koch Outstanding Woman of the Year Award. In 2003, Washington was honored by the BCA with a lifetime achievement award.

Washington had plenty of success on the court as well. She coached at Kansas for thirty years. In 1983, she became the first black woman to coach the U.S. team in international competition. In 1996, she was named an assistant coach of the U.S. Olympic basketball team. She was named BCA Coach of the Year twice. She won the Big Eight Coach of the Year twice. Under Washington, Kansas won the Big Eight title four times. In 1997, Kansas won the Big 12 championship and Washington was named Big 12 Coach of the Year. Washington led Kansas to nine straight NCAA Tournament appearances. For 11 straight seasons, she helped Kansas win at least 20 games.

In 2002, she coached her 850th game. She recorded her 550th victory in 2003. Unfortunately, Washington was forced to retire in 2004 for medical reasons; however, there is no doubt that she continues to have an impact on the game of basketball. It is ultimately Marian Washington the person who will be most cherished.

Even though she has retired, she continues to mentor young student athletes. Not only is she a pioneer in the sport world, she is a true leader who has established a body of work for the ages.

Vivian Stringer

In every sport, there are certain figures that are credited with having some type of profound impact on the sport itself. In the National Football League there is Vince Lombardi. The National Basketball Association has Red Auerbach. In men's college basketball, UCLA coach John Wooden is considered a pioneer of the game. He had a way of teaching his players not only the game of basketball but also the game of life. If one were to look for that type of figure in women's college basketball, one of the names that likely would be at the top of the list is Vivian Stringer.

Coach Stringer began her love for basketball growing up in a small town in Pennsylvania. She grew up at a time when women and sports did not seem to coincide. She had to sneak around to play basketball to avoid being frowned upon by others. Stringer got her debut in college basketball in 1971 as a coach for the little-known school, Cheyney State. She helped put the school on the map by leading them to the inaugural NCAA women's basketball championship game, beating much bigger schools in the process. She moved on to coach at Iowa, taking her teams to the Final Four as well in 1993. She then moved on to coach at Rutgers in 1995, where she is currently still the coach. She made history in 2000 when she led Rutgers to a Final Four appearance as well. In fact, of the 23 NCAA women's basketball tournaments that have been played, Stringer has been a part of 17 of them. She became the first basketball coach to lead three different schools to Final Four appearances. Last season she became the fourth women's coach to ever reach 700-career wins.

Along with her long tradition of winning comes a resume that is just as long. She has garnered numerous awards and accomplishments. She has been the recipient of 14 different Coach of the Year awards. Three of those awards have been National Coach of the Year honors. She has won the NAACP Jackie Robinson Award. In 2002, the US Sports Academy created the Vivian Stringer Medallion Award of Sport for Women's Coaching. She was an honoree for Black Women in Sports at the Smithsonian Institute. In 2003, *Sports Illustrated* named Stringer one of the "101 Most Influential Minorities in Sports."

Vivian Stringer also has had an impact on an international level. She has participated in six different tournaments or games on an international scale. She was an assistant coach for the 2004 Olympic Team that won the gold medal.

During her 33 years of coaching, one of the traits that have set her apart is her dedication to her players and the game. This dedication has been transferred to anyone who has had the opportunity to interact with Vivian Stringer, including many who have gone on to play professional basketball. Whether it was taking Cheyney State to the championship game or pushing her players to exceed in their desired endeavors, she was always pushing them to be all they could be.

Leroy Walker

The youngest of thirteen children, Leroy Walker was born in Atlanta, Georgia, on June 4, 1918. He attended Benedict College in Columbia, South Carolina. As a student athlete at Benedict, Walker was named as an All-American in football and was a national-caliber sprinter in track and field. Walker's jersey number, 11, was retired by the university, and he was elected into the Benedict Athletic Hall of Fame.

After graduating from Benedict, Walker completed graduate school at Columbia University. He then became the first African American to earn his doctoral degree from New York University in the field of exercise physiology and biomechanics. Walker later returned to Benedict to teach physical education and exercise physiology.

As a coach at North Carolina Central University (NCCU), Walker became known as one of the top track and field coaches in the nation. During his time at NCCU, Walker coached 12 Olympians, 40 national champions, and 111 All-Americans. On the Olympic level, he coached national teams from Kenya, Jamaica, Ethiopia, Trinidad, Tobago, and Israel.

Walker became the first African American to coach a U.S. Olympic team when he led the men's track and field team in the 1976 Olympics in Montreal.

After gaining nation prominence in coaching, Dr. Walker served as the chancellor of North Carolina Central University. From 1973 to 1976, he also served as the chairman of the AAU's track and field committee. Walker was president of TAC from 1984 to 1988, before being named president of the United States Olympic Committee. He was inducted into the U.S.A. Track and Field Hall of Fame in 1983, and the U.S. Olympic Hall of Fame in 1987.

Cleveland "Cleve" Abbott

Cleveland Abbott is a coach who has blazed a path for others to follow. After graduating from South Dakota State University in 1916, Abbott began his illustrious career as coach and athletic director at the Tuskegee Institute. He was hired by Booker T. Washington to serve as an agricultural chemist and coach at the Institute. He started in 1923 as the director of the Department of Physical Education.

During his time at Tuskegee, Abbott coached football, basketball, tennis, and track and field teams to a total of 61 conference or national titles. As coach of the football team, he compiled a record of 202-95-27 over 32 seasons. He coached his teams to six Black College national championships and 12 Southern Intercollegiate Athletic Conference championships. As coach of the women's track and field team, Abbott earned 14 national outdoor titles and coached 49 athletes to individual titles. He coached six U.S. Olympic athletes and two gold medalists.

Abbott held his positions at Tuskegee until his death in 1955. Posthumously, he has been elected into several Halls of Fame. In 1968, the South Dakota State Hall of Fame named Abbott as its second inductee. Next was the Tuskegee Hall of Fame in 1975, and then the Southern Intercollegiate Athletic Conference inducted him to its Hall of Fame in 1992. Abbott was elected into the Alabama Sports Hall of Fame in 1995, and the USA Track and Field Hall of Fame in 1996. That same year, the football stadium at the Tuskegee Institute was renamed Cleve L. Abbott Memorial Alumni Stadium. In 2005, the American Football Coaches Association selected Abbott to receive The Trailblazer Award. This award recognizes individuals for their overall impact on their institutions and the game of football.

Ed Temple

An All-State athlete in track, basketball, and football, Edward Temple was the first African American at his high school to be the captain of his team. He attended Tennessee State University and graduated with B.A. and M.A. degrees in health and physical education. Temple coached the women's track and field team for 44 years, during which 40 of his athletes competed in the Olympics and earned a total of 23 medals.

Temple was selected as the head coach for the U.S. Women's track and field teams for both the 1960 Olympics in Rome and the 1964 Olympics in Tokyo. He also served as an assistant coach for the 1980 Olympic games. Temple coached the Pan American Games in 1959 and 1975, the Pan American Junior Games in 1982 and 1986, the first World Junior Championships in 1986, and several international competitions.

Currently an associate professor of sociology and social science at Tennessee State University, Temple led athletes to 34 national team titles, 30 Pan American medals, and 23 Olympic medals during his 43-year tenure as head coach.

Temple is a member of the Tennessee Sports Hall of Fame, the Pennsylvania Sports Hall of Fame, the Ohio Valley Conference Hall of Fame, and the Black Athletes Hall of Fame. He was elected into the Tennessee State University Hall of Fame and in 1989 was inducted into the U.S.A. Track and Field Hall of Fame. He has been presented with the Key to the City in Paducah, Kentucky, as well as in Hanford, California, and Nashville, Tennessee.

Tennessee State University bears the Edward S. Temple Track, and the NCAA Track and Field Coaches Association established the Edward Temple Award.

In conclusion, the African American coaches and administrators identified in this chapter have gained national recognition for their teaching and coaching excellence. They remain strong activitists for the concepts of social justice, diversity, and tolerance in sport and in the wider society.

▲▼ Suggested Readings ▲▼

Cunningham, G. B., & Sagas, M. (2005). Access discrimination in intercollegiate athletics. *Journal of Sport & Social Issues, 29*(2), 148–163.

Doherty, A. J., & Chelladurai, P. (1999). Managing cultural diversity in sport organizations: A theoretical perspective. *Journal of Sport Management, 13*, 280–297.

Fink, J. S., Pastore, D. L., & Reimer, H. A. (2001). Do differences make a difference?: Managing diversity in Division IA intercollegiate athletics. *Journal of Sport Management, 15*, 10–50.

▲▼ Study Questions ▲▼

1. What is diversity?

2. Describe how the concept of diversity came to be studied.

3. Identify and describe trends regarding hiring practices in collegiate athletics.

4. Discuss the importance of having minorities in leadership positions in college and professional sports.

5. Describe the effects diversity has had in the realm of professional sports.

References

Adler, N. J. (1991). *International dimensions of organizational behavior* (2nd ed.). Belmont, CA: Wadsworth Publishing.

Armstrong, K. L. (2002). *A different world: Situational complexities of the African-American female student athlete.* North American Society for Sport Management Conference. Alberta, Canada.

Brooks, D., & Althouse, R. (1993). Racial imbalance in coaching and managerial positions. *Racism in college athletics: The African American athlete's experience* (pp. 101–142), Morgantown, WV: Fitness Information Technology.

Bruening, J. E. (2005). Gender and racial analysis in sport: Are all the women white and all the blacks men? *National Association for Kinesiology and Physical Education in Higher Education, 57,* 330–349.

"Buying Power of Black America—2003."(n.d.). Retrieved from http://www.targetmarketnews.com.BuyingPower04 .htm

"Colin Powell to Commemorate 50th Anniversary of Desegregation of U.S. Armed Forces" (n.d.). Retrieved from www.trumanlibrary.org/news/colinpow.htm

Cox, T. (1994). *Cultural diversity in organizations: Theory, research & practice.* San Francisco: Berrett-Koehler Publishers.

Cunningham, G. B., & Sagas, M. (2005). Access discrimination in intercollegiate athletics. *Journal of Sport & Social Issues, 29*(2), 148–163.

Cunningham, G. B., & Sagas, M. (2004). Racial differences in occupational turnover intent among NCAA Division IA assistant football coaches. *Sociology of Sport Journal, 21,* 84–92.

DeSensi, J. T. (1994). Multiculturalism as an issue in sport management. *Journal of Sport Management, 8,* 63–74.

Doherty, A. J., & Chelladurai, P. (1999). Managing cultural diversity in sport organizations: A theoretical perspective. *Journal of Sport Management, 13,* 280–297.

Fink, J. S., & Pastore, D. L. (1999). Diversity in sport? Utilizing the business literature to devise a comprehensive framework of diversity initiatives. *Quest, 51,* 310–327.

Fink, J. S., Pastore, D. L., & Reimer, H. A. (2001). Do differences make a difference? Managing diversity in Division IA intercollegiate athletics. *Journal of Sport Management, 15,* 10–50.

Fullerton, H. N. (2000) Labor force projections: 1986–2000. *Monthly Labor Review,* 19–29.

Greenhaus, J. H., Parasuraman, S., & Wormely, W. M. (1990). Effects of race on organizational experiences, job performance, evaluations, and career outcomes. *Academy of Management Journal, 33,* 64–86.

Guttman, A. (1993). *EEO law and personnel practices.* Newberry Park: Sage.

Ilgen, D. R., & Youtz, M. A. (1986). *Factors affecting the evaluation and development of minorities in organizations.* In K. Rowland & G. Ferris (Eds.), *Research in personnel and human resource management: A research annual* (pp. 307–337). Greenwich, CT: JAI Press.

"Jackie Robinson" (n.d.). Retrieved from www.historicbaseball.com/players/r/robinson_jackie.html

Johnston, W. (1991). Global work force 2000: The new world labor market. *Harvard Business Review, 69,* 115–127.

Joplin, J. R. W., & Daus, C. S. (1997). Challenges of leading a diverse workforce. *The Academy of Management Executive, 11*(3), 32–37.

King, B. (2005). Reaching today's fans: Delivery of sports info continues to evolve as fans demand more. *Sports Business Journal, 17,* (14).

Kraut, A. I. (1996). *Organizational surveys: Tools for assessment and change.* San Francisco: Jossey-Bass Publishers.

Lapchick, R. L. (2005). *Race & Gender Report Card. Institute for Diversity and Ethics in Sport.* Orlando FL: Devos Sport Business Management Program, University of Central Florida.

NCAA. *2003–04 Student-athlete Race and Ethnicity Report.* Indianapolis, IN.

Roberts, L .L., Konczak, L .J., & Hoff Macan. (2004). Effects of data collection method on organizational climate survey results. *Applied H.R.M. Research, 9*(1), 13–26.

U. S. Census (n.d.). Retrieved from http://quickfacts.census.gov/qfd/states/12000.html and http://www.census .gov/ipc/www/usinterimproj/natprojtbola.xls

Weatherspoon, F. D. (1988). *Equal employment opportunity and affirmative action.* New York: Garland Publishing Company.

Wright, P., Ferris, S. P., & Hiller, J. S. (1995). Competitiveness through the management of diversity: Effects on stock price valuation. *Academy of Management Journal, 38,* 272–287.

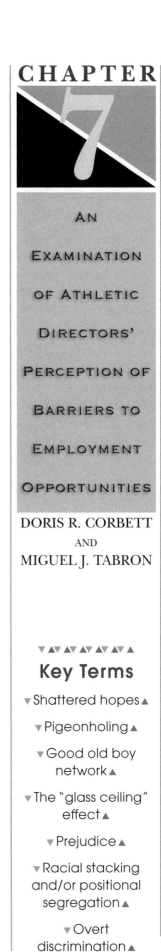

DORIS R. CORBETT
AND
MIGUEL J. TABRON

Doris R. Corbett and Miguel Tabron explore how employment barriers facing minority women and men shape their underrepresentation in leadership in coaching and sport administration positions. In their chapter "An Examination of Athletic Directors' Perception of Barriers to Employment Opportunities," they refocus the significant legislation and judicial decisions impacting employment for minorities. Next, they examine barriers to access and to advancement in leadership and administrative positions, covering a substantial body of the literature of discrimination and prejudice. Notably, Corbett and Tabron are specifically seeking to understand the nature of athletic directors' perceptions of African American coaches. Finally, these authors explore various initiatives that are believed to have a potential positive influence on promoting diversity in coaching.

Abstract ▼ For most people who are not closely associated with sport, there is the belief that sport is the one institution in the American culture where fair play exists, and that it is the best environment in which people of color, particularly African-Americans, can be involved. The truth is, however, that the world of sport is neither better nor worse than the rest of society. For many African-Americans who seek advancements in sport beyond the playing fields (i.e., as a coach, or athletic director in Division I sport), the institution of sport is seen as un-American or anti-democratic, and an environment in which hopes and dreams to become coaches, athletic directors, general managers, and owners of sport are viewed as unattainable pipe dreams for most of those who are indeed highly qualified. This chapter focuses on the issues of race barriers to employment opportunities in sport by examining the perceptions held by those in leadership positions of power and control of sport, mainly focusing on athletic directors. A discussion is provided from an historical perspective regarding the impact of judicial decisions to effect social change. The ability to participate in sport has been intrinsically linked to the political history of the American society. And, as such, one must consider the vast discrepancy between the number of African-Americans who participate as players in relation to those who serve in the administration of sport as coaches and athletic directors. An examination of the perception of racial discrimination and athletic directors' perceptions of the African-American coach as a manager shows the way legislation was used by athletic directors and administrative leaders to deny blacks leadership and managerial access. The chapter concludes by emphasizing strategies designed to make a difference that will allow for equality within the coaching and management of sport at the collegiate level.

▲▼▲▼▲▼

College and professional sports are viewed by the lay public as being color-blind institutions that reward talent with social mobility, recognition,

Key Terms

▼Shattered hopes▲

▼Pigeonholing▲

▼Good old boy network▲

▼The "glass ceiling" effect▲

▼Prejudice▲

▼Racial stacking and/or positional segregation▲

▼Overt discrimination▲

and employment access. However, the research literature reveals a number of employment barriers that seem to limit the opportunities for African Americans to
enter the coaching profession (Coakley, 1994; Davis, 1994, Hoose, 1989; Sage,
1993; Sailes, 1993). For instance, Sage (1993) identified racial stratification as one
of the most significant barriers facing African American coaches. The higher levels or positions of authority where the greatest power, prestige, and material rewards reside are more insulated from direct scrutiny. Those who control access to
positions of authority tend to employ subtle ways of maintaining discriminatory
practices (Sage, 1993).

An historical overview of significant legislation and judicial decisions affecting employment opportunities for minorities provides additional insight into the
barriers African Americans face when seeking leadership opportunities. During
the 1950s and 1960s black civil rights leaders increasingly turned to the courts and
Congress to counter the rampant and flagrant forms of racial discrimination occurring in America. As a result, a number of major legislative decisions were rendered
that helped elevate the citizenship status of minorities, particularly African Americans (Pinkney, 1984). In the summer of 1963, the march on the nation's capital
gave added impetus to the Civil Rights movement and aided in the passage of the
Civil Rights Act of 1964. The Civil Rights Act was the most comprehensive legislation enacted by Congress during the 20th century and was aimed at protecting the
civil rights of blacks and other minorities in employment, education, housing, and
other areas of daily life.

One of the most significant articles of the aforementioned act is Title VII,
which encompasses the area of employment including hiring, training, wages and
benefits, and terminations. Title VII prohibits employers with 15 or more employees either from intentionally discriminating against employees on the basis of race,
color, religion, sex, or national origin or from acting in ways that simply have the
effect of being discriminatory. Under this rubric, therefore, it is illegal for an employer to deprive or deny any individual of employment opportunities. This legislation does, however, allow employers in limited situations to impose hiring restrictions based on sex, national origin, or religion if such characteristics are bona
fide occupational qualifications (Kaplan & Lee, 1995; Shropshire, 1996).

When attempting to enforce Title VII in the workplace, employees can usually
challenge an organization's employment practice by alleging either disparate treatment or disparate impact. According to Shropshire (1996) disparate treatment
refers to purposeful discrimination in the workplace. The key issues addressed
under discrimination claims filed under disparate treatment are: evidence of intentional discrimination on the job site and proof that an employment opportunity is
denied because of one's race, color, religion, sex, or national origin (Kaplan &
Lee, 1995). Federal and state legislation and judicial decisions protecting the civil
rights of minorities have provided improved employment opportunities and working conditions for African Americans in predominantly white institutions. Nevertheless, as Davis (2000) posits, traditional civil rights legislation is not as effective
a mechanism for protecting the rights of African Americans from the onslaught
of racism and other manifestations of discrimination.

The most harmful aspects of employment discrimination facing African
Americans today frequently exist through forms of tokenism, racial stacking, and
stratification. These forms of discrimination create formidable barriers, which

often exclude or restrict African Americans from gaining equal access to employment opportunities on par with white Americans. Throughout most of the mid 1990s, African American employees were more likely to be over-represented in jobs where pay, power, and prestige were the lowest. Only a small number of African American managers have moved beyond middle levels of authority and control in most companies and institutions (Dovidio & Guertner, 1986; Wilson, 1987; Shropshire, 1996).

The Constitution, Bill of Rights, and the Declaration of Independence all claim to embrace the basic notions of equality, liberty, and justice for all. Nonetheless, many people still have difficulty accepting the principle of equal opportunity for minorities when making personnel decisions, allocating resources, and prioritizing rewards and recognition within their organizations. As it relates to the world of professional sport, white coaches are considered coaches, whereas their black counterparts, who have never attained equivalence with the numbers of black athletes participating in those programs, are considered recruiters (Saperstein, 2001). Lapchick (1997) reported that between 1995 and 1996, 1,523 associate and athletic director positions existed at NCAA colleges. The minority representation was as follows: black men (6%), "other minority" men (2%), black women (2%) and other minority women (0.2%). It would appear that corporate America's apparent loss of interest in the critical self-analysis needed to unmask covert forms of employment discrimination (D' Souza, 1995) is being mirrored in the sporting fraternity with disconcerting clarity. Corporate America does not appear overtly receptive to measures that assure greater equality for minorities (D' Souza, 1995). Shropshire (1996) wrote that while the laws have radically changed to eliminate and remedy past employment discrimination since the 1950s, the plain fact is that discriminatory employment practices and barriers continue to exist in America.

Identifying the Barriers to Employment Opportunities for African American Coaches

African Americans face a number of impediments to their advancement as coaches and administrators. African American women, for example, are serially relegated to roles that do not require leadership. Instead they can be located as coordinators and assistants to the major decision makers (Abney, 2000). Negative stereotypes regarding African Americans as a whole have been one of the most widely accepted explanations for their limited advancement in the coaching profession. Steele (1990) makes the point that although the topic of white intellectual superiority and African American intellectual inferiority is a sensitive issue, the physicality of the African American athlete does tend to support the belief that the African American athlete is mentally and intellectually inferior to the white athlete (Davis, 2000; Hoose, 1989; Sailes, 1991, 1993, 1998). Conceptions about the "dumb jock" stereotype targeted at African American athletes are embedded in racial stereotyping.

These distortions are related to positional segregation (often referred to as stacking), which has emerged as a challenging phenomenon in sport. Stacking is one of the persistent patterns of discrimination in collegiate and professional athletics and is more recognizable in sports such as baseball and football (Corbett & Patterson, 2002). Stacking is a form of positional segregation whereby a disproportionate number of minorities (more specifically, African Americans) are found in certain team positions that are less esteemed and less visible (Spence, 1999; Corbett and Patterson, 2002). Black players are routinely selected for positions that demand speed and agility and not for those associated with cognitive abilities (Hoose, 1989; Spence, 1999) or leadership (Smith & Henderson, 2000). Even when black players do perform in positions traditionally reserved for white players, their accomplishments are still not taken seriously by coaches (Wiggins, 1989). But perhaps Spence (1999) captured the currents of racism with his suggestion that many think that "the perfect athlete has the black body and the white mind" (pp. 58). These unspoken and often spoken myths are not isolated to black athletes. They inform the climate and systems that minority coaches and administrators must negotiate. Racial stratification in sport is one of the most significant barriers facing African American coaches. Sage (1993) described the stacking of blacks in non-central coaching positions as an employment barrier that limits the opportunities for African American coaches to enter the coaching profession. The result is that black coaches are restricted from the higher levels of the collegiate coaching profession where the greatest power and prestige reside. Racist attitudes contribute to the discriminatory practice of channeling African Americans away from the central (leadership and/or decision-making) positions in college and professional sport (Coakley, 1994; Eitzen & Sage, 1996; Leonard & Smith, 1997; Schneider & Eitzen, 1986). For example, black athletes are less visible in the leadership positions of quarterback and center in football, and pitcher and catcher in baseball. In Table 1, Corbett and Patterson (2002) report the position distribution of African American Major League Baseball players from 1960–2001. African Americans are shown to be disproportionately positioned in the outfield positions:

> The scarcity of blacks in central positions (e.g., quarterback, center, pitcher) on the playing field continues off the field. It is inevitable that the myths that undergird an ideologically racially segregated society, and which by extension create divisions among members of different ethnic groups, will create fault lines in the administrative and professional world of coaching (Sailes, 2000).

In an attempt to map coaching career patterns, Anderson (1993) traced college career head football coaching mobility and reached the conclusion that "becoming an assistant coach is often a prerequisite to becoming a coordinator, and becoming a coordinator is a prerequisite to becoming a head football coach, and becoming a head football coach is frequently a prerequisite to becoming an athletic

Table 1. Distribution of African American Major League Baseball Players 1960–2001: Percentage by Position

	P	C	1B	2B	3B	SS	LF	CF	RF
1960	3.57%	9.38%	18.75%	12.50%	18.75%	12.50%	6.25%	31.25%	25.00%
1970	5.95%	0.00%	37.50%	12.50%	16.67%	8.33%	35.42%	50.00%	54.17%
2001	3.03%	1.08%	8.62%	18.64%	2.94%	10.45%	31.17%	51.72%	23.81%

Corbett and Patterson, 2002

director." This model appears to be linear, simplistic, and built on previous coaching experience. Anderson (1993) reached the conclusion that race functions to keep African Americans from entering the pool from which head football coaches are selected. The research finding revealed that white assistant coaches were twice as likely to have played the quarterback position in college (Anderson, 1993). These are widely considered to be "the thinking positions" (Spence, 1999). Latimer and Mathes (1985) found that African American coaches play and coach peripheral athletic positions (e.g., running backs, wide receivers) at a higher rate than their white counterparts. In effect, the centrality argument claims that central/leadership positions beget leadership positions, with whites more likely to occupy central positions. The research by Corbett and Patterson (2002), Anderson (1993), and Latimer and Mathes (1985) demonstrates the impact negative stereotyping can have for African American athletes and coaches.

Lombardo (1978) noted two different stereotypes regarding African American males, namely the "brute" and the "Sambo" stereotypes. The "brute" typifies the African American male as over-reactive, primitive, violent, temperamental, uncontrollable, and sexually powerful. The "Sambo" stereotype characterizes the African American as benign, childish, fun-loving, good-humored, immature, inferior, exuberant, lazy, comical, impulsive, uninhibited, and lovable. These labels were created by whites to protect their superior position in society and to disparage African American males in such a way as to keep them in non-consequential positions. The "brute" and the "Sambo" stereotypes intentionally separated the African American from intellectualism and mental control. White society places importance on intellectualism and subsequently removes the African American from equal status by characterizing him with primitive physical attributes, while ascribing such traits as industry and intelligence to its own members (Harris, 1990). The belief that intellectualism does not exist among African Americans has kept management and coaching positions in Division I college and professional sports mostly white (Coakley, 1994; Leonard & Smith, 1997). In fact this contention remains so rife and unchallenged that former Los Angeles Dodgers general manager Al Campanis felt composed enough to postulate to a televised audience that blacks may not possess the "necessities" for managerial positions in professional baseball (Hoose, 1989).

Campanis's comfort in advancing such prejudicial characterizations can perhaps best be explained by Wiggins (1989), who avered:

> Blacks are thought to possess natural athletic ability in speed, quickness, and jumping ability; traits that many coaches believe cannot be taught—you are either born with these qualities or you do without them. That they excel in sport, then, has little to do with their work ethic or their intellect according to this perspective. This view allows blacks to be outstanding athletes without negating the belief that they are lazy and ignorant; in fact, it reinforces the belief in their indolence and incognizance (p. 158–185).

Owing to these labels, Lombardo (1978) disapproved of the basketball performances by the Harlem Globetrotters, citing them as events that perpetuated the "Sambo" stereotype in sport and surrendered the integrity and positive image of African Americans in general and African American athletes in particular. Even today, the display of bravado and rhythmic dance movements that are commonly seen in the football end-zone are viewed as representations of the "Sambo" stereotype.

Such negative typecasting implicitly provides a framework whereby discrimination becomes a norm for non-athletic positions in professional sports. Brooks and Althouse (1993) identified two forms of discrimination that have denied blacks equal employment opportunity in the coaching profession:

▲ Overt discrimination, which occurs when athletic directors and head coaches ignore qualified African American applicants for top spots in athletic departments and coaching staffs.

▲ Prejudice. which is represented by a fear that white fans and alumni will react negatively if an African American is placed in charge of a football or basketball program.

In a survey of over 200 African American corporate professionals, Cose (1993) identified ten major employment barriers African Americans perceived experiencing while employed in predominantly white organizations. Those barriers include:

▲ *Inability to fit in*: White employers in quest of black workers seek African Americans who are frequently perceived to be quiet-spoken and non-threatening.

▲ *Lack of respect*: Regardless of their career accomplishments, black professionals constantly have to prove they are worthy of respect. Whites, on the other hand, are granted respect not because of merit or qualifications, but solely because of race.

▲ *Low expectations*: Blacks often feel their employment careers are blocked and there is little or no room for professional development and growth within the organization. A common perception held by many black professionals is that white males will attempt to halt their achievement, draining away motivation and enthusiasm for the job.

▲ *Shattered hopes*: Black employees frequently see white co-workers moving up the corporate ladder and conclude that skin color is the only legitimate explanation.

▲ *Pigeonholing*: Jobs within the organizational structure are frequently classified by race. "Logic" dictates that certain managerial tasks are to be handled by blacks, while others are best left for whites.

▲ *Good old boy network*: In the face of unfamiliarity and uncertainty, the hiring process serves as an important protective buffer when white males are seeking supervisors and employees. The hiring of blacks in key leadership positions is usually forbidden because it is necessary for blacks first to prove themselves before being considered for a top position within an organization.

▲ *The "glass ceiling" effect*: Within every organization pyramid there are fewer positions at the top. Jones (1986) reported the more visible the job assignment, the fewer the opportunities for African Americans. Consequently, black employees frequently find themselves competing against other blacks for a small number of positions available within the apex of the organization. Often, the first black employee who finds a crack through the "glass ceiling" will attempt to fend off rather than help other black employees.

▲ *Prejudice*: A fear that white fans and alumni will react negatively if an African American is placed in charge of a football or basketball program.

▲ *Experience*: African Americans are considered to have limited coaching experience although African Americans may have coached as assistant or head coaches on the Division I level for one year or more (NCAA, 2003).

▲ *Alumni*: Alumni, former coaches, former players, former students, and former professors play a role in determining the selection of head coaches and tend to hold preferences for individuals who look like themselves. Shropshire (1996) noted in a 1994 study that most post-secondary institutions do not have specific hiring criteria and qualifications from which they select coaches. Unlike the academy where there is the threshold requirement of a particular degree in a specific discipline, athletic administrators tend to use extremely subjective criteria to evaluate potential coaching candidates. Rosellini (1987) suggested that the ultimate barrier for African American coaches is not the lack of skill or coaching potential, but rather lingering prejudices that are deeply rooted in the American culture.

The Perception of Racial Discrimination

The question of racial discrimination arises when one considers the vast discrepancy between the number of African Americans who participate as players relative to those who help coach and run athletic departments. Greenlee (1998) points out that the "number of African Americans hired as head coaches does not come anywhere close to the number of African American athletes who play the games" (p. 23–24).

Tabron (2004) examined institutional and social factors that are perceived as barriers to employment opportunities for NCAA Division I African American male head basketball coaches. The study included senior athletic directors employed at the 83 major National Collegiate Athletic Association (NCAA) Division I institutions in seven of the major conferences during the 2003 basketball season. It was found that across seven conferences investigated, certain patterns were evident. African Americans were largely represented as assistant basketball coaches and are significantly underrepresented as head coaches and athletic directors.

In table 2, Tabron (2004) shows the number of NCAA Division I institutions affiliated with each conference, the number of African American head coaches, assistant coaches, and senior athletic directors employed across the seven conferences.

Tabron (2004) concluded that athletic directors perceived employment opportunities to be equal for African Americans. However, some inconsistencies within responses of athletic directors existed in Tabron's 2004 study. Athletic administrators believed equal opportunity is available regardless of color, yet athletic administrators also agreed that the lack of black administrators limits employment opportunities for African Americans. Tabron's results were consistent with Hill's (1995) study and findings that networking and professional contacts do enhance the professional development of African American coaches. Young (1990) reported that advancement opportunities are greatly enhanced for African American

Table 2. A Status Report of the Representation of African American Basketball Coaches in Division I in 2003

Basketball Conferences	Number of NCAA Institutions	Number of Head Basketball Coaches	Number of African American Head Basketball Coaches	Number of Assistant Coaches	Number of African American Assistant Coaches	% of African American Assistant Coaches	Senior Athletic Directors	African American Senior Athletic Directors
ACC	9	9	3	27	11	40.7	1	0
Big East	14	14	3	42	14	33.3	1	0
Big 10	11	11	2	33	12	36.3	1	0
Big 12	12	12	1	36	13	36.1	1	0
Conference USA	15	15	0	45	22	48.8	1	0
PAC 10	10	10	3	30	11	36.6	1	0
SEC	12	12	2	36	17	47.2	1	0

Note: Only 14 African American head coaches are represented in these conferences, and there are no African-American Senior Athletic Directors (Tabron, 2004)

coaches when supportive networking systems are in place. Understandably, institutions with a diversity plan have more African American assistant coaches. Hill's (1995) study found that 90% of coaches believe that a diversity plan is necessary to eliminate subjective hiring practices.

On the field, sports have as much equal opportunity as anything America has to offer. Off the field, sports are very segregated. The facts are as follows:

▼ As of 2001, there were no African Americans or Latinos who were majority owners in Major League Baseball, the National Basketball Association, or the National Football League (Harrison, 2004).

▼ Only 2% of assistant director positions are held by African American women (National Collegiate Athletic Association, 2004).

▼ Between 2003 and 2004 only 7.2% of directors of athletics at the collegiate level were African American (National Collegiate Athletic Association, 2004).

▼ Of all senior women administrators, only 9.1% were black (National Collegiate Athletic Association, 2004).

▼ At historically black colleges and universities, a mere 3% of athletic directors were women.

Why has desegregation been so slow at the collegiate and professional level of sports organizations? Answers to this question vary, but it would appear that when people in positions of power recruit candidates for top management and coaching positions, they look for people who hold views similar to their own. The "hire people who look like me" logic is one reason that fraternity brothers, fellow alumni from college, or people who grew up together in neighborhood communities often hire each other. Those who share similar backgrounds are "known quantities"; they are people with whom personal connections can be made or already exist. If those doing the hiring are white males, it is more likely that they may raise more questions about the job qualifications of those who come from different racial or ethnic backgrounds (Coakley, 2001).

The relative absence of African Americans in critical teaching and leadership positions reflects in part the institutional racism that is endemic in Western societies, including the United States. It is slowly receding, but far too slowly, especially considering the enormous over-representation of minorities in key American sports (Coakley, 2001).

Athletic Directors' Perception of the African American Coach

Mondy and Premeaux (1993) defined perception as a fixed tendency to interpret information in a particular way. They believe that differences in past experiences, educational background, emotions, values, beliefs, and other factors can indirectly or directly affect an employer, supervisor, or employee's personal perception of what is actually taking place in the workplace. Ivancevich and Matteson (1990) described perception as "the cognitive process by which an individual gives meaning to the environment" (p.71). Consequently, perception not only can influence how an employee perceives what is taking place in the workplace, but also has been found to dictate thought processes, attitudes, and behavior.

The perception of the effectiveness of African Americans as coaches/managers has been an issue among white administrative leaders. Certain management or leadership positions within a corporate or institutional structure have traditionally been off limits to African Americans (Coakley, 1994). The stereotypical profile for an executive level position within an organization is perceived to be intellectualism and mental control. African Americans have not been perceived to satisfy the stereotypical profile for an executive level or head coaching position. Whites are reluctant to hire African Americans into management and head coaching positions in professional and major college sport because they do not have confidence in the intellectual capabilities of African Americans to manage or coach professional or major college ball clubs. (Former executive for the Los Angeles Dodgers Al Campanis exemplified this practice when he exhibited racial stereotyping in sport on national television; Hoose, 1989). As a result, African Americans are systematically channeled away from team leadership positions in favor of white players. Coaches are reluctant to entrust the leadership of the team to African Americans because they believe African Americans are not intelligent enough to be successful team leaders.

Many of the myths regarding African Americans suffer from scientifically unacceptable assumptions that are not validated by research. Sport socialization and sport participation patterns of African Americans in American sport arise from the social constraints placed upon them by the dominant culture (Coakley, 1994; Eitzen & Sage, 1996; Leonard & Smith, 1997; McPherson, 1989; Sailes, 1987; Sokolove, 1988).

Sailes (1998) collected and recorded prevailing myths held by college students about African American student athletes over a ten-year period. The listing of myths collected reflected an informal qualitative approach, providing insight about the attitudes held about the African American athlete. The myths reported by Sailes' students are representative of the Psychological Theory in action.

The Psychological Theory (Sailes, 1998) suggests that African Americans are incapable of fulfilling the leadership roles of quarterback in football, pitcher in baseball, or point guard in basketball. As stated earlier, Al Campanis typified the belief of management in Major League Baseball on national television when he said that African Americans might not have the "necessities" to become managers and field coaches in Major League Baseball (Hoose, 1989). The Psychological Theory claims that African Americans do poorly under pressure and are not good thinkers (Sailes, 1998). This rationale explains the scarcity of black athletes in individual sports such as tennis, skating, gymnastics, and swimming. It does not, however, account for the fact that athletes, managers, coaches, and other leaders of African American heritage have won national championships and individual titles (Sailes, 2000).

The social application of the Psychological Theory results in African Americans not being given management and leadership positions in collegiate and professional sports. Underpinning these actions is whites' fear of African Americans invading the white status quo and attitudes about African American competence. They continue to create barriers to African American success in the administration of sport (Sailes, 1998).

According to Anderson and South (1993), white administrators seldom judge African Americans solely on the basis of character and merit. Instead, the researchers conclude that race continues to have a significant influence on the career employment opportunities for African Americans in predominantly white environments (Anderson, 1993).

Establishing a Support System

Within certain enclaves of the black community (particularly in working class communities), sport is perceived as an avenue to social and upward mobility. Upward mobility is believed to be more easily achieved when network resources and mentors are available. In college athletics and professional sports, African American coaches/administrators must have at least one mentor and network resources to gain upward mobility. Network contacts established through mentoring can significantly enhance the professional experience (Schweitzer, 1993). It stands to reason that a mentor with a high position can help one's career better than a mentor who is not in a power position. Young (1990) found that 98.9% of athletic administrators agreed that networking enhances personal and professional development. Athletic administrators agreed that recommendations by network contacts often overrule a candidate's experience in a job search. Advancement opportunities are enhanced for African American coaches when supportive networking systems are in place (Young, 1990).

The concept of networking to gain influential employment status is by no means a new philosophy. Networking involves the use of contacts for information, advice, support, or job referrals (Sisley, 1990). Houzer (1974) identified the lack of networking opportunities, mentors, and role models as impediments to the advancement of African American women in professional occupations in sport. Abney (2000) contended that because few women hold positions in athletic departments to begin with, there is a dearth of mentor/mentee relationships among African American women. She asserted that this trend is likely to continue since this scarcity means that there are few mentors available as models for black student athletes, who have the best chance of progressing to the positions of administrators and coaches. Coakley (2001) posited that in addition to advanced education, experience, knowledge of training and strategies of sport organizations, skill in interpersonal relations and connections with people who can provide job recommendations are vital to the professional progression of African Americans. It is further asserted that such skills are imperative "because sport as a social institution reflects the basic values within society" (Coakley, 2001).

Gerdy (1994), however, pointed out that evolution, albeit minimal, is under way in the forms of opportunities for student athletes to access new internships and postgraduate scholarship at the institutional, conference, and national levels. Although such developments need to increase in scope, they do provide the window of opportunity that current African American student athletes will become future coaches, conference commissioners, and athletic administrators.

Brooks, Althouse, and Brown (1990) distinguished four mobility paths toward leadership in an athletic career. These were identified as: internships, the professional route, opportunity, and mentorship. Grenfell and Freischlag (1990) identified five factors that contribute to coaching success: administrative support, communication skills, dress, public image, and membership in a professional organization.

It is no secret that the NCAA has a poor record in hiring African American coaches and administrators. Wulf (1988) surveyed the NCAA and found alarming results indicating that the strategies and ideas to promote African American coaches and administrators are not getting any better. White athletic directors routinely go on record supporting equal opportunities for African American basketball coaches. Most postsecondary institutions do not have specific hiring criteria and qualifications from which they select coaches (Shropshire, 1996). Without a clear hiring criterion, athletic directors can use subjective criteria to evaluate potential coaching candidates.

The question that remains a concern for sport social scientists is: How can basketball and football empower and not oppress African American coaches? Sailes (2000) argued that "the fears and anxieties of white America has caused it to subjugate other cultures and ethnic groups within this country to inferior status and to create the caste system of inequities that has kept us apart for decades." How can African American coaches rise above the invisible glass ceiling, that subtle form of workplace discrimination that erects organizational, attitudinal, and social barriers that effectively keep minorities from advancing up the career ladder (Morrison et al., 1987)? National Football League coaches Marvin Lewis (Cincinnati Bengals), Dennis Green (Arizona Cardinals), Herm Edwards (New York Jets), Tony Dungy (the Colts), Lovie Smith (Chicago Bears), and Romeo Crennel (Cleveland Browns), Princeton Basketball Coach John Thompson, Temple University Basketball Coach John Chaney, University of Washington Head Football Coach Tyrone Willingham, Rutgers University Women's Basketball Coach Vivian Stringer, University of Washington Basketball Coach Lorenzo Romar, University of Oklahoma Basketball Coach Kelvin Sampson, University of Oregon Basketball Coach Ernie Kent, University of Kentucky Basketball Coach Tubby Smith, Georgetown Hoyas Women's Basketball Coach Terri Williams-Flournoy, and Athletic Director Daryl

Gross of Syracuse University all have shown that African American coaches can win and be successful at the highest level at predominantly white institutions and at the professional sport level. These coaches and administrators of sport were able to win games, attract fans, and embrace the alumni.

Former Georgetown University head basketball coach John Thompson, in questioning the lack of minorities in front-office positions, remarked that an African American is "competent as a player, but so incompetent that his knowledge leaves him once he graduates from a university" (*Jet Magazine*, 1998, pp. 52–56). African American athletes have taken collegiate and professional sports to a higher level, but "when it comes to who coaches, who manages, and who gets administrative positions, athletics is strictly a white man's game" (Greenlee, 1998, pp. 23–24). When African Americans get a chance to coach in Division I programs, they usually are taking over programs that have a losing record. For example, Willingham became Washington's coach after it went 1-10 in 2004. Croom took over at Mississippi after a 2-10 season, and Dorrell started at UCLA after its 8-5 season in 2002. According to Lapchick (2005), "In the history of Division I teams prior to the 2005 season, which extends more than a century, there have been 11,764 team schedules played. Of those teams, only 85 have been led by African American head coaches" (p. 2). Since the implementation of the Rooney Rule, which requires teams to interview people of color as part of their hiring process, the National Football League has done better in hiring African Americans as head football coaches.

The NCAA and the Black Coaches Association (BCA) have taken positive initiatives to increase the number of black head coaches. One project of the BCA has been the publication of "The Hiring Report Card," which measures and exposes "colleges and universities and their expressed or implied commitment to hiring diversity in collegiate football coaching" (Harrison, 2004, pp. 1–17). In this scenario, the "Hiring Report Card" operates on a grading scale of A, B, C, D, or F and issues the appropriate grade to academic institutions commensurate with the level of their adherence to the BCA "Hiring Report Card" guidelines over the course of the hiring process (Harrison, 2004). The theoretical underpinning for the "Hiring Report Card" is homologous reproduction theory, which posits that people reproduce their environment to mirror themselves (Kanter, 1977; Lovett & Lowry, 1994). The BCA affirms that while "the systemic reproduction of primarily one racial and ethnic group is not necessarily malicious, [it is] indeed problematic in terms of equity, access and opportunity for non-status quo groups" (Harrison, 2004, p. 11). This project therefore is designed to spotlight and expose these imbalances with the ultimate objective of their being expunged from normative hiring practices. Such schemes are in concert with the BCA's 18-year history of improving the employment opportunities and overall professional development of ethnic minority professionals (Harrison, 2004). Over this period the organization has used boycotts and protests as part of their action plan to address the hindrances that impede the access of minority professionals.

The Makings of a Brighter Future

Sports may bring people together, but they do not automatically lead people to question the way they think about race or ethnicity or the way they relate to those from other racial or ethnic groups. For example, white team owners, general managers, and athletic directors in the United States have worked with African American athletes for decades, yet only in recent years have African Americans been hired as coaches. It has taken social and legal pressures to force those in power positions to act more affirmatively when it comes to hiring procedures that would include African Americans (Coakley, 2001). African Americans are still underrepresented in coaching and administrative positions because people in power do not easily change their ideology and the social structure that support their positions of power (Shropshire, 1996).

For racial and ethnic relations to be improved through sports, those who control sport teams and sport events must make an organized and concerted effort to bring people together in ways that will encourage them to confront and challenge racial and ethnic issues. These efforts must be initiated and supported by whites as well as members of ethnic minorities (Oglesby & Schrader, 2000).

In 2001 and 2002, the NCAA budgeted $4.5 million to support the development of ethnic minorities and women coaching candidates by funding 17 different programs that would increase the pool of qualified individuals, enhance professional development and career advancement, and assist the membership in hiring ethnic minorities and women. Another $4.2 million was requested for fiscal years 2002–03 and 2003–04 (NCAA Division II Governance, September, 2000, p. 5).

In August 2002, the Minorities Opportunity Interest Committee (MOIC) conducted a comprehensive study on ethnic diversity of football coaching. The MOIC concluded that specific initiatives in four major areas will make a positive impact on diversity in football as well as other athletic staffs at the Division I level. These initiatives will increase the pool of potential candidates, increase exposure opportunities for ethnic minority coaches at all levels, provide professional development opportunities for ethnic minority coaches, and strengthen the hiring process. There is no national policy or program that will assure success, because hiring decisions can be made only at the campus level.

In order to remedy the paucity of African American representation as coaches and athletic directors in Division I colleges and universities, the following initiatives are proposed:

1. Increase the pool of potential candidates.
   a. Increase the permissible number of graduate assistant coaches at Division I institutions to three from the current limit of two.
   b. Create a matching grant program for Division I institutions to assist with costs associated with adding the third graduate assistant.
   c. Develop materials that highlight coaching as a career to student athletes as part of the Commitment to Career Development program.
   d. Partner with the National Association of Basketball Coaches and the Black Coaches Association to develop programs to recruit ethnic minorities to the coaching profession.

2. Increase exposure opportunities for ethnic minority coaches at all levels.
   a. Sponsor networking opportunities for selected minority coaches with directors of athletics and chief executive officers at selected meetings, including the NCAA convention, National Association of Collegiate Directors of Athletics, and the American Council on Education Convention.
   b. Develop a program to identify ethnic minority head coaches at Division I, II, and III programs.

c. Create candidate profiles for ethnic minority head coaches at all levels to be placed on the NCAA Black Coaches Association (BCA) and other higher education organization's web sites.

d. Create a database of ethnic minority head coaching candidates to be accessed by NCAA member institutions.

3. Provide professional development opportunities for ethnic minority coaches.

a. Develop a Coaches Academy of comprehensive workshops to include interview preparation, networking, resume building, media training, etc. for minority coaches at all levels.

b. Develop an Executive Mentor Program to assign veteran high-profile head coaches with selected minority head and potential head coaches for networking and one-on-one skills enhancement.

4. Strengthen the hiring process.

a. Require written comprehensive institutional diversity plans that include steps the institution uses in the hiring process to ensure a diverse athletic staff. The plan should be kept on file in the offices of the director of athletics.

b. Require institutions to submit the hiring process utilized for all athletic staffs as part of the NCAA Division I certification process.

c. Require that at least one ethnic minority student athlete be involved in the hiring process for head coaching vacancies.

d. Require senior athletic administrative staffs and head coaches at Division I institutions to attend a diversity education workshop at least once every three years to enhance their understanding and valuing of diverse staffs and issues of diversity (NCAA News, 2002).

In order for equality to occur within the coaching profession, athletic administrators must do the hard things and make some hard choices. They must admit that there is a problem with the current system and specific hiring criteria must be put into place. Coaches must understand how to use their resources for advancement opportunities. African American coaches must expand their network of professional associations. According to Brooks, Althouse, and Brown (1990) power is embedded in the recruiting network structure. In an effort to maximize the chances to be hired for a head coaching position, and to avoid token interviews for coaching opportunities, African American coaches must identify appropriate power brokers.

To rise above the invisible glass ceiling, it is necessary for athletic directors and university presidents to change their ideology regarding the role of the African American coach and support and empower African American coaches so they may have a fair chance to succeed. All effort must be taken to break down the "old boy" subculture and "old boy" hiring network (Sperber, 1990). Such networks are rooted in both institutional racism and sexism that aim to keep the lines of power, communication, authority, and prestige sequestered with male, white authority and out of the reach of both women and men of color (Abney, 2000). The importance of visible African Americans as coaches and athletic directors cannot be underscored enough. Their participation in basketball and football can reduce some of the barriers many African American athletes experience. Increased minority opportunities at the collegiate level will help professional sport teams to identify successful candidates to fill similar positions in their organizations.

▲▼ Suggested Readings ▲▼

Harrison, C. K. (2004). The Score: A hiring report card for NCAA Division I and IAA football head coaching positions. Hiring report card no. 1 (2003–04). http://www.bcasports.org/Assets/PDF/2004_BCAHiringReport_Football.pdf

Spence, C. M. (1999). *The skin I'm in: Racism, sports and education.* Halifax: Fernwood Publishing.

▲▼ Study Questions ▲▼

1. How have racial stereotypes impeded the advancement of African Americans interested in a sport management career?

2. Describe and define racial stacking or positional segregation.

3. Identify five major employment barriers to African Americans working in predominantly white sporting organizations or institutions.

4. What are the mobility paths toward leadership in an athletic career?

5. What role does networking play in improving advancement possibilities in sport?

References

Abney, R. (2000). The glass ceiling effect and African American women coaches and athletic administrators. In D. Brooks & R. Althouse (Eds.), *Racism in college athletics: The African American athlete's experience* (pp.119–130). Morgantown, WV: Fitness Information Technology, Inc.

Anderson, A., & South, D. (1993). Racial differences in collegiate recruiting, retention, and graduation rates. In D. Brooks & R Althouse (Eds.), *Racism in college athletics: The African American athlete's experience* (pp. 79–99). Morgantown, WV: Fitness Information Technology, Inc.

Anderson, D. (1993). Cultural diversity on campus: A look at intercollegiate football coaches. *Journal of Sport and Social Issues, 17*(1), 61–66.

Brooks, D. & Althouse, R. (1993). Racial imbalance in coaching and managerial positions. In D. Brooks & R. Althouse (Eds.), *Racism in college athletics: The African American athlete's experience* (pp. 101–141). Morgantown, WV: Fitness Information Technology, Inc.

Brooks, D., Althouse, R., & Brown, R. (1990). Black coaching mobility: An investigation of the stem and branch structural model. Unpublished paper presented at the North Central Sociology Meeting, Louisville, KY. March 22–23.

Coakley, J. J. (1994). Employment barriers in coaching and off the field jobs in sports. *Sport in society issues & controversies* (7th ed.). St. Louis: Times Mirror/Mosby.

Coakley, J. J. (2001). Sports are tied to cultural ideology. *Sport in society: Issues & controversies* (7th ed.). St. Louis: Times Mirror/Mosby.

Coakley, J. J. (2001). Using social theories: What can they tell us about sport in society? *Sport in society: Issues & controversies* (7th ed., pp. 30–53). St. Louis: Times Mirror/Mosby.

Corbett, D., & Patterson, W. (2002). The social significance of sport: Implications for race and baseball. In W. Simons (Ed.), *The Cooperstown symposium on baseball and American culture* (pp.169–181). Jefferson, NC: McFarland & Company, Inc., Publishers.

Cose, E. (1993). *The rage of a privileged class.* New York: Harper Collins.

D' Souza, D. (1995). *The end of racism.* New York: The Free Press.

Davis, T. (1994). Intercollegiate athletics: Competing models and conflicting realities. *Rutgers Law Journal 25*(2), 269–327.

Davis, T. (2000). Race, law and college athletics. In D. D. Brooks & R. C. Althouse (Eds.), *Racism in college athletics: The African-American athlete's experience* (2nd ed., pp. 245–263). Morgantown: W.VA: Fitness Information Technology.

Dovidio, J. F., & Gaertner, S. L. (1986). *Prejudice, discrimination, and racism.* Orlando, FL: Academic Press, Inc.

Doran, P. (2002). Behind the numbers: Black coaches and black athletes. Retrieved January 18, 2003 from *http://www.chronicle.duke.edu/vnews.*

Eitzen, D. S., & Sage, G. H. (1996). *Sociology of North American sport.* Dubuque, IA: Wm. C. Brown.

Gerdy, J. R. (1994). You reap what you sow. *Black Issues in Higher Education, 11,* 30–31.

Greenlee, C. (1998). In sports, those making the off-the-field decisions remain overwhelmingly white. *Black Issues in Higher Education, 4,* 23–24.

Grenfell, C., & Freischlag, J. (1990). Developmental pathways of men's and women's college basketball coaches. Paper presented at the AAHPERD convention. Boston MA.

Harrison, C. K. (2004). The Score: A hiring report card for NCAA Division IA and IAA football head coaching positions. *Hiring report card no. 1 (2003–04).* Retrieved 5th November, 2005 from http://www.bcasports.org/Assets/PDF/2004_BCAHiringReport_Football.pdf

Hill, O. F. (1995). Examining the barriers restricting employment opportunities relative to the perceptions of African-American football coaches at NCAA division I-A colleges and universities. Paper presented at the Black Coaches Association National Convention, Orlando, Florida.

Hoose, P. (1989). *Necessities: Racial barriers in American sports.* New York: Random House.

Houzer, S. (1974). Black women in athletics. *The Physical Educator, 30,* 208–209.

Is There a Double Standard for Blacks in Sport? (May 4, 1998). *Jet Magazine,* pp. 52–56.

Ivancevich, J. M., & Matteson, M. T. (1990). *Organizational behavior and management* (2nd ed). Homewood, IL: Richard P. Irwin.

Jones, Jr., E. W. (1986). Black managers: The dream deferred. *Harvard Business Review,* 84–93.

Kanter, R. M. (1977). Some effects of group life: Skewed sex ratios and responses to token women. *American Journal of Sociology, 82,* 965–1006.

Kaplan, W. A., & Lee, B. A. (1995). *The law of higher education.* San Francisco: Jossey-Bass Publishers.

Lapchick, R. (2005). Black coaches win big. Retrieved 5th November, 2005 from *http://sports.espn.go.com/espn/page2/story?page=lapchick/050922.*

Lapchick, R. E. (1997). *1997 racial report card: College special edition.* Boston: Northeastern University Center for the Study of Sport in Society.

Latimer, S., & Mathes, S. (1985). Black college football coaches' social, educational, athletic and career pattern characteristics. *Journal of Sport Behavior, 8*(3), 149–162.

Leonard, W. M., & Smith, E., (1997). Twenty-five years of stacking research in major league baseball: A theoretical assessment. *Sociological Focus.*

Lombardo, B. (1978). The Harlem globetrotters and the perception of the black stereotype. The *Physical Educator, 35*(2), 60–63.

Lovett, D., & Lowry, C. (1994). "Good old boys clubs" and "good old girls" clubs: Myth or reality? *Journal of Sport Management, 8,* 27–35.

McPherson, B. (1989). *The social significance of sport: An introduction of the sociology of sport.* Champaign, IL: Human Kinetics.

Mondy, R. W., & Premeaux, S. R. (1993). *Management: Concepts, practices, and skills,* (6th ed.). Boston: Allyn and Bacon.

Morrison, S., White, R. P., Velsor, E. V., & The Center for Creative Leadership. (1987). *Breaking the glass ceiling.* Reading, MA: Addison Wesley Publishing Company.

National Collegiate Athletic Association (2002). *2002–03 NCAA Division I Manual.* Indianapolis, IN: The National Collegiate Athletic Association.

The Division II Update (September, 2000). NCAA Division II Governance, Vol. 4, Issue 3, p.5.

Oglesby, C., & Schrader, D. (2000). Where is the white in the rainbow coalition? In D. Brooks & R. Althouse (Eds.), *Racism in college athletics: The African-American Athlete's experience* (pp.279–93). Morgantown, WV: Fitness Information Technology, Inc.

Pinkney, A. (1984). *The myth of black progress.* New York: Cambridge University Press.

Rosellini, L. (1987, July). Strike one and you're out (Racism in sports). *U.S. News and World Report,* pp. 52–57.

Sage, G. H. (1993). Introduction. In D. Brooks & R. Althouse (Eds.), *Racism in college athletics: The African American athlete's experience.* (pp. 1–17). Morgantown, WV: Fitness Information Technology, Inc.

Sailes, G. (2000). The African American athlete: Social myths and stereotypes. In D. Brooks & R. Althouse (Eds.), *Racism in college athletics: The African American athlete's experience* (2nd ed., pp. 53–64). Morgantown, WV: Fitness Information Technology, Inc.

Sailes, G. (Ed.), (1998). *African Americans in sport.* New Brunswick, NJ: Transaction Publishers.

Sailes, G. (1993). An investigation of academic accountability among college student athletes. *Academic Atlantic Journal, 2,* 27–29.

Sailes, G. (1991). The myth of black sports supremacy. *Journal of Black Studies, 21,* 480–487.

Sailes, G. (1987). A socioeconomic explanation of black sports participation patterns. *The Western Journal of Black Studies, 11*(4), 164–167.

Saperstein, A. (2001). The color of college athletics, part 1: Barriers still exist for black coaches. Retrieved 28th October, 2005 from *http://daily@u.washington.edu.*

Schneider, J., & Eitzen, S. (1986). Racial segregation by professional football positions, 1960–1985, *Sociology and Social Research, 70,* 259–262.

Schweitzer, C. A. (1993). Mentoring future professionals. *Journal of Physical Education, Recreation, and Dance, 64*(7), 50–52.

Shropshire, K. (1996). In black and white: Race and sports in

America. Retrieved March, 1996 from *http://www.nyu.edu.*

Sisley, B. (1990). A time to network-how to assist yourself and others. *Journal of Physical Education, Recreation & Dance, 61*(3), 61–64.

Smith, E., & Henderson, D. A. (2000). Stacking in the team sport of intercollegiate baseball. In D. Brooks & R. Althouse (Eds.), *Racism in college athletics: The African American athlete's experience* (pp. 65–83). Morgantown, WV: Fitness Information Technology, Inc.

Sokolove, M. (1988). Are Blacks better athletes than Whites? *Inquirer: The Philadelphia Inquirer Magazine,* pp. 16–40.

Spence, C. M. (1999). *The skin I'm in: Racism, sports and education.* Halifax: Fernwood Publishing.

Sperber, M. (1990). *College Sports, Inc.: The athletic department vs. the university.* New York: Henry Holt and Company.

Steele, S. (1990). *The content of our character.* New York: St. Martin's Press.

Tabron, M. (2004). An examination of athletic directors' perception of barriers to employment opportunities. Unpublished master's thesis, Howard University, Washington, DC.

Wiggins, D. K. (1989). Great speed but little stamina: The historical debate over black athletic superiority. *Journal of Sport History, 16,* 158–185.

Wilson, W. J. (1987). *The truly disadvantaged: The inner city, the underclass, and public policy.* Chicago: University of Chicago Press.

Wulf, S. (1988). Opportunity knocks (NCAA to work for Black Coaches). *Sports Illustrated, 68*(19), 22–25.

Young, D. (1990). Mentoring and networking: Perceptions by athletic administrators. *Journal of Sport Management, 4,* 71–79.

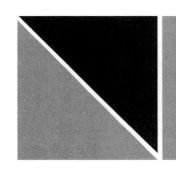

SECTION FOUR
Media, Media Images, and Stereotyping

Every year American sport fans and spectators seek and are subjected to an endless array of media commentary, broadcasting, and sport journalism. Much of the time *what they get* from the media is about African American women and men athletes, but *what is gotten is seldom given* by African Americans in media positions. The chapter by Doris R. Corbett and Aaron Stills, "African Americans and the Media: Roles and Opportunities to Be Broadcasters, Journalists, Reporters, and Announcers," begins with a discussion of eight African Americans identified as leaders or exemplary contributors to sport journalism and the sport broadcast industry. The chapter turns to issues of diversity, sexism, and gender and racial workplace discrimination in the media, and their findings suggest that African Americans are concentrated in competition-level positions, and less represented in studio and other media-type positions. The final section explores likely ways to explain their findings.

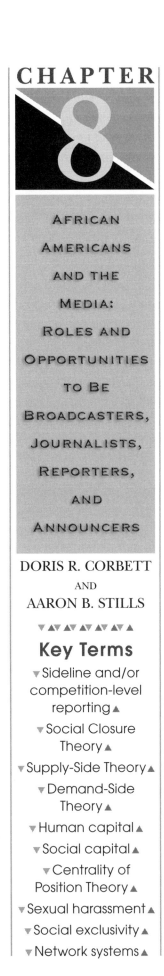

CHAPTER

8

AFRICAN
AMERICANS
AND THE
MEDIA:
ROLES AND
OPPORTUNITIES
TO BE
BROADCASTERS,
JOURNALISTS,
REPORTERS,
AND
ANNOUNCERS

DORIS R. CORBETT
AND
AARON B. STILLS

Key Terms

▾ Sideline and/or competition-level reporting ▴
▾ Social Closure Theory ▴
▾ Supply-Side Theory ▴
▾ Demand-Side Theory ▴
▾ Human capital ▴
▾ Social capital ▴
▾ Centrality of Position Theory ▴
▾ Sexual harassment ▴
▾ Social exclusivity ▴
▾ Network systems ▴

Abstract ▾ This chapter explores media role opportunities for African Americans. The prevailing research literature is reported, documenting the current status of African Americans in a variety of media positions associated with sport. The chapter reports on a few selected African American leaders who have contributed to the profession of sport journalism, discusses relevant issues of diversity, sexism, and gender and racial workplace segregation in the sport media, and proposes several theoretical perspectives to explain segregation in sportscasting. Findings in the research literature suggest that African Americans are concentrated in competition-level reporting positions and are underrepresented as studio analysts and play-by play announcers. African Americans are most likely to be found performing competition-level reporting, followed by studio analysis. They are less likely to work as play-by-play announcers. Additionally, African Americans are delimited to broadcasting roles associated with football, basketball, and baseball. African Americans are more often found in what might be considered the peripheral or dispensable roles such as sideline reporting or competition-level reporting than in other specialties, such as play-by-play announcer or studio host. Typically, African Americans are not included as sportscasters to cover most sports such as auto racing, bowling, golf, ice-skating, and tennis. These roles have been set aside for white broadcasters.

Introduction

Opportunities for African Americans to secure positions as sports writers and sportscasters have been extremely limited until recently. Although black former professional athletes have been able to obtain studio analyst positions, the top journalism play-by-play announcer jobs have usually been reserved for white males. In 1989 CBS sportscaster James Brown said, "I firmly believe people hire in their own likeness, so that's what network executives always have done . . . All we're asking for is an opportunity to succeed and fail like everyone else" (Sport News You Can Use, p.1).

As the minority landscape changes and more Hispanic and Asian minorities become involved in the larger sporting community (Women's Sports Foundation, 2003), the likelihood is greater that the media will be expected to appropriate more of its financial investment to accommodate these sport interest groups (Corbett, 2001). The issues of diversity or lack of it in the sports media are many and are represented by exclusionary practices involving access to media network systems.

Social exclusivity in the sport media is a way of encouraging only a select group of acceptable participants to practice an array of professional skills in the media. The ethnic and gender skewness in the media profession has been explained in several ways. Lafky (1993) credits the skewness to social exclusion from professional networks. She found that women journalists have less access to professional networking organizations than their male colleagues. Seeing that these networks tend to consist of white men, it is imaginable that African Americans also have limited access to them.

According to Deuze (2000), these networks function as important sources for news and career advancement. Those who are excluded from the network systems are significantly hampered from making professional connections that are necessary to get the required work accomplished. To what extent sexual harassment is a factor affecting African Americans in the sport media is not known. The hiring and promotion practices in the sport media field and the choices that black men and women make as to whether to enter or leave sport journalism as a profession are influenced by many social forces (Claringbould, Knoppers, & Elling, 2004).

Only in the past several years have sportscasters such as Robin Roberts and Bryant and Greg Gumbel moved into prestigious network positions. Profiles of early African American contributors to the profession of sport journalism and the broadcast industry are provided here to illuminate the nature of those early beginnings of pioneers in the field such as Frank Young, Wendell Smith, Sam Lacey, Bryant Gumbel, Stuart Scott, Robin Roberts, James Brown, and Greg Gumbel.

Profiles of Pioneer African American Sport Journalists

▲▼ Frank "Fay" Young ▲▼

Frank "Fay" Young was recognized as America's first full-time black sportswriter (Sternberg, 2001, p. 332). He worked as an unpaid sportswriter for the *Chicago Defender* from 1907 to 1915 covering black athletes in a black newspaper. Young played an important role in baseball's National Negro League (NNL) as the official statistician and scorer, secretary, and director of publicity for the Negro American League that formed after the NNL disbanded (Sternberg, 2001, pp.332–333).

Background

Recognized as America's first full-time black sportswriter (Sternberg, 2001, 332) Young played an important role in baseball's National Negro League (NNL) as the official scorer and statistician, and was the secretary and director of publicity for the Negro American League.

(Continued on next page)

▲▼ Frank "Fay" Young ▲▼ *(continued)*

Profile

From 1907 to 1915, Young worked as an unpaid sportswriter for the *Chicago Defender* putting together the first-ever sports page that covered black athletes in a black newspaper.

Through his columns in the *Defender*, such as "It's All in the Game," "Fay Says," and "The Stuff Is Here," he lobbied for the integration of Major League Baseball.

Perspective

In one column Fay wrote:

"It isn't necessary for us to sit by the thousands watching 18 men perform in the national pastime, using every bit of strategy and brain work to have it all spoiled by thinking it is impossible to have any other people officiating but pale faces. Give us a chance. The sooner it comes the better I will like it. (Sternberg, 2001, p. 335)

▲▼ Wendell Smith ▲▼

Wendell Smith, an African American sportswriter, used his position to object to the segregation that existed at the time in professional sports. Smith played a major role in facilitating the desegregation of professional baseball in 1946. He is remembered for his uphill struggle that led to Jackie Robinson's signing with the Dodgers in 1947. He suggested Robinson to Brooklyn Dodgers' coach Branch Rickey for the "great experiment," traveling and rooming with Robinson during the baseball player's early Dodgers career.

Background

Smith was born in 1914 and raised in Detroit, Michigan. He was the only African American student at Southeastern High School in the motor city, played on the school's baseball team, and was a leading pitcher on an American Legion team. Smith played baseball at West Virginia State College at Charleston.

Profile

After college graduation in 1937, Smith worked at *The Pittsburgh Courier* as a sportswriter and as the sports editor.

Smith recommended Robinson to Brooklyn Dodgers' coach Branch Rickey for the "great experiment." Smith traveled and roomed with Robinson during the baseball player's early Dodgers career.

A legendary sportswriter for the *Pittsburgh Courier*, he was the first African American inducted into the Writers Wing of the Baseball Hall of Fame.

Perspective

In his column, Smith crusaded for the right of the Negro League players to a tryout and denounced the Red Sox for blocking their way. "This is Boston," he began, "cradle of America's democracy . . ." After citing Boston's key role in the Revolution, he continued, "I have three of Crispus Attucks descendants with me. They are Jackie Robinson, Sammy Jethroe and Marvin Williams. All three are baseball players, and they want to play in the major leagues. . . . We came here to Boston—the cradle of democracy—to see if perchance a spark of the Spirit of '76 still flickers in the hearts and minds of the owners of the Boston Red Sox and Boston Braves. . . . We have been here nearly a week now, but all our appeals for fair consideration and opportunity have been in vain. . . . But we are not giving up! We are Americans, the color of our skin to the contrary . . . and we are going to stick to our guns! (Smith, 1945, p. 24)

▲▼ Sam Lacy ▲▼

Sam Lacy is recognized as a pioneer in baseball journalism and is credited with playing a central role in the desegregation of professional baseball.

Background

Recognized as a pioneer in baseball journalism, he was one of the first African Americans to be inducted into the Writers Wing of the Baseball Hall of Fame. He was a recipient of the J. G. Taylor Spink Award.

Profile

Lacy's career in print journalism began in the 1920s at the *Washington Tribune*. He was manag-

(Continued on next page)

▲▼ Sam Lacy ▲▼ *(continued)*

ing editor and sports editor of the paper from 1934 to 1939.

Lacy was Assistant National Editor for the *Chicago Defender* from 1940 to 1943.

He was columnist and sport editor for the weekly *Baltimore Afro-American* for over half a century.

Perspective

Sam Lacy, sports editor of the *Baltimore Afro-American*, noted in 1960 that "the African American player was much quicker to sign a contract than white players, and in comparison, was woefully underpaid." (Lacy, 1960, p. 30)

▲▼ Bryant Gumbel ▲▼

Bryant Gumbel attended Bates College in Lewiston, Maine, where he played football and baseball, majored in history, and wrote sports columns for the school newspaper, *The Bates Student*. Gumbel began his television career in October 1972, when he was named a sportscaster for KNBC-TV out of Los Angeles. He first worked for NBC Sports in the fall of 1975 as co-host of its NFL pre-game show *Grandstand* with the late Jack Buck. From 1975 until January 1982 (when he left to do the *Today Show*) Gumbel hosted numerous sporting events for NBC, including those of Major League Baseball, NCAA Basketball, and the National Football League. Gumbel returned to sportscasting for NBC when he hosted the prime time coverage of the 1988 Summer Olympics from Seoul and the PGA tour in 1990. After stepping down from the *Today Show* in 1997, Gumbel moved on to CBS, where he hosted various shows before becoming the co-host of the network's morning show *The Early Show* on November 1, 1999. Gumbel left *The Early Show* in 2002 and is currently concentrating mostly on his duties as host of HBO's investigative series *Real Sports with Bryant Gumbel* (a show that he has hosted since 1995).

Background

Bates College, Lewiston, Maine, Liberal Arts, BA, 1970
1982 Named anchor *Today*
1984 Headed *Today* team broadcasting live from Moscow
1989 Hosted NBC's two-hour prime time special, The R.A.C.E.
1997 Hosted the prime time newsmagazine *Public Eye with Bryant Gumbel*
1997 Named as host of the telecast of the primetime Emmy Awards
1999 Returned to morning television hosting CBS' *The Early Show*

Profile

TV host, newscaster, sportscaster, magazine editor
1972 Joined KNBC-TV Los Angeles as sportscaster
1975 Joined NBC Sports as host of the NFL pre-game show
1980 Named sports reporter, *Today*

1982 Named anchor, *Today*
1984 Headed *Today* team broadcasting live from Moscow
1988 Anchored NBC Sports telecast of the Summer Olympics from Seoul, Korea
1990 Returned part-time to NBC Sports broadcasting golf
1995 Hosted *Real Sports With Bryant Gumbel* for HBO

On being a journalist:

"I'm always amused with people in this business who get so lofty: 'I realized I wanted to be a journalist when I was six.' I didn't. Until I was 21, the only thing I ever worried about was what I was going to be doing that weekend. But growing up, the imperative was to be a professional."

On being called arrogant:

"I think nothing in this country happens absent of race. I do think there are a great number of Americans who are more comfortable with blacks (as) comics, jokesters, always laughing, never taking the world or themselves too seriously. I can think of very few, if any, well-known African American men in this business who were not accused of arrogance. Do I think it's a coincidence? No. I think in this business people get where they are because they have to make certain decisions, judgments, they have to take certain stands. And I do think it less than amusing that Ted Koppel runs his shop in a tight fashion and is concerned about the graphics, concerned about who his producer is, gets tough with his director, and that shows his professionalism, his attention to detail. But if I do that, suddenly I'm a meddler, or I'm arrogant, or I'm conceited, or I make enemies. I don't get it." (Nelson 1997, p.1; *Jet* September 29, 1997, p.1)

▲▼ Stuart Scott ▲▼

Stuart Scott is a sportscaster for ESPN and an anchor on *SportsCenter*. Following graduation from the University of North Carolina, Chapel Hill, Scott worked as a reporter at a small South Carolina television station for six years. In 1993, he joined the cast of *SportsCenter* and has been there since.

Background
Graduated with a degree in speech communication

Profile
First black male Anchor on ESPN's *SportsCenter*.

From 1987 to 1988, worked as a news reporter and weekend sports anchor at a TV station in Florence, South Carolina, on ESPN.

August 1993 joined ESPN 2 as *SportSmash* anchor.

In 1994 became co-host ESPN2's *SportsNight*.

Perspective
"I've tried to make it OK to have a more laid-back style that is a little more reminiscent of the African American subculture. I use words and expressions that are just more relaxed. You don't hear anyone describing Rich Eisen as doing his 'Jewish guy from Long Island shtick.' I think we associate 'hip' too much with being black, and it's not. It's just more young, carefree. That's why ESPN hired us, because we were a little different." (*The Dallas Morning News*, July 5, 1998)

▲▼ Robin Roberts ▲▼

Television broadcaster Robin Roberts co-anchored ABC's popular morning show *Good Morning America*. Roberts' father was one of the Tuskegee Airmen. She grew up in Pass Christian, Mississippi, where she played basketball and tennis among other sports, and graduated from high school as the class salutatorian. She attended Southeastern Louisiana University, graduating *cum laude* in 1983 with a degree in communications. She also played on the university's women's basketball team, ending her career as the school's third all-time leading scorer with 1,446 points and 1,034 career rebounds, putting her into the school's Athletic Hall of Fame.

Roberts began her career in 1983 as a sports anchor and reporter for WDAM-TV in Hattiesburgh, Mississippi. In 1984, she moved to WLOX-TV in Biloxi, Mississippi. In 1986, she became sports anchor and reporter for WSMV-TV in Nashville, Tennessee. She was also a sports anchor and reporter at WAGA-TV in Atlanta, Georgia, from 1988 to 1990. She joined ESPN as a sportscaster in 1990. Roberts co-anchored *Good Morning America*. Later that year, she anchored a series of reports from the Mississippi Gulf Coast after it was devastated by Hurricane Katrina. Roberts has earned three Emmy Awards for her sportscasting work at ESPN.

Background
She was a Mississippi State bowling champion at age 10. Played basketball at Southeastern Louisiana University becoming the school's third best female scorer and rebounder. Graduated with honors in 1983.

Spent two years as a weekend sports anchor at the ABC affiliate in Biloxi, MS, and two years in Nashville, TN. At age 29, she became ESPN's first on-air black woman hosting ESPN's overnight *Sports Center*.

Profile
Roberts joined the *Sunday SportsDay* and *NFL Prime Time* Shows. First woman to host an NFL pregame show. For ABC, she has done play-by-play in golf and women's and men's college basketball.

In 1995, Roberts joined ABC's *Wide World of Sports* and played a primary role in ESPN's coverage of the 1996 Summer Olympics and 1998 Winter Olympics.

Top female sportscaster at ESPN and ABC. Covered women and men's college basketball for both ESPN & ABC.

In April 2002, joined the ABC's *Good Morning America* team.

Perspective
She was ESPN's first on-air black anchorwoman, the first black female host of *Wide World of Sports*, and the first woman ever to host a network televised National Football League pregame show. Roberts stated, "I'm very proud to be the first, and I'm not going to make any excuses for that. But it's a ticklish position because you want to be known for who you are and not just gender or race. I say with all the humbleness I can, I'm qualified and I'm prepared for this assignment." (*The Atlanta Journal*, June 19, 1996, p. F2)

▲▼ James Brown ▲▼

One of the most widely recognized and admired sports commentators in the country, James Brown (more familiarly known as "JB") hosted *The NFL Today* on CBS. JB joined the ranks of play-by-play announcers for the NCAA basketball coverage on CBS.

JB's sports and entertainment career spans more than two decades. He joined FOX Sports in June 1994, following ten years with CBS Sports. Among the highlights of his hosting assignments are three Super Bowls, the 1992 Winter Olympics in Albertville, France, and the 1994 Winter Olympics in Lillehammer, Norway, the NBA finals, ten years of NCAA tournament coverage, and the NHL pregame show. While at CBS he co-hosted *CBS Sports Saturday/Sunday*, a weekend anthology series. Today, in addition to co-hosting *The NFL Today*, JB hosts *The James Brown Radio Show* on Sporting News Radio. He is a reporter/correspondent for HBO's *Real Sports with Bryant Gumbel* and a boxing host for PPV, the pay-per-view division of Time Warner Sports (HBO).

Background

Played basketball at famed DeMatha High School, Washington, D.C. All-American in 1968–69 and had a grade point average of 3.7, and was senior class president. He had more than 250 scholarship offers. Graduated from Harvard University in 1973 with a degree in American government.

Was drafted in the fourth round by the American Basketball Association by the Atlanta Hawks and by Denver. Was released by Atlanta before the season started.

Profile

Joined CBS and did play-by-play for men's basketball; was midday host for the 1992 Winter Olympics; did play-by-play coverage of freestyle skiing at the 1994 Winter Olympics.

Hosted Fox's NHL pregame show; hosts *Coast to Coast* (syndicated radio show) and a syndicated television show addressing black issues; and contributed to HBO's *Real Sports*.

Perspective

"I tell young blacks with sportscasting aspirations that nothing is going to be handed to them. They have to be willing to work for $50 a week if that's what it takes, just to get experience. They have to be willing to take gofer jobs to learn the business. They have to work hard and be prepared." (*Los Angeles Times*, April 2, 1993)

"I firmly believe people hire in their own likeness, so that's what network executives always have done … All we're asking for is an opportunity to succeed and fail like everyone else." (*The Washington Post*, June 22, 1989)

▲▼ Greg Gumbel ▲▼

Considered one of the best in sports television, Greg Gumbel hosted *The NFL Today* on CBS from 1990 to 1993 and *The NFL Show* on NBC. Greg was the lead play-by-play announcer for CBS Sports' coverage of the National Football League for six years, he called the thrilling action at Super Bowl 38 in Houston and Super Bowl 35 in Tampa. He is the first network broadcaster to both call play-by-play and host the Super Bowl. He hosted Super Bowl 26 in Minneapolis, Super Bowl 30 in Tempe, and Super Bowl 32 in San Diego. He has seen tours of duty at Chicago's WMAQ-TV, ESPN, the Madison Square Garden Network, CBS Sports, NBC Sports and, now, again at CBS. His play-by-play resume includes the NFL, NBA and college basketball, Major League Baseball, and the College World Series Championship. At various times he was the voice for the NY Yankees, the NY Knicks, the Philadelphia 76ers, the Cleveland Cavaliers, and the Seattle Mariners. As host, he has covered NFL and college football, Major League Baseball, the Daytona 500, the World Figure Skating Championships, the 1992 Winter Olympics in Albertville, France, and the 1996 Summer Olympics in Atlanta. Greg also served as the primetime anchor for the record-setting 1994 Olympic Winter Games from Lillehammer, Norway.

(Continued on next page)

▲▼ Greg Gumbel ▲▼ (continued)

Background

Born in New Orleans and moved to Chicago in the fourth grade. Attended Loras College in Dubuque, Iowa, where he played baseball. Graduated in 1967 with a degree in English.

Profile

Sports announcer for a Chicago TV station. First network TV job in 1981 with *Sports Center*. Left ESPN in 1986 and went to the Madison Square Garden Network for three years where he covered college basketball.

In 1989 joined MSG to broadcast Yankees games. Hosted a morning show on the radio station WFAN. In 1988, CBS hired him to do NFL play-by-play. While at CBS Gumbel served as the play-by-play announcer for the NBA Cavaliers, did play-by-play for college basketball, and did daily CBS radio talk show. In 1990, began hosting *The NFL Today* (the pregame, halftime, and postgame program). He was co-anchor of the weekday morning coverage of the 1992 Winter Olympics and anchor for prime time coverage of the 1994 Winter Olympics. While at NBC he was involved in *NFL Live; Baseball Night in America;* figure skating coverage, and the 1996 Summer Olympics for NBC as daytime anchor.

Perspective

"I think being minority had something to do with my first TV job and with being hired seven years later at ESPN. But it wasn't a factor in keeping those jobs, or in being hired by MSG and then CBS." (*The Boston Globe*, April 2, 1993)

These early American media icons have prepared the way for other African Americans to follow. Their legacy reflects a clearly defined philosophy that is highlighted in the profiles' "Perspectives" section.

Early African American Leaders and Contributors to the Profession of Sport Journalism and the Broadcast Industry

The sportscaster heroes and heroine cited above share several common distinctions that led to their success: (a) they packed for success in life by getting an education and knew that graduation was only the beginning, (b) they set high standards, and (c) they had the strength to believe in themselves. In order to reach their goals they were able to capitalize on change, demonstrating a willingness to move from city to city, or network to network. The upward climb is an indication that they recognized the power of networking and created connections that counted. Several noteworthy themes resonate from each of the early African American sport journalists, such as: be prepared, work hard, recognize the importance of being a professional, and build on the talents given and knowledge gained.

These media pioneers recognized and understood that their presence was not fully welcomed in the sport media industry, yet they persevered despite the disrespect displayed by corporate media. These icons challenged the industry despite the insensitivity to issues of diversity, sexism in the sport media, and workplace segregation by gender and race.

The situation has not improved significantly. The number of network top play-by-play announcers is few (Pepper, 2006; CBS-TV—3 WSHM, p. 1; Executive Summary: Broadcasting, 1995–2000, p.1). There have been strides, but the number of top African American sport journalists in general has remained almost the same as a decade ago (CBS-TV—3 WSHM, p. 1; Executive Summary: Broadcasting, 1995–2000, p.1). With the large number of college students earning degrees in journalism and former professional athletes seeking positions in the field, one would expect that the talent pool exists (Pepper, 2006). When behavior in the corporate arena does not embrace selected groups into the workplace, supply-side, demand-side, and social closure theoretical explanations have been used to assist in understanding the norm.

Theoretical Perspectives to Explain Segregation in Sportscasting

Researchers (Okamoto & England, 1999; Reskin & Roos, 1990; Tomaskovic-Devey; 1993a; Tomaskovic-Devey & Skaggs, 2002) have used supply-side and demand-side explanations to describe occupational segregation. A theoretical grasp of both of these points of reference can provide a better understanding of the nature of position segregation that exists within the sports media (Coventry, 2004).

The supply-side explanation focuses on the human capital theory. Peter Husz (1998) said that the time, experience, knowledge, and abilities of an individual, or of a structure such as the corporate sport media, can be used in the production process of human capital. Expenditures on education, training, and medical care produce human capital because you cannot separate a person from his or her knowledge, skills, health, or values.

Husz (1998) defines human capital as consisting of a number of components, such as time and experience. There is reason to believe that human capital consists of a much larger number of components, which may include routine, age, wisdom, and self-esteem (Becker, 1993). With this understanding of the theory of human capital, it is evident that the group that actually possesses this human capital is under-defined (Becker, 1993). In the sport media culture, white men are typically considered the proprietors of human capital. There is no doubt that with the increasing diversity in our society, the perceived bearers of human capital must change to include and embrace women and people of color.

Several studies (Becke, 1993; Schonewille, 2001; Schultz, 1992) have focused on schooling and training as the criteria for defining the worth of human capital to a professional entity such as the corporate sport media. However, social capital has value in the production of human capital. Social capital includes social networks and cultural assets, and unlike human capital, social capital includes more than just time, experience, knowledge, and abilities.

Becker (1993) posits that a good working definition of human capital might be all time and experience that are not restricted to any particular form of learning and are embedded in the labor force. For example, Becker's perspective on human capital would allow for the abilities, knowledge, experience, education, training, social networks, and cultural assets of former professional African American athletes to have greater value as human capital in the sport media industry. Position segregation takes a slightly different variation on the question of gender.

Polachek (1981) suggested that the difference between the work role of men and women is due to differences in the workplace investment in the human capital devoted to the position, job, or occupation. Polachek (1981) wrote that women are in lower-level positions than men because employers view the nature of their workplace investment or human capital as less valuable and significant to the work place. The supply side explanation therefore sees a lesser need to prepare African American men and women in the sport media industry because they are thought to have less work experience and less education. The corporate logic would therefore question bringing people into the industry whose human capital is not felt to enhance the larger organization (Polachek, 1981).

Theorists (Baca Zinn, Hondagneu-Sotelo, & Messner, 2000; West & Zimmerman, 1987) contend that society's gender role socialization processes play a major role in explaining women's orientation to focus more on family. Okamoto and England's (1999) research indicates that at an early age, boys and girls are socialized to conform to different preferences and skills that are socially acceptable by gender. The literature puts forward the idea that because women are expected to focus more on the family, they will choose occupations that require limited travel and would therefore make it easier to combine work and family responsibilities.

In sports broadcasting, a number of positions (reporters, play-by-play announcers, game analysts, and sideline reporters) involve travel to the site of the competition. If travel were a primary concern for women sportscasters, they would most likely seek positions as anchors, hosts, and studio analyst that would require broadcasting from one location.

Demand-side theories propose that employers typically determine who will be hired in a particular job and consequently play a significant role in ethnic and gender segregation. Stereotypes about what constitutes male and female work continue to be factors that employers use when making occupational assignments (Becker, 1971; Coventry, 2004). Oppenheimer (1968) submitted that stereotypes determine the nature of male and female dominance in certain occupations.

Academic scholars (Goode, 1982; Murray, 1988; Weber, 1968) on the other hand have argued that the "social closure" perspective prevails, contending that those in the most advantageous positions are diligent in their efforts to preserve the privileges their group members enjoy. Research (Bonacich, 1972, 1976; Edwards, 1979; Reskin & Roos, 1990; Tomaskovic-Devey, 1993a, 1993b; Tomaskovic-Devey & Skaggs, 1999) has shown that white males in high-status leadership positions have discouraged employers from hiring women and men of color for high-ranking positions. As a result, women and people of color are relegated to marginal jobs for which they are often overqualified. Marginal positions do not provide access to higher level position opportunities. Women and people of color are commonly found working in public relations and personnel positions that do not lend themselves to higher level management roles (Sokoloff, 1992; Madrid, 2001). They are working in positions that might be considered the peripheral or dispensable roles, such as sideline reporting or competition-level reporting, rather than in other specialty positions, such as play-by-play announcer or studio host. Competition-level reporting includes sideline reporters of football and basketball, the pit reporters in racing, and the on-course reporters in golf. Clearly, sideline reporting and competition-level reporting provide more sports broadcasting jobs and thus more opportunities for networks to integrate women and blacks into their broadcasting teams (Ring, 2002; Tierney, 2002).

The media networks are more inclined to hire people of color for specific responsibilities within sports broadcasting. The Center for the Study of Sport and Society (2001) research shows that African Americans and Latinos are found in only a small percentage of television and radio broadcasting jobs. A general perusal of television sport broadcasting might leave the perspective that African Americans hold a large number of the sport broadcasting positions. Eitzen and Sage (2003) along with Kouvaris (2000) pointed out that current broadcasting teams are composed of "a serious-play-by-play man, a former player, and an attractive female reporter on the sideline" (p. 1), and that people of color are more likely to be game analysts than play-by-play announcers, and even more likely to be studio analysts. There are nearly twice as many game analyst jobs as studio analyst positions available. The role of analyst can be inferred to be a position of expertise; conversely, it can represent a stereotype for people of color as ex-jocks who are placed in analyst roles and are not given the chance to do "serious" play-by-play announcing (Kouvaris, 2000). This explanation is consistent with the "centrality of position theory" (Corbett & Patterson, 2002) and the "social closure theory," which maintains that blacks are relegated to the peripheral and marginal sport positions (Weber, 1968, Goode, 1982; Murray, 1988).

Coventry (2004) examined whether women and people of color are segregated into specialties within television sports broadcasting (e.g., anchor, reporter, studio host, play-by-play announcer, game analyst, studio analyst, and competition-level reporter). Findings from the study indicate that sex and racial segregation exists inside television sports broadcasting, with women and people of color congregated in marginal positions. Coventry (2004) found that women are more likely to be reporters and sideline or competition-level reporters, while people of color have a greater chance of being studio analysts and competition-level reporters. Coventry's (2004) findings endorse the social closure theory, which contends that those with privilege statuses act to maintain their privilege by placing others in lower positions (Goode, 1982; Murray, 1988; Weber, 1968). Coventry's (2004) research results reveal that women and people of color are confined to competition-level reporting despite their education, age, and/or experience.

The Center for the Study of Sport (2001) found that African Americans account for 16% of the NBA radio and television broadcasters, but none of the National Hockey League (NHL) positions. Research by the Center for the Study of Sport (2001) indicates that sportscasters of color are generally restricted to basketball, football, and baseball. African Americans are not included as sportscasters to cover most sports such as auto racing, bowling, golf, ice-skating, and tennis. These roles have been set aside for white broadcasters. By allowing African American ex-jock players to serve as analysts in the major sports of football, basketball, and baseball, networks can give the impression that they have racially integrated their broadcasts (Coventry, 2004) while retaining white men in the role of "serious play-by-play" announcer.

Issues of Diversity in the Sport Media

In the United States, there is a history of racism and segregation (Hacker, 2003; Omi & Winant, 1994) in sport and the media (Andrews & Jackson, 2001; Billings, 2004; Eastman & Billings, 2001; Hoberman, 1997; Sailes, 1986; Shropshire, 1988; Wilson, 1997). Fewer than 2% of the sports journalists are black (Wolper, 2005). The lack of diversity in the sport media reverberates around problems inherent in how the media conduct business.

The lack of diversity calls into question the integrity of the industry. Sport reporters in the media conform to role definitions in position assignments and tend to be associated with specific groups of people. Those making selection and hiring decisions base their choices on ethnic and gendered criteria that they attribute to those positions (demand-side theory). As a result, the same type of person tends to be hired for specific positions, and others are not considered. Ethnic minorities and women tend to be found in positions lower on the organizational ladder, whereas white men tend to be found disproportionably in the top positions (Claringbould & Van der Lippe, 2002).

Research conducted by Claringbound, Knoppers, and Elling (2004) found that journalists reported that more ethnic minorities are not hired because their writing ability is inadequate. Claringbound, Knoppers, and Elling (2004) concluded that for minorities to have added value as newscasters and reporters, they must not only write well, but must have access to resources less accessible to white men.

The lack of diversity is reflected in the nature and type of coverage that professional African American players receive, especially in American professional football and basketball. Research conducted by Gist (1993) explored effects of social skewness by race and gender in media organizations. The results indicate that minorities and women are underrepresented as quoted sources in new stories and that coverage of issues considered important to minorities and women is minimal.

Although ethnic minorities are underrepresented in the sport media industry, some network journalists believe that affirmative action programs should not be implemented to improve minority position opportunities in the sport media. They are against affirmative action programs because they see them as compromising professionalism. The current hiring and selection criteria to select media personnel are believed to be neutral, objective, and fair (Claringbound, Knoppers, & Elling, 2004). The usefulness of affirmative action programs to resolve the problem of minority underrepresentation in the media is controversial. It is argued that change should not be pushed by policy, but should occur without intervention, and not through any specific recruitment campaign or affirmative action policy (Claringbound, Knoppers, & Elling, 2004).

Gist (1993) concluded that media coverage tends to be biased, and it is linked to the underrepresentation of ethnic minorities and women in the newsrooms. Gist (1993) reported that minorities were more visible in news stories that are negative or stereotypically positive, but not in the many kinds of neutral or generally positive stories.

The lack of diversity promotes the perception that blacks can't write well enough to be journalists, are not effective enough as leaders to be named as editors to manage reporters, and are not sufficiently articulate to be announcers. The low number of African American sports editors at U.S. dailies fosters inadequate coverage (Andrews & Jackson, 2001; Eastman & Billings, 2001; Wolper, 2005). Sport coverage emphasizes stories about black athletes' underprivileged upbringing and fails to portray a comprehensive understanding of the miscellany and complexities of black family life (Wolper, 2005). Although black men and women dominate the sport of basketball and American football, the cultural landscape they represent is not accurately portrayed (Wolper, 2005).

The impudence shown by corporate media can be seen in a variety of ways. For example:

▼ In reports on African American athletes, first names are typically used, while last names are used in the headlines about white players (Billings, 2004; Billings & Eastman, 2002; Dubriel, 2005; Rada & Wulfemeyer, 2005; Messner, Duncan, & Jensen, 1993; Rainville & McCormick, 1977).

▼ Subtle and not so subtle stereotyping is often communicated in the sport media's discourse surrounding African American athletes. For example, the African American athlete is commonly defined as "naturally gifted," while white athletes are referred to as "field generals" (Billings, 2004; Billings & Eastman, 2002; Entine, 2001; Rada & Wulfemeyer, 2005; Stone, Perry, & Darley, 1997).

▼ There is considerable focus on African American athletes as vicious and aggressive, yet equal time is rarely given to white athletes who perpetrate similar behavior (Billings, 2004; Czopp & Monteith, 2006; Leonard, 2004; Rada & Wulfemeyer, 2005; Rainville & McCormick, 1977; Sabo & Jansen, 1994).

▼ Black coaches who receive bad press are more likely to have their careers ruined than are white coaches (Gaston, 1986; Hughes, 2004; Sabo & Jansen, 1994).

A 2006 Radio and Television News Directors/Ball State University report showed that black presence increased slightly in radio news, although the overall representation of minorities in radio newsrooms decreased by more than 8% in the past decade. The report indicates an increase in minority journalists in TV newsrooms, with journalists of color representing 22.2% of the TV news workforce, up a full percent from 2005. The findings from the survey point out that the growth came almost entirely from an increase in Hispanic and Asian Americans (The 2006 Radio & Television News Directors/Ball State University Report, http://www.cbs 3online.com/business/3295371.html). The increases by Hispanic and Asian Americans offset a 0.8% drop in African Americans. President Bryan Monroe, National Association of Black Journalists (NABJ) asserted that "as stations seek to diversify their news staffs, such progress should not come at the expense of African American (The 2006 Radio & Television News Directors/Ball State University Report, http://www.cbs3online.com/business/3295371.html). Barbara Ciara, NABJ's Vice President for Broadcasting and an anchor/managing editor at WTKR-TV in Norfolk said, "I hope this survey is not an indication that the broadcast industry is just trading one race off for another instead of making a true effort to really diversify our nation's newsrooms" (Radio & Television News Directors/Ball State University Report, 2006). One area of concern is the lack of growth among black general managers. The survey indicates that 93% of general managers of television stations are white, and four out of five were men (Radio & Television News Directors/Ball State University Report, 2006). The lack of gender diversity has contributed to male dominance in the way sport is covered. Ciara contends that "if there is no improvement in diversity among the people in charge of overseeing hiring practices, . . . it makes sense that we resemble a rocking chair . . . lots of movement yet never moving forward" (Radio & Television News Directors/Ball State University Report, 2006).

Sexism in the Sport Media Industry

Sexual Harassment in the Sport Media

Sexual harassment is a recognized social problem in sport (Cense & Brackenridge, 2001; Brackenridge, 1997; Fasting, Brackenridge, & Sundgot Borgen, 2004; Fasting, Brackenridge, & Sundgot Borgen, 2003; Fasting, Brackenridge, & Walseth, 2002;

Holman, 1995; Kirby & Greaves, 1996; Leahy, Pretty, & Tenenbaum, 2002; Lackey, 1990; Lenskyj, 1992; Volkwein, Schnell, Sherwood, & Livezey, 1997). The research evidence clearly documents that sexual harassment exists in sport, that both women and men are harassed, and that women are more often harassed than men. Still, the full extent to which sexual harassment is a problem in the media is yet to be determined. In a definition of sexual harassment taken from the 1997 Netherlands Olympic Committee and Confederation of Sports Code of Conduct, "sexual harassment" is defined as follows (Fasting, Brackenridge, & Sundgot-Borgen, 2003):

> "Sexual harassment" is any form of sexual behavior or suggestion, in verbal, non-verbal or physical form, whether intentional or not, which is regarded by the person experiencing it as undesired or forced. (pp. 84–96)

It is important to recognize that sexual harassment consists of unwelcome sexual advances for sexual favors, and other verbal or physical conduct of a sexual nature when:

- ▼ Submission to conduct or communication is made either explicitly or implicitly as a provision or condition for an individual to maintain or secure employment;
- ▼ Submission to or rejection of conduct by an individual is used as a factor in decisions affecting that individual; or
- ▼ Sexual conduct unreasonably interferes with an individual's work and creates an intimidating, hostile, or offensive working environment.

Examples of behavior that are representative of sexual harassment include (Fasting, 2005):

- ▼ Disparaging or humiliating jokes and comments of a sexual nature
- ▼ Non-verbal behavior such as whistling, sexual gawking, or leering
- ▼ Unsolicited and unwanted sexual suggestions about one's body, clothes, or private life
- ▼ Unsolicited and unwanted telephone calls or letters with sexual content
- ▼ To be shown or to receive pictures or things with unwelcome and uninvited sexual content
- ▼ To ridicule or make sexist jokes about women in general
- ▼ Repeated undesirable and unwelcome sexual proposals or invitations concerning sexual behavior
- ▼ Unwelcome touching of a sexual nature such as: pinching, attempted kissing, unwanted body pressing and body contact
- ▼ Forced sexual behavior or action
- ▼ Rape or attempted rape

To date, there is no evidence to support a claim that sexual harassment toward African Americans is a factor in determining the occupational media positions held by relatively few African Americans. This is an area where further research investigation is needed to determine the extent and nature of sexual harassment in the sport media.

Sport and the mass media are two of the most recognized hegemonic social institutions with significant influence on the cultural practices in society (Duncan & Brumett, 1993; Sage, 1998). The power of sport and the mass media has contributed to the overpowering perpetuation of male dominance in the nature of media coverage that has largely barred, curtailed, and made light of the achievements of sportswomen (Buysse, 1992; Eitzen & Zinn, 1989; McKay & Rowe, 1987). The domination of sport by men has created an environment whereby sport has become almost synonymous with masculinity (Kane, 1989). The media have reinforced the ideology that sport is a masculine domain (Daddario, 1994; Kane & Disch, 1993). The process by which sport has become viewed as a male entitlement has been accomplished largely through the efforts of the media. In 1997 Graber noted that the media "present a set of cultural values that their audiences are likely to accept in whole or in part as typical of American society. The media thus help to integrate and homogenize American society" (p. 3).

The media uphold male hegemony by maintaining limited positions for women in the newspaper sports departments as reporters, photographers, and editors (Schell & Rodriquez, 2000). The exclusion of women personnel from key positions in the media has the effect of providing inequitable and limited coverage of women in sport.

In an effort to achieve more equitable coverage for women in sport, some research scholars have suggested that the addition of more women to newsrooms would make a difference (Schell & Rodriquez, 2000; Wann et al., 1998). Studies have not been definitive in showing that female and male editors, writers, and photographers are equally likely to provide inequitable coverage of girls and women in sport. Studies in this area are inconclusive on this point. According to Pedersen, Whisenant, and Schneider (2003), both male and female journalists underrepresent the coverage of girls' athletics.

From the research (Buysse, 1992; Daddario, 1994; Kane & Disch, 1993; Eitzen & Zinn, 1989; Kane, 1989; McKay & Rowe, 1987), it appears that regardless of gender, the American culture endorses male domination of both sport and the media. The social ethos indicative of the sport media is characterized by the criticism regarding women sideline reporters made by Andy Rooney of CBS' *60 Minutes.* Rooney commented, "A woman has no business being down there trying to make some comment about a football game." And, "most of the women are there because they're good-looking, not because they know the game" (Rooney, 2002).

If African Americans and women are going to access power and the privilege to report sport free of racial and gender bias, the culture of sport must change. The perceived nature of sport and the media as a white masculine domain will diminish only when sport newsrooms avail themselves of men and women who subscribe to the thesis that all people, regardless or race or gender, should receive an equal opportunity to report and cover sport without being subjected to gender and racial workplace segregation.

Gender and Racial Workplace Segregation

Workplace segregation by gender and race has been a part of the American fabric for generations (Beller, 1984; Jacobs, 1989; Padavic & Reskin, 2002; Reskin & Roos, 1990). Traditionally, white men and women have occupied a place in the labor market superior in status to the working positions held by black women and men. During the Industrial Revolution, black men and women were relegated to oc-cupations that offered low pay and poor working conditions (Padavic & Reskin, 2002). However, at the close of the 20th century, occupational, racial, and gender workplace segregation had declined significantly. In far greater numbers people of color are entering occupations not traditionally open to them. It is more common to see racial and ethic groups members entering professions such as law, medi-cine, and the corporate world today than in previous decades. At the start of this new millennium and the 21st century, women and men of color continue to be seg-regated or separated into different media occupations (Beller, 1984; Jacobs, 1989; Reskin & Roos, 1990).

According to researchers (Bonacich, 1972; 1976; Edwards, 1979; Reskin & Roos, 1990) jobs that are high in pay require advanced skills, have good benefits, and are consigned or set aside for white men. Historically, African Americans have been confined to positions that are service oriented. Characteristically, black women were employed as maids, cooks, waitresses, childcare and health-related providers, and teachers. Black men worked as service and manual laborers as jan-itors/custodians, waiters, doormen, railroad porters, sanitation/garbage collec-tors, stock clerks, bus drivers, sawmill workers, gardeners, farm laborers, preachers, and educators.

Even today, post the Civil Rights Era, African American men and women con-tinue to hold positions primarily in the service industry, as governmental civil ser-vants, construction workers, mechanics, secretaries, salespersons, personnel staff, and Internet technologists. There are many exceptions to this list. African Amer-icans can be found in executive positions in all fields of endeavor whether busi-ness, politics, law, medicine, education, religion, science, or the military. On the other hand, when blacks achieve occupational prominence outside of sport, the success is believed to be an exception to the rule rather than the norm.

In summary, African Americans media roles and opportunities to be broadcast-ers, journalists, reporters, and announcers continue to be limited. A few famous ex-coaches and players provide viewers with the impression that African Americans are strongly represented in a variety of media roles. The presence of a few highly visible individuals of color may suggest to some viewers that African Americans play a significant role in the sport media without being aware that the privileged positions are still held by white men in specialties, such as play-by-play announcer and studio host.

As reported in the chapter, research evidence supports the fact that:

▼ Social exclusivity in the sport media is a way of encouraging only a select group of acceptable participants to work in the sport media as broadcast-ers, journalists, reporters, and announcers.

▼ Sexual harassment exists in sport; however, the extent to which it is a factor affecting African Americans in the sport media is not known.

▼ The African American sport media pioneers recognized and understood that their presence was not welcome in the sport media, yet they endured.

▼ Supply-side, demand-side, and social closure theories provide a theoreti-cal understanding to explain segregation in sportscasting.

▼ Gender and racial segregation exists inside television sports broadcasting, with women and people of color congregated in marginal positions.

- ▼ Women are concentrated in positions as sideline or competition-level reporters rather than studio analysts and play-by-play announcers.

- ▼ People of color have a greater chance of being studio analysts and competition-level reporters. There are fewer opportunities to work as play-by-play announcers.

- ▼ Sportscasters of color are generally restricted to basketball, football, and baseball.

- ▼ African Americans are not included as sportscasters to cover most sports such as auto racing, bowling, golf, ice-skating, and tennis.

- ▼ By allowing African American ex-players to serve as analysts in the major sports of football, basketball, and baseball, networks can give the impression that they have racially integrated their broadcasts.

- ▼ Sport coverage emphasizes stories about black athletes' underprivileged upbringing and fails to portray a comprehensive understanding of the range, scope, and complexities of the sport experience and black family life.

- ▼ The lack of gender diversity has contributed to male dominance in the way sport is covered.

- ▼ As more and more television and radio sports broadcasting outlets become available, there will be greater employment opportunities for African American men and women. However, despite the increases in employment opportunities, African Americans will remain largely in marginal positions.

Strategies That Will Have an Impact on Increasing the Minority Pool of Applicants in the Sport Management Field (Sport Reporting, Journalism, Broadcasting, and Announcing)

The challenge for the media to address diversity issues in sport media starts within media itself. Professional organizations like the National Association of Black Journalists (NABJ) and national surveys such as the "2006 Radio and Television News Directors/Ball State University Report" may continue to make recommendations to bring about equitable changes, but acceptance of proposed changes can take a long time, and even after approval, may often be of low priority for enactment. Also, the culture of the corporate sport media does not fundamentally embrace issues of equity. It is therefore crucial that people involved in sport media be aware of the need for an approach to strategically increase the minority pool of applicants in the sport management field of sport reporting, journalism, broadcasting, and announcing. The lessons learned over the past years lead to the following suggestions of best practices or strategies that will have an impact for increasing the minority pool of applicants for sport media positions:

Seek diversity in the media's top management that controls the selection process for sport reporters, journalists, broadcasters, and announcers. It is incredible to observe the number of developmental internship programs including those within sport whose primary decision-making body lacks significant diversity in race and gender. Without members who possesses direct experiences from a variety of social perspectives, decision makers will likely make decisions based on their own experience or based on research often generated by similar group members. In order for the reporting of sport to be reflective and inclusive of all people who are consumers of sport, the very top levels of sport and the media, its decision makers, its sport reporters, journalists, broadcasters, and announcers must be representative of a body of people that depicts an inclusive and diverse sport media. Diversity in the media's top management ensures that individuals served are in fact participants in how sport is reported. If indeed diversity is valued, those at the highest levels must practice diversity.

Promote diversity early in the game. The sport media industry must include a variety of members from all levels of the sport community at the table when decisions are to be made about the needs for new sport media personnel. The groups invited to the table should represent the diversity of the entire community. If there is a potential for tension among various members of the community, such as among different ethnic groups (Asian, Hispanic, or black), men and women, or people of different social classes, it is important to create an atmosphere where people will feel comfortable talking with each other.

Promote diversity in staff/volunteers/trainers in the sport media. Engaging diverse staff members where blacks and women have been excluded from leadership opportunities in the media is challenging. Often the candidates who may appear to be the "best" in curriculum vitae or during an interview come from similar backgrounds. Seek to engage a well-rounded sport media staff made up of individuals who make different contributions based on their own personal experiences.

Seek ways to include a democratic process in the way sport stories are covered. Sport and the media can provide ample opportunities to present messages around the question of fair play, peace, and justice by the manner in which they cover the array of controversial sporting stories involving African American athletes.

Consider diversity in programming. Coverage of sport should be respectful and representative of the local community, and not solely representative of the male sport programs and white sporting institutions.

Encourage the development of tools and systems for monitoring and evaluating the nature of the sport coverage of black athletes. The sport media industry has a responsibility to monitor and evaluate the nature of the sport coverage that minority group members receive in order to guard against the promotion of unfair, inappropriate, stereotypical, and biased reporting.

This list is merely a beginning for how to have an impact on increasing the minority pool of applicants for sport media positions. It is up to sport media executives to constantly monitor and manage their own particular sport industry operations to promote and protect the rights of all people, including blacks and other minorities, to share in the opportunities to function as ambassadors of sport as reporters, journalist, broadcasters, and announcers.

▲▼ Suggested Readings ▲▼

Andrews, D. L., & Jackson, S. J. (2001). *Sport stars: The cultural politics of sporting celebrity.* New York: Routledge Taylor & Francis Group.

Billings, A. (2004, October-December). Depicting the quarterback in black and white: A content analysis of college and professional football broadcast commentary. *Howard Journal of Communications, 15*(4), 201–210(10). New York: Routledge, Taylor & Francis Group.

Billings, A. C., & Eastman, S. T. (2002). Selective representation of gender, ethnicity, and nationality in American television coverage of the 2000 summer Olympics. *International Review for the Sociology of Sport, 373*(4), 351–370.

Brackenridge, C. H. (1997) "He owned me basically": Women's experience of sexual abuse in sport. *International Review for the Sociology of Sport, 32*(2), 115–130

Corbett, D. R. (2001). Minority women of color: Unpacking racial ideology. In G. L. Cohen (Ed.), *Women in sport: Issues and controversies* (2nd ed., pp. 291–310). Reston, VA: National Association for Girls and Women in Sport, an Association of the American Alliance for Health, Physical Education, Recreation and Dance.

Corbett, D. R., & Patterson, W. (2002). The social significance of sport and its implications for race and baseball. In W. Simons (Ed.), *The Cooperstown symposium on baseball and American culture* (pp. 169–181). Jefferson, NC: McFarland and Company, Inc., Publishers.

Coventry, B. T. (2004). On the sidelines: Sex and racial segregation in television sports broadcasting. *Sociology of Sport Journal, 21*, 322–341.

Czopp, A. M., & Monteith, M. J.(2006). Thinking well of African Americans: Measuring complimentary stereotypes and negative prejudice. *Basic and Applied Social Psychology 28*(3), 233–250.

Daddario. G. (1994). Chilly scenes of the 1992 Winter Games: The mass media and the marginalization of female athletes. *Sociology of Sport Journal, 11*(3), 275–288.

Murray, R. (1988). *Social closure: The theory of monopolization and exclusion.* New York: Oxford University Press.

Okamoto, D., & England, P. (1999). Is there a supply side to occupational sex segregation? *Sociological Perspectives, 42*, 557–582.

Rada, J. A., & Wulfemeyer, T. (2005). Color coded: Racial descriptors in television coverage of intercollegiate sports. *Journal of Broadcasting & Electronic Media, 49*(1), 65–85.

Rowe, D. (1999). *Sport, culture and the media: The unruly trinity.* Philadelphia: Open University Press.

Sokoloff, N. J. (1992) *Black women and White women in the professions: Occupational segregation by race and gender, 1960–1980.* New York: Routledge.

Tomaskovic-Devey, D. (1993b). *Gender and racial inequality at work: The sources and consequences of job segregation.* Ithaca, NY: ILR Press.

▲▼ Study Questions ▲▼

1. Define the following key terms: Sideline and/or Competition-Level Reporting, Social Closure Theory, Supply-Side and Demand-Side Theory, Centrality of Position Theory, Human Capital, Social Capital, Sexual Harassment, and Social Exclusivity.

2. Identify early African Americans in the sport media.

3. What are the diversity issues in the sport media?

4. How has the corporate media demonstrated a lack of respect and sensitivity to how it covers African Americans in sport?

5. What effect does the presence of African Americans in the media have on how sport is reported?

6. What theoretical explanations can be given to understand the status of African Americans in the sport media?

References

Andrews, D. L., & Jackson, S. J. (2001). *Sport stars: The cultural politics of sporting celebrity.* Routledge Taylor & Francis Group.

Baca Zinn, M., Hondagneu-Sotelo, P., & Messner, M. A. (Ed.). (2000). *Gender through the prism of difference* (2nd ed.). Boston: Allyn and Bacon.

Becker, G. S. (1971). *The economics of discrimination.* Chicago: University of Chicago Press.

Becker, G. S. (1993). *Human capital, a theoretical and empirical analysis with special reference to education.* National Bureau of Economic Research. Chicago: The University of Chicago Press.

Beller, A. H. (1984). Trends in occupational segregation by sex and race, 1960–1981. In B. F. Reskin (Ed.), *Sex segregation in the workplace: Trends, explanations, remedies* (pp. 11–26). Washington, DC: National Academy Press.

Billings, A. (October-December, 2004). Depicting the quarterback in black and white: A content analysis of college and professional football broadcast commentary. *Howard Journal of Communications, 15*(4), 201–210(10). New York: Routledge, Taylor & Francis Group.

Bonacich, E. (1972). A theory of ethnic antagonism: The split labor market. *American Sociological Review, 37,* 547–59.

Bonacich, E. (1976). Advanced capitalism and Black/White race relations in the United States: A split labor market view. *American Sociological Review, 41,* 34–51.

Brackenridge, C. H. (1997) "He owned me basically": Women's experience of sexual abuse in sport. *International Review for the Sociology of Sport, 32*(2), 115–130

Buysse, J. M. (1992). Media constructions of gender differences and hierarchy in sport: An analysis of intercollegiate media guide coverage photographs (Doctoral dissertation, University of Minnesota, 1992). *Dissertation Abstracts International, 53*–09A, 3138–3325.

Cense, M., & Brackenridge, C. H. (2001). Temporal and developmental risk factors for sexual harassment and abuse in sport. *European Physical Education Review, 7*(1), 61–79.

Center for the Study of Sport and Society. (2001). *Racial and gender report card.* Boston: Northeastern University.

Claringbould, I., Knoppers, A., & Elling A. (December 2004). Exclusionary practices in sport journalism. *Sex Roles, 51*(11/12), 709–718.

Claringbould, I. E. C., & Van der Lippe, T. (2002). Women in executive positions. *Tijdschrift voor Arbeidsvraagstukken, 3,* 257–268.

Corbett, D. R. (2001). Minority women of color: Unpacking racial ideology. In G. L. Cohen (Ed.), *Women in sport: Issues and controversies* (2nd ed., pp. 291–310). Reston, VA: National Association for Girls and Women in Sport, an Association of the American Alliance for Health, Physical Education, Recreation and Dance.

Corbett, D. R., & Patterson, W. (2002). The social significance of sport and its implications for race and baseball. In W. Simons (Ed.). *The Cooperstown symposium on baseball and American culture* (pp. 169–181). Jefferson, NC: McFarland and Company, Inc., Publishers.

Coventry, B. T. (2004). On the sidelines: sex and racial segregation in television sports broadcasting. *Sociology of Sport Journal, 21,* 322–341.

Czopp, A. M., & Monteith, M. J. (2006). Thinking well of African Americans: Measuring complimentary stereotypes and negative prejudice. *Basic and Applied Social Psychology, 28*(3), 233–250.

Daddario. G. (1994). Chilly scenes of the 1992 Winter Games: The mass media and the marginalization of female athletes. *Sociology of Sport Journal, 11*(3), 275–288.

Deuze, M. (2000). Onderzoek journalistiek in Nederland [Research journalism in the Netherlands]. Retrieved October 22, 2003 from http://users.fmg.uva.nl/mdeuze/publ13.htm.

Dubriel, J. G. V., (2005) *The television portrayals of African Americans and racial attitudes, communications.* Master's thesis, Georgia State University.

Duncan, M. C., & Brummett, B. (1993). Liberal and radical sources of female empowerment in sport media. *Sociology of Sport Journal, 10*(1), 57–72.

Eastman, S. T., & Billings, A. C. (2001, October). Biased voices of sports: Racial and gender stereotyping in college basketball announcing. *Howard Journal of Communication 12*(4), 183–201.

Edwards, R. (1979). *Contested terrain.* New York: Basic Books.

Eitzen, D. S., & Sage, G. H. (2003). *Sociology of North American sport* (7th ed.). Boston: McGraw-Hill.

Eitzen, D. S., & Zinn, M. B. (1989). The de-athleticization of women: The naming and gender marking of collegiate sport teams. *Sociology of Sport Journal, 6*(4), 362–370.

Entine, J. (2001). *Taboo: Why black athletes dominate sports and why we're afraid to talk about it.* New York: Public Affairs

Fasting, K. (April, 2005). Research on sexual harassment and abuse in sport, Norwegian School of Sport Sciences, Oslo. Retrieved September 23, 2006 from http://www.idrottsforum.org/articles/fasting/fasting050405.html

Fasting, K., Brackenridge, C., & Sundgot Borgen, J. (2004). Prevalence of sexual harassment among Norwegian female elite athletes in relation to sport type. *International Review for the Sociology of Sport, 39*(4), 373–386

Fasting, K., Brackenridge, C., & Sundgot Borgen, J. (2003) Experiences of sexual harassment and abuse amongst Norwegian elite female athletes and non-athletes. *Research Quarterly for Exercise and Sport, 74*(1), 84–96.

Fasting, K., Brackenridge, C., & Walseth, K. (2002). Consequences of sexual harassment in sport for female athletes. *The Journal of Sexual Aggression, 8*(2), 37–48.

Gaston, J. C. (June, 1986). The destruction of the young black male: The impact of popular culture and organized sports. *Journal of Black Studies, 16*(4), 369–384.

Gist, M. E. (1993). Through the looking glass. In P. J. Creedon (Ed.), *Women in mass communication* (pp. 104–117). London: Sage.

Goode, W. J. (1982). Why men resist. In B. Thorne with M. Yalom (Eds.), *Rethinking the family* (pp. 131–47). New York: Longman.

Graber, D. A. (1997). *Mass media and American politics* (5th ed.). Washington: Congressional Quarterly, p. 3.

Hacker, A. *Two nations: Black and white, separate, hostile, unequal.* New York: Scribner, 2003.

Hoberman, M. (1997). *Darwin's athletes: How sport has damaged black America and preserved the myth of race.* New York: Houghton Mifflin Co.

Holman, M. (1995). Female and male athletes' accounts and meanings of sexual harassment in Canadian interuniversity athletics. Ph.D. thesis, University of Windsor: Ontario, Canada.

Hughes, G. (2004). Managing black guys: Representation, corporate culture, and the NBA. *Sociology of Sport Journal, 21*, 163–184.

Husz, M. (1998). *Human capital, endogenous growth, and government policy.* New York: Peter Lang Publishing, Inc.

Jacobs, J. A. (1989). Long-term trends in occupational segregation by sex. *American Journal of Sociology, 95*, 160–73.

Jet Magazine. (1997, September 29). Bryant Gumbel speaks out on racism in TV.

Kane, M. J. (1989). The post Title IX female athlete in the media. *Journal of Physical Education, Recreation and Dance, 60*(30), 58–62.

Kane, M. J., & Disch, L .J. (1993). Sexual violence and the reproduction of male power in the locker room: The "Lisa Olson incident." *Sociology of Sport Journal, 10*(4), 331–352.

Kirby, S., & Greaves, L. (1996) *Foul play: Sexual abuse and harassment in sport.* Paper presented at the Pre-Olympic Scientific Congress, Dallas, USA, 11–14 July.

Kouvaris, S. (2000, November 10). Wanted: Blonde bombshell. *Sam Kouvaris' Weekly Commentary.* Retrieved January 12, 2002, from http://www.samsportsline.com/features-commentary/commentary -11-10-2000.html

Lackey, D. (1990). Sexual harassment in sport. *The Physical Educator, 47*(2), 22–26.

Lacy, S. (1960, November). *Negro History Bulletin* (p. 30).

Lafky, S. A. (1993). The progress of women and people of color in the U.S. journalistic workforce: A long, slow journey. In P. J. Creedon (Ed.), *Women in mass communication* (pp. 87–101). London: Sage.

Leahy, T., Pretty, G., & Tenenbaum, G. (2002) Prevalence of sexual abuse in organized competitive sport in Australia, *Journal of Sexual Aggression, 8*(2), 16–36.

Lenskyj, H. (1992). Unsafe at home base: Women's experiences of sexual harassment in university sport and physical education. *Women in Sport and Physical Activity Journal, 1*(1), 19–34.

Leonard, D. J. (2004). The next M. J. or the next O. J.? Kobe Bryant, race, and the absurdity of colorblind rhetoric. *Journal of Sport and Social Issues, 28*(3), 284–313.

Madrid, A. (2001). Missing people and others: Joining together to expand the circle. In M. L. Andersen & P. H. Collins (Eds.), *Race, class, and gender* (4th ed., pp. 23–28). Belmont, CA: Wadsworth.

McKay, J., & Rowe, D. (1987). Ideology, the media and Australian sport. *Sociology of Sport Journal, 4*(3), 258–273.

Messner, M. A., Duncan, M. C., & Jensen, K. (1993, March). Separating the men from the girls: The gendered language of televised sports. *Gender and Society, 7*(1), 121–137.

Murray, R. (1988). *Social closure: The theory of monopolization and exclusion.* New York: Oxford University Press.

Nelson, J. (1997). Gumbel's New Gamble. *USA WEEKEND Magazine.* Retrieved July 14, 2006, from http://www.usaweekend.com/97_issues/970907/970907cov_st_Bryant_gumbel.html

Okamoto, D., & England, P. (1999). Is there a supply side to occupational sex segregation? *Sociological Perspectives, 4*, 557–582.

Omi, M., & Winant, H. (1994). *Racial formation in the United States: From the 1960s to the 1990s.* New York: Taylor and Francis Group.

Oppenheimer, V. K. (1968). The sex-labeling of jobs. *Industrial Relations, 7*, 219–234.

Padavic, I., & Reskin, B. (2002). *Women and men at work* (2nd ed.). Thousand Oaks, CA: Pine Forge.

Pedersen, P. M., Whisenant, W. A., & Schneider, R. G. (2003). Using a content analysis to examine the gendering of sports newspaper personnel and their coverage. *Journal of Sport Management, 17*, 376–393.

Pepper, B. (2006, July). The RTNDA/Ball State University Annual Survey of Women and Minorities in the Newsroom shows some of the highest highs and the lowest lows. Retrieved July 7, 2006 from http://www.cbs3online.com/business/3295371.html.

Polachek, S. W. (1981). Occupational self selection: A human capital approach to sex differences in occupational structure. *Review of Economics and Statistics, 63*, 60–69.

Rada, J. A., & Wulfemeyer, T. (2005). Color coded: Racial descriptors in television coverage of intercollegiate sports. *Journal of Broadcasting & Electronic Media, 49*(1), 65–85.

Radio and Television News Directors/Ball State University Report. (2006). Retreived from www.cbs3online.com/business/3295371.html.

Rainville, R. E., & McCormick, E. (1977). Extent of covert racial prejudice in pro football announcers' speech. *Journalism Quarterly, 54*(1), 20–26.

Reskin, B. F., & Roos, P. A. (1990). *Job queues, gender queues: Explaining women's movement into male dominated occupations.* Philadelphia: Temple University Press.

Ring, T. (2002). Round the horn . . . with Tim Ring: Did you ever notice? *Sportscasting Jobs.* Retrieved December 11, 2002, from http://www.sportscastingjobs.com/round horn3.asp

Rooney, A. (2002, October). Rooney laments remarks about women sideline reporters. *USA Today.* Retrieved July 10, 2006, from http://www.usatoday.com/sports/2002-10-21-rooney-remark_x.htm.

Sabo, D., & Jansen, S. C. (1994). Seen but not heard: Black men in sports media. In M. Messner & D. Sabo, *Sex, violence, and power in sports: Rethinking masculinity* (pp. 150–160). Freedom, CA: The Crossing Press.

Sage, G. H. (1998). *Power and ideology in American sport: A critical perspective* (2nd ed.). Champaign, IL: Human Kinetics.

Sailes, G. A. (1986). The exploitation of the black athlete: Some alternative solutions. *Journal of Negro Education, 55*(4), 439–442.

Schell, L. A., & Rodriguez, S. (2000). Our sporting sisters: How male hegemony stratifies women in sport. *Women in Sport and Physical Activity Journal, 9*(1), 15–34.

Schonewille, M. (2001). *Does training make a difference? Institutional environment and returns to human capital.* Paper for the International Labour Market conference at Aberdeen, University of Nijmegen.

Schultz, P. T. (1992). *The role of education and human capital in economic development: An empirical assessment.* Paper presented at the conference on Economic Growth in the World Economy, Institut für Weltwirtschaft, Kiel.

Shropshire, K. L. (1988). *In black and white: Race and sports in America.* New York: NYU Press.

Smith, W. (1945, November 3). Sports spurts. *Pittsburgh Courier-Journal.*

Sokoloff, N. J. (1992) *Black women and white women in the professions: Occupational segregation by race and gender, 1960–1980.* New York: Routledge.

Sport News You Can Use. "Television Sportscasters (African American)," Issue 44, p.1. Retrieved July 21, 2006.

Sternberg, J. (2001). Frank A. "Fay" Young. In R. Orodenker (Ed.,) *Dictionary of literary biography: American sportswriters and writers on sport, 241,* 332–341. Detroit: The Gale Group.

Stone, J., Perry, W., & Darley, J. M. (1997). "White men can't jump": Evidence for the perceptual confirmation of racial stereotypes following a basketball game. *Basic and Applied Social Psychology, 19*(3), 291–306.

The 2006 Radio and Television News Directors/Ball State University Report, (2006, July 7). CBS—TV – 3 WSHM—Business—Survey shows Blacks continue to decline in TV news. Retrieved July 7, 2006 from http://www.cbs3online.com/business/3295371.html

Tierney, M. (2002, October 29). Is it time for sideline reporters to go away? *The Atlanta Journal-Constitution.* Retrieved December 11, 2002, from http://www.accessatlanta.com/ajc/columns/tierney/102802.html.

Tomaskovic-Devey, D. (1993a). The gender and race composition of jobs and the male/female, White/Black pay gaps. *Social Forces, 72,* 45–76.

Tomaskovic-Devey, D. (1993b). *Gender and racial inequality at work: The sources and consequences of job segregation.* Ithaca, NY: ILR Press.

Tomaskovic-Devey, D., & Skaggs, S. (1999). An establishment-level test of the statistical discrimination hypothesis. *Work and Occupations, 26,* 422–445.

Tomaskovic-Devey, D., & Skaggs, S. (2002). Sex segregation, labor process organization, and gender earnings inequality. *American Journal of Sociology, 108,* 102–129.

Volkwein, K., Schnell, F., Sherwood, D., & Livezey, A. (1997) Sexual harassment in sport: Perceptions and experiences of American female student-athletes. *International Review for the Sociology of Sport, 23*(3), 283–295.

Wann, D. L., Schrader, M. P., Allison, J. A., & McGeorge, K. K. (1998). The inequitable newspaper coverage of men's and women's athletics at small, medium, and large universities. *Journal of Sport and Social Issues, 22*(10), 79–87.

Weber, M. (1968). *Economy and society: An outline of interpretative sociology* (G. Roth & C. Wittich, Trans. and Ed., 3 volumes). New York: Bedminister.

West, C., & Zimmerman, D. H. (1987). Doing gender. *Gender and Society, 1,* 125–151.

Wilson, B. (1997). "Good blacks" and "bad blacks": Media constructions of African-American athletes in Canadian basketball. *International Review for the Sociology of Sport, 32*(2), 177–189.

Wolper, A. (March, 2005). One black list that shouldn't be short. *Editor & Publisher, 138*(3), 28. Retrieved February 16, 2007, from http://apse.dallasnews.com/news/2005/031005ethics.html

Women's Sports Foundation (2003). Report: Title IX and Race in Intercollegiate Sport. New York: www.WomensSportfoundation.org.

CHAPTER
9

MAINSTREAMING
AND INTEGRATING
THE SPECTACLE
AND SUBSTANCE
OF SCHOLAR-
BALLER®:
A NEW
BLUEPRINT
FOR HIGHER
EDUCATION,
THE NCAA,
AND SOCIETY

C. KEITH
HARRISON
AND
JEAN BOYD

▼ ▲▼ ▲▼ ▲▼ ▲▼ ▲▼ ▲

Key Terms

▼NCAA: The National
Collegiate Athletic
Association▲

▼Academic Reform
Movement (ARM)▲

▼Scholar-Baller▲

▼Culture▲

▼Higher education▲

▼Critical Race
Theory▲

▼Representation▲

Tʜis next chapter is unique. Keith Harrison and Jean Boyd's chapter, "Mainstreaming and Integrating the Spectacle and Substance of Scholar-Baller®: A New Blueprint for Higher Education, the NCAA, and Society" summarizes the recent NCAA reform policy addressing athletic eligibility, matriculation, and graduation of student athletes, called the *Academic Reform Movement* (ARM). But in the context of NCAA's efforts to promote policy, these authors also note that the commercialization and entertainment value of sports usually overrides any academic and educational accomplishments of individual athletes. This assessment, then, lends to the creation of what is called the "Scholar-Baller Paradigm." The avowed purpose of the Scholar-Baller Identity Model (SBIDM) is the dissemination of relevant incentives to student athletes through fashion and identity consumption patterns aimed at shattering the stereotyping that obstructs the personal, social, cultural development, and educational achievements, in particular, of African American student athletes. The authors articulate how to forge a proactive collegiate environment that is acquired through the Scholar-Baller curriculum.

Abstract ▼ The purpose of this chapter is to theoretically and empirically capture the cultural divide between education and sport and entertainment in American society. The NCAA Academic Reform Movement has evolved from holding individuals accountable to presently monitoring institutions and their retention and graduation success of college student athletes. This movement will require a deeper examination of how culture influences academic attitudes and lifelong learning. Based on empirical data from different methodologies, this chapter proposes that student athletes, especially African American males, are often stereotyped with few strategies to empower their academic and athletic identities. The Scholar-Baller Paradigm is designed to help athletes escape the stereotyping that confines their talents to athletics and hinders personal, social, cultural, and educational development. The new paradigm extends the dominant athletic visuals to include academic excellence. This reframing must be sensitive to the needs of the student athletes themselves. Part of integrating them into the university community will involve fusing their desires, connections, technologies, and artifacts (including video games, language, and fashions) with academic reform initiatives and policies. A key component of the NCAA Academic Reform Movement is the concept of contemporaneous penalties in which "real-time" evaluations will be made in order to improve the academic retention and matriculation rates of student athletes in all sports. A contemporaneous reward system for academic achievement that acknowledges and extends itself to popular culture should also be examined, in addition to traditional recognition artifacts (e.g., trophies, plaques, and certificates). Urban and hip-hop culture have moved into the center of American popular culture. This makes it possible to imagine a synergy of education, sports, and entertainment creating a new paradigm in which athletics, education, and popular culture are united into an indissoluble whole.

Introduction

In 2006, the National Collegiate Athletic Association (NCAA) celebrated its 100th centennial as the marquee infrastructure of competitive athletics in American higher education. Coincidentally, this celebration is concurrent with the new policy known as the Academic Reform Movement (ARM) by the leaders at the national office and membership institutions across the nation. "The NCAA academic reform effort has been a multiphase approach to ensuring student athlete academic success and has been informed by a substantial body of research" (Franklin, 2006, p. 4). The reform effort has occurred in three distinct phases: (1) initial academic eligibility standards; (2) progress toward degree standards; and (3) coaches and institutions being held accountable for the academic performance of their student athletes. These phases have prompted a unique "real-time" system by the NCAA that monitors retention, matriculation, and graduation.

Dr. Myles Brand, president of the NCAA, has created with his constituents the Academic Progress Rate (APR), a formula of accountability for all student athletes in the NCAA membership. This Academic Reform Movement and this formula are timely when considering the private and public debates about commercialism, academic fraud, graduation rates, exploitation of student athletes, and issues of gender and racial equity (Duderstadt, 2000; Gerdy, 2000). These debates are some of the negative highlights of the NCAA, mostly related to academic reform.

Academic reform is not a new dilemma when examining college sports and higher education. Since the NCAA was established, academic reform has been part of the policy initiatives in terms of changing the culture of retention and graduation. College boards and task force committees have been created from 1906 to present to address the academic accountability of student athletes. Faculty, administrators, college presidents, and students have historically been involved in this process (Smith, 1988). In the last couple of decades, Propositions 48, 42, and 16 have all been policy reforms that have been altered and tweaked to "fit" the culture of college athletics and the student athletes that participate while on athletic scholarship. The irony of the ARM is that the presence of African Americans (mostly males), who were legally prevented from integrating sport earlier in history, cultivated much of the discourse and many of the modern developments of reforming college athletics (Watterson, 2000). This was specifically tied to those African American participants from more urban and lower income perspectives (Edwards, 2000; Lapchick, 2001).

The context of African American representation as student athletes in the NCAA membership will be addressed later in this chapter. In general, the theory and practice of issues related to all student athletes have been preoccupied with pre-college cognitive characteristics within the SAT/ACT requirements and core classes in secondary education—before student athletes enter college. This is in contrast to other approaches that address socialization and systematic reward systems that acknowledge positive academic behavior from student athletes (Harrison & Boyd, 2005).

Although men's and women's athletics recognize academic all-conference and national scholar-athletes, these achievements are often unseen by the public, peers of student athletes, and other campus professionals such as administrators and faculty. This raises some theoretical and practical issues to consider about the future of academic and athletic policy outcomes in American higher education.

Ultimately, this chapter bridges representation theories developed by Stuart Hall (2003) and John Singer's (2005) timely article and contribution to Critical Race Theory (CRT) in addressing "epistemological racism in sport management research." Singer stated the following:

> Sport management scholars must begin to recognize the significance of race and ethnicity as viable epistemological considerations in research inquiry. Because CRT focuses on issues of justice, liberation, and the empowerment of people of color in a society based on white supremacy (i.e., Eurocentrism), the purpose of this article is to provide sport management scholars and students with insight into how CRT's epistemological and methodological bases could be applied to critical areas of research in our field. The article concludes with some practical suggestions for how we can address epistemological racism in our sport management research and education. (p. 464)

How will the ARM reach the goals it seeks to achieve? What are the cultural and social forces that remain untapped as educational resources that may empower youth and young adults who participate in athletics? What innovative approaches to bridging the gap between academics and athletics would impact the retention of student athletes and alter the historical stereotypes of many athletic populations? These are the central questions this chapter synthesizes and addresses at the practical and theoretical levels. We begin the chapter with an important historical context of the academic and athletic gaps in American higher education.

Intercollegiate Athletics History: Sport and Entertainment but Not Education

According to the seminal text *Sports and Freedom: The Rise of Big-Time College Athletics (1988)* by sport historian Ronald Smith, the myth that education was a high priority was less a reality than the issues and problems documented at universities such as Harvard University in 1885. Harvard developed the Athletic Committee concept in large part because Princeton, Yale, and other major eastern colleges and universities had begun to encounter problems that would later become embedded in higher education based on "athletic ills" on campus.

The next section synthesizes some of the examples of these ills. Academic policy reform committees, compiled mostly of faculty members, expressed concerns about the number and intensity of athletic contests disturbing serious academic work (Smith, 1988) (i.e., Division I football contests during the week and no longer restricted to Saturday), ungentlemanly behavior (i.e., fights off campus), injuries and brutality (i.e., paralysis due to the violent nature of football), unhealthy moral influences of big city games (i.e., gambling), financial inducements to attend college (i.e., booster and alumni slush funds or material "hook-ups"), and waste and extravagance under student management (i.e., students missing class, drinking excessively, and partying all day and participating with ESPN's College Game Day).

With the exception of injuries and brutality, these issues remain a challenge for higher education and college athletics (Duderstadt, 2000; Sperber, 1990). In particular, the influence of commercialism and its impact on the academic progress of student athletes in revenue sports is a key factor. Although faculty began to intervene with the cultural and social problems of intercollegiate athletics, a massive compromise between students' love of athletics and faculty's concern for educational integrity has never systemically occurred. This treaty between academics and athletics and the communication lines among university administrators, faculty, coaches, and the athletic departments themselves can be attributed to the lack of inter-institutional control (Smith, 1988). These disconnects between education, athletics, and popular culture are depicted in 22 photos and cartoons chronicled in *Sports and Freedom* (Smith, 1988).

These images and representations are central to addressing the timeline of the ARM and the APR formula by the NCAA and how cultural and social forces have been used and not used as resources that influence the mindsets of student athletes. Simply defined, the APR is a real-time assessment of a team's academic performance, which awards two points each term to scholarship student athletes who meet academic-eligibility standards and who remain with the institution. A team's APR is the total points earned by the team at any given time divided by the total points possible.

The following is a summary of a few selected photos and cartoons most applicable to the issue of academic accountability by student athletes. Sport managers and sport management students should be aware of the stigmas student athletes have faced over time. Sport managers and students of sport studies can become more aware of and begin critically to deconstruct traditional academic and athletic messages in the culture, and possibly even construct new ones. The importance of understanding contemporary student athlete messages is discussed later in this chapter. For now, we turn to a brief analysis of historical photographs that appeared in *Sports and Freedom* (Smith, 1988). The first point in each section is the historical context; the second point is our critical analysis and application to contemporary athletics and higher education:

1. Intercollegiate track and field began as an outgrowth of the annual college regatta in 1873. Participation was stimulated by offers of expensive silver trophies, with some participants known as "pot hunters."

   Faculty and other educators could have developed incentives for participation in the track and field contest by rewarding those student athletes with high marks in school with rewards beyond the silver trophies. Examples include books and other intellectual necessities, as well as distinctive rewards for those who were "true" student athletes.

2. Some faculty members, including Professor Woodrow Wilson at Wesleyan College in the 1890s, helped coach football and other sports.

   Some faculties value the student athlete experience and have learned life lessons themselves from participating in sport as a student athlete, coach, researcher, or administrator.

3. Few college presidents spoke out against the excesses of intercollegiate athletics, though Harvard's Charles Eliot was an exception. He wanted football banned but could not gather enough support among the forces that controlled it.

The NCAA is the key organization if any significant cultural change is to take place; however, the NCAA needs cultural partnerships at various levels from external and internal organizations. According to Gerdy (2000), "The most likely source of outside influence would be a body of highly influential leaders in higher education, highly visible and respected business leaders, and a few powerful political leaders, with the sponsorship and political influence of a coalition of educational organizations and foundations behind it" (p. 228).

4. Well before the 20th century, the "dumb jock" was caricatured in contrast to the sickly looking "brain." Thomas Nast, the superb cartoonist, may have been first, in 1879, to do so.

As of 2005, the "dumb jock" caricature is still embedded in the culture and few mainstream outlets promote the scholar-athlete in concert with entertainment and advertising slogans.

5. Athletes from an early time were often more concerned with participation in sports than with academics. Fielding H. Yost, the legendary coach, transferred from the West Virginia Law School to Lafayette in order to play in a game against Pennsylvania in 1896.

Until the recent Academic Reform Movement, the cultural and commercial emphasis has always been on sports versus academics. The recent NCAA policies should cultivate new attitudes and behaviors about academics and athletics—possibly a cultural shift in the lifestyle of the student athlete in American higher education.

In sum, the historical context of academic reform has focused more on policy and athletic recognition (absent from commercial educational praise) than on the cultural factors that are most influential on the outcomes and practical basis behind the legislation. The commercialization and representation curve of college sports is often critiqued as a negative aspect of the NCAA and higher education (Sperber, 1990). However, some critics, such as Gerdy (1997), see the opportunity for empowering student athletes, educating the public, and changing the stereotype through the same cultural forces that create narrow perceptions of student athletes. Gerdy stated the following:

> Television needs college athletics every bit as much as college athletics needs television. Network executives know college sports well. Televised college athletics is a hot property. The public wants to see sports and will continue to watch them even if more time is carved out of broadcasts to promote educational themes. More time and money should be spent developing creative ways to advertise education. (p. 116)

The next section takes a more in-depth look at Gerdy's notion by analyzing the cultural forces in what is known as the "triangle of success" (Harrison & Boyd, 2005). Sport managers and sport management students are challenged in particular to think of and create new ways of presenting academic and athletic success for public consumption.

A Theoretical Basis: Representation and Social Communities that Reinforce Education and Break the "Trinary"

Scholar-Baller and the Triangle Equation[1]: Education, Entertainment, and Sport = A "Brand" New Day

Hall (2003) contended that language constructs meanings based on the "Circuit of Culture" that conveys values. What follows is the application and overview of Hall's major representation theories and concepts from this circuit, applied to a new "brand" and representation in college athletics and higher education—the scholar-baller. The components include representation (i.e., athletics), regulation (i.e., shaping mindsets through television), consumption (i.e., the public, alumni, and higher education), production (i.e., stakeholders and advertisers), and identity (i.e., outcome of this cyclical machine). As Hall (2003) explained, "We do not have a straightforward, rational or instrumental relationship to meanings. They mobilize powerful feelings and emotions, of both a positive and negative kind. We feel their contradictory pull, their ambivalence. They sometimes call our very identities into question" (p. 10). In terms of education, sport, and entertainment, the meanings attached to the student athlete lack continuity, synergy, and communication. For example, the commercial and mainstream advertising for college sports often has little to do with campus life, academic achievement, and other institutional rituals with value beyond athletics (Gerdy, 1997, 2000). One important question due to this fact is: How might these cultural messages reinforce that student athletes are "truly" student athletes? Currently the messages reinforce the glamour of college sports and athleticism, not education. For the most part, the emphasis is more athlete student when representing college sports. This is not an accident when we consider the documented history of collegiate athletics and the way sport has been represented—it has produced the meaning of athletics through a specific language, discourse, and image.

As college athletics have become more and more commercial (Duderstadt, 2000; Sperber, 1990), they have grown into the institutionalization and marriage of sport and entertainment. What is most powerful is that American college athletics operate in higher education, an institution founded on the values of liberal education and intellectual development. Thus, three spaces or what we might call a "trinary" exists in terms of representation: education, sport, and entertainment. While the latter two have become increasingly intertwined, the reality is that binaries in general still represent win/lose or zero sum identities (i.e., student or athlete). In order for student athletes to use the "triangle of success," they must identify the educational, sporting, and entertaining priorities they face as one unified lifestyle. This has the potential for a win/win/win trilogy and cultural capacity to achieve Hall's (2003) theoretical suggestion:

> We should perhaps learn to think of meaning less in terms of "accuracy" and "truth" and more in terms of effective exchange—a process of translation, which facilitates cultural communication while always recognizing the persistence of difference and power between different "speakers" within the same cultural circuit. (p. 11)

---

1. The triangle symbol is parallel to Rocawear, Inc.'s "diamond" sign that is popular with youth and young adults. The diamond's meaning could integrate education, sport, and entertainment into one lifestyle, similar to that of the scholar-baller.

This translation is captured by using "scholar-baller"(someone who succeeds academically and socially) as the language to communicate that being educated, athletically talented, and presented in mass entertainment can exist as one logo, versus choosing only one identity in the "trinary" of higher education, elite sport competition, and pop culture, with many student athletes becoming pop culture icons through mass media and entertainment (e.g., Reggie Bush, the 2005 Heisman Trophy Winner for Division I football). Scholar-Baller challenges the meaning of these cultural messages by serving as a counter-strategy to intervene in representations and to reconstruct stereotypical images of student athletes with a new "brand" and broader meaning(s) of what it means to be a student athlete.

Closely related, entertainment (i.e., music and fashion) tends to construct identities that are focused on other binary cultural representations, instead of including academic achievement and long-term gratification messages. These short-term success messages that parallel athletic marketing and promotion are known in the hip-hop world as "making it," "bling-bling," or "blowin' up"—what some hip-hop artists have coined as the phenomenon of "get rich or die trying" (Boyd,

Figure 1.

2003). A great example can be seen in three advertisements that contain messages from two cultural leaders in hip-hop and business, Russell Simmons and Sean "Puffy" Combs (see www.defjamuniversity.com, www.badboy.com, and Figure 1). Although all three advertisements are powerful in terms of projecting self-empowerment and achieving goals, none is explicitly overt in terms of detailing how specifically to "further your knowledge," "get money," or define and historicize the meaning of Sean Combs' fist raised in the air, as the image promotes Sean John clothing apparel (Figure 1). Tommie Smith and John Carlos were demonized at the 1968 Olympics for raising their fists in the air on the victory stand in Mexico City, and now Sean Combs can raise his fist as a major advertisement in Times Square.

Sport and entertainment in reality have numerous representations that collaborate, partner, and coexist in popular text(s), but all are disconnected from education. This phenomenon has major implications for student athletes who are players in the larger game of big-time college sports and mass entertainment. The binary theories that Hall (2003) established through his critique, cited earlier in this chapter, mean that there is a natural conflict between student athlete and being a student first. Further complicating this tension and disconnect between student and athlete is that entertainment and mass commercialization have created a hyper-masculine, hyper-athletic, and anti-intellectual text in most instances of popular representations of high-profile student athletes in American higher education (Burstyn, 1999; Willis, 1998).

Why is this disconnect so crucial when analyzing the Academic Reform Movement and the power of cultural forces such as athletics and music? Coleman (1960) theorized and empirically supported a hypothesis that links to the Scholar-Baller Paradigm of magnetizing education, sport, and entertainment at the macro (structural) and micro (individual) levels as one lifestyle and social identity. In other words, cultural communities and organizations such as the NCAA, hip-hop entities such as Phat Farm or Bad Boy, film/modern cinema, and finally the student athletes themselves would all be on the same cultural page—reinforcing a unified lifestyle. Coleman (1960) articulated an important analysis of the connecting of these impressionable social worlds:

> In effect, then, what our society has done is to set apart, in an institution of their own, adolescents for whom home is little more that a dormitory and whose world is made of activities peculiar to their fellows. They have been given as well many of the instruments which can make them a functioning community: cars, freedom in dating, continual contact with the opposite sex, money, and entertainment, like popular music and movies, designed especially for them. The theory and practice of education remains focused on *individuals*; teachers exhort individuals to concentrate their energies in scholarly directions, while the community of adolescents diverts these energies into other channels. The fundamental change which must occur is to shift the focus; to mold social communities as communities, so that the norms of the communities themselves reinforce educational goals rather than inhibit them, as is at present the case. (pp. 337–338).

The relevance of Coleman's study with current theories and research will be further analyzed after the Scholar-Baller Identity Model (SBIDM) is examined in the next section.

The Scholar-Baller Identity Model (SBIDM)

The Scholar-Baller Identity Development Model (SBIDM) of persistence is a simplified longitudinal version of reality that specifies the conditions and varying factors presumed to influence whether a student athlete matriculates and graduates from a given institution of higher education. SBIDM identifies the student athlete's accumulative processes prior to and during college entry, various interaction patterns, and the relationship among those patterns within the college environment and the persistence decision; it has some roots in Tinto's model of attrition. In order to conceptualize SBIDM, we contend that there are several important issues to define: matriculation, identity formation, variable selection, and the interrelationships among selected variables.

From our perspective, matriculation is a process in which student athletes make consistent, annual progress toward a degree. The goals of matriculation are to ensure that student athletes complete their course requirements in a specific degree program, develop a philosophy of life, and achieve their educational objectives. In the early stages of the matriculation process, student athletes may struggle to form positive identification with the college environment (Erickson, 1987). As such, we integrate the identity framework of Erickson into SBIDM, which is assumed to yield early identification of student athletes who enter from diverse cultural backgrounds. In doing so, we expect that if student athletes develop a positive self-identity and integrate into selected college environments, they will increase the likelihood of being college persisters.

Furthermore, since the college environment encompasses both an academic and social sphere, it is important to separate what Tinto (1975) interpreted as the "normative and structural integration in the academic domain of the college from that in the social domain of the college" (p. 92). This distinction is necessary because students may connect with the academic domain, increasing the likelihood

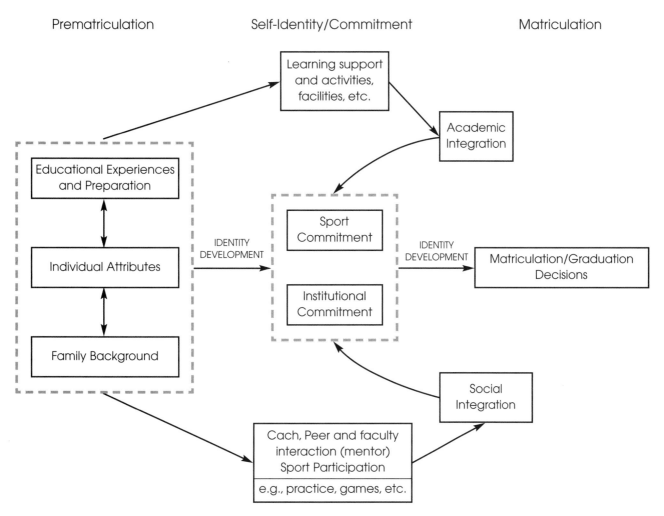

Figure 2. Scholar Baller Identity Development Model

of academic success and varying forms of persistence behavior; the same would hold true for integration into the social domain.

Separating both the academic and social sphere infers that student athletes who connect with the academic domain do not have to integrate socially in order to persist. This is conceivable, according to Tinto, yet "one would expect a reciprocal functional relationship between the two modes of integration such that excessive integration in one domain would, at some point, detract from one's integration into the other domain" (p. 92). Nonetheless, integration achievement may vary from individual to individual depending on the level of positive self-identity and to what extent integration, either socially and/or academically, is personally relevant to one's own culture (Settles, Sellers, & Damas, 2002).

Precollege Characteristics

Selected precollege or input characteristics are included in the longitudinal, theoretical model because they appear to relate to the college persistence and academic achievement of the student athlete. The most significant precollege characteristics shown to relate to persistence and academic achievement include family background, educational experiences and preparation, and individual characteristics.

Family background characteristics have shown to influence students' expectations about college, as well as their likelihood of interacting in certain college environments (Astin, 1993a; Lang, Dunham, & Alpert, 1988) Student athletes with higher socioeconomic status (defined as a composite of mother's and father's educational attainment, as well as students' estimate of their parents' income) are associated with higher persistence and graduation rates (Sellers, 1989, 1992). Further, the quality of relationships within the family and the degree of support and mentoring shown by the parent(s) or guardian toward the students' academic and athletic prowess are all important factors for educational attainment and college persistence, as well as sport commitment (Sedlacek & Adams-Gaston, 1992). Relationships within the family and even peer educational encouragement also, to some extent, influence the long- and short-term educational and sport goals of the student athlete (Sedlacek & Adams-Gaston, 1992). Thus it appears that the family's expectations of college are as vital to the student athlete's success as the student athlete's own expectations about college.

Included in family background are varying forms of culture. Cultural factors are imperative for any meaningful responsive evaluations of student athletes (Hood, 2004). The types and magnitude of culture one secures, as defined by the institution entered, play an important role in student athletes' persistence and performance in college. Put another way, the more cultural capital students bring to the institution and also inherit during their academic journey within the college environment, the more likely they will be college persisters (Bourdieu, 1986). In this sense, the existing structures of institutions of higher education do not represent cultural diversity, and thus could affect one's ability to persist in college (Tierney, 1993).

Precollege *academic experiences and preparation* are related to college performance. High school GPA, for instance, continues to be a strong predicator of academic achievement in college (Astin, 1993a, 1993b; Seller, 1992). Teacher support and academic advising, among other characteristics within the high school environment, are also associated with one's college aspirations and expectations (Comeaux, 2005). By contrast, disparities in access to advanced placement classes, honors courses, and other college preparatory services for high school students in underserved communities have proven to affect college access as well as persistence and full participation within the college environment for many student athletes and their non-athlete peers (Allen et al., 2002).

Furthermore, academic characteristics may directly or indirectly affect the student athlete's sport commitment (Simons et al., 1999). For example, a high school student athlete who becomes academically ineligible as a result of failing grades would not be able to participate in his or her sport. This situation would not necessarily affect immediate or future sport commitment despite being academically ineligible, because the student would have opportunities to pursue desired outcomes—to participate in sport—after improving his or her academic status.

Individual Characteristics

Individual characteristics are shown to be associated with college persistence and academic achievement. Noncognitive characteristics such as academic motivation (Lang, Dunham, & Alpert, 1988; Lawrence, 2001; Simons, Van Rheenen, & Covington, 1999), academic self-concept (Sedlacek & Adams-Gaston, 1992; White & Sedlacek, 1986), mental health (Petrie & Russell, 1995; Sellers, Kuperminc, & Wadell, 1991), and educational goals (White & Sedlacek, 1986) are related to academic performance. In addition, Simons and Van Rheenen (2000) also found that noncognitive variables of athletic-academic commitment, feelings of being exploited, academic self-worth, and self-handicapping excuses were all associated with college performance. Long- and short-range educational goals are an integral part of understanding persistence in college as well. Student athletes, for example, interested in attaining a doctoral degree would more than likely fare better than student athletes whose expectations are only to complete a four-year degree.

Finally, the type of sport, race/ethnicity, gender, and level of competition appear to be associated, to some extent, with matriculation and graduation (NCAA, 2005a). That is, (1) male football and basketball players perform less well academically than other athletes as measured by grades and graduation rates; (2) black student athletes tend to come from poorer backgrounds and are the least prepared academically; (3) female athletes exhibit academic preparation/performance similar to that of their nonathletic peers, and considerably better than that of their male counterparts; and (4) the higher the level of competition (Division I vs. Division II and III), the less likely the athletes will compare favorably with nonathletes.

Environmental Characteristics

College environmental characteristics are associated with academic success for student athletes (Comeaux, 2005). The environment encompasses all that happens to student athletes during the course of their educational programs, which may influence their desired educational outcomes—to matriculate and graduate (Astin, 1993a). As is the case with precollege characteristics, matriculation and graduation are the results of a longitudinal process that includes the interaction of environmental characteristics with the academic and social domains. As such, it has been well documented that the more time and energy that student athletes devote to learning and the more intensely they engage within the college environment both academically and socially, the greater their potential outcomes for achievement, satisfaction with educational experience, and persistence in college (Pascarella & Terenzini, 1991; Tinto, 1987). Such environmental characteristics as interactions with faculty, study time with other students, and volunteer work, among other activities, influence academic success.

Longitudinal Process of Interactions

The SBIDM employs "Input-Environment-Outcome" (I-E-O) for understanding and explaining the accumulative processes and interaction patterns on student athletes' outcome (Astin, 1993a). "Inputs" refer to the student athlete's entering or precollege characteristics, "environment" is that which the student athlete is exposed to during college, (i.e., faculty, peers, college coaches, etc.) and "outcomes" are the student athlete's characteristics after interacting with the environment, in this case, matriculation and graduation (Astin, 1993a).

The framework for the analysis of student athlete matriculation is derived from studies that have examined precollege characteristics of student athletes and on this basis have attempted to predict the likelihood that the student athlete will matriculate and graduate at a given institution of higher education (Astin, 1993ab; Comeaux, 2005; Sellers, 1992). Precollege characteristics (family background, educational experiences and preparation, and individual attributes) interact with one another and are likely to influence initial institutional commitment (commitment of matriculation and graduation) and sport commitment (commitment of developing various athletic skills; e.g., leadership; see Figure 2).

Environmental characteristics also play an integral role in the likelihood that the student athlete will matriculate and graduate at a given institution (Comeaux, 2005). In line with Tinto's Model (1975) on student attrition, within the academic domain, utilizing such services as tutoring, the library, faculty office hours, and so on increases the likelihood of student development, higher academic performance, and *academic integration*, which is expected to influence institutional commitment. In the social domain, peer group interaction and faculty interaction, among others social factors, result in *social integration*, which is likely to influence institutional commitment. And lastly, student athletes' involvement in team practices and games, various community services activities, and interaction with coaches in the social system also result in *social integration*, which in turn influences their sport commitment.

Various Forces that Impact Persistence

The SBIDM is a practical illustration of the matriculation process across institutions of higher education. It indicates information about the student athlete that, if it were known, would likely reveal student athlete's probability of matriculation and offer reasons for success. The SBIDM, to reiterate, identifies three classes of variables—precollege variables, environmental variables, and outcome variables— that have direct or indirect effects on intent to matriculate and graduation. The SBIDM also allows us to identify classes of variables related in a causal sequence. It is also important to note that the degree of institutional factors such as institutional racism, the instructional image, administrative policies and decisions, institution size, and academic standards are influential in the academic and social integration and identity development of student athletes. Moreover, coaches demand an incredible amount of the student athletes' time with practices, travel, team meetings, and game schedules that structurally inhibit their academic presence on campus. Thus, unlike traditional students, student athletes are burdened with many pressures that are vital to their academic success. Unless student athletes are able to develop a strong sense of positive identification with the self and the college environment early on, there are potential barriers and constraints that increase the likelihood of their voluntary or involuntary withdrawal from the college or university.

Breaking Timeless Stereotypes of Student Athletes: Fusing Cultural Forces

Coleman (1960) exposed gaps in the United States educational system nearly 50 years ago that are still major challenges today. The intention of Coleman's (1960) methodology was to study schools that had quite different status systems, yet the similarities were far more striking than the differences. In a questionnaire, male students were asked, "How would you most like to be remembered in school: as an athletic star, a brilliant student, or most popular?"

The data from this study revealed the results of examining the status systems of the adolescent communities in ten high schools in the Midwest and the effects of these status systems upon the individuals within them. The findings indicated:

▼ The schools were remarkably grouped somewhat off-center, showing a greater tendency for the students to say "star-athlete" than either of the other choices.

▼ In almost every case, the leading crowd tended in the direction of the athlete—in all cases away from the ideal of the brilliant student.

▼ For the leading crowds as well, as for the students as a whole, the uniformity was remarkably great.

▼ The uniformity was not so great in the absolute positions of the leading crowds but in the direction they deviated from the student bodies.

▼ Overall, the data indicated the importance of athletic achievement as an avenue for gaining status in the schools.

The cultural phenomenon of athletic glory and popularity continues in present-day athletics in higher education. This cultural context of athletic emphasis versus academic excellence suggests that student athletes may not always find themselves in an academically supportive or unbiased performance context. This is historical for student athletes in terms of being stereotyped and stigmatized as "dumb jocks" based on their participation in athletics. For African American student athletes, there are specific and unique effects of being stereotyped (Lapchick, 2000). The remainder of this section focuses on theoretical and practical issues related to strategies that may help break common stereotypes that student athletes face.

Recent research about collegiate culture and education validates some of Coleman's (1960) major findings but also extends his inquiry in other related ways (i.e., qualitative methods, studies on race and gender in sport). For example, Donnor (2005a) departed from extant inquiry and reductionism of academics and athletics by examining a more holistic picture of the scholastic education of African American male student athletes. This particular study explored the academic preparation of 17 African American male college football student athletes and revealed "specific actions taken by parents and teachers. In examining the scholastic education experiences of black male student athletes from this viewpoint, this study revealed the conditions (i.e., race, socioeconomic, and institutional) that shaped individual behavior outside of sport" (Donnor, 2005b, p. 2). In short, this study created new knowledge instead of continuing the "critical shortcoming of conventional studies and their inability to delineate the attributes of individual black males irrespective of sport" (Donnor, 2005, p. 2). While Donnor's findings are less generalizable to a broader context of student athletes, the results still reveal a deeper meaning about attributes developed by African American male student athletes at some institutions. Among these attributes are academic success and the self-perception of intellectual prowess.

Martin (2005) has also contributed to examining less stereotypical attributes instead of continued reliance upon research that consistently calls attention to the problems and shortcomings of African American men in higher education. As Martin (2005) stated, "Most of the published research regarding their experiences at highly selective institutions disproportionately focuses on low retention rates, dismal graduation statistics, and other maladjustments to higher education" (p. 2).

The high-achieving African American male student athlete is "rarely highlighted in the higher education literature, thus making his reflections of success seemingly insignificant and unknown" (Martin, 2005, p. 1). Other scholars have examined this phenomenon of academic success and cultural expression in terms of African American female student athletes with research and commentary stretching beyond traditional epistemologies (Bruening, 2003, Sloan-Green, 1981; Smith, 2000; Suggs, 2003). This raises the question: what strategies are available to assist student athletes? Steele et al. (2002) noted that there are few empirically established individual strategies that empower "targets" with skills and responses that can mitigate the effects of being stigmatized (Aronson, Fried & Good, 2002; Major et al., 2000). This may help explain and interpret some of the other research related to academic and athletic identities that have followed Coleman's earlier data. First, Settles et al. (2002) found in their investigation of student athletes (N = 200):

▾ Despite the correlation they found between role interference and well-being, much of that relationship could be explained by other demographic and role importance factors.

▾ In general, both the academic and the athletic roles appeared to be highly central identities for the student athletes in this sample.

▾ No relationship between level of interference and well-being was found for student athletes who viewed being a student and an athlete as a single role.

Yopyk and Prentices's (2005) findings are also pertinent to the theories and research related to academic and athletic identity. In their two studies at Princeton, which consisted of student athletes (N = 37) and members of three all-male a capella singing groups (N = 30), they found:

▾ In terms of test performance, athletes primed with their athlete identity performed less well on the test than did athletes primed with their student identity or with no identity.

▾ Both singers and athletes who were primed with their extracurricular identity attempted fewer problems on the test and gave fewer correct answers, but athletes less successfully solved those problems they did attempt.

▾ As expected, athletes primed with their athlete identity reported significantly lower academic self-regard than did athletes primed with their student identity. Likewise, athletes primed with no identity reported lower self-regard than did athletes primed with their student identity. There was no difference between the athlete-prime and no-prime conditions, and no differences for singers across conditions.

One area of inquiry that may be helpful to understanding various intellectual debates about student athlete identity roles (that has not received much empirical attention) is the use of self-affirmation (i.e., academic success) processes (Steele,

1998). Although there is still some debate in the literature, the ability to reflect on positive self-attributes may provide a buffer against the threat imposed by the salience of a negative stereotype in a performance context. For example McIntyre et al. (2003) reported that providing women with feedback about achievements by females—a group level affirmation—enhanced the performance of female college students on a math test when they were under stereotype threat. Based on these assumptions and findings, Scholar-Baller as a concept and unique affirmational strategy intends to help targets such as student athletes disarm the threat they experience when negative stereotypes are salient in a performance context.

One stigma intervention is based on the new individualized affirmation concept of the scholar athlete model (Harrison, 2002). Research decades after Coleman's (1960) indicated that intelligence and athleticism are considered to be mutually exclusive at the high school level (Chandler & Goldberg, 1990; Nixon, 1982), and there is some evidence to suggest this is the case for intercollegiate student athletes (Harrison, 1998, 2002). The purpose of Scholar-Baller is to eliminate this dichotomy for student athletes by helping them reconceptualize the mental and physical aspects of their self-concept (Harrison & Boyd, 2005; Stone & Harrison, 2005). As was mentioned earlier in this chapter, entertainment has further complicated the dichotomy into a "trichotomous" identity struggle. With this reality in mind, sport managers and athletic leaders have the unique opportunity to fuse education, sport, and entertainment into one unified message.

This possibility is summarized by Gerdy (1997): "Athletic departments produce an incredible amount of material promoting their teams—media guides, game programs, and posters. Athletic events themselves offer an opportunity to address a captive audience on campus. But once again, the messages and themes associated with these publications and events are almost exclusively sports related" (p. 118). Scholar-Baller serves as a cultural intervention package that athletic managers can use to promote broader characteristics of the student athlete.

The goal of this Scholar-Baller intervention is to help student athletes integrate their academic and athletic self-concepts into one positive superordinate self-image (Steele, 1997). The hypothesis is that when a threat to their academic self-concept is imposed by the salience of a negative stereotype in the classroom, the integrated "scholar athlete" conception of self can then serve as an affirmational resource that reduces their concern and empowers them to perform well in the testing context (Steele et al., 2002). One of the major reasons the salience of education is less than that of sport and entertainment is that the education does not engage and/or inspire the masses of youth and young adults at the magnitude and with the frequency that music and athletics do. The section that follows discusses how hip-hop youth link culture to the scholar-baller concept.

Hip-hop as a Positive Cultural Force

The spread of hip-hop in present society is similar to Coleman's (1960) observation about rock and roll and to the influence of popular culture as a whole. Today, entertainment (i.e., music, film, fashion, video games) and hip-hop influence the attitudes and values of youth and young adults on a global scale (Boyd, 2002; Keyes, 2004). Any serious academic reform movement must acknowledge the realities of various cultural artifacts that teach values and influence social perceptions. West (2004) stated the following:

> Although hip-hop culture has become tainted by the very excesses and amorality it was born in rage against, the best of rap music and hip-hop culture still expresses stronger and more clearly than any cultural expression in the past generation a profound indictment of the moral decadence of our dominant society. (p. 179)

Examples of cultural artifacts include PlayStation (NCAA college version), music on iPods and CD players (hip-hop and other genres), and the public consumption of major and big-time college athletics as they continue to be embedded in America's psyche (e.g., March Madness and the Bowl Championship Series [BCS]). All of these examples serve as translators of the engagement with popular culture and athletics and with what youth and young adults learn and internalize as social reality.

Dyson (2005) critiqued the power and influence of entertainment. "Even more than their predecessors, hip-hop artists play a critical role in circulating the meanings and messages of urban black culture. Hip-hop stars and impresarios like Sean "P. Diddy" Combs (Sean John), Jay-Z (Rocawear) and Russell Simmons (Phat Farm) have branded their products—compact discs, films and especially fashion lines—across a number of media, proving that black urban styles have global reach in the international marketplace" (p. 113). This is why urban culture and its related styles have become institutionalized and mainstream. The challenge is to mainstream the academic and educational identities through this same representational system, as discussed in Hall's research earlier in this chapter. The importance of styles should be acknowledged in this quest for change.

Patillo-McCoy (2000) analyzed one type of representational system and the targets for consumption of its product: "Styles are generated by the strong messages delivered in advertising, and transformed through local processes of re-definition. It is clear that Nike has made a strategic pitch to the African American community, especially its youth, and that Nikes have in turn been incorporated into a dialogue of symbols for courtship, for self-esteem, for aesthetic enjoyment, for gang affiliation" (p. 166). Educational styles are normally created outside the medium of sport and entertainment and tend to be conservative and less innovative (Meier, 1995). Public service announcements (PSA's) and Public Broadcast Service (PBS) are exemplars of the traditional educational representation system.

In terms of visibility, non-revenue sports do not receive the attention that revenue sports enjoy. However, the student athletes who participate still co-exist on campus and in a society that privileges athletic participants. This is why organizations such as the National Association for Academic Advisors for Athletics (N4A) have been formed, as well as educational intervention programs such as CHAMPS/Life Skills. These two important entities will be analyzed in the context of meeting the cultural needs of today's student athlete.

First, N4A is comprised mostly of academic advisors, assistant athletic directors, and associate athletic directors who direct student athlete services: tutoring, advising, study hall, and monitoring of academic eligibility through higher education's athletic departments. Although these are important developmental infrastructures, the limitation of this model (for the most part) has been its inability to address the dichotomy of academics and athletics in a culturally influential capacity that significantly impacts a quality education, graduation rates, and career development in the revenue sports. Both authors of this chapter have attended several N4A meetings, and the dominant theme is that "everyone knows the problem of student athlete retention," especially in revenue sports, but what do leaders, administrators, and faculties do to change it? This remains the question, and the next program we will discuss has addressed part of this question.

Second, the CHAMPS (Challenging Athlete's Minds for Personal Success)/ Life Skills program was created in 1991 through the collaboration of the NCAA Foundation and the Division I-A Athletics Directors' Program. It was not until the summer of 1994 that 46 NCAA institutions participated in the first orientation for administrators from around the country. Since then, approximately 40 member institutions and conferences have joined the CHAMPS/Life Skills Program each year.

Participating institutions in the CHAMPS/Life Skills Program are provided with instructional materials and supplemental resources that support a student athlete's development in five areas: academics, athletics, personal development, career development, and community service. The stated mission of this program is "to provide services and support to the membership, public and media to develop and enhance the life of the student athlete through educational programs and resources focusing on gender equity, student athlete welfare and life skills" (NCAA CHAMPS/Life Skills Pamphlet, 2005b, p. 1). The components of the program are extensive, thus only those aspects that address culture on campus versus a broader societal level will now briefly be analyzed in contrast to the Scholar-Baller program.

First, the objectives that CHAMPS/Life Skills strives to fulfill are relevant for college sports and higher education. However, the mission statement focuses on gender equity, student athlete welfare, and life skills. Scholar-Baller focuses on culture, race, gender, and lifelong learning with a foundation on diversity. In other words, promoting respect for diversity among student athletes is not limited to tolerance, but includes valuing the diversity of student athlete profiles in terms of social class, perceptions of education and life, and respecting how the construction of self has been developed by each student athlete. Second, ownership by student athletes of their academic, athletic, and social responsibilities can be realized only by enhancing and creating new partnerships among the NCAA, member institutions, and social communities—this is the purpose of education (Coleman, 1960; Meier, 1995).

This is precisely the theory of representation and *shared* meaning discussed by Hall (2003) as noted previously in this chapter. All of this social and cultural synergy will be difficult to achieve if the consciousness of each student athlete is not raised to a level of self-respect. After self-respect has been achieved, student athletes will be on the road to becoming lifelong players and leaders in the greatest game of all, life. In sum, the Scholar-Baller differs from N4A and CHAMPS/Life Skills strategies because of its theoretical and practical applications to the social communities that shape the mindsets of student athletes in American culture.

Examining deeper narratives at the practical level must be substantiated by rigorous theoretical and cultural frameworks that reveal the true experiential aspects of student athlete perceptions and lifestyles about education. This is key for sport management scholars, practitioners, and students seeking to understand student athletes from diverse backgrounds and social origins. The next section addresses the notion of how Scholar-Baller can theoretically and practically illuminate some of these realities.

Critical Race Theory and Critical Scholar-Baller Theory and Application (CSBTA)

Singer (2005) summarized the defining elements of CRT and, more pertinent to this chapter, a foundation for a Critical Scholar-Baller Theory and Application (CSBTA) when he stated, "CRT challenges ahistoricism and insists on a contextual/historical examination of the law and acknowledgement of the experiential knowledge of people of color in analyzing the law and society" (p. 469). This is key when hearing the narratives of student athletes in high-profile sports such as football, but especially African American males who are often stereotyped because of sport participation and racial category. Often, marketing and advertising from athletic departments exclude the cultural perspective of student athletes and, in general, perspectives outside the dominant ideology of whiteness and mainstream society (Armstrong, 1998).

CSBTA models Singer's (2005) provocative challenge that "sport management scholars must begin to recognize the significance of race and ethnicity as viable epistemological considerations in research inquiry" (p. 464). As an extension and case example of CRT's growing body of knowledge, CSBTA extends the CRT framework by legitimately challenging traditional approaches. This is the long-term goal of intellectualism and scholarship in terms of sport studies, to examine alternative and other scholarly and applied approaches that overlook racial and culturally based emancipatory research and best practices sport management, athletic administration, and the educational training of students as future leaders or researchers in these areas (Singer, 2005). CSBTA parallels the themes of CRT's focus on issues of justice, liberation, and the empowerment of people of color in a society that has historically resisted multiculturalism, inclusion, and diversity. The following is research from a single institution to illustrate some of the major points synthesized earlier in this paragraph. It also addresses alternative research approaches suggested by some of the scientists, scholars, and researchers mentioned in the section on recent campus climate literature and student athletes, focusing on African American males and females.

Based on a narrative study (N = 17) by Harrison (2004) of the 28 total student athletes (11 of the players were unavailable at the time of the study) who displayed the Scholar-Baller patch during the 2004 NCAA Division I football season, the following is a summary of the African American male "voices" and counter storytelling as they name their own reality and engage in dialogue that enables them to reflect on their situation and what can be done to change and improve it (Singer, 2005). The following are the compiled narratives and stories from the African American male football players (there were five non-African American players with narratives that are not the present focus) in the study (Harrison, 2004; N = 12):

> It's something to be proud of. It informs people that athletes these days are not one dimensional. We can excel in different aspects of life. Personally, being a black college athlete the blessing doubles, because it gives us a change of pace, instead of the "coming from the hood" story the media loves to tell. This gives them something positive to talk about. It changes the goal of those we influence—they not only want to come play ball . . . now they want to come play ball and get a degree. That's what it

Figure 3. "Thinkman"
(Scholar-Baller® Jersey Patch)

means to me; it says look at me, not only am I on a Division I football team and an athletic specimen, I am also a scholar and if I no longer had football I would excel in whatever area I choose to pursue. I am well rounded. I am trained for all aspects of life. I am no longer a boy. I have become a man. (African American male student athlete, junior)

To me it feels really good to be a Scholar-Baller because to me it lets me tell people that hey I'm a good student as well as a football player. And it makes me feel real good in the inside. I think it's really cool that we are the first school to ever do this because now we could lead by example and set certain standards for other schools to reach. (African American male student athlete, graduate student with athletic eligibility/fifth year senior)

It's nice to be able to be recognized as being a good student. It is not often that student athletes get recognized for their academics. Especially football players get the stereotype of being dumb jocks. So, it is nice to be recognized. (African American male student athlete, junior)

It feels good because of the stereotypes that have been set about f-ball players and that we can't be smart, but society always changes. Happy to represent by wearing the patch. (African American male student athlete, sophomore)

Our bodies endure the grind of two-a-days and the outcome is athletic performance at a high level. With academics the playing field is the classroom and the course material are the plays. What happens if one doesn't know the plays on the field? They're benched! It's different with academics, except you're benched in the game that matters—life. (African American male student athlete, freshmen)

I am glad that there is finally a program that recognizes the positives in academics. Usually people are always focused on the negatives! Football players don't do this. . . . And don't do that . . . just a bunch of haters. Finally a program that recognizes and rewards the *student athlete* for good work. (African American male student athlete, senior)

It feels good because it took work to accomplish it and not everyone has a Scholar-Baller patch. Also it shows that academics are taken seriously. I also believe that the few who have one get an extra level of respect from others. They see that the people who have one work a bit harder than others, because it is not easy to be successful on the field and carry high marks in school. (African American male student athlete, junior)

It feels good to be recognized for something positive. Many people think of football players as dumb, so this was a way to prove that they were wrong. It gave me something to push for. (African American male student athlete, sophomore)

I think it is unique to be recognized on the field for my academic achievements. It's a good feeling to be a "pioneer," so to speak, of this trend. (African American male student athlete, junior)

It's an honor really! I believe the Scholar-Baller identity will take off. I can't lie; it's been sort of an adjustment for me to recognize my education on the football field. But I'm proud to do it, I'm proud of it. I work hard on and off the field to be the best football player I can be, and to achieve Scholar-Baller status I must do the same, in and outside the classroom. This is history, being the first NCAA school to represent Scholar-Baller! It's an honor and I strive to continue achieving this academic status. (African American male student athlete, sophomore)

I feel good to know that I am a part of something that will eventually blow up. I really think it shows people on the outside how much work student athletes put into their academics. It is also a personal honor to be recognized for something other than ball. (African American male student athlete, senior)

I felt good wearing the patch on my jersey because people also could know that I can get it done on the field and in the classroom. Football players usually never get noticed for what they do in the classroom nationally, but after the patches came out, people started to notice it. Compete with Passion and Character (CPC) Nationwide! (African American male student athlete, junior)

As Martin (2005) suggested, "the paucity of research regarding African American male student athletes who perform well academically is highly problematic" (p. 1). He theorized that his study would assist college administrators in marketing and promoting more emphasis of academic success of student athletes; faculty, in mentoring student athletes; coaches, in reinforcing the value of education; and officials within the NCAA, in creating effective programming (e.g., see *Coach Carter* film screening in the conclusion of this chapter) and interventions (e.g., Scholar-Baller) that will aid in reversing the current perceptions of African American male student athletes in higher education (Harrison & Boyd, 2005; Martin, 2005).

The narratives reveal themes of pride and liberation and acknowledge how deficit perspectives on student athletes influence how they see themselves. This is why Martin's (2005) non-traditional research design and findings are key, as they break tradition by examining African American male student athletes with a cumulative grade point average at or above a 2.8 and on schedule to graduate in five years or less. Martin (2005) found the following to be most characteristic of academic achievement by student athletes in his study (N = 27):

1. Having a host of peers, family, professors, and academic advisors as sources of support

2. Having pride and working diligently in all of their scholastic endeavors

3. Engaged in campus and community organizations and other purposeful out-of-class activities that enable them to bond with the institution beyond their athletic obligations

4. Equating masculinity with having strong, upstanding, and moral character

5. Not characterizing masculinity through their athletic accomplishments, material possessions, or popularity among the women they were dating

6. Not desiring to be defined by the "jerseys on their backs," as they characterized themselves as men with aspirations and identities that stretch beyond the realm of athletics

These findings, coupled with the Scholar-Baller narratives, are key, because with Critical Race Theory they inform sport scholars, students, and sport managers of

> a framework or set of basic insights, perspectives, and methods that could help sport management scholars identify, analyze, and change those structural and cultural aspects of sport that maintain subordinate and dominant racial positions in and out of various sport organizations. CRT and qualitative research could allow us to better understand how these structures and practices negatively impact people of color in sport organizations, and what needs to be done to ameliorate the social conditions of these individuals. (Singer, 2005, p. 471)

Harrison's (2004) and Martin's (2005) findings are most pertinent because they are counter-stereotypical in a culture that often sees African American male student athletes as intellectually inferior to all other students on campus (Sailes, 1993). What follows in the next section is a single-institution analysis of the Scholar-Baller implementation in the culture of Division I athletics. Recent research and policy analysis by Bell (2005) indicated that "with support, encouragement, and interest, student athletes can be successful in challenging courses if those lacking academic skills are given the support they need, and if each student can discover where his 'spark' lies" (pp. 3–4).

The Triangle: A Community of Scholar-Ballers

Scholar-Baller is a committed team of educators, practitioners, professional athletes, and entertainers dedicated to educating today's youth about the importance of academics using sports and entertainment. Established in 1995, Scholar-Baller evolved in response to concerns that the student athlete's athletic role increasingly superseded the student role. In order to address this issue, the founding members of Scholar-Baller developed a paradigm to bridge the education and sport gap that utilizes student athletes' common passion for sport and entertainment.

The implementation of the Scholar-Baller program at Arizona State University (ASU) has been a collaborative effort between Dr. C. Keith Harrison, director of the Paul Robeson Research Center for Academic and Athletic Prowess, Jean Boyd, associate athletic director for student athlete development, and the ASU football coaching staff, led by head coach Dirk Koetter (2001–2006). The Scholar-Baller Paradigm teaches that performing well in school and earning a bachelor's degree are victories that last a lifetime. As a result, the Scholar-Baller program has produced unprecedented outcomes in student retention and academic achievement. What follows is a summary of the program's results, which help buttress the theoretical claims asserted earlier in this chapter. This implementation approach is multifaceted and consists of identity and curriculum intervention, academic team competition, single-institution analysis, and descriptive statistics of the progress in terms of matriculation and graduation at Arizona State University. The process of Scholar-Baller has consistently taken place during summer practices and in in-season/off-season meetings twice a week during the academic school year. The Scholar-Baller intervention focuses on critical pedagogy and "transformative knowledge by engaging the student athletes in experiences of values, character, morals, attitudes, outlooks, and so on" (Pugh & Bergin, 2005, p. 19). What produces the results that follow are weekly lesson plans and internal team competition in academic performance. This all begins during two-a-day practices where 15 of the 47 lessons plans are taught in a two-week period.

In three fall semesters previous to the arrival of Dirk Koetter and his staff and Jean Boyd's appointment as coordinator of football academics, the freshmen classes averaged a grade point average (GPA) of 1.67 (1998, 1.74; 1999,1.70; 2000,1.57). In the three fall semesters after Coach Koetter's arrival, the freshmen classes averaged 2.40 GPA (2.55, 1.91, and 2.31).

In the year previous to Coach Koetter's arrival, the frosh cohort average GPA for the fall semester was 1.57 with 10 student athletes under 1.00. In Coach Koetter and Jean Boyd's first year of the Scholar-Baller intervention, the frosh cohort earned an average GPA of 2.55 with all student athletes over 1.00 and only 4 of 17 under 2.00, with the lowest GPA being 1.75. The cumulative GPA of the football program overall significantly improved as well, and following the summer of 2002, the team cumulative GPA for scholarship student athletes was 2.60, up from 2.23 the previous two years. The cumulative GPA for the fall semesters over the same period of time increased each year from 2.23 to 2.31 to 2.38 to 2.40. Seventy-four percent of all football student athletes who played for Coach Koetter have either graduated or are still competing or finishing school. Overall, Coach Koetter's three recruiting classes have an 84% retention rate. One key aspect of this success is that players are randomly assigned teammates in groups of eight to ten student athletes, and the teams with the highest GPA's are recognized and praised for competing at the highest academic levels. This is where the core values of Scholar-Baller are taught.

The core values of the program are self-respect, perseverance, industry, vision, success, and humility. Adherence to these values in the contexts of academic and social achievement is what makes someone a "baller." To become a Scholar-Baller, student athletes must achieve a minimum GPA of 3.0. Professional athletes who have earned a bachelor's degree and others who demonstrate a commitment to the Scholar-Baller value system are also recognized as Scholar-Ballers. As a Scholar-Baller, the student athlete is awarded motivational gear that has the logo of ThinkMan (see Figure 3) or ThinkWoman. This logo is rare in that it represents the fusion of education, sport, and entertainment. The logo represents a well-rounded student athlete who has a positive lifestyle encompassing a lifelong commitment to learning.

Scholar-Baller is a reality due to its curriculum intervention and mentoring program. The curriculum is a culturally innovative and incentive-based program that bridges the gaps between academic and social achievement, athletics and popular culture. Upon completion of the program, all students have a new perspective for what it means to be a "baller." The six principles of the curriculum are:

▼ Identity (Self and Social)

▼ The Competitive Spirit/Compete with Passion and Character (CPC)

▼ The Scholar-Baller Paradigm

▼ Purpose/Vision/Mission/Goals

▼ Decision-Making System

▼ Vision, Industry, Self-Respect, Perseverance, Success, and Humility

The following is a synthesis of each of the six principles of the Scholar-Baller curriculum:

Principle One: Identity is something that many individuals pride themselves on. This is an extremely important concept as it relates to being a student athlete. Most student athletes take pride in who they are and what they stand for as athletes. The challenge that many institutions face is getting their student athletes to create an identity as "student" and "athlete." Because of the many differences in individuals who attend institutions across the nation, it becomes very challenging to foster the idea of one unified and shared meaning of this identity. Many student athletes view athletics as their ticket to a life of fame and fortune. As a result, they place a greater emphasis on being athlete. If student athletes come from environments where education is not a priority, they attend a college or university on athletic scholarships and their focus tends to be less on academics and more on athletics. This is sometimes the result of not being able to identify with the importance of academics and athletics as synergistic and inclusive in terms of excellence and cultural performance.

The goal of the self-identity principle is to educate students about stereotype threat processes and to introduce the concept of the scholar athlete self-identity. Getting students to engage in self-exploration through visualizations and workbook exercises accomplishes these goals. There are two major themes: social identity and values clarification. These themes will evolve through self-exploration to assist students in seeing how they identify themselves, as being "just" athletes or more rounded individuals, as well as to assist students in creating a stronger sense of self. A lesson will also address the incorrect assumptions that stereotypes like the "dumb jock" create, and will carefully explain the process of stereotype threat using the educational approach described by some scholars (Steele, 1997; Stone & Harrison, in prep.). Finally, students will critically assess their own balancing act of being a student and athlete and will be exposed to new strategies for managing the balancing act.

Principle Two: This principle focuses on competition and what it means to compete with passion and character (CPC). This principle will identify where competition takes place and will reiterate that competition takes place not only in the sports world, but also in the classroom. Students will investigate why it is important to obtain as much education as possible, learn the statistics that compare income for college graduates versus non-college graduates, learn the percentage of student athletes who go professional versus those who do not, and even more important, learn about those who are professionals in the world outside of physically participating in athletics. It will also highlight both the manifest and latent consequences of earning a college degree. The principle will be completed by presenting the rules necessary to compete in NCAA sports and how these rules relate to competition in both academics and sports.

CPC is a difficult concept to grasp for many student athletes. A good number of student athletes in our society have gravitated to the notion of becoming a profession athlete. As a result, many have become disinterested in academics. They figure that if LeBron James or Kobe Bryant entered the NBA draft fresh out of high school they will have the opportunity to do the same. They totally ignore the statistics that indicate that fewer than 2% of collegiate athletes actually make it onto a professional roster (Edwards, 2000; Lapchick, 2001). It takes a peer, coach, or administrator who has a passion for teaching and acquiring knowledge to act as a model for these student athletes to relay the message of what it means to "Compete with Passion and Character."

Principle Three: This is probably the most important principle of the Scholar-Baller curriculum, "The Scholar-Baller Paradigm/Standard." This concept is fueled by the energy of many individuals, past and present, who have exemplified the true meaning of self-respect, perseverance, industry, vision, success, and humility. Scholar-Baller is a committed team of educators, administrators, professional athletes, and entertainers dedicated to educating today's youth about the importance of academics through their interest in sport and entertainment.

Through educators, athletic administrators, counselors, and most importantly coaches, it is imperative that Scholar-Baller provide student athletes with multiple opportunities to acquire knowledge. Simply put, Scholar-Baller has a unique leadership opportunity that is unparalleled to that of any other profession: to use the power of sport and entertainment to educate today's youth and young adults. Through this paradigm, the Scholar-Baller team provides innovative approaches by teaching students and student athletes in a language and culture that are relevant to their concept of self.

The Scholar-Baller Paradigm is also designed to challenge student athletes to create entirely different images of themselves. Their major task is to establish a self-identity beyond the playing field or basketball court. Student athletes need positive heroes and role models they can emulate to help them create positive self-identities. Such models are essential to student athletes; therefore, role modeling is something that is greatly emphasized by the Scholar-Baller Paradigm.

This principle focuses on the desirability of the Scholar-Baller image. It begins with a definition and with contemporary examples like Pat Tillman (former pro football player and American hero), Dhani Jones (graduate of the University of Michigan and pro football player of the Philadelphia Eagles), and players from their own teams. The principle then focuses on Paul Robeson, the original Scholar-Baller, and the "Ball Like Paul" phrase, which means to excel in all aspects in the game of life. The session concludes with the students listening to a Scholar-Baller guest speaker. This assists in the embodiment of the concept, as well as lending credibility to it by demonstrating that being a Scholar-Baller is a positive goal.

Principle Four: For students, athletes, or businessmen, there are certain criteria that are necessary to be successful. Each of these individuals must have the ability to perform at the highest level at all times. As a result, a certain amount of planning is imperative for such individuals to become successful in their respective environments. In this fourth principle of becoming a Scholar-Baller, there are four concepts that must be investigated: vision, purpose, mission, and goal-setting. Each of these concepts gives student athletes or any other individuals the blueprint for success because these concepts offer structure to their lives. This principle will also help student athletes to take personal responsibility for their future.

Principle Four focuses on defining and exploring important life goals. It helps student athletes set, establish, and maintain realistic and powerful short- and long-term goals. They think critically about the difference between internal and external motivators and are encouraged to reevaluate their academic goals for staying in school (i.e., change the emphasis from passing to stay eligible to not being personally satisfied with just passing). Lastly, the principle closes with each student creating a personal mission statement, along with a list of goals of how to achieve and maintain that mission.

Principle Five: A student athlete's ability to make decisions in every aspect of life is critical to achieving overall success. Student athletes are faced with choices on a daily basis; it is imperative that they have a solid decision-making system. This principle focuses on how to make better decisions. It emphasizes the power of one decision that can create a domino effect as a direct result. It explains a decision-making rubric system, which asks the student athletes to critically identify if their decisions are in concert with their goals. This principle uses contemporary examples of positive and negative decisions made by personalities and identities in education, sport, and entertainment. One approach that consistently enables student athletes to become more aware of their goals and choices is to personalize the scenario. Dialogues and vignettes about eligibility for participation in athletics based on life decisions off the field are specific activities that allow players to connect with the reality that choices shape the future of their lives forever.

Principle Six: The sixth and final principle of becoming a Scholar-Baller is "Compete; Live the Scholar-Baller Way." This principle has a direct influence on coaches, teachers, counselors, administrators, and student athletes themselves. Most important, cultural changes on the entire campus and social environment are the goal. In many instances, "Living the Scholar-Baller Way" will revitalize certain individuals, who have been given these tools, to take life more seriously, not only competing on the playing field, the basketball court, or the baseball diamond, but also having that competitive spirit in the classroom. This principle is the most important of all because it truly defines what the Scholar-Baller program is all about: Getting student athletes to compete and live the Scholar-Baller way.

By living the Scholar-Baller way, these student athletes will be given the skills to compete in the game of life. They will have the confidence needed to attack any obstacle that life has to offer. These student athletes will have earned the right to be considered Scholar-Ballers.

This principle summarizes and reiterates the main points of the previous principles. Students connect with a panel of faculty, who provide tips for success in the classroom, including study skills, test taking, time management, and how to interact with professors.

This principle also connects pop/hip-hop culture to the students by emphasizing the marriage of hip-hop and sport. This principle re-discusses the issues of character, how it is defined, and its significance. It introduces the character quotient, which focuses on the concept that having a strong character will take an individual further in life than will a weak character. Finally, this section uses college situations and distractions in which character is revealed, exemplifying both strong and weak characters.

Summary

In this chapter, the Academic Reform Movement (ARM) and Academic Progress Rate (APR) by the NCAA are put into a historical context in which systemic problems such as academic accountability can be understood as a multi-layered, multi-faceted challenge by higher education and society. A timeless theme of academic reform has been the lack of institutional control, the primary focus on the new educational policies in place (Smith, 1988). It is important and timely that the NCAA has created a policy and shift in formally holding institutions accountable for the welfare of student athletes, regarding not only eligibility, but also matriculation and graduation.

Additionally, the representational system of education, sport, and entertainment is explained and labeled the "tri-nary," and Scholar-Baller as an intervention and symbol for these three cultural forces is synthesized. By creating a synergy of shared meaning in one symbol such as Scholar-Baller, the cultural forces of education, sport, and entertainment no longer compete with the desires of youth and young adults. On the contrary, all three constructs via Scholar-Baller reinforce a unique energy that embraces learning, no matter which domain is being consumed by the individual.

Third, the SBIDM is presented in order to contextualize the various theoretical and practical components that influence retention in terms of psychosocial issues in higher education. There is a scarcity of student athlete development theories in the higher education literature and few models of student athlete matriculation have been developed. (Some attention has been given in the psychological and sociological fields.)

Also, recent empirical findings are presented on stereotypes and counter-stereotypes specifically applied to the plight of African American student athletes. In general, this body of emerging knowledge related to the phenomenology of African American student athletes (especially males) reveals key factors that positively affect the academic performance of African American student athletes.

For instance, Gragg (2003) found in his qualitative study of Southeastern Conference (SEC) football student athletes (N = 18) the following positive factors of educational persistence: family/significant other influence, institutional commitment, teammate influence/peer acceptance, self-motivation, fraternity influence, and spirituality. This is juxtaposed with obstacles to positive academic performance, found in Gragg's study: unhealthy team subcultures, institutional barriers, racism, lack of positive interaction with campus and community constituents, and personal challenges. It is important to remember that much of the qualitative data synthesized in our chapter was conducted on predominantly white campuses. More qualitative research in the future should examine African American and other ethnic group student athlete experiences at historically black colleges and universities (HBCU's).

Lastly, the Scholar-Baller community at Arizona State University is examined as a single-institution self-study of the program since its implementation with significant results in academic retention, matriculation, and graduation rates. The Scholar-Baller Paradigm compels dramatic cultural change that transforms and unifies, when defining aesthetic understanding(s) in both research and everyday life. As Pugh and Bergin (2005) stated, "Transformative experience and aesthetic understanding both emphasize acting on subject matter ideas in everyday contexts and undergoing an expansion of perception and value" (p. 20). This transformative perception of self and worldview is more salient when there is synergy and transfer within the triangle of success—education, sport, and entertainment. The final section of this chapter presents a vision for the future of the previously analyzed topics.

The Future

On January 13, 2005, the "trinary" and triangle of success celebrated a collaborative moment. Scholar-Baller and its team of educators, Rush Philanthropic led by Ellen Haddigan and Russell Simmons, and the NCAA represented by Senior-Vice President Bernard Franklin all partnered together for a film screening of *Coach Carter* for over 300 urban and inner-city youth in New York City. Educational and critical dialogue followed, with a panel and group discussion about the influence of sport and entertainment on the educational aspirations of youth and young adults in America.

In the film *Coach Carter* (2005) many of the student athletes/players sported the latest name brands in urban hip-hop wear (Phat Farm, Sean John, Roca Wear, Ecko, and Nike). As we have articulated throughout this chapter, these identities are produced and consumed by the meanings and connotations that go with this type of attire—the baller and player lifestyle. By designing a cultural reward system through institutions like the NCAA and higher education, Scholar-Baller has the opportunity to symbolize academic excellence as well as athletic prowess. This type of campus and societal "coolness" in concert with America's cultural forces of entertainment (e.g., hip-hop, country music) and college athletics can shape new and progressive attitudes about education in modern society. This would enable students and student athletes to have at least a *common* meaning and perception to reach their goals. In essence, commerce will be used to highlight education while also being culturally salient to values typically learned through sport and entertainment.

The desires of youth and young adults in the modern world would be communicated in harmony while stretching across a boundary yet to be systematically embedded in the visceral cultures of sport and entertainment—education. This communication would enable the Scholar-Baller Paradigm to be more than a passing fad or traditional educational service announcement that lacks innovation and style. In order for this to transpire, Dr. Myles Brand's leadership of the Academic Reform Movement must continue to be taken seriously and enforced with a cultural sensibility for partnerships and alliances that are most influential in the lives of young people who participate in athletics and students in general.

Russell Simmons, the godfather of hip-hop, can continue to be a stakeholder in this Academic Reform Movement. Author and close friend of Simmons, Nelson George (1998), offered these words:

> Having cracked the forty mark in 1997, Russell is at one of those psychological crossroads where his relevance to contemporary hip-hop will be challenged, both by the constant emergence of new musical trends and by unpredictable cultural shifts. His many nonmusic initiatives are a response to the business opportunities hip-hop's maturation affords him. (p. 88)

Regardless of their success, Nelson George continues to challenge Simmons and other cultural leaders in the hip-hop communities to evolve. The potential synergy for a *unifying* message with college sports is only one idea of this (r)evolution. Both sport (e.g., NCAA, leisure activities, professional sport) and entertainment (e.g., hip-hop, video games, film) have the power and influence to positively and predictably shift cultural attitudes about their respective entities and more importantly education. However, it is impossible to predict all of the positive outcomes of this three-prong marriage of education, sport, and entertainment.

We do know as a society that not all young people are negative about the future and do aspire to opportunities that can liberate them as United States and global citizens. As West (2004) articulated, "Some young folk do persevere and prevail: those who are dissatisfied with mere material toys and illusions of security. They hunger for something more, thirst for something deeper. They want caring attention, wise guidance, and compassionate counsel. They desire individuality, community and society" (p. 177). Finally, it is time for education to gain ground in the sprint of sport and entertainment to reach the finish line of representation. Sport managers can make a difference in the "representation race" between academics and athletics to inform the public and broaden its perceptions about student athletes' accomplishments in the classroom and off the field of play. If we continue in this direction, our society may have the opportunity to mainstream and integrate the spectacle and substance of Scholar-Baller, a new blueprint for higher education, the NCAA, and society.

▲▼ Suggested Readings ▲▼

Bowen, D., & Levin, S. (2003). *Reclaiming the game: College sports and educational values.* Princeton, NJ: Princeton University Press.

Elligan, D. (2004). *Rap therapy: A practical guide for communicating with youth and young adults through rap music.* New York: Kensington, Publishing Corp.

George, N. *Hip-hop America.* New York: Penguin Putnam Inc.

Ginwright, S. (2004). *Black in school.* New York: Teachers College Press.

Marx, K. (1955). *Craft idiocy.* Out of print. On-line.

Meier, D. (1995). *The power of their ideas.* Boston, MA: Beacon Press Books.

Patillo-McCoy, M. (1999). *Black picket fences: Privilege and peril among the Black middle class.* Chicago: Chicago University Press.

Prosser, J. (1998). *Image-based research.* Bristol, PA: Falmer Press, Taylor & Francis Group.

Ross, C. (2004). *Race and sport: The struggle for equality on and off the field.* Ole Mississippi Press. Oxford, MS: University Press of Mississippi.

Sparks, D., & Robinson, S. K. (1999). *Lessons of the game.* Los Angeles, CA: Game Time Publishing.

Svare, B. (2004). *Reforming sports: Before the clock runs out.* Delmar, NY: Bordalice Press, Sports Reform Press.

Thelin, J. (1994). *Games colleges play: Scandal and reform in intercollegiate athletics.* Baltimore, MD: The Johns Hopkins University Press.

West, C. (2004). *Democracy matters.* New York: The Penguin Press.

White, H. (2003). *Believe to achieve.* Hilsboro, OR: Beyond Words Publishing.

▲▼ Movies ▲▼

Finding Forrester (2000)
Coach Carter (2005)
He Got Game (1998)
Varsity Blues (1997)
The Program (1993)

▲▼ Music ▲▼

Higher (1994). Ice Cube.
I Can (2002). Nasir Jones.
Drugs, Basketball and Rap (2005). Talib Kweli.
I Wish (1996). Skee-Lo.
It All Falls Down (2004). Kanye West.

▲▼ Study Questions ▲▼

1. What is the history of the Academic Reform Movement in higher education and how does the NCAA currently address this issue?

2. What is Scholar-Baller and how does it complement the Academic Reform Movement?

3. Explain the triangle of success and the importance of education, sport, and entertainment existing as one lifestyle and cultural approach to human excellence.

4. How has Arizona State University collaborated with the Scholar-Baller program and what results and patterns of behavior change have they seen?

5 How might Scholar-Baller influence the future of higher education, the NCAA, and entertainment?

References

Adler, P., & Adler, P. (1985). From idealism to pragmatic detachment: The academic performance of college athletes. *Sociology of Education, 58,* 241–250.

Allen, W. R., Bonous-Hammarath, M., & Teranishi, R. (2002). Stony the road we trod: The black struggle for higher education in California. *CHOICES,* University of California, Los Angeles.

Armstrong, K. L. (1998). Ten strategies to employ when marketing sport to Black consumers. *Sport Marketing Quarterly, 7*(3), 11–18.

Aronson, J., Fried, C. B., & Good, C. (2002). Reducing the effects of stereotype threat on African American college students by reshaping theories of intelligence. *Journal of Experimental Social Psychology, 38,* 113–125.

Astin, A. (1993a). *Assessment for excellence.* Phoenix, AZ: American Council on Education & The Oryx Press.

Astin, A. (1993b). *What matters in college?* San Francisco: Jossey-Bass.

Bourdieu, P. (1986). The forms of capital. In J. G. Richardson (Ed.), *Handbook of the theory and research for the sociology of education* (pp. 241–258). New York: Greenwood Press.

Boyd, T. (2002). *The new HNIC: The death of Civil Rights and the reign of hip-hop.* New York: NYU Press.

Bruening, J. E. (2000). *Phenomenal women: A qualitative study of silencing, stereotypes, socialization, and strategies for change in sport participation of African American female student athletes.* Doctoral dissertation, The Ohio State University, Columbus.

Burstyn, V. (1999). *The rites of men: Manhood, politics, and the culture of sport.* Toronto, Ontario: University of Toronto Press.

Chandler, T. J. L., & Goldberg, A. D. (1990). The academic All-American as vaunted adolescent role-identity. *Sociology of Sport Journal, 7,* 287–293.

Coleman, J. (1960). The adolescent subculture and academic achievement. *The American Journal of Sociology 65*(4), 337–347.

Comeaux, E. (2005). Environmental predictors of academic among student athletes in the revenue-sport sports of men's basketball and football. *The Sport Journal, 8* (ISSN: 1543-9518).

Comeaux, E., & Harrison, C. K. (under review). Conceptual model of Scholar Baller success: Implications for college persistence, theory, and practice in higher education.

Donnor, J. (2005a). Towards an interest-convergence in the education of African-American football student athletes in major college sports. *Race, Ethnicity, and Education 8*(1), 45–67.

Donnor, J. (2005b). *Going somewhere: Understanding the contributory role of teachers and parents in the secondary education of African American football student athletes.* Research paper abstract submitted to American Educational Research Association (AERA) Sports and Education.

Edwards, H. (2000). Crisis on the eve of Black athletes. *Society, 37*(3), 9–13.

Engstrom, C., & Sedlacek, W. (1991). A study of prejudice toward university student athletes. *Journal of Counseling and Development, 70,* 189–193.

Erickson, E. (1987). *The human life cycle.* In S. P. Schlein (Ed.), A way of looking at things: Selected papers from 1930–1985 (pp. 595–610). New York: Norton.

Franklin, B. (2005, March). *The NCAA Academic Reform Movement (ARM).* Presentation given to graduate class Higher Education (HED) 691 Educational Leadership and Diversity in Sport, Arizona State University, Tempe, Arizona.

Franklin, B. (2006, March). *College athletics as a model for promoting academic integrity in higher education.* Presentation given to graduate class Higher Education (HED) 691 Educational Leadership and Diversity in Sport, Arizona State University, Tempe, Arizona.

Gerdy, J. (2000). *Sports: The All-American addiction.* Oxford, MS: Ole Miss Press.

Gragg, D. (2003). *Factors that positively affect academic performance of African-American football student athletes who graduate from Southeastern Conference institutions.* Doctoral dissertation, University of Arkansas.

Grundy, P. (2001). *Learning to win: Sports, education, and social change.* Chapel Hill: University of North Carolina Press.

Hall, S. (2003). *Representation: Cultural representations and signifying practices.* London: Routledge.

Harrison, C. K. (1998). Themes that thread through society: Racism and athletic manifestation in the African American community. *Race Ethnicity and Education, 1,* 63–74.

Harrison, C. K. (2002). Scholar or baller: A photo and visual elicitation with student athletes. *NASPAJ, 8*(1), 66–81.

Harrison, C. K. (2004). Narratives of Scholar-Ballers. Robeson Center data set of student athletes.

Harrison, C. K., & Boyd, J. (2005). Scholar-Baller. *World Encyclopedia of Sport, 3,* Great Barrington, MA: Berkshire Publishing.

Hood, S. (2004, Summer). A journey to understand the role of culture in program evaluation: Snapshots and personal reflections of one African American evaluator. *New Directions for Evaluation, 102,* 21–37.

Hooks, B. (2004). *We real cool: Black men and masculinity.* New York: Routledge.

Keyes, C. (2004). *Rap music and street consciousness.* Urbana, IL: University of Illinois Press.

Lang, G., Dunham, R.G., & Alpert, G. P. (1988). Factors related to the academic success and failure of college football players: The case of the mental dropout. *Youth and Society, 20,* 209–222.

Lapchick, R. (2000). *Smashing barriers: Race and sport in the millennium.* Lanham, MD: Madison Books.

Lapchick, R. (2005). *Racial and Gender Report Card.* Orlando: University of Central Florida.

Lawrence, S. M. (2001). The African-American athlete's experience with race and sport: An existential-phenomenological investigation. Paper presented at the North American Society for the Sociology of Sport Annual Meeting in San Antonio, Texas, November, 2001.

Major, B., Quinton, W. J., McCoy, S. K., & Schmader, T. (2000). Reducing prejudice: The target's perspective. In S. Oskamp (Ed.), *Reducing prejudice and discrimination* (pp. 211–237). Mahwah, NJ: Lawrence Erlbaum Associates.

McIntrye, R. B., Paulson, R.M., & Lord, C.G. (2003). Alleviating women's mathematics stereotype through salience of group achievements. *Journal of Experimental Social Psychology, 39,* 83–90.

McNutt, K. (2002). *Hooked on hoops: Understanding Black youths' blind devotion to basketball.* Chicago, IL: African American Images.

NCAA (2005a). *Graduation Rates of Division I Athletics.* Indianapolis, IN: NCAA publications.

NCAA (2005b). *NCAA CHAMPS/Life Skills Pamphlet.* Indianapolis, IN: NCAA publications.

Nixon, H. (1985). The athlete as scholar in college: An exploratory test of four models. In A. Dunleavy, A. Miracle, & C. R. Rees (Eds.), *Studies in the sociology of sport.* Fort Worth, Texas: Texas Christian University Press.

Pascarella, E., & Terenzini, P. (1991). *How college affects students: Findings and insights from twenty years of research.* San Francisco: Jossey-Bass.

Petrie, T. A., & Russell, R .K. (1995). Academic and psychological antecedents of academic performance for minority and non minority college football players. *Journal of Counseling and Development, 73,* 615–662.

Pugh, K., & Bergin, D. (2005). The effect of schooling on students' out-of-school experience. *Educational Researcher, 34*(9), 15–23.

Rueda, R. (2004–05). An urban education view of culture and learning. *USC UrbanEd, Fall/Winter,* 20–25.

Sailes, G. (1993). An investigation of campus stereotypes: The myth of Black athletic superiority and the dumb jock stereotypes. *Sociology of Sport Journal, 10,* 88–97

Sedlacek, W., & Adams-Gaston, J. (1992). Predicting the academic success of student athletes using SAT and noncognitive variables. *Journal of Counseling and Development, 70,* 724–727.

Sellers, R. M. (1989, August). The role of motivation in the academic preparation of student athletes. Presented at the annual meeting of the Association of Black Sociologists, San Francisco.

Sellers, R. M., Kuperminc, R., & Wadell, A. (1991). Life experiences of black student athletes in revenue-producing sports: A descriptive empirical analysis. *The Academic Athletic Journal,* 20–38.

Sellers, R. M. (1992). Racial differences in the predictors of academic achievement of student athletes of Division I revenue-producing sports. *Sociology of Sport Journal, 1,* 46–51.

Settles, I. H., Sellers, R. M., & Damas, A. (2002). One role or two? The function of psychological separation in role conflict. *Journal of Applied Psychology, 87,* 574–582.

Simons, H., Van Rheenen, D., & Covington, H. (1999). Academic motivation and the student athlete. *Journal of College Student Development, 40*(20), 151–161.

Simons, H., & Van Rheenen, D. (2000). Noncognitive predictors of student athlete's academic performance. *Journal of College Reading and Learning, 30*(2), 167–193.

Sloan-Green, T. (1981). *Black women in sport.* Reston, VA: American Alliance of Health, Physical Education, Recreation and Dance.

Smith, Y. (2000). Sociohistorical influences on African American elite sportswomen. In D. Brooks and R. Althouse (Ed.), *Racism in college athletics* (pp. 173–197). Morgantown, WV: Fitness Information Technology.

Smith, R. (1988). *Sports and freedom: The rise of big-time college athletics.* New York: Oxford University Press.

Steele, C. (1997). A threat in the air: How stereotypes shape intellectual identity and performance. *American Psychologist, 52,* 613–629.

Steele, C. M., Spencer, S. J., & Aronson, J. (2002). Contending with group image: The psychology of stereotype and social identity threat. In M. P. Zanna (Ed.), *Advances in experimental social psychology* (Vol. 34, pp. 379–440). San Diego, CA: Erlbaum Publishers.

Stewart, J. (1998). *Paul Robeson: Artist and citizen.* New Brunswick, NJ: Rutgers University Press.

Stone, J., & Harrison, C.K. (in prep.). The dumb jock meets the Scholar-Baller: How stereotypes shape the academic performance of college student athletes. Review paper in preparation.

Suggs, W. (2001). Left behind: Title IX and Black women athletes. *Chronicle of Higher Education,* A35–A37.

Tierney, W. (1993). *Building communities of difference in higher education in the twenty-first century.* Westport, CT: Bergin & Garvey.

Tinto, V. (1975). Dropout from higher education: A theoretical synthesis of recent research. *Review of Educational Research 45,* 89–125.

Tinto, V. (1987). *Leaving college: Rethinking the causes and cures of student departure.* Chicago: University of Chicago Press.

Watterson, J. (2000). *College football: History, spectacle, controversy.* Baltimore, MD: Johns Hopkins University Press.

White, T. J., & Sedlacek, W. (1986). Noncognitive predictors: Grades and retention of specially admitted students. *The Journal of College Admissions, 3,* 20–23.

Willis, D. (1998). *The image and Paul Robeson.* In J. Stewart (ed.) Paul Robeson: Artist and citizen. New Brunswick, NJ: Rutgers University Press.

Yopyk, D., & Prentice, D. (2005). Am I an athlete or student? Identity salience and stereotype threat in student athletes. *Basic and Applied Social Psychology, 27*(4), 329–336.

O thello Harris' essay, "*Taboo*'s Explanation of Black Athlete Dominance: More Fiction than Fact," focuses on the contention that "blacks have racially linked genetic advantages over whites." Harris systematically refutes claims that African Americans possess biological characteristics that are advantageous for sport performance. As Harris sees it, race is a social construct and, as such, hardly qualifies as a universal biogenetic foundation with which to explain differential patterns of sport participation, let alone differential expectations and treatment of athletes. In the end, Harris is deeply concerned by the ease with which sports managers, sports announcers, and others in the business foster stereotypes, many of which are then used by fans to explain sports performance.

CHAPTER

10

TABOO'S

EXPLANATION

OF BLACK

ATHLETE

DOMINANCE:

MORE FICTION

THAN FACT

OTHELLO HARRIS

Abstract ▼ I focus on the contention that blacks have racially linked genetic advantages over whites by reviewing the basis for the persistence of such claims that are made, particularly by "claims-makers" such as Jon Entine's *Taboo* and their agencies, refuting claims that blacks possess biological characteristics advantageous for sport performance. Race is a social construct; its application to an athletes' performance is best understood as a product of specific historic periods and particular political practices. Continued efforts to use race in constructing images of athletes should concern sports administrators, broadcasters and announcers, sports managers and others who make decisions about personnel and associates who make attributions about sport performances with obvious references to biological race.

▲▽▲▽▲▽

African American males are so conspicuous as outstanding participants in many of the major American sports that countless observers have come to equate "athlete" with African Americans. In fact, the term athlete is often used as code for "black" by coaches and announcers when describing past and expected player performances.[1]

Questions about how we can account for the disproportionate sports excellence by a group of individuals are old and enduring. Before boxing became the domain of African Americans and Latinos, Irish, Jewish, and Italian men were believed to dominate boxing for presumably the same reasons—they had more "natural" talent. Social Darwinist thought during the late 19th and early 20th centuries served as scientific justification for the exclusion of African Americans from many American sports (Harris, 1997).

---

1. Sports announcers often use "athlete" or some derivation of the term to describe African Americans. As an example, during the 2004/2005 NCAA season, Jay Bilas, an ESPN commentator for college basketball, rarely discussed an important upcoming or past game without referring to one or more of the African American players as "long and athletic." This descriptor is rarely used for white athletes, especially white American athletes.

Key Terms

▼Race▲

▼Biological race▲

▼Civil Rights movement▲

▼Race as a social construct▲

▼Racial purity▲

▼Social Darwinism▲

▼*Plessy vs. Ferguson*▲

▼One-drop rule▲

▼Self-fulfilling prophecy▲

▼Pygmalion coach▲

During the late 1800s and the early 1900s much of the western world believed in Social Darwinism—the idea that natural selection served to elevate some groups into positions of dominance, while simultaneously subordinating others (Jaret, 1995). According to sociologist Herbert Spencer, who coined the phrase, humans were enmeshed in a process of "survival of the fittest," (Gonzales, 1993) with whites on top. Pseudoscientific studies which reported that African Americans are less intelligent than whites because of various biological differences, such as smaller brains with less complex convolutions and lower, narrower frontal lobes, were used to support the belief that whites were superior to other groups (Feagin & Feagin, 1996). Furthermore, whites' natural superiority was not confined to intellectual pursuits; rather it extended to athletic ability, as whites were also believed to be physically superior to African Americans. It is for this reason that many believed that a black challenger to the heavyweight title was an unlikely occurrence. During that time, Irish boxers such as John L. Sullivan, "Gentleman" Jim Corbett, and Bob Fitzsimmons, who dominated the top ranks of their profession, were believed to illustrate the "fact" that whites were endowed with athletic skills that African Americans lacked. In later years, the same beliefs would prevail about Jewish and Italian boxers.

When John Taylor, an African American track star from the University of Pennsylvania, competed in the 1908 Olympics, he was said to be outstanding because he was built more like a white runner (Wiggins, 1997). Equating athletic talent with whites was true not only of the boxing and track events. Prior to Jackie Robinson's re-integration of professional baseball,[2] one of the reasons given for the exclusion of African Americans from "America's game" was black ballplayers' lack of talent (Tygiel, 1997). However, as African Americans gained prominence as athletes, the search for a race-based explanation for athletic accomplishment resulted in a different conclusion: they were believed to be outstanding because they were black. Now, what needed to be determined was how they differed—what was the source of their sporting prowess? In the search for answers, African American athletes, such as the great cyclist Major Taylor, who raced in the late 19th and early 20th centuries, and the incomparable 1936 Olympian Jesse Owens, were probed and measured by scientists eager to examine whether African Americans had distinctive physical attributes including, but not limited to: a longer or shorter leg (either would be interpreted to sufficiently determine an advantage for black athletes); the size and shape of the calf muscle; the length and breadth of the foot; the presence of a protruding heel bone; and the size of the thigh. After comparing Owens to his athletic peers, the noted anthropologist W. Montague Cobb (1936) concluded, "There is not a single physical characteristic which all the Negro stars in question have in common which would definitely identify them as Negro" (p. 56). This did not seem to satisfy those who felt otherwise.

Three decades after Cobb's observation, African Americans, who were already a sizable share of the professional boxers, began to appear in much larger numbers in other major sports such as basketball, baseball, and football. Their pres-

---

2. Jackie Robinson is widely credited with breaking the color line in professional baseball and/or with being the first African American to play major league (white) baseball. Although his accomplishment is a momentous historical event, Native American and Latino baseball players preceded him in the majors (Tygiel, 1997), and Moses "Fleetwood" Walker, an African American, was a major leaguer some 60 years before Robinson suited up for the Brooklyn Dodgers (Zang, 1995).

ence and performances also increased in the Olympic Games. (David Wiggins, in *Glory Bound*, argues that the debate about the source of black athletic performance seemed to increase each Olympic year.) This recognition of the increase in stellar performances by black athletes prompted Martin Kane (1971), a senior writer for *Sports Illustrated*, to devote a lengthy discussion to the physiological, psychological, and historical advantages enjoyed by African Americans that make them better suited for sport. Kane's thesis was confuted by Edwards (1972) and public debates of that sort seemed to fade, at least for a short time.

However, during the decade of the 1980s, several events converged that reopened the public discussion about race and athletic performance. In April, 1987, Al Campanis was invited to appear on the television show *Nightline* in a celebration of the 40th anniversary of Jackie Robinson's historic inclusion as a major league baseball player. Campanis was vice-president for player personnel for the Los Angeles Dodgers, the team that had selected Robinson to be the first African American major leaguer in the 20th century. But the celebration turned awkward for many, and appalling to some, when Campanis was asked by (host) Ted Koppel to explain why there were no black managers, general managers, or owners in professional baseball. Campanis stated:

> I truly believe [African Americans] may not have some of the necessities to be, let's say a field manager or perhaps a general manager . . . why are black men or black people not good swimmers? Because they don't have the buoyancy . . . They are outstanding athletes, very God-gifted, and they're wonderful people . . . They're gifted with great musculature and various other things. They are fleet of foot. And this is why there are a lot of black major league ballplayers. Now as far as having the background to become club presidents or presidents of a bank . . . I don't know. (Harris, 1991, p. 25).

Less than one year later, sports personality, Jimmy "the Greek" Snyder, commenting on race and sports, declared African Americans to be better athletes than whites because of breeding. During slavery, he argued, "the slave owner would breed his big black with his big woman so the he could have a big black kid" (Harris, 1991, p. 25). From this breeding, Snyder argued incoherently, "the black athlete" inherited bigger thighs that made him a superior athlete.

In 1989, Tom Brokaw hosted (and Jon Entine produced) an NBC special, *Black Athletes: Fact and Fiction*, which purported to examine why black athletes are successful. Near the end of the show, Brokaw concluded that the reasons for black athletes' success were "complicated and sensitive," even as he tried to reduce the explanations to a physiological one—that "blacks have a genetic edge."

Laurel Davis was one of a number of scholars who disagreed with Brokaw's presentation and conclusion. Davis (1990) argued that the preoccupation with exploring genetic differences linked to race is racist, as it is "founded on, and naturalizes racial categories as fixed and unambiguous biological realities, obscuring the political processes of racial formation" (p. 179). Another scholarly critique of the show by Mathisen and Mathisen (1991) argued that Brokaw's claims were racist, as was his presentation of the "data." They allege that although Brokaw's claims suggested he would be objective, his insistence on the conclusion that blacks have a genetic edge, the way he presented and validated bioscientists' claims over others', and his refusal to consider contrary evidence—even when presented on his show—all indicate his uncompromising bias in the direction of a physiological explanation (Mathisen & Mathisen, 1991).

However, not all feedback was critical of the show and its conclusions. For example, Roger Stanton, who published *Basketball Weekly* and *Football News*—two outlets whose subjects were undoubtedly primarily black—responded to *Black Athletes* by declaring black athletes as lacking in discipline. They are, he said, unwilling to work hard, which disqualifies many of them for the quarterback position. He further stated that "if you gave 20 white college players and 20 black college players an IQ test, the whites would outshine the blacks every time" (Harris, 1991, p. 25). What, then, would be the source of black athletes' continued dominant performances in the sports that Stanton covers? It appears that he, like Brokaw, Snyder, and Campanis, believes that there are biological advantages enjoyed by black athletes. If not, it would be difficult to explain, using Stanton's claims, how African Americans could be unintelligent and undisciplined, while turning in many or most of the superb athletic performances in some sports.

One can see from the above that there continues to be interest in explaining black athletic performance as a biological reality. Interestingly, however, there seem to be few who show much concern with understanding the biological bases of athletic performances of once racial, now ethnic groups (e.g., Italians, Jews, and Irish), and few who seem to be stumped by Australians' and Germans' domination of sports such as swimming or Canadians' continued domination of professional hockey—even as professional hockey has drawn many more players from Europe. Yet, the question of black dominance in sport is still perplexing to some.

Taboo

One of the most recent attempts to return to a biological answer to "racial variations" in success at some sports is Jon Entine's *Taboo*. First, it should be stated that Entine set out to "prove" or to provide incontrovertible evidence that blacks have racially linked genetic advantages over whites.[3] Entine begins by stating that "elite athletes who trace all or most of their ancestry to Africa are by and large better than the competition" (p. 4). In the next paragraph, after dismissing social explanations, he presents his thesis for the first time: "The decisive variable is in our genes—the inherent differences between populations shaped over many thousand of years of evolution" (p. 4). His suppositions include the following:

▼ Blacks have innate advantages over whites, Asians, and Native Americans. Their specific advantage depends on whether they trace their ancestry to West or East Africa.

▼ Elite athletes who trace all or most of their ancestry to Africa are, by and large, better than the competition.

▼ Black Hispanic ballplayers are the most likely to make it to the big leagues, followed by players of mixed black and white heritage, then whites, with Mexicans having the toughest time.

Entine also makes what he considers to be important distinctions between people

---

3. With the exception of "Hispanics," Entine largely fails to discuss where other groups—those who are neither black nor white—fit in his racial sports hierarchy.

of West African ancestry and East African descendants: According to him, those of West African ancestry have:

▼ less subcutaneous fat on arms and legs,

▼ more lean body and more muscle mass,

▼ smaller chest cavities,

▼ narrower hips and lighter calves,

▼ a longer arm span,

▼ faster patellar tendon reflex,

▼ greater body density, and

▼ more fast-twitch muscles.

These differences, Entine claims, make "West African blacks" superior in anaerobic activities, which include sprinting, football, and basketball. These differences are also barriers to their success at swimming and "cold-weather and endurance sports" (p. 269).

By contrast, East African descendants have:

▼ superior fatigue resistance coded into their genes,

▼ more efficiency as runners,

▼ more durability as runners, and

▼ perfect aerobic potential as runners.

East Africans, Entine claims, are genetically programmed for endurance events but lack the explosiveness and jumping ability of their African brothers from the west of the continent.

Thus, we are told that "nearly all of the sprints are won by runners of West African descent" (p. 31).[4] But, how is Entine able to determine the racial make-up of "black" athletes? It seems highly unlikely that he has investigated the origins of the hundreds of athletes who he infers trace their ancestry to West Africa. Nor is there evidence that Entine has even bothered to ask each of, or most of, these athletes about their ancestry. Nowhere is there evidence that Entine has gathered—scientifically or even "unscientifically"—data on the proportion of each athlete's ancestry that comes from Africa (or Europe or Asia for that matter). This is an especially significant omission in multi-racial and multi-ethnic societies.

Historically, in America and elsewhere, there has been much miscegenation as a result of marital and non-marital unions. Given the large admixture of much of the world's population, and especially the forced and voluntary mixing of residents of the United States, how do the labels "black" and "white" tell you conclusively about one's genetic make-up? How does Entine know how "black" athletes

---

4. Entine also claims that genetic advantages cause East and North Africans to dominate the middle and long distance races, even as he points out that "Mexicans, mostly Native Indians, are strongest at the longer races, 10,000 meters and the marathon . . . [and] East Asians—Chinese, Koreans and Japanese—are competitive at the event requiring the most endurance, the marathon" (p. 34). This exemplifies the way Entine ignores his own "findings" in favor of a narrow genetic explanation for his thesis. What, genetically, do East Africans, North Africans, Mexicans, Chinese, Koreans, and Japanese have that whites lack, which makes them all (except whites) excel at distance running? Moreover, why the decision to ignore a "racial explanation" for Mexican, Chinese, Korean, and Japanese excellence in distance running in a treatise obsessed with racial explanations for sport performance?

trace their ancestry? It appears he uses the time-worn definition of race, which, simply put, implies that "you know one when you see one."

Who Is Black? (Or White Women Can Have Black Babies, but Black Women Can't Have White Babies.)

According to Entine, most of us can determine one's ancestry by looking at that person. To support this statement, he provides a quote from a physiology professor who claims, "Given one person each from Sweden, Nigeria, and Japan . . . none of us would have any trouble deciding at a glance which person was from which country" (p. 96). While this might seem, on the surface, to be true, in fact, many people might have trouble determining the country of origin (as indicated above) and one's ancestry by simply looking at an individual. The statement above assumes that one's ancestry is written on one's face (or breasts, buttocks, or penis, to name some of the other features Entine uses in his book to illustrate "human racial variation"). In other words, for Entine, people are distinctly different, thus ethnic and/or racial identification are not problematic. But this statement should cause one to question, are there no "white Nigerians," "Canadian Japanese," or "black Swedes," to use a few examples, all of whom could be mixtures of two or more groups? To ask the question a different way, is the popular actress Charlize Theron *either* white or South African but not both? More to the point, how do we determine racial groups? What criteria do we employ to assign individuals to different groups, and how does this reflect biological rather than social definitions?

Entine adopts the beliefs that spawned the many uses of biological race: that human groups are different by nature, and that there is a line of separation between them. It is these beliefs that at one time held that Americans of Irish, Jewish, and Italian descent were separate "races." This once popular "scientific" belief has all but disappeared from most Americans' thinking and those once distinct racial groups are now seen as a part of the larger, more diverse "white" racial category. Yet, the search for biological race and racial differences continues, including the idea of a "pure" race.

This concern with racial purity is demonstrated by the one-drop rule. During post-Reconstruction America, whites, especially in the South, became increasingly anxious about ensuring racial purity (Davis, 1991). How would one classify the offspring of interracial unions? In places where children were required to take on the "race" of the mother, this was not a problem for the children of black women and white men—they were black like their mothers. Thus, in this context, *black women and white men had black children* and racial purity was unchallenged. Or course, these children were *biologically* just as white as they were black, but their classification was black.

During the early 20th century, some states determined that the predominance of blood must be white for one to be classified as white (as in three-quarters white equals white, but one-half white did not equal white). Hence, the offspring of interracial unions were black, irrespective of the race of the mother. When most Southern states adopted the one-drop rule, any drop of black blood, any black ancestor, made one black (Davis, 1991).[5]

---

5. It appears that this one-drop rule—one black ancestor makes you black—applies only to African Americans. One Greek ancestor does not make one Greek.

When Homer Plessy, who was reported to be seven-eighths white, was denied seating in the white passenger section of a railway car in Louisiana, the preponderance of white in his background did not matter. Irrespective of his "white appearance" and despite the fact that he thought he was indiscernible from whites, the fact that he had any black heritage at all made him black. From this, one could expect that many people who are considered black are likely as much white as black, if not more so. This would seem to have major implications for any findings that "genetic" or even "phenotypic" factors determine race and racial differences in performance, since genetic and phenotypic factors have not been the overriding factors in assigning individuals to racial categories.

Part of the problem with seeing white and seeing black has to do with how we see black and white—that is, what we look for. Most of us learn to look for any sign of blackness as an indication that one is black. However, having one white feature (whatever we take black and white features to be) does not result in defining one as white, as Homer Plessy and later Susie Phipps found out.[6]

One of the major flaws of Entine's work is that he adopts, rather than contests, the one-drop rule, even as he says skin color and facial features are problematic in determining race. For example, he purports to list the ancestry of world record holders in running events. All of them, he claims, are from Africa—West Africa, East Africa, or North Africa. But, given the way "black" has been and continues to be determined, many of these athletes are likely as much from "European stock" as they are African. Entine fails to consider this as he attempts to demarcate "African stock" and "European stock." It appears that he uses skin color (and the one-drop rule) to determine one's race.

That skin color is a poor indicator of one's racial makeup can be indicated by the variation in skin color—sometimes, great variation—by siblings of the same two parents. It is not unusual in African American families (at least as socially determined) to find brothers and sisters who vary from very light complexion to very dark complexion. This is true, also of non-black families, although we are often not attuned to seeing differences in color among those lightest in color. Still, if skin color is supposed to tell us something about how African or European one is, wouldn't darker black athletes dominate lighter black athletes in all anaerobic activities? This, obviously, is not the case.

The one-drop rule is further illustrated in *Taboo* (chapter eight), in which Entine, naming Tiger Woods a "mutt," claims that his "father, Earl, is half African American, one-quarter American Indian, and one-quarter Chinese. His mother, Kutilda, is half Thai, one-quarter Chinese and one-quarter white" (p. 98). Then Entine claims that to African Americans (but curiously not to whites or other groups) and to most of the media Tiger Woods is black. Entine's silence on Woods' racial status—indeed on Tiger's genetic makeup—is in fact not surprising given his use of the one-drop rule throughout his book. And, Entine is not alone; in fact many people, especially in America, use the one-drop rule when determining the racial makeup of athletes (present and former) such as Herman Edwards,

6. Homer Plessy, a Louisianan, was the plaintiff in the famous United States Supreme Court case in 1896 that allowed states to continue the practice of having separate (but supposedly equal) accommodations for whites and African Americans. Nine decades later, Susie Phipps was denied "white" classification because in Louisiana one was designated "black" if he or she was $\frac{1}{32}$nd black—that is, had one black great, great grandparent.

Derek Jeter, James Blake, Tiger Woods, and Hines Ward. All are or have been described as black athletes, although the former three have white mothers and the latter two have mothers of Asian descent. Do they get their racial status from their
fathers? If Edwards, Jeter, and Blake had white fathers and black mothers, would
their classification be different? Not likely, because it is widely believed that "white
women can have black babies, but black women can't have white babies." This is an
extension and continuation of the practice of white racial purity—anything that
is not "pure white" is not white. White is only white while black can include white.
This kind of logic may indicate much about social race, but it has obvious shortcomings and little utility for discerning biological race, which Entine attempts to
do throughout his book.

Race as a Social Construct

Race is a meaningful construct, but it falls miserably short as a biological construct.
Biological race is based on the idea that groups of people have different biological
characteristics that we can use to divide them into different races. To do this, we key
on physical types, believing that people with different physical appearances belong to different groups. However, this presents two significant problems. First,
the "markers" that we use for physical types are arbitrary, not universal. By way of
example, in the United States, skin color and the shape of one's lips are important, but in Latin America hair texture, eye color, and stature are indicators of
"race" (Ritzer, Kammeyer, & Yetman, 1987). Why these markers? Why would skin
color tell you more about one's race—biologically—than, for example, the length
and shape of one's fingers or the thickness of one's eyebrows? What makes skin
color, for Americans and some others, the important determinant of race? Biologically, there is no justification for using one set of markers over another since no
markers allow us to clearly draw racial boundaries with any certainty.

Second, there is great variation within any one group on any characteristic
we (could) use to determine race. That is, there is no characteristic that is found
in one race but not others. Entine says eyes differ between races, but eye color and
eye shape vary, often greatly, within members of the same "racial group." Furthermore, eye shape and eye color, much like other markers, cross "racial groups. Begley (1995) points out that epicanthic eye-fold, or "Asian eye" is prevalent among
!Kung San (Bushmen) as well as Japanese and Chinese. Another "Asian characteristic," the shovel-shaped incisors, is also found among Swedes and Native Americans. One could also use the presence of the sickle-cell trait (which would pair Italians and Greeks with equatorial Africans), blood type, or lactose tolerance as ways
to classify races and we would end up with very different "races" (Begley, 1995),
that would be no more or less valid than our use of skin color to determine genetic
differences among groups. Although they might result in different definitions of
"race," they would (like skin color) make the concept of biological race problematic.

Societies take what they deem to be important physical differences (individual differences are ignored when making "racial distinctions") and create racial
categories from them. The choice is arbitrary, yet consequential, for as Thomas
and Thomas (1928) warned, "if men define situations as real, they are real in their
consequences" (p. 572). Thus, whether or not race has biological bases, if people

believe there are differences between groups, they will act on those perceived differences. These different perceptions may result in different expectations not only for different individuals but also for different groups of individuals.

Sport offers an interesting setting for the illustration of how others' expectations affect behavior. Horn, Lox and Labrador (2001), in a discussion of the self-fulfilling prophecy, argue that coaches develop expectations for athletes based, in part, on personal cues such as race, ethnicity, gender, and socioeconomic status. Coaches' expectations influence their treatment of athletes. For example, the Pygmalion coach will spend less time and less quality time with athletes he or she does not believe to be talented. This coach will also differ with regard to the type and frequency of feedback provided. Low expectancy athletes will receive less frequent, less appropriate, and less beneficial feedback. Thus, they conclude, coaches' feedback and expectations may be the cause of, not just the correct prediction of, athletes' behavior. Therefore, the differences we see in sport performance may be a reflection of coaches' and others' expectations, not necessarily real or "natural" differences in ability. And, this is only one of a number of social factors that affect sporting practices.

Any purported racial explanation of sport performance that does not take into account social factors—how race is determined socially and how socially determined race has an impact on differential expectations and treatment of athletes—does little to advance our understanding of patterns of sport participation. Explanations of that sort rely on archaic, often primeval hypotheses about race and behavior. Race is not a static biological phenomenon. Rather, it is an evolving historical construct rooted in struggles over power. To reduce race to genotype is misguided. To equate race, based on genotype, with athletic skill is absurd.

Confusion and Contradictions

One of the major problems with *Taboo* is that Entine presents sprinting and distance running (and baseball, basketball, boxing, etc.) as purely physical activities. They are, very much, social activities. They depend on social factors, including the availability of resources and how those resources are distributed or made available differently, as well as the encouragement, discouragement, and expectations of others. Writers such as Entine would have us believe that people are equally exposed to activities, training, expectations, and rewards but people of African descent are better able to take advantage of these activities because of physical distinctiveness.[7] However, it is a mistake to reduce human behavior to biological differences. As Coakley reminds us, "the effects of genes cannot be disassociated from the environment in which other factors influence the expression of those effects . . . [because] genes do not exist and operate in environmental vacuums" (2001, p. 250).

---

7. Even a purely economic explanation for "race" differences in sport participation fails to adequately capture the diversity within any one "racial" or "ethnic" group. For example, those who seek to explain the paucity of African Americans as golfers, hockey players, tennis players, figure skaters, and so forth, often claim that African Americans lack the wealth and resources to participate in these activities. While wealth and resources may help to explain this difference, they fail to account for the great range in wealth and resources among African Americans. In other words, while African Americans tend to have lower incomes and less wealth in comparison to whites, there are many African Americans who are wealthier than most whites and some are wealthier than nearly all whites. (This group would include persons such as Oprah Winfrey, Russell Simmons, Bob Johnson, and so forth.)

Taboo also suffers from a number of other problems. These would include the author's confusion about important concepts and numerous contradictions in his work. I begin with a discussion about conceptual obscurity.

Although Entine's book proclaims the significance of race in sport performances—the decisive variable, he says, is in our genes—he is unable to determine what constitutes race. To quote Entine:

> Race—based on ancestry and marked by skin color, ethnicity and geography—is a fuzzy concept. This fuzziness is compounded by the historical reality that theories about race have been frequently superficial and almost always reflective of a social agenda, whether stated or unrecognized. (p. 9)

Thus, Entine appears to understand that race is not measurable in the way that income, education, and other variables can be specified. He further seems to understand that racial markers and the ideologies that buttress them are the products of specific historical periods and particular political practices. One would expect this to be followed by a critique of the existing beliefs about race as evident and unclouded. Instead, sadly, Entine exhibits an uncritical acceptance of the very ideas he appeared to be prepared to challenge by insisting that race ("a fuzzy concept") is the determinative factor in sports performance. Later in the book, while defending "the fuzzy logic of race," Entine says that while "races reflect a continuous biological reality, they are not a discontinuous classificatory system. The boundaries are always blurry" (p. 110). Yet, Entine seems clear in his ability to designate individuals as descendants of West Africa (and he distinguishes them from descendants of East Africa) on the basis of skin color.

This leads to a second example of conceptual confusion. Entine acknowledges that phenotypes are confusing markers of race and provides, as an example, the range in skin color of Africans from white to ebony. In Entine's words, "the most conspicuous of traits, skin pigmentation, dominated the views of late eighteenth century scientists as it does our popular consciousness today" (p. 101). Despite this confession, Entine feels comfortable making unfettered claims about race and sport using phenotypes as his mechanism for determining, in an uncomplicated way, who descends from which part of the world.

His use of phenotypes is, indeed, confusing given that physical appearance often masks (or highlights) some, or even much of one's background. In other words, as was the case with Homer Plessy, what we see in an individual may be little more than a portion of that individual's makeup, often the portion that we deem (socially) significant. This tells us little about one's genetic makeup—which is the basis of Entine's argument. Thus, the use of phenotypes to stand for genetic differences between races is untenable.

One of the most glaring problems with Entine's book is that he ignores, often without comment, evidence that contradicts his findings. For example, Entine asserts that sport is a natural laboratory where innate differences are on display. Since running requires no special skills or coaching, he claims, the decisive factor in running performance is in our genes.

Yet, he fails to adequately address European and Asian dominance of some women's track events. As St. Louis asks, "Why are the women's Olympic 100 meter finals not all black events? Why are we unable to trace the 'racial ancestry' of all the holders of women's world track running records to Africa?" (2003, p. 81).

Entine's superficial coverage of this finding leaves him making a few social attributions: black females have had to battle sexism and racism, and East Germans used performance-enhancing drugs.[8] This raises numerous questions about Entine's assertions. How is sport a "natural laboratory" when clearly other factors—including drugs, nutrition, opportunities, resources, and so forth—affect sport performance? Why would social factors, some of which Entine briefly mentions, be confined to female athletic performance?

The challenges faced by African American females are very different from those faced by African American men and by white (and other) women. But, in part, they reflect a combination of racial and gendered attitudes about the recruitment, retention, coaching, and training of groups of individuals. If practices resulting from these attitudes have, for years, denied opportunities for African American females, wouldn't social practices such as the preference for recruiting and training Latino men for baseball or African American men in some sports also affect sport performance?

Another example of the way Entine ignores contradictory evidence is his assertion that Chinese women, too, are excellent at middle distance running. Kenyans, he declares, have innate talent. Why only Kenyans? Why is there no assertion of innate talent that allows Chinese women to outrun Europeans, Mexicans, and others?

In the end, Entine is never able precisely to define race (the foundation for his argument), to specify which traits allow us to divide populations into "racial categories" or which traits people of African descent have that others lack (even as he claims there are two different kinds of Africans), or to identify "African traits" that lead specifically to excellence in sprints, distance running, football, basketball, baseball, and boxing.[9] Thus, his work on the racial/genetic basis of sport performance is more fiction than fact. This should concern sports managers, sports administrators and others who make decisions about sports personnel, sports announcers who often use race in constructing images of athletes, and sports fans and others who make attributions about sport performances with obvious or subtle references to biological race.

▲▼ Suggested Readings ▲▼

Davis, F. J. (1991). *Who Is Black? One nation's definition.* University Park, PA: Penn State Press.

St. Louis, B. (2003). Sport, genetics, and the "natural athlete": The resurgence of racial science. *Body and Society, 9*(2), 75–95.

---

8. African American athletes, both male and female, have been accused of using or have been found to have used performance-enhancing drugs. Yet, for Entine, this does not raise questions about black "natural" advantages in sport.

9. Even if one wanted to accept the argument that West Africans have more fast-twitch fiber, could that possibly account for the various activities black players are involved in as offensive linemen, defensive linemen, running backs, receivers, cornerbacks, quarterbacks, linebackers, and so on in football, not to mention the many skills required of athletes in the other sports mentioned above?

▲▼ Study Questions ▲▼

1. What is the difference between race as a biological construct and race as a social construct?

2. What constitutes "white" in America? What constitutes "black" in America? How do these constructs challenge the idea of biological race?

3. What are some of the problems authors such as Entine have when trying to argue that differences in sports performances reflect biological (racial) differences?

References

Begley, S. (1995, February, 13). Three is not enough. *Newsweek*, pp. 67–69.

Cobb, W. M. (1936). Race and runners. *The Journal of Health and Physical Education* (Jan.), 3–7, 52–56.

Davis, L. R. (1990). The articulation of difference: White preoccupation with the question of racially linked genetic differences among athletes. *Sociology of Sport Journal, 7*(2), 179–187.

Davis, F. J. (1991). *Who is Black? One nation's definition.* University Park, PA: Penn State Press.

Edwards, H. (1972). The myth of the racially superior athlete. *Intellectual Digest* 2 (March), 58–60.

Entine, J. (2000). Taboo: Why black athletes dominate sports and why we are afraid to talk about it. New York: Perseus Group Books.

Feagin, J. R., & Feagin, C. B. (1996). *Racial and ethnic relations* (5th ed.). Upper Saddle River, NJ: Prentice-Hall.

Gonzales, J. L., Jr. (1993). *Racial and ethnic groups in America* (2nd ed.). Dubuque, Iowa: Kendall/Hunt Publishing Co.

Harris, O. (1991). The image of the African American in psychological journals, 1895–1923, *Black Scholar, 21*(4), 25–29.

Harris, O. (1997). The role of sport in the Black community. *Sociological Focus, 30*(4), 311–319.

Horn, T. S., Lox, C. L., & Labrador, F. (1998). The self-fulfilling prophecy theory: When coaches' expectations become reality. In J. M. Williams (Ed.), *Applied psychology: Personal growth to peak performance* (pp. 63–81). Mountain View, California: Mayfield.

Kane, M. (1971). An assessment of "Black is best." *Sports Illustrated, 34* (February 1), 18–32.

Mathisen, J. A., & Mathisen, G. S. (1991). The rhetoric of racism in sport: Tom Brokaw revisited. *Sociology of Sport Journal, 8*(2),168–177.

Ritzer, G., Kammeyer, K. C. W., & Yetman, N. R. (1987). *Sociology: Experiencing a changing society* (3rd ed.). Boston: Allyn and Bacon, Inc.

St. Louis, B. (2003). Sport, genetics, and the "natural athlete": The resurgence of racial science. *Body and Society, 9*(2): 75–95.

Thomas, W. I., & Thomas, D. S. (1928). *The child in America: Behavior problems and programs.* New York: Alfred A. Knopf.

Tygiel, J. (1997). *Baseball's great experiment: Jackie Robinson and his legacy.* NY: Oxford University Press.

Wiggins, D. K. (1997). *Glory bound: Black athletes in White America.* Syracuse, NY: Syracuse University Press.

Zang, D. (1995). *Fleet Walker's divided heart: The life of baseball's first black major leaguer.* Lincoln, NE: University of Nebraska Press.

In the last chapter of the section, Louis Harrison, Jr., and Leonard Moore explore differences in racial identity and athletic identity of white (termed "European" Americans) and African American athletes. Equipped with theoretic underpinnings of a black identity development process, they explore the socialization of African Americans, a process called *Nigrescence*, which allows us to understand a transformation of perception and self-evaluation from Euro- to Afro-centric identity. In the authors' terms, this is the metamorphic process by which African Americans "become black." Further, the degree to which individuals identify with the athletic role or how individuals label themselves as athletes represents the concept of athletic identity. The researchers ask: How do these identities reflect each other? Is there a difference among whites and African Americans? Does the socialization process progress evenly, smoothly, or can it be stalled, and what are the consequences? Harrison and Moore theorize that the interactions of these identity constructs have a significant influence on sport *preference*, on patterns of *participation*, and possibly on *performance* itself.

CHAPTER
11

WHO AM I?
RACIAL
IDENTITY,
ATHLETIC
IDENTITY,
AND THE
AFRICAN
AMERICAN
ATHLETE

LOUIS
HARRISON, Jr.
AND
LEONARD N.
MOORE

▼ ▲▼ ▲▼ ▲▼ ▲▼ ▲▼ ▲
Key Terms
▼ Racial identity ▲
▼ Athletic identity ▲
▼ African Americans ▲

Abstract ▼ This chapter is an attempt to integrate and apply literature on African American racial identity theory and related investigations in the development of sport and physical activity in African American youth. Studies isolating race as a biological or genetic variable, particularly with regard to sport superiority, have a historically inauspicious and questionable reputation (Wiggins, 1997). The over representation of African Americans in particular sports phenomena has been researched via genetics, anthropocentric measures, physiology, sociology, and psychology. The development of this vast array of theories testifies to the interest in, speculation on, and complexity of this phenomenon. This chapter provides yet another compelling perspective.

This psycho-social attempt at an explanation of the African American sports experience interconnects research from racial identity research (Cross, 1995) and athletic identity (Brewer, Raalte, & Linder, 1993). This chapter examines the Cross model of African American racial identity, and its relation to the development of athletic identity, and gives theoretical implications for the development of sport and physical activity in African American youth.

Introduction

Studies isolating race as a biological or genetic variable, particularly with regard to sport superiority, have a historically inauspicious and questionable reputation (Wiggins, 1997). Even geneticists reiterate the fact that their research does not subscribe to the idea of race as a biological or genetic identity ("Census, Race & Science," 2000). Speaking from the geneticists' perspective, the lines of demarcation between races have been profoundly and increasingly blurred. Only relatively recently have the terms biracial and multiracial been accepted as demographic indicators that give at best imprecise clues as to the racial lineage of an individual. Hidden is the fact that most if not all of the people in this country can be classified as biracial or multiracial if an accurate ancestral trace is performed.

In the U.S. there are some classified as African American who have more features common to Europeans than to Africans. The study of the genetic and biological basis for race has been deemed fruitless and is composed of "loose and leaky" categories that defy logic and are inherently inconsistent (Dole, 1995). According to LaVeist (1996), race is a social, rather than a biological factor that is based on somewhat superficial appearances, but reveals a common socio-political history. Race is a category in the social world that refers to people with similar biological characteristics, but relates more comparably to their social experiences (Sun, 1995). People of different races experience different world views and opportunities, are given different identities and statuses, and demonstrate different behavior. Categorizing people by race has a profound meaning and impact on those assigned to those categories by others or themselves (Anderson & South, 1993). Being African American has more to do with shared experiences than shared genetic material.

Many have embraced the idea that racial differences in sport performance are a product of biological and genetic differences among the races (Entine, 2000; Wiggins, 1997). A rather subtle assumption is that whiteness is the norm and any variation from the norm is problematic and warrants scientific study. Thus Scandinavian skiers' domination of that sport in the Olympic games does not stimulate the volume of research that does African American overrepresentation in basketball. This race logic encourages people to view sport performances in racialized terms, that is, in terms of skin color, and leads people to explain the sport success or failure of people with dark skin in racial terms (Coakley, 2004).

Recent work such as Entine's (2000) *Taboo* tend to reinforce this idea of biological determinism that obscures the empirical realities of how race and racism influence patterns of identity, social distinction, and among other things, sport participation patterns and performance. Biological determinism also neglects the powerful influence and lasting impact of the legacy of slavery, the history of race relations, and racial interactions (or the lack thereof) in this country.

Although discourse regarding racial and ethnic differences brings unique challenges to the study of sport and physical activity, the dialogue is of critical importance. Even though it may be politically correct and acceptable to display behaviors and attitudes that embrace a color-blind perspective, many social scientists and philosophical views indicate the social reality that "race matters," especially when it comes to sport (see Coakley, 2004, pp. 283–323; Eitzen & Sage, 2003, pp. 285–306). Though America prides itself on being a cultural melting pot, noted author and curriculum theorist William Pinar (1994) warned:

> We say "we are what we know." But, we are also what we do not know. If what we know about ourselves—our history, our culture—is distorted by delusions and denials, then our identity—as individuals, as Americans—is distorted. (p. 245)
>
> All Americans are racialized beings; knowledge of who we have been, who we are, and who we will become is a story or text we construct. (p. 247)

Yet to be examined are issues concerning "whiteness" in the sport domain. According to Johal (2001), "In popular and academic debates focused around sport and race . . . the term race is reduced to, or conflated with being black" (p. 155). The overwhelming and one-sided focus on African Americans' sporting ability (Entine, 2000) has privileged European Americans as the norm by which other racial/ethnic groups are to be judged (Carrington & McDonald, 2001). Whiteness has largely escaped critical scrutiny (Kusz, 2001; Long & Hylton, 2002). Consequently, this results in the hyper-visibility of African American athletes, while European American athletes appear as merely the norm (Gallagher, 2003). Confounding to this concept of "invisibility" are many years of research in which the race/ethnicity of participants has gone unknown, resulting in many "norms" produced with white European American males as the sample in question yet unquestioned in terms of generalizability to other populations. Tate (2003) postulated:

> The fact that "whiteness" has gone unexamined for so long is a function of the power of paradigmatic thinking in the social sciences. The predominant viewpoint in the social sciences has been that people of color lack many of the characteristics associated with being white, thus the focus of scholarship has been on documenting these differences or examining interventions designed to remedy these so-called deficiencies. (p. 121)

African American Racial Identity Development

Every person journeys through the process of self-definition in terms of values, personal and social importance, and meaning attached to being a part of a particular racial group. The definitions and construction of these groups may change over time but there are important and appreciable differences in the experiences of people that vary by racial categorization (Tatum, 1997). While European Americans have the luxury of trying on several identities, the reality is that they can still return to the privilege that comes with paler pigmentation (Belcher, 2003). The formation of self-identity is an outgrowth of social interactions with family, friends, school activities, group and social affiliations, and other influences in the environment. Identities are tried, tested, and examined until comfortable to bring about a sense of stability in the individual to make life predictable (Cross, 1995). Even though change in one's surroundings is often accepted and sometimes welcomed, a significant change in identity can be troubling and difficult to handle.

Cross (1995) set forth the metamorphic process through which African Americans "become black." This process involves a change in the perception and evaluation of the self in terms of being "black" and is called *Nigrescence* (Cross, 1995; Helms, 1985). Nigrescence is described as a re-socialization experience that changes one's perspective or racial identity from Eurocentric to Afrocentric (centered or grounded in African American culture). Cross' model of African American racial identity development provides a discursive and analytical structure that can logically be applied to the development of sport and physical activity preferences and participation to support the comprehension of the relationship of racial identity development and sport (Harrison, Harrison, & Moore, 2002). Cross, Parham, and Helms (1991) attributed the range of application of this model to the fact that several theorists in different parts of the country were formulating parallel models independently. This strongly suggests that African American racial identity development is a nationally generalizable model. This model has even been employed with slight modifications for the people of South Africa (Hocoy, 1999).

The original four-stage process has been modified to a five-stage theory through review of research findings on racial identity development (Cross, 1995). Nigrescence is not an outgrowth of normal physical growth and development. It is a process by which African Americans, a people who are assimilated, deculturalized, and in many cases miseducated, develop into more grounded, self-loving, Afrocentric persons. Though the Cross model is rather involved and complex, the following are condensed summaries of Cross' revised Nigrescence model (Cross, 1995) with inclusion of sport and physical activity applications (Harrison et al., 2002).

Pre-Encounter

In the pre-encounter stage the individual exhibits a racial attitude that ranges from racelessness to anti-black. They may not deny being physically of African American descent, but consider it to be unimportant in their lives or, in some cases, an unfavorable trait that they have to live with. In some cases, the individual may display a negative attitude toward African Americans and internalize the negative stereotypes of white racists. African Americans in this stage will seldom exhibit any racial pride and even blame other African Americans for their own racial problems. Their sport and physical activity choices are likely focused on traditionally European American activities as they strive to eschew identification with activities that are stereotyped for African Americans. They are likely to choose to participate in activities that provide greater opportunity for contact with European Americans. This stage may be extended or revisited by some African American males who enjoy social success because of athletic talent (Brown et al., 2003). American culture often embraces African American athletes, thus young African Americans gifted with athletic ability may be shielded for some time from the experiences that may trigger racially uncomfortable encounters.

Stage 2: Encounter

The encounter stage is stimulated by a sequence of occurrences or circumstances that force the individual's present outlook or world view from the comfort of race neutrality to the uneasiness and reality of living in race-conscious society. These encounter episodes push the individual outside his or her comfort zone and cause discomfort, apprehension, or even depression.

The opportunity to experience encounter episodes is surprisingly common. A powerful example of an encounter episode can be found in the *Autobiography of Malcolm X* (Haley, 1965). The author noted the response of a European American teacher when Malcolm confided in the teacher his aspiration to be a lawyer. The teacher responded, "A lawyer—that's no realistic goal for a nigger" (p. 36). Though Malcom was an A student and president of his class, the teacher made him keenly aware of his race and the accompanying restrictions on his future career possibilities.

Though blatant examples of racist attitudes may not be as common today, there are still many opportunities to experience encounter incidents. Talented African American athletes, in many instances, enjoy a large degree of social acceptance in predominantly European American settings. This relationship can be severely strained when the athlete's playing days are over or younger and more talented athletes are recruited. When African American athletes are no longer useful to their formerly adoring fans, they may become just other members of the African American community. This often strips the athletes of their privileged status and renders their once tolerated actions and behaviors as reason to shun them. Furthermore, encounters with law enforcement officers who are unaware of the African American athletes' status are common (Slansky, 1997) and also provide for encounter opportunities.

In this stage individuals will seek additional information and validation for their newly emerging identity, which may be accompanied by emotion, guilt, and anger generalized toward whites. Even though important changes are taking place in the individual's identity, there may be insignificant outward manifestation.

Stage 3: Immersion-Emersion

The immersion-emersion stage of Nigrescence is delimited by the demolition of the previous identity and the formation of a new Afrocentric identity. During this process the new self is not yet clearly defined. Symbols such as styles of dress, hairstyles, and involvement in particular organizations and political groups typify those in this stage. It is at this crucial stage that African American youth recognize and magnify the difference between themselves and their European American peers and begin to segregate themselves. This is not just an attempt to be "black," but it comes as a consequence of having different experiences and seeing the world through different lenses. It manifests itself through disengaging from European Americans who "don't get it" and identifying with other African Americans who do (Tatum, 1997). This develops an informal support group and gives them an opportunity to be with peers who know how to be "black." During this stage of racial identity development participation in "black sport" or physical activities that connect the individual with "blackness" are likely sought out in an effort to completely immerse themselves in "blackness."

After immersing one's self in the cocoon of blackness, through realigning his or her attitude and posture, the individual emerges from this oversimplified external ideological perspective to a more reflective and profound understanding of African American issues.

Stage 4: Internalization

Internalization represents a calmer sense of contentment with the self that soothes the internal struggle of the previous stages. Militant and extremist attitudes are transformed into thoughtful inspection and scrutiny of oppression and racism. The individual is committed to continual development of love and acceptance of African American communities. Sport and physical activities are no longer viewed through racial lenses but simply as exercise or recreation rather than a source of identity.

Stage 5: Internalization-Commitment

Finally, Nigrescence develops into a forging of this new world view into tangible efforts to further the cause of blackness. Nigrescence theory suggests that this commitment to sincere involvement in activities that further causes that are of interest to the African American community is the only partition between the previous stage and this one. For instance, the individual may commit to remaining physically fit via any mode that is attractive and available rather than being overly concerned with the Afrocentricity of the mode.

Though this explanation of Nigrescence is rather oversimplified (see Cross, 1995, for a complete description), it provides a brief glimpse into the racial identity development of the African American related to sport and physical activity. The activation and consummation of the Nigrescence experience is not the same for all African Americans. In some highly unlikely situations the individual may never develop past the pre-encounter stage while others progress through all stages before reaching adulthood. Plummer (1995) indicates that African American adolescents from nurturing environments display primarily internalization attitudes and are prepared by their parents with the skills necessary to function in a predominately European American environment. It is doubtful that today's African American adolescent begins Nigrescence development at the pre-encounter stage as encounter episodes are numerous, especially for African American adolescents.

Athletic Identity

Concurrent with the development of racial identity, many African American youth undergo the development of an athletic identity. The ascendance to elite levels in sport requires long hours of intense and dedicated practice. Thus, to rise to this level, participants must exhibit strong levels of commitment and dedication to their sport. The level of commitment and importance individuals assign to their roles as athletes, and the degree to which the athletes identify with, or view themselves in the role of athletes, has been termed *athletic identity* (Brewer et al., 1993). For many youth, sport participation and the development of sport skills are important aspects of life and powerful determinants of social acceptability. This is especially important during adolescence when family influence dissipates, peer approval escalates, and group affiliations often develop around sport (Payne & Isaacs, 2005). This is particularly true for African American males for whom sport performance often becomes an opportunity to display masculinity. For many African American males, and increasingly females because of the recent rise in professional opportunities for women, racial identity and athletic identity may develop along parallel pathways (Brown et al., 2003; Harrison et al., 2002).

Development of superior athletic identity has advantages. An athlete with elevated athletic identity tends to narrow his or her external activities to focus on athletic pursuits. High levels of athletic identity have been correlated with better athletic performance, positive psychological consequences during training, and enhanced body image (Horton & Mack, 2000).

Conversely, there are also disadvantages that are related to high levels of athletic identity. Athletes with elevated athletic identity experience increased social isolation and decreased social activity (Horton & Mack, 2000). Additionally, Brewer et al. (1993) indicated that high-athletic-identity athletes have their identities severely threatened by injury. These athletes have to cope with changes in status or career choices and with serious injury that often leads to negative psychological and emotional reactions. In fact, Brewer contended that the higher the athletic identity, the more severe the athlete's depression in experiencing a career-ending injury. Webb et al. (1998) demonstrated that elevated athletic identity was related to retirement difficulties, particularly when the retirement was due to injury. Because of the intense focus on athletic pursuits, these individuals often have few other sources of self-worth and often disregard alternative career options. Ryska (2002) added that individuals with high athletic identity, a high ego orientation, and low perception of ability were prone to avoidance of challenges.

Intersection of Athletic and Racial Identity

Although athletic identity has been examined theoretically and empirically, few studies have explored the relationships and influence of race in athletic identity development. Recent research indicates that African American males have higher levels of athletic identity than European American males (Harrison, Moore, Burden, & Kennedy, 2004). This study was limited to college athletes; however, other research has indirectly corroborated this concept. Lee (1983) found that in high school athletes, and Harrison et al. (1999) in middle school students, African Americans had significantly higher aspirations toward athletic careers than their European American counterparts. This is not surprising when one recognizes that the most accessible role models for African American youth are athletes. What is surprising is that this research reports a statistically significant difference in the athletic identity of African American and European American athletes attending the same university and on the same athletic teams. This research seems to indicate that African Americans identify more intensely with the athletic role and narrow their focus to concentrate more on athletic activities than other pursuits. In fact, in a qualitative study, European American athletes and former athletes indicated that they were often steered away from athletic pursuits. That appeared to lower their athletic aspirations and possibly their athletic identity (Harrison, Azzarito & Burden, 2004). Influential members in these athletes' environment and the potent persuasion of stereotypes communicated messages that were interpreted by the athletes as strong derogations that deflated the sport aspirations of these participants. Oftentimes messages from parents, coaches, and other valued members of the European American athlete's social circle can have a depressing impact on the athlete's athletic identity. *Washington Post* writer Michael Wilbon's (2002) experience exemplified this point when he recalled this incident:

Fifteen years ago when I was still playing pickup basketball, a white kid in upper Northwest was the best ball handling guard in the neighborhood. He probably was one of the best in the city, and he was 13. Suddenly and inexplicably, he stopped showing up to play. I ran into his parents one evening at the grocery store and asked why he had stopped coming to the playground. And the father said, "He's just a skinny white kid. Why should he waste his time playing against all those black players?" (p. D 04)

On the other hand, African American parents seem to embrace the sport dreams of their children and encourage their participation. Often for African American athletes and their parents, sport participation may offer one of the few perceived exits from the prison of poverty. Even in middle-class African American families sport celebrity status may appear to be one of the few domains where an African American can get "respect." Middle-class parents who may have grown weary of bumping their heads against the proverbial "glass ceiling," the subtle discrimination and institutional racism of the corporate world, may seek significance in the respect accorded African American athletes.

Sport participation may be one of the few domains where being African American does not put one at a disadvantage. The strong and pervasive stereotypes surrounding the perceived superiority in sport performance by African Americans has made particular sports an African American domain. While in many other areas of American life people of color experience discrimination, successful performances in particular sports (e.g., basketball, football, track) by a significant number of African Americans has led many to believe in the innate abilities of African American athletes (Entine, 2000). Whether such innateness is real or imagined, this thought process has placed the African American athlete in advantageous positions with regard to perception of performance (Horn & Lox, 1993; Johnson & Hillian, 1999; Solomon, et al., 1996).

African American sport participation has developed into a unique style that seeks to separate and advance athletes' "blackness" as a stylistic option and creative part of their performance (Majors, 1990). Majors has noted that in the African American community sport performance for males has evolved into a display of masculinity. According to Majors, many African American males who are deprived of traditional venues for exhibiting masculinity (e.g., wealth, possessions) have developed unique expressive sport styles that set them apart from their European American counterparts. Harrison et al. (2002) suggested that sport is one of the few places where an African American man can be a man.

Sport Stereotypes in Identity Development

Sport choices and participation and persistence patterns are likely linked to racial identity attitudes. Viewing a sport as identity-appropriate may strongly influence participation, practice, and persistence in the sport or activity of choice (Harrison, Lee, & Belcher, 1999). African American youth with immersion identity attitudes would likely consider basketball, football, and track and field as appropriate for participation while excluding themselves from sport that they deem as "white" sports. It is likely that these attitudes foster the development of skills, interests, and competencies in a rather narrow range of "black" activities to the exclusion of most others.

Obvious to this idea is the influence of sports that are stereotyped as being "black." Stereotypes are defined as reliance on the characteristics of a group to predict their behavior. Stereotypes are often overgeneralized, erroneous perceptions, but they are resistant to change (Meyer, 1993). Though often inaccurate, stereotypes substantially influence the way we regard other groups of people as well as our own group. Stereotyping is an efficient cognitive function that organizes and simplifies information, preserves important social values, helps to maintain group beliefs and justify collective actions, and sustains positive group distinctiveness.

Stereotyping that operates in the self-concept precipitates self-stereotyping, which changes individuals into psychological group members (Oakes, Haslam, & Turner, 1994). This process of self-stereotyping is meshed in the development of social identity. Social identity deals with the tendency to maintain an optimistic view of the self through identifying with and establishing favorable comparisons between one's own group and other groups (Crocker & Luhtanen, 1990). Self-stereotyping as a function of social identity derives from an awareness of group membership and a desire to develop collective self-esteem. This can be observed in the self-segregation of many young African Americans, especially adolescents in immersion stage (Tatum, 1997).

African American youth's experiences with negative stereotypic attitudes, however well intentioned they may be, prompt them to gravitate to places where they feel "safe" from further racial affronts. Recalling a personal high school experience, this author had a high school physics teacher who commented, "You're the best colored student I've ever had." Though this was likely an attempted compliment, one can easily decipher the underlying message. Tatum added that encounters like these may lead to sharing of experiences with European American friends who try to diminish the significance of the encounters, using phrases such as "I'm sure he didn't mean it that way" or "Don't be so sensitive." When one's feelings are routinely invalidated, a normal response is to disengage and turn to someone who will understand and validate these feelings. This is more likely to happen with someone who has similar experiences. Other European American students may be well intentioned but ill equipped to respond in supportive ways. This, along with many other commonalities such as style of dress, vernacular, neighborhoods, and so on, leads to self-segregation of African American youth.

In the African American community, the overwhelming success of African American athletes in particular sports is a potent influence on the development of elevated collective self-esteem and obviously perpetuates positive self-stereotypes in the realm of sport (Harrison, 2001). The process of self-stereotyping is selective, and individuals of stereotyped groups often immerse themselves in the group identity (Biernat, Vescio, & Green, 1996). This apparently allows the group members to better protect their collective self-esteem. Again, we can see this concept illustrated in the self-segregating behavior of many African American youth in sport settings. This in essence is a racial identity survival strategy. Often majority group members will downplay and minimize the experiences of African Americans;

therefore, to protect their self-esteem, the African Americans tend to gravitate toward others with similar experiences that can affirm their own. In many instances, those who don't share these experiences, "just don't get it."

Research indicates that racial identity and self-esteem are meaningfully correlated for African Americans, but not for European Americans (Goodstein & Ponterotto, 1997). An explanation for this phenomenon is that living in a society where being African American evokes so many negative stereotypes, it is easy to understand why there is ardent identification with a positive stereotype. The African American athlete stereotype has an unequaled history that is also pervasive among the general population (Wiggins, 1997) . Several research studies (Harrison, 1999; Harrison, Azzarito, & Burden, 2004; Horn & Lox, 1993; Johnson, Halliman, & Westerfield, 1999) give evidence of the perception of superior performance of African Americans in basketball. When given the equivalent information while listening to a radio broadcast of a basketball game, the participants rated players identified as African American as having more athletic ability while players identified as European American were rated as having more basketball intelligence and hustle (Stone, Perry, & Darley, 1997). Psychological evidence also suggests that racial stereotypes can significantly influence intellectual (Steele, 1997; Steele & Aronson, 1995) and athletic performance (Stone, Lynch, Sjomeling, & Darley, 1999). Because stereotypes and self-stereotypes are thought to form the basis of group identity, and thus, African American racial identity, it is tenable to come to the conclusion that developing particular sport skills may occur as a result of the development of African American racial identity.

Fusing Sport, African American Masculinity, and Popular Culture

The meshing of African American racial identity, stereotypes, and athletic identity is also interwoven with today's popular culture. The impact of these potent influences may limit the attainable aspirations of African American youth. Research findings indicate that African American adolescents' physical activity choices are significantly different from and less eclectic than those of European American adolescents (Harrison, Lee, & Belcher, 1999). Implicit in this is the generalization of these racial and sport attitudes to the limiting of future career opportunities. The development of narrow and limited sport and possible career identities for African American youth has likely impacted the Nigresence process.

Ogbu (1990, 2004) investigated attitudes toward academic achievement in African American adolescents. It was found that these adolescents, who are in many instances in immersion stage, see their peers who achieve academically as "acting white." Thus, to attain success in the academic realm or to expend effort studying and doing school work was part of an identity reserved for European Americans. Hence, for many African Americans, the Nigresence process may initiate a divergence from academic attainment. Recently, the "acting white" theory has been challenged and suggested to be more complicated and less homogenous than previously thought (Spencer et al., 2001), but the preference for particular sport by race is fairly well documented (Harrison, 1999; Heath, FACSM, Macera, Eaker, & Wheeler, 1991).

This may also be related to the disproportional funneling of African American youth into participation in particular sports as the most viable way of achieving economic success. Previous research suggests that African American males demonstrate higher aspiration for participation in particular sports (Harrison, Lee, & Belcher 1999; Lee, 1983). These aspirations often persist into adulthood for many African American males. For example, a college athlete related an event where tryouts for a semi-professional basketball league drew crowds of over 300 African American men. Many of these men were significantly beyond their prime athletic years and ranged up to forty years old. In several instances these authors have encountered young African American males who were not skilled enough to get appreciable playing time on their college teams leaving their more promising academic careers behind to prepare for tryouts for professional sport teams. These young men seemed incapable of moving from their athletic selves and developing other facets of their identity. In many instances these athletes' "hoop dreams" and "football fantasies" turn into academic and career nightmares.

Since African American youth display higher ambitions in the sport realm, and many aspire to professional sport careers, the relevant question is to consider whether these youth, particularly males, have negative perceptions of occupations outside sport. How do these perceptions influence or affect the individual in later identity development stages? Cornel West (1993) stated that African American males should have alternate forms of expression through which to navigate oppression, racism, and patriarchal power structures. African American males are attracted to sport and entertainment because these are the vessels that offer them stylistic options. Hip-hop has been defined as a sub-culture of the larger African American culture denoted by its unique music, language, style of dress, and attitude (McLead, 1999).

The merger of hip-hop culture and particular sports, especially basketball, has virtually defined many African American athletes. African American youth in their most malleable stages of identity development can readily observe sport superstars and emulate their styles of clothing, hair, demeanor, language, and playing skills. This is particularly attractive when we can readily observe the superstars "playing by their own rules," something successful African Americans in corporate America can rarely do. These young people may find it difficult to identify with a successful African American dressed in a suit, carrying a briefcase, driving a BMW, and working in a high-rise building. But they can identify with an athlete with tattoos, braids, wearing hip-hop garb, driving a Hummer with spinner rims, and defying the rules of the establishment. Such behavior would not be tolerated in corporate America. African American youth struggling to be successful in the academic domain will more easily identify with athletes like Lebron James, Kobe Bryant, or Allen Iverson rather than an African American corporate executive, engineer, or scientific researcher. If a young African male has not been very successful academically, it is easy to understand his identification with a sport star earning millions of dollars for playing basketball.

Another reason these young people readily identify with sport stars is because of the inaccurate perception of few obstacles to athletic success. Corporate success requires academic success and the adoption of a "sell out" attitude (that is, the loss of African American identity and pursuit of academic excellence) and label. Media images and peer influences send strong messages to African American youth that sport success is easily attainable and available to any African American youth who "got game." Unfortunately, it is more attractive for a 12-year-old

African American male to spend 10 years training and preparing for a minuscule chance at being a professional athlete than to spend that same time preparing to become a professional businessman, scientist, or educator. These young people learn at an early age that in this country, being an educated African American is not nearly as attractive to the masses as being a professional athlete. European Americans will embrace, support, and encourage African American athletes in their athletic pursuits while questioning the authenticity, quality, and skills of educated African Americans. Unless these barriers are removed, athletics will continue to occupy a central place in the African American life simply because it is one of the few places where an African American man can be a man (Harrison, Harrison, & Moore, 2002).

Cause for Conflict: Interaction of Racial and Athletic Identity

In the study of African American racial identity there have been theoretical questions as to the stability of the construct. If racial identity is not constant or stable, of what use is it in influencing the sport choices of African Americans? If racial identity changes are manipulated by situational factors or circumstances, of what import are they? Research suggests that African American racial identity is relatively stable. While other dimensions of identity change in response to varying contexts and situations, the racial component of African American racial identity remains relatively stable. Since race is one of the most often used variables in categorization, it is almost always an important factor in social interactions. It is especially critical in situations in which race is a perceived significant issue (Shelton & Sellars, 2000)

The question is how do the constructs of racial and athletic identity interact? What occurs when one develops a well-developed athletic identity? What happens when an African American develops a strong affinity and identity in the realm of sport? Posited here is that the African American racial identity prompts and augments the growth of athletic identity in particular sports. But what happens when athletic identity dominates? The results of two studies (Brown et al., 2003; Harrison et al., 2004) suggest that stronger athletic identity is associated with an immature racial identity and conversely, lower athletic identity is correlated with advanced racial identity. That is, in African Americans, racial and athletic identity are somewhat negatively correlated. A possible explanation is that talented African American athletes may be shielded from the harsh realities of racism and discrimination because of their athletic status. This can possibly impair the development of the Nigrescence process, or possibly reverse it, rendering the perception of the athlete color-blind. It has been suggested that while competing in elite-level intercollegiate and professional athletics, African American athletes are often "given a pass" that protects them from daily bouts with racism and discrimination and allows their athletic identities to come to the forefront (Brown et al., 2003).

During the 1960s, the height of the Black Power movement, African American athletes experienced blatant racism such as obvious stacking, stereotypic remarks by sports commentators, racial team quotas, and policing of social activities and events (Spivey, 1983). This led to accelerated racial identity development and a significant degree of African American athlete activism. In recent times there has been relatively little public activism on the part of African American athletes. Although blatant racist activity seldom occurs, African American athletes learn that public displays of activist attitudes may have serious repercussions that may impair their opportunity to enter the professional realm.

Concluding Remarks

The recent Affirmative Action Supreme Court hearings on race-based college admissions is illustrative of the challenges faced by African American athletes (Malveaux, 2004). When race-based admissions policies were challenged at the Universities of Texas, Michigan, and Georgia, no one suggested that it was a form of reverse discrimination to admit to the school student athletes who didn't meet the new admission standards. In fact, many student athletes are exempt from these new standards. The message these universities are sending is that in order for them to be competitive, scholarship athletes should need to meet only the lower NCAA criteria for admission. While many universities are raising admission standards, many of these same institutions are utilizing athletic affirmative action giving athletes admittance to classrooms by way of basketball courts and football fields. The academic dilemma created here is that these same athletes are expected to compete in the classrooms with other students who have a distinct academic advantage.

There is also an implicit message to America that African American students want to attend a major university. If they are lacking athletic talent, they must meet rigorous admissions criteria, but students who entertain through participation in sports that generate revenue for the university can be admitted with lower standards. It confirms again that African Americans who conform to the black athletic stereotype are welcomed, while others must prove their academic worthiness. It also illustrates that while America welcomes the African American athlete, it is ambivalent at best toward the academically able African American student. Why can't the African American pre-med student be admitted with a lower ACT score? Could it be because white America views this as an opportunity taken from a more qualified white person, while the black basketball player is just fulfilling his stereotypical role.

The challenge for university athletic departments is not to ignore or reject African American male confidence and expression by directing them out of sport. The real challenge is to discover how to invest the African American athlete's academic preparation and career development paths with comparable zeal. Those who administer athletics should strive to provide as much reinforcement for academic achievement as for athletic accomplishments (Harrison, Holmes, Moore, & Manning, 2000). Plausibly more research on racial identity theory and the Nigrescence process will reveal possible interventions. It is also important that European Americans promote, embrace, and endorse African American racial identity development and academic achievement with the same enthusiasm accorded athletic competency. Finally, research into the understanding of the perceptions of young African American youth and behaviors that correlate with, exert influence upon, and impact their perceptions of academic achievement and success in the context of sport should be encouraged.

▲▼ Suggested Readings ▲▼

Brown, T. N., Jackson, J. S., Brown, K. T., Sellers, R. M., Keiper, S., & Manuel, W. J. (2003). "There's no race on the playing field": Perceptions of racial discrimination among white and black athletes. *Journal of Sport and Social Issues, 27,* 162–183.

Harrison, L., Jr. (2001). Understanding the influence of stereotypes: Implications for the African American in sport and physical activity. *Quest, 53,* L97–114.

Ogbu, J. U. (2004). Collective identity and the burden of "acting white" in black history community, and education. *The Urban Review, 36,* 1–35.

Steele, C. M. (1997). A threat in the air: How stereotypes shape intellectual identity and performance. *American Psychologist, 52,* 613–629.

Tatum, B. (1997). *"Why are all the black kids sitting together in the cafeteria?" And other conversations about race.* New York: Basic Books.

▲▼ Study Questions ▲▼

1. How might sport and physical activity choices vary in the different stages of racial identity?

2. Why do many African American youth experience the immersion/emersion stage of racial identity during adolescence?

3. How does the development of racial identity impact athletic identity in many African American male youth? Why would this process differ in European Americans?

4. How does the existence of strong sport stereotypes affect racial and athletic identity in African American male youth?

5. How can racial identity development be used to explain self-segregation in African American youth? How can this impact sport selection and participation?

6. How can racial and athletic identity operate to promote a disproportionate funneling of African American youth into sport?

7. Explain the following sentence: "Sport is one of the few places where an African American man can be a man."

8. How can sport be considered an accepted place for "affirmative action"? How can this work to the detriment of African American athletes? What can be done to alleviate this situation?

References

Anderson, A., & South, D. (1993). Racial differences in collegiate recruiting, retention, and graduation rates. In D. Brooks & R. Althouse, *Racism in college athletics*. Morgantown, WV: Fitness Information Technology.

Bandura, A. (1982). Self-efficacy: Mechanism of human agency. *American Psychologist, 37*, 122–147.

Belcher, D. (2003). European Americans and Identity Development. Presentation at the National AAHPERD Convention (April, 1–5), Philadelphia, PA.

Biernat, M., Vescio, T. K., & Green, M. L. (1996). Selective self-stereotyping. *Journal of Personality and Social Psychology, 71*(6), 1194–1209.

Brewer, B. W., Raalte, J. L. V., & Linder, D. (1993). Athletic identity: Hercules' muscles or achilles heel? *International Journal of Sport Psychology, 24*, 237–254.

Brown, T. N., Jackson, J. S., Brown, K. T., Sellers, R. M., Keiper, S., Manuel, W. J. (2003). "There's no race on the playing field": Perceptions of racial discrimination among white and black athletes. *Journal of Sport and Social Issues, 27*, 162–183.

Carrington, B. & McDonald, I. (2001). *Race, sport and British society*. London: Routledge.

Census, race and science (2000). *Nature Genetics, 24*, 97–98.

Coakley, J. J. (2004). *Sport in society: Issues and controversies*. Boston: McGraw-Hill.

Crocker, J., & Luhtanen, R. (1990). Collective self-esteem and in-group bias. *Journal of Personality and Social Psychology, 58*, 60–67.

Cross, W. E. (1995). The psychology of Nigrescence: Revising the Cross model. In J. G. Ponterotto, J. M. Casas, L. A. Suzuki, & C. M. Alexander, *Handbook of multicultural counseling*. Thousand Oaks, CA: Sage.

Cross, W. E., Parham, T. A., & Helms, J. E. (1991). The stages of Black identity development: Nigrescence models. In R. E. Jones (Ed.), *Black psychology*. New York: Harper & Row.

Eitzen, D. S., & Sage, G. H. (2003) *Sociology of North American sport*. Boston: McGraw-Hill.

Entine, J. (2000). *Taboo: Why black athletes dominate sports, and why we are afraid to talk about it*. New York: Public Affairs.

Gallagher, C. A. (2003). Miscounting race: Explaining white's misperception of racial group size. *Sociological Perspectives, 46*(3), 381–396.

Goodstein, R., & Ponterotto, J. G. (1997). Racial and ethnic identity: Their relationship and their contribution to self-esteem. *Journal of Black Psychology, 23*, 275–292.

Haley, A., & X, M. (1964) *The autobiography of Malcom X*. New York: Balantine.

Harrison, C. K., Holmes, S., Moore, D., & Manning, T. (2000). *The effects of media ads on intercollegiate student-athletes: Exposure to athletic and professional occupational imagery*. Paper presented at the North American Society for the Sociology of Sport Annual Meeting (November 2–5), Colorado Springs, Colorado.

Harrison, L., Jr. (1999). Racial attitudes in sport: A survey on race-sport competence beliefs. *Shades of diversity: Issues and strategies*: A Monograph Series, 2.

Harrison, L., Jr. (2001). Understanding the influence of stereotypes: Implications for the African American in sport and physical activity. *Quest, 53*, 97–114.

Harrison, L., Jr., Azzarito, L., & Burden, J., Jr. (2004). Perceptions of athletic superiority: A view from the other side. *Race, Ethnicity, & Education, 7*, 149–166.

Harrison, L., Jr., Harrison, C. K., & Moore, L. (2002). African American racial identity and sport. *Sport Education and Society, 7*, 121–133.

Harrison, L., Jr., Lee, A., & Belcher, D. (1999). Race and gender differences in sport participation as a function of self-schema. *Journal of Sport and Social Issues, 23*, 287–307.

Harrison, L., Jr., Moore, L. N., Burden, J., Jr., & Kennedy, E. (2004). *Athletic Identity: The Relationship of Race, Gender and Athletic Status*. Paper presented at the annual meeting of the American Alliance for Health Physical Education, Recreation and Dance, New Orleans, LA.

Heath, G., FACSM, Macera, C., Eaker, E., & Wheeler, F. (1991). Physical activity patterns in a bi-racial semi-rural population. *Medicine and Science in Sport and Exercise, 23*(suppl), S105.

Helms, J. E. (1985). An overview of Black racial identity theory. In J. E. Helms, *Black and White racial identity: Theory, research, and practice*. New York: Greenwood.

Hocoy, D. (1999). The validity of Cross's model of Black racial identity development in the South African context. *Journal of Black Psychology, 25*, 131–152.

Horn, T. S., & Lox, C. (1993). The self-fulfilling prophecy theory: When coaches' expectations become reality. In J. M. Williams (Ed.), *Applied sport psychology* (pp. 68–81). Mountain View, CA: Mayfield.

Horton, R. S., & Mack, D. E. (2000). Athletic identity in marathon runners: Functional focus or dysfunctional commitment? *Journal of Sport Behavior, 23*, 101–119.

Johal, S. (2001). Playing their own game: A South Asian football experience. In B. Carrington & I. McDonald (Eds.), *"Race," sport and British society* (pp. 153–169). New York: Routledge.

Johnson, D. L., Hallinan, C. J., & Westerfield, R. C. (1999). Picturing success: Photographs and stereotyping in men's collegiate basketball. *Journal of Sport Behavior, 22*, 45–53.

Kusz, K. W. (2001). I want to be the minority! The politics of youthful White masculinities in sport and popular culture in 1990s America. *Journal of Sport and Social Issues, 25*, 390–416.

LaVeist, T. A. (1996). Why we should continue to study race . . . but do a better job: An essay on race, racism and health. *Ethnicity and Disease, 6*, 21–29.

Lee, C. C. (1983). An investigation of the athletic career expectations of high school athletes. *The Personnel and Guidance Journal, 61*, 544–547.

Long, J. G., & Hylton, K. (2002). Shades of white: An examination of whiteness in sport. *Leisure Studies, 21*, 87–103.

Majors, R. (1990). Cool pose: Black masculinity and sports. In M. A. Messner & D. F. Sabo (Eds.), *Sport, men, and the gender order: Critical feminist perspectives* (pp. 109–114). Champaign, IL: Human Kinetics.

Malveaux, J. (2004, December 3). A bad sign: Colleges enroll fewer blacks. *USA Today*, 13A.

McLead, K. (1999). Authenticity within hip-hop and other cultures threatened by assimilation. *Journal of Communication, 49*, 134–150

Nicholls, J. G. (1984). Achievement motivation: Conceptions of ability, subjective experience, task choice, and performance. *Psychological Review, 91*, 328–346.

Oakes, P. J., Haslam, S. A., & Turner, J. C. (1994). *Stereotyping and social reality.* Cambridge: Blackwell.

Ogbu, J. U. (1990). Minority education in comparative perspective. *Journal of Negro Education, 59*, 45–55.

Ogbu, J. U. (2004). Collective identity and the burden of "acting white" in black history, community, and education. *The Urban Review, 36*, 1–35.

Payne, V. J. G., & Isaacs, L. D. (2005). *Human motor development: A lifespan approach.* Boston: McGraw-Hill.

Pinar, W. F. (1994) *Studies in the postmodern theory of education.* New York: Peter Lang.

Plummer, D. L. (1995). Patterns of racial identity development of African American adolescent males and females. *Journal of Black Psychology, 21*, 168–180.

Ryska, T. A. (2002). The effects of athletic identity and motivation goals on global competence perceptions of student-athletes. *Child Study Journal, 32*, 109–129.

Shelton, N. J., & Sellers, R. M. (2000). Situational stability and variability in African American racial identity, *Journal of Black Psychology, 26*, 27–49.

Slansky, D. A. (1997). Traffic stops, minority motorists, and the future of the Fourth Amendment. *Supreme Court Review,* annual, 271–329.

Solomon, G. B., Wiegardt, P. A., Yusuf, F. R., Kosmitzki, C., Williams, J., Stevens, C. E., & Wayda, V. K. (1996). Expectancies and ethnicity: The self-fulfilling prophecy in college basketball. *Journal of Sport and Exercise Psychology, 18*, 83–88.

Spencer, M. B., Noll, E., Stoltzfus, J., & Harpalani, V. (2001). Identity and school adjustment: Revisiting the "acting white" assumption. *Educational Psychologist, 36*, 21–30.

Spivey, D. (1983). The Black athlete in big time intercollegiate sports, 1941–1968. *Phylon, 44*, 116–125.

Steele, C. M. (1997). A threat in the air: How stereotypes shape intellectual identity and performance. *American Psychologist, 52*, 613–629.

Steele, C. M., & Aronson, J. (1995). Stereotype threat and the intellectual test performance of African Americans. *Journal of Personality and Social Psychology, 69*, 797–811.

Stone, J., Lynch, C. I., Sjomeling, M., & Darley, J. M. (1999). Stereotype threat effects on black and white athletic performance. *Journal of Personality and Social Psychology, 77*(6), 1213–1227.

Stone, J., Perry, Z. W., & Darley, J. M. (1997). "White men can't jump": Evidence for the perceptual confirmation of racial stereotypes following a basketball game. *Basic and Applied Social Psychology, 19*, 291–306.

Sun, K. (1995). The definition of race. *American Psychologist, 50*, 43–44.

Tate, W. (2003) The "race" to theorize education: Who is my neighbor? *Qualitative Studies in Education, 16*(1), 121–126.

Tatum, B. (1997). *"Why are all the black kids sitting together in the cafeteria?" And other conversations about race.* New York: Basic Books.

Webb, W. M., Nasco, S. A., Riley, S., & Headrick, B. (1998). Athletic identity and reactions to retirement from sports. *Journal of Sport Behavior, 21*, 338–362.

West, C. (1993). *Race matters.* Boston: Beacon Press.

Wiggins, D. K. (1997). "Great speed but little stamina": The historical debate over black athletic superiority. In S. W. Pope (Ed.), *The new American sport history: Recent approaches and perspectives* (pp. 312–338). Urbana, IL: University of Illinois Press.

Wilbon, M. (2002, May 5). To NBA's European stars, "big white stiff" doesn't translate. *The Washington Post*, p. D 04.

SECTION FIVE
Intersection of Race, Sport, and Law

Our attention to the intersection of race, sport, and law is portrayed through three chapters dealing with various forms of discrimination committed against African American athletes. Timothy Davis's two chapters, "The Persistence of Unconscious Racism in College Sport" and "Academic Inequality and the Impact of NCAA Rules," remind us that the law has been an instrument of the intercollegiate athletic establishment throughout its history, and African American college students have been the victims. He presents race as a variable that influences the promulgation of NCAA rules and regulations, and in particular, the implementation of the NCAA's initial eligibility rules. The record shows that judicial action has primarily served as a device to foster external accountability of NCAA rules, causing the NCAA to improve its policies. In the end, however, Davis provides us with an account of the persistent racism in collegiate athletics, and tells why traditional civil rights laws have been mostly ineffective for protecting interests of the African America college athletes. Given the constraints of traditional civil laws and often of judicial hostility to affirmative action for African American athletes, coaches, and administrators, Davis proposes legal and non-legal strategies for eliminating racism in college sports.

Abstract ▼ This chapter examines the intersection of race and law in intercollegiate athletics. It examines whether racism continues to adversely affect the interests of African American administrators and coaches engaged in college sports. Notwithstanding the persistence of racism in college sports, traditional civil rights laws are largely ineffective vehicles for protecting the interests of African Americans. The limited utility of these laws is a product of evidentiary standards that plaintiffs must meet to prevail in traditional civil rights suits. These standards and the covert nature of the racism that imbues college sports create obstacles that are difficult for plaintiffs to traverse. Given the constraints placed on traditional civil rights laws, this chapter examines alternative approaches—legal and nonlegal—to remedying the harm that racism inflicts upon African Americans in college sports.

CHAPTER

12

THE

PERSISTENCE

OF

UNCONSCIOUS

RACISM IN

COLLEGE

SPORT

TIMOTHY DAVIS

▼ ▲▼ ▲▼ ▲▼ ▲▼ ▲▼ ▲

Key Terms

▼Antidiscrimination norms▲

▼Circumstantial evidence▲

▼Common Law▲

▼Direct evidence▲

▼Invidious discrimination▲

▼Judicial review▲

▼Prima facie evidence▲

▼Racial animus▲

▼Rational basis standard of review▲

▼Stereotype *▲

▼Strict scrutiny standard of review▲

*(Thomas & Rich, 2005, p. 304).

Introduction

Race, Sport, and Values

As social institutions, law and sport are instrumental in shaping societal values. Whether manifested in the doctrines that constitute a body of law or the formal and informal rules and customs that govern a particular sport, these institutions also reflect societal values and mores. Positive values commonly fostered and reflected by sport include advancement through merit, equality, opportunity, and fair play. This conceptualization of the values associated with sport is laden with notions of meritocracy that are weaved into judicial reasoning. In a leading Title IX gender discrimination case (*Hoover v. Meiklejohn*, 1977), the court stated, "It must also be made clear that the mandate of equality of opportunity does not dictate a disregard of difference in talents and abilities among individuals. There is no right to a position on an athletic team. There is a right to compete for it on equal terms" (p. 171).

Thus sport is often "envisioned as embodying the dominant themes of freedom and individual achievement. It comports with the belief that conceives of 'meritocracy as a system in which beliefs and burdens are distributed in accord with one's deeds—presumably the products of rational choice—rather than characteristics over which one has no apparent control.'" (Davis, 2003, p. 338)

Given this conceptualization of sport and the resulting belief that sport rises above the biases that afflict other important social institutions, sport has historically been viewed as the "common carrier" of the aspirations of those seeking upward mobility (Davis, 2003, p. 338). Yet throughout America's history, events occurring within sport have called into question the accuracy of this premise. Notably, racial segregation that precluded African Americans from participating in sports in player and administrative capacities "contradicted the idealized belief that sport . . . constitutes a venue in which those who possess the requisite ability can have free access to all of the benefits that can be derived from successful athletic participation" (Davis, 2003, p. 338).

Events occurring after the re-integration of the major professional sports leagues, and the collegiate conferences and associations after World War II, challenge not only the prevalence of merit as the core value within sport, but also sport as a forum within which racial and gender equity exist. The following recent illustrations of racial and gender inequity in sport reveal an institution that is not insulated from the struggles for equity that reside within the larger society. These examples also demonstrate the changing nature of the racial equity debate within sport, which has evolved beyond its historical focus on access to participation opportunities for athletes.

Racial Inequity in Sport

Despite dramatic progress in the hiring of African American head NFL coaches, African Americans and other racial minorities lag far behind their white counterparts in high/senior level management positions within the NFL and other professional sports leagues. For example, very few persons of color hold president, chief executive officer, general manager, and team vice president positions in the NFL. Thus barriers persist in the hiring of African Americans to coaching and administrative positions in the NFL (Lapchick, 2006b).

Turning to college sports, the challenge of achieving racial equity in intercollegiate athletics includes, but is not confined to, access to employment opportunities. For example, one scholar opined that addressing racial equity in collegiate sport should not ignore the controversial issue of whether African American male basketball and football student athletes are economically exploited:

> With the clear dominance (65 percent) of African-American males in Division I basketball, for example, the current diversion of profits generated from that enterprise to other uses raises serious questions of potential exploitation. . . . Those revenues, in turn, largely fund the entire operations of the NCAA. To compound matters, Division I basketball also generates significant profits for member institutions, with profits per institution averaging $1.6 million in 1994. While other intercollegiate sports typically operate at a loss, Division I football, like basketball, tends to be profitable, generating an average profit of $3.9 million per institution. The profits generated as a result of the labors of male athletes of color, therefore, largely fund the NCAA and support other predominantly non-minority sports at the institutional level. This use of revenues largely generated by male athletes of color for purposes other than supporting the efforts of those minority athletes to obtain an education raises questions of exploitation or, perhaps even, conversion. (Smith, 1996, pp. 9, 348–349).

Another scholar added that "to the extent that legal rules underlying gender equity compel the creation of additional non-revenue sports for women in educational institutions, Black student athletes, and Black males in particular, have been required to fund them" (Mathewson, 1996, p. 240).

Multiple variables, such as the convergence of poverty and race, and gender and race, also contribute to inequity in sport. For example, questions have been raised regarding whether African American women student athletes have benefited from the increased opportunities for women student athletes spawned by Title IX in college sports. The predicament of African American women in sport has been described as follows:

> I have already demonstrated that Black women do suffer from the confluence of gender and racial discrimination forces in the sports context. Let me summarize. Black women have had to overcome two specific prohibitions: "No Blacks Allowed" and "No Women Allowed." Black women are adversely affected by both signs, yet taking down the former sign does not prevent or remedy the harm caused by the latter. Nor does removing the latter prevent or remedy the harm caused by the former. Finally, removing both signs does not remedy the harm caused by the effect of both signs together (Mathewson, 1996, p. 253).

▲ ▼ ▲

> Black women are caught in a world that Title IX does not fully address. As I have discussed above, young athletes develop in three systems (the playground, amateur athletics sponsored by educational institutions, and amateur athletics sponsored by non-educational institutions). No law governs participation opportunities on the playground. But athletes develop in the amateur systems and move up to higher levels as they do. The number of sports in which black girls can develop competencies is a function of where they live and their socio-economic circumstances. Suppressed opportunities at the lower levels affect the number of athletic choices available at higher levels. There are opportunities in basketball and track that are not very expensive to produce, but the number of those opportunities at the upper levels is somewhat finite. (Mathewson, 1996, pp. 265–266. See also Dees, 2004, p. 265, noting that the "marked over representation in basketball and track highlights the disturbing under representation of black women in other sports such as ice hockey, golf, tennis, synchronized swimming, volleyball, and rowing.")

Questions regarding racial and cultural inequity and insensitivity also lie at the heart of efforts by Native Americans and their supporters to eradicate the use of Native Americans as mascots, nicknames, and logos for amateur, collegiate, and professional sports teams. Their litigation efforts have met with mixed results. An attempt to eradicate the use of the NFL's Washington franchise's "Redskins" name on the ground that it constituted a disparagement under federal copyright law was unsuccessful (*Pro-Football, Inc. v. Harjo*, 2003). On the other hand, a court ruled against the University of Illinois' attempt to preclude certain student and faculty from contacting prospective student athletes in order to inform them of the controversy regarding the university's use of a Native American mascot (*Crue v. Akin*, 2004). Notwithstanding these mixed results and contrasting views on this controversial issue, the campaign to end the use of Native American names and mascots has been successful. A 2003 study revealed that between 1969 and 2001, more than 1,200 schools, at all levels of sport, had discontinued the use of Native American mascots.

In early 2005, the NCAA completed a review of self-analyses undertaken by its member institutions that continue to use Native American mascots, nicknames, and logos. The purpose of the analysis was to determine whether such use is offensive. In August 2005, the NCCA Executive Committee approved a policy that "prohibits NCAA colleges and universities from displaying hostile and abusive racial/ethnic/ national origin mascots, nicknames or imagery at any of the 88 NCAA championships." Unless the 19 schools identified made changes prior to February 1, 2006 they would not be able to host future NCAA championships(Brown, 2005, p. 1). At the time the policy went into effect, institutions that had been selected as predetermined sites to host an NCAA championship competition would be permitted to do so but would be required to cover up references to Native Americans. The policy allows institutions to appeal the categorization of their school as one "whose mascots are considered hostile or abusive" (Brown, G., 2005, p. 1). Several institutions, including Florida State University, have established to the satisfaction of the NCAA's Executive Committee that their use of a Native American name, mascot, or symbol is not offensive. Others such as the University of North Dakota had their appeals rejected (Aronauer, 2005). The NCAA's rejection of North Dakota's appeal prompted the university to file a lawsuit challenging the NCAA's policy. In November 2006, a state court judge granted the university an injunction that permitted it to host a post-season football game notwithstanding its use of the "Fighting Sioux" nickname. The injunction will stay in effect until the case goes to trial or is otherwise resolved.

Finally, the quest for racial equity in sport extends beyond national boundaries. One illustration, in which racial and economic variables converge to create inequity in sport, involves what some have characterized as the economic exploitation of the young Latinos who aspire to professional baseball careers in the United States (Marcano & Fidler, 1999). As described by these commentators, the inequitable treatment of Latino baseball prospects allegedly manifests in "MLB scouts getting Latino children to sign blank pieces of paper as 'contracts' to play professional baseball; MLB teams paying no or only paltry signing bonuses for Latino baseball prospects; and, MLB teams systematically discouraging Latino baseball prospects from retaining agents" (p. 532).

The forgoing examples demonstrate that the quest for racial equity at all levels of sport continues. The remainder of this chapter will highlight the intersection of law, sport, and racial inequity as it relates to barriers to hiring opportunities for African Americans in sport. It begins, however, with a brief discussion of the source of the continued marginalization of people of color in certain aspects of intercollegiate sport.

The Intersection of Law, Sport, and Racial Inequity

The Persistence of Unconscious Racism in Collegiate Sport

No single variable is responsible for the continued marginalizing of African Americans in some aspects of college sport. Yet the failure of African Americans to achieve full equality remains, in part, a product of the unconscious racism that results from the "internalization of stereotypes concerning Black athletes" (Davis, 1995, p. 644). A stereotype is "a conventional, formulaic, and oversimplified conception, opinion, or image" (Thomas & Rich, 2005, p. 317). Prior to World War II, stereotypes of African Americans as not being serious, but rather "docile, subservient, good-natured, childlike and slightly exotic" were used to exclude African American athletes (Lombardo, 1978, p. 61). Their athletic accomplishments were often defined in terms of "natural ability" and other stereotypes that belittled individual effort and achievement (Coakley, 1994). Today, derogatory images persist, but in more subtle forms (Davis, 1995). These images and myths ultimately rest on beliefs that the success of African American athletes results more from innate physical skills than from hard work and determination (Wiggins, 1993).

Under-Inclusion in Collegiate Coaching Positions

African Americans student athletes constitute a disproportionate percentage of Division I basketball and football players as compared to the percentage of African Americans at Division I institutions. As it relates to access for African Americans to coaching opportunities, a different picture emerges. With the exception of basketball, coaching positions in the premier Division I sports have remained largely closed to African Americans and Latinos. As Table 1 depicts, in 2004–05 African Americans accounted for 57.8% and 45.4% of Division I male basketball players and football players, respectively. On the other hand, Table 1 also shows that at the beginning of the 2005 season African Americans at the Division I level held 25.2% of head basketball and 0.5% of head baseball coaching positions. At the beginning of the 2005 season, there were 3 African American Division I-A head football coaches. At the beginning of the 2006 football season, the number of African American Division I head football coaches had grown to 6, which represented 6.1 percent. The higher percentage is depicted in Table 1. Table 2 depicts similar disparities in Division I women's sports. In his *2005 Racial and Gender Report Card for College Sports*, Dr. Richard Lapchick (2006a) found that:

> Whites dominated the head coaching positions held on men's teams at each level. Whites held 90.6, 89.5 and 93.4 percent of all head coaching positions in Divisions I, II and II respectively. African-Americans accounted for 7.3, 4.4 and 4.1 percent respectively in each division. Asians represented 0.4, 0.7 and 0.6 percent at each level. Latinos held 1.1, 3.6 and 1.5 percent of the positions in each division. Native Americans accounted for less than 1 percent of total head coaches at each level. (p. 5)

▲ ▼ ▲

> In fact, African Americans were so underrepresented as head coaches, that once again, the percent [sic] of women coaching men's teams actually exceeded that of African Americans in Division III (4.3 percent versus 4.1 percent). In Division II, the percentage of women coaching men's teams almost matched the percentage of African-Americans (3.5 percent versus 4.4 percent). (p. 13)

With respect to both men's and women's sports, it is not necessary that the numbers of African Americans in coaching and administrative positions mirror the percentage of African American student athletes participating in particular sports. Gaps, however, of the magnitude of those reported are disturbing because they suggest barriers to entry into the coaching ranks.

*Under-Inclusion in Collegiate
Administrative Positions*

Examining access to athletic administration, Dr. Richard Lapchick's 2005 report and a 2004 NCAA study reported that African Americans are underrepresented in the upper echelons of collegiate sports and NCAA management. Information obtained from the *NCAA's 2003–2004 Race and Gender Demographics of Member Institutions' Athletics Personnel Report* shows minimal gains and even some losses since 1995, when the report was first compiled (NCAA, 2004a). A summary of the report indicates that although the percentage of African Americans in administrative positions increased from 5.1 % to 6.6% in 2003, the gains were not made in the power positions, such as athletic directors, and associate and assistant athletic directors (NCAA, 2004a). "Rather, the largest increase for black men was realized in the positions of equipment manager, ticket manager and intern" (NCAA, 2004). As for African American women, the most notable progress was made at the senior women administrators and academic advisor levels (NCAA, 2004a).

The *2005 Racial Report Card*, prepared by Dr. Lapchick (2005a), revealed progress had been made since the NCAA issued its 2004 report. Overall, however, the report reached findings similar to the earlier NCAA report with regard to the absence of African Americans from upper level administrative positions in college sport (Lapchick, 2006a, pp. 15–17). Dr. Lapchick acknowledged the breakthroughs in Division IA such as the hiring of the first African American athletic directors in the SEC and Big East, Damon Edwards and Daryl Gross, respectively, and an overall increase in the number of African American athletic directors at the Division IA level. For example, he concluded that "when considering all divisions combined, the athletic director position was one of the whitest positions in all of sport when HBCUs [historically black colleges and universities] were excluded" (Lapchick, 2006a, p. 16).

Table 3 provides an overview of minorities in leadership roles at Division I institutions.

Table 1. African Americans as a Percentage of Male Student Athletes (2004–05) and Head Coaches (2005–06) in Division I Basketball, Football, and Baseball

Male Student-Athletes (2004–05) Division I

	Basketball	Football	Baseball
White	31.90%	47.70%	83.70%
Black	57.80%	45.40%	6.50%
Latino	1.50%	2.30%	5.40%

Male College Head Coaches (2005–06) Division I

	Basketball	Football	Baseball
White	73.80%	92.70%	95.90%
Black	25.20%	6.10%	0.50%
Other	1.0%	1.20%	3.60%

Based on information found in Lapchick, R. (2006a). Excluding historically black colleges.

Table 2. Racial Composition of Female Student Athletes (2004–05) and of Head Coaches for Division I Women's Teams (2005–06)

Female Student-Athletes (2004–5) Division I

White	70.5%
Black	15.4%
Latino	3.3%
Asian	2.2%
Native American	0.4%

College Head Coaches (2005–6) Division I

White Men	54.3%
White Women	35.3%
Black Men	3.6%
Black Women	3.0%

Based on information found in Lapchick, R. (2006a). Excluding historically black colleges.

Table 3. Minorities in Leadership Roles

| | All Institutions | | | Historically Black Institutions Excluded | | |
Position	1995–96*	2003–04	Change	1995–96*	2003–2004	Change
Overall Percentages						
Director of Athletics ▲▲▲▲▲▲▲▲▲▲▲7.5	7.2	-0.3	2.7	3.0	0.3
Associate Director of Athletics ▲▲▲▲8.2	8.1	-0.1	6.1	6.6	0.5
Assistant Director of Athletics ▲▲▲▲▲▲8.5	8.7	0.2	6.7	6.8	0.1
Senior Woman Administrator▲▲▲▲▲▲▲9.1	9.1	0.0	3.2	4.9	1.7
Academic Advisor ▲▲▲▲▲▲▲▲▲▲▲20.9	22.5	1.6	18.2	19.9	1.7
Overall +	*8.4*	*9.1*	*0.7*	*5.1*	*6.6*	*1.5*
Division I Percentages						
Director of Athletics▲▲▲▲▲▲▲▲▲▲▲▲10.1	9.3	-0.8	3.7	3.4	0.3
Associate Director of Athletics ▲▲▲▲9.1	9.7	0.6	7.2	7.8	0.6
Assistant Director of Athletics ▲▲▲▲▲▲9.5	10.0	0.5	8	8.2	0.2
Senior Woman Administrator▲▲▲▲▲▲▲8.4	14.1	5.7	2.4	8.3	5.9
Academic Advisor ▲▲▲▲▲▲▲▲▲▲▲22.8	24.1	1.3	20.5	22.3	1.8
Overall +	*9.0*	*10.7*	*1.7*	*6.2*	*8.2*	*2.0*

*Baseline year of the study   + all athletics administrative staff

(NCAA, 2004b, p. 10)

Reasons for Underrepresentation

Other chapters in this book address in detail the variables that may contribute to the small number of African Americans in coaching and administrative positions in collegiate sports (Brooks, Althouse, & Tucker, 2007; Polite, 2007; Corbett, 2007). One notable variable, however, is stereotypes. "The inequality of access for Blacks to the administration of college athletics demonstrates the persistent influence of a particular racial stereotype: the Black athlete as inferior to the White athlete regarding intellectual and leadership abilities" (Davis, 1995, p. 657).

In a recent article, two commentators addressed the question of why sports teams are integrated in entry level positions (*i.e.*, players) but not at the managerial levels (*i.e.*, coaches and administrators), and why the managerial levels of certain sports (*e.g.*, basketball) are more integrated than others (*e.g.*, football). They argue that with winning as their goal, sports organizations will hire the best players that they can find based upon objective performance criteria. According to Professors Thomas and Rich, to select players on the basis of any other criteria would place a team at a competitive disadvantage (Thomas & Rich, 2005). At the managerial level, a different picture emerges. Unintentional racism, more so than overt racism, combined with institutional complexity that increases the difficulty of measuring a candidate's relative qualifications, limits opportunities. Professors Thomas and Rich further stated that at the managerial levels the decision-making process "is replete with ambiguity and uncertainty. This uncertainty encourages the use of stereotypes, attributions, and decision frame biases to simplify this subjective decision process. These biases work to the detriment of minority promotion candidates" (Thomas & Rich, 2005, p. 319). Applying their analysis to college and professional football, Thomas and Rich concluded that these unintentional biases operate to limit the managerial opportunities for minorities.

Assuming that racism affects African Americans adversely in college sport, an obvious inquiry is what legal mechanisms are available to redress the harm. More specifically, is there a role for the law to play in addressing the harm caused by adherence to stereotypes and unconscious racism? The remainder of this chapter examines the role of the law in redressing the under-inclusion of African Americans and other ethnic minorities at coaching and administrative levels of college athletics. It concludes that given the limited effectiveness of traditional antidiscrimination norms to achieve racial equity for coaches and administrators, non-legal alternatives may hold greater promise for redressing the adverse consequences of the unconscious racism that permeates college athletics.

Traditional Antidiscrimination Norms and Access to Athlete Administration

In seeking redress for barriers to entry and promotion, coaches and administrators would more than likely turn to Title VII and Section 1981 of the Civil Rights Act. Title VII prohibits discrimination in employment. Section 1981 is broader in scope in that it applies to the making, performance, and enforcement of all contracts, not just employment contracts. As the following discussion reveals, the nature of the proof required to establish a cognizable Title VII or Section 1981 action limits the potential effectiveness of these antidiscrimination norms.

Title VII Analysis
Title VII of the amended Civil Rights Act of 1964 renders it unlawful for an employer

> to fail or refuse to hire or to discharge any individual, or otherwise to discriminate against any individual with respect to his compensation, terms, conditions, or privileges of employment, because of such individual's race, color, religion, sex or national origin.

The thrust of Title VII is to prohibit employers from discriminating against any individual with respect to that individual's compensation or privileges of employment.

With respect to allegations that racism impedes access to employment opportunities in college sports, two types of Title VII cases appear particularly relevant:

1. disparate treatment actions, in which plaintiffs allege intentional discrimination on account of race; and

2. disparate impact actions, in which plaintiffs allege the use of employment practices that appear to be neutral but unjustifiably discriminate against members of a protected group.

Disparate Treatment

In a Title VII claim based on disparate treatment, a plaintiff alleges that he or she has been treated less favorably than his or her peers on account of race. To prevail on such a claim, the plaintiff must prove discriminatory purpose on the part of the employer (Modjeska, 1993). Thus the key to proving disparate treatment is intent to discriminate (*St. Mary's Honor Center v. Hicks*, 1993; *Anderson v. Douglas & Lomason Co., Inc.*, 1994).

A plaintiff can prove discrimination by producing direct evidence of racial animus. As noted by Professor Kenneth Shropshire, "This would be the rare smoking gun event where the employer says, for example, 'We don't want to hire you because you are black'" (Shropshire, 1996, p. 64). Professor Shropshire further noted that where direct evidence of discriminatory intent is unavailable, a plaintiff can establish discriminatory intent pursuant to a formula approved by the United States Supreme Court (*McDonnell Douglas Corp. v. Green*, 1973). There the court held that a prima facie case of racial discrimination can be established by showing that a) the plaintiff belongs to a racial minority; b) the plaintiff applied and was qualified for a vacant employment position; c) the employer rejected the plaintiff despite his or her qualifications; and d) after the plaintiff's rejection, the employer continued to accept applications of persons similarly qualified (*McDonnell Douglas Corp. v. Green*, 1973; *Washington v. Garrett*, 1993). Defendants can rebut evidence of discriminatory intent (whether direct or indirect) by proving the allegations are false or by establishing a nondiscriminatory reason for rejecting the African American applicant. The burden of proof would then shift to the plaintiff to establish that the proffered reason was a pretext for racial discrimination. In other words, a plaintiff would have to establish a discriminatory intent behind the defendant's motives.

The requirement that the plaintiff prove discrimination is a formidable obstacle to prevailing in a Title VII disparate treatment case. As noted by one legal scholar, only in cases of extreme discrimination can a plaintiff demonstrate the requisite intent to discriminate, short of an admission of culpability by the defendant (Suggs, 1991). As discussed below, the manner in which hiring decisions are made in college sport makes it unlikely that prospective African American coaches or administrators will be able to prove that discriminatory motivation lies behind a college's negative promotion or hiring decision.

Disparate Impact

In 1971, the Supreme Court held that Title VII, in addition to banning intentional discrimination, also bans neutral employment practices that have a disparate impact on blacks, unless those practices are shown to be justified by business necessity (*Griggs v. Duke Power Co.*, 1971). In this regard, the Court stated that facially neutral practices that "operate as 'built-in headwinds' for minority groups and are unrelated to measuring job capability" violate Title VII regardless of the employer's good intent or lack of discriminatory intent (*Griggs v. Duke Power Co.*, 1971, p. 432). The Court further stated:

> The objective of Congress in the enactment of Title VII is plain from
> the language of the statute. It was to achieve equality of employment

opportunities and remove barriers that have operated in the past to favor an identifiable group of White employees over other employees. Under the Act, practices, procedures, or tests neutral on their face, and even neutral in terms of intent, cannot be maintained if they operate to "freeze" the status quo of prior discriminatory employment practices. (p. 432)

To prevail in this type of case, a plaintiff must establish, by statistics, that the practice at issue resulted in a substantially disproportionate under-representation of statutorily protected persons. However, a plaintiff cannot sustain an action simply by proving the existence of a racial or other imbalance in the employer's work force. A disparate impact claimant must also demonstrate that this imbalance was caused by a specific discriminatory practice and "that each challenged employment practice causes a disparate impact" (*Wards Cove Packing Co., Inc. v. Atonio*, 1989, p. 657).

The most viable suits in this area are those brought by a party denied a job opportunity based on a discriminatory selection device or hiring practice. Examples of employment practices that might be deemed discriminatory because of their consequences include standardized tests and educational requirements (Shropshire, 1996).

To summarize, a plaintiff alleging disparate impact must establish that (1) an employment practice causes a disparate impact, and (2) the defendant cannot demonstrate the practice is related to the job at issue and that the practice is consistent with its business needs (*Civil Rights Act of 1991*, 1994).

Features of sports-hiring create significant evidentiary barriers to sustaining a Title VII disparate treatment or disparate impact claim. In making hiring decisions in sports, employers typically will not use a selection device or specific hiring practice. Indeed, an NAACP study revealed an absence of hiring or promotion practices in sports that amount to disparate impact or treatment (Shropshire, 1996). In this regard, Professor Shropshire concluded: "Employers in sports tend to use a series of subjective criteria, varying among employment decisions, with no elements necessarily being weighed more heavily than others. With no unique practice to target as discriminatory, it is difficult to bring an action under Title VII no matter what the statistics show regarding the under representation of any group at any job level" (p. 65).

It is important to note, however, that the use of subjective hiring criteria will not provide an absolute shield against a Title VII disparate impact claim. In *Watson v. Fort Worth Bank & Trust*, 1988, the United States Supreme Court held that subjective criteria under which employers or their agents have substantial discretion in identifying desired traits or characteristics are subject to disparate impact theory. In deciding that subjective criteria are subject to impact analysis, the Supreme Court noted the difficulty in showing what is sufficient to make out a prima facie case. This difficulty was expressed by another court as follows: "The difficulties are obvious: how does one show that the application of variable concepts such as 'experience' create racial disparity between those hired and those qualified for jobs?" (*Atonio v. Wards Cove Packing Co., Inc.*, 1993, p. 1498).

Once again plaintiffs are confronted with a formidable obstacle: establishing the requisite relationship between particular subjective employment practices and disparities in the work force (*Johnson v. Uncle Ben's, Inc.*, 1992). Subjective criteria are subject to the requirement that the plaintiff identify the specific criteria and demonstrate that it is responsible for the statistical disparity (*Atonio v. Wards Cove Packing Co., Inc.*, 1993).

Given these evidentiary requirements, African Americans will face serious impediments to prevailing on a disparate impact theory. The controversial hiring in the mid-1990s of Rick Neuheisel, who is white, rather than Bob Simmons, who is African American, as head football coach for the University of Colorado, illustrates this point. In justifying its hiring of the less experienced Neuheisel, Colorado officials made reference to various subjective criteria. As one commentator wrote, "Neuheisel was the right hire at Colorado because he was an extraordinary coaching prospect, and because, not incidentally, he was a good fit for Colorado, a maverick campus, and for Boulder, a cosmopolitan college town along the picturesque Flatirons. Bob Simmons wasn't rejected; he just wasn't the No. 1 choice" (Frei, 1995, p. 26).

The hard-to-quantify factors on which hiring decisions are based in sport were identified by former University of Colorado President Judith Albino as including "proven coaching ability, recruiting ability, management skills, communication skills, public relations skills and ethical standards" (Willis, 1995, p. 1). She concluded that "over all, we found that our appraisal of [Neuheisel] was the highest of those we interviewed. . . . Any one of the four candidates could have done the job. But we weren't in the business of picking an acceptable coach. We were in the business of picking the best possible coach" (Willis, 1995, p. 1).

Case Analysis

Jackson v. University of New Haven

Two recent cases also illustrate the formidable barriers that those asserting claims for racial discrimination in sport must overcome. In *Jackson v. University of New Haven*, 2002, an African American applicant for a coaching position brought suit asserting disparate treatment and disparate impact racial discrimination in violation of Titles VI and VII. In 1999, the head football coach for the University of New Haven resigned to take another position. An advertisement seeking his replacement listed the various requirements including "successful collegiate coaching experience . . . ." (*Jackson v. University of New Haven*, 2002, p. 157). From the 36 applications submitted, the university decided to interview six candidates, all of whom had previous collegiate coaching experience and were white. Jackson, who had minor league but no collegiate coaching experience (he had earned several coach-of-the-year honors in this capacity), was not one of the six selected. One of the six white applicants, a former assistant coach at the University of New Haven, was eventually selected.

The university argued that the previous college coaching experience requirement was necessary to ensure the coach was well-versed with NCAA rules and regulations and in order for him to manage the football team successfully. Jackson argued the previous coaching experience requirement amounted to racial discrimination in violation of Titles VI and VII. Alleging disparate impact and disparate treatment, Jackson asserted that "the challenged qualifications had a discriminatory effect upon African Americans (disparate impact) and that the defendants intentionally discriminated against him based on his race (disparate treatment) (*Jackson v. University of New Haven*, 2002, pp. 158–159).

In assessing the viability of Jackson's disparate treatment claim, the court first articulated the applicable test. According to the court:

> A plaintiff alleging disparate treatment based on race and national origin must first establish a prima facie case of discrimination. . . . The burden then shifts to the defendant to offer a legitimate, non-discriminatory rationale for its actions. . . . Finally, if the defendant does offer a non-discriminatory reason for its decision, the burden again shifts to the plaintiff to show that the defendant's stated reason is a mere pretext for discrimination. (*Jackson v. University of New Haven*, 2002, pp. 160)

The court adopted the four-prong test articulated in *McDonnell Douglas Corp. v. Green* (1973) to determine whether Jackson had presented a prima facie case of discrimination. In concluding that Jackson had failed to establish a prima facie case of discrimination, the court focused on the third prong of the test—whether a plaintiff is qualified for the employment he or she sought. The court's conclusion, that Jackson was not qualified for the New Haven coaching position because he did not possess collegiate coaching experience, demonstrates the evidentiary difficulties plaintiffs are likely to encounter. It also displays the deference courts will afford employers in selecting employment criteria and the difficulty unsuccessful coaches will encounter in establishing a disparate treatment claim. The court found that the prior coaching experience requirement was reasonable on its face. Relatedly, the court stated that "deference must be given to the defendants in selecting college coaching experience as a qualification for the position of head coach. Nor is it appropriate for this Court to mandate that the defendants equate Jackson's experience in coaching minor league football with college coaching experience" (*Jackson v. University of New Haven*, 2002, pp. 161–162).

The court also ruled against Jackson on his disparate impact claim. In so doing, the court stated that a prima facie case of disparate impact requires proof that "a specific policy or practice of the defendant has had a disproportionate negative impact on the plaintiff's protected class. . . ." (*Jackson v. University of New Haven*, 2002, pp. 161–162). To make this showing, a plaintiff must, "(1) identify a policy or practice, (2) demonstrate that a disparity exists, and (3) establish a causal relationship between the two" (p. 164). In support of his claim, Jackson presented evidence showing that only 10% (1 out of 10 candidates) of white versus 50% (2 out of four) of the African American candidates for the New Haven coaching position did not have college coaching experience. The court found that this statistical evidence, given the small size of the sample (14 total applicants), was insufficient to establish a causal relationship between the employment criterion and its impact on African Americans (*Jackson v. University of New Haven*, 2002, pp. 164–165).

Richardson, Jr. v. Suggs

In *Richardson, Jr. v. Sugg*, 2004, Nolan Richardson, head coach of the University of Arkansas at Fayettville's men's basketball coach from 1985 until his termination in 2002, filed a discrimination lawsuit against the university. Richardson alleged "he was fired because of his race and because he spoke out on matters of public concern (race)" (*Richardson, Jr. v. Sugg*, 2004, p. 922). With respect to his racially motivated employment termination claim, Richardson asserted disparate treatment—he received less favorable treatment than white head coaches at UAF with respect to the scope of his duties and authority and to his pay. The court rejected Richardson's Title VII based disparate treatment claim. According to the court, Richardson failed to produce sufficient evidence to establish intentional discrimination.

Richardson also alleged a freedom of speech claim under which he asserted he was terminated in retaliation for making comments regarding the university's recruitment of African American athletes, the difficult social environment that confronted African American athletes at the university, and the low graduation rates of African American in contrast to white athletes. In rejecting this claim, the court recognized the rule that speech regarding matters of public concern may not be restricted by the government (*Richardson, Jr. v. Sugg*, 2004, p. 941). It concluded that his comments regarding the social environment at Fayettville were not made as an attempt to raise social consciousness of the public. The court found that Richardson failed to produce evidence that the school had restrained him or acted in retaliation for his comments regarding graduation rates (*Richardson, Jr. v. Sugg*, 2004, p. 943). In 2006, A federal appellate court agreed and affirmed the decision of the trial court (*Richardson, Jr. v. Sugg*, 2006).

Jackson and *Richardson* illustrate the difficulty African Americans encounter in challenging allegedly racially discriminatory hiring and promotion decisions. One reason for such difficulty is the absence of objectively quantifiable factors on which employment decisions are made. As revealed in Jackson, such a challenge is all the more difficult to establish inasmuch as courts, which presume to lack the requisite expertise, are reluctant to second-guess hiring decisions in sports (Shropshire, 1996).

Voluntary Affirmative Action Plans

The limited effectiveness of the law as a means of diversifying the positions of authority in college athletics underscores the critical role of college presidents and athletic directors in achieving this goal. As noted by Professor Shropshire, the limited utility of the law and the impact of the old-boy network lead inevitably to the conclusion that "[a]ffirmative action must be taken for more African Americans to become a part of these hiring networks" (Shropshire, 1996, pp. 114–115).

The National Collegiate Athletic Association (NCAA) has undertaken affirmative initiatives to increase the number of minorities in administrative positions at its member institutions and conference. One program, the Leadership Institute for Ethnic Minority Males was developed by the NCAA's Minority Opportunities and Interests Committee. It "represents the NCAA's commitment to address the critical shortage of senior-level ethnic minorities involved with athletics programs at member institutions and conference offices" (NCAA, 2006a). Program participants undergo a twelve-month "leadership and skills development experience" (NCAA, 2006a). A parallel program exists for minority females, the Leadership Institute for Ethnic Minority Females (NCAA, 2006b).

The NCAA has also developed a program, in conjunction with the American Football Coaches Academy and the Black Coaches Association, aimed at addressing the paucity of minorities in football coaching ranks. "The NCAA Coaches

Academy program was created by the NCAA Minority Opportunities and Interests Committee in 2003 to assist ethnic minority football coaches with career advancement through skills enhancement, networking and exposure opportunities and to raise awareness regarding the substantial pool of talented ethnic-minority coaches" (NCAA, 2007).

Notwithstanding laudable efforts by organizations such as the NCAA and BCA, increased diversity at coaching and administrative levels will be achieved only from within institutions. In this regard, college presidents must be willing to hire African American coaches and athletic directors even if it means disturbing the racial sensitivities of alumni and boosters. College presidents and athletic directors must be willing to hire minorities for senior level administrative positions in order to open up the hiring networks that inform those in decision-making positions of the existence of all qualified applicants. As Professor Shropshire (2004) noted, apart from continued negative impact of racial stereotypes on the willingness of institutions to hire coaches and administrators of color, the importance of hiring networks cannot be ignored:

> Most who have looked at hiring and promotion problems in sports have concluded that the heart of the problem—beyond discrimination—is the network used to hire at various levels. As with most other American enterprises, these networks have not traditionally included people of color. The primary participants have been white males. Even if one can successfully have a decline in racist attitudes . . . , accessing jobs [in power positions] through traditional networks remains problematic. The world of sports, unlike traditional businesses, is not one where jobs are posted and people apply. It is one where someone knows someone because they played or coached together, or some other relationship previously existed with someone not too far removed from the potential candidate. (p. 203)

Learning from the NFL's Experience

The current predicament in collegiate sport is not unlike that in the NFL prior to 2004. Before a major breakthrough in 2004, African Americans were largely shut out of head coaching positions in professional football. A September 2002 report by attorneys Cyrus Mehri and the late Johnnie Cochran concluded that "African American football players are victims of discrimination with respect to hiring and firing notwithstanding their superior coaching performance" (Cochran & Mehri, 2002). Addressing the difficulty encountered by African American head coaching prospects in the NFL, the report stated,

> Our report describes several manifestations of such limited opportunities, including the higher bar set for black coaches before they are seriously considered for top coaching positions ("moving goal posts") and the tendency to quickly terminate black coaches. In case after case, NFL owners have shown more interest in—and patience with—white coaches who don't win than black coaches who do. (p. ii)

The report deftly placed the plight of black NFL coaching prospects within the larger societal context:

> The parallels between the struggles of African-Americans at [major US corporations] and within the NFL coaching ranks are striking. For years, we have discovered and documented how minority professionals are forced to significantly outperform their white counterparts to advance half as far. And even those employees who break through the glass ceiling are afforded far less room for error than similarly situated whites. The same is true for NFL coaches. (p. i)

After the report was released, Cochran and Mehri suggested they might initiate legal action against the NFL if the league failed to undertake efforts to increase the representation of African Americans as head coaches of its 32 franchises. As a result of external pressure and efforts undertaken within the NFL, the number of African American head football coaches in the NFL has increased dramatically since the report was released in early 2003. Shortly after the release of the Cochran & Mehri report, an NFL committee designed to address the issue of diversity issued guidelines referred to as the Rooney Rule, as a part of its policy to foster greater opportunities for African Americans to gain head coaching positions. Under the Rooney Rule, at least one person of color must be interviewed as a candidate for each NFL head coach vacancy. The Rooney Rule was the result of a collaborative effort on the part of those with leadership positions in the NFL, including the Commissioner's Office, owners, and committees established to address the dearth of coaches of color. As of July 2006, African Americans filled an all-time high of seven of the NFL's head coaching positions. African Americans also fared well in NFL assistant coaching positions. During the 2005 season, African Americans held 152 assistant coaching positions in the NFL. (Lapchick, 2006b). A similar policy adopted by Major League Baseball resulted in an increase in the number of managers of color.

Whether recent progress in the NFL will become longstanding such that it constitutes a part of the NFL culture remains uncertain. Nevertheless, the NFL experience underscores that progress can be made as a result of affirmative means undertaken to open up hiring networks to all qualified candidates, including persons of color.

Conclusion

The foregoing discussion suggests that given the proper set of circumstances, traditional and nontraditional antidiscrimination norms may provide mechanisms for confronting the harm caused by racism in college athletics. Yet, as a general proposition, it is fair to conclude that the role of the law—if the focus is on existing antidiscrimination statutes—will be limited. For example, there will likely be few instances where an African American coach can proffer the evidence of racial animus necessary to prevail in a Title VII claim.

Consequently, litigation strategies for addressing the unconscious racism that African Americans will encounter in seeking coaching and administrative positions in intercollegiate athletics will require honest and creative approaches that transcend traditional doctrinal boundaries. Limitations inherent in a litigation strategy for effecting social change moderate its effectiveness in achieving racial equity in intercollegiate athletics. As noted by Professor Smith, the principal role of litigation may be as supplemental to non-litigation strategies. Ultimately, achieving racial equity in sports will require a shift in attitude. Those in power positions in intercollegiate athletics must commit to achieving racial equity. This will require recognizing and moving beyond the stereotypes and assumptions that underlie the unconscious racism that permeates college athletics.

▲▼ Suggested Readings ▲▼

Anderson, P. (1996). Racism in sports: A question of ethics. *Marquette Sports Law Journal, 6,* 357–408.

Davis, T. (2003). Breaking the color barrier. In E. Ward (Ed.), *Courting the Yankees* (p. 335). Durham: Carolina Academic Press.

Davis, T. (1995). The myth of the superspade: The persistence of racism in college athletics. *Fordham Urban Law Journal, 22,* 615–698.

Dees, A. J. (2004). Do the right thing: A search for an equitable application of Title IX in historically black colleges and university athletics. *Capital University Law Review, 33,* 219–290.

Grant, O. B. (2003). African American collegiate football players and the dilemma of exploitation, racism and education: A socio-economic analysis of sports law. *Whittier Law Review, 24,* 645–661.

Mathewson, A. D. (1996). Black women, gender equity and the function at the junction. *Marquette Sports Law Journal, 6,* 239–266.

Shropshire, K. L. (2004). Minority issues in contemporary sports, *Stanford Law & Policy Review, 15,* 189–211.

Shropshire, K. L. (1996). *In black & white: Race and sports in America.* New York: New York University Press.

Smith, R. K., & Walker, R. D. (2001). From inequity to opportunity: keeping the promises made to big-time intercollegiate student-athletes, *Nevada Law Journal, 1,* 160–206.

Smith, R. K. (1996). When ignorance is bliss: In search of racial and gender equity in intercollegiate athletics. *Missouri Law Review, 61,* 329–392.

Suggs, R. E. (1991). Racial discrimination in business transactions. *Hastings Law Journal, 42,* 1257–1323,

Yarbrough, M. V. (1996). If you let me play sports. *Marquette Sports Law Journal, 6,* 229–238.

▲▼ Study Questions ▲▼

1. Describe the ways in which racism negatively affects the interests of African Americans in college athletics.

2. Describe the historical transformation of racism in college athletics.

3. What variables contribute to the racism that persists in present-day college athletics?

4. Given that racial discrimination negatively affects the interests of African Americans in college sports, why are traditional civil rights laws of limited effectiveness as vehicles for combating it?

5. Inasmuch as traditional civil rights legislation is of limited utility in ameliorating racism in college athletics, identify alternative means of recourse.

References

Anderson v. Douglas & Lomason Co., Inc., 26 F.3d 1277 (5th Cir. 1994), *cert. denied*, 513 U.S. 1149 (1995).

Arlosoroff v. National Collegiate Athletic Ass'n., 746 F.2d 1019 (4th Cir. 1984).

Aronauer, R. (2005, Sept. 29). NCAA denies U. of North Dakota's request to be exempted from policy on Indian mascots. *Chronicle of Higher Education.*

Atonio v. Wards Cove Packing Co., Inc., 10 F.3d 1485 (9th Cir. 1993), *cert. denied*, 513 U.S. 809 (1994).

Brooks, D., Althouse, R., & Tucker, D. (2007). African American coaching mobility models and "the global market place." In D. Brooks & R. Althouse (Eds.), *Diversity and social justice in college sports.* Morgantown, WV: Fitness Information Technology, Inc.

Brown, G. T. (2005, August 15). Policy applies core principles to mascot issue. *NCAA News, 42,* 1, 19.

Civil Rights Act of 1871, 42 U.S.C. § 1983 (1988), Civil Rights Act of 1870, 42 U.S.C. § 1981 (1994).

Corbett, D. (2007). An examination of athletic directors' perception of barriers to employment opportunities. In D. Brooks, and R. Althouse, R. *Diversity and social justice in college sports.* Morgantown, WV.: Fitness Information Technology, Inc.

Coakley, J. A. (1994). *The sociology of sport.* Dallas, TX: Taylor Publishers.

Cochran, J., & Mehri, C. (2002, September 10). Black coaches in the National Football League: Superior performance, inferior opportunities. Retrieved from www.findjustice.com/cases

Coral Construction Co. v. King County, 941 F.2d 910, 931 (9th Cir. 1991), *cert. denied*, 502 U.S. 1033 (1992).

Davis, T. (1995). The myth of the superspade: The persistence of racism in college athletics. *Fordham Urban Law Journal, 22,* 615–698.

Davis, T. (2003). Breaking the color barrier. In E. Ward (Ed.), *Courting the Yankees* (p. 335). Durham: Carolina Academic Press.

Dees, A. J. (2004). Do the right thing: A search for an equitable application of Title IX in historically black colleges and university athletics. *Capital University Law Review, 33,* 219–290.

Dixon v. Margolis, 765 F. Supp. 454 (N.D. 111.1991).

Edwards v. Jewish Hospital of St. Louis, 855 F.2d 1345 (8th Cir.1988).

Evans v. Newton, 382 U.S. 296 (1966).

Frei, T. (1995, October 30). Separate ways. *Sporting News.*

Griggs v. Duke Power Co., 401 U.S. 424 (1971).

Harris, O. (1993). African American predominance in collegiate sport. In D. Brooks & R. Althouse (Eds.), *Racism in college athletics: The African American athlete's experience* (pp. 51–74). Morgantown, WV: Fitness Information Technology, Inc.

Hoover v. Meiklejohn, 430 F. Supp. 164 (D. Colo. 1977).

Jackson v. University of New Haven, 228 F.Supp.2d 156 (D. Conn. 2002).

Johnson v. Uncle Ben's, Inc., 965 F.2d 1363 (5th Cir. 1992), *cert. denied*, 511 U.S. 1068 (1994).

Lapchick, R. (2006a). *The 2005 racial and gender report card: College sports.* DeVos Sport Business Management Program: Orlando, FL: University of Central Florida.

Lapchick, R. (2006b). *The 2005 racial and gender report card: National Football League.* DeVos Sport Business Management Program: Orlando, FL: University of Central Florida.

Large eligibility differences noted by race, income (1998, February 2) *NCAA News,* p. 1.

Lombardo, B. (1978). The Harlem Globetrotters and the perpetuation of the Black stereotype. *Physical Educator, 35,* 60–63.

Marcano, A., & Fidler, D. (1999). The globalization of baseball: Major League Baseball and mistreatment of Latin American baseball talent. *Indiana J. Global Legal Studies, 6:* 511.

Mathewson, A.D. (1996). Black women, gender equity and the function at the junction. *Marquette Sports Law Journal,* 6, 239–266.

McDonnell Douglas Corp. v. Green, 411 U.S. 792 (1973).

Metro Broadcasting, Inc. v. FCC, 497 U.S. 547 (1990), *overruled in part* by Adarand Constructors, Inc. v. Pena, 115 S. Ct. 2097 (1995).

Modjeska, A. C. (1993). *Employment discrimination law* (3rd ed.). Deerfield, IL: Clark Boardman Callaghan.

Mott, R. D. (1996, January l5). Delegates reject modification to initial eligibility standards. *NCAA News,* p. 7.

National Collegiate Athletic Association (2004a, August 30). National collegiate athletic association report shows little change for minorities in leadership roles. *NCAA News Online.* Retrieved from http://www2.ncaa.org/media_and_events/association_news/ncaa_news_online/2004/08_30_04/association_wide/4118n08.html

National Collegiate Athletic Association (2004b). Minority Opportunities and Interest Committee's Biennial Study, 2003–04 Race and Gender Demographics of NCAA Member Institutions' Athletics Personnel. Retrieved from http://www.ncaa.org/library/research/race_demographics/2003-04/2003-04_race_demographics_athletics_personnel.pdf> (last visited 2/1/007).

National Collegiate Athletic Association (2006a). *Leadership Institute for Ethnic Minority Males.* Retrieved from http://www1.ncaa.org/membership/ed_outreach/prof_development/leadership_institute.html (last visited February 2, 2007).

National Collegiate Athletic Association (2006b). *Leadership Institute for Ethnic Minority Females.* Retrieved from http://www1.ncaa.org/membership/ed_outreach/prof_development/leadership_institute_for_ethnic_minority_females.html (last visited February 2, 2007).

National Collegiate Athletic Association (2006c). *2006–07 NCAA Division I Manual.* Indianapolis, IN: National Collegiate Athletic Association.

National Collegiate Athletic Association (2007, January 3). NCAA to host first future coaches academy for prospective head football coaches. *Press Release.* Retrieved from http://www.ncaa.org/wps/portal/!ut/p/kcxml/04_Sj9SPykssy0xPLMnMz0vM0Y_QjzKLN4j3NQDJgFjGpvqRqCKO6AI-YXARX4_83FR9b_0A_YLc0NCIckdFAEuT364!/delta/base64xml/L3dJdyEvUUd3QndNQSEvNElVRS82XzBfTFU!?CONTENT_URL=http://www2.ncaa.org/portal/media_and_events/press_room/2007/January/20070103_fut

ure_coaches_academy_rls.html (last visited Feb. 2, 2007).

Nowak, J., & Rotunda, R. (1995). *Constitutional law* (5th ed.). St. Paul, MN: West Publishing Co. Parish.

Polite, F. G. (2007). Minority opportunities in college athletics: A business imperative? In D. Brooks & R. Althouse, *Diversity and social justice in college sports.* Morgantown, WV: Fitness Technology Inc.

Richardson, Jr. v. Sugg, 448 F.3d 1046 (8th Cir. 2006).

Richardson, Jr. v. Sugg, 325 F.Supp.2d 919 (E.D. Ark. 2004).

St. Mary's Honor Center v. Hicks, 509 U.S. 502, 1113 S. Ct. 2742 (1993).

Shropshire, K. L. (1996). *In Black and white: Race and sports in America.* New York: New York University Press.

Shropshire, K. L. (2004). Minority issues in contemporary sports, *Stanford Law & Policy Review, 15,* 189–211.

Smith, R. K. (1996). When ignorance is not bliss: In search of racial and gender equity in intercollegiate athletics. *Missouri Law Review, 61,* 329–392.

Smith, R. K., & Walker, R. D. (2001). From inequity to opportunity: Keeping the promises made to big-time intercollegiate student-athletes. *Nevada Law Journal, 1,* 160–206.

Suggs, R. E. (1991). Racial discrimination in business transactions. *Hastings Law Journal, 42,* 1257–1323.

Suggs, W. (2003, Jan. 17). Jock majors. *The Chronicle of Higher Education,* A33.

Thomas, R. E., & Rich, B. L. (2005). Under the radar: The resistance of promotion biases to market economic forces, *Syracuse Law Review, 55,* 301.

Title VII of the Civil Rights Act of 1964, as amended by the Civil Rights Act of 1991, 42 U.S.C. Section 2000e *et seq.* (1995).

U.S. Constitution, amend 14, 1.

Village of Arlington Heights v. Metropolitan Housing Development Corp., 429 U.S. 252 (1977).

Washington v. Davis, 426 U.S. 229 (1976).

Washington v. Garrett, 10 F.3d 1421 (9th Cir. 1994).

Watson v. Fort Worth Bank & Trust, 487 U.S. 977 (1988).

Wiggins, D. K. (1993). Critical events affecting racism in athletics. In D. Brooks & R. Althouse (Eds.), *Racism in college athletics: The African American athlete's experience* (pp. 23–49). Morgantown, WV: Fitness Information Technology, Inc.

Willis, G. (1995, Jan. 1). College football coaching picture (In black and white). *New York Times.* Sec. 8, p.1.

Abstract ▼ Historically, a mindset nurtured by negative stereotypes resulted in the exclusion of African American student athletes from the academic mainstream in many predominately white colleges and universities. Vestiges of such a mindset continue to adversely affect and devalue the African American student athlete's educational interests. Given the limited role of traditional antidiscrimination norms and common law doctrine to ameliorate this harm, those adversely affected must turn to alternatives to a litigation strategy in order to promote the educational interests of African American student athletes. A controversial issue that has surfaced in college sports is the extent to which race is a variable that influences the promulgation of NCAA rules and regulation. In particular, controversy surrounded the promulgation and implementation of the NCAA's initial eligibility rules, Propositions 16 and 48, and whether they disparately affected African American student athletes. Litigation asserting that the standardized test component of the initial eligibility was a manifestation of racial discrimination against African Americans student athletes met with mixed results. A recent favorable ruling on behalf of plaintiffs challenging the test component, however, was an important factor contributing to the NCAA's making fundamental changes to its initial eligibility rules.

Introduction

This chapter examines the impact of race on the interests of African American student athletes as it relates to: (1) the alleged neglect of their academic interests; and (2) the alleged disparate impact of NCAA rules and regulations. It explores the role the law has played and may yet play in ameliorating the impact of race in these two contexts.

Race, Academics, and the African American Student Athlete

The essence of the contractual relationship between a scholarship student athlete and his or her university is premised on a bargain in which the university gives the student athlete a scholarship in exchange for the student athlete's promise to participate in a particular sport. The scholarship represents an opportunity for student athletes to obtain an education and to develop their athletic skills. A tension that has resided throughout the era of the scholarship athlete is to what extent economic and athletic interests jeopardize the academic achievement of student athletes. This tension manifests in a range of conduct, from institutions' failure to make adequate academic resources available to student athletes to academic advisors performing work for student athletes, that ultimately undermines student athletes' academic achievement. A concern that emerges is whether educational institutions engage in exploitation when they fail to do all within their power to ensure that educational benefits are received by their student athletes (Smith & Walker, 2001).

The question of academic inequity is particularly acute in the case of African American Division I football and basketball players. The specter

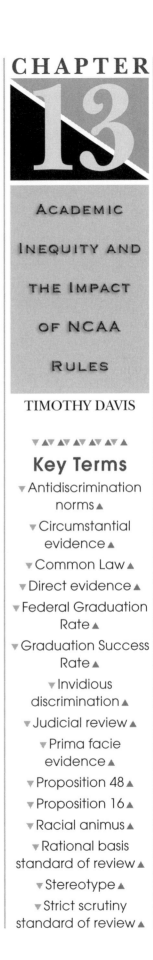

CHAPTER

13

ACADEMIC
INEQUITY AND
THE IMPACT
OF NCAA
RULES

TIMOTHY DAVIS

▼▲▽ ▲▽ ▲▽ ▲▽ ▲▽ ▲

Key Terms

▼Antidiscrimination
norms▲

▽Circumstantial
evidence▲

▽Common Law▲

▽Direct evidence▲

▽Federal Graduation
Rate▲

▽Graduation Success
Rate▲

▽Invidious
discrimination▲

▽Judicial review▲

▽Prima facie
evidence▲

▽Proposition 48▲

▽Proposition 16▲

▽Racial animus▲

▽Rational basis
standard of review▲

▽Stereotype▲

▽Strict scrutiny
standard of review▲

of academic inequity arises, in part, because African American student athletes are disproportionately responsible for generating the profits in these revenue-producing sports that fund non-revenue-producing sports and the NCAA's operations (Smith & Walker, 2001).

There also persists the lingering question of race as it relates to academic inequity in the case of the African American student athlete. Historically, it was clear that a mindset nurtured by stereotypes resulted in the exclusion of "African American student athletes from the academic and social mainstream in many predominately white colleges and universities" (Davis, 1995, p. 699). Do lower graduation rates for African American student athletes in contrast to white student athletes continue to reflect a devaluation of the African American athlete's educational interests (Harris, 1993)? Male African American football and basketball players are graduating at rates that exceed those they achieved prior to the enactment of Proposition 48 in 1986. Despite impressive gains, however, graduation rates for African American male student athletes in revenue-producing sports continue to lag behind those of other male student athletes.

Before examining graduation rate data, a brief discussion of two graduation computation models is in order. The Federal Graduation Rate measures the number of student athletes who graduate within six years of when they enter college. The federal methodology has been criticized for not making adjustments for variables that would result in higher institutional graduation rates. For example, the federal methodology has been criticized for including within its graduation computation, as non-graduates, student athletes who leave their institutions in good academic standing. In response to such criticism, the NCAA developed an alternative methodology, the Graduation Success Rate (GSR), which is viewed as providing a more accurate assessment of graduation rates since it makes adjustments for variables such as student athletes who leave an institution in good academic standing and those who transfer into an institution. The following discussion includes statistics based on both methodologies.

While depicting improved graduation rates for African American student athletes, both graduation rate methodologies reveal a persistent gap in the graduation rates for African American and white student athletes. According to the federal rate, graduation rates increased from 33% to 48% for male African American student athletes who entered college in 1984 and 1999, respectively (DeVos Sport Business Management Program, 2006a, p. 1; NCAA News, Nov. 20, p. 20). With respect to the revenue-producing sports, the federal rate revealed that 42% of Division I male African American basketball players who entered college in 1999 graduated within six years (the GSR was 51%). This figure is lower than the 52% federal graduation rate for white Division I male basketball players (the GSR was 76%), and the 56% federal rate for all male student athletes who matriculated in 1999 (the GSR was 70%) (NCAA, 2006, Nov. 20, p. 20). African American football players who entered college at Division I-A institutions in 1999 posted a 49% federal graduation rate in contrast to a 64% rate for their white counterparts (NCAA, 2006, Nov. 20, p. 20). The GSR was 56% and 79%, respectively for Division I-A African American and white football players.

These statistics raise the question of whether too little is expected academically of the African American student athlete. Some assert that African American student athletes have become commodities serving the financial interests of the institutions for which they compete (Davis, 1995). As evidence, critics point to the dominance of African Americans in the revenue-producing sports (Smith, 1996). In particular, critics also point to the graduation rates of African American student athletes at some of the more athletically successful institutions. Using Graduation Success Rate data, a study by Dr. Richard Lapchick revealed the following: 38 (66%) of the men's teams that participated in the NCAA's men's 2006 basketball tournament graduated 70% or more of their white basketball student athletes; yet only 21 (33%) of these institutions graduated 70% or more of their African American basketball student athletes. This report also showed that 43 (74%) tournament teams graduated 60% or more of their white male student athletes, while 28 (44%) of these teams graduated more than 60 percent of their male African American basketball student athletes (DeVos Sport Business Management Program, 2006b, p. 2). Dr. Lapchick concluded that "race is an ongoing academic issue, reflected in the continued gap between graduation rates for white and African-American student athletes. While the rates for both groups have improved over the last few years, a significant disparity remains between graduation rates for white and African-American basketball student-athletes" (DeVos Sport Business Management Program, 2006b, p. 3).

The NCAA recently has undertaken measures aimed at reducing the likelihood that a student athlete will leave college after his or her eligibility has expired without having developed educationally in a substantively meaningful way. In May 2004, as a part of what it characterized as Division I academic reform measures, the NCAA implemented incentive/disincentive legislation, Academic Progress Rate, aimed at penalizing institutions whose athletes fail to measure up to certain academic requirements. In 2002, the NCAA heightened its satisfactory progress rules, which require a student athlete to demonstrate that he or she is making progress toward a degree in order to maintain athletic eligibility, for the specific purpose of increasing graduation rates for Division I football and men's basketball players (Suggs, 2003). Pursuant to these revised rules, student athletes must declare a major at an early stage during their college careers and complete a substantial amount of their major coursework within the first few years of college.

To the extent that student athletes generally benefit from these measures, African American student athletes may profit from them as well. Critics question, however, whether a well-intended reform, such as heightened satisfactory progress rules, will negatively affect academic achievement by encouraging student athletes to take "jock majors" that allow them to "maneuver through the maze of academic requirements and remain eligible to compete . . . [T]he march toward tougher standards and . . . , higher graduation rates begs a crucial question, however: Do numbers matter if players are being sent into academic programs that won't give them a meaningful education or marketable skills?" (Suggs, 2003, pp. A33–34).

In conclusion, economics and race converge so as to devalue the African American student athlete's academic interest. This devaluation raises concerns regarding the exploitation of African American student athletes who provide valuable services yet arguably leave their institutions of higher learning without having obtained the academic preparation necessary for them to cope successfully with the life issues they will encounter following their college careers. Notwithstanding the real harm that ensues from this devaluation, it is unlikely that traditional antidiscrimination norms will provide a means of redress.

Academic Opportunity for Student Athletes: A Section 1981 Analysis

42 U.S.C. §1981 prohibits racial discrimination in the contracting process. Notwithstanding the student athlete's contractual relationship with his or her institution, the utility of Section 1981 is dubious to redress alleged racially based harm suffered by African American student athletes. Section 1981, like most antidiscrimination statutes, proscribes only intentional acts of racial discrimination (*Edwards v. Jewish Hosp. of St. Louis*, 855 F.2d 1345; 8th Cir. 1987). Therefore, to sustain a Section 1981 claim, it would be incumbent upon the student athlete to show that the institution's conduct was motivated by race. However, except in rare instances, the academic neglect of African American student athletes appears to result from unconscious rather than deliberately overt forms of racial discrimination.

Given the inherent nature of the racism implicated, the African American student athlete is situated like many other plaintiffs alleging discrimination in the contracting process. Section 1981 claimants encounter an intent element that represents an almost insurmountable hurdle to establishing their claim. Indeed, African Americans' inability to rely on established antidiscrimination laws to achieve racial justice illustrates the limitations inherent in an antidiscrimination legal framework that fails to take into account unconscious racism (Lawrence, 1987; Green, 1990). For example, in urging that the equal protection doctrine come to grips with unconscious racism, Professor Charles Lawrence (1987) commented as follows:

> Traditional notions of intent do not reflect the fact that decisions about racial matters are influenced in large part by factors that can be characterized as neither intentionally, in the sense that certain outcomes are self-consciously sought, nor unintentionally, in the sense that the outcomes are random, fortuitous, and uninfluenced by the decision maker's beliefs, desires, and wishes. (p. 322)

In summary, traditional antidiscrimination law as a tool to combat unconscious racism in collegiate sport will be of limited effectiveness. Consequently, a broad range of legal and non-legal approaches to combating racial inequities in college sports must be considered. These approaches include resort to common law doctrine, NCAA rule-making, state and federal legislation, and political action (Smith, 1996; Davis, 1995).

Alternative Approaches to Combating Discrimination in Collegiate Sport—Common-Law Doctrine

African American student athletes might resort to common-law doctrine in challenging the devaluation of their academic opportunity. For instance, student athletes have challenged the failure of their institutions to provide them with an educational opportunity pursuant to breach of contract and educational malpractice claims.

One such approach has been taken with respect to using the common law to protect the academic interests of student athletes. For instance, in *Ross v. Creighton University* (1992), a student athlete was recruited to play basketball at Creighton in exchange for a basketball scholarship. He achieved a grade point average of only 0.54 during his last semester at Creighton. Ross did not graduate and departed from the university after his four years of playing eligibility were exhausted. He left Creighton with the reading skills of a seventh grader and the overall language skills of a fourth grader (*Ross v. Creighton University,* 1992). Ross sued seeking to impose an obligation on the university to provide him with an educational opportunity. He alleged that the university had engaged in conduct that obstructed the minimal opportunity that he had to obtain substantive educational benefits during his college career. In asserting the existence and breach of such a duty, Ross asserted claims based on common-law tort and contract theories such as educational malpractice, negligent admission, intentional infliction of emotional distress, and breach of implied and express contract. The court's rejection of Ross' educational malpractice and breach of contract claims was influenced by several policy considerations, including: the unavailability of a standard of care to evaluate educators; the difficulties in establishing the cause of the student athlete's inability to develop academically; and the lack of judicial expertise to intervene in such matters (*Ross v. Creighton University,* 1992).

Similar allegations were made by Terrell Jackson in his lawsuit against Drake University. In *Jackson v. Drake University* (1991), an African American student athlete recruited by Drake University to play basketball brought suit alleging that the institution engaged in conduct that amounted to a breach of contract and educational malpractice. Jackson also alleged that a pattern of abusive conduct by Drake's basketball coach constituted a civil rights violation pursuant to 42 U.S.C. Section 1981 (*Jackson v. Drake University,* 1991). With respect to the breach of contract and educational malpractice claims, Jackson alleged that Drake engaged in a pattern of conduct that undermined both his ability to play basketball and to succeed academically. The court refused to impose a duty on Drake to provide an educational opportunity. The court reasoned, in part, that the judiciary lacks the experience to define a clear standard of care by which to measure a university's conduct (*Jackson v. Drake University,* 1991).

The forgoing cases demonstrate the judicial reluctance to adopt theories that protect the academic interests of student athletes. In addition to judicial refusal to acknowledge such theories, other limitations reside in a litigation-based strategy to combat racial discrimination. Litigation is financially and emotionally costly. Litigation also requires resources that may not be readily available to student athletes. Moreover, the very nature of litigation is such that it provides redress on a case-by-case basis. Consequently, a litigation strategy effectuates change slowly. "Given its expense and interstitial nature, therefore, litigation is a weak strategy for bringing racial . . . equity to intercollegiate athletics. Indeed, its major virtue may simply be that it can encourage an important dialogue regarding equity issues, which may ultimately help facilitate meaningful reform at the broader legislative or rulemaking level" (Smith, 1996, p. 367).

Given these limitations to litigation as a strategy for achieving racial equity in college sports, other alternatives must be pursued. While most of these strategies are untested, they may warrant consideration either singularly or in combination. Such strategies include the following:

1. Extending the term of athletic-related scholarships from one year to five years.

2. The initiation of congressional hearings regarding racial equity in college sport that would specifically focus on exploitation and access (Smith, 1996).

3. State legislative hearings exploring issues of racial equity (Smith, 1996).

4. NCAA legislation prohibiting freshman eligibility to compete in intercollegiate athletic competition.

5. Development at the institutional level of detailed and comprehensive plans to create racial equity.

6. Requiring that NCAA legislation be subjected to racial impact studies that would consider the racial implications of proposed legislation.

7. Requiring institutions to account for funds generated in the revenue-producing sports—basketball and football—as a means of avoiding the exploitation of African American student athletes (Smith, 1996).

8. Recognition by state legislatures that student athletes possess certain contract and torts claims as a means of holding their institutions accountable for providing educational opportunity and avoiding exploitation.

9. Collaboration between the NCAA and its member institutions to identify and develop academic assistance programs geared toward the complete education and development of student athletes.

10. Distribution of larger percentages of revenues generated from intercollegiate athletic competition for academic development of student athletes.

None of the suggestions above will be without their own difficulties. However, they offer promise for addressing the range of problems stemming from racism in college athletics.

Disparate Impact of NCAA Rules?

A principal function of the National Collegiate Athletic Association (NCAA) is the promulgation of the rules and principles with which its member institutions must comply (Davis, 1995). It is through the NCAA's rule-making and enforcement processes that the association articulates adherence to values long perceived as fundamental to intercollegiate athletics—educational primacy and amateurism. These values are articulated in the NCAA's statement of its primary purpose: "to maintain intercollegiate athletics as an integral part of the educational program and the athlete as an integral part of the student body and by so doing, retain a clear line of demarcation between intercollegiate athletics and professional sports" (NCAA, 2006, art. 1.3.1, p. 1).

With respect to the amateurism value, NCAA bylaws enumerate the requirements with which a student athlete must comply in order to retain amateur status. For example, student athletes are prohibited from accepting pay for the use of their athletic abilities (NCAA, 2006). Athletes who enter into representation agreements with sports agents may jeopardize their amateur status and the ability to compete in intercollegiate athletics. With respect to the educational value, the NCAA considers intercollegiate athletic programs as "vital component[s]" of an institution's education program (NCAA, 2006, art. 2.5, p. 4). Rules reflecting the educational value include those regulating initial eligibility (NCAA Manual, 2006).

Critics question the legitimacy of amateurism and educational values as providing the cornerstone for NCAA rules in the context of big-time intercollegiate sports and the commercialism that permeates it. In addition, although the NCAA's uniform rules and regulations are premised on the notion of color blindness, they have been assailed as racially and culturally insensitive to ethnic minorities. Rules that allegedly reflect racial or cultural bias include: (a) NCAA initial eligibility standards, (b) amateurism rules, (c) anti-celebration rules, and (d) rules that restrict the money student athletes are permitted to earn from employment.

An incident involving a violation of NCAA amateurism rules that occurred in the mid-1990s raised questions of racial insensitivity, pay-for-play, and economic equity. In 1995 Donnie Edwards, a former UCLA football player, was suspended for one game and ordered to make full restitution for accepting $150 in groceries from a sports agent. Under NCAA rules, an athlete can lose his or her eligibility to compete by accepting cash or other benefits from professional sports agents. Edwards denied that he knew that the groceries were from an agent, but acknowledged that there were times when he did not have the money to buy food. The NCAA concluded that the suspension was warranted (Wilner, 1995).

Reacting to the NCAA's decision, Edwards urged a one-day boycott of college football players to protest their alleged exploitation (Springer, 1995). According to Edwards, "A lot of minority student athletes who play football or basketball have parents who don't have any money. We're lucky to get a scholarship. But once we get here, what do we do? The money we get is not enough to even live on, especially in Westwood" (Springer, 1995, p. E5). Edwards added, "Look at how much money they make from college football alone, all those TV deals, the shoe deals, the jersey deals. There's a lot of money around here. Who's getting it? All the schools. Who's being exploited? Us" (Springer, 1995, p. E5).

Responding to criticism, the NCAA relaxed limitations on earnings by student athletes. At their 1997 convention, the delegates adopted Proposal 62, which later became NCAA Article 12.4.1 and allows student athletes to earn compensation during the school year for work actually performed (Farrell, Fernandez, & Niland, 1997, p. 5; NCAA Manual, 2006, art. 12.4.1, p. 74).

Disparate Impact of NCAA Initial Eligibility Rules

NCAA initial eligibility rules have generated the most controversy regarding their disparate impact on African American student athletes because of the rules' alleged racial and socio-economic bias. The perceived unfairness of NCAA initial eligibility rules also illustrates the racial tensions surrounding the academic experiences of African American student athletes. NCAA initial eligibility rules constitute the standards that determine which student athletes are eligible to receive athletic related financial aid and compete for their institutions. In 1986, the NCAA's initial eligibility rules known as Proposition 48 went into effect. Proposition 48 required that a student athlete achieve a minimum GPA of 2.00 in a least 11 designated high school courses (core courses). In addition, it required a minimum combined score of 700 on the SAT or 15 on the ACT. Commenting on the purpose of Proposition 48 requirements, one court stated, "Division I members implemented Proposition 48 to address the perception that its member schools were exploiting athletes 'for their talents without concern for whether they graduated'" (*Cureton v. NCAA*, 1999, p. 110).

In 1992, Proposition 48 guidelines were replaced by the more stringent requirements of Proposition 16, which increased the number of core courses in which a student athlete had to maintain a minimum GPA. It also created a formula pursuant to which eligibility would be based on a combination of the individual student athlete's high school GPA and his or her standardized test score results.

Critics assert that the NCAA initial eligibility rules historically have disparately impacted African American student athletes because of the standards' racial and socioeconomic bias. Critics challenged Proposition 48 as racist in part because of the projected negative impact on African American enrollment (Mott, 1996).

They argued heightened standards would limit the African American student athletes' access to college. Critics also contended that standardized tests are fundamentally flawed in that they are culturally biased against African Americans. Proponents argued that stricter initial eligibility rules would aid in restoring academic integrity to colleges and universities; according to proponents, the educational mission of institutions of higher education had been undermined by scandals arising within intercollegiate athletics. Heightened requirements might be an effective vehicle in helping to provide student athletes with a reasonable opportunity of obtaining a meaningful degree (Mott, 1996; Davis, 1991).

Both opponents and proponents of the initial eligibility requirements were correct. Graduation rates for all student athletes, including African Americans, increased in the aftermath of Propositions 48 and 16. At the same time, the number of student athletes declared ineligible due to the requirements had a more substantial impact on African American than on white student athletes.

In 2002, the NCAA adopted legislation, effective 2005, that modified its initial eligibility rules. The new legislative retains the Proposition 16 formula approach by which eligibility is based on a combination of GPA and standard test scores. The new requirements, however, deemphasize the standardized test score component of initial eligibility rules by eliminating the cutoff score for this requirement. For example, a student with a 3.0 GPA needs to score only a 620 on the SAT to be eligible for athletic competition and financial aid during his or her first year. The minimum SAT score ranges from 400 for students with a GPA of 3.550 or above to a maximum of 1010 for students with a GPA of 2.0. In commenting on the reasons for the change, NCAA President Miles Brand stated:

> The goal of developing the most recent eligibility models was to maximize graduation rates while minimizing disparate impact. . . . We believe that eliminating the test score cut will increase access and that the new progress-toward-degree benchmarks—particularly in student athlete's first two years—will put athletes on track to graduate at even higher rates than they already do. (NCAA, 2003)

The following table is an excerpt from the NCAA's Division I Manual. It demonstrates, in part, the extent to which the NCAA's revised initial eligibility rules deemphasize the standardized test score component.

The decision to lessen the significance of the standardized test component of the NCAA's initial eligibility rules was also the result of a successful legal chal-

Table 1. Freshman Academic Eligibility Requirements

Core GPA	SAT	Sum ACT
3.550 & above	400	37
3.525	410	38
3.500	420	39
3.475	430	40
3.450	440	41
3.425	450	41
▲ ▼ ▲ ▼		
2.100	970	82
2.075	980	83
2.050	990	84
2.025	1000	85
2.000	1010	86

(NCAA Division I Manual, 2006, art. 14.3.1.1.1, pp. 148–150).

lenge. This case and the other significant legal challenge to the validity of the NCAA's initial eligibility rules are discussed below.

Legal Challenges to Initial Eligibility Rules

Cureton v. NCAA

In January 1997, Trial Lawyers for Public Justice, a public-interest group, filed a lawsuit alleging that the NCAA's eligibility requirements discriminate against African American athletes. In the lawsuit, *Cureton v. NCAA* (37 F. Supp.2d 687, E.D. Pa. 1999), four African American student athletes alleged that they were unlawfully denied educational opportunities as freshmen by virtue of NCAA initial eligibility rules. Plaintiffs had failed to achieve the minimum standardized test score required to receive an athletic scholarship and to compete in intercollegiate competition during their first-year at a Division I institution. They sought to invalidate the minimum standardized test component of Proposition 16 and to permanently enjoin the NCAA from using it.

Plaintiffs turned to Title VI as their basis for recovery. Title VI provides that "[n]o person . . . shall, on the ground of race, color, or national origin, be excluded from participation in, be denied the benefits of, or be subjected to discrimination under any program or activity receiving Federal financial assistance" (Title VI of Civil Rights Act of 1964, 42 U.S.C. Section 20000d et seq [1995]). Specifically, they alleged that Proposition 16 utilized a minimum test score requirement that had "an unjustified disparate impact on African American student athletes" in violation of Title VI (*Cureton v. NCAA*, 1999, p. 111).

The federal district court held that the NCAA's initial eligibility rule unjustifiably discriminated against African American student athletes in violation of Title VI. Relying on data, much of it from NCAA-sponsored studies, the court concluded that Proposition 16 disproportionately affected African American student athletes and permanently enjoined its enforcement. As an example, the court pointed to NCAA data that revealed that in 1996, 21.4% of African American student athletes failed to meet Proposition 16 requirements, in contrast to 4.2% of white student athletes.

It also noted a decrease from 23.6% to 20.3% in African American student athletes enrolled in Division I institutions for 1994–96. The court concluded that according to the data, this decrease was attributable to these student athletes not having satisfied Proposition 16 requirements (*Cureton v. NCAA*, 1999). The court reached this result even though it acknowledged that increasing student athlete graduation rates—a principal justification offered by the NCAA—is a legitimate educational goal. Nevertheless the NCAA failed, according to the court, to produce evidence that established a relationship between using particular cutoff scores of 820 and 68 on the SAT and ACT, respectively, and its goal of achieving enhanced graduation rates.

The NCAA appealed the lower court decision. The Third Circuit Court of Appeals agreed with the NCAA and reversed the trial court decision in favor of the plaintiffs (*Cureton v. NCAA*, 198 F.3d 107, 3rd Cir. 1999). In ruling in favor of the NCAA, the Third Circuit did not address the merits of whether the standardized test component of the Proposition 16 improperly discriminated against African American student athletes. The appellate court focused on the question of whether the NCAA was subject to Title VI regulations. (Only parties who receive federal funds are subject to Title VI regulations). In this regard, the appellate court found that Title VI applied only to specific programs or activities using federal funds and not to a college or university in its entirety. The court concluded that since the NCAA did not exercise controlling authority over member institutions' ultimate decisions about student athletes' eligibility to participate in athletics, it was not subject to the regulations.

An important development occurred after the *Cureton* decision. In *Cureton*, plaintiffs relied on a disparate impact rather than an intentional discrimination theory in pursuing their Title VI action against the NCAA. In an unrelated case, the United States Supreme Court had an opportunity the interpret Title VI's regulations so as to determine the nature of the actions that plaintiffs can assert. In *Alexander v. Sandoval* (2001), the Supreme Court found that individuals may pursue Title VI claims alleging intentional discrimination, but not disparate impact discrimination.

At the time it was decided, *Cureton* was a very significant discrimination case involving the NCAA and it was heralded as major victory for the NCAA. It seemed to immunize the centerpiece of the NCAA's academic reform measures—initial eligibility rules—from litigation. Subsequent developments, however, have proved that this success was short-lived.

Pryor v. NCAA

In 1999, Kelly Pryor, an African American student athlete, signed a Letter of Intent to play varsity soccer at San Jose State University. Similarly, Warrant Spivey, an African American student athlete, signed a Letter of Intent to play football at the University of Connecticut (*Pryor v. NCAA*, 2002). Pursuant to an express condition contained therein, their Letters of Intent were rendered void when neither athlete was able to satisfy the standardized test component of Proposition 16's eligibility requirements. Pryor petitioned for a waiver on the basis of a learning disability and was afforded partial qualifier status, which allowed her to retain her scholarship but prohibited her from competing in team games. The University of Connecticut petitioned on behalf of Spivey on the ground that he was prepared for its academic requirements. The NCAA denied this petition and a subsequent appeal.

Thereafter, both Pryor and Spivey sued the NCAA alleging that its adoption of Proposition 16 intentionally discriminated against them on account of race in violation of Title VI and Section 1981. Pryor also asserted claims based upon her learning disability. The following discussion will focus solely on Pryor and Spivey's Title VI claim, which closely resembled the claim asserted in *Cureton*. The principal difference was that in *Cureton* plaintiffs alleged disparate impact, and in *Pryor* plaintiffs alleged purposeful discrimination.

Relying considerably on evidence obtained during the *Cureton* proceedings, the *Pryor* plaintiffs supported their race discrimination claim by pointing to NCAA generated documents. To illustrate that Proposition 16 was not race neutral, the plaintiffs pointed to an interrogatory response in which the NCAA identified the promotion of higher graduation rates for black student athletes, which would narrow the gap between black and white student athletes' graduation rates, as the goal of Proposition 16 (*Pryor v. NCAA*, 2002). The essence of the plaintiffs' complaint was as follows:

> Proposition 16 achieves the NCAA's stated goal of improving graduation rates for black athletes relative to white athletes by simply "screen[ing] out" greater numbers of black athletes from ever becoming eligible in the first place, *i.e.*, from ever receiving athletic eligibility and scholarship aid. . . . [A]lthough the NCAA knew that Proposition 16 would have a more adverse impact on black student athletes than on white student athletes, the NCAA went ahead and adopted Proposition 16 anyway, based on its "misguided view" toward affecting African American student athletes' graduation rates by denying [scholarship] eligibility to greater numbers of black student athletes. (*Pryor v. NCAA*, 2002, p. 556)

The federal trial court rejected plaintiffs' Title VI claim by concluding that even though Proposition 16 did have a disparate impact on African American student athletes, the NCAA had not intended to intentionally discriminate against African American student athletes when it adopted the legislation. According to the trial court, "The NCAA adopted Proposition 16 in spite of its impact on black athletes, not because of that impact" (*Pryor v. NCAA*, 2002, p. 564). In articulating the standard for determining whether plaintiffs had asserted a cognizable Title VI claim, the court stated that plaintiffs were required to prove that the NCAA adopted Proposition 16 with the intent to impose adverse consequences on African American student athletes. The trial court concluded that purposeful discrimination was not established since Proposition 16 is a facially neutral policy and policies that incidentally, in contrast to intentionally, create a racially disparate impact do not violate Title VI.

The appellate court disagreed. It found that the evidence established that the NCAA intended to harm black student athletes when it adopted a policy that would prevent some of them from receiving a scholarship:

> The NCAA expressly considered race and how Proposition 16 would affect African-American athletes when it adopted this policy. Further, though the NCAA may have intended this race-based consideration for the "laudable" goal of increasing graduation rates for black student athletes, the . . . policy was actually adopted to harm black athletes by preventing them from ever receiving college athletic scholarships and eligibility in the first place. Moreover, contrary to the assertions made in the NCAA's brief, none of the case law it cited, much less Supreme Court case law, absolves a decision-maker from liability simply because it considered race for the "benevolent" purpose of helping a particular racial group. (*Pryor v. NCAA*, 2002, pp. 560–61)

The *Pryor* court's ruling that plaintiffs presented a prima facie case that the NCAA's initial eligibility rules were intentionally discriminatory marked a rare instance in which plaintiffs had mounted a successful legal challenge to a NCAA eligibility rule. The saga of the NCAA's initial eligibility rules also demonstrates the important role of the judicial system as external means of accountability. The possibility of further judicial intervention propelled, in part, the NCAA's decision to drastically alter its initial eligibility standards.

Conclusion

As articulated in the NCAA bylaws, athletics must be an integral part of the educational mission of colleges and universities. Notwithstanding this laudable principle, a pervasive tension residing within big-time intercollegiate athletics is the conflict between the economic interests of institutions and the academic pursuit of student athletes. This tension manifests in ways that negatively affect many student athletes. The conflict takes on particularly acute significance, however, in the case of the African American student athlete. The devaluation of the academic interests of some African American student athletes undermines their ability to realize a meaningful collegiate academic experience. Although recent NCAA reforms may stymie this devaluation, they alone will not be sufficient to give preeminence to academic interests. An array of strategies including legal and legislative must be undertaken to promote the educational pursuits of African American student athletes.

In addition to questions regarding the devaluation of their academic interests, African American student athletes have had occasion to critically assess NCAA rules and regulations. In particular, lawsuits contesting the legality of the standardized test component of the NCAA's initial eligibility rules focused attention on the disparate impact of these and other rules on African American student athletes. In the case of NCAA initial eligibility rules, African American student athletes turned to the judicial system as an external means of holding the NCAA accountable for the impact of its regulations on them. Success, albeit limited, in the judicial system was sufficient to prompt the NCAA to modify its initial eligibility rules so as to deemphasize standardized tests. This demonstrates the role of judicial intervention in influencing NCAA policymaking.

▲▼ Suggested Readings ▲▼

Clark, L. D. (1993). New directions for the Civil Rights Movement: College athletics as a civil rights issue. *Howard Law Journal, 36,* 259–289.

Davis, T. (1995). A model for institutional governance for intercollegiate athletics. *Wisconsin Law Review,* pp. 599–645.

Davis, T. (1995). The myth of the superspade: The persistence of racism in college athletics. *Fordham Urban Law Journal, 22,* 615–698.

Davis, T. (1996). African American student-athletes: Marginalizing the NCAA regulatory structure? *Marquette Sports Law Journal, 6,* 199–227.

Green, L. S. (1984). The new NCAA rules of the game: Academic integrity or racism? *St. Louis University Law Journal, 28,* 101–151.

Grant, O. B. (2003). African American collegiate football players and the dilemma of exploitation, racism and education: A socio-economic analysis of sports law. *Whittier Law Review, 24,* 645–661.

Lufrano, M. R. (1994). The NCAA's involvement in setting academic standards: Legality and desirability. *Seton Hall Journal of Sports Law, 4,* 97–141.

Munczinski, A. (2003). Interception: The courts get another pass at the NCAA and the intentional discrimination of Proposition 16 in Pryor v. NCAA. *Villanova Sports and Entertainment Law Journal, 10,* 389–414.

National Collegiate Athletic Association (2006). *2006 Graduation-Rate Report for NCAA Division I Schools.*

Oates, E. D. (2000). Cureton v. NCAA: The recognition of Proposition 16's misplaced use of standardized test in the context of collegiate athletics as a barrier to educational opportunity for minorities. *Wake Forest University Law Review, 35,* 445.

Shropshire, K. L. (1997). Colorblind propositions: Race, the SAT and the NCAA. *Stanford Law and Policy Review, 8,* 141–157.

Smith, R. K., & Walker, R. D. (2001). From inequity to opportunity: Keeping the promises made to big-time intercollegiate student-athletes. *Nevada Law Journal, 1,* 160–206.

Smith, R. K. (1996). When ignorance is bliss: In search of racial and gender equity in intercollegiate athletics. *Missouri Law Review, 61,* 329–392.

Waller, J. M. (2003). A necessary evil: Proposition 16 and its impact on academics and athletics in the NCAA. *DePaul Journal of Sports Law and Contemporary Problems, 1,* 189–206.

▲▼ Study Questions ▲▼

1. How does unconscious racism affect the academic achievement of African American student athletes?

2. What does the gap between the graduation rates of African American and white student-athletes reflect?

3. Identify strategies that might be employed to enhance the academic achievement of African American student athletes.

4. How has the NCAA changed its initial eligibility rules?

5. What factors contributed to the NCAA's decision to change its initial eligibility rules?

References

Alexander v. Sandoval, 532 U.S. 275 (2001).

Coakley, J. A. (1994). *The sociology of sport.* Dallas, TX: Taylor Publishers.

Civil Rights Act of 1871, 42 U.S.C. Section 1983 (1988).

Civil Rights Act of 1870, 42 U.S.C. Section 1981 (1994).

Cureton v. NCAA, 198 F.3d 107 (3rd Cir. 1999).

Cureton v. NCAA, 37 F. Supp.2d 687 (E.D. Pa. 1999).

Davis, T. (1995). The myth of the superspade: The persistence of racism in college athletics. *Fordham Urban Law Journal, 22:* 615–698.

Davis, T. (1995). A model of institutional governance for intercollegiate athletics. *Wisconsin Law Review, 1995,* pp. 599–645.

Davis, T. (1996). African American student athletes: Marginalizing the NCAA regulatory structure? *Marquette Sports Law Journal, 6,* 199–227.

Davis, T. (1991). Absence of good faith: defining a university's educational obligation to student-athletes. *Houston Law Review, 28,* 743–790.

DeVos Sport Business Management Program (2006a, April 6). New study reveals marked improvement for the graduation rates for African-American student-athletes. Press release.

DeVos Sport Business Management Program (2006b, March 15). Academic progress/graduation rate study of Division I NCAA Women's and Men's Basketball Tournament Teams reveals marked improvement in overall graduation rates but large continuing disparities of the success of male and female and white and African-American student-athletes. Press release.

Edwards v. Jewish Hospital of St. Louis, 855 F.2d 1345 (8th Cir.1988).

Farrell, K., Fernandez, J., & Niland, B. (1997, January). Convention listened to concerns of athletes. *NCAA News, 5.*

Frei, T. (1995, October 30). Separate ways. *Sporting News.*

Harris, O. (1993). African American predominance in collegiate sport. In D. Brooks & R. Althouse (Eds.), *Racism in college athletics: The African American athlete's experience* (pp. 51–74). Morgantown, WV: Fitness Information Technology, Inc.

Haworth, K. (1997, January 17). Suit says NCAA's eligibility standards discriminate against Black students. *The Chronicle of Higher Education,* p. A46.

Jackson v. Drake University, 778 R Supp. 1490 (S.D. Iowa 1991).

Lawrence, C. R. (1987). The id, the ego and equal protection: Reckoning with unconscious racism. *Stanford Law Review, 39,* 317–388.

Lufrano, M. R. (1994). The NCAA's involvement in setting academic standards: Legality and desirability. *Seton Hall Journal of Sports Law, 4,* 97–141.

Modjeska, A. C. (1993). *Employment Discrimination law* (3rd ed.). Deerfield, IL: Clark Boardman Callaghan.

Mott, R. D. (1996, January 15). Delegates reject modification to initial eligibility standards. *NCAA News,* p. 7.

National Collegiate Athletic Assocation (1998, February 2). Large eligibility differences noted by race, income. *NCAA News.* Retrieved from http://www.ncaa.org/wps/portal/!ut/p/kcxml/04_Sj9SPykssy0xPLMnMz0vM0Y_QjzKLN4g3NPUESUGYHvqRaGLGphhCjggRX4_83FR9b_0A_YLc0NCIckdFACrZHxQ!/delta/base64xml/L3dJdyEvUUd3QndNQSEvNElVRS82XzBfMTVL?New_WCM_Context=/wps/wcm/connect/NCAA/NCAA+News/NCAA+News+Online/1998/Association-wide/Large+eligibility+differences+noted+by+race%2C+income+-+2-2-98 (last visited February 2, 2007).

National Collegiate Athletic Association (2003, Sept. 1). Athletes graduation rates continue to climb. *NCAA News 1,* 11.

National Collegiate Athletic Association (2006). 2006–07 NCAA Division I Manual.

National Collegiate Athletic Association (2006, Nov. 20). Federal rate shows Division I athletes ahead of student body. *NCAA News, 43,* 24.

Nowak, J., & Rotunda, R. (1995). *Constitutional law* (5th ed.). St. Paul, MN: West Publishing Co.

Pryor v. NCAA, 288 F.3d 548 (3rd Cir. 2002).

Ross v. Creighton University, 957 F.2d 410 (7th Cir. 1992).

Smith, R. K. (1996). When ignorance is not bliss: In search of racial and gender equity in intercollegiate athletics. *Missouri Law Review, 61,* 329–392.

Smith, R. K., & Walker, R. D. (2001). From inequity to opportunity: Keeping the promises made to big-time intercollegiate student-athletes. *Nevada Law Journal 1*(1), 160.

Springer, S. (1995, October 20). UCLA's Edwards says athletes don't get enough money to live on, and he wants to see drastic measures taken. *S.F. Chronicle,* p. E5.

Suggs, W. (2003, Jan. 17). Jock majors. *The Chronicle of Higher Education,* A33.

Title VI of Civil Rights Act of 1964, 42 U.S.C. Section 2000d *et seq* (1995).

Title VII of the Civil Rights Act of 1964, as amended by the Civil Rights Act of 1991, 42 U.S.C. Section 2000e *et seq.* (1995). U.S. Constitution, amend 14, 1.

Willis, G. (1995, Jan. 1). College football coaching picture (in black and white). *New York Times.*

Scott Brooks and Linda Kim take on the controversy of salary compensation for student athletes, and center their chapter on the question of whether or not African American athletes who are the predominant players in big-time, revenue sports are being exploited and therefore deserve some compensation. Building on the historic context in which black athletes were recruited, as well as the impact of professionalization in sports, they explore how a change in the status of black student athletes to professional student athletes would affect their life experiences on American college campuses. The bottom line, as they see it, is that the NCAA operates as a cartel and black student athletes have been (and continue to be) recruited for winning and profit, not for pursuing productive academic experiences. In this vein, compensation in some fashion would be appropriate as principles of reciprocity and fairness, as well as a basis for an improved quality of life as student athletes.

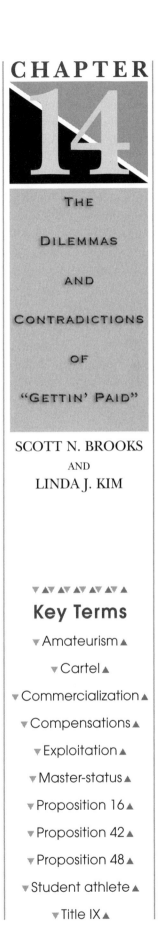

CHAPTER 14

THE DILEMMAS AND CONTRADICTIONS OF "GETTIN' PAID"

SCOTT N. BROOKS
AND
LINDA J. KIM

Key Terms

▼ Amateurism ▲

▼ Cartel ▲

▼ Commercialization ▲

▼ Compensations ▲

▼ Exploitation ▲

▼ Master-status ▲

▼ Proposition 16 ▲

▼ Proposition 42 ▲

▼ Proposition 48 ▲

▼ Student athlete ▲

▼ Title IX ▲

Abstract ▼ Much has been written on both sides of the debate on compensation for student athletes, yet a comprehensive statement that considers historical context as well as current conditions for black athletes is missing. We look at the historical context in which black athletes have been recruited as a base for understanding the relationship between black student athletes and colleges and universities. Next, we discuss the current conditions in which the professionalization of sports has led to increasing exploitation of black athletes and increasing (although still small) opportunities in sports. These circumstances reflect black conditions generally, as race, class, and gender remain significant to the quality of life of individuals in America. Last, we highlight how a change in the status of black student athletes to professional student athletes would undoubtedly affect their life experiences on campus, negatively and positively. There are the moral and social charges from some academics, coaches, students, and others who cling to the notion that education is a privilege and a sufficient compensation in its own right; however, we suggest compensation is due as principles of reciprocity and fairness, and to improve the quality of college life of black student athletes, particularly those who come from poor, inner-city backgrounds.

Introduction

Think back to your days on the playground. You're a team captain and have first pick. Whom do you pick? You want to pick your best friend, but at the same time you want to win and have fun. It's not that you can't have fun if you lose, but losing can be embarrassing and the other team members, particularly those one or two persons who like to boast, will have bragging rights and possibly ridicule you for losing. This adds to the pressure of picking; you struggle to pick a team that will win yet will include as many of your friends as possible. After the teams have been chosen, a new problem arises. Who plays in what position? Again, you have to worry about sparing feelings. Some of the people you have chosen were picked because they were friends and not for their ability. Others were chosen because they were leftovers, or because of their singular ability or multiple abilities. The fact remains that people have to play some position and often they will want to take on roles they may not be equipped to do very well. The person whom you expected to play in the outfield wants to play pitcher or first base, and someone else wants to play shortstop because that's the position they play on their t-ball or Little League team even though you know that that person won't be good there.

In many ways, this dilemma of playground kickball is analogous to collegiate sports. Coaches recruit players for different reasons, and black[1] athletes have typically been recruited to add "athleticism" and to improve the opportunity for winning. They are generally not recruited as "friends" (as in the example above) or to enhance the intrinsic fun value. They are selected because they are believed to be good and will improve a team's performance and chances at winning. Therefore, discussions regarding improving the conditions and environment of college sports and the academic experiences for black student athletes fall largely on deaf ears. Black student athletes (and student athletes generally) are not actually to be taken seriously as students, their job is to perform on athletic fields, and reform policies are focused on getting athletes into college (eligibility and financial inducements to attend one school over another) rather than helping them stay in college and graduate. However, college is an experience and should not simply be reduced to a job. Unfortunately, for the majority of black student athletes who are not able to enjoy their college experience because of a lack of financial resources, their participation *is* a job, and some compensation is therefore reasonable and necessary.

In *USA Today's* sports page cover story for March 30, 2001, titled "In their own words," some male college basketball players were told that the NCAA (National Collegiate Athletic Association) signed a multi-year $6 billion contract (with NBC) and then asked whether student athletes should be compensated. According to the responses reported, nine of the eleven players felt that they should be compensated.[2] Some responses considered merchandise sales and the lack of athletes' compensation, as well as the need to make funds available for athletes from "inner cities." Of course this survey was not administered in a random manner, because only a handful of students whose teams made the NCAA Division I tournament were captured. Nor can it be discerned whether these players felt compensa-

---

1. Blacks will be used as a more inclusive term instead of African Americans because black athletes include non-American students of African descent.
2. "We sell Nike, all these clothing, jerseys with my number on it, and I see none of it," one player said, echoing Chris Webber's comments for why he entered the draft after his sophomore year. One of the other two players was against receiving a wage personally, but made it a point to say, "For the players that it's really necessary that they get some aid, I think it should be there. Some of the guys from the inner cities could really use a stipend, and I think something could be worked out. But for most of us, we get our schooling and we get support to do something we love to do, and that's good enough."

tion was due because of the amount of money that colleges make from their play on the hardwood or simply because some players from poor backgrounds carry a financial strain while in college. Still, two points must be made about the preceding quotes and article: (1) discussions regarding student athletes are distinctly gendered, speaking primarily about males and largely ignoring females; and (2) (male) student athletes see the hypocrisy of profit making and student athlete amateurism, particularly where African American male athletes are concerned, because a significant number are poor and many are not graduating.

This chapter briefly reviews the historical context of black student athletes, then highlights today's college experience of the black student, and concludes with implications for compensating black student athletes. Our point here is that black student athletes (women and men) have a quantitatively and qualitatively different college experience than their white counterparts in multiple ways that generally does not lead to a leveled playing field, upward mobility, or improved quality of life. We do not see this as a simple problem. It is the responsibility of colleges and universities, black student athletes, and the black community to strive and demand more of the experience. Universities need to take the student athletes seriously, working to improve their long-term quality of life, black student athletes need to understand what might be gained through academic excellence and plan long-term for mobility, and local black communities need to re-emphasize the necessity of taking full advantage of the college opportunity.

THE NCAA: Cartel or Free Opportunity?

The explicit core purpose of the NCAA is to govern competition in a fair, safe, equitable and sportsmanlike manner and to integrate intercollegiate athletics into higher education so that the educational experience of the student athlete is paramount (NCAA, "Mission," n.d.); its core values emphasize the importance of both academics and athletics, with athletics described as "supporting" the higher education mission. The marriage of athletics to academics espouses the NCAA's historical view of amateurism, as opposed to professionalism, whereby athletes are student athletes and students first. However, it is plain to see by all of the television and marketing revenue, coupled with poor graduation rates, that the term "student athlete" is a misnomer. Thus, some scholars have described collegiate athletics as a cartel or monopoly, a violation of anti-trust legislation, because it has become a profit engine and market with only one player—the NCAA (made up of its member schools), and makes its own rules that others must subscribe to in order to play. The NCAA is a governing body that is made up of more than 1,250 member schools over five divisions of competition. Consider the enormous power that the NCAA holds: it makes contracts with television companies, owns the licensing of collegiate merchandise, and creates and enforces its own rules for play, equipment specifications, eligibility, coaches' salaries, scholarships, and much more (Becker, 1985; Fleischer, Goff, & Tollison, 1992; Brown, 1993, 1994; Zimbalist, 2001/1999). Kids who are not ready to play professionally but want to play after high school have few to no options because of the NCAA cartel. Schools that want to compete outside of the NCAA are either marginally accepted as pre-season practice dummies or are considered complete outcasts. Moreover, the NCAA boasts an operating budget of more than $520 million for 2005–06 and revenues of over $435 million from television and marketing fees and $27 million from the Division I men's basketball championship tournament for 2004–05 (*NCAA Budget & Finances 2005–2006*). Also, while black women athletes graduate at a rate of 56%, equivalent to that of all college students, a trending improvement and increase over the last two decades, the graduation rate for black men athletes is less than 50%, and basketball players, in particular, have dismally low graduation rates of 41%.[3]

For the student who reads Marx, collegiate sports are an obvious form of exploitation. The capitalists reap profits on the backs of an exploited class, one that is not given the right to unionize and cannot develop a class consciousness to protect itself and go against the profiteers because of the monopoly held by collegiate sports. A Marxist analysis is strengthened after race, gender, and class have been added to the picture. Estimated revenues earned by colleges and universities vary widely, but Brown (1993) found that top-level college football players each earned their schools roughly $540,000 per year or more than $2 million for four years. Similarly, Noll (1991) calculated that in the 1986–87 season, a star quarterback on a mediocre team earned the school $200,000 that year and "good" players added an incremental $150,000 per year on average. As mentioned before, the discussion of student athletes is generally limited to men, and those involved in college's "cash" or high-revenue sports (football and men's basketball) are disproportionately black, male, and from the inner city. Thus, persons from the most economically, socially, educationally, and politically marginalized communities are carrying the most weight for the multi-million dollar college sports enterprise. Moreover, the labor of black men benefits universities, while black women's labor, limited primarily to basketball, is invisible or considered negligible. University prestige is increased, which benefits the white establishment, including all graduates, past, present and future and other student athletes, in non-cash sports, who are overwhelmingly white.

The Beginnings of Collegiate Competition

The relationship between athletics and higher education has not always been exploitative. Early on, athletics were student-run, with no paid coaches or conferences or governing boards. But even then corporate interests influenced intercollegiate rowing competitions, and alumni and other ringers were used. In 1859, Brown, Harvard, Yale, and Trinity formed the College Rowing Association, and then other conferences were created in other sports, including football. Football surpassed rowing and other collegiate sports in popularity by the 1880s, bringing in large gate revenues and enlarging the names of schools (Zimbalist, 2001/1999). In 1905, under pressure from President Roosevelt, the NCAA was formed as a way to regulate recruiting practices and then to reduce violence in football; in fact, the nose of Roosevelt's son had been broken in a Harvard freshman football game. Between 1920 and 1940, college football grew tremendously and 40 new large stadiums were built around the country. These greater investments and popularity also brought forth an indomitable pressure to win. Scandals increased and the Carnegie Commission issued a report in 1929 that found that "the heart of the problem facing college sports was commercialization: an interlocking network that

---

3. These statistics are gathered from the latest data for those students entering college in 1997–98 and found on the NCAA website.

included expanded press coverage, public interest, alumni involvement and recruiting abuses" (Thelin, 1994, p. 26). It seems as if little has changed, and with larger investments and emphasis on winning, football and other sport programs looked for competitive advantages, which came in the form of black labor.

The Black Student Athlete

The question posed is whether or not black student athletes are being exploited and therefore deserve some compensation. Based upon the varied experiences of athletes, collegiate athletics is both exploitation and opportunity, and it is up to the athletes as to whether or not they take advantage, or better yet, are able to make something of the opportunity. Making something of the opportunity is affected by the school, administration (academic and athletic), coaches, and the student. Sports are huge profit engines when successful, and a public relations machine at worst when unsuccessful. The issue of amateurism began before blacks competed in significant numbers (Shropshire, 2000); however, the demographics make for undeniable implications concerning the current situation in college sports. Although colleges changed the organization of athletics, from student-run groups to more professional organizations with paid coaches and administrators and administrative organizations, white students were always welcome and eligible for college (although one might argue that student populations were skewed by class). Blacks were not always welcome at predominantly white institutions and undoubtedly their athletic value aided their presence. The high proportion of black female and male athletes in basketball and males in baseball and football (also called the "cash sports") come from poor inner-city communities, and without sports involvement they very often would not be eligible for or attend predominantly white colleges and universities. Considering this point then, blacks were not first students, but rather athletes first—"gladiators," as Harry Edwards (1969) says—recruited and admitted to participate in collegiate sports to increase the wins and the public image of the university. What this suggests is that black student athletes should not be considered in the same light as white student athletes. Black student athlete amateurism must be put in a context that highlights the initial profit and success motivation that guided the decision to include black athletes.

They're Fast: Natural Athletes and Black Gladiators

In 1966, the so-called "[basketball] game that changed sports" took place in which an all-black starting five of Texas Western (now University of Texas—El Paso, or UTEP) played against the historic Adolph Rupp, University of Kentucky's Hall of Fame coach, and his all-white team for the national championship. This was the first time that an all-black starting five (generally considered the team's top five players) had made it to the national championship. UTEP won, outlasting Rupp's Kentucky team, and ending the Kentucky dynasty. This game is held as a beacon of racial victory because blacks then were not seen as smart, mentally tough, or disciplined enough to beat whites in a rigorous contest. Even Rupp held to these views, which is why for many Civil Rights advocates he stood as the athletic counterpart to Bull Connor, the notorious and infamous sheriff who used dogs to attack and fire hoses to spray down blacks in the South (Fitzpatrick, 1999). Today, all-black starting fives are more commonplace than all-white starting fives on the nation's best basketball teams, and many coaches and the general public still believe that blacks are the greatest athletes; therefore, blacks continue to be recruited for their "natural" and "God-given" abilities and talents rather than for their character, intelligence, and work ethic.

In a special issue of *Sport Illustrated* (November 1997), Bobby Bowden, Florida State's future Hall of Fame football coach, spoke of a white player as a *phenomenon* (our emphasis) because of outstanding leaping ability, speed, and strength that he generally associated with black players.[4]

In October of 2005, Fisher DeBerry, the football coach at the Air Force Academy, echoed similar sentiments, but with a different tone, after a 48-10 loss to Texas Christian University (TCU). DeBerry noted that TCU had more black players than his team, which he believed gave TCU an advantage.[5] Longtime and historic coach Joe Paterno of Penn State was sympathetic to DeBerry and claimed that black athletes had affected football through their superior athleticism.[6]

NCAA Reforms and Inaction

Black athletes are recruited for their ability to win games, not because of affirmative action or to give blacks an opportunity to level the playing field. If recruiting more blacks were about equality and integration, college sports would fit a race fantasy where black and white athletes were treated similarly. Instead, there is a history of disparate treatment. Historically, black athletes have dealt with Jim Crow and with differing expectations of behavior, performance, and racial group responsibility (i.e., being role models). At the same time, the NCAA has focused more attention on whether student athletes are given financial inducements than on whether students are given inferior educations (Purdy, Eitzen, & Hufnagel, 1982). Reform policies and enforcement by the NCAA are focused overwhelmingly on how student athletes get in.

Proposition 48 was passed by the NCAA national convention as an attempt to set an academic standard and address the protests by some faculty that student athletes received undue favorable treatment and admission. Proposition 48 stipulated that student athletes had to have a minimum 2.0 high school GPA in 11 core courses and a combined 700 on the math and English sections of the SATs (and the correlate ACT scores). Black coaches, in particular, denounced Proposition 48 as racist because the SAT was culturally biased, favoring white middle-class students, and Proposition 48 was softened in partial response to this issue (Zimbalist, 2001). Student athletes who had earned the minimum GPA but not the SAT score or vice versa were considered "partial" qualifiers and eligible for full scholarship although they were ineligible to practice and ineligible to play on

---

4. Bowden added, "But there ain't many like him. And my thinking is that there's a whole lot more blacks who can do that than white guys . . . you see better catches, runs, tackles—anything involving mobility, toughness, anything physical . . . You ask what [blacks have] brought to the table? They've brought better athletes."

5. DeBerry said, "[TCU] had a lot more Afro-American players than we did and they ran a lot faster than we did. Afro-American kids can run very well. That doesn't mean that Caucasian kids and other descents can't run, but it's very obvious to me that they run extremely well."

6. "Poor [Air Force coach] Fisher DeBerry got in trouble, but the black athlete has made a big difference. They have changed the whole tempo of the game. Black athletes have just done a great job as athletes and as people in turning the game around."

a college team during their first year. The partial qualifier, also called "special admit," gained full eligibility after satisfactory progress and an illustration of ability to do college coursework. However, the NCAA did not monitor the coursework and progress closely, and student athletes were encouraged to take or were simply put into junk or "jock" courses to become eligible and help athletic programs (Fleisher et al., 1992). To address the growing corruption, Proposition 42 was adopted in 1989, banning the full scholarship to partial qualifiers. Again this was taken on by many prominent black coaches of men's basketball programs who felt that the proposition would have a disproportionate impact on black student athletes who would not do as well as whites on the standardized tests. This time the protest had little impact, and in fact many football and basketball coaches found a silver lining and loophole. NCAA rules limited the number of "full grants-in-aid" (95 for football and 15 for basketball), but black special admits often qualified for federal and state funds previously designated for non-athlete students who were needed and promising. Programs could bring in students, without using their own money. In 1992, Proposition 16 created a sliding scale in which a student with a higher GPA in core courses could be eligible with a lower minimum score on the SAT or ACT, and partial qualifiers could practice with the team (but not play until eligible) and receive full scholarships. The increasing importance of core courses necessitated close scrutiny and so the NCAA established the NCAA Eligibility Clearinghouse in 1993 to evaluate the curricula of over 24,000 high schools around the country. Of course, the variety of school curricula makes direct comparisons difficult and thus evaluation has regularly been slow, superficial, and inaccurate, causing overall eligibility to plummet, and as expected, having the greatest effect on the eligibility of poor black students. In one year, 1995 to 1996, ineligibility rose from 16.3 percent to 26.9 percent.[7] Yet, even with stricter admission policies and academic standards, the greatest growth in the number of those who graduate belongs to black women student athletes, as reported above, and reports of the failure of some prominent basketball programs to graduate black male basketball players has yielded little to no sanctions and actions by the NCAA.

Dilemmas and Contradictions of Gettin' Paid

Everett C. Hughes, a prominent sociologist, wrote an article titled, "Dilemmas and Contradictions in Status (1945)," which proposed that people interact with others, particularly strangers, based upon perceived notions of status, expectations, and appropriate behavior, that people have multiple identities (we are some things to certain people and other things to other people), and that sometimes these multiple identities appear to contradict one another, presenting dilemmas for some people as they meet others. For blacks, the mark of oppression is said to be the "master-status," or individual characteristics and traits that trump all other status-determining qualities. In this way, a black person (woman or man) who is a physician is a black physician and not simply a physician. Women experience a similar status issue; they are women doctors or women athletes or smart women. The implicit idea is that they are somehow like a man, because of what they are

---

7. In Zimbalist (2001[1999]), taken from *NCAA News*, February 2, 1998, p.1.

capable of doing. Phrases like "she can throw like a man" or "she's as good as any man" capture this sentiment well. Of course, black women (note the distinction "black" in front of "women") carry the double bind of being black *and* women such that when they are doctors, they are black women doctors, jobs held most by whites and men, and when they are nurses or flight attendants or teachers, jobs traditionally held by white women, they are black nurses or black flight attendants or black teachers. Likewise, black gays and lesbians, when identified or speculated as such, are further marginalized. This is not simply a theoretical point. Status accompanies individuals but group-affiliated and defined characteristics and traits lead to unequal pay, differential rates of arrest, varied assumptions of intellectual ability, and treatment in "neutral" settings.

For black student athletes, the designation of being college students is trumped by their racial and gender affiliation and athlete status.[8] They are black and then athletes, neither of which garners much deference or respect in the traditional fields of power. They are not white, are thought to be largely from "urban" or "inner-city" neighborhoods (these terms are used as code words for black), are from poor and working-class backgrounds, and are not considered intelligent or worthy of respect outside of the gridiron or off their field of play. Bottom line, they are viewed as entertainers instead of real college students.

Considering the existing relations between students and universities, and at the risk of sounding overly dramatic, compensation will lead to a status change from student athlete to paid athlete, and, in turn, the academic role for many current student athletes, particularly males, will further decline and increase the pressure for their performing consistently.[9] At the same time, being a paid group introduces a host of other social dilemmas, such as the opportunity, although an unlikely one, for athletes to become their own collective bargaining unit or union, for the highest-paid athletes to compete with professors and administrators for status and affect institutional rank, and for athlete's to gain power in relation to coaches and others who now wield relatively unilateral control.[10]

Athletes-in-Residence

If student athletes were to be paid, they would become paid athletes, and the line between "student" and "athlete" would change drastically. Some student athletes would continue to be students, but many would be reduced to being simply ath-

8. Some research has found that athletic identity trumps racial identity for blacks, but not whites (Brown, Jackson, Brown, Sellers, Keiper, & Manuel, 2003). However the authors of this chapter find this puzzling and not to be the case based on those athletes who they have spoken with.

9. Adler and Adler (1989) discuss student athletes as having three role identities, the social, athletic, and academic roles. Essentially these roles make up their college lives and speak to the different groups of which they are a part and to the differing expectations of them. They belong to the general student population and have a position in the social hierarchy. They also have a specific role as a member of the athletic department, with a cast of characters that overlaps little with their social and academic groups. Last, they are students and therefore interact with professors, academic counselors, and others directly involved with student affairs.

10. Max Rafferty's chapter in Scott (1971) highlighted the conflict between coaches' unilateral power and athletes' freedom of expression that occurred in the 1960s. Because of the mounting external and internal tensions on college campuses, athletes won some victories, but the tide has turned since the 1980s, when college coaches began earning additional income from athletic apparel companies and the accessible supply of talented athletes boomed with modern recruiting and scouting: coaches wield more power because they earn more money and athletes are more expendable.

letes or athletes-in-residence. In practice, many folks might see this as nothing new.[11] Compensation, however, would make the athlete-in-residence status explicit.

With compensation and less reason to take on the academic role, the social role of student athletes might worsen. Like other students, now they attend classes with regularity and irregularity, take exams, walk on campus, and eat at the cafeteria, and they rely upon the other students for support, friendship, tutors, dates, and so on. Student athletes are generally very popular figures at schools with big-time athletics because of the visibility of sports; it is a common thing for regular students to try to get to know the student athletes who perform on television and/or in front of large audiences. Student athletes are somewhat accessible and more down-to-earth than the normal stars found on television or on stages because they, too, are students. At certain schools, there is a pride among non-athlete students in the commonness of athletes, particularly at schools known for tough academic standards and high selectiveness and lower competitive level athletic programs. Here, the athletes are regarded with esteem because they work while being enrolled in school; they do real schoolwork and have regular, non-jock majors, in addition to their athletic obligation, which is essentially perceived to be a tough full-time job. But if athletes earned a wage, what would motivate them to join sororities and fraternities or other campus clubs? Why would they continue to live in dorms (at least initially) or act as college students? They could possibly afford to live as young professional persons, in different, more upscale housing, date different folks, and shed the college life. A change in status would change the common ground between athletes and other students, and athletes could take on new and different roles in the college community.

Possible Effects on Title IX

Given the necessity to enforce Title IX (a legislative measure to balance the athletic opportunities for women in college), black women athletes would also face the special resentment of being paid, as women who are already discriminated against.[12] Even now, women are not perceived as "legitimate" athletes in the eyes of many men. They do not fit the ideal of femininity or traditional female gender-role expectations.[13] At the same time, many laypersons do not give female college athletes the respect they are due as athletes. Women athletes are not considered "superhuman" or better than most persons at their sport of choice, because they are viewed as not as good as men, although this is clearly not true. Men, in general,

---

11. There is a wealth of research on role conflict/role strain for athletes, and it is inconclusive (Edwards, 1969, 1974; Stein & Hoffman, 1978; Coakley, 1982; Adler & Adler, 1985; Lewis, 1993; Lance, 2004). One side maintains that the sports role/identity often leads to role engulfment in which athletes in "big time" sports programs must cope with team and external demands on time and pressures that work against social and academic roles. The other side typically finds that satisfaction in sports achievement leads to greater happiness and motivation to excel in other areas. Interestingly, Lance (2004) found that female student athletes perceived more role conflict between academic and athletic expectations than did male student athletes.
12. Title IX governs the overall equity of treatment and opportunity in athletics while giving schools the flexibility to choose sports based on student body interest, geographic influence, budget restraints, and gender ratio. It is not about sameness, i.e. offering the same sports or spending the same amount for men and women, but is a matter of insuring that women have equal opportunities as men on a whole, not on an individual basis.
13. See Coakley (2001) for a discussion on gender-role expectations.

see themselves as the norm and standard; if a woman can't beat a man, then she is simply a woman athlete, not an athlete. Of course it is rare that women student athletes compete with men to challenge this; the assumption is that they are good if they are compared only against other women. Where there is support for paying student athletes, it starts with the assumption that these young men are deserving of pay or special status because they are special, better than most men at what they do, and therefore also worthy of special attention, television coverage, and commendations. In the media, women are covered less and receive scant attention generally.[14] Many believe that women do not deserve special status because they are not better than men. Thus, it seems obvious that universities and colleges would want to pay more for male athletes because their participation yields higher revenues, but this is poor rationale considering the gender gap in wages for women inside and outside of sports, which speaks directly to society-wide gender discrimination and inequality. For example head coaches of men's basketball programs receive greater compensation than coaches of women's programs, at the same schools, for doing a comparable job. In a similar vein, the status difference between paid student athletes could create problems.

Athletes as Staff

Compensation adds to the uniqueness of black athletes and potentially exacerbates the gross resentment by some professors and students that already exists. Athletes, male athletes in particular, have a certain amount of respect and fame on campus, which is not to be confused with people taking them seriously. They are seen as "cool" guys, great athletes, and people with extraordinary bodies, determination, and strength. But if they are black, they are not considered "most likely to be president or a CEO." With gettin' paid though, they might really threaten the social order of campus life, because they in fact would be engaged in a career and could push for being taken more seriously by the administration, faculty, and other students. Student athletes, big stars specifically, could push the limits of their new status and expect faculty to treat them more as equals because of their physical stature and staff positions.

Paying students could place athletes above other students as valuable enough to pay and not charge for admission (if tuition scholarships are to continue). As employees, they would be higher on the hierarchy scale. Bringing in money, they would have to be considered a significant part of a university's status, rather than simply academics, and could even be included in rankings of institutions (i.e., rankings of sport programs as a measure of school status and prominence). Many feel that affirmative action has been a favor to blacks, enabling white America to assuage black activism, but athletes would be seen for their legitimate contributions to academia. Black student athletes could then be explicit contributors to the intellectual endeavor of elite institutions, at the same time that their white counterparts, male and female, would be paying to receive what these institutions offer. Academics and the price of information sold to students would be in direct and public competition with the legs, arms, and "instincts of dumb black jocks" for university prestige. The appropriate question for why a student would choose one school over another might be: Is it the books or the sports? Moreover, the two-

---

14. See Messner, Duncan, and Cooky (2003) for a discussion on the difference in gender treatment in television/media coverage.

sided role of higher learning institutions would be unveiled. Colleges and universities play different roles and have different impacts on different people, regardless of the myth that a college education is the best decision and insures middle-class attainment and success.

A new class would be created on college campuses, which would come with legal rights, such as the right to unionize or come together for a common cause. This would translate into power. Moreover, employment would go up for a group with historically low employment rates. Black males, in particular, who are typically expected to drop out of school after chasing a pipe dream, would instead attend college and gain something else: a paycheck. And their chase might bear fruit for many more people, creating a class of workers whose status would change from being gladiators to being paid employees.

The Down Side

Receiving a wage could lead to worsening treatment of student athletes by universities and colleges and to worsening outcomes (e.g., even lower graduation rates, short-term contracts/scholarships and frequent firings, as well as decreasing funding for educational supports such as tutoring and study tables). Reform has already brought about change in athletic scholarships, which are no longer guaranteed. Instead, coaches and players renew contracts annually, a practice that has been rather automatic but might become an effective and useful tool to remove athletes who take school seriously or who simply fall out of favor. As staff members, they could be treated as other staff persons and could be fired and replaced with little to no notice leading to greater possibilities for interpersonal conflict between a coach under pressure and an underperforming young man.[15] Athletic administrators and coaches would, more than likely, still be the power wielders (as in professional sports) and could also use the paycheck to control student athletes. Some student athletes claim coaches do this already; coaches threaten to take away an athlete's scholarship as a means of control and coercion. Thus, pay could contribute to even more role conflict and strain for student athletes, because coaches would be controlling the livelihood of young athletes.

Cutting Out the Middle Man: Coaches and Athletic Programs

Coaches, their staffs, and athletic departments would likely be the most affected by compensation of student athletes. Although the power now held by coaches varies widely from program to program and division to division, it seems rare that a single or even a group of student athletes has the power to affect the future of a coach. The obvious reasons for this: coaches can be long-term employees and an investment, whereas a student athlete has only four years of eligibility, and the supply of athletes is fairly high because of the improved and vast recruiting networks and information available. Thus, the compensation of athletes by colleges and universities could change the possible social order. Gettin' paid lifts the title of amateur that is currently placed on athletes and eliminates the prohibition of contracts between athletic apparel companies and athletes. Compensation would lead to additional opportunities for student athletes to earn an income, which would be

---

15. This also speaks to the player-coach problems found elsewhere, like the Latrell Sprewell—P. J. Carlesimo conflict in 1997, in which Sprewell explained, "There was just a buildup of anger and frustration and having it all bottled up and not being able to express myself. At that point, it just came to a head."

tough to monitor and regulate. This would lead to under-the-table, disproportionate incomes among players, as well as create resentment among teammates, teams, and races. Moreover, this could affect the money coming into the university via institutional contracts with athletic companies. If deals were made between athletic departments and companies based on athletes, then the athletes would become more powerful and would gain leverage to influence certain decisions, such as the future of a coach/coaching staff. This must scare the NCAA, athletic departments, coaches, and universities.

Conclusion

The problem, as we see it, is that the NCAA operates as a cartel, and black student athletes continue to be recruited for the sole purpose of profit making and winning and to improve the bottom line. The focus has been on getting blacks into college to play and perform well, and not on ensuring that they have good and productive academic experiences. Although the traditional notion of sports as a tool to mental and physical fitness remains, the program of collegiate athletics stretches the point. Black student athletes rarely earn the benefit of the relationship financially because of their master status of marginality. Black labor has always been paid less than white labor and women less than men. For the student athlete, the job of being an athlete most often supersedes academic responsibilities, and less than 1% goes on to professional athletic careers. Black athletes are used up and spit out, no better for the wear because they lose their marketability outside of the athletic realm and they do not gain work skills.

A Better Question

The basic question is: Does collegiate athletics exploit or offer an opportunity (for black student athletes)? The obvious answer is that most individual athletes gain much less from their efforts than do the universities for which athletics serves primarily as a public relations machine, turning universities and colleges into brand names. And yet, some student athletes have gained much by taking advantage of the opportunity. This leads us to the more relevant question perhaps: How do more black student athletes take advantage of the exploitation and turn it into opportunity?

Compensation (the authors say this cautiously) in some fashion is appropriate because of how much black student athletes contribute to the student life, revenues, and legacies of "big time" sports colleges and universities, while at the same time some students struggle or seek "alternative" compensation in order to live well. However, compensation must not be considered simply as a way to reinforce the status assignment of black jocks. Instead, compensation needs to be part of a plan that works to eradicate exploitation both in the short and long terms. The NCAA earns profit via direct negotiation and earnings from television contracts, merchandising, and other avenues and thus should compensate players. Moreover, the inequality among schools and men's and women's athletics is currently exacerbated by alumni contributions, which are difficult to track and are used nar-

16. Eligibility is no more than five years with a medical redshirt year, which is a NCAA-approved stoppage of eligibility for athletes who become injured. Eligibility requirements differ according to year of athlete and circumstances.

rowly by schools toward specific teams. Funneling all contributions through the NCAA or some other body, and limiting contributions directly to schools and specific programs, would be an administrative and financial management nightmare, but might insure more equality and financial controls. NCAA control of payments would allow for better regulation and monitoring of payments—any other payments would be violations. Toward improving the quality of life for black student athletes, minimal benefits could also be given, similar to those given to employees, such as childcare allowance or vouchers and even retirement funds or pensions based upon athletes' tenures and/or contribution to earnings (estimated value to a team's revenue) and tied to the NCAA earnings over time.

But the issue of compensation is somewhat shortsighted while the exploitation of black student athletes is two-fold. One is financial, which is what the authors think of mostly in terms of exploitation, but the other is consideration of how student athletes fare in life after college. Gettin' paid comes with baggage. When people are accustomed to interacting along certain status lines, change sometimes creates irrevocable consequences. For black student athletes, and student athletes in general, compensation may open Pandora's box and lead to many new issues, challenges, and problems without solving the initial problem at the heart of this matter.

Solving the Real Problem

The mythical singular role of college, to gain an education, is false. College, for white students who are resource and network heavy, reproduces social class and status, guaranteeing white-collar jobs and a high quality of life. But for black student athletes, it is increasingly a momentary shining of their talent with an ultimate return to their low economic social position. Therefore, a plan to reform athletics that simply addresses financial remuneration is incomplete. Instead, reform needs to be based on an understanding that money is not enough. Upward mobility must be the goal, and black student athletes need to be equipped to benefit from their college experience. Programs need to be built, implemented, measured, and monitored that lead to a first job, truly changing the life course and opportunities of black student athletes and the families counting on them. Mandatory programs need to include skill building, networking, guidance, and preparation for continuing education. Most colleges and universities already have these resources in career counseling offices but do not fully equip, encourage, or empower black student athletes to make full use of these services. The student athletes do not know what to do after college, how to go about their after-college plans, and so on. The goal must be to make college an opportunity for all, regardless of their athletic promise. The possibility of becoming a professional athlete is not expanding for black athletes, particularly in basketball, because more and more European athletes are being recruited to American colleges/universities and are being drafted into the professional ranks. Black student athletes need to get more out of their college experience than airtime and cover stories, nets and trophies, and sweat suits and Nikes. They need to understand fully what they are getting into as student athletes and gain skills, experience, and confidence that will carry them through their entire lifetimes.

▲▼ Suggested Readings ▲▼

Benson, K. F. (2000). Constructing academic inadequacy: African American athlete's stories of schooling. *The Journal of Higher Education, 71*(2), 223–246.

Fizel, J., & Fort, R. (Eds.) (2004). *Economics of college sports.* Westport, CT: Praeger Publishers.

Gerdy, J. R. (2000). *Sports in school: The future of an institution.* New York: Teachers College Press.

Knight Foundation. (2001). *A call to action: Reconnecting college sports and higher education.* Miami, FL: John S. and James L. Knight Foundation

Murphy, S., & Pace, J. (1994). "A plan for compensating student athletes." *Education and Law Journal, Spring 1994,* 167–186.

Sailes, G. (Ed). (1998). *African Americans in sport.* New Brunswick, NJ: Transaction Publishers.

Shropshire, K. L. (1985). *In black and white.* New York: New York University Press.

Zimbalist, A. (2001). *Unpaid professionals* (Rev. ed.). Princeton, NJ: Princeton Press.

▲▼ Study Questions ▲▼

1. What types of reforms would you develop and implement to improve the plight of black student athletes?

2. What types of reforms would you develop to ensure equity for female student athletes?

3. What types of changes in the NCAA would improve the experiences of student athletes?

4. How might colleges/universities change to improve the experiences of black student athletes?

5. What are some advantages and disadvantages of compensating student athletes that have not been brought up by the authors?

6. What are some of the implications of the commercialization of college sport?

7. Do you think student athletes should be compensated? Why or why not?

References

Adler, P. & Adler, P. (1989). The gloried self: The aggrandizement and constriction of self. *Social Psychology Quarterly, 52*(4), 299–310.

Becker, G. (1985, September 30). College athletes should get paid what they are worth. *Business Week*, p. 18.

Brown, R. W. (1993). An estimate of the rent generated by a premium Division I-A college football player. *Economic Inquiry, 31*(4), 671–684.

Brown, R. W. (1994). Measuring cartel rents in the college basketball player recruitment market. *Applied Economics, 26*, 27–34.

Brown, T. N., Jackson, J. S., Brown, K. T., Sellers, R. M., Keiper, S., & Manuel, W. J. (2003). 'There's no race on the playing field': Perceptions of racial discrimination among white and black athletes. *Journal of Sport & Social Issues, 27*(2), 162–183.

Coakley, J. J. (2001). *Sport in society.* Boston: McGraw-Hill.

Edwards, H. (1969). *The revolt of the black athlete.* New York: Free Press.

Edwards, H. (1973). *Sociology of sport.* Homewood, IL: Dorsey Press.

Elliot, C. (1883). *Report of the President and Treasurer of Harvard College, 1882–1883.*

Fitzpatrick, F. (1999). *And the walls came tumbling down.* Lincoln, NE: University of Nebraska Press.

Fleischer, A., Goff, B., & Tollison, R. (1992). *The NCAA: A study in cartel behavior.* Chicago: University of Chicago Press.

Hughes, E. C. (1945). Dilemmas and contradictions of status. *American Journal of Sociology, 50*, 353–59.

Lance, L. M. (2004). Gender differences in perceived role-conflict among university student athletes. *College Student Journal, June*, 179–190.

Lewis, M. (1993). Athletes in college: Differing roles and conflicting expectations. *College Student Journal, June*, 195–202.

Messner, M. A., Duncan, M. C. & Cooky, C. (2003). Silence, sports bras and wrestling porn: The treatment of women in televised sports news and highlights. *Journal of Sport and Social Issues, 27*, 38–51.

Moore, D. L., Wieberg, S., Allen, K., Becker, D., & Whiteside, K. (2001, March 30). In their own words. *USA Today*, pp. 1C-2C.

NCAA Budget & Finances 2005–2006 Budget. Retrieved December 5, 2005, from *http://www2.ncaa.org/portal/about_ncaa/budget_and_finances/*

NCAA News, (1998, February 2) p. 1.

NCAA Mission Statement. Retrieved December 5, 2005, from http://www2.ncaa.org/about_ncaa/overview/mission.html

Rafferty, M. (1971). Interscholastic athletics: The gathering storm. In J. Scott (Ed.), *The athletic revolution* (pp.13–22). New York: Free Press.

Snyder, E. E., & Spreitzer, E. (1983). *Social aspects of sport.* Englewood Cliffs, NJ: Prentice-Hall, Inc.

Stein, P,. & Hoffman, S. (1978). Sports and male role strain. *Journal of Social Issues, 34*, 136–150.

Thelin, J. R. (1994). *Games colleges play.* Baltimore: Johns Hopkins University Press.

SECTION SIX
Sport Administration/ Management: Intersection of Race, Class, and Gender

The participation of black women in sport must be understood in a context of double prejudice—race and gender—that has historically limited their participation in sport. "Beyond Tokenism to Empowerment: The Black Women in Sport Foundation," undertaken by Linda Sheryl Greene and Tina Sloan-Green, chronicles the significance of the participation of African American women athletes in every aspect of sport and reaffirms their struggle to eliminate tokenism encountered by minority women in sport participation. Their purpose is to expose myths about race and gender discrimination and to foster the participation of black women in every aspect of sport, including power positions. Although the Black Women in Sport Foundation (BWSF) was founded in 1992, the chapter chronicles more than 30 years of pioneer civil rights reflected in the collective efforts of Sloan-Green and Greene, and a close company of advocates including Carol Oglesby, Nikki Franke, Alpha Alexander, and other significant colleagues who conferenced, caucused, and lobbied for a broader role in sport. The BWSF has promoted achievements of African American women in sports, has created mentoring opportunities for exposure of women to non-traditional sports, and continues to be a leader in advancing the number of African American women in every aspect of sport, including intercollegiate sports.

CHAPTER 15

BEYOND TOKENISM TO EMPOWERMENT: THE BLACK WOMEN IN SPORT FOUNDATION

LINDA SHERYL GREENE
AND
TINA SLOAN-GREEN[1]

▼ ▲▼ ▲▼ ▲▼ ▲▼ ▲▼ ▲
Key Terms
▼Tokenism▲
▼Title IX▲
▼AIAW▲
▼Intersectionality▲
▼Athletics▲
▼African American women▲

1. Both authors thank Elizabeth O'Callaghan, Ph.D. candidate, Educational Administration, School of Education, University of Wisconsin-Madison, for her editorial assistance.

Abstract ▼ There is relatively little written about the role of black women in sport. A short book entitled *Black Women in Sport*, authored by Tina Sloan-Green, Carole Oglesby, Alpha Alexander, and Nikki Frank (Green, Oglesby, Alexander, & Frank, 1981) discussed the myths surrounding the participation of black women in sport, as well as the double prejudice—race and gender—that has historically limited the participation of black women in sport (Oglesby, 1981). In the past, the public has been aware of only a few highly visible athletes such as Wilma Rudolph (*Women in History*, n.d.) and Althea Gibson (Gray & Lamb, 2004). However, invisibility was partially ameliorated when Alpha Alexander conducted a study to answer questions about black women participation in intercollegiate athletics that showed very small numbers of minority women participating in intercollegiate sport as athletes, administrators, and coaches (Alexander, 1978).

Although incorporation of the Black Women in Sport Foundation (BWSF) occurred in 1992, the genesis of the Black Women in Sport Conference can be traced to 1974, when Temple University hired Tina Sloan-Green to teach physical education and coach women's varsity lacrosse, field hockey, and badminton. Title IX (1972) prohibited sex discrimination in education programs or activities receiving federal financial assistance. Under pressure to add high-quality coaches for women's teams, Temple hired Sloan-Green. This chapter recounts the struggle of Sloane-Green and Greene, along with a network of remarkable friends gathered over more than 30 years, on behalf of African American women in sport. The BWSF was established to eliminate that invisibility and tokenism. Its purpose is to facilitate and advance the number of black women in every aspect of sport, including power positions, and to realize achievements, specifically in intercollegiate sports.

Beyond Tokenism to Empowerment:
The Black Women in Sport Foundation

There is relatively little written about the role of black women in sport. A short but path-breaking book, *Black Women in Sport*, authored by Tina Sloan-Green, Carole Oglesby, Alpha Alexander, and Nikki Frank (Green, Oglesby, Alexander, & Frank, 1981), discussed the myths surrounding the participation of black women in sport, as well as the double prejudice—race and gender—that has historically limited the participation of black women in sport (Oglesby, 1981). This double prejudice was also reflected in the lack of research and documentation of achievements of black women in sport (Oglesby, 1981). In the past, the public has been aware of only a few number of highly visible athletes such as Wilma Rudolph (Women in History, n.d.) and Althea Gibson (Gray & Lamb, 2004). However, invisibility was partially ameliorated when Alpha Alexander, a candidate for a master's degree in physical education at Temple University, conducted a study to determine the answers to questions about black women's participation in intercollegiate athletics (Alexander, 1978). Alexander encountered significant obstacles, as the queried institutions were unable to supply the number of minority women involved in sports participation. The institutions also did not have data on minority women who might make up the available pool for administrators or coaches. The data that was available showed very small numbers of minority women participating in intercollegiate sport as athletes, administrators, and coaches. Therefore, the Black Women in Sport Foundation (BWSF) was established to eliminate that invisibility and tokenism[2] and to foster the participation of black women in every aspect of sport, including power positions (Greene, 1991; Evans, 1998).

Alhough the incorporation of BWSF occurred in 1992, the genesis of the Black Women in Sport Conference can be traced to 1974 when Temple University hired Tina Sloan-Green to teach physical education and coach women's varsity lacrosse, field hockey, and badminton. Title IX (1972), added to the federal law in 1972, prohibited sex discrimination in any education program or activity receiving federal financial assistance. Although it was added to the federal code in 1972, its effective date was July 21, 1975. Before the effective date, the Office of

---

2. Tokenism refers to a policy or practice of limited inclusion of members of a group that results in a higher level of visibility for that group. This may result in differential performance demands, as well as marginalization of the token from the dominant group (Kanter, 1977). The inclusion often masks a discriminatory intent and usually creates a false appearance of inclusive practices, whether intentional or not (Wikipedia, n.d.). See Greene (1991) for a discussion of applying the term to African American females.

Civil Rights of the United States Department of Health, Education, and Welfare developed and promulgated regulations that, among other things, required equal opportunity for members of both sexes interested in participating in athletic programs offered by institutions (Office of Civil Rights of the United States Department of Health, Education, and Welfare, 1975). The regulations required that institutions consider a number of factors to determine whether the institutions were providing equal opportunity in athletic programs. They included the nature and extent of sports programs offered, provision of equipment, game and practice scheduling, travel and per diems, coaching and academic tutoring, compensation and assignment of coaches and tutors, locker rooms, practice and competitive facilities, medical and training facilities, housing and dining facilities, and publicity (45 C.F.R § 86.41, 1999). Under pressure to add high-quality coaches for women's team, Temple hired Sloan-Green.

Sloan-Green was a world-class athlete and an experienced coach. She had been a member of United States National Teams in lacrosse 1968–1972 and field hockey in 1969 (Alexander & Franke, 1981). She received a bachelor's degree from West Chester College and a master's degree in physical education from Temple University. Thereafter she became a high school physical education teacher and coach, first in Unionville, Pennsylvania, and then in Philadelphia. She coached lacrosse, basketball, and swimming, and later coached lacrosse and basketball at Lincoln University in Pennsylvania.

Carol Oglesby, sport sociologist, was an early advocate for black women in sport.

Upon her arrival, Sloan-Green met Nikki Franke, a graduate assistant in the Department of Physical Education. Franke started Temple's women's fencing team in 1972. Franke had been All-American fencer in her senior year at Brooklyn College. She was the United States National Champion in women's foil in 1975, a Pan American Games silver medalist in 1975, a member of the United States Olympic team in 1976, a Pan American Games bronze medalist in 1979, and a member of the United States Olympic Team in 1980. Sloan-Green and Franke had a lot in common. They were trailblazers, world-class athletes, and coaches in virtually all-white sports.

Also at Temple was Professor Carole Oglesby, a sport sociologist who had begun to incorporate an investigation of women's roles into sport sociology. Dr. Oglesby, Sloan-Green, and Franke became colleagues and began to discuss the role of black women in sport. Dr. Oglesby was a senior colleague with involvement in a number of national organizations. Oglesby introduced Sloan-Green and Franke to various organizations in which black women had yet to be significantly involved. These organizations included the National Association for Girls and Women in Sport (NAGWS), The American Association of Health, Physical Education, and Recreation, (AAHPER), and the Association of Intercollegiate Athletics for Women (AIAW) (Willey, 1996).

Both Sloan-Green and Franke were dismayed to discover that they were the only black women attending these meetings. Even more disappointing to them was the fact that none of the meetings addressed the needs, or the empowerment, of black women in sport.

In 1976, to fill this vacuum, Sloan-Green, Franke, and Oglesby offered the first workshop on Black Women in Sport. The workshop was offered as a continuing education program of Temple University. It was specifically designed to respond to the needs of Philadelphia coaches and teachers, many of whom were black and who were coaching young black women. The materials focused on the issues inner-city coaches faced as they sought to lead girls to better performance on and off the courts and fields. Both high school and college coaches attended this workshop.

Sloan-Green and Oglesby were not content with the failure of existing women's sport organizations to address issues of racial discrimination and differential access to sports opportunity. At the AIAW 1977 Delegate Assembly they introduced a resolution that proposed the establishment of AIAW Commission on the Status of Minority Women. The commission would complete a study on the status of minority women within the AIAW and provide recommendations for action. The AIAW Delegate Assembly approved the resolution.

The study was conducted by Alpha Alexander in 1977 and completed in 1978. Dr. Alexander was another woman who became a significant participant in the BWSF. Alpha Alexander was then a candidate for a master's degree in physical education at Temple University and did the study in conjunction with her work on her degree. Alexander encountered significant obstacles as the queried institutions were unable to supply the numbers of minority women involved in sports participation. The institutions also did not have data on minority women who might make up the available pool for administrators or coaches. The data that was available showed very small numbers of minority women participating in intercollegiate sport as athletes, administrators, and coaches. In addition, she recommended that the AIAW conduct additional research on degrees and professional occupations of minority women athletes, investigate the status of minority women within the AIAW, maintain an annual data collection, and involve minority women as athletes, administrative personnel, and coaches within their institutions (Alexander, 1978). Her study became her master's thesis for her degree in sports administration (Alexander, 1978).

The commission made several important recommendations to address the specific needs of minority women in sport. In particular, the commission recommended that the AIAW officially encourage minority women to come together to exchange ideas and identify needs, develop and encourage efforts to include minority women in those sports with almost nonexistent minority participation, encourage workshops relevant to minority women, and establish a permanent Committee on the Status of Minority Women (CSMW).

The Association of Intercollegiate Athletics for Women (AIAW) did establish the CSMW. The members included two of the women who had authored the report, Vivian Acosta of Brooklyn College and Marion Washington of the University of Kansas. Other committee members included Sharon Chatman of San Jose State University, Myra Miyasoto of California State University, Stephanie Scyleyer of the University of Alabama, and Vivian Stringer of Cheyney State. Sloan-Green served as chair. The CSMW played an important role in creating more involvement of minorities on all levels by the co-sponsorship of workshops on Minority Women in Sports.[3] The CSMW also raised the consciousness of many on the extent to which work remained to fully include minority women in the budding effort to secure greater sports opportunities for women. As a result of increasing conflict with the NCAA over the control of women intercollegiate sport in the post Title IX era, and an unsuccessful antitrust lawsuit against the NCAA, the AIAW dissolved in 1983 (Cain, 2001).

In 1978, Sloan-Green, Franke, Oglesby, and Alexander met Linda Greene, who had joined the Temple University Law School faculty as a new assistant professor. Greene had graduated from UC Berkeley Law School and had been a civil rights and constitutional lawyer at the most important civil rights law firm in the United States, the NAACP Legal Defense and Education Fund (LDF) in New York City. LDF was headed by Thurgood Marshall, who won the historic *Brown v. Board of Education* (1954) case, as well as many other important racial discrimination decisions.[4] Greene joined the LDF after law school, and spent three years litigating civil rights cases all over the country. She spent a year as a deputy city attorney in the City of Los Angeles, where she specialized in civil and constitutional rights policy. Greene had also been a nationally ranked 800-meter and 400-meter track and field athlete as an undergraduate at California State University Long Beach. From 1965–1967, she competed in an Amateur Athletic Union (AAU)–sponsored club called the Long Beach Comets, coached by Ronald Allice.[5] In her last year of law school, 1974 Greene celebrated Title IX by joining the first University of California-Berkeley women's track team and resumed her 800-meter competition. While practicing law in New York, she continued to compete in long-distance road races and in cross country meets.

Greene met Sloan-Green during her first days at Temple University at the university's day care center where they both left their young children during the school day. They began to share conversation on a wide range of topics. Greene and Sloan-Green soon learned that they had common interests in family, sports, and equality.

Sloan-Green introduced Greene to Franke, Oglesby, and Alexander. In addition to teaching civil procedure, constitutional law, and employment discrimination, Greene added a legal and civil rights dimension to the on-going conversation about equality in sport for minority women. Sloan-Green introduced Greene to other black women who were interested in greater opportunity for black women in sport.

---

3. Two conferences were endorsed by AIAW: 1) The 1980 National Minority Women in Sport Conference held at Howard University in Washington D.C.; and 2) The 1981 Second Annual Conference on Minority Women in Sports held at Michigan State University in East Lansing, Michigan.

4. See Kluger (1975) for a history of the LDF and its legal legacy.

5. Coach Allice was a high school physical education and history teacher at Compton High School who coached an AAU women's team called the Long Beach Comets. At the time that Greene graduated from high school, there was only one university in America that provided track and field competition and scholarships for women, Tennessee State University in Nashville, Tennessee. The coach of Tennessee State was Ed Temple, and the program produced Olympians including Wilma Rudolph, Mae Faggs, Wyomia Tyus, Edith McGuire, and Madeline Manning Mims. Her high school did not offer track and field for girls. Aided by a male high school classmate who trained her in cross country the summer after she graduated from high school, Greene met Allice while she raced cross country as an unattached athlete during her freshman year in college. Ronald Allice is currently the head coach of men's and women's track and field at the University of Southern California. (Allice, R., personal communication, May 19, 2006).

In particular, Philadelphia high school girls' basketball coaches with outstanding teams had long lamented the fact that girls' teams were unable to compete in the celebrated City Title Championships that pitted the best Philadelphia public school team against the best Philadelphia Catholic League team. In October of 1979, Lurline Jones, a renowned coach at Philadelphia's University City High School, filed a complaint with the Office of Civil Rights (OCR) of the Department of Health, Education, and Welfare alleging that the practice of denying girls City Title Championships violated Title IX. After investigation, in January 1980 the OCR concluded absence of City Title Championships for girls did violate Title IX (Dodd, D., personal communication, 1980). Led by the University City High School girls' basketball coach Lurline Jones, coaches and female athletes asked Greene to represent them in a federal court lawsuit to extend the City Title Championships to Philadelphia Public League and Catholic League schools. With Gillian Gilhool as co-counsel, Greene filed suit in federal court to secure City Title Championships competition for girls (*Jones et al. v. Marcase*, 1980). After several months of litigation, the federal judge presiding over the case told the parties that it was not possible to continue City Title Championships for Philadelphia Public and Catholic League boys while denying them to girls. Upon the receipt of this clear signal that the judge was prepared to rule in favor of the plaintiffs and either enjoin the championship or order it extended to prep girls, the archdiocese announced the end of Catholic League participation in the City Title Championship tradition.[6] Thereafter, the court declared the controversy moot. This was not the expected result. The goal had been to expand competition for all prep girls in the Philadelphia area.

The victory was pyrrhic, a battle won but a war lost. However, the lawsuit, one of the earliest to apply Title IX to athletics, resulted in increased visibility for the Temple Cohort and increased their determination to focus on the development of a strategy to increase sports opportunity for black girls and women. It was clear that lawsuits would be a necessary but insufficient means to increase opportunities for black women. The OCR complaint and the federal court lawsuit were forms of advocacy that resulted in greater activism and increased public awareness of the disparity in competitive opportunity for black women. But the real challenge would be to develop support for the idea that increased opportunity for black women was a necessary component of an agenda of empowerment for women in athletics. That meant involvement with people and institutions who shared a commitment to increased opportunity.

Conferences were one important means to development of a consensus in favor of increased opportunities. In 1980, there were two important conferences on black women in sport. The first was the National Minority Women in Sports Conference, held at Howard University. The conference materials explicitly acknowledged that the first 1976 Black Women in Sport Workshop at Temple University laid the foundation for the Howard Conference. The conference was also endorsed by the National Association for Girls and Women in Sport and by the Association

---

6. On May 19,1980, the Monsignor Francis N. Schulte, Superintendent of Schools for the Archdiocese of Philadelphia, announced the withdrawal of the archdiocese from City Title Championships. The statement offered several reasons for the termination of archdiocesan participation, including the adequacy of current sport competition, the desire for local suburban competition rather than city competition, the problem of violence, and the cost of security.

for Intercollegiate Athletics for Women. The conference committee included Sloan-Green and Alexander from Temple University, Professor Doris Corbett of Howard University, and Dr. Dorothy Richey of the College of Allegheny County. The conference programs addressed numerous issues from image and stereotypes to the role of black women in nontraditional sports, black women as coaches and administrators, and black women as professional athletes. The conference also provided an opportunity for the Committee on the Status of Minorities within AIAW to report on the results of its work.

In addition, in 1980, Greene, Sloan-Green, and Oglesby organized a Black Women in Sport Workshop at the University of Iowa. The workshop took place over three days and combined history, sociology, and legal perspectives on the role of black women in sport. At the workshop, the Temple Cohort worked with other black women including Dr. Nell Jackson, a former Olympic sprinter and the assistant athletic director at Michigan State University, and Dr. Dorothy Richey, a professor at the College of Allegheny County. These women would all figure prominently in the development of the organization that became the Black Women in Sport Foundation.

Although Greene left Temple University in 1981 to become an associate professor at the University of Oregon Law School, she remained in contact with her Temple colleagues. They continued to work together and support one another's efforts. They also included other women such as Richey and Jackson who had become athletic administrators in an era in which few women held those roles. In 1986, Sloan-Green, Franke, Richey, and Jackson came to Howard University for a conference. Linda Greene, who was living in Washington D.C. and teaching at Georgetown University, hosted a dinner at her home where they discussed their common interest in an expansion of the roles of black women in sport. They continued to discuss ways to influence the development of a consensus that full black female participation in the widest range of athletic ventures was a necessary component of equality for females in athletics. They discussed their own experiences and observed that few black women occupied positions in which they could make policy rather than advocate change to policymakers. They decided that another avenue for the advancement of the opportunity agenda would be full participation in sport administrative and policy roles. They vowed that they would not only seek a broader role in sport for themselves as individuals, but that they would also do everything possible to support each other in that quest.

In 1989, Alexander, who at that time was the Director of Health Promotion at the YWCA, kept her promise. Dr. Alexander, then a United States Olympic Committee (USOC) Board Member, urged the USOC to appoint some black women to USOC committees. At that point, only a small number of blacks and women participated in the governance and committees of the USOC. Dr. Alpha Alexander used her leverage as a member of the USOC Board to urge President Robert Helmick to appoint Alexander, Sloan-Green, and Greene to important USOC committees. Alexander became a leader in the USOC Community Based Organization Committee. She also became chair of the powerful USOC Member Services Committee, which allocated funds to national sports governing bodies and other USOC member organizations. Sloan-Green served on the Olympic Festival Committee and along with Greene, fresh from a three-year stint as Counsel to the United States Senate Judiciary Committee, was appointed to and eventually chaired the

USOC Legislation Committee, the policy committee of the USOC Board. The decade-long dream for a broader role in sport was becoming a reality.

Now, after almost 14 years of friendship and collaborative activity, Sloan-Green, Alexander, Franke, and Greene were ready to create a formal organization called the Black Women in Sport Foundation. Greene recruited Charisse Lillie, a black woman and a prominent Philadelphia lawyer, to serve as the lawyer for the new non-profit organization. Lillie, like Greene, had been one of a handful of black women teaching law in 1978. In 1991, Lillie was a partner at Ballard-Spahr, one of the most important law firms in Philadelphia. She convinced her firm to provide legal services to the fledgling organization on a pro bono basis. The high quality of legal services facilitated the development of an organization that observed all the required legal formalities from corporate filings and taxes to oversight of contracts and other matters. The affiliation with Lillie and her law firm increased the organization's stature and contributed measurably to its stability. The Black Women in Sport Foundation, a 501(c)(3) corporation, was founded to facilitate the involvement of black women in every aspect of sport.

The initial board members also included other women of great talent and energy. For example, Dr. Alpha Alexander served as the initial vice president and continues to serve in the role. She was a vice president of health promotion at the YWCA and a member of the Board of the Directors of the United States Olympic Committee. Dr. Ann Koger, a prominent tennis coach and administrator at Haverford College, served as the initial secretary of the board and the Project Challenge Chair. Dr. Cassandra Jones was a high school teacher specializing in urban sports programming. Dr. Lucille Hester, a prominent sports program director, political organizer, and sister of Olympian Bob Hayes, provided fundraising and program expertise and developed BWSF programs in the Washington, D.C. area. Dr. Marcia Oxley, also a founding board member, worked from the University of the West In-

The Black Women in Sport Foundation Board of Directors (2006)

Name	Position on BWSF Board	Title
Tina Sloan Green	President	Professor Emeritus, Temple University
Alpha Alexander	Vice President	Associate Professor, Lane College
Nikki Franke	Secretary	Associate Professor, Temple University
Linda S. Greene	Treasurer	Law Professor, University of Wisconsin
DawnMarie Montgomery-Otis	Board Member	Vice President, PNC Bank
Ernestyne J. Adams	Honorary Member	Professor Emeritus, Temple University
Lucille Hester	Board Member	Project Director, National Youth Sports Program
Cassandra Jones	Board Member	CEO and President, Next Step Associates
Marcia Oxley	Board Member	Tutor, Erdison Teachers Training College, Barbados
Lynnore Lawton Thames, Esq.	Board Member	Paralegal, ESPN Inc. Legal Department
Rochelle M. Taylor	Board Member	President, National Youth Sports Corporation
Sheila A. Ward, Ph.D., MPH	Board Member	Associate Professor, Norfolk University
Stephanie Franklin-Suber, Esq.	Legal Counsel	Ballard, Spahr, Andrews, and Ingersoll

dies in Barbados and focused on the development of BWSF international alliances and programs. As a result of Oxley's work and her international networks, the BWSF is recognized internationally and has been invited to participate in significant international sport meetings and conferences. Lynnore Lawton Thames brought expertise in public relations and marketing as a result of her employment in the legal department at ESPN.

Subsequent board members contributed significant expertise and energy to BWSF programs. An important focus of BWSF has been the development of professional development programs that focus on black women as coaches. Women with considerable program development experience joined the board and spearheaded the initiative called The Next Step Programs. These board members include Rochelle Taylor, a board member with senior NCAA experience who now is president of the National Youth Sports Corporation; Felicia Hall, a former WNBA vice president and program development consultant; and Sheila Ward, a professor at Norfolk and health-sports expert. DawnMarie Montgomery Otis, then a senior banking officer with Merrill Lynch, provided financial expertise and investment advice while Mitchell and Titus, one of the countries largest black accounting firms, provided advice as well as some pro bono services.

The activities of the Black Women in Sport Foundation have been facilitated by a strong commitment to strategic planning. In 1997, led by Linda Greene, BWSF devoted significant time to a strategic planning process in order to assess its achievements and more sharply focus its activity. The board adopted the following strategic objectives: (a) increase public awareness of the BWSF; (b) increase the number of the black girls and women served by BWSF activities; (c) establish BWSF as the preeminent source of information on the expanding roles of black women in sport; (d) increase sport career awareness and opportunity for black girls and women; (e) restructure and improve governance; (f) increase collaboration with corporate and institutional partners and develop new partners; and (g) establish a national office of the BWSF that is open to the public.

The accomplishments of the Black Women in Sport Foundation are numerous. It has developed grassroots programs for young women that combine instruction in nontraditional sports with mentoring programs. In most cases, these programs have combined sports instruction and competition in sports in which black children have not traditionally participated (e.g., tennis, fencing, golf, and lacrosse) with academic enrichment programs and mentoring activities. For example, in 2002 BWSF conducted several "Gear Up" programs for 7–9th graders designed to develop awareness and readiness for undergraduate programs. In 1995, mentoring clinics were held for golf and tennis in numerous sites nationwide as well as lacrosse clinics for middle school girls. The programs have served thousands of young African American women. During 2004 and 2005 the BWSF provided at least 30 programs serving almost 3,000 African American girls between the ages of five and 18 years old. (See Appendix.)

The Black Women in Sport Foundation has also developed a body of educational literature and videos that permit its message of black female participation in every aspect of sport to be widely disseminated. One of the important missions of the BWSF is facilitating the development of resources for and about black women. As a result, curricular innovation has been an important emphasis of BWSF. In

1993, with funding from Greg Hartley, vice president of the Sporting Goods Manufacturing Association, the BWSF produced the video *Amazing Grace: Black Women in Sport*. The 25-minute educational video, narrated by Robin Roberts, the prominent black female sports and newscaster, featured black women of significant athletic achievement including Althea Gibson, Florence Joyner-Griffin, Wilma Rudolph, and other prominent black females. In order that educators might be able to incorporate the video into their work with girls, BWSF paired this video with a training manual (Black Women Sport Foundation, 1996). A second video, *After the Whistle Blows* (1999), highlighted the accomplishments of black female athletes beyond the playing field, in athletic administration, policy, and management. Sloan-Green and others have developed college courses with unique content, including a "Black Women in Sport" course. Sloan-Green and Alexander wrote a chapter on black women in sport entitled "Sheroes over the Rim" (Green & Alexander, 2000).

The conferences conducted by the Black Women in Sport Foundation emphasized new opportunities for black women in sport. A unique feature of each conference was the selection of a powerful theme that defined the conference focus. As noted above, the first Black Women in Sport Workshop was held in August of 1976 and was organized by Tina Sloan-Green with Nikki Franke and Carole Oglesby. There were subsequent workshops in the 1980s that played an important role in reinforcing the legitimacy of a broader role for black women in sport. As a formal nonprofit, the BWSF had its first national conference in October 1996. The conference was sponsored by the Athletic Footwear Association. The 1996 conference theme was "The Black Woman in Sport, Shaping Power Strategies for 2001." The second conference in 1997 adopted the theme "Passing the Baton: Mentoring Women for a New Millennium." The 2000 conference broke new ground through its focus on strategic objectives and the success of BWSF in securing a large number of financial sponsors for the conference.[7] The 2002 conference, with the theme "Celebrating the Achievements of Black Women in Sports," was the largest ever. In 2002, there were 300 participants from 20 states and three countries.

These conferences served many roles. They were sites and spaces in which the interests of black women, often marginalized at other gatherings or relegated to a diversity panel, were the focal point of the entire event. As such, they represented an example of emancipatory activity, that is, activity whose primary purpose is the empowerment and interests of black women. The conferences broadened the perception of conference attendees because the conferences themselves, as well as the participants, presented tangible examples of BWSF's vision of black women as leaders in

---

7. The sponsors of the 2000 Black Women in Sport Conference included *Sports Illustrated for Women*, the accounting firm of Mitchell and Titus, *Health Quest Magazine*, Keystone Mercy Health Plan of Philadelphia, Norton Communications, October Gallery, Penn State University Athletic Department, *SportsBusiness Daily*, Temple University Athletic Department, Temple University Book Store, Temple University Department of Health Studies, Tribune Society of the Courts in the State of New York, Inc., Zavelle's Bookstore. Youth sponsors included C.O.E. D.E. Inc (Community Operation for Economic Development and Education), Gamma Sports, Juneteenth Coalition–Ron Brown, LongStreth Women's Sports Specialist, Philadelphia Academies, Inc, Philadelphia Department of Human Services-Prevention Services, Philadelphia School District Communities in Schools, Philadelphia School District-Fels Cluster/New School, Philadelphia School District-Gear Up/University City Cluster, Philadelphia Visitors, and Convention Bureau, Santelli Fencing Equipment, Support Community Outreach Program (SCOP), Julie Senko, Sisters in Sport Science, Amy Taylor, Temple University College of HPERD Alumni Association, United States Tennis Association/Middle States Tennis Association.

the formulation of an agenda for their future. The conferences also provided opportunities for the professional development of black women.[8]

The promotion of the achievements of black women in sport has a significant part of the activities of the BWSF.[9] One purpose of this activity is to honor these black females whose extraordinary sports achievements have not been recognized. The other purpose is to provide real-life examples of extraordinary achievement, role models who will inspire young and mature black women alike to adopt the highest aspirations. In November of 2004, the BWSF partnered with the Women Sport Project and the Pennsylvania Historical and Museum Commission to dedicate a historical marker to the life of Ora Washington (1898–1971), an eight-time American Tennis Association National Crown Winner and a basketball center.[10]

Black Women in Sport Foundation has also focused on the development and maintenance of relationships with many other organizations. These organizations include the Women's National Basketball Association, the National Basketball Association, Nike, the United States Tennis Association, the United States Golf Association, the National Hockey League, the National Collegiate Athletic Association, The Philadelphia School District and other school districts, The Women's Sports Foundation, the BCA, Methodist Services for Children and Families, the NCAA, National Consortium for Academic and Sports, Association of Black Women in Higher Education, and the American Association of University Professors. These relationships often involve funding for BWSF programs, sponsorships of conferences and events, exchange of information and expertise, education on issues important to black women, partnership in the delivery of programs, and BWSF participation in the governance and consultation on the design of programs.

BWSF Board members recently reflected on the significance of BWSF's work generally and, more specifically, in their lives. Cassandra Jones emphasized the manner in which the BWSF has expanded opportunity for both young people and adults:

> BWSF has successfully sustained the work with grassroots communities and has exposed young people . . . to experiences that have enriched their lives . . . BWSF has also . . . empowered adults who have not traditionally been reached through workshops and conferences. Our interns have gone on to become leaders in their field . . . (Jones, C., personal communication, August 8, 2005).

Ottley said that her involvement with BWSF helped her to see the intersection between sports and business. "Although my career is in business, BWSF opened my eyes to the possibility of sports marketing and management. I see great opportunities in the sports field" (Ottley, personal communication, August 25, 2005).

---

8. For example, the 1999 Annual Black Women in Sport Foundation Conference (October 8–10) featured a workshop entitled "The Business of Sport."
9. For example, the 2002 10th Anniversary Black Women in Sport Foundation Conference (October 11–12) had the theme "Celebrating the Achievements of Black Women in Sports."
10. Ora Washington competed in basketball during 1930 for a YMCA-sponsored team called the Germantown Hornets, and in 1930s as a member of a barnstorming team called the Philadelphia Tribune Girls. She was the top black tennis player during the thirties, winning many single and doubles titles. In 2004, she was honored with a State Historic Marker by the Philadelphia Historical and Museum Commission, The Women's Sport Project, and the Black Women in Sport Foundation.

Robin Turner has found inspiration from the educational mission of BWSF:

> Through working with the BWSF, I realized that I wanted to educate minority students about various untapped scholarships and help them gain access to career opportunities that are not easily accessible to minorities. (Turner, R., personal communication, August 25, 2005)

Katie Henderson, a special education teacher, praised the Black Women in Sport Foundation for its development of her leadership skills and the enhancement of her love for children (Henderson, K., personal communication, August 23, 2005). Dr. Angelia Nelson is ecstatic about the mentoring work of the BWSF. She began her affiliation with BWSF as an intern and is now the director of a sports foundation. She said the following:

> The Black Women in Sport Foundation has played a major role in my career as executive director of the Dawn Staley Foundation. It was through my affiliation with the BWSF as an intern that I had the opportunity to meet with Nike representatives and be offered the opportunity to work with one of their athletes. Furthermore, Tina Sloan-Green has been extremely supportive and a wonderful mentor. (Nelson, A., personal communication, August 25, 2005)

Rochelle Taylor, former NCAA Director of Professional Development, current President, National Youth Sports Corporation, said that BWSF had increased black female awareness of the breadth of sports opportunity:

> BWSF has provided exposure to issues facing black women in sport; increased participation of black girls in sport and increased exposure opportunities for black women considering careers in sport. Opportunities for athletes have been increased as more black girls have been exposed to nontraditional sports and are exposed to women excelling in all aspects of sport. (personal interview, August 11, 2005)

Professor Nikki Franke, a founding member, emphasized the importance of BWSF in the exposure of black women to non-traditional sports as well as the mentoring programs that provide opportunities for black female college students to mentor and lead young black girls (personal interview, August 24, 2005). Dr. Alpha Alexander, also a founding member, cited the work of the BWSF in the development of grassroots community sports organizations as well as BWSF's work in promoting participation in nontraditional sports and careers (personal interview, August 23, 2005).

Several themes emerge from the reflections of these women. Foremost, they believe that this success was due to the determination of the founders to create a grassroots, working board dedicated to the creation of significant change in the sports opportunity for black women. Although all the women involved on the board had significant talent as well as a track record of prior significant achievements, they all realized that they would not be able to make significant contributions in the world of sports as individuals working alone. They conceived BWSF as an institution that would provide a space in which it would be routine to recognize and celebrate black female sport achievement rather than to treat black females as invisible except when they participate in stereotypical roles. They also intended to establish the routine expectation that the next generation of black women will shatter the white glass ceiling that exists in all sports institutions. The success of this effort is illustrated in the chart that follows, which lists past and present BWSF board members and their work in the world of sports.

Table 1. Black Women in Sport Foundation Board Profile

Board Members	Positions	Dates Served	
Tina Sloan Green	President, Executive Director	1992–2005	Video production; sport mentoring programs
Alpha Alexander	Vice President	1992–2005	Board comp; video production
Linda Greene	Past Treasurer/ Member	1992–2005	Legal
Ann Koger	Past Secretary	1992–1994	Project Challenge; Amazing Grace Manual
Nikki Franke	Member/Secretary	1992–2005	Web site
Cassandra Jones	Member/Secretary	1992–2005	Educational consultant
Ernestyne Adams	Member/Emeritus	1994–	Sport counseling
Lynnore Thames	Member	1997–present	Public relations/marketing
DawnMarie Montgomery Otis	Treasurer	1999–present	Merrill Lynch
Marcia Oxley	Member	1992–2005	International network
Felicia Hall	Member	2000–2003	Next Step conference support
Sheila Ward	Member	2000–present	Researcher: Next Step proposal and health disparities
Rochelle Taylor	Member	2000–present	Next Step conference support
Lucille Hester	Member	1993–present	Youth sports; Howard Legends Reception; conference support; Angela Murphy scholoarship
Stephanie Franklin Subir	Counsel	2004–present	
Deidre Downes	Assistant Counsel	2004–present	
Charisse Lillie	Counsel	1992–2004	

Dr. Carole Oglesby, an early mentor of several of the black women who founded BWSF, credits those women with her evolution from a secure professional with "white liberal baggage," devoid of any sense of responsibility for racism, to a white person who understood her role in the sustenance of racism.

> My family ties were in rural Oklahoma. . . . The professional colleagues of color I met in Philadelphia at Temple, and graduate students of color I worked with there, were the ones who helped me to finally get some of the way past my racism and for that I will ever be in their debt. These were, not coincidently, the women (especially Tina Sloan-Green and Alpha Alexander) who also built and fostered the Black Women's Sport Foundation . . . I know for me, however, if it had not been for the women of color who worked before and into and beyond the Black Women's Sport Foundation, we would not (as a women's sport movement) be *near* to the place we find ourselves now. Where we are is far from perfection but they simply had to do what they did and they did

it with grace, enthusiasm, generosity, and love. (personal communication, September 9, 2005)

The work of the Black Women in Sport Foundation has been based upon a combined gender-race critique of sports institutions and sports in society. The intellectual and activist work of the black women in sport movement, later BWSF, is analogous to the academic work of Dr. Harry Edwards more than 30 years ago. He offered a critique of sports institutions that espouse meritocracy yet continue to exclude discrete identifiable groups, including minority women, from participation in the ranks of privilege, leadership, and power (Edward, 1997). In addition, the focus of the BWSF on the role of sports institutions in the subordination and exclusion of black women[11] is similar to a later emerging critique adopted by the black female legal scholars who urged the exploration of the phenomena associated with the intersection of race and gender.[12] Such a critique explores the ways in which black males and females experience similar as well as unique forms of indifference, marginalization, and tokenism.[13] Intersectionality analysis rejects essentialism assumptions, assumptions that the experience of all women is identical, and instead demands an exploration of the precise experiences of groups and subgroups to determine whether subordination exists and to determine whether equality has been achieved.

Although the BWSF has achieved a great deal, there is still much to be done. A November 2001 Chronicle of Higher Education Report noted that black women have yet to benefit from the collegiate competitive and scholarship opportunities available in sports other than basketball or track and field (Suggs, 2001). Black women are only 2.7% of those participating in the sports that are now available to women athletes. Over 70% of the women participating in intercollegiate sport are white. Donna Lopiano, president of the Women's Sport Foundation admitted: "The plight of women of color, who are in double jeopardy, is oft times on the back burner." Tina Sloan-Green stated, "I'm not going to say that black women haven't benefited, but they have been left out of the full promise of gender equality in sport" (Suggs, 2001).

In 1981, Tina Sloan-Green predicted that, though there would be progress in the future decade, many barriers would remain:

> There will be great barriers to increasing the numbers of black females in high authority sport occupations. Racism and sexism continue to influence hiring practices, but, how many black head coaches, athletic directors, sport promoters and commentators have been seen in the past twenty years. As coaching female athletes becomes more lucrative financially and socially, the white male, the black male, and the white female will compete with the black female for the jobs. Lack of sufficient experience will be the cited reasons for not hiring black females. Those black

---

11. As early as 1981, Professor Sloan–Green and others addressed the particular forms of discrimination in sport experienced by black women. See Oglesby (1981) and Green (1993) for more information.

12. Long after the black women who founded the Black Women in Sport Foundation began to act to eliminate the invisibility and exclusion experienced by black women in sport, scholars began to address the phenomenon of intersectionality (e.g., Austin 1989; Trent, 1989; Harris, 1990; Crenshaw, 1991; Yarbrough, 1997; Greene, 1999).

13. More recent works explore this intersection of race and gender in the context of sport (e.g., Mathewson, 1996).

females hired will be super-qualified. The current trend . . . will continue over the next decade without significant affirmative action efforts.
(Green, 1981)

Sloan-Green's words, written in 1981, are not significantly different from the observation of a recent Princeton graduate who wrote her senior thesis on the racial
inequality in intercollegiate athletics in the post–Title IX Era (Lattimer, 2005).
Chanel Lattimer wrote on racial inequality in women's intercollegiate athletics
and observed that despite Title IX's effect on the growth in women's intercollegiate athletics, a racial disparity exists. She concluded:

> This disparity is defined as the under representation of African-American
> women in "non-traditional" sports—sports outside of basketball and
> track and field—as compared to their Caucasian counterparts. Despite
> the increase in various women's athletic programs, African-American
> females continue to primarily participate in basketball and track and
> field; where they make up one-quarter and one-fifth of college athletes
> respectively (Lattimer, 2005).

Lattimer's conclusions are consistent with those of a study done by Dr. Alexander
in 1978. The results demonstrate that racial inequality existed in the early days of
Title IX legislation and continues to this day. Additionally, these findings support
criticism of the beneficial role of Title IX in the lives of African American female
athletes.

Despite these dismal statistics, BWSF remains committed to the goal of increasing the involvement of black women in every aspect of sports. Some have criticized BWSF for its persistent commitment to the empowerment of black women
through an organization exclusively devoted to the interests of black women in
full participation in every aspect of sport. Sloan-Green has responded this way:

> The Black Women in Sport Foundation has led the way in the promo-
> tion and provision of opportunities for black women. We are willing to
> work with any one and any organization that shares our passion for a
> broader role for black women in sport. The future success of the BWSF—
> and all black women in sport—will be based on a compelling agenda
> that focuses on the needs of black women without limitations as to their
> class, economic status, or educational status. The Foundation must also
> find continuous and secure funding in order to insure the continuity
> and sustainability of its programs. The organization will continue to
> thrive if it continues to attract courageous black women who care less
> about personal gain and more about the good of the whole, who respect
> individual excellence without jealousy, and who cultivate allies among
> all—including men and white women—who share our vision and our
> goals. The work of the Black Women in Sport Foundation will be com-
> plete when there is no need for BWSF. Our work will be done when we
> routinely see black girls and women who excel in every aspect of sport—
> as athletes in all sports, as coaches, administrators, professors, policy
> makers, broadcasters, managers, and owners. (personal communication,
> November 18, 2005)

▲▼ Suggested Readings ▲▼

Cain, P. (2001). Women, race and sports: Life before Title IX. *Journal of Gender, Race and Justice, 4,* 337.

Crenshaw, K. (1991). Demarginalizing the intersection of race & sex: A Black feminist critique of anti-discrimination doctrine, feminist theory and antiracist politics. In A. Phillips (Ed.), *Feminism and politics* (pp. 314). Buckingham, England: Open University Press.

Evans, T. (1998). In the Title IX race toward gender equity, the black female athlete is left to finish last: The lack of access for the "invisible" women. *Howard Law Journal, 42,* 105.

Gray, F. C. & Lamb, Y. R. (2001). *Born to win: The authorized biography of Althea Gibson.* Hoboken, NJ: John Wiley and Sons, Inc.

Yarbrough, M. (1977). A sporting chance: The intersection of race and gender. *South Texas Law Review, 38,* 1029–1035.

▲▼ Study Questions ▲▼

1. In 1992 the BWSF was officially incorporated. What was the mission of the organization? What programs were created to fulfill the mission?

2. Some critics believe that since the BWSF targets black women, this is a discriminatory practice. Sloan-Green disagrees with the critics. Explain her argument.

3. Name and explain the contributions to BWSF of at least five board members.

4. Compare and analyze the results of the studies conducted by Alexander and Lattimer.

5. What were the initial recommendations of the AIAW Commission on the Status on Minority Women? Were the recommendations successfully followed? Why or why not?

6. What were the events and reasons that led Greene to file suit in federal court to secure City Title Championships Competition rights for girls in Philadelphia? What was the title of the suit? Was the suit successful?

7. What were two the important conferences on Black Women in Sport in 1980? What did they hope to accomplish? Were they successful in accomplishing their goals?

8. Why did the 2000 BWSF conference break new ground? What was historically significant about the 2002 conference?

9. What are some of the organizations that the BWSF has relations with? Do you consider these organizations to be influential?

10. What percentage of women participating in intercollegiate sports are not white? Based on your answer do you think racial inequality exists for women in sports today?

References

Alexander, A. (1978). *Status of minority women in the Association of Intercollegiate Athletics for Women.* Unpublished master's thesis, Temple University, Philadelphia, PA.

Alexander, A. & Franke, N. (1981). Her story of Black sportswomen. In T. Green, C. Oglesby, A. Alexander, & Frank, N. (Eds.), *Black women in sport* (pp. 36). Reston, VA: National Association of Girls and Women in Sport.

Austin, R. (1989). Sapphire bound! *Wisconsin Law Review,* 539.

Black Women in Sport Foundation (Producer). (1988). *Amazing grace: Black women in sport* [Videotape]. (Available from Black Women in Sport Foundation, 4300 Monument Avenue, Philadelphia, PA 19131-1690).

Black Women in Sport Foundation (1992). *Amazing grace: Black women in sport (student workbook).* Philadelphia, PA: Black Women in Sport Foundation.

Black Women in Sport Foundation (Producer). (2000). *After the whistle blows* [Videotape]. (Available from Black Women in Sport Foundation, 4300 Monument Avenue, Philadelphia, PA 19131-1690.)

Cain, P. (2001). Women, race and sports: Life before Title IX. *Journal of Gender, Race and Justice, 4,* 337.

Crenshaw, K. (1991). Demarginalizing the intersection of race & sex: A Black feminist critique of anti-discrimination doctrine, feminist theory and antiracist politics. In A. Phillips (Ed.), *Feminism and politics* (pp. 314). Buckingham, England: Open University Press.

Edwards, H. (1997). The end of the "Golden Age" of black sports participation? *South Texas Law Review 38,*1007.

Evans, T. (1998). In the Title IX race toward gender equity, the black female athlete is left to finish last: The lack of access for the "invisible" women. *Howard Law Journal, 42,* 105.

Gray, F. C., & Lamb, Y. R. (2001). *Born to win: The authorized biography of Althea Gibson.* Hoboken, NJ: John Wiley and Sons, Inc.

Green, T., Oblesby, C., Alexander, A., & Franke, N. (Eds.). (1981). *Black women in sport.* Reston, VA: National Association of Girls and Women in Sport.

Green, T. (1993). Future of the African-American female athlete. In D. Brooks & R. Althouse, (Eds.) *Racism in college athletics.* Morgantown, WV: Fitness Information Technology, Inc.

Greene, L. (1991). Tokens, role models and pedagogical politics: Lamentations of an African American female law professor. *Berkeley Law Journal, 6,* 81.

Greene, L. (1999). From tokenism to emancipatory politics: The conferences and meetings of law professors of color. *Michigan Journal of Race and Law, 5*(43), 161.

Harris, A. (1990). Race and essentialism in feminist legal theory. *Stanford Law Review, 42,* 581. *Jones et al v. Marcase,* No.80-0811 (E.D. Pa. 1980).

Kanter, R. M. (1977). *Men and women of the corporation.* New York: Basic Books.

Kluger, R. (1975). *Simple justice.* New York: Alfred A. Knopf.

Lattimer, C. (2005). *All, is that all? An exploration of African-American women in intercollegiate athletics post Title IX.* Unpublished abstract, Princeton University, Princeton, New Jersey.

Mathewson, A. (1996). Black women, gender equity, and the function at the junction. *Marquette Sport Law Journal, 6,* 23.

Office of Civil Rights of the United States Department of Health, Education and Welfare. (1975, September). *Memorandum to chief state school officers, superintendents of local educational agencies and colleges and university presidents. Subject: Elimination of sex discrimination in athletic programs.* Washington, DC: Office of Civil Rights.

Oglesby, C. (1981). Myths and realities of Black women in sport. In T. Green, C. Oglesby, A. Alexander, & Frank, N. (Eds.), *Black women in sport* (pp. 1–3). Reston, VA: National Association of Girls and Women in Sport.

Public Welfare and Human Services Nondiscrimination on the Basis of Sex in Education Programs and Activities Receiving or Benefiting from Federal Financial Assistance, Athletics, 45 C.F.R § 86.41 (1999).

Sloan-Green, T., & Alexander, A. (2000). Sheroes over the rim. In K. Shropshire & T. Boyd (Eds.) *Basketball Jones: America above the rim (Fast Track)* (pp. 176). New York: New York University Press.

Suggs, W. (2001, November 30) Left behind: Title IX has done little for minority female athletes because of socioeconomic and cultural factors, and indifference. *The Chronicle of Higher Education,* A35.

Title IX, Education Amendments of 1972, 20 U.S.C. § 1681 *et seq.* (1972).

Tokenism (n.d.). In *Wikipedia, The Free encyclopedia.* Retrieved June 2, 2006 from Wikepdia website: http://en.wikipedia.org/wiki/Tokenism.

Trent, S. (1989). Black women and the constitution: Finding our race, asserting our rights. *Harvard Civil Rights-Civil Liberties Law Review,* 24.

Willey, S. (1996). *The Governance of women's intercollegiate athletics: Association for Intercollegiate Athletics for Women (AIAW), 1976–1982.* Unpublished doctoral dissertation, Indiana University, Bloomington, Indiana.

Women in History (n.d.). Wilma Rudolph biography. Retrieved June 2, 2006 from Lakewood Public Library Web site: http://www.lkwdpl.org/wihohio/rudo-wil.htm.

Yarbrough, M. (1977). A sporting chance: The intersection of race and gender. *South Texas Law Review, 38,* 1029–1035.

▲ *Appendix*▼

Black Women in Sport Foundation
2004–2005 Sites

Site	Location	Director/ Principal	Program Name	# of Participants	Ages
Fall/Spring					
Discovery Charter School	5070 Parkside Aveue Suite 6200 Philadelphia PA 19131	Ms. Solomon	Extended Day Program	60	5 to 12
Martha Washington	766 North 44th Street Philadelphia PA 19104	Carolyn Jackson	After School	32	
Lotus Academy	340 East Haines Street Philadelphia PA 19144	Ina Walker	In School Program	150	5 to 12
Girard College	2101 South College Avenue Philadelphia PA 19121			50	
Methodist Services	4300 Monument Road Philadelphia PA 19131	Tabitha DeJesus	After School	50	
	4300 Monument Road Philadelphia PA 19131	Tina Sloan-Green	Harriet Davis Adult League	30	Over 35
Monument Village	4300 Monument Road Philadelphia PA 19131	Anne Rice-Burgess	After School	20	10 to 17
Grover Washington	201 East Olney Avenue Philadelphia PA 19120	Rashida Stamps	Beacon After School	30	
SISCOM	Norris Square 173 West Norris Street Philadelphia PA	Paige Taylor	Sisters in the Community	20	8 to 12
	Paul Lawrence Dunbar Elementary School 1750 North 12th Street Philadelphia PA 19122	Paige Taylor	Sisters in the Community	20	8 to 12
	Zion Baptist Church 3600 North Broad Street Philadelphia PA 19140	Paige Taylor	Sisters in the Community	25	7 to13
	Lighthouse 152 West Lehigh Avenue Philadelphia PA 19133	Paige Taylor	Sisters in the Commuity	20	8 to12
Stetson Middle School	3200 B Street Philadelphia PA 19134	Kathleen Fitzpatrick	Beacon After School	20	8 to12

▲ *Appendix* *(continued)* ▼

Site	Location	Director/ Principal	Program Name	# of Participants	Ages
Summer					
Gear-Up	Locke Elementary School 4550 Haverford Avenue Philadelphia PA 19139	Traci Green		54	
Girard College	2101 South College Avenue Philadelphia PA 19121			15	
New Covenant	7500 Germantown Avenue			44	
Salvation Army	Broad & Brown			60	
HERO	17th & Tioga			24	
Martha Washington	766 North 44th Street Philadelphia PA 19104	Carolyn Jackson	Summer Camp	50	
Methodist Services	4300 Monument Road Philadelphia PA 19131	Tabitha DeJesus	Day Camp	200	5 to 13
Chester Education	2600 West 9th Street			24	
GoGirlGo	Girl Scouts of South Eastern Pennsylvania Philadelphia PA 19118	Sheila Williams	GoGirlGo	75	
	B&V Outreach 1518 North Broad Street Philadelphia PA 19121	Veronica Norris	GoGirlGo	25	10 to 16
	Shelbourne Community Center 3 Curley Street Roslindale MA 02131	Alfreda Harris	GoGirlGo	130	8 to 18
	Hardy Middle School, Washington D.C. 20090	Lucille Hester	GoGirlGo	375	10 to 14
	Baltimore City Public School 200 East North Avenue Room 305 Baltimore MD 21202	Jessica Ivey	GoGirlGo	148	9 to 12
	Sisters 'n Sport Marion College, Butler University and University of Indianapolis	Rochelle Taylor	GoGirlGo	238	10 to 18
	Lane College 545 Lane Avenue Jackson TN 38301	Dr. Alpha Alexander	GoGirlGo	450	9 to 17

▲ *Appendix* (continued) ▼

Site	Location	Director/ Principal	Program Name	# of Participants	Ages
GoGirlGo *(continued)*					
	Triple Threat Entourage 5725 Jefferson Street Philadelphia PA 19131	Da'Lia Starkey	GoGirlGo	17	10 to 17
	Goulds Park Recreation Center 11350 SW 216 Street Miami FL 33170	Marilyn Stephens Franklyn	GoGirlGo	60	9 to 15
	Widener University 1 University Place Chester, PA 19013	Marcine Davis Pickeron	GoGirlGo	15	12 to 14
SISCOM	Temple University 1801 North Broad Street Philadelphia, PA 19122	Paige Taylor	Sisters in the Community	90	7 to 13
Sickle Cell	Camp Nock-A-Mixon Pennsylvania	Dr. Chavis	Camp Free to Be Me	200	5 to 17

Fritz Polite explores sports as a bridge to global marketing. In Polite's assessment it is the sports event in different venues that connects together an evolving hundred billion dollar industry across national boundaries. Sports are being played out through an array of sports marketing packages that promote the market for different sports organizations (media, event promoters, sponsors, fans, and sport leagues). "The Globalization of Sport: A Bridge to Advancing Cultures" draws attention to economic and technological forces driving development, but also considers exploitation, racism, and social injustices. Polite turns to *NFL International* for a closer look at a sport organization engaged in global marketing of sports.

CHAPTER 16

THE GLOBALIZATION OF SPORT: A BRIDGE TO ADVANCING CULTURES

FRITZ G. POLITE

Abstract ▼ The world in which we live is constantly evolving toward a more global community. This phenomenon is predicated on advanced technologies, sophisticated methods of communication, and the prevalence of expanding international markets. International events bring together people from different countries and different racial, ethnic, and religious backgrounds, promoting understanding and friendships across social divides (Eitzen, 2003). A fundamental shift is taking place that is focused on a world economy versus a national economy. A self-contained national economy mindset may create modes of isolation from existing global partnerships. These would include creating barriers to trade, investment opportunities, financing, and international exposure. This fundamental globalization shift has had an especially significant impact on sport and the visibility of the global aspects of sport. There is a cultural convergence that is merging into an interdependent global economic system that is interconnected by the broader social and economic demands of the international community. This chapter discusses the concept of global marketing, drivers and barriers to globalization, and the international scope of sport, and presents a case study of NFL Europe and its relationship to the model of global expansion. The globalization of sport as a bridge to advancing cultures along with the connecting of the world via sporting events is also discussed.

Introduction

The world has historically experienced exponential growth in the exchange of services, ideas, and goods. The desire for bigger, better, new, and improved has motivated people to attempt to move their services, ideas, and goods around the world. This movement has led to increased interaction among countries, which has contributed significantly to the synergy of cultures that has been described as the global human community. *Webster's Dictionary* defines globalization as "the process that renders various activities and aspirations worldwide in scope or application" (Chandra, 2002).

Key Terms

▼ Globalization ▲

▼ Global marketing ▲

▼ Global sport marketing ▲

Countries have historically traveled and spread themselves across continents. The emergence of the New World (1400–1500) created an array of goods, services, philosophies, and ideas. This concept of mixing different societies, economics, politics, and technologies expanded the process of multiculturalism, diversity, languages, and most importantly, multiple discourses of thought. There may be a direct connection to these concepts in the global reach of sport and the aspects of global sport marketing. The effects of globalization are readily apparent in most American professional sports leagues. The National Basketball Association has been at the forefront of the international movement and has been largely affected by the influx of foreign talent in American sports. Steve Nash, a Canadian, was selected as the Most Valuable Player for the 2004–2005 season. One of the league's most marketable athletes, Yao Ming, is from Shanghai, China, and was introduced to the world of the NBA in 2002. The $7'6''$ center has consistently led the league as the top vote getter globally in the NBA All-Star voting, receiving more than 2.3 million votes. Conversely, the influence of NBA basketball in Asia has affected the Chinese culture, where in 2005 the top-selling NBA player jerseys were those of Tracy McGrady and Allen Iverson. China has more than 1.3 billion people with a consistent positive rise in disposable income; many advertisers as well as globally branded companies have been drawn to this large demographic segment. Companies such as Amway, Nike, Reebok, McDonalds, Adidas, and Sony have joined the group of major players in attempting to gain valuable international market shares.

The expanding segment of free trade has had a positive impact on the economic growth and development of most developed countries. This has in turn increased the overall consumption of globally produced goods and services in the international market. Interestingly, the world's two most populous countries, China and India, have experienced a rise in household incomes along with greater consumption spending power (Chanda, 2002).

Global Marketing

As globalization has altered the way in which business is conducted, the door has been opened for the concept of global marketing. Through advances in technology, the sale of products is no longer exclusive to any one geographic region. Production facilities and distributorships enjoy the ability to place any product, anywhere, at any time. Where demand for a certain product may not have previously existed, the use of global marketing can create and drive the demand for market expansion. It is, however, important to understand the difference between globalization and global marketing. Although global marketing may have a strong impact on globalization, it is only a contributing factor (McAuley, 2004).

Global marketing may be defined as the creation and implementation of marketing strategies on a global scale. Yip specified that that global marketing consisted of "globally uniform approaches to elements of the marketing mix" (Yip, 1997). The concept of "selling the same things in the same way everywhere" was furthered by the global strategy concept of Levitt (1983). Differentiation in advertising provides an element of uniqueness, but strategies that utilize uniformity may be easily adapted as the target market varies.

The effectiveness and practicality of global marketing depends on several factors. A global marketing scheme may not be conducive for all companies. Large-scale organizations may find global concepts more useful than organizations that are smaller and geographically limited. The extent of global coverage is a determining factor for the usefulness of a global marketing campaign. Companies with greater global coverage and a greater share in the global market have more of a need to coordinate their marketing activities.

Nationality and, more specifically, cultural orientation play a significant role in the use of global marketing. Yip's 1997 study concluded that "companies from countries that perceive their cultures to have global appeal are more likely to extend domestic marketing approaches into a global approach. In contrast, companies from countries that perceive their cultures to lack global appeal are more likely to adapt their marketing approaches for specific countries."

Global marketing strategies are most effective when the needs of the customers are standardized. The more similar the customer needs and tastes in different countries, the more scope there is to market globally standardized products and services and to use a globally uniform marketing mix (Levitt, 1983).

Globalization

The ongoing process of globalization is fundamentally altering the world in which we live. No longer do distance, language, and culture dictate the way in which society and business operate. National economies are no longer isolated from one another, but instead work together as an interdependent global economic system to present new opportunities in new markets. This shift has provided great stimulation to much of the world's economy and acted as the catalyst for many of the trends seen in the world economy today.

The technology boom of the late 20th century paved the way for worldwide economic and business reform. Communication is now instantaneous, overseas travel is readily available, and the cultural identity of one country easily permeates into that of another. As advances in technology have led to lower costs and greater efficiency in the production of goods and services, the resulting economic benefits have had an impact on much of the global community.

As the impact of globalization has altered the world's economy, so too has it altered the world of sport. Large scale international competitions such as the Olympics and the World Cup feature a growing number of nations and competitors. The 2002 World Cup in South Korea featured four countries that made their World Cup debut: China, Ecuador, Senegal, and Slovenia. In 2006, the World Cup was held in Germany and included six first-time participants: Angola, Cote d'Ivoire (Ivory Coast), Ghana, Trinidad and Tobago, Togo, and Ukraine. The economic impact of hosting such an event can generate long-term benefits for the host cities and countries. Locations that previously have been labeled as undesirable are now contenders to host some of the largest sporting events in the world. South Africa, once a breeding ground for political turmoil, was selected to host the 2010 World Cup.

The world of sport and the way it is managed, marketed, and consumed have been dramatically altered by globalization. It is a world in which Major League Baseball's Seattle Mariners are owned by Nintendo of America, a Japanese company;

and Manchester United, the world's most popular soccer team, is owned by American billionaire Malcolm Glazer. It is a world in which the popularity of athletes such as Tiger Woods, David Beckham, and Michael Jordan crosses continents and transcends all societal bounds. As the world has essentially become smaller, the global economy has bloomed, and so too has the world of international sport.

Drivers and Barriers to Globalization

Factors that work to advance or restrict the progression of economic globalization were identified by Khor (2001). There were several drivers identified as aiding in the development of globalization.

Compared to past generations, the state of the world has changed at lightning speed. The emergence of technology, the drive for economic prosperity, more competition, higher standards of living, and expanded forms of communication have all contributed significantly to the vast expansion of sport as a driver to globalization.

Given the opportunity, the increased accessibility of information has made it easier for providers and consumers to find the services and products that are available. This allows products to saturate new markets, which in turn drives up the demand for those products. This exchange of information is a result of increased connectivity through technology. It is now feasible to immediately communicate with individuals on the other side of the globe. This connectivity allows for the various phases of the development and production process to take place anywhere. These advances in communication and technology have allowed global consumers to emerge by identifying global market segments.

Additionally, as international trade barriers have been removed or reduced, the marketplace has reflected an increased number of goods and services available around the globe. The manufacturing and marketing of sports and sporting goods has taken on monumental proportions. This expanding of international marketplaces has created multiple synergies of companies. This is reflected in the merging of the sport apparel companies Adidas and Reebok. This merger attempts to maximize the defined international market places by extending the market brand via multiple products. The emergence of Under Armour into the international sporting goods arena is another example of the expanding market place. These companies focus on the capacity to think globally and critically about the international market and about long-term global profits. This involves establishing specific goals that require an understanding of cross-cultural communication and intercultural issues.

Finally, globalization is driven by the size of the investment required. As information and technology spread, the possibility of smaller production runs emerges but the relative unit of financial and human investment increases (McAuley, 2004).

Factors that act as barriers to globalization include consumer tastes, local market conditions, and culture. Consumer tastes make it difficult for standardized products to succeed. As consumer tastes vary, standardized approaches must adapt. There is a need to take into account the local market's needs for particular national or regional identities, the role of individualism in the target market, and the degree of nationalism inherent in local purchase behavior. Perhaps the most important barrier is culture. Culture-specific adaptation is sometimes necessary in order to maximize the economic potential for a company (McAuley, 2004).

Technology

One of the most powerful forces for transmitting thoughts, ideas, and products around the world is advanced technology. The revolution of information technology played a key role in the 20th century. The computer, television, and telephone and the advancement of the Internet have significantly changed the way in which information is gathered, distributed, and received. In our current society, large amounts of information can be processed in multiple formats to include text messages, video, television, voice, and Internet, with just the flick of a button. Another significant factor has been the decline in the cost of communicating. This has contributed to vast growth and benefit to the international community. It has allowed multiple modes of communication to be viewed and shared in a much more global context. This information explosion is being shared by the world. Inventions, innovations, and new concepts continue to refine these methods of communication, further extending the capabilities of the world communication systems. Satellite television, cable television, cell phones, and digital technology have affected this transformation of technology immensely.

Global Sports Marketing

Global sports marketing is a broad concept that encompasses many facets. According to the *Global Entertainment and Media Outlook: 2005–2009*, published by PricewaterhouseCoopers, sports marketing includes gate revenues for live sporting events, rights fees paid by broadcast and cable television stations to cover those events, merchandising, sponsorships (including naming rights and payments to have a product associated with a team or league), and other packages with rights to sports events or programming. The estimated economic impact of the global sports market is projected to reach $111.1 billion by 2009.

Two companies that have achieved worldwide success in the global sport market are Nike and Adidas. Founded by Phil Knight and Bill Bowerman in 1971, Nike has become the world's largest and most profitable footwear and athletic apparel company. Nike's annual revenues exceeded $13.7 billion in 2005 (Barbaro, 2006).

Although based in Beaverton, Oregon, Nike has taken a global approach in becoming one of the world's most recognizable brands. The company, along with its famous "swoosh" logo and "Just Do It" tagline, has been associated with many of the world's most famous athletes, including Michael Jordan, Lance Armstrong, Tiger Woods, and Lebron James. Nike has also engaged in sponsorship agreements with several of the world's premier soccer clubs, including the national teams of the United States and Brazil, and four of Europe's premier soccer teams: Manchester United (England), Arsenal (England), Juventus (Italy), and FC Barcelona (Spain). In 2006, Nike further extended its reach and became the official sponsor of the national cricket team of India (Digi-help).

Adidas has emerged as Nike's closest rival in the global sports market. A German sports apparel manufacturer, Adidas was started in 1949 by German shoemaker Adolf Dassler. Much like Nike, Adidas has come to be recognized by its logo: three parallel stripes. With over $9 billion in annual revenues, Adidas is the worldwide leader for the world's most popular sport, soccer (adidas-group, n.d.).

Adidas is the official sponsor of the World Cup, the premier soccer event in the world. Since 1970, it has been the official supplier of all match balls used in

World Cup play. The company paid $350 million to extend those sponsorship rights through 2014. Additionally, Adidas sponsors more than twenty different national teams, as well as professional soccer teams in North America, South America, Europe, and Asia. Internationally, it also sponsors teams in rugby, cricket, and Australian Rules football.

In the United States, Adidas is a major sponsor of several professional sports leagues and teams. Beginning with the 2006–2007 season, Adidas is the official supplier of all uniforms and sideline apparel for the National Basketball Association, the Women's National Basketball Association, and the National Basketball Development League. It is also the official supplier of uniforms and game balls for Major League Soccer. In 2005, Adidas announced a contract extension that would cement it as the official athletic apparel and footwear company of the New York Yankees through the 2013 season (Adidas, 2005). It is also the official sponsor of several major collegiate athletics programs, including UCLA, Nebraska, Indiana, Tennessee, Kansas, and Notre Dame.

After acquiring industry competitor Reebok in 2006, Adidas' market share reached 28%, just shy of the 30.9% controlled by Nike (Barbaro, 2006).

The Olympics

The modern Summer Olympic Games have been held on four continents, with Africa, South America, and Antarctica having never been selected as a host. The United States has hosted the Games eight times, more than any other country. The Summer Games have been held in St. Louis, Missouri (1904), Los Angeles, California (1932 and 1984), and Atlanta, Georgia (1996). The United States has hosted the Winter Olympic Games four times: in Lake Placid, New York (1932 and 1980), Squaw Valley, California (1960), and Salt Lake City, Utah (2002). The Olympic Games have incredible marketing implications over several industries. According to the International Olympic Committee's *2006 Marketing Fact File*, marketing revenues totaled over $4 billion during the four-year period leading up to and including the 2004 Summer Olympic Games in Athens, Greece. Of the total revenue amount, broadcast rights accounted for 53%, followed by corporate sponsorship (34%) and ticketing (11%). Licensing and other revenues accounted for 2% of total revenues.

The Olympic Partners, or TOP Sponsors, are the official sponsors for their given product or service category. TOP Sponsors receive exclusive marketing rights on a worldwide basis for their product category and may use any Olympic imagery in their marketing campaigns. TOP Sponsors for the 2006 Winter Olympics Games in Torino, Italy, included The Coca-Cola Company (non-alcoholic beverages), McDonalds (retail food services), Kodak (film/photographics and imaging), Johnson & Johnson (health care products), Atos Origin (information technology), General Electric (power and lighting), Lenovo Group (computing equipment), Manulife Financial (life insurance/annuities), Omega (timing, scoring, and venue results services), Panasonic (audio/TV/video equipment), Samsung (wireless communication equipment), and Visa International (consumer payment systems).

The Olympics experienced an incredible boost with the overwhelming success of the 1996 Olympic Games held in Atlanta, Georgia. Over 8.3 million tickets were sold to 271 events in 26 sports. The Atlanta Games, or Centennial Games, marked the 100th anniversary of the modern Olympic Games and featured 10,320 athletes from 197 countries (www.olympic.org). Sydney, Australia, was selected as the host city for the 2000 Summer Olympics and was accessible to 3.6 billion people through 400 hours of television coverage. Countries totaling 199, represented by 10,651 athletes, competed in Sydney (www.olympic.org). The 2004 Summer Olympics in Athens, Greece, boasted the highest number of athletes ever to compete in the Olympic Games. A total of 11,099 people competed in 28 sports in 301 events. These games also featured the highest number of countries, as each of the 201 National Olympic Committees was represented. Ticket sales in Athens were far below what had been projected, at a mere 3.8 million, but the television coverage expanded to 1200 hours of coverage available to 3.9 billion people worldwide.

Asia and Europe will host the next sessions of the Summer Olympics. Beijing, China, will host the Games in 2008, after easily beating out the other bidding cities. The 2012 Olympic Games were awarded to London after a very close vote with runner-up Paris, France, and third-place Madrid, Spain.

World Baseball Classic

The inaugural World Baseball Classic was held in the spring of 2006. The 18-day tournament featured 16 of the top baseball teams from around the world. Seven different venues hosted games in Arizona, Florida, California, Puerto Rico, and Japan. Despite early political problems surrounding Cuba's involvement in the tournament, the World Baseball Classic was widely considered a huge success. Spectators numbering 737,112 attended the Classic's 39 games, including 42,696 at the championship game between Japan and Cuba (Fatsis, 2006). This event was monumental in that it was the first time outside of the Olympics that teams had gathered from around the world to compete in a baseball tournament. The scope was global as well as international and was considered a major success in terms of touching the uniqueness of the global market.

National Basketball Association

At the forefront of the globalization in professional sports, the NBA has stretched its global appeal far beyond the borders of the United States. The league's 1995 expansion placed franchises in Toronto and Vancouver, the first NBA franchises outside of the United States' borders. The influx of international talent has also bolstered the appeal of the league to other parts of the world. As of 2006, 82 international players from 38 countries and territories were on NBA rosters (Boeck, 2006). International interest is especially strong in Europe and Asia, which have accounted for the majority of international players. One of the league's most marketable stars is Houston Rockets center Yao Ming. Ming, a native of China, was a star in the Chinese Basketball Association. The 7'6" center was the first pick in the 2002 NBA Draft. While Ming was the highest profile Chinese player to be drafted, he wasn't the first. In 1987, the Atlanta Hawks made China's Sung Tao the first Asian player drafted to the NBA. Wang Zhi Zhi became the first Chinese player to step on the court for an NBA team in 2001, when he played with the Dallas Mavericks. Mengke Bateer was next when he joined the Denver Nuggets in 2002 (Blinebury, 2004).

The NBA began broadcasting games in China in 1987. By the 2005–2006 season, 24 Chinese stations were broadcasting games to over 30 million viewers each week. In major markets such as Shanghai, Beijing, and Guangzhou, Chinese fans could see six different games a week (Blinebury). Two preseason exhibition games between the Houston Rockets and Sacramento Kings were held in Shanghai and Beijing in 2004 (Cody, 2006).

The interest in China extends far beyond Yao Ming. Among the best-selling NBA jerseys in China, Yao ranks third behind Tracy McGrady and Allen Iverson. Other NBA players have been sought out by Chinese sponsors. In January of 2006, Cleveland Cavaliers guard Damon Jones signed an endorsement contract with Li-Ning, the largest sports apparel company in China. Jones became the first NBA player to sign an endorsement deal with a Chinese company (Robbins, 2006).

NFL International

NFL International has several programs that have spread the exposure of American football on a global scale. One such program is NFL Canada, which handles the interests of the National Football League in Canada.

One of the most successful programs of NFL International is the American Bowl. Since 1986, the NFL has held preseason exhibition games in countries outside of the United States. The game is always the fifth preseason game for those teams selected to participate. The purpose of the American Bowl is to promote American football in other countries (NFL, 2002a). Since 1986, the American Bowl has been held in 12 cities in different countries around the world: London, Tokyo, Montreal, Berlin, Barcelona, Mexico City, Toronto, Monterrey, Dublin, Vancouver, Sydney, and Osaka.

Table 1. American Bowl Results

Date	Location	Result
August 3, 1986	London, England	Chicago 17, Dallas 6
August 9, 1987	London, England	L.A. Rams 28, Denver 27
July 31, 1988	London, England	Miami 27, San Francisco 21
August 5, 1989	Tokyo, Japan	L.A. Rams 16, San Francisco 13 (OT)
August 6, 1989	London, England	Philadelphia 17, Cleveland 13
August 5, 1990	Tokyo, Japan	Denver 10, Seattle 7
August 5, 1990	London, England	New Orleans 17, L.A. Raiders 10
August 9, 1990	Montreal, Canada	Pittsburgh 30, New England 14
August 11, 1990	Berlin, Germany	L.A. Rams 19, Kansas City 3
July 28, 1991	London, England	Buffalo 17, Philadelphia 13
August 3, 1991	Berlin, Germany	San Francisco 21, Chicago 7
August 4, 1991	Tokyo, Japan	Miami 19, L.A. Raiders 17

Table 1. **American Bowl Results** *(Continued)*

Date	Location	Result
August 2, 1992	Tokyo, Japan	Houston 34, Dallas 23
August 15, 1992	Berlin, Germany	Miami 31, Denver 27
August 16, 1992	London, England	San Francisco 17, Washington 15
August 1, 1993	Tokyo, Japan	New Orleans 28, Philadelphia 16
August 1, 1993	Barcelona, Spain	San Francisco 21, Pittsburgh 14
August 7, 1993	Berlin, Germany	Minnesota 20, Buffalo 6
August 8, 1993	London, England	Dallas 13, Detroit 13 (OT)
July 31, 1994	Barcelona, Spain	L.A. Raiders 25, Denver 22 (OT)
August 7, 1994	Tokyo, Japan	Minnesota 17, Kansas City 9
August 13, 1994	Berlin, Germany	N.Y. Giants 28, San Diego 20
August 15, 1994	Mexico City, Mexico	Houston 6, Dallas 0
August 5, 1995	Tokyo, Japan	Denver 24, San Francisco 10
August 12, 1995	Toronto, Canada	Buffalo 9, Dallas 7
July 27, 1996	Tokyo, Japan	San Diego 20, Pittsburgh 10
August 5, 1996	Monterrey, Mexico	Kansas City 32, Dallas 6
July 27, 1997	Dublin, Ireland	Pittsburgh 30, Chicago 17
August 4, 1997	Mexico City, Mexico	Miami 38, Denver 19
August 16, 1997	Toronto, Canada	Green Bay 35, Buffalo 3
August 1, 1998	Tokyo, Japan	Green Bay 27, Kansas City 24 (OT)
August 15, 1998	Vancouver, Canada	San Francisco 24, Seattle 21
August 17, 1998	Mexico City, Mexico	New England 21, Dallas 3
August 8, 1999	Sydney, Australia	Denver 20, San Diego 17
August 5, 2000	Tokyo, Japan	Atlanta 20, Dallas 9
August 19, 2000	Mexico City, Mexico	Indianapolis 24, Pittsburgh 23
August 27, 2001	Mexico City, Mexico	Dallas 21, Oakland 6
August 3, 2002	Osaka, Japan	Washington 38, San Francisco 7
August 2, 2003	Tokyo, Japan	Tampa Bay 30, New York Jets 14
August 6, 2005	Tokyo, Japan	Atlanta 27, Indianapolis 21

http://www.nfl.com/international

NFL International currently broadcasts to 235 countries around the world. Their broadcasts are carried through 62 broadcasters and are available in 31 languages (NFL, 2002b). That coverage was recently expanded to incorporate more of the European market, where the NFL Europe league is featured. NFL Europe is comprised of six teams in Western Europe and is a descendant of the World League of American Football, which was established in 1990.

CASE STUDY
NFL Europe (NFLE)

American football is one of the largest professional sports in the United States, as measured by attendance and television spectators. This professional product has now expanded into the global markets of Europe, Central America, Far East, and Mexico. The National Football League Europe (NFLE) has evolved into a potential global entity. Thus far, the results have been mixed. Although there have been several players who have benefited from the league (Kurt Warner), the league has struggled to gain major support from European corporations and media outlets. The multi-billion dollar sports revenue cycle is dependent upon the relationship between sponsors, fans, products, media, and event promoters. The European club American Football system has grown at an unprecedented rate. American Football is now being played in 15 European nations, with over 75,000 members spread over 650 teams. Boone and Kurtz (1995) identified brand equity as the extended value a brand entity gives to a marketplace. It is this new brand concept that makes the NFLE substantially different from the previous attempt of the World League of American Football (WLAF). This globalization of the sport of American football as a viable product became a purpose of the National Football League and its leadership.

The Original World League of American Football

The Beginning—1991 & 1992

When the USFL folded in 1986, it was the end of spring football, as it had become known, in the United States. It was also the end of the attempted rival league to the NFL. That changed in the spring of 1991 when the NFL took the matter into its own hands.

After years of intense planning and development, the spring of 1991 brought a new league to the world, the World League of American Football. The WLAF was the forerunner to the current league known as NFL Europe. The WLAF was an NFL-backed venture that was created with two main goals in mind. This league was to be a "developmental" league for the NFL as well as to help spread the sport of American football throughout the world. The top executives of the league were convinced they were going to make history, as well as break major ground in the globalization of American football.

After many final hectic months of planning, the league did not have the normal allotment of time needed to conduct extensive planning meetings, player workouts, and an inaugural draft of those players. It was decided to hold a major, unique 17-day football extravaganza in Orlando, Florida. It has been said that the over 1000 league personnel involved in this event will never forget this experience.

The birth of the WLAF is regarded to be February 8, 1991 as everyone affiliated with the World League converged on Orlando. Staffs of all three league offices (New York, Dallas, and London), all 10 franchises, and all of the sponsors were present. They all met face-to-face for the first time at this event scheduled to last until February 24. There was a vast list of tasks and topics to tackle, and one person was put in charge of making sure everything ran smoothly. Les Miller, a former Director of Scouting for the NFL's San Diego Chargers, was appointed the World League's special events coordinator for the Orlando meetings and the inaugural draft. He is quoted as saying, "It was truly a mind-boggling thing to put together."

League business executives and team front office staffs were busy sitting through a series of extensive planning meetings as they attempted to establish policies that would set the league's future business plan as well as shape the future of football around the world. Decisions that were made during this time period had a significant impact on the future of the league.

At the same time, the league's football operations staff members and the teams' coaching staffs were busy evaluating the huge pool of player talent that had responded to the league's call for applicants. The league's scouts initially reviewed the NFL draft classes of 1988, 1989, and 1990 for talent prospects. They looked at players who made it in the NFL for a year or possibly two, or those who made it all the way until final cuts before the season. They were truly surprised as how many players fell into that category. Of the 10,000 football players who are produced annually by the U.S. college system, it is estimated that 2000 of those are high-quality players who can play at a higher level. Of those, roughly only 330 are even drafted by the NFL's teams. And a large number of them do not last even through training camp.

The league's player personnel office reportedly received over 4,000 resumes from player hopefuls wanting a chance to prove their skills and to make an attempt to get back into the NFL. The WLAF again made history by inviting over 700 prospects to attend the testing combines in Orlando. This number is double that of the approximate 350 top prospects that attend the NFL's yearly scouting combine in Indianapolis. The numbers were justified by the league's plan to test over 65 players for each of its ten teams as well as for 60 players for Team Dallas, which was an 11th team that served as a practice squad pool for the league throughout its inaugural season of 1991. The league also made a big step in its international player efforts by adding an additional 40 players via its Operation Discovery program. This program was initiated to find the best amateur players in Europe. The league was dedicated to the globalization of American football.

The football extravaganza in Orlando was concluded by yet another WLAF milestone in football history. The league's inaugural player draft was conducted by player position and each of the 10 clubs were granted a first choice in one of the 10 sections drafted. The league's executives had found another way to tout the league as a groundbreaking organization. This was characterized as the kind of innovative approach that would become the future hallmark of the WLAF.

When the WLAF first kicked off in the spring of 1991, league officials placed three teams in Europe, one in Canada and six teams in the U.S. With the placement of teams outside of the continental United States, league officials felt it gave a true international flair, and hence the name World League. Southern cities in the United States had not had their own teams since the USFL failed. Those cities were Birmingham, Alabama, San Antonio, Texas, and Orlando, Florida. The league decided to try their luck in places like Raleigh-Durham, North Carolina, and Sacramento, California, as well as New York City.

Opening weekend in 1991 looked promising when one considers attendance numbers recorded for the initial four games played. On the European continent, 23,169 people attended the first game in WLAF history in Frankfurt, Germany. The Frankfurt Galaxy hosted the London Monarchs. In Barcelona, Spain, over 19,200 Barcelonans attended the first WLAF game on Spanish soil when the Dragons took on the NY/NJ Knights in Olympic Stadium de Montjuic. League officials were thrilled that close to 45,000 Europeans attended the first games in league history to watch a sport they understood nothing about. Back in the U.S., two other league opener games were played. Approximately 53,000 fans attended the first game of the Birmingham Fire, at Legion Field, versus the Montreal Machine, the league's only team located in Canada. An estimated crowd of over 15,000 people attended the Sacramento Surge's inaugural game versus the Raleigh-Durham Skyhawks at Hughes Stadium, a junior college field.

The league's 10 teams would go on to play a total of 53 games over 12 weeks, and the London Monarchs would eventually emerge as the first-ever World Bowl Champions, defeating the Barcelona Dragons 21-0 in front of a record crowd of 61,108 spectators at London's famed Wembley Stadium. A veteran London sports writer is quoted as calling the World Bowl I "as fine a celebration as ever seen at Wembley." World Bowl I was history, almost 25 years to the day after the NFL and AFL came to an agreement to merge, and in front of a crowd that fell only approximately 830 short of the attendance number of the first Super Bowl held in Los Angeles in 1967. The three European teams drew five of the WLAF's 10 largest crowds in 1991. The London Monarchs, who closed the season with a 9-1 record and as winners of the first World Bowl, had the largest following with an average home crowd of 40,500. WLAF and NFL executives were convinced that this league had a big future, especially in Europe. By late fall in 1991 signs of the European potential were confirmed when the Barcelona Dragons fan club had swelled to close to 33,000 members, the Frankfurt Galaxy had already sold over 9,000 season tickets for their second season, and the London Monarch announced upwards of $300,000 worth of merchandise sales during the World Bowl and the months after it. In December of 1991, the WLAF had been promised a minimum three-year extension and numerous changes were in the works. A new team based in Columbus, Ohio, would replace an unsuccessful team in Raleigh-Durham. The Operation Discovery plan, which placed foreign-born athletes on each team, had been scrapped for all of the league's North American teams, but would be continued with its three European clubs.

In 1991, the three Europe-based teams had a combined 24-6 record while posting a combined 11-1 record against North American teams at their home venues. No North American team managed to be better than 5-5 during the 1991 season and the Raleigh-Durham Skyhawks lost all 10 of their games. Prior to the 1992 season draft, it was rumored that the league would insure that the American teams would not be inferior again. All three European teams had losing records in 1992, while five of the seven North American teams had successful, winning seasons.

Some critics of the league believed that Barcelona, London, and Frankfurt were the only reason that the NFL allowed the WLAF to go forward with its 1992 season.

The original WLAF had an extraordinary fan following in Europe as well as in cities like Birmingham, but due to a major lack of fan support in the other North American cities, interest in the league quickly died, which led to the eventual demise of the World League after just two seasons. True football fans saw the league as less than minor league due to a lack of stars. Others saw it as a big joke. The staff working in this league as well as the players all put in their best efforts. Many of the players assigned to the teams were playing their hearts out in an attempt to get another true shot at the NFL.

The original WLAF was not without support. The World League had a favorable television deal with USA Network. The TV arrangement called for USA Network to broadcast one game a week, usually on Monday or Thursday night. ABC also supported the league and broadcast one game each Sunday to its U.S. audience. Despite the TV arrangements and favorable interest, as well as loyal and supportive fans in many cities, the league was failing.

At the end of its second season, during the summer of 1992, the NFL and the WLAF league officials decided it was time to rethink their strategy and put the league to rest. The growing labor unrest within the NFL and a court ruling that the NFL's free agency system violated antitrust laws were said to be big factors in the league's decision to suspend WLAF operations. The league was rumored to have lost close to $20 million in its initial two seasons.

Initially plans were to close down for one season (1993). All intentions were to return strong for a new season in the spring of 1994. During the break in the action, the NFL maintained offices and staff in its three European locations, which had been league owned and operated from the time of its inception. League personnel in Frankfurt, Germany, in London England, and in Barcelona, Spain continued to work on the league's youth and amateur football efforts, as well as support of the NFL's American Bowl series of international pre-season games.

The 10 Original WLAF Teams (1991–1992)

Barcelona Dragons   ▼   *Barcelona, Spain*

Played in the European Division. Home stadium was the Montjuic Olympic Stadium with a seating capacity of 55,000. Team owner was Joseph M. Figueras, and the general manager was Andrew Brandt. The only coach in the history of the Barcelona

Dragons was Jack Bicknell. In 1991 the Dragons finished the season as an 8-2 Wildcard qualifier for the playoffs and reached the inaugural World Bowl in London's Wembley Stadium. They lost the World Bowl to the London Monarchs. The Dragons finished the 1992 season with a 5-5 record winning the European Division. Overall record after the two seasons was 13-7.

Birmingham Fire ▼ *Birmingham, Alabama*

Played in the North American West Division. Home stadium was Legion Field with a seating capacity of 55,000. The owner was Gavin Maloof, and the general manager was Michael Huyghue. The only coach in the history of the Birmingham Fire was Chan Gailey. In 1991 the Fire won the North American West Division with a 5-5 record. The Fire finished the 1992 season with a 7-2-1 record and was a Wildcard qualifier for the playoffs. Overall record after the two seasons was 12-7-1. Birmingham was one of the more successful teams in North America. It was able to win both on the field and in the box office. The Fire's tie of London in Week 4 of the 1992 season is one of only two tie games in the history of the World League.

Frankfurt Galaxy ▼ *Frankfurt, Germany*

Played in the European Division. Home stadium was the Waldstadion with a seating capacity of 53,000. Team owner was the WLAF, and the team's first general manager was Oliver Luck. The first coach in the history of the Frankfurt Galaxy was Jack Elway, the father of former Denver Broncos Quarterback John Elway.

   In 1991 the Galaxy finished the year with a 7-3 record in the highly competitive European Division. Despite having the third best record in the league, the team did not qualify for the playoffs. Frankfurt has the distinction of scoring the first points in World League history when the Galaxy's nose tackle tackled a London running back in the end-zone for a safety. Although the team scored the first points, it was not able to win its first game, falling to the Monarchs 24-11. The Galaxy finished the 1992 season with a 3-7 record. Overall record after the two seasons was 10-10. The Frankfurt Galaxy is the only team of the original 10 WLAF teams that still exists, now playing in the NFL Europe League.

London Monarchs ▼ *London, England*

Played in the European Division. Home stadium was the famous Wembley Stadium with a seating capacity of 63,500. Team owner was the WLAF, and the team's first general manager was Billy Hicks. The first coach in the history of the London Monarchs was Larry Keenan. In 1991 the Monarchs finished the year with a 9-1 record, won the European Division, and ultimately won the first World Bowl. The Monarchs were led by QB Stan Gelbaugh and dominated WLAF competition on their way to the World Bowl Trophy. Gelbaugh returned to the Monarchs in 1992, but he was unable to find the success he had found in 1991. After an almost perfect season in 1991, London fell to the bottom of the European Division in the 1992 season with a 2-7-1 record in its second season. Overall record after the two seasons was 11-8-1.

Montreal Machine ▼ *Montreal, Canada*

Played in the North American East Division. Home stadium was the Montreal Olympic Stadium with a seating capacity of 61,000. Team owner was Roger Dore, and general manager was Gordon Cahill. The only coach in the history of the Montreal Machine was Jacques Dussault. In 1991 the Machine finished the season with a 4-6 record. The Machine finished the 1992 season with a 2-8 record. Overall record after the two seasons was 6-14. The WLAF decided to bring pro football back to Montreal after the CFL team there folded because of financial troubles. Although the team was not very successful on the field, it was very successful in the ticket sales category.

New York/NJ Knights ▼ *New York, New York*

Played in the North American East Division. Home stadium was Giants Stadium in East Rutherford, New Jersey, with a seating capacity of 75,000. Team owner was Robert F.X. Sillerman, and the general manager was Reggie Williams, a former NFL player now a sports executive with Disney Companies. The only coach in the history of the NY/NJ Knights was Darrel "Mouse" Davis. The Knights provided excitement to the league when Mouse Davis brought his run-and-shoot offense to the league. In 1991 the Knights finished the season with a 5-5 record and won the North American East Division. The Knights finished the 1992 season with a 6-4 record. Overall record after the two seasons was 11-9. The WLAF awarded New York with a franchise to insure that there was at least one large television market in the United States.

Ohio Glory ▼ *Columbus, Ohio*

(1992 Season only)

Played in the North American East Division. Home stadium was Ohio Stadium with a seating capacity of 91,000 plus. Team owner was the WLAF, and the general manager was Peter Hadazy. The only coach in the one-year history of the Glory was Larry Little. In 1992 the Glory finished the season with the league's worst record of 1-9. Ohio was awarded the franchise after the Raleigh-Durham team folded during the 91-92 off-season. The Glory did improve on the Skyhawks 1991 league worst record of 0-10 by one game.

Orlando Thunder ▼ *Orlando, Florida*

Played in the North American East Division. Home stadium was the Florida Citrus Bowl with a seating capacity of 70,000. Team owner was Raj Bhathal, and the team's first general manager was Lee Corso. The Thunder was coached in 1991 by Don Matthews, who was replaced by Galen Hall for the 1992 season. Hall would go on to coach the Düsseldorf Rhein Fire upon the WLAF's return in 1995. In 1991 the Thunder finished the season with a 5-5 record. The Knights finished the 1992 season with an 8-2 record, won the North American East Division, and advanced through the playoffs to World Bowl II. The Thunder lost to the Sacramento Surge in World Bowl II. Their overall record after the two seasons was 13-7. The Thunder team members are usually remembered for their neon green jerseys, worn during the two seasons of their existence.

Raleigh/Durham Skyhawks ▼ *Raleigh, North Carolina*

(1991 Season only)

Played in the North American East Division. Home stadium was Carter-Finley Stadium with a seating capacity of 45,000. Team owner was George Shinn, and the general manager was Wayne Thompson. The only coach in the one-year history of the Skyhawks was Roman Gabriel. In 1991 the Skyhawks finished the season with the league's worst record of 0-10. The Skyhawks were the laughingstock of the WLAF during the 1991 season, and the team disbanded after their first season. Thankfully pro football in the Carolinas was not harmed, and the Carolina Panthers of the NFL are now very successful in the region.

Sacramento Surge ▼ *Sacramento, CA*

Played in the North American West Division. Home stadium was Hughes Stadium with a seating capacity of 23,000. The owner was Fred Anderson and the general manager was Mike Keller. The only coach in the history of the Sacramento Surge was Kay Stephenson. The Surge finished the 1991 season with a 3-7 record and was not a strong contender. That changed for the 1992 season as the Surge posted an 8-2 record en route to a win in World Bowl II. Their road to the championship game included a dramatic last-second field goal to beat Barcelona in the first-round play-offs. The success of Sacramento led to the Canadian Football League's awarding the city with a team after the WLAF folded. They, like most other CFL teams in the U.S., failed due to a lack of support. Overall record after the two seasons was 11-9.

San Antonio Riders   ▼   *San Antonio, Texas*

Played in the North American West Division. Home stadium was Alamo Stadium with a seating capacity of 25,000. Owner was Larry Benson and the general managers were Tom Landry, Sr., and Tom Landry, Jr. The only coach in the history of the Riders was Mike Riley. The Riders finished the 1991 season with a 4-6. The 1992 season ended with a 7-3 record, and like Frankfurt of 1991, they did not make the playoffs despite a 7-3 record. QB Jason Garrett who later went on to play for the Dallas Cowboys led the Riders during their 1992 campaign. Overall record after the two seasons was 11-9.

The Rebirth/Return of WLAF

Late in the fall of 1994, the remaining personnel on staff in Europe received the information that the league would indeed return after a two-season hiatus in the spring of 1995. The World League was re-born, and with an interesting twist. League officials had determined that the market interest was supportive of an all-European effort and the league was in discussion with numerous potential joint venture partners that would support their all-European format. The WLAF returned in 1995, adopting the simple name of World League and without any North American teams. All six teams were fully owned and operated by the league and its partners on the European continent. The World League was to consist of the three existing teams from its original format as well as three new teams located in Düsseldorf, Germany; Amsterdam, the Netherlands; and Edinburgh, which would compete as a Scottish branded team.

Upon the return of the World League, the level of support from the NFL was even more extensive than in the early 1990s. One of the original thoughts of the league during the 1991 and 1992 seasons was that the NFL teams would automatically find players who could gather playing experience within the ranks of the WLAF. They could work on their playing skills by actually getting on-field playing time. WLAF league officials were expecting NFL teams to send players to do just that; however, the NFL teams initially were not very supportive of this effort. At the end of the 1991 NFL season, only 19 WLAF alumni finished the season on NFL rosters. With the re-birth of the league there were guidelines set in place for a required support of the league.

Upon the league's return, extensive effort was put into the NFL player allocation plan, which provided NFL teams with various benefits. All NFL teams were required to allocate a set number of players to the World League and later the NFL Europe League. Initially the NFL mandated that each WLAF team allocate six players per team. This was eventually changed to require only three players per team, and most teams continue to send a higher number of players due to the roster spot advantages offered to them by the league. On an average, NFL teams allocated well over 200 players per season to NFL Europe. NFL teams were granted roster spot exemptions throughout the team's fall training camps for their support of the European league.

Teams allocating players to the European League were granted one additional roster spot per player allocated. This allowed teams to carry extra bodies all the way through training camp, not requiring them to meet final roster numbers until the final cuts. Teams sending six players to Europe were permitted to have six additional players on their rosters through the final cuts stage.

In time, the initial success of the league subsided. From 1995 to 2003, franchises in Germany remained viable, but the other franchises began to struggle. Part of the struggle had to do with the structural constraints. The league was an expensive proposition and presented little chance of breaking even in the future. The league was also constrained by the small number of teams and the short length of the season. The six teams were too spread out, which prevented the league from reaching the following it desired. The distance also made it difficult for television broadcasts to penetrate markets on a nationwide basis. Perhaps because of that lack of exposure, the media never gave the league the credibility that a major professional sports league commands.

In its latest phase of reorganization, NFL Europe decided to focus on markets that had proven successful in the past. The England Monarchs folded in 1998, the Barcelona Dragons shut down in 2002, and the Scottish Claymores played their last season in 2004. These teams were replaced by franchises in Berlin, Cologne, and Hamburg. With those changes, five of the six teams in NFL Europe were located in Germany, with the sixth team in Amsterdam. The league decided to utilize the existing fan bases in Germany as a means of fostering a national interest. With five teams in one country, constant competition presented the opportunity for rivalries to flourish. After refocusing on Germany, NFL Europe set a record for attendance in 2005. The league averaged 18,965 fans per game, a 19% increase in attendance over 2004. The Hamburg Sea Devils, Berlin Thunder, and Cologne Centurions all set single-game attendance records in the last two weeks of the 2005 season. (http://www.nfl europe.com/news/story/8541737).

The NFL Europe targeted a younger demographic than other professional sports leagues. The average age of a fan at an NFL Europe game was 27 years of age, and 50% of fans who attended games were between the ages of 12 and 29. Spectators who attended the game were 70% male and 30% female. The average income of NFL Europe fans is higher than the incomes of other comparable sports fans. These fans had more disposable income, and they were very sociable in nature. NFL Europe fans were also willing to come a long way for the experience, as spectators traveled an average distance of ninety kilometers to attend a game. Approximately 550,000 people attend NFL Europe games each season (Smith, 2005).

The league has increased its exposure by maximizing its availability through numerous media outlets. The majority of NFL Europe coverage comes

Table 2. NFL Europe attendance, 2005	
Amsterdam Admirals	12,877
Berlin Thunder	6,848*
Cologne Centurion	14,231*
Frankfurt Galax	29,377
Hamburg Sea Devils	17,920*
Rhein Fir	22,532
NFL Europe League	18,965

NFLEurope.com
* Denotes franchise record

through the local or regional markets. Newspapers publish an estimated 80,000 articles about the league on a yearly basis. Radio is used for team and league-wide promotion, and each team has a strong partnership with at least one radio station. Television coverage is available in over 80 countries, and all 30 regular season games are broadcast on NFL Network. In January of 2006, NFL Europe and ARD, the number one television network in Germany, entered into an agreement to broadcast NFL and NFL Europe games. The broadcast agreement included coverage of all five NFL Europe teams in Germany (NFL Europe, 2006a).

NFL Europe aims to create a top-level sports product, while offering high-class entertainment. The league has several sponsors, including Gatorade, Ridell, Reebok, Wilson, Skoda Auto, and Yello Strom, the league's official sponsor (NFL Europe 2006b). Game day experiences focus on fan relations and may consist of pre-game parties with partners and sponsors, the actual game, and then a post-game party.

The Teams after the 1995 Return

London/England Monarchs

Team Location: London, England

Date Founded: December 6, 1990

Date Disbanded: June 25, 1998

Championships: World Bowl I Champions—1991

Home Stadiums: Stadium on White Hart Lane (25,000) 1995–1996
　　　　　　　Stadium at Stamford Bridge (30,000) 1997
　　　　　　　London Crystal Palace Athletics Arena (23,000) 1998—3 Games
　　　　　　　Birstol Ashton Gate Stadium (20,000) 1998—1 Game
　　　　　　　Birmingham's Alexander Stadium (15,000) 1998—1 Game

General Managers: Gareth Moores 1995–1996, Alton Byrd 1997–1998

Head Coaches: Bobby Hammond 1995–1996, Lionel Taylor 1996–1998

Famous Past Player: Former Chicago Bear—William "The Refrigerator" Perry—1996 Season

Barcelona Dragons

Team Locations: Barcelona, Spain

Date Founded: December 5, 1990

Date Disbanded: October 28, 2003

Championships: World Bowl V Champions—1997

Home Stadiums: Olympic Stadium de Montjuic (54,000) 1991–2001
　　　　　　　Mini Estadi—F.C. Barcelona (17,000) 2002–2003

General Managers: Andrew Brandt 1991–1992, Jordi Vila-Puig 1995–1997, Marco Fuste 1998–2000, Rafael Cervera 2001–2003

Head Coaches: Jack Bicknell 1991–1992 & 1995–2003 (only head coach in franchise history)

Scottish Claymores

Team Location: Edinburgh, Scotland

Date Founded: August 1, 1994

Date Disbanded: October 21, 2004

Championships: World Bowl IV Champions—1996

Home Stadiums: Murrayfield Stadion-Edinburgh (67,000)
            Hampden Stadium-Glasgow 2001

General Managers: Sandy Waters 1994–1995, Mike Keller 1995–1997,
            Richard M. Regan Jr. 1997–1998, Will Wilson 1998–2001,
            Steve Livingstone 2001–2004

Head Coaches: Larry Kuharich 1994–1995, Jim Criner 1995–2000, Gene Dahlquist
    2001–2003, Jack Bicknell 2004

Famous Past Player: Gavin Hastings—Former Great Scottish Rugby Star—Kicker 1996
    Season

NFLE Today

Amsterdam Admirals

Team Location: Amsterdam, Netherlands

Date Founded: July 27, 1994

Championships: World Bowl XIII Champions—2005

Home Stadiums: Olympisch Stadion (38,000) 1995–1996
            Amsterdam ArenA (51,328) 1997–Present

General Managers: Darrell Roland 1994–1995, Bill Peterson 1995–1999
            Ronald Buys 1999–2005, Stefaan Eskes 2005–Present

Head Coaches: Al Luginbill 1995–2000, Bart Andrus 2001–Present

Famous Past Players: Kurt Warner, QB Super Bowl MVP, Jake Delhomme QB Carolina
    Panthers, Adam Vinatieri, Kicker N.E. Patriots Super Bowl winner, first former
    World League Player to score points in a Super Bowl (January 26, 1997)

Interesting Fact: The team was named after and in celebration of Amsterdam's sea-
    farers who were very prosperous during the golden age years of 1580–1720.
    Ships were led by admirals who set sail from Amsterdam to conduct trading all
    over the world.

Berlin Thunder

Team Location: Berlin, Germany

Date Founded: June 13, 1998

Championships: World Bowl Champions—2001, 2002, 2004

Home Stadiums: Jahn-Stadion (25,000) 1999–2002
            Olympiastadion (74,400) 2003

General Managers: Michael Lang 1998–2004, Joe Cealera 2005–Present

Head Coaches: Wes Chandler 1998–2000, Peter Vaas 2000–2003, Rick Lantz
    2004–Present

Cologne Centurions

Team Location: Cologne, Germany

Date Founded: December 19, 2003

Championships: None

Home Stadium: Rhein-Energie-Stadium (50.997) 2004–Present

General Managers: Jacques Orthen 2004–2005, Hauke Wilkens 2005–Present

Head Coaches: Peter Vaas 2004–2005, David Duggan 2006–Present

Frankfurt Galaxy

Team Location: Frankfurt, Germany

Date Founded: December 18, 1990

Championships: World Bowl Champions—1995, 1999, 2003 and 2006

Home Stadiums: Waldstadion (57,000) 1991–2005
Commerzbank Arena (48,500) 2005–Present

General Managers: Oliver Luck 1991–1992, Christoph Heyne 1994–1998, Tilman Engel 1998–Present

Head Coaches: Jack Elway 1991–1992, Ernie Stautner 1995–1997, Dick Curl 1998–2000, Doug Graber 2001–2003, Mike Jones 2004–Present

Hamburg Sea Devils

Team Location: Hamburg, Germany

Date Founded: November 24, 2004

Championships: None

Home Stadiums: AOL Arena (55,000) 2005–Present

General Manager: Kathrin Platz 2004–Present

Head Coach: Jack Bicknell 2005–Present

Rhein Fire

Team Location: Düsseldorf, Germany

Date Founded: August 1, 1994

Championships: World Bowl Champions—1998, 2000

Home Stadiums: Rheinstadion (57,000) 1995–2002
Arena AufSchalke (60,601) 2003–2004
LTU Arena (51,500) 2005–Present

General Managers: Olivier Luck 1995, Alexander Leibkind 1996–2004, Sammy Schmale 2005–Present

Head Coaches: Galen Hall 1995–2000, Pete Kuharchek 2001–2005, Jim Tomsula 2005–Present

Table 3. History of NFL Europe teams

Franchise	Years of Operation
Birmingham Fire*	(1991–1992)
Sacramento Surge*	(1991–1992)
San Antonio Riders*	(1991–1992)
Montreal Machine*	(1991–1992)
New York/New Jersey Knights*	(1991–1992)
Orlando Thunder*	(1991–1992)
Raleigh-Durham Skyhawks*	(1991)
Ohio Glory*	(1992)
London Monarchs*	(1991–1997)
Barcelona Dragons*	(1991–2003)
Frankfurt Galaxy*	(1991–Present)
Scottish Claymores	(1995–2004)
Amsterdam Admirals	(1995–Present)
Rhein Fire	(1995–Present)
England Monarchs	(1998)
Berlin Thunder	(1999–Present)
Cologne Centurions	(2004–Present)
Hamburg Sea Devils	(2005–Present)

* Denotes World League of American Football franchise

Timeline: Former World League/NFLE Players on NFL

July 1992—At the opening of NFL Training Camps, 219 of the former 360 World League players had been signed to NFL contracts.

September 1994—On NFL Opening Day team rosters included 43 players who had World League experience.

September 1995—NFL Opening Day rosters include 72 players with World League experience.

September 1996—NFL Opening Day rosters include 116 former World League players, a new record number.

September 1999—NFL Opening Day rosters include 180 players with NFL Europe experience.

January 2000—Former Amsterdam Admirals QB Kurt Warner, now with the NFL's St Louis Rams, is named NFL Season MVP. He is one of 11 former NFLEL quarterbacks who have started games at the NFL level.

December 2000—NFL season concludes with yet again another record number of 187 former NFLEL players on NFL team rosters. In addition, four former NFLEL players are selected to participate in the Pro Bowl.

December 2001—NFL season concludes with a record number of 217 former NFLEL players on team rosters. Ten former NFLEL quarterbacks started in games during the 2001 NFL season.

Febuary 3, 2002—Former Amsterdam Admirals Kicker Adam Vinatieri kicks a 48-yard field goal as the time expires in Super Bowl XXXVI to give his New England Patriots a 20-17 victory over the St. Louis Rams. Former Admirals quarterback Kurt Warner has won his second MVP award. Warner is one of four former NFLEL players again selected for the Pro Bowl.

December 2002—NFL season concludes with another record number—257 former NFLEL players on team rosters; again the Pro Bowl selections number has gone up—to eight former NFLEL players participating.

January 26, 2003—Super Bowl XXXVII takes place with 18 former NFLEL players on the two competing teams' rosters. Game winning quarterback Brad Johnson of the Tampa Bay Buccaneers is a former London Monarch.

December 2003—NFL season concludes with 232 former NFLEL players appearing on team rosters.

February 1, 2004—Again, Adam Vinatieri kicks a field goal as time expires to give the Patriots a last-second victory over the Carolina Panthers in Super Bowl XXXVIII. In addition, in this game former Amsterdam and Frankfurt QB Jake Delhomme starts as QB for the Panthers and becomes the fourth former NFLEL quarterback to start in five years in the Super Bowl.

December 2004—NFL season concludes with a new record of 266 former NFLEL players on NFL team rosters. This number includes eight starting quarterbacks and five Pro Bowl selected players.

December 2005—NFL season concludes with 236 former NFLEL players on team rosters, including three Pro Bowl selected players.

Febuary 5, 2006—Super Bowl XL kicks off with 10 former NFLEL players on the rosters of the Pittsburgh Steelers and the Seattle Seahawks.

Timeline: NFL Player Allocation to Europe

February 1995—NFL teams allocate a total of 37 players to World League teams. The New Orleans Saints sends a league high of seven players to Europe.

February 1996—NFL teams allocate a total of 72 players to World League teams.

February 1997—A record 28 NFL teams allocate a new record number of 112 players to World League Teams.

January 1998—World League is renamed NFL Europe League to strengthen the relationship between the NFL and the game in Europe.

February 1999—29 NFL teams allocate yet another record number of 152 players to NFL Europe.

February 2000—After a three-phase allocation process, a total of 153 NFL players are allocated to NFL Europe.

November 2000—The NFL team allocation program has been reorganized and all 32 NFL teams have agreed to allocate at least six players each to NFL Europe.

March 2001—NFLE training camp opens with again a record number of 229 players allocated by NFL teams to participate in the NFL Europe experience.

February 2002—Again a record number of 257 players from NFL teams are allocated to NFL Europe.

▲▼ Suggested Readings ▲▼

Ragus, M. W., & Brueno, B. J. (2002). *The power of cult branding*. Prima Venture Publishing.

Parks, J. B., & Quarterman, J. (2003). *Contemporary sport management*. Champaign, IL: Human Kinetics.

Rosner, S., & Shropshire, K. L. (2004). *The business of sports*. Sudbury, MA: Jones & Bartlett Publishers.

Mullin, B. J., Hardy, S., & Sutton, W. A. (2007). *Sport marketing* (3rd ed.). Champaign, IL: Human Kinetics.

▲▼ Study Questions ▲▼

1. Why might global marketing strategies be more conducive for some companies and not for others?

2. Discuss the role of cultural orientation in terms of global marketing.

3. Identify and discuss components of global sports marketing as evidenced by NFL Europe.

References

Adidas Group. Consolidated Balance Sheet. Retrieved February 3, 2006 from www.adidas-group.com/en/investor/key_financial_data_balance_sheet/default.asp

Adidas Press Release. (2005, April 1). Adidas announces partnership extension with New York Yankees.

Barbaro, M. (2006, January 30). Sports sneaker wars are going international. *The New York Times*. (retrieved April 29, 2007 from http://www.iht.com/articles/2006/01/30/news/sneakers.php.1

Blinebury, F. (2004, October 10). China's budding dynasty. *Houston Chronicle*, p. 21.

Boeck, G. (2006, April 20). Team-first, back-to-basics foreigners changing NBA. *USA Today*, p. 1a.

Boone, L., & Kurtz, D. (1995). *Contemporary marketing* (8th ed.). Fort Worth: The Dryden Press.

Campbell Jr., R., & Kent, A. (2002). Brand extension evaluation: The case of NFL Europe. *Sport Marketing Quarterly, 11*(2), 117–120.

Chandra, N. (November 19, 2002). Coming together: Globalization means reconnecting the human community. *Yale Global Magazine*. Retrieved April 29, 2007 from http://yaleglobal.yale.edu/about/essay.jsp.

Cody, E. (2006, February 15). The NBA has become a leading export to China. *Washington Post*, p. E1.

Digi-help. Nike beats Adidas, Reebok to win Indian cricket team endorsement rights. Retrieved Febuary 6, 2006 from http://www.digi-help.com/pub/nike-indian-cricket-sponsorship.asp

Eitzen, D. S., (2003). *Fair and foul: Beyond the paradoxes of sport*. Lanham, MD: Rowman and Littlefield Publishers, Inc.

Fatsis, S. (2006, March 22). After a few foul balls, World Tournament ends up being a hit. *Wall Street Journal—Eastern Edition*, p. B1–B3.

International Olympic Committee. Athens 2004. Retrieved March 12, 2006 from http://www.olympic.org/uk/games/past/index_uk.asp?OLGT=1&OLGY=2004

International Olympic Committee (2006). *2006 Marketing Fact File*.

Khor, M. (2001). *Rethinking globalization*. London: Zed Books

Levitt, T. (1983). The globalization of markets. *Harvard Business Review*, May–June, pp. 92–102.

McAuley, A. (2004). Seeking (marketing) virtue in globalisation. *The Marketing Review, 4*, 253–266

National Football League: NFL International. (May 8, 2002a). NFL International historical results. Retrieved March 6, 2006 from http://www.nfl.com/international/story/6699961

National Football League: NFL International. (May 8, 2002b) International Programming. Retrieved March 6, 2006 from http://www.nfl.com/international/intl-program

NFL Europe. (January 12, 2006) NFLEL sets attendance record. Retrieved March 6, 2006 from http://www.nfleurope.com/news/story/8541737

NFL Europe League. (2005) PowerPoint Presentation. Steve Smith, Annual NFLE League Meetings, New York, NY.

NFL Europe (January 12, 2006a). Super Bowl on ARD. Retrieved March 6, 2006 from http://www.nfleurope.com/news/story/9160859

NFL Europe (January 12, 2006b). Sponsors. Retrieved March 9, 2006) from http://www.nfleurope.com/sponsors

PricewaterhouseCoopers. (2005). *Global Entertainment and Media Outlook: 2005–2009*.

Robbins, L. (2006, January 15). Shoes make the man a lot of money. *New York Times*, Section 8, p. 2-2

Yip, George S. (1997). Patterns and determinants of global marketing. *Journal of Marketing Management, 13*, 153-164.

K etra Armstrong's chapter explores the predominant sports consumption patterns and tendencies of African Americans. Her chapter offers insight into this topic by using a blend of historical and contemporary issues and factors. She presents the term *the economy of Blackness*, to describe the manner in which the economic attractiveness of African American consumers and the subculture of hip-hop influence sport marketing practices. She employs a sociocultural foundation for contextualizing African Americans' consumption of sport and concludes that, indeed, Race Matters!

CHAPTER
17

AFRICAN

AMERICANS'

CONSUMPTION

OF SPORT:

RACE

MATTERS!

KETRA L.
ARMSTRONG

▼ ▲▼ ▲▼ ▲▼ ▲▼ ▲▼ ▲

Key Terms

▼ Sport consumption ▲

▼ Sport fanship ▲

▼ Race ▲

▼ Ethnicity ▲

▼ African American
or black ▲

▼ HBCU: Historically
black colleges
and universities ▲

▼ PWU:
Predominately
white universities ▲

▼ Racial similarity ▲

▼ Racial
consciousness ▲

▼ Racial
endorsement ▲

Abstract ▼ The focus of this chapter is the impact of race on African Americans' consumption of sport. This chapter begins with an overview of African Americans' sport consumption preferences, patterns, and tendencies. The chapter offers an introduction to the economical and sociological perspectives of sport consumption, and reviews African Americans' sport consumption patterns and tendencies based on these paradigms. The chapter will then take you through a historical journey of the African American sport fan experience from being one of discrimination to one of affirmation. Next, you will learn about the economic attractiveness of African American consumers and the use of hip-hop as a means by which sport organizations have sought to facilitate business with African American consumers (and the markets/consumers they influence). The chapter will conclude with a summary of three core themes that illustrate the significance of race (and race-related constructs such as ethnicity) to African Americans' consumption of sport.

Introduction

Individuals have myriad ways of consuming sport—among them are: (a) sport media consumption, such as watching sports or sport-related shows on television, reading about sports in newspapers, magazines, and other periodicals, and listening to sport on the radio and other media technology devices; (b) visiting sport sites on the worldwide web and Internet; (c) purchasing sport merchandise, apparel, and equipment; (d) actively participating in different sport activities; and (e) attending live sport events as spectators. Based on the myriad ways in which sport may be mass consumed, sport consumption is an activity engaged in by people throughout America and throughout the world (Wilcox, 1994). Understanding the benefits consumers seek from sport consumption and identifying individuals' motives and enjoyment for consuming sport are paramount to the development of successful sport management and sport marketing practices. However, not only is the process of identifying the myriad of sport consumption motives and benefits a challenge in and of itself, but complicating this challenge is the cultural diversity among sport consumers.

America is a multicultural nation undergoing a dramatic increase in the racial and ethnic diversity of its inhabitants (Humphrey, 2005). Subsequently, multiculturalism is redefining what it means to be an American. Schreiber and Lenson (2001) reported that ethnic American consumers of color were increasing in population seven times as fast as the non-ethnic majority. Additionally, the economic clout of consumers of color is noteworthy. For example, Humphrey (2005) estimated that the combined buying power of African Americans, Asians, and Native Americans will be $1.7 trillion (representing a gain of 268%) in 2010.

As Schreiber and Lenson (2001) asserted, the sociodemographic shifts in America represent a critical moment for American business in that it has required businesses to increase their understanding of the impact of race on business success. The impact on race is also evident in the business of sport, as well as in sport consumption patterns and tendencies in consumers of color. Sport consumption is a multicultural phenomenon in that people from various cultures and traditions (African, Asian, Hispanic, and Native American descent) have recognized and utilized sport consumption for its many (physical, social, cultural, psychological, economical, and/or political) benefits (Wilcox, 1994). As such, sport businesses are not exempt from understanding the racial dynamics that underlie the nuances of sport consumption. Herein lies the impetus for this chapter, which focuses on the racial dynamics of African Americans' consumption of sport.

Overview of African Americans' Consumption of Sport

Sport Preferences

A review of the dearth of literature available on African Americans' consumption of sport reveals interesting trends and patterns. First and foremost, African Americans have long been reported to have a fondness and special affinity for the sport of basketball (Coakley, 2007; ESPN-Chilton Sports Poll, 1999; Kaplan & Lamm, 2000; Lapchick, 2005; Simmons, 1994; Sachs & Abraham, 1979). African Americans have typically participated in and attended basketball games in general and NBA games in particular at a rate that exceeds their representation in the population (Simmons, 1994; Lapchick, 2005) and they have considered themselves more avid fans of men's and women's basketball than have Caucasians (Kaplan & Lamm, 2000).

Basketball does not appear to be the only sport of preference for African Americans, as Kaplan and Lamm (2000) also reported that African Americans considered themselves more avid fans of football (a finding also reported by the 1999 ESPN-Chilton Sports Poll), boxing, and tennis than did Caucasians. Coakley (2007) also commented on African Americans' propensity to participate in college and professional football and basketball, Major League Baseball, track and field, and boxing. Kaplan and Lamm (2000) reported that African Americans were 134% more likely than Caucasians to identify themselves as tennis fans. Sports that were not preferred among African Americans and yet were preferred among Caucasians (as avid fans) were figure skating, ice hockey, and auto racing (Kaplan & Lamm, 2000). Thus, research has revealed that African Americans appear to have differentiating preferences for different types of sports.

Sport Attendance

Interest and preference for sports do not automatically translate into actual sport attendance. For instance, although the ESPN-Chilton Sports Poll (1999) reported that 58% of African Americans were interested in college football and 70% of African Americans were interested in college basketball, 69% of them had not attended any college football games the previous year and 72% had not attended any college basketball games the previous year. Moreover, the ESPN-Chilton Sports Poll (1999) reported that 94% of African Americans did not own season tickets for college sport teams. It is not surprising that interest in a sport does not lead to sport attendance, because attending sport events requires a greater level of personal and financial commitment from consumers (time, money, travel, inconvenience, and so on). Nonetheless, African Americans have attended basketball games in general and NBA games in particular at a rate that exceeds the norm, i.e., relative to their composition in the population (Simmons, 1994).

Another interesting finding emerges when African Americans' attendance at historically black colleges and universities (HBCU) sports is considered. The African American HBCU sport attendance picture is not as bleak as it is for "mainstream" or predominately white universities (PWU) sports. Although attendance rates of African Americans at most professional and PWU sport events is generally abysmal (Armstrong, 1998; 2001), they are avid fans of HBCU sports, most notably HBCU football classics. Many of the African American consumers of HBCU sports have no direct HBCU affiliation (in that they are not HBCU students, employees, or alumni), yet they have attended HBCU football classics in record-breaking numbers, setting new sport venue records, including at the New Orleans Super Dome (76,753 spectators), the Hoosier Dome in Indianapolis (61,129 spectators), and the Liberty Bowl Stadium (62,380 spectators) in Memphis, Tennessee (Armstrong, 1998). Thus, as is the case for African Americans' interests and preferences in sport, they also appear to have distinguishing sport attendance desires.

Sport Media Consumption

The ESPN-Chilton Sports Poll (1999) revealed that 78% of African Americans had watched a college football game on television the previous year and 80% had watched a college basketball game on television during the previous year. Bernstein's (1999b) study comparing Hispanics' sport media consumption with that of African Americans and non-Hispanic/whites actually illustrated that African Americans exhibited the highest media consumption frequency. African Americans watched Major League Baseball games, National Basketball Association games, and National Football League games at a rate that was higher than that of Hispanics and non-Hispanic/whites. Bernstein(1999b) also revealed that: (a) Hispanics watched boxing on television at a slightly higher frequency than African Americans, and substantially higher rate than non-Hispanic/whites, and (b) Non-Hispanic/whites watched National Hockey League games on television at a rate that was slightly higher than that of African Americans and Hispanics. Armstrong (2002a; 2002b) also revealed that the predominant behavior and method of consuming sport for African American consumers was watching sports on television.

Based on these general sport consumption patterns and tendencies of African American consumers, the question that begs an answer is: What are the underlying factors contributing to African Americans' consumption of sport (i.e., their under-consumption of some sports and their over-consumption of others)?

Theoretical Foundations of Sport Consumption

Economics of Sport Consumption

There are several theoretical approaches to understanding the role of consumption for individuals and/or societies. One approach is that offered by Veblen (1975), which is rooted in economic thought. Veblen asserted that one's esteem was proportioned with one's wealth. Bourdieu (1984) offered a related perspective of the economics of consumption and posited goods as a means by which different classes define and establish their place in the larger social structure. Thus, from an economic perspective the significance of consumption resides within the socioeconomic status of the individual and is largely based on economically derived goals and motivations.

The economic perspective of sport consumption would posit African Americans' consumption of sport as a manner of their socioeconomic/financial demography. This would infer that African American professionals (doctors or lawyers) would consume sport at a rate and manner similar to that of their Caucasian doctor and lawyer counterparts because of the similarity of their socioeconomic status. Support for the premise of the economics of sports consumption was provided by Rudman's (1986) study of the relationship between race, social structure, and sport orientation. Rudman (1986) sought to examine whether sport attitudes and orientations between African Americans and Caucasian were due to racial factors, factors related to socioeconomic structure of society, or an interaction between race and the status quo within society's socioeconomic power structures and processes.

Rudman's (1986) results supported beliefs about differences in African Americans' and Caucasians' orientations toward sport, such as that African Americans were more likely than Caucasians to become vicariously involved in sport outcomes and were more likely to incorporate sport into their daily activities. However, race-specific (regression) analyses suggested that the differences between African Americans' and Caucasians' sport attitudes may have been due to an interaction between the individuals' race and social structure. In other words, sport attitudes and orientations were similarly dependent upon age, education, family structure, and thus, overall socioeconomic status/social class distinction. For example, age and socioeconomic status had similar effects on sport attitudes: (a) as African Americans and Caucasians aged, sport became less important, and (b) as education decreased, both African Americans and Caucasians were likely to become emotionally involved in sport and posit sport as a vehicle for dealing with social problems. Two exceptions to these general patterns were revealed such that the influence of education and having children were more pronounced in influencing the sport orientations of African Americans than they were for Caucasians. Nonetheless, Rudman (1986) surmised that the differences in sport orientations between African Americans and Caucasians were primarily rooted in individuals' socioeconomic status.

Sociology of Sport Consumption

Douglas and Isherwood (1979) and Corrigan (1997) contended that goods serve a role in the creation and maintenance of social relations. Thus, in contrast to the economic perspective, it is the sociological perspective which posits that the significance of consumption resides not merely in the socioeconomic status of the individual but at the social and cultural levels. Affiliation or membership in a cultural group has a pervasive influence on an individual's sense of self and the sociocognitive process in which motives and behaviors are internalized and operationalized (Markus & Kitayama, 1999). Sport is a social product that is typically socially consumed in the presence of others. Moreover, sport consumption offers a social space that influences consumers' identity such that they often make concerted efforts to cultivate psychosocial attachments to sport teams and other sport spectators associated with the sport consumption experience (Armstrong, 2002a). Consequently, sport consumption often communicates social and cultural meaning, provides a platform for social and cultural interaction, and serves as a form of social and cultural distinction for its consumers.

Evidence of a social and cultural relations influence on sport consumption was provided by Spreitzer and Snyder (1990). The purpose of their research was to further the research by Rudman (1986) on the role of sport in the African American community. As stated earlier, Rudman (1986) concluded that African Americans' and Caucasians' sport orientations were primarily a function of their socioeconomic status. Spreitzer and Snyder (1990) revealed results that countered those of Rudman (1986) in that: (a) African American and Caucasians differed considerably on their orientation toward sport, and (b) when controlling for socidemographic variables (age, income, education, and place of residence) the significant impact of race remained. Spreitzer and Snyder (1990) reported that: (a) sports were more salient to African Americans than they were to Caucasians and (b) African Americans were generally more likely to express positive attitudes and sentiments about sport, such as sports being valuable for psychosocial development, sport competition as a positive experience, professional sports as a desirable career, and athletes as good role models.

These findings led Spreitzer and Snyder (1990) to conclude that race was not a proxy for socioeconomic status, as sports were apparently a distinctive source of social cohesion within the black community. Spreitzer and Snyder (1990) also concluded that sport might be one of the "expressive spheres of life" (p. 57) where African Americans may express cultural nuances. Sailes (1998) also commented on sports as a venue for personal empowerment whereby some African American athletes "tended to engage in electric self-expression" (pg. 123). Moreover, Sailes (1998) supported the contention for social and cultural variables at the rudiment for the sport orientations of African American athletes. The findings by Spreitzer and Snyder (1990) and Sailes (1998) evidenced how sport consumption may function to make visible particular categories that are relevant in a given culture (as discussed by Douglas & Isherwood, 1979, and Corrigan, 1997). Goldsmith (2003) also concluded that race-related factors influenced African Americans' participation in sports. These findings collectively support the sociological bases of sport consumption for African Americans.

Sport Consumption in Black and White: From Discrimination to Affirmation

From Discrimination . . .

United States' sport history is rife with examples of racial and ethnic exclusion (Coakley, 2007). African American consumers were prevented from attending sport events in early years because of discrimination and segregation laws. Hoose (1989) reported that African Americans fans were forced to sit in distant segregated areas, had to drink from "Blacks only" fountains, and had to use the "Blacks only" restrooms. They were allowed to purchase food only from Black vendors and tickets from the Black ticket windows, and they were allowed to enter the stadiums only through the gates reserves for Blacks. In addition to the segregated process of the sport service delivery, a brick wall served as a structural barrier to confine their experience and to separate African American fans from Caucasian fans.

Hoose (1989) reported that as late as 1962, practices of segregation and discrimination influenced Blacks' professional sport spectating experience. According to Avans (2001), in 1978 the Minnesota Twins were moved from Washington, D.C., to Minnesota in part because there were significantly fewer African Americans in Minnesota and the owner would not have to depend on African Americans for fan support. In Staples' (1987) article titled "Where Are the Black Fans?" he recounted the racism prevalent in professional ballparks that discouraged African Americans' attendance. He described one scenario in which a grandfather was "apologizing grimly for the presence—and the smell—of the large number of Blacks he found [at the baseball stadium]," telling his grandson, "Don't be scared . . . I told you there'd be some dark people here" (p. 27).

. . . To Affirmation

In response to and simultaneously with demographic changes and a growing vitality and Black self-consciousness, Black institutions emerged as viable social forces for African American consumers (Lomax, 1998). These institutions were attractive to African Americans who preferred to avoid the prejudice in racially hostile environments. A desire for Black separatism fostered a renaissance of entrepreneurship that gave rise to Black sports: namely professional baseball (at the professional level), historically Black colleges and universities (HBCU) sports at the collegiate level, and as Lomax (1998) described, an all-Black YMCA at the community level. Such institutions played a pivotal role in establishing a sense of racial pride and community spirit because they represented means by which African Americans could counter discrimination, by deemphasizing the focus on integration and instead focusing on organizing their own enterprises (Lomax, 1998).

African Americans played sports among themselves and formed their own professional leagues marked with their own creative cultural style. The Negro Baseball Leagues were the mainstay for African Americans' consumption of sport. [Note: For a more exhaustive review of the commercial and entrepreneurial success of the Negro Baseball Leagues, see Lomax's (2003) *Black Baseball Entrepreneurs 1860–1901: Operating by Any Means Necessary.*] According to Ogden and Hilt (2003), many of the Negro Leagues achieved commercial success and attracted a faithful core of ardent fans from the burgeoning Negro population (Peterson, 1970; Lomax, 1998). The Negro League East-West All Star game played annually in

Comiskey Park was a national market attraction and one of the League's biggest money makers ("The Negro League History 101"). During the first few decades of the 20th century, baseball was a salient sport in the African American community and served as a means by which African Americans created collective identity and civic pride, despite the racism that pervaded the dominant culture and thus excluded African Americans' sports participation (Ogden & Hilt, 2003). However, as the financial solvency of Negro Leagues dissipated and the number of Negro Leagues players dwindled (to participate in integrated major and minor leagues), so did the number of African American fans at sport events. African American fans started attending Caucasian major league sports in significant numbers in 1946, when Jackie Robinson signed with the Brooklyn Dodgers. The historical segregated sport fan experience undoubtedly influenced African Americans' contemporary desires and intentions to consume sport in segregated and/or integrated settings. Such racially distinct sport consumption environments exist today and offer a platform for further insights on African Americans' consumption of sport.

For example, according to Gouke (1987) there are typically two distinct consumption markets: one primarily for the general "mainstream" consumers and one for predominately Black consumers. Although both African Americans and Caucasians typically consume the mainstream products, African Americans are the primary consumers of the "Black" products. The racial distinctiveness of consumer markets discussed by Gouke (1987) also exists in college sports. For example, mainstream and predominately white universities (PWU) sports are sport events offered for the masses and thus, typically, have a racially integrated consumer fan base. In contrast, historically Black colleges and universities (HBCU) sports are sport events that are consumed primarily by a niche market of African American consumers and thus have a predominately Black consumer fan base. Just as the overall packaging of the consumption experience for PWU sports is reflective of the consumers who comprise their primary target markets (racially integrated mass appeal of the product, racially integrated fan base, and mass appeal product extensions such as entertainment), (in stark contrast) the overall packaging of HBCU sports is also reflective of their niche market (racially/culturally targeted appeal of the product, preponderance of members from the black racial/ethnic group, and racially/culturally infused product extensions and entertainment).

Armstrong (2002a) described the packaging of HBCU sports as one that "fosters a distinct atmosphere reflecting African heritage, culture, and tradition" (p. 268). HBCU classic events (which are akin to some PWU bowl games) are particularly racially and culturally heightened events. Burwell (1993) described HBCU football classics as a "radical departure" (p. 5C) from the predominant image of college football and fosters a unique and Afrocentric sport experience. HBCU football classics have been described as "an Ebony Fashion Fair . . . Soul Train . . . a country revival and a family reunion all set to the funky tempo and sultry gyrations of black college marching bands and dance teams" (Burwell, 1993, p. 5C). Armstrong (2002a; 2003) revealed that not only does a viable niche market for HBCU sports exist, but many of the HBCU consumers are frequent consumers of HBCU sports and are infrequent consumers of mainstream (PWU and professional sports), inferring a symbolic appeal of HBCU sports to African American consumers.

As illustrated in this discussion, African Americans' sport fanship has obviously changed over the years. It has evolved from one of discrimination (Evans,

2001), in which African Americans were discriminated against for attending integrated/mixed-race sports to one of affirmation (Armstrong 2002a), such that they have made concerted efforts to patronize culturally relevant sports products and experiences that welcome, celebrate, and affirm salient artifacts of racial/ethnic identification with the African American culture.

The Economy of Blackness! African American Consumers, Urban Consumers, and Hip-Hop

African American Consumers' Economic Attractiveness

Sport organizations have typically targeted Caucasian middle-class consumers with children, based on the premise that this would garner the greatest amount of profits. However, the economic viability of African American consumers fostered a change in that mentality. Humphrey (2005) estimated that African American consumer spending power (after tax, disposable income) of $761 billion (in 2005) will increase to more than $1 trillion in 2010. Even more impressive, Humphrey (2005) reported that the buying power of African Americans and Hispanics will exceed the Gross Domestic Product of Canada, which is the ninth largest economy in the world. Additionally, African American consumers have very attractive consumption patterns in that they tend to shop and make purchases more frequently than other consumers, they are generally a younger consumer market, and they exhibit product loyalty (Humphrey, 2005; Schreiber & Lenson, 2001). Consequently, many businesses have increased their understanding of the African American consumer market, and the sport market is no exception.

Even during the latter days of segregation, sport organizations and franchises began to take notice of the economic attractiveness of the African American consumer market. For instance, the substantial increase in African American fans (and thus increase in on-site sales) at the games of the Brooklyn Dodgers during the inaugural season of Jackie Robinson's entrance into Major League Baseball prompted a change in segregation in some ballparks (Evans, 2001). Some of the owners around the League began to realize the promise of increased revenues from African American attendance and changed their management and marketing practices accordingly. Evans (2001) reported that during a St. Louis Cardinals game, so many African Americans were in attendance that the segregated stadium sections reserved for them were not adequate to seat them all. Because a lack of seats meant a loss of revenue, the St. Louis Cardinal management eliminated restrictive segregated seating and allowed African Americans to purchase any seats they could afford (regardless of their location in the stadium). Although this policy was not enforced throughout the League for fear of upsetting Caucasion fans, it provided a historic illustration of the economic viability of African American consumers and sport management's response to it in times of sociocultural transition and unrest.

The economic attractiveness of African American consumers and their active spending patterns have also been very critical to the success of black college sport events (such as HBCU football classics). For example, the economic impact on the local cities that host HBCU football classics has been in the millions and has made substantial and direct increases in the bottom line of the hotel, restaurant, travel, and retail industries (Armstrong, 2001; Davidson & Jaffee, 1992). Among the implications of Black consumer spending at HBCU sports are: (a) the creation of jobs for Black residents; (b) the patronizing of Black businesses; (c) the provision of services to the Black community relative to community education, empowerment, and social uplift; (d) the creation of student scholarships; and (e) substantial donations to the educational and athletic missions of various HBCUs (Armstrong, 2001).

Young Urban African American Consumers

Not only does the African American consumer market represent an economically attractive market collectively, but contemporary sport managers have also begun to recognize and target the viability of an independent and unique sub-segment of African American consumers: the emerging young and affluent urban African American consumer. Although the diversity within the multiracial urban consumer market is recognized, in the context of this chapter, urban consumer pertains to the predominantly African American/Black consumers who are at the fore of this sweeping cultural revolution.

Urban African American consumers tend to be brand-loyal consumers and tend to buy well beyond their means, such that their purchases often defy their incomes (Schreiber & Lenson, 2001). The young urban African American consumer market comprises an economically viable target that is trend-setting, has a propensity to shop, and exerts a formidable influence on mainstream consumption patterns, particularly in the realms of music, fashion, sports, and language (Newsome & Gallop-Goodman, 1999; Schreiber & Lenson, 2001). "Selling to urban youths sells to more than urban youth, . . . affluent suburbs . . . kids . . . have adopted the style and music of the inner-city and hip-hop youth" (Schreiber & Lenson, 2001, p. 23). Urban American styles may also be witnessed in international markets such as Tokyo, Hamburg, and Paris, as the "with-it up-to-date young people there wear dreadlocks, American style street jeans, and other trappings of American urban life" (Schreiber & Lenson, 2001, p. 23). Thus, appealing to young urban African American consumers may offer entry into other (secondary) markets as well.

To illustrate this point: One of the more pervasive cultural extractions of the urban African American market to the mainstream market is hip-hop (Williams, 2005). Although young urban African Americans gave birth to hip-hop, there are an estimated 45 million hip-hop consumers between the ages of 13 and 34, and over 70% of them are Caucasian.

Hip-Hop Revisited

The term *hip-hop* was born in and reflects the burgeoning African American youth-oriented culture that originated in the Bronx, New York, during the 1970s (McLeod, 1999). Hip-hop symbolizes the voice of many urban Black youth and is reflected in the culture of their music, clothes, language, and overall way of life (Dyson, 1996; Midol, 1998). Traditionally, the powers that be in the United States have acted more in opposition to rather than support of the hip-hop movement (Midol, 1998). When hip-hop first appeared it was perceived as "too black, too strong" (Basu & Werbner, 2001, p. 244). "Mainstream marketing people say they don't understand today's hip-hop culture. They don't understand what urban youth is wearing, what it is doing. They don't understand the music. They don't understand the words of the songs these young people are listening to" (Schreiber & Lenson, 2001, p. 2).

However, as sport marketers have increased their understanding of: (a) the social and economic viability of young urban African American consumers; (b) their affinity to sport; (c) their loyalty as consumers and attractive purchase patterns coupled with their response to style and fashion; (d) their influence on general "mainstream" consumption patterns; and (e) the need for targeted marketing activities to appeal to them, sport marketers have likewise increased their understanding of the socioeconomic influence of hip-hop and the nuances of its consumers. Consequently, the integration of sport, fashion, and music has become even more pronounced, and sport is being concertedly marketed with a hip-hop appeal. Skateboarders, snowboarders, and other non-traditional sport participants were early adopters of hip-hop culture (Speiger, 1996); however, the sport industry soon followed and began to engage in marketing and management strategies to capitalize on hip-hop's sociocultural and economic profitability.

The contemporary manner in which sport organizations have sought to attract African American consumers in general and young urban African American consumers in particular is under the auspices of the culture of hip-hop. The fusion of sport and hip-hop has influenced sport consumption in myriad ways. Among them are: (a) sport merchandise and apparel, (b) sport event production, and (c) sport media.

Sport Merchandise/Apparel

The urban market is a particularly fertile ground for athletic retail (Silverman, 1999) and this fact has not been lost on sport retailers as they have infused hip-hop into their fashion consciousness and thus their retail and merchandising strategies. For example, Converse developed a "Smooth" brand of sneaker endorsed by rap artist "Master P" that sold out. Based on the success of the rap artists' influence on sales, Converse later launched "The MP" and "Chuck Authentic," which were also quite successful (Newsome & Gallop-Goodman, 1999). Former National Basketball Association player Hakeem Olajuwan was one of the athletes who realized that urban consumers were being exploited to purchase expensive basketball shoes (in fact, a number of violent outbursts ensued in inner city areas over the possession of sport apparel such as shoes and jackets). He (consciously) launched a line of shoes that were affordable to inner city youths, costing approximately $20. The shoes were not a success; urban youths did not buy them because they lacked "sizzle" and were not associated with the style of marketing that communicated an "urban" flair or appeal. Further, many of them equated price with "style points" and value. Thus, the shoes were perceived as "cheap," and were never a hit with the "in crowd." This scenario illustrates the difficulty of competing with the effectiveness of the symbolism created by the intensive urban-laden/sociocultural style of marketing.

When rap stars began wearing National Hockey League (NHL) jerseys, the NHL experienced an increase in merchandise sales from $200 million to more than $1 billion (Bernstein, 1999b). Perhaps the most glaring illustration of the sport industry's response to the economic viability of the urban African American market and the hip-hop culture is the marketing attention urban consumers have received from NASCAR. NASCAR has long been characterized as having a "redneck" appeal, and an ambience of white, male, blue-collar, with scantily clad women in halter-tops and bikinis (Silver, 1995). In an attempt to dispel the image of NASCAR being an all-white sport, NASCAR hired a firm that specializes in attracting inner city shoppers to launch a new line of colorfully designed NASCAR jackets with a "look" and fashion consciousness that will attract urban consumers (Bernstein, 1999b). Therefore, it was the hope of NASCAR that such culturally crafted race jackets would be a fixture in African American communities (Bernstein, 1999b).

It must be noted that the fashion consciousness in sport is not lost on young urban African American consumers. This author interviewed a young African American male at an inner city recreational center wearing a jersey of a professional football franchise. When asked if he were a fan of the team he replied, "No." When asked if he was a fan of the player whose number was on the jersey he was wearing, he replied, "Not really." When asked why he was wearing the jersey, he replied, "I like the look. The colors are smooth." Many designers have also sought to enter the urban markets with colorful and fashionable merchandise that feature a "sports" look. Kani, the African American designer who catapulted hip-hop urban wear, also manufactures golf wear. FUBU, a very popular fashion designer that caters to urban consumers also has a line of sports gear, "FUBU Sports."

Sport Event Production

Live performances of hip-hop/rap stars are frequently featured in the production of pre-game, half-time, during game, and post-game sport event promotions at the high school, collegiate, and professional levels. Hip-hop is also infused in the production of ancillary sport event programs such as sport news/entertainment/magazine format initiatives (such as *Inside Stuff* of the National Basketball Association, *Under the Helmet* of the National Football League, and various other related sport ventures). The sport logos that were once blurred out in "gangster" rap videos are now glamorized, and many sport personalities and professional athletes now make cameo appearances in such videos. Also, bits of the "slanguage" and lyrics of hip-hop music are often infused into the promotion and the delivery of sport broadcasts and sport event productions.

Sport Media

Electronic and print media have also marketed the coupling of hip-hop and sports. Black Entertainment Television (the longstanding media entity targeted to black viewers) has also glamorized the partnering of sport and hip-hop as evidenced in their *Mad Sports* program (which is an informational and entertaining sports show that integrates hip-hop music and sport via entertaining highlights, news, and human interest features). *Mad Sports* also features a video countdown of professional athletes presenting their favorite rap/hip hop musical videos. *The Source*, the magazine of hip-hop music, culture, and politics has a sister publication that is solely devoted to sport, *The Source Sports*. Further, *The Source Sports* launched its annual Athlete of the Year Award. *Slam* magazine, also a sport publication widely read by hip-hop and rap fans, is packaged with hip-hop and rap nuances and an appeal to urban consumers.

Coca-Cola Company featured two legendary hip-hop "MC's" (KRS-One and MC Shan) in their series of NBA Sprite commercials. The commercials glamorized one of the most pronounced forms of expressions and rites of passage in the hip-hop genre by having the artists engage in a free-style rap battle. According to Spreigler (1996), the commercial was praised throughout the rap world and beyond. Major League Baseball (MLB) launched a commercial advertisement featuring rhythm and blues singer Aretha Franklin and rapper L. L. Cool J endorsing MLB. Major League Soccer (MLS) also employed the talents of rap group Run D.M.C. to promote MLS. These practices illustrate the role of hip-hop, rap, and R&B music in creating a celebration and affirmation of Black culture, hip-hop, and sports.

Sociological Premises of Sport Marketing and Hip-Hop: A "Functional Conflict"

Is the increasing infusion of hip-hop in marketing to attract African American consumers an effective strategy? What are the merits of this approach? What are the dangers of this approach? Research on the empirical effectiveness of employing hip-hop nuances to reach African American and other urban consumers is lacking and still in the infancy stage. However, since hip-hop represents a sociocultural movement (albeit with political and economical undertones), the effectiveness of hip-hop may be examined from a sociological perspective. Sociological theories are often employed as approaches to understanding the dynamics of the inner workings of the institution of sport, the consumers it serves, and the consumers that serve it. As such, sociological theories provide a viable lens through which to examine the effectiveness of hip-hop sport marketing. Coakley (2007) remarked:

> The best theories are those we understand so clearly that they help us make sense of our experiences and the social world. When we study sport in society, the best theories are those that describe and explain aspects of social life in logical terms that are consistent with systematic observations of the social world. Theories enable us to see things from new angles and perspectives, understand more fully the relationship between sports and social life, and make informed decisions about sports and sport participation in our lives, families, communities, and societies. (p. 31)

Two theories that may help to make sense of the contemporary hip-hop approach to sport marketing are (a) functionalist theory and (b) conflict theory. The limited space allotted for this chapter will not allow for an exhaustive discussion of these two theories. Please refer to Coakley's *Sport and Society* (2007, 9th ed.) for a detailed discussion. Following is a brief overview of each theory relative to the hip-hop infusion into the marketing of sport.

Functionalist Theory Analysis of Hip-Hop Sport Marketing

According to Coakley (2007), functionalist theory focuses on how sports offer positive contributions and assistance to society and how sports also positively influence the individuals participating therein. As such, functionalist theory assumes that the values in society are shared among the various constituents in the social system, and sport serves as a vehicle to maintain stability and order. Consequently, functionalist theory provides an underpinning from which to examine how sport as a social institution may be maintained as it is.

From a functionalist theory perspective, infusing tenets of hip-hop into sport marketing illustrates intercultural accommodation, which refers to attempts to use symbols (verbal and non-verbal) that are relevant to message recipients to enhance communication and ultimately influence their attitudes and behaviors. In so doing, hip-hop is the accommodation used to accentuate the "cultural" connectedness with urban consumers. Based on the functionalist perspective, appealing to urban consumers may be posited as a means for the sport organizations to demonstrate respect for the urban African American community, which subsequently will diversify the base of sport consumers. By increasing the patronage among urban African American consumers in general and ethnic minority consumers in particular, such strategies may be deemed positive contributors to sport being utilized as a tool for social integration and cultural diversity.

From a functionalist perspective, the hip-hop style of sport marketing also offers positive benefits to the respective sport organizations. For example, the communication of "shared" values between the respective sport organizations and urban African American consumers, along with the promotion of a culture of consumption among urban African American consumers, will contribute to the positioning of the respective sport organization as a socially responsible entity. Such positioning among the lucrative urban African American market will undoubtedly contribute to the growth of sport as an industry. Functionalist theorists may contend that the hip-hop style of marketing illustrates how the needs of both constituencies are met and how both the sport organizations and urban consumers are contributing to a symbiotic relationship that maintains and promotes the good in and the stability of the consumption of sport. The functionalist perspective would suggest an increase in the hip-hop style of marketing to (a) further attract African American and urban consumers (offering them the benefits of sport consumption) and (b) further diversify and expand the consumer base of African Americans for the respective sport organizations (allowing them to serve a multicultural, underrepresented, and often socially disenfranchised segment of society).

Conflict Theory Analysis of Hip-Hop Sport Marketing

In contrast to the optimistic view functionalist theorists have of sport, conflict theorist have a more pessimistic view. Conflict theory assumes that economic factors shape societal functions and structures, and it illuminates the exploitive and perilous nature of sport. It examines the detrimental aspects of the capitalistic nature of sport and seeks to awaken the consciousness of those exploited by the system of sport (Coakley, 2007). From a conflict theorist perspective, employing a hip-hop style of marketing sport is exploitive. Branding, product positioning, and other sport marketing strategies that utilize a hip-hop appeal seek to accentuate the cultural connectedness of sport (merchandise) to the urban African American community have promoted a culture of consumption that has contributed to consumer exploitation. By specifically appealing to urban consumers' affinity to sports and their propensity to shop, the hip-hop style of marketing has accentuated style over substance, making many consumers unaware of the economic implications of their sport consumption desires and patterns.

Conflict theorists would also argue that applying the latest fashion trends to sport merchandise and imbuing sport ventures and promotions with an underlying hip-hop appeal are quick-fix economic "silver bullets," and may not necessarily translate into an increase in urban consumers' active or vicarious sport involvement beyond the actual merchandise purchase. For instance, when rap stars began wearing NHL jerseys, although the NHL merchandise sales increased dramatically from $200 million to more than $1 billion, very little change occurred in the urban representation of the NHL fan base (Bernstein, 1999a). Thus, as conflict theory would purport, this practice did not facilitate long-term relationships with urban African American consumers.

Conflict theorists would opine that the use of hip-hop as a vehicle for foray into the urban African American market should be done with a sincere sense of care, respect, and responsibility for urban consumers and the communities of which they are products. For example, as the conflict theorists would surmise, there is still a grave need for many sport companies and organizations that use hip-hop to reach African American consumers to involve urban African American consumers in the retail and distribution of sport. Creating profitable businesses and partnerships in urban areas would be a way of translating urban consumer spending on sport into economic prosperity in the consumers' own communities.

Examining the tenets and practices of hip-hop sport marketing from the functional and conflict theory perspectives suggests that both theories (as suggested by Coakley, 2000) "help us ask questions and seek information that enable us to see sports in new ways, understand the relationship between sports and social life, and make informed decisions about sports and sport participation in our lives, families, communities, and societies" (p. 31). Based on the merits and dangers in which hip-hop sport marketing affects African American consumers, it may be appropriately deemed a "functional conflict."

Black' Consumption of Sport: Race Matters!

What underlying force(s) is(are) driving African Americans' patterns of sport consumption? What is it about basketball that makes it so salient to the African American community? Why do African Americans patronize HBCU sports in record-breaking numbers? Why has hip-hop become a viable strategy for marketers seeking to attract African American consumers? These questions will now be explored.

As stated earlier in this chapter, historically, racial segregation and laws rooted in racial discrimination adversely influenced the African American sport consumer experience. Today, African American consumers have more choices in their sport consumption desires relative to consuming racially integrated sports (PWU and professional sports) or racially segregated sports (HBCU); nonetheless, the impact of race remains.

A person's race generally exerts a notable influence on that person's thoughts, attitudes, and behaviors including those that pertain to sport consumption. Race may affect sport consumption at the collective and individual levels because of the manner in which race meshes with ethnicity. Racial influences may be internal (factors within individuals that may influence their sport consumption behaviors), external (factors that are prevalent in the sport setting or environment that may influence sport consumption behaviors), or a combination thereof. Racial influences are often difficult to discern; nonetheless, they persist and profoundly influence sport consumer behavior. There are three central (and related) race-based themes that may underlie African Americans' consumption of sport: racial similarity, racial consciousness, and racial endorsement.

Racial Similarity

The racial aesthetics associated with a product often elicit a perceived similarity that influences consumers' product preferences and choices (Armstrong, 2002a). Consumers may perceive racial similarity with sport consumption in a myriad of ways. For example, Harrison (1995) discussed the manner in which racial similarity/racial awareness via the self-schema phenomenon (which refers to cognitive generalizations of self based on racial aesthetics) was a major determinant of sport activity choices of African American youths. African American sisters Venus and Serena Williams provided a "looking glass" for many African American youth such that they saw someone who looked like them (i.e., their racial similarity) excel in a sport that was not perceived to be for Blacks. The visibility of the Williams sisters made the sport of tennis accessible and acceptable for other African Americans. Tiger Woods (although a self-proclaimed multi-raced individual) had a similar effect on African American youth relative to their increased interest in golf because his visibility provided a measure of racial similarity.

Bilyeu and Wann's (2002) interviews with African American college students about their motivations for sport consumption revealed that racial similarity (with African American coaches and quarterbacks) was an important reason for them to watch, read, or discuss sports. Further support of the salience of racial similarity to African Americans' sport enjoyment was offered by Sapolsky (1980) in his demonstration of African American viewers' disposition to watch African American athletes. He revealed (via an experimental study that edited the competing teams to be all-Caucasian and all-African American) that the African American viewers enjoyed baskets by African American players significantly more than they did those by the Caucasian players. Additionally, having the African American team win was significantly more important than having a close contest.

Research (see Armstrong 2002a; Armstrong & Stratta, 2004) has indicated that African American sport fans choose to be in settings that are more racially segregated such that there is a predominance of other African American fans and the sport experience is one that is also racially/culturally imbued. Armstrong and Strata (2004) revealed that African American spectators' attendance frequency was significantly higher for the professional women's basketball games of the team that had the greater composition of African American players and management personnel, and was located in a market that had a significant population of Black residents. Racial similarity may be a driving force behind African Americans' noteworthy consumption of HBCU sports. HBCU sports obviously provide and reinforce racial similarity for African American consumers (predominantly African American athletes, coaches, and spectators) that undoubtedly encourages their patronage and loyalty.

The importance of racial similarity to African American consumers may also be viewed from a historical perspective. For instance, African Americans' attendance at professional sports primarily began with the integration with Major League Baseball in 1946 when Jackie Robinson was signed by the Brooklyn Dodgers. During his rookie season, African Americans' attendance at the Dodgers' games increased by 400%, setting a new record for Ebbets Field (Evans, 2001).

Racial similarity also influences how African Americans may respond to persuasive sport communications. Armstrong (2000) revealed that having an African American spokesperson present a message to African American students elicited biased processing of the message such that the students' attitudes were similar to the African American spokesperson regardless of the merits (strong or weak) of the arguments contained in the message. In contrast, having a Caucasian messenger as a spokesperson of the same messages elicited objective processing such that the students' attitudes were only favorable when the Caucasian spokesperson's message was strong and had merit.

These findings collectively illustrated how racial similarity may affect African Americans' attitudes and preferences regarding sport consumption, their sport consumption patterns and tendencies, and the means of communicating sport-related issues to African American students.

Racial Consciousness

In addition to the impact of racial aesthetics and racial similarity based on physical resemblance or surface characteristics, as previously discussed, is the impact of race on an individual's consciousness from a spiritual, emotional, or ideological level. In fact, racial similarity often influences individuals' consciousness based on underlying inferences and attitudes associated with race. Because African Americans are generally required to function and operate as minorities within Eurocentric majority in most settings in the U.S., one of the challenges many African American consumers face is one of whether to retain aspects of their Afrocentric racial/ethnic group consciousness or assimilate their consciousness into the dominant Eurocentric culture. Armstrong (2002a) reported that African American consumers generally tend to have strong identification with their racial/ethnic group. Additionally, African American consumers' high levels of identification with the Black ethnic group significantly influenced their HBCU sport attendance frequency and their attendance at sport events in general. Bilyeu and Wann (2002) also supported the notion of racial kinship in sport. Their findings revealed that the feeling of being racially represented and feeling that the sport represented their culture were important reasons for African American students to watch, read, and discuss sports. The racial consciousness of African American students interviewed by Bilyeu and Wann (2002) was displayed in their feeling that supporting certain teams and players translated into supporting their culture and players who have overcome racial obstacles.

The racial consciousness of individuals is often manifested in their interests, desires, motivations, and information processing strategies. Bilyeu and Wann (2002) revealed that African Americans' attendance (in comparison to other spectators) was more motivated by the opportunity to escape from the routines of the day. This finding was consistent with the premise that minorities and stigmatized groups often display more stress symptoms than do groups in the majority who are not stigmatized and are of higher economic status, and sport appeared to offer a platform of escape. Armstrong's (2002b) research countered the premise of Bilyeu and Wann (2002), and that of other researchers such as Hansen and Gauthier (1989) and Zhang, Smith, Pease, and Jambor (1997). She revealed that the racial and cultural affiliation with Black athletes, Black spectators, and the overall Afrocentric environment were more influential to Black HBCU basketball spectators' sport consumption tendencies than were motives such as group entertainment, an opportunity for a psychological escape, or the economic or psychological investment in (i.e., identification with) the team/event. Armstrong (2003) revealed that cultural motives, such as to see Black bands perform, to see Black athletes, the cultural/Afrocentric atmosphere, and to support HBCU sports were more influential on the attendance decisions of black spectators at HBCU football than were sport motives, such as being a fan of football or the quality of the teams competing.

Research (James & Ridinger, 2002; Robinson & Trail, 2005) has revealed pronounced gender differences in the sport orientations and motivations of their predominately Caucasian samples; however, such gender differences have not been revealed among African American spectators (Armstrong 2002a; 200b; Davidson & Jaffee, 1992). In fact, whereas "mainstream" sport consumer research has revealed that males are the predominant consumers of male sports, Armstrong revealed that African American females actually attended HBCU sports at a frequency that was greater than that of males. These findings suggest that the role the cultural packaging of HBCU sports plays in the socialization of its consumers is not tempered by African American fans' gender. The Afrocentric cultural appeal of HBCU sports is effective because it represents a racial consciousness (racial centrality, racial salience, and racial affirmation) for African American consumers.

Racial consciousness may also apply to urban African American consumers' response to the infusion of hip-hop into sports. Hip-hop and its packaged nuances have garnered a favorable (and profitable) position among many African American and urban consumers, largely because they (the musical flavor, lyrics, and lifestyles depicted and portrayed) collectively represent a consciousness of racial authenticity that captures a slice of reality for many urban African American consumers. Thus, race appears to activate the spiritual, emotional, and ideological consciousness of African American/black consumers that may influence their consumption of sport.

Racial Endorsement

In addition to the manifestations of race from a physical resemblance perspective or a deeper spiritual or ideological perspective, aesthetics of race may also imbue a product with an appeal or personality such that it becomes a racial endorsement. In fact, it may be surmised that racial similarity (previously discussed) may invoke a racial consciousness (previously discussed) that leads to racial endorsement. As discussed previously, based on the frequency with which African American consumers support basketball (actively and vicariously), basketball appears to be a sport that is racially endorsed. Schurr, Wittig, Ruble, and Ellen (1988) revealed that race was statistically significant in explaining the differences between college basketball game attendees and non-attendees; games were frequently attended by African American men (race effect) and African American women (race x gender effect). Boyd (1997) also discussed the racial/aesthetic appeal of basketball to the African American culture in his assertion that basketball was "a cultural space where aesthetics, politics, and an overall sense of Blackness could be communicated to both marginal and mass audiences" (p. 134).

Appiah (2000) equated basketball to jazz and hip-hop and indicated that it is "culturally marked as Black" (p. 612). Basketball is apparently associated with the cool pose phenomenon and appears to be a racially sanctioned activity for African American men. Although the notion of the cool pose phenomenon generally references African American males' style, it may relate to African American women's style as well. For example, Armstrong and Stratta (2004) revealed that the number one motive for the black spectator's decision to attend a professional women's basketball game (featuring an all-black team) was the basketball action, perhaps inferring that the spectators enjoyed the black women's style of play. Moreover, Armstrong and Stratta (2004) revealed that black spectators were overrepresented and white spectators were underrepresented at the respective professional basketball game featuring the black female players.

Based on: (a) visibility of the racial aesthetic of Blackness witnessed among basketball players in the U.S., and (b) the stylistic aesthetic appeal of the game of basketball to the African American culture, it is not surprising that basketball is racially endorsed as a site for cultural reproductions for Black athletes and a platform for cultural celebration among the fans consuming the overall basketball experience. The infusion of more Black athletes into other sports is also influencing the image of those sports as racially endorsed. For example, as discussed previously, having the style, flair, and "flavor" of Venus and Serena as they play tennis has marked it as a "cool" sport (Kaplan & Lamm, 2000) and one that is not so elitist but also acceptable for African American youth.

Racial endorsement also applies to sport products. Sport products have been packaged with racial markers such that they become identified with African American culture. The strategy behind infusing hip-hop into sports such as the NHL jerseys, the merchandising of NASCAR jackets, the racial overtones of Nike advertisements, the promotion of Converse sneakers by African American rap artists, and so on was to communicate racial endorsement for the respective products to African American consumers. Nike has been particularly successful in creating print and electronic advertisements that are laden with racial/cultural markers constituted and drawn from the worlds and realities of African American consumers. It has been reported that African American purchases accounted for 30% of Nike sales (Woodard, 1990).The racial endorsements of products have not been lost on African American adolescents as they have identified the existence of a distinctive "Black" style that is being communicated in television commercials for Nike basketball shoes (Wilson & Sparks, 1996). Therefore, it is likely that African American consumers will patronize sport events, experiences, and products that are perceived to be sanctioned by the African American community and thus racially endorsed.

Chapter Summary

To recap, this chapter provided a review of research on African Americans' consumption of sport and indicated that they have discriminating taste preferences for certain sports. Although they are generally interested in a variety of sports, with the exception of HBCU sports and the sport of basketball (collegiate or professional), African Americans are more likely to watch sports on television than they are to attend live events. One way in which contemporary sport managers have sought to increase sport consumption among African American consumers (and the consumers they influence) is through a hip-hop style of sport marketing (which is evident in sport merchandise and apparel, sport event production, and sport media) that theoretically represents a functional conflict. Three central themes that may explain African Americans' consumption of sport are racial similarity, racial consciousness, and racial endorsement.

Conclusion

America is a nation transformed by the fulfillment of its own ideals such that never have its population and culture been more vibrant and diverse (Time, 2004). America is no longer defined and shaped exclusively by white Anglo-Saxons, but increasingly by African Americans, Asian Americans, and Hispanic Americans. This new mainstream is transforming how America will work, play, learn, and spend in the coming decades. Any company or institution that fails to understand it will be left behind (Time, 2004).

"Race itself signifies differently and is lived differently between different discursive and cultural locations" (Alcoff, 1999, p. 33). Structural and economic factors undoubtedly interact with many of the social and psychological factors discussed in this chapter to influence African Americans' sport consumption. As such, it was not the intent of this author to universalize the experiences of all African American consumers. Instead, the focus of this chapter was on the collective consciousness manifested and illustrated in the predominant consumption patterns of African American consumers. Nonetheless, one reality that is apparently not lost on many African American sport consumers (urban residing or otherwise) is the salience of race. African Americans' affinity for racial regard, racial centrality, and racial salience in their consumption of sport evidences an underlying influence of race.

Therefore, the answer to the question posed at the outset of this chapter—What are the underlying factors contributing to African Americans' consumption of sport?—may lie in Cornel West's (1994) declaration of the salience of race to Blacks in America. As illustrated throughout this chapter regarding African Americans' consumption of sport: indeed, *Race matters!* Social scientists have long concluded that racial dynamics pervade various facets of life and the social institutions that are necessary to sustain and improve quality of life. Sport is a salient social institution and is a site for racial manifestations and affirmations. This means that contemporary sport managers need to increase their understanding of the racial (and ethnic) dynamics of sport consumption. This requires sport managers to respect and respond to: (a) the micro level influences of race on consumers' thoughts and actions relative to sport consumption, (b) the influence of the macro level racial environment in which the sport consumption takes place, and (c) the manner in which sport management practices and activities communicate racial meaning.

▲▼ Suggested Readings ▲▼

Coakley, J. (2007). *Sports in society* (9th ed). New York: McGraw-Hill.

Lomax, M. (2003). *Black baseball entrepreneurs 1860–1901: Operating by any means necessary.* Syracuse, NY: Syracuse University Press.

Sailes, G. (1998). *African Americans in sport: Contemporary themes.* New Brunswick, NJ: Transaction Publishers.

▲▼ Study Questions ▲▼

1. What are the different ways in which individuals may consume sport?

2. Identify some of the unique patterns of African Americans' consumption of sport.

3. Compare and contrast the economic and sociological perspectives of examining African Americans' consumption of sport.

4. Discuss the evolution of the African American sport consumer experience from discrimination to affirmation.

5. What are your thoughts about using hip-hop to reach African American and urban consumers? Discuss the pros and cons from a functional and conflict theory perspective. Is hip-hop sport marketing good for African American consumers?

6. Discuss the three central themes of race that underlie African Americans' consumption of sport and provide evidence of each.

7. What role(s) does sport consumption play in the lives of African American consumers?

References

Alcoff, L. M. (1999). Philosophy and racial identity. In M. Blumer & J. Solomon, *Ethnic and racial studies today* (pp. 31–44). London: Routledge.

Appiah, K. A. (2000). Racial identity and racial identification. In L. Black & J. Solomos (Eds.), *Theories of race and racism* (pp. 607–615). London: Routledge.

Armstrong, K. L. (1998). Ten strategies to employ when marketing sport to Black consumers. *Sport Marketing Quarterly, 7*(3), 11–18.

Armstrong, K. L. (2000a). African-American students' responses to race as a source cue in persuasive sport communications. *Journal of Sport Management, 14,* 208–226.

Armstrong, K. L. (2001). Black consumers' spending and historically black college sport events: Marketing implications, *Sport Marketing Quarterly, 10*(2), 102–111.

Armstrong, K. L. (2002a). An examination of the social psychology of Blacks' consumption of sport. *Journal of Sport Management, 16*(4), 267–288.

Armstrong, K. L. (2002b). Race and sport consumption motivations: A preliminary investigation of a Black consumers' sport motivation scale. *Journal of Sport Behavior, 25*(4), 309–330.

Armstrong, K. L. (2003, Spring/Summer). An exploratory examination of Black consumers' motivation to attend an Ohio HBCU football classic. *Future Focus,* 17–24.

Armstrong, K. L., & Strata, T. M P. (2004). Market analyses of race and sport consumption. *Sport Marketing Quarterly, 13*(1), 7–16.

Basu, D., & Werbner, P. (2001). Bootstrap capitalism and the culture industries: A critique of invidious comparisons in the study of ethnic entrepreneurship. *Ethnic and Racial Studies, 24*(2), 236–262.

Bernstein, A. (1999a, October 11–17). NASCAR's fashion grabs inner city fans. *Sports Business Journal, 2*(25), 1, 10.

Bernstein, A. (1999b, November 1–7). Study: Hispanic tastes are varied, strong. *Sports Business Journal, 37.*

Bilyeu, J. K, & Wann, D. (2002). An investigation of racial differences in sport fan motivation. *International Sports Journal,* 93–106.

Bourdieu, P. (1984). *Distinction: A social critique of the judgment of taste* (translated by Richard Nice). London: Routledge & Kegan Paul.

Boyd, T. (1997). The day the niggaz took over: Basketball, commodity, culture, and black masculinity. In A. Baker & T. Boyd (Eds.), *Out of bounds* (pp.123–142). Bloomington, IN: Indiana University Press.

Burwell, B. (1993)). Bayou Classic gives tradition a new beat. *USA Today,* November 26, 5C.

Coakley, J. (2007). *Sports in society* (9th ed.). New York: McGraw-Hill.

Corrigan, P. (1997). *The sociology of consumption.* Thousand Oaks, CA: Sage Publications.

Davidson, L. S., & Jaffee, B. L. (1992). *Visitor spending at the 1991 Circle City Classic.* Unpublished report, Indiana University.

Douglas, M., & Isherwood, B. (1979). *The worlds of goods: Towards an anthropology of consumption.* London: Allen Lane.

Dyson, M. E. (1996). *Race rules: Navigating the color line.* Reading, MA: Addison-Wesley.

ESPN-Chilton Sports Poll (1999). *Demographic Data.* Author.

Evans, A. S. (2001). Blacks as key functionaries: A study of racial stratification in professional sport. In A. Yianikis & M. J. Melnick's (Eds.), *Contemporary issues in sociology of sport* (pp. 211–218). Champaign, IL: Human Kinetics.

Goldsmith, P. A. (2003). Race relations and racial patterns in school sport participation. *Sociology of Sport Journal, 20*(2), 147–171.

Gouke, C. G. (1987). *Blacks and the American economy.* Needham Heights, MA: Guinn Press.

Hansen, H., & Gauthier, R. (1989). Factors affecting attendance at professional sport events. *Journal of Sport Management, 3,* 15–32.

Harrison, L. (1995). African Americans: Race as a self-schema affecting physical activity choices. *Quest, 47,* 7–18.

Hecht, M. L., Collier, M. J., & Ribeau, S. A. (1993). *African American communication: Ethnic identity and cultural interpretation.* Newbury Park, CA: Sage.

Hewitt, J. P. (2000). *Self and society: A symbolic interactionist social psychology* (8th ed.). Needham Heights, MA: Allyn and Bacon.

Hoose, P. M. (1989). *Necessities: Racial barriers in American sports.* New York: Random House.

Humphrey, J. M. (2005). The multicultural economy 2005: America's minority buying power. *Georgia Business and Economic Conditions, 65*(3). Athens, GA: Selig Center for Economic Growth, The University of Georgia

James, J. D., & Ridinger, L. L. (2002). Female and male sport fans: A comparison of sport consumption motives. *Journal of Sport Behavior, 25*(3), 260–278.

Kaplan, D., & Lamm, M. (2000). Poll: Blacks surpass whites in devotion to tennis. *Sports Business Journal, 2*(49), 1, 53.

Lapchick, R. (2005). *The 2004 racial and gender report card.* Orlando, FL: Institute for Diversity and Ethics in Sports at University of Central Florida.

Lomax, M. E. (1998). Black entrepreneurship in the national pastime: The rise of semiprofessional baseball in Black Chicago, 1890–1915. *Journal of Sport History, 25*(1), 43–64.

Markus, H. R., & Kitayama, S. (1999). Culture and the self: Implications for cognitive, emotion, and motivation. In R. F. Buameister (Ed.), *The self in social psychology* (pp. 339–367). Philadelphia: Psychology Press.

Midol, N. (1998). Rap and dialectical relations: Cultural, subculture, power, and counter-power. In R. Genevieve (Ed.), *Sport and postmodern times* (pp. 333–343). Albany, NY: State University of New York Press.

Mowen, J. C. (1995). *Consumer behavior* (4th ed). Englewood Cliffs, NJ: Prentice Hall.

The Negro League History 101. Retrieved from NegroLeagueBaseball.com on August 8, 2005.

Newsome, M., & Gallop-Goodman, G. (1999, December). Your guide to cashing in on the young urban market. *Black Enterprise,* 159–164.

Ogden, D. G., & Hilt, M. L. (2003). Collective identity and basketball: An explanation for the decreasing number of African-Americans on America's baseball diamonds. *Journal of Leisure Research, 35*(2), 213–227.

Peterson, R. (1970). *Only the ball was white.* Englewood Cliffs, NJ: Prentice-Hall, Inc.

Robinson, M. J., & Trail, G. T. (2005). Relationships among spectator gender, motives, points of attachment, and sport preference. *Journal of Sport Management, 19,* 58–80.

Rudman, W. (1986). The sport mystique in the Black culture. *Sociology of Sport Journal, 3,* 305–319.

Sachs, M. L., & Abraham, A. (1979). Playground basketball: A qualitative, field examination. *Journal of Sport Behavior, 2*(1), 27–36.

Sailes, G. (1998). An examination of basketball performance orientations among African American males. In G. A. Sailes (Ed.), *African Americans in sport: Contemporary themes* (pp. 121–130). New Brunswick, NJ: Transaction Publishers.

Sapolsky, B. S. (1980). The effect of spectator disposition and suspense on the enjoyment of sport contests. *International Journal of Sport Psychology, 11,* 1–10.

Schurr, K. T., Wittig, A. F., Rubble, V. E., & Ellen, A. S. (1988). Demographic and personality characteristics associated with persistent, occasional, and non-attendance of university male basketball games by college students. *Journal of Sport Behavior, 9*(1), 3–17.

Schreiber, A .L., & Lenson, B. (2001). *Multicultural marketing: Selling to the new America.* Lincolnwood (Chicago), IL: NTC/Contemporary Publishing Group, Inc.

Simmons Market Research Bureau, Inc. (1994). *Study of media and markets: Sports and leisure, 10*(9), Part P.

Silver, M. (1995, July 24). A day at the races. *Sports Illustrated, 83*(4), 18–24.

Silverman, D. (1999, February). Bright sites, big cities. *Sportstyle,* 70.

Speigler, M. (1996, November). Marketing street culture: Bringing hip-hop style to the mainstream. *American De-*

mographics, 29–32.

Spreitzer, E., & Snyder, E. (1990). Sports within the Black subculture: A matter of social class of distinctive subculture. *Journal of Sport and Social Issues, 14,* 48–58.

Staples, B. (1987, May 17). Where are the Black fans? *The New York Times Magazine,* 27–31.

Time. (2004, September 20). Selling ethnicity, Inc.: Why business needs to design strategies to reach the new mainstream. *Time Magazine Archive (online).* Retrieved from www.time.com/time/archive on March 30, 2006.

Vleben, T. (1975). *The theory of the leisure class.* New York: August M. Kelly.

West, C. (1994). *Race matters.* New York: Vintage Books.

Williams, H. (2005). How Blackness became "universal." Retrieved from http:www.popandpolitics.com/articles on September 14, 2005.

Wilson, B., & Sparks, R. (1996). "It's gotta be the shoes": Youth, race and sneaker commercials. *Sociology of Sport Journal, 13,* 398–427.

Woodard, W. M. (1990, November). It's more than just the shoes. *Black Enterprise, 17.*

Zhang, J. J., Smith, D. W., Pease, D. G., & Jambor, E. A. (1997). Negative influence of market competitors on attendance at professional sport games: The case of minor league hockey team. *Sport Marketing Quarterly, 6*(3), 31–40.

▲ *Epilogue* ▼

Looking Toward the Future: Developing a Shared Community

In the first essay of this book David Wiggins traced the nature of the critical events related to sports from slavery to the modern professional and to Olympic sports that have influenced the status of African American athletes at both the amateur and professional levels of sport. This final essay by Earl Smith, a highly regarded past president of the North American Society of the Sociology of Sport, and his colleague Angela Hattery is an absorbing study that scrutinizes race relationships in American society and contemporary big-time sports. In the Introduction, George Sage noted how, one after another of the essays included in the book bring into focus an understanding of the consequences of pervasive social stereotyping that African Americans have experienced. In this essay, Smith and Hattery show how such stereotyping has stifled the potential of African Americans, including through its grip on sports. In particular, they propose that the shaping of African American Civil Society must be understood as a direct result of segregation from other institutions (education, law, politics, medicine, business), and sports must be seen as a possible route to success for athletes, entertainers, players, and so on. Within sports itself, stereotyping and discrimination are reflected in such issues as access to coaching and leadership positions, life after the game, sport and black identity, and the economic and social problems that are embedded in relations between American society and the African American Civil Society.

AFRICAN

AMERICAN

COMMUNITY:

THE DYNAMICS

OF RACE,

CLASS,

GENDER, AND

COMMUNITY

EARL SMITH
AND
ANGELA
HATTERY

The problem of the twentieth century is the problem of the color line.

—W. E. B. Du Bois (1903, p. 13)

Since the beginning of the nation, white Americans have suffered from a deep inner uncertainty as to who they really are. One of the ways that has been used to simplify the answer has been to seize upon the presence of African Americans and use them as a marker, a symbol of limits, a metaphor for the "outsider." Many whites could look at the social position of African Americans and feel that color formed an easy and reliable gauge for determining to what extent one was or was not American. Perhaps that is why one of the first epithets that many European immigrants learned when they got off the boat was the term "nigger"—it made them feel instantly American. But this is tricky magic. Despite his racial difference and social status, something indisputably American about Negroes not only raised doubts about the white man's value system but aroused the troubling suspicion that whatever else the true American is, he is also somehow African American.

—Ralph Ellison
"What America Would Be Like Without Blacks" (1970/1995, pp. 582–583)

Introduction

The future for African American athletes is inextricably linked to the future of African American Civil Society. Whereas we live in a society that has opportunities for all, it has been shown that many of these opportunities are disproportionately arranged so that they are parceled out along lines of (a) race, (b) class, and (c) gender.

This chapter takes a look into the future and, as sociologists rather than futurists, we take this look through a lens based on the empirical realities of the past. Our examination is based on empirical facts and it is from that vantage point that we make our analysis.

At the beginning of what we attempt to do, it needs to be noted that our discussion in this chapter is located within the realm of North American sociology. The focus of the discipline, at times referred to as the scientific study of the human condition, is the proper locale for the study of the future of sport in African American Civil Society. Sociologists study human life, the life chances of individuals and groups, and they also study societal institutions like the family, religion, and the corporate structure.

Recently, there has emerged a systematic focus on the institution of sport. Unlike other social scientists, who, for example, focus on the behavior of individuals, as sociologists, we are interested here in examining and exploring the relationship between two structures: (a) the institution of sport and (b) African American Civil Society. How do these two institutions interact? How do these institutions shape each other? How do the intersections of these institutions differ from the intersections of other institutions (such as the institution of sport and the White community or the institution of education and the African American community)? What are the consequences and outcomes of the intersection of sport and the African American community and are these consequences positive or negative or both? These are the issues that will be explored in this chapter. Though our focus will be on institutions, we will draw on individual examples to illustrate our points to be made.

Specifically, this chapter takes as its charge the erasure of the tragic social stereotype that has plagued African Americans by limiting their full capabilities in all spheres of American life, including sports (Gossett, 1965; Graves, 2001). The

American image of African Americans as athletes, dancers, musicians, clowns, and criminals has also been encouraged by the almost total invisibility of African Americans in other roles besides the ones mentioned here. At a national level they are simply invisible and in many cases do not even exist.

It is also unfortunate that the juxtaposition of athletics versus academics is accepted in almost all quarters when it comes to the men and women who attend institutions of higher learning, such that many believe that African American men and women attend college only for sports and not for a serious education.

Yet in the environment of today's athletic world, we ask: Is the blanket acceptance of mediocre students who may be attending college only as an avenue to a career in professional athletcis (see Press & Washburn, 2000) the price we ultimately pay for the quest of having winning intercollegiate sport teams? When John B. Slaughter was president of the University of Maryland he seemed to be saying as much when he argued that stopping freshmen with poor grades from playing sports would hurt the chances of many institutions to field competitive athletic teams (Hughes, 2001).

This issue is so pervasive that it upsets the normal run of things related to academics. Its concern is so deep that former all-pro National Football League player David Meggyesy (2000) could write, "Looking at graduation rates for incoming National Football League (NFL) players, of the 221 rookies on NFL teams in 1998 only 13, or 6 percent, had graduated." And, sadly these patterns continue today. (See the NFL Professional Development website for the latest statistics: http://www.nfl.com/player-development/story/6190917.)

The patterns are similar in professional basketball. In the 2005 NBA draft, for example, fewer than half, 43%, of the players drafted never graduated from college and nearly a quarter, 23%, of the players drafted in the first round never *went* to college (they were foreign or high school players). Eight players in the first round (26%) and seven players in the second round (23%) had completed four years of college. In fact, the number 8 pick (Channing Frye) is the highest pick to have completed four years of college

This is problematic for a number of reasons, including the fact that when African American men underperform in academics, when they fail to be credentialed, they are prevented from finding a position in the world economy (because of being marginalized and out on the periphery) when they reach the end of their sports careers. And this will happen for most by the time they are 22 to 25 years of age (see especially Smith, 2007).

The problems that Meggyesy points out are further exacerbated, it could be argued, by the fact that in big-time intercollegiate sports success comes to those who already have it. Year after year after year, the names of the schools who win at football, basketball, and now women's soccer and field hockey remain virtually the same. Thus, though the majority of programs and institutions suffer from the same problems to some degree, not only the successes but also the problems are concentrated most severely in a small sub-set of these programs and institutions. It is as if Professor Robert K. Merton (1968) had in mind these teams when he coined his neologism, "the Matthew Effect," named after a passage in the Gospel of St. Matthew, which holds that patterns of biased peer recognition of authors of collaborative papers are often skewed in favor of the more established scientist. He put it this way:

> For unto everyone that hath shall be given, and he shall have abundance; but from him that hath not shall be taken away even that which he hath. (1968, p. 56)

We take these concerns seriously, about life after sports, about scrutiny, and about the failure of the collegiate sport institution (the NCAA-sanctioned programs) to deliver an education and academic credentials (when earned) to student athletes, especially African American males. We build in this chapter an examination of these topics and their impact on African Americans and the African American community at large, who seem to place at the center of ambition and even of the quintessential American dream—SportsWorld.

SportsWorld

According to *New York Times* sportswriter Robert Lipsyte, there exists an alternative world to the one we live in and he has named it "SportsWorld" (Lipsyte, 1995). In SportsWorld, there are athletes, managers, owners, who are involved in the managing and playing of contested games. For those at the top, the league owners, team owners, and even managers, SportsWorld is almost exclusively about business and making money. And while these games may have changed over the years, that is, the rules, the equipment, the uniforms, the slang, and the players, SportsWorld still offers refuge from the real world for the men and women who play these sports. Just as important, we argue, SportsWorld plays a significant role in shaping daily American culture, especially in the African American community. Want proof? Simply look at the clothing lines of many signature designers; all are in some way connected to the world of sport. Even automobile makers have special cars that in some way link to sports.

SportsWorld and African American Civil Society

It is widely accepted among scholars of race and ethnicity that anti-black forms of discrimination continue in American society. Joe Feagin in his American Sociological Association Presidential Address (2000) asserted as much (see also Bonilla-Silva 2001, 2003). We argue here that the exalted institution of sport is not immune from this disease that continues to plague American culture and society. For example, we note that African American men are *overrepresented* in the ranks of players in both intercollegiate (NCAA) and professional football (NFL) and basketball (NBA), yet they are *underrepresented* in other positions in these institutions. For example, though African American men make up half of the athletes playing football and more than 75% of the athletes playing basketball on the typical NCAA Division 1 campus, they make up only 1–10% of the male student body on these same campuses (Smith, 2007). Similarly, though African American men make up nearly half of the players in the NFL, and despite the historicity of SuperBowl XLI and two African American head coaches, there are fewer than ten African American men coaching NFL teams (Smith, 2007).

Lipsyte's (1995) critique centers on the argument that African Americans have long made contributions to this American SportsWorld culture that have remained unrecognized. We note that this is similar to the failure of White America to recognize the contributions African Americans made in building the American economy and in fighting in all American wars from the American Revolution to both World Wars to Vietnam to Iraq, with many of these important contributions coming during the 300 years of chattel slavery (see Kaplan, 1986).

Lipsyte (1995) offers a reasoned assessment of this contribution without the tone and hype of others who seem to feel that African American athletes are not conciliatory enough for the great opportunity they have been given to populate the ranks of "sport entertainers." One of the key issues that Lipsyte (2000) and we are raising is the question of what, if anything, SportsWorld owes African Americans (individuals and community) in return for their contributions. It begs the question: Do participation in and reaping the benefits of the institution of SportsWorld end with injury and/or retirement? If so, should they?

Life after Participation in SportsWorld: Does the Institution Owe the Player Anything from a Job to a Private Life to a Chance?

For a long period of time Boston Celtic superstar Bill Russell stayed away from the press and the public because he felt that the scrutiny of his private life was unfair. He felt he played the game both fair and at the highest level (and honestly) but that he also wanted, in the end, a private life.

A similarly private person, the former Los Angeles Laker superstar Kareem Abdul-Jabbar, had a somewhat different aspiration. After a stellar career as the center of the Lakers and arguably one of the best basketball players of the 20th century, he was told that before he could enter the collegiate or professional ranks as a coach he needed to take a basketball position at an Arizona high school on an Indian reservation to get some coaching experience under his belt. He was told over and over that he needed to build up his resume "as a coach" if he expected to get in the game at the NBA level. In contrast, the Boston Celtic superstar Larry Bird became a pro head coach *having never coached a game in his life*. Both Russell and Abdul-Jabbar struggled to build post-athletic careers even though there is no argument that both were the best at what they did during their time in SportsWorld.

Former Seattle Mariner, Detroit Tiger, and San Diego Padre baseball player Ruppert Jones, after 12 seasons as a pro, had no future plans. After a job offer of selling insurance that came from his neighbor, Jones is now enjoying life and happy to be a salesperson. Yet, he says: "I don't have a college education. So the satisfaction at making a success in something other than athletics is extra sweet"(*USA Today*, 2002).

Many ex-athletes find themselves in the same boat as Jones after their career playing days are over. They ask themselves, "What am I going to do now?"

Looking at the end of the career of "the fastest man alive," Florida A&M and Dallas Cowboys star Bob Hayes, further illustrates our argument that the treatment of athletes in retirement is very clearly shaped by race (and gender). While attending Florida A&M, a historically black college, Hayes won the gold medal in the 1960 Rome Olympics. He then turned that feat into a lucrative professional career with "America's" team, the Dallas Cowboys. To be sure, "Bullet Bob" Hayes had a storied career and led the way for many a track star into the National Football League. Yet, he died just another poor, black man, no longer able to cash in on his athletic prowess despite the fact that the opportunity structure, at least for him, had appeared to open up, as it had in the larger economy, such that *most* young African American men worked normal 40-hour-week jobs, though in positions that were not so flattering or lucrative.

In days gone by, ex-athletes could go to work in their respective communities in institutions such as the car wash. Today, with the changes that took place in the middle of the 20th century (1950s), principally the movement from an industrial to a post-industrial service economy, many institutions that were staples in the world of work in America have become obsolete and many have disappeared from North America altogether. The car wash itself is now automated. In fact, Minnesota Twins Hall of Famer Kirby Puckett used to remark that after retiring from baseball he wanted to open a series of carwashes around the Twin Cities area and call them "Kirby's Truck Wash."

When we look back on the research and writing that the first author has done over the last decade as well as the trials and tribulations of African American athletes, we find that much of what was a glorious beginning with Jackie Robinson has failed to come full circle. The commercial enterprise that has become the institution of sport has never become the place where African Americans can aspire to be *on a permanent basis*, after their skills have waned, even if only to escape the ghetto of poor life chances.

An accomplished amateur and professional tennis star and political activist who chronicles his life in his autobiography, *Days of Grace* (Ashe, 1993), Arthur Ashe once said that it is important in our lives to understand the dynamics that drive societal forces. This is firmly a sociological concern and was especially important to Ashe after he was forced to divulge on Wednesday, April 8, 1992, that he was HIV (human immunodeficiency virus) positive. (See the case of Earvin "Magic" Johnson as well.) That afternoon Ashe held a public news conference, hosted by Home Box Office television network (HBO), to tell the world that he was HIV-positive. After the news was out, the private side of a retired athlete's life was open like a book for all to see. Ashe's family life, his relationship with his daughter, Camera, his relationship with his wife, Jean Moutoussamy, and everything about him—especially his future—became an open book for interpretation, speculation, degradation, and inspection. From that day forward until his death on February 6, 1993, the life of this great champion was suspect.

The question that Ashe's life experience raises is this: Do African American athletes, however great and famous, ever reach a point where they can integrate into mainstream American life, without the ever-present scrutiny of their private lives and the over-attention to their race and ethnicity? If Arthur Ashe can't achieve these ends, who can?

African Americans are involved as players in all levels of sport (collegiate, Olympic, professional), and the days of the all-white teams that dominated the sport enterprise (intercollegiate and professional) will never again exist, especially in the big sports of basketball, baseball, and football (Price, 1997). Yet African Americans, ex-athletes or pure businessmen, are not represented among the power-brokers in the institution of sport. They are not represented among NCAA Division I athletic directors, they are not represented among professional head coaches, and they do not own either leagues or teams. (We note here that Robert Johnson, who made his money in the print media and later as the founder of BET, is the *only* owner of a professional team in the major sports—football, basketball,

Hofstra College basketball team, 1959–1960.

or baseball. He owns the Charlotte Bobcats, the newest team in the NBA.) For a lengthy discussion, see Smith, 2007, especially chapter 8.

SportsWorld Is Big Business: The Athletic Industrial Complex (AIC)

These issues are even more profound in the context of modern-day, 21st-century intercollegiate sport, which is such big business that even the athletes have become expendable commodities. In high schools all over the country boys and girls are preparing for "careers" in sport instead of preparing for a life of learning that would lead to successful careers in anything they would choose. (See the four-part series in *Sports Illustrated* starting with Volume 97, No. 20, November 18, 2002. What is interesting is the feature story by Kelley King entitled "Ultimate Jock School," which features the IMG sport academies in Bradenton, Florida. These institutions profess sport first, academics second). And, the likelihood that a student will graduate from high school and be prepared to enter college is significantly shaped by race.

There is also a significant race/ethnic difference in the percentage of students who leave high school eligible for college admission. About 40% of White students, 23% of African American students, and 20% of Hispanic students who started public high school graduated "college-ready" in 2002 (Greene & Winters, 2005).

Table 1. High School Graduation Rate Data by Race/Ethnicity

	African Americans	Hispanics	Whites
Regular HS Diploma	56%	52%	78%
Eligible for College Admission	23%	20%	40%
Attended College	52%	50%	65%
Earned BA	18%	16%	31%

Sources: Greene and Winters 2005; U.S. Department of Health and Human Services 1997

Many people falsely assume that these problems of academically under-prepared students heading to college to play sports are limited to the realm of "big-time" college athletics. Yet, even schools like Williams College in Massachusetts, a small, competitive, liberal arts college, has to adjust its admission standards to ensure that the entering class is not dominated by student athletes recruited to Williams to play sports. It is important to note that at small colleges that field the same number of competitive teams, an entering class of 400 students may be constructed such that 20% are student athletes, whereas at large, state universities student athletes may comprise only 1 or 2% of each entering class. And though we do not assume that student athletes at Williams are academically under-prepared, the point is that even at the level of small colleges the model of big-time sports has taken hold.

All of the above affects the African American athletes especially hard. These athletes, many from impoverished backgrounds with weak family structures, start at an early age to hone their athletic skills with the hopes of landing in the professional leagues some day. The lure of life as a professional athlete, now depicted in off-the-court shows such as MTV's *Cribs*, has resulted in an increasing number of high school student athletes foregoing the education that awaits them in college and taking the shortcut to the pros. This phenomenon has been taken to new heights lately with some of these athletes jumping straight from high school to the National Basketball Association and with multi-million dollar contracts for those few likely to land a team position. The current rage is LeBron James, who was a star high school basketball player at St. Vincent–St. Mary High School in Akron, Ohio. Before being picked first in the NBA draft by the Cleveland Cavaliers, James was being touted as the best high school player ever and his high school reaped the financial benefit of this sport prowess as ESPN televised on pay-per-view TV several games, giving St. Vincent–St. Mary's $10,000 to $15,000 per game. All of the games that James played in at the end of his high school career were sold out.

Other examples include the pro teams' choosing, in the 2001 draft, Kwame Brown, Tyson Chandler, and Eddy Curry before they picked college graduate and proven winner Shane Battier of Duke University. In the 2004 NBA draft, eight of the first 19 picks were either high school athletes or foreigners, sending the message that college does not matter. Dwight Howard made $1.8 million in compensation for his first three years as a pro. It is important to note that Howard became the third high school player taken as the first overall pick in the National Basketball Association draft, ahead of established and trained collegiate players. Finally, in the 2005 NBA draft, seven high school students were drafted in the first round. [We note, however, that this practice has recently been prohibited by the league ownership and the 2005 NBA draft marked the last time athletes could be drafted into the NBA straight out of high school and at the age of 17 or 18.]

If we pay attention to the composition of the last three or four intercollegiate "Final Four" basketball tournaments and the last three or four NBA drafts, it becomes evident that the infusion of foreign players has become a reality, thus making it more difficult for young African American men to (a) pick up an education at the college level that also gives them credentials and (b) satisfy their dream of playing professional basketball (Smith 2007).

This reality has become a frustration for African Americans as it was recently portrayed in the on-camera exchange between the basketball all-star Charles Barkley and Kenny Smith while they were announcing a NBA game. Barkley bet FOX Sports broadcaster Smith that Chinese player Yao Ming would not score more than 18 points in his inaugural NBA season. The next night Ming scored 20 points. In the end, though, Smith allowed Barkley off the hook and brought to the studio a donkey, whose tail Barkley kissed. Looking on in the studio was Minnesota Governor Jesse Ventura. What this exhange demonstrates is the high level of frustration for African Americans who once thought of the NBA as an automatic escalator out of the ghetto. Yet, American society continues to recklessly send the message to young African American males, in essence saying, "You do not need an education to be successful in life. Just learn how to do something with a ball."

Harry Edwards considers this a myopic approach and one that ultimately damages individuals by setting the stage for their exploitation. It also damages communities, he argues, because it takes the focus of young people off of academics and other pursuits, and narrowly focuses them on an arena (sports) where the probability for success is minute. In many ways, we agree.

Every summer literally hundreds of African American parents take their young men to the Wake Forest campus for football and basketball camp. On the other side of campus, White parents take their children for science, foreign language, and debate camp. Wake Forest University has one of the highest ranked debate teams among all colleges and universities nationally, and of the hundreds of young men and women in attendance at camp, few are African American. Why are these camps so segregated? How can we explain this phenomenon when it involves children who are too young to have been already selected in or out of other options based on talents and skills? (Most of these observations were made by one author across a long time period. This pattern was seen in a 15-year tenure at Washington State University and a 4-year tenure at Pacific Lutheran University. For 10 years, the same pattern was seen at Wake Forest University. One author's two sons went to sport camps and science camps, thus giving him the chance to observe up close and analyze sociologically the patterns discussed.)

One popular explanation focuses on individual choice: African American parents push their children toward sports, whereas White parents, at least middle-class and affluent Whites, push their children toward academic pursuits. And, this is in part true.

Certainly we see the outrageous behavior of many parents who drive hundreds and sometimes thousands of miles so that their *10-year-olds* can compete in the AAU sponsored national tournament for basketball or baseball. Parents of "elite" athletes pay tens of thousands of dollars annually and pull their children out of mainstream schools so that they can attend academies like IMG in Florida, work out at Bela Karoli's gym in Houston, Texas, or train at the Olympic complex in Colorado Springs, Colorado. And, for the parents of high-profile college athletes, the desire for and anticipation of the big contracts their sons will someday sign often lead them to spend outrageous amounts of money before their sons are drafted. For example, while still in high school, and anticipating the NBA contract that would come his way, LeBron James "bought" his mother a Hummer. While a sophomore at Wake Forest, Chris Paul behaved similarly. Finally, Reggie Bush, Heisman Trophy winner in 2005, faces an NCAA investigation in regards to an arrangement between his parents and San Diego businessman Michael Michaels, who is alleged to have given his parents a $750,000 house to live in during his final year at USC (ESPN, 2006).

But, sometimes the over-involvement and anticipation of the parent negatively impacts the athlete. It is important to examine the case of another Wake Forest basketball hopeful, Eric Williams. During his junior year at Wake Forest, Williams's mother acted as Eric's agent and negotiated his exploration of his NBA draft status. Determining that he would make more money if he returned to play his senior year at Wake Forest, Eric's mother made the decision that he would return. In the end, Williams performed poorly his senior year and was not drafted. We are not suggesting that he should have gone into the draft at the end of his junior year, nor are we suggesting that his mother should not have been involved in his decisions. We are suggesting that in some cases the interests of the parents of student athletes contradict the interests of the athletes themselves (Smith, 2007; see also Friend, 2002, for a discussion of LeBron James and his parents).

We're also suggesting that whereas most parents would never give their children advice to drop out of college at the end of their junior year and try to enroll in medical school early (hastening the onset of the kinds of paychecks we associate with the medical profession), parents of elite athletes often think they know more than coaches, scouts, and advisors with regards to their children's prospects. This is, we think, what Edwards was talking about.

However, it is also important to recognize that the majority of scholars who argue from the position Edwards established are intellectuals and people for whom the choice *appears to be:* athletics or academics. Yet, the construction of this choice is shaped by social class. The truth is that for the vast majority of American families, White or African American, the choices for their children are not between being a *professional athlete* or being a *professional* (medical doctor, college professor, lawyer, etc.), but rather they are between being a *professional athlete* or being a *blue-collar or low-wage service sector worker.*

Most of the athletes and their families that we described above did not make a decision to push a young man into the singular pursuit of sport when he might otherwise have become the next Harry Edwards (who rose out of the ghetto via his own hard work and opportunities that opened up for him as a student athlete) or Colin Powell by attending the best schools and earning a post-graduate degree. Rather, these young men come primarily out of families and communities where work is vanishing (Wilson 1996). And with the jobs goes access to the "American Dream."

Block and colleagues (2006) demonstrated that the coupling of incredible inflation in the cost of housing, health care, and higher education (the costs of which have quadrupled) with the decline in real wages (minimum wage has doubled, rather than quadrupled, in value in the last 25 years) has severely limited the access working Americans have to the American Dream. Block and colleagues argued that the dream that was within the reach of working Americans during the 20th century is out of reach for all but the affluent in the 21st century. Through much of the 20th century, working families, even those working at the bottom of the salary ladder, could afford a portion of what they call The American Dream. For example, a conscientious working family could achieve the American Dream in 1973 by taking on a few extra hours at work, saving carefully, and so on. Today, the typical working class family is living on two minimum wage incomes, earning less than half of what is necessary to achieve the American Dream. And blocked access to the American Dream is felt disproportionately by African American families (Hattery & Smith, 2007). The inability to buy into the American Dream has a significant impact on the priority many African American families place on athletic pursuits.

Arguing from the perspective of the average American, who can no longer buy into the American Dream by working full time, who cannot afford to send his or her children to college (at $40,000 per year) and therefore has no hope that they will enter the professions, the intense and myopic focus on sports does not seem so foolish or shortsighted.

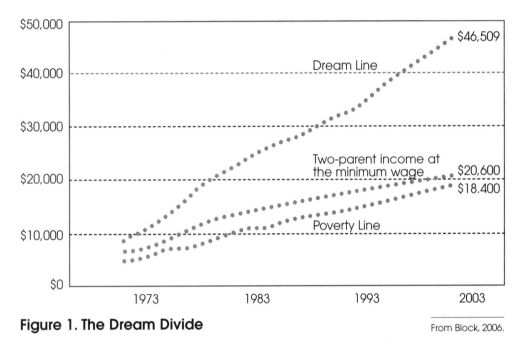

Figure 1. The Dream Divide

From Block, 2006.

In short, when African American parents push their children toward sports, by enrolling them in football camp or driving them around the country to compete in AAU basketball, they may be making what looks to them like a good decision given the ratio of athletic to academic scholarships, given the quality of schools most African American children are forced to attend, given their perceptions of access for African Americans to institutions of higher learning, and given their perceptions of the accessibility African Americans have to certain professions.

In fact, the data suggest that African Americans, like White Americans, would be better off preparing their children for the intellectual and academic life of college as it is this pathway that leads most Americans, including African Americans, to the American Dream.

We argue that until access is truly open in all institutions, we cannot begin to analyze individual choices, as they are constrained severely by the structural limitations. And, these limitations, even those that have been partially lifted, are perceived to be real and thus they become real.("If men define situations as real, they are real in their consequences." See W. I. Thomas & Dorothy Swaine Thomas, 1928. *The Child in America*. New York: Knopf. Quote on page 572.) These constraints and barriers shape human behavior at both the individual and group levels.

The (Negative) Impact of African American Male Athletes as Role Models

In looking back over the extensive time that the first author has spent researching the institution of sport, we argue that our society has become sport crazed to the extent that anything goes in the name of sports. Automobiles are sold using sport as the metaphor for success. The message is rather simple: If you buy this car, then you are successful. Sex, once a private matter, is now sold both directly and indirectly in the name of sport. Sexual images are everywhere and as a society we have grown cynical or bored or accepting of virtually anything—even rape—in regards to the sexual behavior of celebrated athletes, movie stars, and even politicians as high up as a former United States president. Kobe Bryant, whether he was guilty or not of rape, had sex with a stranger less than an hour after meeting her. We argue that Kobe Bryant should have been put on administrative leave beginning with his arrest. Furthermore, his contract re-negotiations (he signed on July 16, 2004 for $136 million across seven years) should have been put off until after the trial. In retrospect it should be noted that the Lakers had two chances to do the right thing: (1) to place Bryant on administrative leave and (2) hold off on any further discussion of his future contract with the team. They failed on both accounts! (Smith & Hattery, 2006a).

Author bell hooks reports in her book *We Real Cool* (2004) that acts like this one by African American men underscore the stereotype about African American males and sexuality. She put it thus:

> Undoubtedly, sexuality has been the site of many a black male's fall from grace. Irrespective of class, status, income, or level of education, for many black men sexuality remains the place where dysfunctional behavior first rears its ugly head. (p. 87)

Not only do we "tolerate" such abhorrent sexual behavior as Kobe Bryant or Ruben Patterson (who was convicted of raping his children's nanny) but the majority of the sexual activities of athletes, especially African American male athletes, has been glorified. Wilt Chamberlain reportedly had sex with 20,000 different women. Patrick Ewing talked in public and to a grand jury about his visits (along with the entire New York Knicks team) to a famous strip club (The Gold Club) in Atlanta. We have to ask the question then: What impact does this glorification of promiscuous, largely anonymous sex by these high-profile athletes have on the attitudes, behavior, and dreams of young African American men who look to these same athletes as "role models"? We know that in the past decade there has been an increase in the number of cases of rape and battering of high school and college-age girls by their male counterparts (also see Hattery & Smith, 2007).

This is tragic enough, as it ruins so many young lives, but we also argue here that the changes in SportsWorld, namely the high salaries of the athletes and the glorification of their sexual promiscuity, create an even stronger impetus for young, largely African American men to strive for this life and to emulate it at whatever level they can (as high school and college athletes as well as professionals). The results of this kind of role modeling, one we deem as negative, are devastating to the African American community (Smith & Hattery, 2006b).

"Negative" role-modeling is not limited to sexual behavior. In fact, high-profile athletes have been in trouble recently for a number of things, including possession of illegal drugs and even homicide. We argue that when the name of the game becomes all about the money, we see some very unsavory practices. Many blame this on the kind of benefits and cash money that are being thrown around in both intercollegiate and professional sports (Simone, 2003; Benedict, 2004), hence luring the most un-likely "athletes" to try for entry onto athletic teams. Take, for example, the case of Sam Mack, who was arrested on a variety of charges from drugs to armed robbery to accessory to murder. When one program, in an attempt to salvage its reputation, dumped him, he was immediately picked up by another. Controversy surrounded Jerry Tarkanian when he was head coach at UNLV, and his reputation for taking troubled players and junior college transfers was pushed even further amid reports that a player or two came to Las Vegas to play for him after serving time at Rikers Island (Tarkanian, 2003). As long as money runs the game, it appears that the end is not in sight (see Benedict, 2004 for a lengthy discussion of professional athletes and crime and especially college athletes and crime, while the athletes are receiving scholarships).

How, then, can we look past the kind of relationships young men and women seek as they plan for a future in sport when the field they are choosing is deep into trouble? Although there are no easy answers to this difficult question, it is well known that something needs to be done and can be done if, as a society, there is the will to take big risks.

Access to the Opportunity Structure or Cordoning-Off?

To be sure, African American Civil Society has come to rely on the folklore that it is in SportsWorld where the real welcome mat has been placed for African Americans who play sports. Is it? And, what are the ramifications of this? If we take the analogy sociologist Wright provides of cordoning-off, is this in fact a case of cordoning-off of African Americans, especially males, into SportsWorld and thus, by definition, out of the professions and all other aspects of a free and open market economy? How convenient if African Americans accept this willingly and line up to be marched off to this competitive and highly limited sector of the burgeoning economy, for then they are not challenging White Americans for their positions in this larger and over the long term more lucrative market economy. As University of Wisconsin sociologist Erik Olin Wright put it, African Americans are settling for a life of vulnerability, exploitation, marginalization, and being cordoned off. Wright (1998) stated it thus:

> In the case of labor power, a person can cease to have economic value in capitalism if it cannot be deployed productively. This is the essential condition of people in the "underclass." They are oppressed because they are denied access to various kinds of productive resources, above all the necessary means to acquire the skills needed to make their labor power saleable. As a result they are not consistently exploited. Understood this way, the underclass consists of human beings who are largely expendable from the point of view of the logic of capitalism. Like Native Americans who became a landless underclass in the nineteenth cen-

tury, repression rather than incorporation is the central mode of social control directed toward them. Capitalism does not need the labor power of unemployed inner city youth. The material interests of the wealthy and privileged segments of American society would be better served if these people simply disappeared. However, unlike in the nineteenth century, the moral and political forces are such that direct genocide is no longer a viable strategy. The alternative, then, is to build prisons and cordon off the zones of cities in which the underclass lives. (p. 153)

Following sociologist Wright we note that far too many African American males are in prison for crimes that can be argued are not threatening to other members of our society, primarily drug *possession* offenses (Hattery & Smith, 2007).

> **U.S. Prison Population**
> White men: 900,000
> White women: 64,000
> Black women: 84,000
> Black men: 1,000,000
> Total: 2.3 Million
>
> (U.S. Bureau of Justice Statistics, 2006)

Because of the length of sentences and the stigma of felonies, many of these men exit prison with no real alternatives toward shaping a gainful future (see specially Pager, 2003). Before their prison sentences, during the time spent in prison, and after prison, African American males spend an inordinate amount of time thinking about and playing sports. It is an identification that is central to African American Civil Society. Yet, we argue that as long as White Americans create and sustain images and perceptions of and for African Americans that their surest way to the American Dream is through athletics, African Americans will remain cordoned off in an area where very few will make it and most will not. And, they will not try to compete alongside Whites for the money and power that is available in business, the professions, and politics. In the next section of this chapter we explore more fully how this identification unfolds. (For a lengthy discussion of the cordoning-off of African Americans into prisons, ghettos, and SportWorld, see Hattery & Smith, 2007; Smith, 2007.]

Sports and African American Civil Society: Identity Politics

When you attend in person on a crisp fall Saturday afternoon or tune the TV to a high-profile collegiate or professional sports game, especially football or basketball, it is possible to become blinded for a moment by the revelry of the band, the cheerleaders, and the spectacle and forget that you are *in the U.S.*, observing these sports in North America. Why? Sport sociologist Harry Edwards put it this way in 1982:

> This is why, when you turn on television . . . all too often, with the exception of the quarterback and a few other positions, it doesn't look like Georgia playing Texas, it looks like Ghana playing Nigeria. (p. 17)

The essence of this quote is that as more and more African American athletes get involved in organized sports, the more negative consequences from the "Athletic Industrial Complex." In addition, negative images of African American male athletes as thugs and sexually promiscuous will engulf African American Civil Society at a much more intense level than it has previously.

The negative impact and fallout of two events simultaneously (1) this cordoning-off into SportsWorld and (2) the pervasive power of sports in creating identity for African American males is especially devastating as the social and economic order disintegrates for African American Civil Society, thus today creating one of the clearest-ever class divisions in the history of African Americans. Reasons for this are profound and deeply complex. They include the explosion of the number of African American males who sit in county, state, and federal prisons, the numbers of African American men killed at war, and the lack of serious representation in the U.S. Congress and in corporate America. And they include, as the subject closest to this chapter, the lack of representation as coaches, managers, and owners of sport teams. African American Civil Society has been "torn asunder" and observations tell us that the bipolar results are a clearly divided class society within the Black community.

This class gulf, fueled by SportsWorld, means that some African American men are among the most highly paid Americans (even while others of their membership makes up fully *half* of the entire U.S. prison population), yet African Americans have not made inroads in corporate leadership or in national politics. This is perhaps best illustrated by the important distinction between being paid (income) and wealth. Though African American male athletes command exorbitant salaries, they have access to very little wealth, as wealth is more generally accumulated through ownership. The richest Americans, those with the most wealth, are people like Bill Gates (Microsoft) and the Waltons (family of Sam Walton the founder of WalMart) (see especially Hattery & Smith, 2007; Shapiro, 2004).

Outside of the sporting arena these divisions show up for African Americans in ways such as, on the one hand, the growing Black middle class, and on the other, the growing Black underclass. It is the increasing African American underclass that deserves more of our attention as sociologists, for it is in these homes that the increasing aspirations of athletic success are "nurtured." That is to say, more and more of the African American males (and increasingly females) who want to be like Michael Jordan and like Magic Johnson or even "Flo-Jo" Florence Griffith Joyner come from poverty backgrounds.

The following table shows how African Americans and Whites view making it to the next level in sport—the professional ranks, or what the young athletes themselves call "going pro." The following table reports the mean scores on a scale of 1 to 5 with 5 being the most probable and 1 being the least probable.

Table 2. Professional Sports Aspirations	African American	White
Expect to have career in professional sports	4.52	3.28
Believe professional sport is best way to become economically successful	3.08	2.3

Source: K. Beamon and Patricia Bell, University of Oklahoma (2002), unpublished data

No matter what one thinks about sports as the pathway to success for African Americans, in fact, it is not the panacea it seems to be. How then do we explain the phenomenon of so many African American parents pushing their children toward athletics, when in fact the probability for access to the American Dream is so much greater through the pathway provided by the professions? We argue that there are three important forces at work that are necessary in order to understand what otherwise appears to be a foolish choice:

1. First, the media plays a powerful role in shaping perceptions of opportunity. Many studies of race and gender suggest that minorities and women have much less exposure in the media, and when they are portrayed, the range of ways in which they are portrayed is significantly narrower than it is for White men. Glassner (2000) demonstrates, for example, that African American men are depicted in only three primary roles: as an entertainer, as an athlete, and as a criminal. Thus, we argue that regardless of the reality of options for African Americans, the media strongly shapes perceptions and these perceptions become the basis for judgment and action.

2. Second, access to higher education, particularly at elite institutions and professional schools (medical school, law school, MBA programs) has only very recently been opened up for African Americans. And, the price of higher education has risen four times faster than working class wages, such that attendance at elite institutions is restricted to the affluent. Thus, parents who are not affluent and hope their children will be able to go to college must hope that their children will be offered a scholarship in order to make attendance affordable.

   On the Wake Forest campus, there are 4 or 5 times more athletic scholarships than there are academic/merit scholarships. Thus, it is clear that many parents push their children down the road of earning an athletic scholarship because the odds are simply greater of earning one. And, this is particularly the case for African American families whose children, more so than Whites of a similar social class, attend the kinds of underresourced schools that leave them without the skills necessary to perform well enough to earn academic or merit-based scholarships.

3. Third, African Americans have been cordoned off from institutions of higher learning and the professions for so long that even as these institutions open up slightly for African Americans, the perception in the African American community remains that these institutions are not for them. We cite here the poignant example provided by one of our own students, Josh Howard:

Josh Howard attended Wake Forest on an athletic scholarship and is currently contributing significantly to the Dallas Mavericks basketball team. Josh grew up in the segregated section of Winston-Salem known as "East Winston," just a few steps away from the Wake Forest campus, which is surrounded by gates and has gate houses staffed by security officers from 10 p.m. to 6 a.m. Josh recalls that despite passing the Wake Forest gates literally hundreds of times, he never went onto campus, and he had no idea what went on "behind those hedges." (Josh shared this story with *Sports Illustrated*, and with the author in private communication.)

Despite the fact that Wake Forest began admitting African Americans in the early 1970s, the student body remains only 5% to 6% African American. This phenomenon can be explained in part by the story provided by Josh. Even though the "Whites only" sign has been removed from the Wake Forest campus, if African Americans perceive that the campus is not really open to them, except as athletes and custodial staff, they will not pursue their educational goals there, as they do not see this as a viable option toward attaining the American Dream.

In short, the aspirations of many young African American men (and less so women) are out of whack with social reality. The professional teams have *never* been an automatic pathway to accessing the American Dream for African Americans, and with the high specialization necessary to become a star player in today's sports, they never will be.

Few Americans are aware that there are only approximately 1,600 African American men making money playing professional sports, but there are 1,700 African Americans who earn a Ph.D. every year, and there are more than 41,000 African American medical doctors, 25 times more than the number playing professional sports. The Harvard humanities scholar, Henry Louis Gates put it thus (2004):

> Guess how many black athletes are playing professional basketball, football, and baseball combined? About 1400 . . . In fact there are more board certified black cardiologists than there are black professional basketball players. (p. A10)

Although used in a different context, the theoretical dimensions of Steele's "stereotype threat" apply here as well. That is, Steele's (1999) research on stereotype threat is instructive; in discussing academic achievement he maintains that even high-performing, achievement-identified African American students are affected by racist stereotypes of Blacks as being less intelligent than Whites. This is not at all surprising in a racially antagonistic society, in which at every turn African Americans and other underrepresented minority group members must "prove themselves." Athletes are fearful in this way, too, in that they are socialized to succeed, that is, to win. But, that said, research comparing the performance and statistics mounted by White and African American athletes demonstrates clearly that African Americans have to outperform Whites in order to earn a place on the team (Smith, 2007).

Much of this failure is an outcome of the exploitation these young men experience in college. For these men, their athletic prowess is a ticket to a college education that would otherwise be unattainable because they could not afford it, could not get admitted, or both. Yet, once they arrive on campus they find that the access to the education portion of the scholarship deal they signed on to is blocked. On most Division IA campuses, student athletes cannot take classes after 2:00 P.M. so as to meet practice, travel, and competition schedules. This will virtually rule out majors that require labs, field work, or internships.

Second, athletes in sports with heavy travel, such as basketball or golf, may miss 25% or more of their scheduled class meetings. In fact, 2003 marked the 20th anniversary of a U.S. Supreme Court decision that prohibited the NCAA from requiring universities to comply with their plan for televising football games. "The issue without a doubt is the pursuit of money, and what money does in excessive coaches' salaries and greater bonding debt," stated Welch Suggs, sports columnist with the *Chronicle of Higher Education*. "Intercollegiate sports have got to stop this arms race" (2003, p. A32). Finally, these athletes are advised (or required) simply to take enough classes to remain eligible with no attention to progress toward a major or a career. After their eligibility is expired and used up, these athletes are discarded. Many never receive the precious educational credential they (and their parents) were promised as 17-year-old recruits. This is yet another layer of the cordoning-off. Student athletes are effectively segregated from the general student population and are prohibited from the opportunity to earn the same credential, with the same training, as their non-athlete counterparts.

For example, many college and university faculty across the country are aware of the process by which student athletes receive, each semester, their course schedules. A player for Crenshaw High School, Reggie Dymally, always knew he would attend college and took care with his academic work to ensure that this would happen. But as a student athlete, and one of five African Americans on the baseball team, he encountered something contradictory at the University of Hawaii as he suited up to play. Reggie signed up for classes in English, a business course, and a computer science course. This was in 1980. When he received his final course schedule it was changed. He put it this way:

> They changed all my classes. I had a class on how to coach football. I had a class on how to coach soccer. I had a swimming class and a military science class. That was the most asinine thing of all. They taught us how to shoot a rifle. I didn't leave L.A. to learn how to shoot guns . . . It was a terrible insult . . . I was like, no, you want me to play baseball for you, you give me something that's not baseball. People don't see that. They wonder why black athletes don't have an education, but it's not always because they don't want one. Coaches direct you into easy classes so they're sure you'll stay eligible to play—which is different from them being interested in you learning something so you can succeed in life. (Sokolove, 2004, pp.155–156)

In contrast to the past, even a few decades ago, when many student athletes graduated and went on to professional careers in or outside of sports, the Athletic Industrial Complex (AIC) has resulted in a system that rarely provides a ticket out of an impoverished life. Why? Because the AIC transforms the enterprise of collegiate athletics from a way in which students can participate in sports while earning their credentials to a virtual minor league for professional sports, and transforms it, too, from a pastime designed to engender school spirit and camaraderie to a money-making machine.

With virtually no real options available for a career in sport after athletes are no longer playing the games that have consumed a great deal of their time and energy, an enterprise into which they have put all of their hopes and dreams, the future is very grim. They leave the sport with no future and with no other training or credential earned along the way. For African American male athletes, the ubiquitous "Dumb Black Jock" is a continuing racial stereotype that has been soundly embedded in contemporary American folklore. Like many stereotypes, it may not be true, but its persistence makes it even more difficult for athletes, except those who have achieved the highest level of success, to find opportunities outside of SportsWorld. Athletes whose careers ended in college, or who were virtually unknown despite their names on the rosters of professional teams, are quickly forgotten. Who remembers Craig Hodges or even Darryl Henley? (Craig Hodges played on several successful Chicago Bulls basketball teams when the player roster had Scotty Pipen, Dennis Rodman, and Michael Jordan. He faded from view when he started to ask (complain) for more playing minutes, thereby confusing his role as a support player with the role of the superstar. And, can anyone forget Darryl Henley, who had several good years with the St. Louis Rams as a defense player. Henley went to the federal prison at Marion, Illinois, in April 1977 to start a 41-year sentence for trafficking in drugs and plotting the murders of St. Louis rams cheerleader Tracy Donahue and Judge Gary Taylor.)

Those athletes who live on in honor, dignity, respect, and who are the embodiment of being true role models are the very ones we sometimes forget, remembering instead those who make poor yet memorable choices, athletes like Mike Tyson or Ray Carruth. (Mike Tyson is, of course, remembered because he served time in prison for raping Robyn Washington, and then after his release, for biting off Evander Holyfield's ear in a prize fight. Ray Carruth is remembered for setting up the murder of his pregnant girlfriend; their child survived to live life without his mother and with his father in prison.)

Here is the irony: though African Americans are over-represented in Sports-World as players (not coaches, managers, owners, or administrators), and though they are under-represented in fields such as medicine, the odds that an African American will become a medical doctor are 25 times higher than the odds that he or she will play professional sports, and an African American is 75 times more likely to enter the most prestigious professions (medicine, law, and the academy) than to play professional sports (see Smith, 2007). Yet, because of the media focus on professional athletes (not medical doctors) and because of the glorification of the career (we can credit shows such as MTV's *Cribs*, which allows us to see the high life that Shaquille O'Neill and other players live), young African American men "study" to become the next Michael Jordan rather than the next Floyd J. Malveaux, M.D., Ph.D., who specializes in asthma and in closing the racial gap in the treatment of asthma. The effects of this focus are devastating to African American Civil Society.

How? Why? Because African Americans, especially young men, fail to develop their intellectual talents and put all of the energy instead into pursuing an athletic dream that, though more glorious, is riddled with negativity (crime, drugs, and sexual promiscuity) and is also significantly less likely to become reality. And when the singular pursuit of athletics is unsuccessful, many African American men will drop out of the system of education entirely, sometimes even before the end of high school.

From *New York Times* columnist Bob Herbert's very sociological observation on the deeper meaning of the impact of dropping out of high school on both America and on African American Civil Society in particular, we learn the following (July 21, 2005, Op-Ed):

▼ High school dropouts, on average, earn $9,245 less per year than high school graduates.

▼ The poverty rate for families headed by dropouts is more than twice that for families headed by high school graduates.

▼ Dropouts are much more likely to be unemployed, less likely to vote, and more likely to be imprisoned than high school graduates.

For those concerned about the state of leadership in America, and who wonder where the next generation of leaders will come from, I can tell you it's not likely to emerge from the millions upon millions of dropouts we're setting loose in the land. (p. A10)

Hence, it is especially important for African American males who look to athletics as the "ticket out of the ghetto" not to be fooled when they see that three of the first five or six first-round picks in the NBA draft come directly out of high school, delivering the message that schooling is far less important than dunking a basketball. The odds that they will be among the high school students who make it out are more remote than winning the lottery. And certainly their chances to escape the life of poverty in which they grew up are far higher if they complete high school and get some post-secondary education in the form of technical training or a college degree. That, according to Herbert and others, is the real ticket out!

Although the numbers that demonstrate the odds are very clear, it is the stories behind the numbers that speak the loudest. After many, many years of trying to play organized sports and then finding out that there will not be a "rainbow" at the end, many of these young men end up as failures. The players whose lives illustrate this are many. Here we profile two: Lloyd "Sweet Pea" Daniels and Earl "The Goat" Manigault.

Lloyd "Sweet Pea" Daniels has a huge reputation as a legendary playground basketball player from New York City. His biography has him a better player by the age of 15 than Kareem Abdul-Jabbar, Larry Bird, and Magic Johnson all rolled into one. The problem is that even though Daniels' ambitions were high (for playing professional basketball) he had little in the way of self-control and ended up on the heap-pile of discarded players.

One plus in the brief life of Daniels is that many believed in him, including the legendary coach Jerry Tarkanian who, as the head basketball coach at University of Nevada Las Vegas (UNLV), was able to pull strings and get Daniels admitted, even though he never graduated from high school.

Daniels' basketball career ended like so many other young African American men as a result of uncontrollble drug habits, drug dealing, being shot, and ending up in the criminal justice system.

Earl "The Goat" Manigault without question is known to basketball aficionados as one of the greatest players to lace up sneakers. He played in and around New York City. In a powerful book on basketball, *The City Game* by Pete Axthelm, we are provided with one of the first analyses of The Goat under the chapter title "The Fallen Idol: The Harlem Tragedy of Earl Manigault." The Goat's abilities are legendary and even show up in a HBO movie, wherein his feat of taking quarters off the top of the backboard is highlighted.

For us, though, the issue is not this athletic prowess but the failed ability to carry the talent to even greater heights. The Goat became a haunted drug addict and in the end never made it to the NBA even though he held court with the best of his day, including Connie Hawkins and Lew Alcindor (Kareem Abdul-Jabbar).

What is important here, as well, is that the rate of failure for African American males to make it to professional sport teams wreaks havoc inside the African America community, as the preparation for careers out of sports has not been fully developed, in part because access has been denied, to education and to non-sports careers.

SportsWorld: The Future Is Midnight Basketball and AND1, Or Is It?

Scholars have argued that sports and SportsWorld play an important role in the African American community (for a discussion, see Smith, 2007; Harris, 1998).

> Athletics is to the Black community what technology is to the Japanese and what oil is to the Arabs. (Harris, p. 3)

Why? We argue that there are many important and logical reasons. Sports provided leisure and were among the first social and professional realms to be integrated. In terms of the role that sports played as a form of leisure in the African American community, we note that during segregation, for example, the Negro Baseball Leagues provided entertainment for African Americans. The Negro Baseball Leagues provided family entertainment and also a social outlet for courtship. In terms of their second function, sports were important because they offered an opportunity for integration that was otherwise blocked. For example, Major League Baseball was integrated by Satchel Paige and Jackie Robinson 15 years before the official legal end to segregation (in the *Brown v. the Board of Education* decision of 1954) and decades before any real movement toward desegregation in public space, housing, education, or the work place. We note here the long journey toward integration in sports. Boxing, for example is one of the first sports to integrate with Jack Johnson, yet other sports, especially those associated with the country club (tennis, golf, and swimming) and even NASCAR and ice hockey exist in only a limited form of integration even today, in the 21st century.

One of the negative consequences of the integration of Major League Baseball for African American Civil Society was the demise of the Negro Leagues. Because African Americans could not attend Major League Baseball games, they turned to other sports to fill this void in leisure. We note, for example, that based on our general observation, rather than empirical research, we subscribe to the argument made by Robert Putnam (2001) that a decline in social capital in the African American community can be directly linked to the death of bowling leagues. Bowling once served as family recreation in the African American community. Though bowling alleys, like all other public spaces, were segregated by race, they were family friendly. Men and women bowled in leagues (replete with team shirts), and the alley provided space for their children to play and hang out. Thus, bowling provided a mechanism for the maintenance of social capital and family bonds in the African American community.

Despite the death of bowling, the power of sports in creating and shaping identity politics for African Americans can be traced to the fact that sports provided two key things. First, it was one of the first occupations to be integrated. And second, especially in the last 30 years or so, it provided the kind of economic power that served as a "ticket out of the ghetto." Namely, the over-representation of African American males in high-profile, televised sports helps to keep sports and SportsWorld central to the identity politics of African Americans, especially males, and to African American Civil Society more generally.

In order to illustrate the power that SportsWorld has in shaping the identity politics of the African American community, we point to the recent developments of both "Midnight Basketball" and "Streetball."

Midnight Basketball and Community Action

Midnight Basketball (MB) is one community response to complacency and failure among African America males. Never mind that White youth have no attraction to or representation in MB, it is assumed that MB is rooted in African American Civil Society. Douglas Hartmann (2004) studied MB and stated this:

> This reminds us that the connections between basketball and Blackness run so deep and were so taken for granted, they almost do not need saying. (p. 351)

And, in fact, Hartmann argued that MB is not only rooted in African American Civil Society because of the stereotypes and assumptions that African Americans have a penchant for basketball, but that MB and its funding were explicitly tied to crime legislation that targeted low-income African American neighborhoods. Hartmann (2004) demonstrated that members of the U.S. Congress, mostly male and White, found MB to be a good solution to the crime "problem" that they saw exploding in the urban (read "Black") ghettos. Why? Because we all know that African Americans have a penchant for basketball.

An examination of the main "goals" of Midnight Basketball makes this clear. The main goals, as stated in Congressional crime legislation, are:

▼ Provide youth with educational and drug prevention information and presentations weekly

▼ Improve the self-esteem of youth and enhance their interpersonal skills

▼ Continue to build relationships in the community that have a positive role in the lives of youth

▼ Strengthen the relationship between local police and communities

We note that the rules of the MB league require the presence of two uniformed police officers at every venue.

We also note that it's interesting that there are no sport leagues in any other racial or ethnic communities that are explicitly designed to fight crime. There are no Midnight Tennis Leagues in the affluent suburbs designed to keep corporate executives from pilfering their companies (see for example cases at Enron, Tyco, and WorldCom and the cases of executives like Michael Milken and Martha Stewart).

Midnight Basketball was, however, filling another niche as well. Built on the history of the very street courts on which players like Sweet Pea and Earl the Goat became famous, it provided an opportunity for building community identity for low-income African Americans. It came, as it were, to replace the bowling leagues that Putnam (2001) identified as signaling the decline of social capital. Websites that profile MB leagues demonstrate or advertise that the games are a family-friendly place. These sites show pictures of young children who are entertaining themselves while their parents play basketball, which is reminiscent of the bowling leagues.

Indeed, what made Midnight Basketball attractive was that it held the promise of reestablishing both the social fabric and the moral fiber of life for these at-risk young men—the type of improvement that was essentially what George Bush meant to highlight with his thousand-points-of-light vision, a set of ideas that his son would call "compassionate conservatism," and Robert Putnam (2000) would later call "civic engagement." And if Putnam's thesis was formulated as a critique of bowling alone, MB offered precisely the practice of playing basketball together that Putnam took as ideal. This is precisely the way that Chicago Housing Authority Chairman Vincent Lane promoted the program to the public: "We're going to try to move them down the road to being contributing citizens" (Hartmann p. 356).

In the late 1990s, the U.S. Congress cut the funds for Midnight Basketball and corporations took over. "Streetball," which has its roots in the hard courts of New York, the places where Earl the Goat and Sweat Pea became legends, has only recently become institutionalized via a company called AND1. AND1, which started in 1993 as an athletic apparel company, quickly morphed into a sort of "All-Star Wrestling" of basketball when the company executives realized that they could not compete in the market with Nike, Reebok, and Adidas. They decided, instead,

Courtesy of Drew Dionisio

Midnight Basketball provided an opportunity for building community.

to institutionalize a street form of basketball that entered the mainstream consciousness with films such as *Hoop Dreams* (Frey, 2004).

AND1 recruits players (many of whom played in college but did not make it to the NBA) through a series of localized tryouts as well as recently through a "reality series" that has Magic Johnson choosing the next AND1 star. AND1 then stages games in arenas throughout the United States. The players all have nicknames, such as "White Chocolate" that are reminiscent of names like "Stone Cold" that we see in the World Wrestling Federation (WWF).

AND1 "streetball" has strong influences from hip-hop culture as well. It is part athletics and part entertainment. It targets an African American crowd, though it is specifically targeted at young men. The tournaments are played a midnight, just like the Midnight Basketball leagues. The time of the events, the influences of hip-hop, the "street" nature of the tournaments and the price (tickets run just $10–15, whereas NBA tickets are now largely unaffordable by any but the most affluent of Americans) has led to AND1 contributing significantly to the identity of the African American community.

AND1, which again relies on the stereotypes about an African American penchant for basketball, can be seen in contrast to the "extreme" sports movement in the U.S. These extreme sports, which entered the mainstream consciousness through ESPN's televising of the X-Games and include skateboarding, motocross, BMX biking, are all targeted to a White, mainly middle-class audiences, and the participants are drawn from the same demographic. Thus, we argue that sports, as an institution, is not so much reacting to needs in the society but is, in fact, creating preferences in ways that are rooted not only in stereotypes about "likes and dislikes" but also in biological myths about athletic abilities that are shaped by race. (For an extended discussion, see Smith, 2007.)

AND1 provides entertainment, it projects an image, and it offers an opportunity, though like the NBA a very limited one, for young men, primarily African American, to make money playing professional sports. Yet, the "street" images also invoke images of violence, thuggery, and misogyny while not invoking images of intelligence or professional success. Though very popular (and obviously lucrative for the CEOs who are now worth tens of millions of dollars), we ask if this form of sport is beneficial for African American Civil Society, or does it merely reinforce the stereotypes that already limit, by proscribing such narrow and stereotypical ideals, the life chances of many African American young men and women, particularly those from the lower classes?

Conclusion

In closing this chapter let us add that this is not the way we remember the African American athlete or the role that sports has traditionally played in the African American community. We agree with Richard Lapchick (2001), who wrote, "Sports have exploded and become big business. In too many instances, those managing sports have not been able to keep up with the speed of the changes" (p. 323). Much of this change has been the incorporation of African American athletes into sports, and this will continue at all levels. These men and women are heroes in the African American community and beyond. (This is long standing. In the HBO documentary entitled "The African American Athlete," the late Marty Glickman, a teammate of Jesse Owens at the 1936 Berlin Olympics, noted that the German track and field fans went wild over Jesse Owens both in 1936 and in a follow-up trip to Germany many years later.) Their achievements both on and off the fields of play give hope to 33 million African Americans. According to the late Chicago Bears football star Walter Payton, we need to acknowledge that life is "sweet" but that it is also short (*USA Today*, 2003, p. C7).

As we look toward the future with the benefit of hindsight, it is clear that sports can be a rewarding, even profitable experience for many athletes and their families. This includes African American athletes. Yet, we would be wise to be both cautious and careful. *New York Times* columnist Robert Lipsyte (1995) noted that sports have now become a major part of the larger entertainment industry, which can prove to be highly problematic. He put it thus:

> As a mirror of our culture, sports now show us spoiled fools as role models, cities and colleges held hostage and games that exist only to hawk products. The pathetic posturing of in-your-face macho has replaced a once self-confident masculinity. And the truth and beauty of sport itself—a pleasure of the flesh to the participant, an ennobling inspiration to the spectator—seem to have been wiped off the looking glass. (p. A10)

The African American athletes of the 1990s and early in the New Millennium (2000s) have built their prominence and place within the institution of sport on the gains made by their predecessors. And even if this fact is not always acknowledged, there is no way that we would see the Williams sisters in tennis except for the pioneering work of Althea Gibson, or see the phenomenal Tiger Woods in golf if it were not for pioneers like Charlie Sifford and others in the closed world of elite golf. We need to remember that as late as 1961, the constitution of the Professional Golfers Association (PGA) stated that the association was open only to "professional golfers of the Caucasian race." (See, especially, Porter, 1995, p. 306.)

This chapter is an attempt to make sense of the role that sports play in African American Civil Society. Why, with the limited number of professional positions in these games, do African Americans continue to consume time, energy, and resources to become sport greats? This question is important and the answer is hard to find in a packaged context.

African Americans have always viewed the sport playing field as a place where they could compete on even par with the dominant society—a level playing field. And, as it has been shown here, this has not always been true, especially before Jackie Robinson became a Brooklyn Dodger. And, we have argued, the playing field is still not level despite the successes of men like Tiger Woods (Smith, 2007).

We have argued throughout this chapter that despite the doors of opportunity opened by brave souls like Jackie Robinson and the continuous challenges to the remaining barriers by courageous individuals like Tiger Woods, African Americans still find themselves on the margins, the periphery. They are athletes, employees. Opportunities to lead, manage, or own the teams leave African Americans on the outside looking in. No one could have thought that the greatest basketball player ever, Michael Jordan, would be rebuffed by the real owner of "his" Washington Wizards, Abe Pollin, who said to the basketball legend, "You know what, Mike, thanks very much, but we don't need you anymore."

Here is how Michael Jordan put it:

> I came to Washington $3\frac{1}{2}$ years ago excited about the challenge of turning around this franchise. During my tenure, I dedicated myself to bringing excitement, credibility and my love of the game of basketball to Washington. It was well understood that when I finished playing, I would return as president of basketball operations and this was definitely my desire and intention. However, today, without any prior discussion with me, ownership informed me that it had unilaterally decided to change our mutual long-term understanding. I am shocked by this decision, and by the callous refusal to offer me any justification for it.
>
> —Michael Jordan (*USA Today*, May 7, 2003)

This scenario is what really matters in big-time sport. Those who own and control the athletic departments and professional teams also "own" the players. Even managers with fancy titles (e.g., Jordan: President of Basketball Operations) are just workers. And, this position, as noted by many theoreticians, from Marx to Wallerstein, and especially Erik OlinWright, is thus one of vulnerability and marginalization.

Finally, we conclude by noting that the power of SportsWorld is deceptive. On the outside it seems to offer professional and economic opportunity for a group within American society that has been denied entry into the professional and lucrative fields (such as medicine, law, politics, and business) that have always been open to White Americans (although we acknowledge that only recently have these fields been open to women). Sports is perhaps the most "level" playing field, the most integrated of all occupations. And yet, it is deceptive in two critical ways.

1. As noted in the example above: the real power and the real money in SportsWorld are in control and ownership. At the collegiate level this is the rank of head coach of power teams (football and men's basketball), athletic director, and director of the major conferences. At the professional level this is the rank of head coach, manager, but more specifically the team owner and the league presidents. These positions have been almost

exclusively reserved for White men. The "level" playing field does not extend to the field of decision-making, owning, or real power.

2. As we noted earlier in the chapter, the "level" playing field in SportsWorld has created a sense of false consciousness for African Americans that is extraordinarily dangerous. Why? For two key reasons. First, because the "dream" of making it in the professional ranks of sports is illusive. Fewer than 2,000 African American men earn a living in this way. The young African American man who banks on this, especially at the exclusion of other professional tracks (i.e., going to college on an athletic scholarship but never earning the credential), is playing a losing game. The odds are so low that he will ever make it into the professional ranks that he would be better off using his tuition money to play the lottery. The effect of this, however, is primarily at the individual level. More dangerous to African American Civil Society is the collective decision of young men (and to some degree their parents) to purse athletics as the ticket out at the exclusion of other career paths. What this allows for is the cordoning-off of African Americans into this lottery system for the few positions available in professional sports and the simultaneous removal of African Americans from the competition for the small (though relative to athletics extraordinarily high) number of positions in careers like medicine, law, politics, higher education, and most importantly in the fields of business and financial services. This cordoning-off results in a virtual exclusion of African Americans from the positions in American society that are most highly linked with wealth and power. And, from the perspective of those in power, namely White Americans, all of this is accomplished without ever passing a law denying equal access or without ever having African Americans see the ways in which they are being denied access. Yet, the impact on African American Civil Society is not that significantly different than that of the laws of Jim Crow segregation, which denied equal opportunity and left talent undeveloped. It is simply accomplished without laws and relies instead on an ideology that dictates that African Americans are more suited to SportsWorld than to the realms of intellect and power. And, like the Horatio Alger myth, because it masquerades as a system that "appears" to be open, no one is ever the wiser.

When we connect the Du Bois concern with the penchant in African American Civil Society for sports, we end up with the following question: If playing sports is a means, what happens when it ends? (Sokolove, 2004, p. 150).

References

Ashe, A. (1993). *Days of grace.* New York: Alfred A. Knopf.

Axthelm, P. (1970). *The city game.* New York: Penguin Books.

Benedict, J. (2004). *Out of bounds.* New York: Harper and Collins.

Block, F., Korteweg, A. C., & Woodward, K., with Schiller, Z., & Mazid, I. (2006). "The compassion gap in American poverty policy." *Contexts,* 5(2), 14–20.

Bonilla-Silva, E. (2001). *White supremacy & racism in the post–Civil Rights Era.* Boulder, Colorado: Lynne Rienner Publishers.

Bonilla-Silva, E. (2003). *Racism without racists: Color-blind racism and the persistence of racial inequality in the United States.* Lanham, Maryland: Rowman & Littlefield Publishers.

Bowen, W., & Levin, S. (2003). *Reclaiming the game: College sports and educational values.* Princeton, New Jersey: Princeton University Press.

Edwards, H. (1982). Common myths hide flaws in the athletic system. *The Center Magazine*, Jan/Feb., pp. 17–21.

Ellison, R. (1970/1995). What America would be like without African Americans. In J. F. Callahan, (Ed.), *The collected essays of Ralph Ellison*. New York: Modern Library Edition.

ESPN. (2006) Bush says family has done 'absolutely nothing wrong'. April 25, 2006, 5:02 PM ET. http://sports.espn.go.com/ncf/news/story?id=2419079

Feagin, J. (2001). Social justice and sociology in the 21st century. *American Sociological Review, 66*(1), 1–20.

Frey, D. (2004). *The last shot : City streets, basketball dreams*. New York: Mariner Books.

Friend, T. (2002). Next: LeBron James. *espnmag.com.* 5(26). December 10, 2002. http://espn.go.com/magazine/vol5no26next.html

Gates, H. L. (2004). Breaking the silence. *New York Times*, August 1, A10 .

Glassner, B. (2000). *The culture of fear: Why Americans are afraid of the wrong things*. New York: Basic Books.

Gossett, T. (1965). *Race: The history of an idea in America*. Dallas, TX: Southern Methodist University Press.

Graves, J. (2001). *The emperor's new clothes: Biological theories of race at the millennium*. New Jersey: Rutgers University Press.

Greene, J. P., & Winters, M. A. (2005) Public high school graduation and college-readiness rates: 1991–2002. *Education Working Paper No. 8*, February 2005. Manhattan Institute for Policy Research.

Harris, O. (1998). The role of sport in the black community. In G. Sailes (Ed.), *African Americans in sport* (pp. 3–13). New Brunswick, N J: Transaction.

Hartmann, D. (2001). Notes on Midnight Basketball and the cultural politics of recreation, race, and at-risk urban youth. *Journal of Sport and Social Issues, 25*(4), 339–317.

Hattery, A. J., & Smith, E. (2007). *African American families*. Thousand Oaks, CA: Sage.

Hochschild, J. L. (1995). *Facing up to the American dream: Race, class and the soul of the nation*. New Jersey: Princeton University Press.

hooks, b. (2004). *We real cool: Black men and masculinity*. New York: Routledge.

Hughes, R. (2001). "Proposition 48." Paper read at the Annual Meeting of the North American Society for the Sociology of Sport. San Antonio, Texas (p. 27).

Johnson, E. Magic, with Novak, W. (1992). *My life*. New York: Random House.

Kaplan, S. (1986). *The black presence in the era of the American Revolution*. Amherst, Massachusetts: University of Massachusetts Press.

Lapchick, R. (2001). *Smashing barriers: Race and sport in the new millennium*. New York: Madison Books, p. 323.

Lipsyte, R. (1995). The emasculation of sports. *New York Times*, April 2, Section 6, p. 51.

Lipsyte, R., & Eitzen, S. (Ed.). (1984). Sportsworld. *Sports in contemporary society*. New York: St. Martin's Press.

Meggyesy, D. (2000). Athletes in big-time college sport. *Society Magazine*, March/April: 24–28.

Merton, R. K. (1968). The Matthew Effect in science. *Science, 159*, 56–63.

Pager, Devah. (2003). The mark of a criminal record. *American Journal of Sociology, 108*, 937–975.

Porter, David L. (1995). *African American sports greats*. Greenwich, CT: Greenwood Press.

Price, S. L. (1997). What ever happened to the white athlete? *Sports Illustrated, 87*(23), 30–42.

Press, E., & Washburn, J. (2000). The kept university. *The Atlantic Monthly* (March), 39–54.

Putnam, R. (1995). Bowling alone. *Journal of Democracy (6)*1, 65–78.

Shapiro, T. M. (2004). *The hidden cost of being African American: How wealth perpetuates inequality*. New York: Oxford University Press.

Shields, D. (1999). *Black planet: Facing race during an NBA season*. New York: Three Rivers.

Simone, L. (2003). Hold athletes accountable. *The Baltimore Sun*. February 23, 5C.

Smith, Earl. (2007). *Race, sport and the American dream*. Durham, NC: Carolina Academic Press.

Smith, E., & Hattery, A. (2006a). Hey stud: Race, sex, and sports. *Journal of Sexuality and Culture, 10*(2), 3–32.

Smith, E., & Hattery, A. (2006b). Athletes, role-models and criminals: What do we make of this tripartite mess? In B. Lapman and S. Spickard Prettyman (Eds.), *Changing the game: Thinking critically about sport* (pp. 214–225). Rowman and Littlefield.

Sokolove, M. (2004). *The ticket out: Darryl Strawberry and the boys of Crenshaw*. New York: Simon & Schuster.

Suggs, W. (2003). Football, television, and the Supreme Court: How a decision 20 years ago brought commercialization to the world of college sports. *Chronicle of Higher Education*. http://chronicle.com Section: Athletics, Volume 50, Issue 44, p A32.

Tarkanian, J., with Yaeger, D. (2003). *Shark Attack: Jerry Tarkanian and His Battle with the NCAA and UNLV*. New York: Harper Collins.

Thomas, W. I., & Swaine, T. D. (1928). *The child in America*. New York: Knopf.

U.S. Department of Health and Human Services. (1997). *Trends in the well-being of America's children and youth*. Office of the Assistant Secretary for Planning and Evaluation U.S. Department of Health and Human Services.

USA Today (2002). August 2. p. 3C.

USA Today (2003). Walter Payton, deceased running back for the Chicago Bears in his Pro Football Hall of Fame Enshrinement Speech, July 31, 1993. October 28, 2002, p. 7C.

USA Today (2003). May 7.

Wilson, W. (1996). *When work disappears*. New York: Knopf.

Wright, E. O. (1998). Class analysis. In R. Levine (Ed.), *Social class and stratification: Classic statements and theoretical debates*. Lanham, Maryland: Rowman & Littlefield Publishers.

▲ *Summary* ▼

Sport Management—Valuing Diversity

DANA D. BROOKS and RONALD C. ALTHOUSE

As early as 1957, James Mason (University of Miami, Florida) and Walter O'Malley (Brooklyn/Los Angeles Dodgers) discussed the need for focused sport management curricula (Masteralexis, Barr, & Helms, 1998). Records indicate Ohio University (1966) established the first nationally recorded sport management M.S. degree program. Chalip (2006) noted, "Sport management is relatively young as an academic discipline" (p. 1). Yet, by 2006, there were about 200 recognized sport management (undergraduate and graduate) programs in America (Comfort, 2005a; Comfort, 2005b).

According to the National Association for Sport and Physical Education (NASPE), sport management program standards were "developed to provide some level of quality assurance to students enrolling in sport management programs and to the employers hiring graduates of these programs" (AAHPERD). National Association for Sport and Physical Education (NASPE) and the North American Society for Sport Management (NASSM) review sport management programs on a regular basis. Current undergraduate standards are as follows:

Standards for Undergraduate Programs in Sport Management

Standard 1 . . . . Critical Mass & Curricula

Standard 2 . . . . Critical Mass & Faculty

Standard 3 . . . . Socio-Cultural Dimensions in Sport

Standard 4 . . . . Management and Leadership in Sport

Standard 5 . . . . Ethics in Sport Management

Standard 6 . . . . Marketing in Sport

Standard 7 . . . . Communication in Sport

Standard 8 . . . . Budget & Time in Sport

Standard 9 . . . . Legal Aspects of Sport

Standard 10 . . . . Economics in Sport

Standard 11 . . . . Governance in Sport

Standard 12 . . . . Field Experience in Sport Management

Fitness Information Technology (FIT), a Division of the International Center for Performance Excellence, West Virginia University, established the Sport Management Library to provide a comprehensive array of textbooks for students enrolled in sport management programs. Titles in the current Sport Management Library are as follows:

Ammon, R., Southall, R., and Blair, D. (2004). *Sport Facility Management: Organizing Events and Mitigating Risks*

DeSensi, J., and Rosenberg, D. (2003). *Ethics and Morality in Sport Management*

Hall, A., Nichols, W., Moynahan, P., and Taylor, J. (2007) *Media Relations in Sport* (2nd Edition)

Howard, D. R., and Crampton, J. L. (2005). *Financing Sport* (2nd Edition)

Li, M., Eschenfelder, M. J. (2007). *Economics of Sport* (2nd Edition)

Pitts, B. (2003). *Case Studies in Sport Marketing*

Stotlar, D. K. (2005) *Developing Successful Sport Sponsorship Plans* (2nd Edition)

Textbooks were developed to meet the standards and competencies as outlined in NASPE/NASSM. To date, the FIT Sport Library does not contain a comprehensive textbook addressing the issues of social justice and diversity within the sport industry. It is important to note that several of the leading journals in the field recognized the need for future professionals to have a fuller understanding and appreciation of diversity issues within the field.

During the time period from 2003 to 2006 the *Journal of Sport Management* published several research articles targeting social justice and diversity issues within the field of sport management:

1. Sock A. L., and Singh, P. (2005). Occupational Segregation on the Playing Field: The Case of Major League Baseball.

2. Cunningham, G. S., and Sagas, M. (2004). Group Diversity, Occupational Commitment and Occupational Turnover Intentions Among NCAA Division IA Football Coaching Staffs.

3. Chelladurai, P., and Ogasawara, E. (2003). Satisfaction and Commitment of American and Japanese Collegiate Coaches.

4. Armstrong, K. (2002). An Examination of Social Psychology of Blacks' Consumption of Sport.

5. Fink, J. A., Pastore, D .L., and Riemer, H. A. (2001). Do Differences Make a Difference? Managing Diversity in Division IA Intercollegiate Athletics.

It is also important to note that selected articles appearing in the *Sport Marketing Quarterly* (2000 to 2005) provided additional evidence that diversity issues (i.e. race, gender, social class) are legitimate and important research topics within the sport management discipline and profession:

1. Armstrong, K., and Stratton, T. (2004). Market Analysis of Race and Sport Consumption.

2. Dixon, M. A. (2002). Gender Differences in Perceptions and Attitudes Toward the LPGA and Its Tour Professionals: An Empirical Investigation.

3. Cuneen, J., and Spencer, N. (2003). Gender Representation Related to Sport Celebrity Portrayals in Milk Mustache Advertising Campaign.

4. Armstrong, K. (2001). Black Consumers: Spending and Historically Black College Sport Events: The Marketing Implications.

5. Jackson, E., Lyons, R., and Gooden, S. (2001). The Marketing of Black College Sports.

6. Kahle, L., Dalakas, V., and Aiken, D. (2001). The Social Values of Fans for Men's Versus Women's University Basketball.

7. Pons, F., Laroche, M., Nyeck, S., and Perreault, S. (2001). Role of Sporting Events as Ethnoculture's Emblems: Impact of Acculturation and Ethnic Identity on Consumer's Orientation Toward Sporting Events.

Chalip (2006) appropriately stated, "Sport sociologists and sport psychologists have become adept at exposing fallacies in popular wisdom about sport, but they have rarely considered the implications of those fallacies for sport management. It is an unfortunate oversight because fallacious beliefs about sport can have a detrimental impact on sport management research and sport management practice" (p. 10).

The authors of this book include internationally recognized sport sociologists, sport managers, lawyers, sociologists, historians, and coaches. The scholars and practitioners identified the fallacies, misperceptions, stereotypes, and miseducation existing in the sport industry. More importantly, the concepts and principles cited throughout the book provide sport management scholars, practitioners, and students with the tools necessary to bring about positive changes in the industry.

Fink, Pastore, and Riemer (2001) analyzed the extent to which NCAA Division IA athletic directors, senior women's administrators, and associate/assistant athletic directors value diversity and its management in the workplace. Based on the results of this study, the authors concluded that diversity management topics should be discussed more fully within the sport management curricula. It was strongly suggested that current and future sport managers must not only value diversity in the workplace, but they also need to have a knowledge base to provide appropriate diversity leadership training and advocacy within the sport market place. The textbook was written to enhance the student knowledge base about the numerous and complex issues surrounding diversity concepts within intercollegiate and professional sports.

Chapter Highlights

Diversity and Social Justice in College Sports: Sport Management and the Student Athlete represents an excellent addition to the existing sport management textbook library. Authors and co-authors assembled in the book represent leading experts and scholars in their chosen disciplines. The purpose of the textbook was to provide a comprehensive appraisal of the current status of diversity (broadly defined: race, gender, ethnicity) within sport at the college and professional level. More importantly, many of the authors offered tangible suggestions to increase diversity within the organization thus building a shared and valued sport community.

David Wiggins' chapter, "Climbing the Racial Mountain: A History of the African American Experience in Sport," provided the reader with an excellent overview of the historical achievements of African-American athletes.

Hartman (2003) reminded readers, "The notion that sport is a positive, progressive force for African Americans and race relations in general is an idea—or, in social scientific parlance, an 'ideology'—that resonates deeply in contemporary American popular cultures" (p. xi). Counterbalanced to this proposition, the journey of the African American athletes from slavery to modern professional and

Olympic sports has witnessed the joy of competition and the agony of racism and discrimination.

Throughout Dr. Wiggins' historically documented chapter, the author was able to identify notable African American sport performers such as: Isaac Murphy, Marshall Taylor, Fritz Pollard, Paul Robeson, Jesse Owens, Alice Couchman, and Wilma Rudolph. Unfortunately, success on the playing field did not translate to equal access to housing and employment opportunities beyond the playing arena. Wiggins reminded readers, "Although more overt forms of discrimination against African American athletes have decreased over the last few decades, it is apparent that many people still held to their racist beliefs and deep-seated stereotypical notions about African-Americans in both sport and larger society."

Robertha Abney, writing in "African American Women in Intercollegiate Coaching and Administration: Unequal Access" called to question the extent to which African American female coaches have gained parity within the NCAA coaching and administrative ranks. Similarly, Brooks and Althouse (1996) wrote, "The opportunity for women to gain parity in collegiate sports barely exists. Scanty as it is, the literature dealing with African American women athletes reaffirms stereotypes and myths that have had adverse effects in their mobility as well as their personal well being" (p. 51).

Dr. Abney was able to identify the socio-cultural and structural barriers that deny African American women, and other ethnic minority women, the opportunity to gain complete access to all levels of coaching and administration within NCAA member institutions. The passage of Title IX in 1972 provided the legal doctrine by which women would gain high levels of access to high school and college sports. Yet, African-American women tend to lag behind the white females in positions such as head coach and athletic director. This condition led the author to conclude, "As long as racial and sexist practices influence hiring practices, the number of African American women in high authority sport positions will not increase."

After reading this chapter, readers became very aware that, "gender segregation in the labor market, sex discrimination and under representation of women in managerial/ leadership roles are problematic not only in generic business environments but also in sporting organizations" (O'Shea, 2005, p. 38).

Noted sociologists Audwin Anderson and Donald South's chapter, "The Academic Experiences of African American Collegiate Athletes: Implications for Policy and Practice," documented racial differences in educational outcomes (i.e. clustering by academic majors, graduation roles) for college athletes. However, "the marriage between education and athletics is likely to endure foreseeable failure." Given this fact, the authors suggested several structural changes hopefully having a positive impact of the African American coaching experience. Suggested policies included: the establishment of "minor leagues," development of policies that enforce the college educational experiences of student athletes, redistribution of college revenues, and the evaluation of coaching performance beyond games.

Billy Hawkins, Brianne Milan-Williams, and Akilah Cater provided an excellent critique of the post-NCAA eligibility experiences of African American student athletes. The chapter, "From Glory to Glory: The Transition of African American Athletes for College Sports into Athletic Retirement," provides sport management students with knowledge about athletic retirement theories and factors contributing to athletic retirement. The majority of research on the topic, "Retirement for Sports" has been conducted utilizing white athletes. The authors of this chapter described the retirement experiences of 21 African American student athletes. It was concluded that a majority of the athletes were satisfied with their athletic careers and termination from sport participation was due to end of athlete eligibility.

Dana Brooks, Ronald Althouse, and Delano Tucker's chapter, "African American Coaching Mobility Models and the Global Market Place," discussed current NCAA and Black Coaches Association programs and recommendations to increase diversity within NCAA coaching and administrative roles. The authors summarized, "Historically, research focused primarily on the African American athlete's experience and the lack of coaching and other leadership opportunities for African American males and females."

On a somewhat discouraging note, the authors concluded, it is unlikely that the general public will witness a significant increased number of ethnic minority and women NCAA head coaches. Given the scenario, the authors began to question the extent to which the globalization of sport will have a positive impact on coaching opportunities for African American and other ethnic minorities. Coaching opportunities in soccer, Canadian football, NFL Europe football, and the Olympics were discussed. To date, the scholars do not fully understand coaching mobility avenues existing at the global sport level.

Fritz Polite writing in, "Ethnic Minority Opportunities in College and Professional Sports: A Business Imperative," argued convincingly that a diverse minority work force makes good business sense! Dr. Polite asserted that valuing and merging cultural diversity is critical to the ultimate success of the organization. The author concluded, similar to Brooks, Althouse, and Tucker and Robertha Abney's findings, that there is a dearth of Latino, Native American, and African American representation in NCAA coaching and administrative positions. Yet, there have been some success stories. Pioneer and innovative coaches such as Eddie Roberson, Frederick Pollard, Cleveland Abbott, Marion Washington, Vivian Stanger, and Dr. Larry Walker have "set the standard" for coaching excellence.

As previously noted, the role of athletic director is very critical to the ultimate success of the NCAA athletic department. Individuals occupying these positions are highly visible and have financial responsibility for multi-million dollar budgets and athletic facilities. Unfortunately, few ethnic minorities or women currently hold the title "NCAA Athletic Director." Doris Corbett and Miguel Tabron clearly articulated perceived employment barriers facing minority applicants within NCAA member institutions. Building on the concepts presented in "Ethnic Minority Performances in College and Professional Sports A Business Imperative" (by Fritz Polite), the authors of this chapter suggested the following initiatives would result in greater diversity within NCAA coaching ranks: (1) take all appropriate stages to increase the pool of minority applicants; (2) provide great media exposure opportunities for ethnic minority coaches; (3) provide professional development opportunities for coaching; (4) strengthen the hiring process by diversifying the diversity on the search and screen committee and where appropriate, develop university diversity hiring plans.

The number of scholarly publications highlighting the contributions of African American sport broadcasters, journalists, and reporters and announcers is minimal. "African American newspapers and magazines were founded in the

United States as early as 1884," (Brooks & Althouse, 1996, p. 105). As early as 1938, Wendell Smith of the *Pittsburgh Courier* was assigned to cover the Negro Baseball League in America. African American reporters offered positive views of the African American sport experience. Doris Corbett and Aaron Stills' chapter, "African Americans and the Media: Roles and Opportunities to Be Broadcasters, Journalists, Reporters, and Announcers," makes a significant contribution to the sport management literature.

Keith Harrison and Jean Boyd's chapter, "Mainstreaming and Integrating the Spectacle and Substance of Scholar-Baller: A New Blueprint for Higher Education, the NCAA and Society," outlined an innovative analysis of the student-athlete paradigm on the college campuses.

The authors supported current NCAA academic reform efforts leading to higher levels of interconnects between athletes, education, and popular culture. The Scholar-Baller concept represents "someone who succeeds academically and socially." A Scholar-Baller is a student athlete who expects and meets academic and athletic expectations. Contrary to the belief that student-athletes, especially African-American athletes, are commodities and devalue their college education expenses, Sholar-Baller athletes perceive students as student athletes.

"*Taboo*'s Explanation of Black Athlete Dominance: More Fiction than Fact," written by Othello Harris, challenged many of the assertions made by Entine (2000) and addressed the following basic questions: Why are African American athletes desperate to find a certain sport (i.e., basketball and football) as compared to other sports (e.g., volleyball, soccer, tennis)? How are performance differences in sport performances explained? Entine's *Taboo* theory is that blacks have racially linked genetic advantages over whites. Similarly to a surgeon, Harris removed the layers of proposition put forth by Entine in support of his various performance outcome positions. Harris outlined what he perceived to be flaws in Entine's arguments: (1) definition of race, (2) sport as physical and social activities, (3) confusing notion of phenotypes as members of race, and (4) the relationship between race, gender, and sport performance.

"Who Am I? Racial Identity, Athletic Identity, and the African American Athlete," written by Louis Harrison, Jr. and Leonard Moore, provided an excellent critique of African-American racial development, stereotyping, and its relationship with athletic development. The application of racial identity theory and the Nigresence process provide the reader with a better understanding of the role and importance of sport within the African-American community.

Timothy Davis, highly regarded legal scholar, in his two chapters: (1) "The Persistence of Unconscious Racism in College Sport," and (2) "Academic Inequity and the Impact of NCAA Rules," challenged readers to explore controversial sport management and social justice conditions such as: the alleged disparate impact of NCAA rules and regulations and their effect on African American student athletes' participation rates, and how social stereotypes perpetuate racial misunderstanding.

Similarly, by presenting relative court cases, Davis explored the connections between sport and law in college athletics. Davis argued that existing civil rights laws have been ineffective in protecting the interests of African Americans who participate or work in the sport industry. Davis recommended that NCAA college administrators learn from NFL experience when confronted with a lack of diversity in the coaching rank. A significant change in NFL hiring practices, known as the Rooney Rule, mandated that at least one person of color must be interviewed as a candidate for each NFL head coaching vacancy.

Scott Brooks asked the fundamental question: If black student athletes are being exploited, do they deserve some compensation? Brooks' chapter, "The Dilemmas and Contradictions of "Gettin' Paid", presented a point and counter-point debate about a highly emotional topic: Should college student athletes be paid for their services? Discussion of the dilemma of getting paid included: definition of amateurism, black athlete as gladiators, social and academic roles of student athletes on campus, differential pay scales for athletes, negotiations based upon college graduation rates.

Legal scholar Linda Sheryl Green and internationally recognized college coach Tina Sloan-Green provided a historical analysis of the development of the Black Women's Sport Foundation. "Beyond Tokenism to Empowerment: The Black Women in Sport Foundation," is an excellent addition to the gender stacking and sport management literature. Through the chapter the authors were able to provide a journey of the Black Women's Sport Foundation (BWSF) from its incorporation in 1992 to its current status as an internationally recognized organization providing black women with a sense of pride, visibility, and "power." The Black Women's Sport Foundation remains committed to: (1) increasing diversity within the coaching and administrative ranks and (2) providing educational material and programs at all levels of athletics within America. Pioneer female civil rights advocates such as Carol Oglesby, Tina Sloan-Green, Nikki Franke, and Linda Green became the pioneers promoting equality for women in sport.

Sport has become a multi-million dollar global entertainment where athletes are perceived "performers." Fritz Polite's chapter, "The Globlization of Sport: A Bridge to Advancing Cultures," reminds readers that concepts of racism, exploitation, and social justice need to be analyzed and discussed at the global level. Globilization and sports (professional and Olympics) tied with media exposure and technology and permitted African-American superstars such as Michael Jordan, Tiger Woods, and LaBron Jones to become household names throughout the world. Similarly, the Olympic Games became venues in which highly acclaimed ethnic minorities and women were able to demonstrate their athletic prowess.

Professional sports such as American football have not been immune from the impact of globalization. NFL Europe teams provide opportunities for African Americans to continue their football playing careers beyond college. Unfortunately, scholars have failed to investigate the social and cultural experiences of minorities and women who play professional sports outside of America. Several questions come to mind: How are players socialized? To what extend are ethnic minorities prepared for a professional career outside of sport? How are formal and informal networks established to identify and recruit players to participate in a global sport market? Hopefully, these questions will stimulate sport managers and sport sociologists to expand research in these areas.

Derrick Bell's (1992) controversial book, *Faces at the Bottom of the Well: The Permanence of Racism,* argued that race does matter. Racism and discrimination are part of the historical American fabric. Bell identified what he has labeled "racial schizophrenia" in America. Seemingly, middle-class African Americans are not immune from racial practices. Yet, "careful examination reveals a problem to those seemingly arbitrary racial actions; when whites perceive that it will be profitable or at least cost-free to serve, hire, admit, or otherwise deal with blacks on a nondiscriminatory basis, they do so" (p. 7).

Ketra Armstrong's contribution, "African Americans' Consumption of Sport: Race Matters!" provided an excellent insight into the benefits and liabilities of target marketing strategies. Armstrong stated, "Since America as a multicultural nation undergoing a dramatic increase in the social (and ethnic) diversity of its inhabitants, there is a particular need to understand the racial dynamics of the nuances of sport consumption."

Arguing from a conflict perspective and structural-functional theory, the author was able to identify distinctive consumer behaviors of African Americans and whites. African American and other ethnic minorities are gaining a greater share of the sport market. The authors noted that historically black colleges and universities are very much aware of the economic impact of sport mobility and promotions in local economies. Yes, race matters in sport marketing and in the consumption market place. Thus, it is very important for sport managers to learn the importance of concepts such as social justice and diversity.

Nationally recognized sociologist Earl Smith and his colleague Angela Hattery's chapter, "African American Community: The Dynamics of Race, Class, Gender, and Community Sports," provided an outstanding overview of the current and future social conditions existing within the social institution of sport. Specifically, the authors provided an excellent analysis of the relationship between sport and the African American Civil Society. African American Civil Society must still confront discrimination in the workplace, denial of top level managerial positions, and perpetuation of negative stereotypes about African Americans athlete role models.

According to the authors, sport and the sports world are a very integral part of the African American community. Yet, "The impact of African American Civil Society is no different than that of the laws of Jim Crow segregation."

In closing, Charles Barkley (former NBA basketball player), writing in *Who's Afraid of a Large Black Man?*, said, "In so many of the conversations in this book, people acknowledge how much racism and bigotry has cost America, but people also talk about the economic divide being even greater than the racial divide. Obviously, the journey via these conversations center on race in America and how it impacts everybody. But it's not possible to examine the impact of race without it being tied to the broader issue of poverty" (p. xiii, xiv).

Social facets such as race, gender, ethnicity, and social class have tremendous impact on sport consumers and producers (athletes). The primary purpose of this text was to provide sport management students with additional diversity and social justice concepts necessary to better understand and analyze the culture that exists in the global sport market.

References

American Alliance for Health, Physical Education, Recreation and Dance (n.d.). *Sport management standards and review protocol.* Retrieved from www.aahperd.org/naspe.

Armstrong, K. L., & Stratton, T. M. (2004). Market analyses of race and sport consumption. *Sport Marketing Quarterly, 13,* 7–16.

Armstrong, K. L. (2001). Black consumer's spending and historically black college sport events: The marketing implications. *Sport Marketing Quarterly, 10*(2), 102–111.

Armstrong, K. (2002). An examination of social psychology of blacks' consumption of sport. *Journal of Sport Management, 16*(4), 267–288.

Barkley, C. (2005). *Who's afraid of a large black man?* New York: The Berkeley Publishing Group.

Bell, D. (1992). *Faces at the bottom of the well: The permanence of racism.* New York: Basic Books.

Brooks, D., & Althouse, R. (1996). *The African-American resource directory.* Morgantown, WV: Fitness Information Technology.

Chalip, L. (2006). Towards a distinctive sport management discipline, *Journal of Sport Management, 20,* 1–2.

Chelladurai, P., & Ogasawara, E. (2003). Satisfaction and commitment of American and Japanese collegiate coaches. *Journal of Sport Management, 17*(1), 62–73.

Comfort, P. G. (2005a). *Directory of graduate programs in sport management.* Morgantown, WV: Fitness Information Technology.

Comfort, P. G. (2005b). *Directory of undergraduate programs in sport management.* Morgantown, WV: Fitness Information Technology.

Cuneen, J., & Spencer, N. (2003). Gender representation related to sport celebrity portrayals in milk mustache advertising campaign. *Sport Marketing Quarterly, 12*(3), 140–150.

Cunningham, G. B., & Sagar, M. (2004). Group diversity, occupational commitment, and occupational turnover intentions among NCAA Division IA football coaching staffs. *Journal of Sport Management, 18*(3), 236–254.

DeSensi, J., & Rosenberg, D. (2003). *Ethnics and morality in sport management.* Morgantown, WV: Fitness Information Technology.

Farmer, P. J., Mulroney, A. L., & Ammon, R., Jr. (1996). *Sport facility planning and management.* Morgantown, WV: Fitness Information Technology.

Hartman, D. (2003). *Race, culture, and the revolt of the black athlete: The 1968 Olympic protests and their aftermath.* Chicago: The University of Chicago Press.

Howard, D. R., & Crompton, J. L. (2004). *Financing sport* (2nd ed.). Morgantown, WV: Fitness Information Technology.

Jackson, E. N., Lyons, R., & Gooden, S. (2001). The marketing of black college sports. *Sport Marketing Quarterly, 10*(2), 138–146.

Kahle, L., Dalakas, V., & Aiken, D. (2001). The social values of fans of men's versus women's university basketball. *Sport Marketing Quarterly, 10*(2), 156–162.

Li, M., Holfecie, S., & Mahoney, D. (2001). *Economics of sport.* Morgantown, WV: Fitness Information Technology.

Marlene, A. D. (2002). Gender differences in perceptions and attitudes toward the LPGA and its tour professionals: An empirical investigation. *Sport Marketing Quarterly, 11*(1), 44–54.

Masteralexis, L. P., Ball, C. A., & Helms, M. A. (1998). Principles and practice of sport management. Gaithersburg, MD: Aspen Publishers, Inc.

Nichols, W., Moynahan, P., Hall, A., & Taylor, J. (2001). *Media relations in sports.* Morgantown, WV: Fitness Information Technology.

O'Shea, M. (2005, Sept./Oct.) Sport's glass ceiling, *Australian Leisure Management, 50*(38), 40.

Parks, J. B., & Quaterman, J. (2003). Sport management: An overview. In J. B. Parks & J. Quarterman (Eds.), *Contemporary sport management,* 2nd ed. (pp. 5–22). Human Kinetics, Champaign, IL.

Pitts, B. (2003). *Case studies in sport marketing.* Morgantown, WV: Fitness Information Technology.

Pons, F., Laroche, M., Nyeck, S., & Perreault, S. (2001). Role of sporting events as ethnoculture's emblems: Impact of acculturation and ethnic identity on consumers' orientation toward sporting events. *Sport Marketing Quarterly, 10*(4), 231–240.

Sack, A. L., & Singh, P. (2005). Occupational segregation on the playing field: The case of major league baseball. *Journal of Sport Management, 19,* 300–318

Stotlar, D. K. (2005). *Developing successful sport sponsorship plans* (2nd ed.). Morgantown, WV: Fitness Information Technology.

Index

101 most influential minorities in sports, 118, 154
14th Amendment, 24
15th Amendment, 4
27-Year Update, 70–71

A

Abbott, Cleveland, "Cleve" Abbott, 155
academic clustering, 97
academic opportunity for student athletes, 284
Academic Progress Rate (APR), 86, 202, 204, 283
Academic Reform Movement (ARM), 10, 202, 204, 205
academic-athletic conflicts and African American athletes, 9–10
academicians, sports performances, and continued evidence of discrimination, 38–42
academics, 86–88
access denied, 144
access discrimination, 59, 144
Account-Making Model, 101
"acting white," 254
Affirmative Action Plans, voluntary, 275–277
African American athletes and Civil Rights, 23, 37–38
African American coach, athletic directors' perception of, 167–168
African American consumers, urban consumers, and hip-hop, 364–368
African American consumers' economic attractiveness, 364–365
African American leaders and contributors to sport journalism and broadcast industry, 185–186
African American male athletes as role models, 390–391
African American women and intercollegiate sport, 12–13
African Americans as a percentage of male student athletes and head coaches, 268
African Americans as sport consumers, 13–14
After the Whistle Blows, 322
Alexander v. Sandoval, 290
Alexander, Alpha, 314

Amazing Grace: Black Women in Sport, 322
American Bowl results, 340–341
American Dream, 25–27
Amsterdam Admirals, 351
AND 1, 399–402
antidiscrimination norms and access, 270–273
Ashe, Arthur, 384
associate and assistant athletic directors, 148
athletes as staff, 304–305
athletes-in-residence, 302–303
athletic industrial complex (AIC), 385–389, 392, 396
athletics administrative staff
    1995–1996—overall percentages, 55–56
    2001–2002—black women, 61
    2001–2002—overall percentages, 57
Autobiography of Malcolm X, 249

B

Barcelona Dragons, 345–346, 350
Bateer, Mengke, 340
Berlin Thunder, 351
Birmingham Fire, 346
Black Athletes: Fact and Fiction, 235–236
Black Coaches Association (BCA), xii, 10, 40, 59, 72, 120, 122, 153, 170, 275–276
Black Entertainment Television (BET), 367
black student athlete, 299–301
Black Women in Sport, 314
Black Women in Sport Foundation (BWSF), 13, 50, 320–327
    Board of Directors, 320
    Board profile, 325
    2004–2005 Sites, 330–332
Black Women in Sport Workshop, 319
black-bottomed pyramid, 130
Bowden, Bobby, 300
Brand, Myles, 51, 64, 126, 146, 202, 288
Brown v. Board of Education of Topeka, 3, 8, 35, 36, 119, 140, 317
Brown, James, 184
Bryant, Kobe, 390
Buying Power of Black America, The, 145

C

Call to Action, A, 80

campaigns to reintegrate lily-white sport, 32–34

Campanis, Al, 40, 163, 167, 235

Career Assessment Program for Athletes (CAPA), 105

career resources and networks, 58–60

career-track jobs for athletic directors, 120

Carnegie Commission, 298–299

case analysis, 273–275

Central Intercollegiate Athletic Association, 28

centrality of position theory, 188

CHAMPS/Life Skills Program, 100, 111, 217–218

Circuit of Culture, 206

Civil Rights, 23, 37–38

Civil Rights Act of 1964, 160, 270

Civil Society, 380, 382–383, 391, 397, 400

clustering, 62–63, 90

Coach Carter, 227

coaches and athletic programs, 305–306

coaching, 148

coaching opportunities at the global level, 130–135,

　　Canadian Football League, 133,

　　football, 132,

　　NFL Europe, 133–134,

　　Olympic Games, 134

　　soccer, 130–132,

college athletics and issues of race, 79–82

collegiate competition, beginnings of, 298–299

Cologne Centurions, 352

Colored Intercollegiate Athletic Association, 28, 29–30

Combs, Sean, 207, 216

common-law doctrine, 284–286

conferences, 66–68

conflict theory analysis of hip-hop sport marketing, 369–370

consumers, urban, 364–368

cordoning-off, 391–392

Cribs, 386, 397

Critical Race Theory, 203

Critical Race Theory and Critical Scholar-Baller Theory and Application, 218–226

Croom, Sylvester, 123, 140, 144, 149

Cureton v. NCAA, 289

D

Daniels, Lloyd "Sweet Pea," 398

Days of Grace, 384

dead-end positions, 57–58

DeBerry, Fisher, 300

DeFrantz, Anita, 135

demand-side theories, 187

"Dilemmas and Contradictions in Status," 301

discrimination

　access, 59, 144

　in collegiate sport, alternative approaches to combating, 284–286

　racial, perception of, 165–167

　treatment, 144

　within the coaching ranks, 130

disparate impact, 160, 270–274, 289, 290

　of NCAA initial eligibility rules, 287–289

　of NCAA rules 286–287

disparate treatment, 160, 270–274

distribution of African American Major League Baseball players 1960–2001, 162

diversity

　(definition), 142

　and opportunity, 141–142

　in sport, cultural, 143

　in the sport media, 188–190

　and sport participation, 126–28

　strategies (coaching and administrative), 121

dream divide, 389

Du Bois, W. E. B., 79, 139, 379

E

Eastern Negro League, 31

East-West All-Star Game, 32, 362

Ebaugh's Role Exit Theory, 101

economy of blackness, 364

Edwards, Damon, 268

Edwards, Donnie, 287

Edwards, Harry, 37, 39, 85, 140, 326, 387, 388

eligibility requirements, 289

eligibility rules, legal challenges to, 289–292

Ellison, Ralph, 380

employment barriers, 164–165

employment opportunities for African American coaches, barriers to, 161–167

Entine, Jon, 236–243, 246

establishing a support system, 168–170

Evans, Damon, 140, 147

Executive Order 9981, 140
expanding opportunities in college sports, 8–9

F

Federal Graduation Rate, 282
Foster, Andrew "Rube," 31
Franke, Nikki, 315–327
Frankfurt Galaxy, 346, 352
functionalist theory analysis of hip-hop sport marketing, 368–369

G

Gear Up, 321
glass ceiling, 57–58, 252
global marketing, 334–335
global sports marketing, 337–338
globalization, 14–15, 127, 128–130, 333, 335
    drivers and barriers to, 336
    and racism, 128–129
    technology and, 337
globalization, sport, and coaching opportunities, 129–130
Glory Bound, 235
graduation rate, 88–90, 97
    critical appraisal of use of, 89–90
    data by race/ethnicity, high school, 385
    meaning of, 91
Greene, Linda, 317–327
Gross, Daryl, 147, 268
Gumbel, Bryant, 182
Gumbel, Greg, 184–185

H

Hackley, Lloyd, 39
Hamburg Sea Devils, 352
Harkin, Shaun, 132
Harlem Globetrotters, 163
hate crimes, 3
Henderson, Edwin Bancroft, 41
hip-hop, 255, 364–370
    as a positive culture force, 215–217
    revisited, 365–366
hip-hop sport marketing
    conflict theory analysis of, 369–370
    functionalist theory analysis of, 368–369
hiring and dismissal process, 119–120
Hiring Report Card, 121–125, 170
historical listing of African American and Latino Division IA head football coaches, 149

Hoover v. Meiklejohn, 263
Hughes, Everett C., 301
human capital, 186
Human Grieving Model, 101, 105

I

identity
    athletic 250–251
    interaction of racial and athletic, 256–257
    intersection of athletic and racial identity, 251–252
identity development, African American, 247–254
    encounter stage, 248–249
    immersion-emersion stage, 249
    internalization stage, 250,
    internalization-commitment, 250
    pre-encounter stage, 248
    sport stereotypes in, 252–254
identity politics, 392–399
In Black and White: Race and Sports in America, 40
intercollegiate athletic departments, 68–71
intercollegiate athletics history, 203–206
intercollegiate sport: the beginnings, 7–8
Interscholastic Athletic Association (ISAA), 27
intersection of law, sport, and racial inequity, 266–270
interventions (for transition to non-athlete), 105

J

Jackson v. Drake University, 285
Jackson v. University of New Haven, 273–274
James, LeBron, 386
Jay-Z, 216
Jim Crow, 3, 26, 300
Johnson, Jack, 25
Jordan, Michael, 403

K

Knight Foundation, 80
Knight Foundation's Commission on Intercollegiate Athletics, 80, 103
Kubler-Ross, Elisabeth, 101, 105

L

Lacy, Sam, 181–182
Leadership Institute for Ethnic Minority Females, 275
Leadership Institute for Ethnic Minority Males, 275
learning from the NFL's experience, 276–277

legal system and African American college athletes, 11–12

limited opportunities in leadership in sport, 10–11

Lipsyte, Robert, 382

London Monarchs, 346, 350

Lopiano, Donna, 326

Louis, Joe, 25

M

M Street School, 27

Mad Sports, 367

Manigault, Earl "The Goat," 398

Mann Act, 25

markers, 240, 242

"Matthew Effect," 381

McDonnell Douglas Corp. v. Green, 274

media images, 53–54

mentors, 60

Midnight Basketball, 399–402

Miller, Cheryl, 152–153

Ming, Yao, 339, 340

minorities in leadership roles, 269

Minority Opportunities and Interests Committee (MOIC), xi, 11, 64, 72, 124–125, 171, 275–276

Montreal Machine, 346

N

NAACP Legal Defense and Education Fund (LDF), 317

NASCAR, 367

National Association for Academic Advisors for Athletics (N4A), 216–217

National Association for the Advancement of Colored People (NAACP), 33

National Association of Black Journals (NABJ) 194

National Basketball Association, 339–340

National Collegiate Athletic Association, 63–65

National High School Athletic Association, 29

National Interscholastic Athletic Association (NIAA), 29

National Interscholastic Basketball Tournament, 28, 29–30

National Minority Women in Sports Conference, 318

National Negro Baseball League (NNL), 31

National Scholarship Service and Fund for Negro

Students (NSSFNS), 79

Native Americans, 265–266

NBA League Office, 143–144

NCAA presidents and vice presidents in Division IA, 146–147

NCAA reforms and inaction, 300–301

NCAA

academic reforms, 83–86

and athletic retirement, 98–100

Coaches Academy, 275–276

coaching and administrative opportunities, overview,145–146

Committee on Women's Athletics (CWA), xi,

Constitution, xi,

demographics, 144

Diversity Programs, 123

Ethnic Minority Enhancement Postgraduate Scholarship for Careers in Athletics Program, 124

Fellows Leadership Development Program, 124

member institutions, 145

Men's Coaches Academy, 124

Minority Opportunities and Interests Committee (MOIC), xi, 11, 64, 72, 124–125, 275–276

Office of Diversity and Inclusion, xii, 64, 127

purpose, xiii

Self-Study—Minority Issues, 125–126

Strategic Plan, xi

NCAA: cartel or free opportunity? 297–298

NCAA-IA African American athletic directors, 147

Negro American League, 31

Negro Baseball Leagues, 362–363

networking, 168

New York, NJ Knights, 347

Next Step Programs, 321

NFL Europe

attendance, 349

teams, history of, 352

NFL International, 340–341

NFLE Today, 351–352

Nigresence, 7, 248, 254, 256

O

Oglesby, Carole, 315–327

Ohio Glory, 347

Olajuwan, Hakeem, 366
Olympic Committee, United States (USOC), 105, 319
Olympic Games, 30
Olympic Partners, the (TOP Sponsors), 338
Olympic Project for Human Rights (OPHR), 38
Olympics, 338–339
one-drop rule, 238
opportunity structure, access to, 391–392
Orlando Thunder, 347
Owens, Jesse, 26, 234, 402

P

Paterno, Joe, 83, 300
persistence, forces that impact, 212
phenotypes, 242
Phipps, Susie, 239
playing the race card, 119–120
Plessy, Homer, 239, 242
Plessy v. Ferguson, 24
politics, 58
Pollard, Frederick Douglass, 151–152
Pollard, Fritz, 26
position clustering, 62–63
Principles of Student Athlete Welfare, 98–100
professional administration, 148
professional sports aspirations, 393
progress in professional sports, 143
Proposal 62, 287
Proposition 16, 84, 202, 288–291, 301
Proposition 42, 39, 202, 301
Proposition 48, 38–39, 83–85, 202, 287–288, 300
Pryor v. NCAA, 290–292
Public Schools Athletic League (PSAL), 28

R

race, academics, and the African American student athlete, 281–283
race relations
    in American society, 2–5
    in sport, 5–7
race as a social construct, 240–241
race, sport, and values, 265–266
Racial and Gender Report Card, 52, 64, 67, 89, 118, 145, 267–268
racial composition of female student athletes and of head coaches, 268
racial discrimination, perception of, 165–167
racial inequity in sport, 264–266

racism
    in collegiate sport, 266–267
    and sexism, 54
Rainbow Coalition, 120, 121
Raleigh/Durham Skyhawks, 347
rap, 368
Remember the Titans, 36
representation in sport management programs, 150–156
retirement
    African American intercollegiate athletes' experiences with athletic, 106–109
    individual characteristics, 108–109
    insight, 107
    level of competition, 107–108
    post-retirement involvement and career satisfaction, 109
    pre-retirement planning, 108
    reactions to, 104–105
    reasons for, 108,
    social support for, 108,
Rhein Fire, 352
Richardson, Jr. v. Suggs, 274
Roberts, Robin, 183
Robeson, Paul, 26, 27
Robinson, Eddie, 150–151
Robinson, Jackie, 6, 22, 140, 234, 235, 363, 364, 403
role models, 60
Rooney Rule, 277
Rooney, Andy, 192
Ross v. Creighton University, 284–285
Rudolph, Wilma, 8, 30

S

Sacramento Surge, 347
San Antonio Riders, 348
Scholar-Baller Identity Model, 208–212
    environmental characteristics, 211
    individual characteristics, 210–211
    longitudinal process, 211–212
    precollege characteristics, 209
Scholar-Baller Paradigm, 10
scholar-ballers, a community of, 221–226
    six principles of curriculum, 222–226
Scott, Stuart, 183
Scottish Claymore, 351
Section 1981, 284, 285

segregation
    gender and racial workplace, 192–194
    in sportscasting, theoretical perspectives,
        186–194
self-segregation, 253
self-stereotype, 253–254
senior woman administrator, 56, 65–66
separate but equal, 24
sexism in the sport media industry, 190–192
sexual harassment in the sport media, 190–191
Simmons, Russell, 207, 216, 228
Slam magazine, 367
Sloan-Green, Tina, 315–327
Smalls, Biggie, 107
Smith, Ronald, 203
Smith, Wendell, 32–34, 181
Snyder, Jimmy "the Greek," 235
social capital, 186
"social closure" perspective, 187–188
Social Darwinism, 24, 234
social gerontology, 101
social meaning of African American maleness,
        82–83
social mobility, indirect, 98
societal attitude, 52–53
socio-cultural barriers, 52–63
Souls of Black Folk, The, 79
Source Sports, 367
Southern Interscholastic Basketball (SIB), 29
sport
    as cultural practice in American society, 1–2
    behind segregated walls, 27–32
sport, African American masculinity, and popular
        culture, 254–256
sport consumers, African Americans as 13–14
sport consumption, 370–375
    attendance, 359
    economics of, 360
    from discrimination in, 362
    in black and white, 362–364
    overview of, 358–360
    preferences, 358
    racial consciousness in, 372–373
    racial endorsement in, 373–374
    racial similarity in, 371–372
    sociology of, 361
    theoretical foundations of, 360–362
    to affirmation in, 362–364

sport event production, 367
sport journalism and the broadcast industry,
        185–186
sport management
    and diversity, 142–143
    standards for undergraduate programs in, 407
sport marketing and hip-hop, sociological prem-
        ises of, 368–370
sport media, 367–368
sport media consumption, 359
sport merchandise/apparel, 366–367
sport participation percentages of 2000–2001
        NCAA female athletes, 63
sport stereotypes in identity development,
        252–254
sports and African American Civil Society,
        392–399
Sports and Freedom, 203, 204
SportsWorld, 382–383, 397, 399–402
    and African American Civil Society, 382–383
    is big business, 385–389
    life after participation in, 383
stacking, 60–62, 130, 161
status report of the representation of African
        American Basketball Coaches in Division I
        in 2003, 166
stereotype, 53, 252–254, 266–267, 380, 396
stereotype threat, 395
stereotypes of student athletes, 212–215
stereotypes, sport, in identity development,
        252–254
strategies to increase minority pool of applicants
        in sport management, 194–195
streetball, 401
Stringer, Vivian, 154
structural barriers, 54–56
Student-Athlete Right-to-Know Act, 88, 90
success in late 19th-century sport, 23
suggestions for change, 71–72
supply-side explanation, 186–187

T

*Taboo: Why Black Athletes Dominate Sports and Why
        We Are Afraid to Talk About It,* 6, 236, 246
Tao, Sung, 339
Tarkanian, Jerry, 391
Taylor, John Baxter, 26, 30
Temple Cohort, 318, 319

Temple, Ed, 155–156

thanatology, 101

Thinkman, 219

Tigerbelles of Tennessee State, 8, 30

timeline: former World League/NFLE Players on NFL, 353–354

Title IX, 265, 265, 273, 314, 317–318, 327
    possible effects on, 303–304

Title VI, 273, 289–291

Title VII, 160, 270–273

transition from athletic competition, models and theories on, 100–102

transition to non-athlete, contributing factors, 102–104

treatment discrimination, 144

triangle of success, 206

U

U. S. Census Bureau, 145

under-inclusion
    in collegiate administrative positions, 268
    in collegiate coaching positions, 267

underrepresentation, reasons for, 269–270

United States Olympic Committee (USOC), 105, 319

V

Voting Rights Act, 4

W

Walker, Leroy, 134, 154–156

Washington, Marian, 153–154

Washington, Ora, 323

Watson v. Fort Worth Bank & Trust, 272

West Virginia Athletic Union (WVAU), 28

West, Cornel

Westerhaus, Charlotte, 127

who is black? 238–240

Williams, Eric, 388

World Baseball Classic, 339

World League of American Football, 342–348
    original teams, 345–348
    rebirth/return of, 348–350
    teams after 1995 return, 350–351

Y

Young, Frank "Fay," 180–181

Z

Zhi, Wang Zhi, 339

About the Editors

Ronald Althouse is a professor of sociology, former director of WVU's Survey Research Center, and past chairperson of the Division of Sociology and Anthropology. He received a Ph.D. in sociology from the University of Minnesota. Dr. Althouse's research and publications have focused on worker's risk and worker's health, health care delivery, and rural health systems. He has written about safety and miner health, as well as coal management's responsibilities for significantly improving mining operations and making mines safer places to work. Dr. Althouse has contributed to the literature on sport and athletic participation and is committed to efforts focused on social justice in sports. Collaborative research on discrimination in sports has contributed to publication of highly regarded studies on racism in collegiate athletics, particularly the African American athlete's experience.

Dana Brooks is a professor and dean of the School of Physical Education at West Virginia University. He received his B.S. from Towson State University (1973), M.S. (1976) and Ed.D. (1979) from West Virginia University. He has published and presented nationally and internationally in the areas of sport sociology and sport social psychology. He is the co-author of *Racism in College Athletics: The African American Experience* and is project administrator of the National Youth Sport Program at West Virginia University. Dr. Brooks is a member of the North American Society for Sport Sociology and the American Alliance for Health, Physical Education, Recreation and Dance. He received the Dean's Recognition Award from the College of Health Professions, Towson University Alumni Association in 1999; the Martin Luther King Jr. Achievement Award from the WVU Center for Black Culture and Research in 1997; and the WVU Social Justice Award in 1992. Dr. Brooks was also inducted as a Fellow in the American Academy of Kinesiology and Physical Education in September 1999.

About the Authors

Robertha Abney is an associate professor in physical education and sport management, and associate director of Athletics at Slippery Rock University of Pennsylvania. She earned a bachelor's degree at South Carolina State College and an M.Ed. at the University of Pittsburgh. She earned a Ph.D. from the University of Iowa.

Audwin Anderson is an associate professor in the Department of Sociology, Texas State University—San Marcos. He earned a Ph.D. in sociology from Texas A&M University in 1990. Dr. Anderson's scholarship has focused on race relations in a number of different social settings including education, sport, medicine, and the law.

Ketra L. Armstrong is an associate professor and the director of the graduate program in sport management at California State University, Long Beach (CSULB). She is also the president of the National Association for Girls and Women in Sport. Prior to her arrival at CSULB, Dr. Armstrong taught in the sport management program at The Ohio State University. Her research specialization is sport marketing/sport consumer behavior, and her research has been featured in numerous journals. Dr. Armstrong co-authored a manuscript that received the Outstanding Research Award by the Sport Marketing Association. She has conducted research for *Essence Magazine* on black women's fitness, and she received the Young Professional Award from the American Association of Active Lifestyle and Fitness.

In addition to Dr. Armstrong's scholarly pursuits, she has amassed a wealth of practical experience in the sport industry. She is a former Division I athlete (basketball player), Division I collegiate women's basketball coach, and collegiate athletic administrator. Over the years, she has performed integral roles in the research, management, and marketing of, as well as media relations for, numerous community, national, and international sport events. Dr. Armstrong is also a freelance sport broadcaster and a former board member of the National Women's Hall of Fame.

Jean Boyd co-founded Scholar Baller® with Dr. C. Keith Harrison and Cliff Parks. Although Mr. Boyd is currently the associate athletic director for student-athlete development at Arizona State University, he continues to work on a daily basis with football student-athletes to help them develop critical academic and life skills. Mr. Boyd has personal experience as a student-athlete at a Division I college and spent time in the NFL and NFL Europe.

Scott N. Brooks is assistant professor of sociology at the University of California—Riverside. He earned a B.A. from the University of California—Berkeley, an M.A. from California State University at Hayward, and a Ph.D. in sociology from the University of Pennsylvania. His research areas include urban sociology, race and ethnicity, qualitative methods, popular culture, and sociology of sport.

Akilah Carter received two B.S. degrees from University of Houston (UH) (in kinesiology exercise science and psychology), and an M.A. in exercise science from the University of Georgia (UGA). While attending UH, she was a member of the track and field team, specializing in 100m hurdles and long jump. Ms. Carter is a certified personal trainer, a USATF Level I coach, and a former high school track and field and cross country coach. Ms. Carter is currently the assistant director for strength and conditioning at UGA's Recreational Sports Department and is pursuing her Ph.D. in sports studies.

Doris R. Corbett is a professor of sport studies with a research focus on ethics, human rights, and ethnic and gender issues in sport. Dr. Corbett has served as a Congressional Research Fellow at the United States Capitol Historical Society, Washington, DC; distinguished visiting professor at the United States Military Academy at West Point, NY; distinguished visiting professor of sport sociology at Nanyang Technological University, National Institute of Education, School of Physical Education, Republic of Singapore; and distinguished visiting professor at Emporia State University Jones Institute for Educational Excellence, Emporia, Kansas. Dr. Corbett has served as president of both the American Alliance for Health, Physical Education, Recreation and Dance (AAHPERD) and the International Council for Health, Physical Education, Recreation, Sport and Dance (ICHPER.SD) and on numerous review boards and committees. She has conducted workshops, seminars, and delivered keynote and main addresses throughout the United States and the world. Dr. Corbett has authored myriad chapters and refereed journal articles, as well as two books and one monograph, and is the recipient of a number of honors and recognitions.

Timothy Davis is the John W. & Ruth H. Turnage Professor of Law at Wake Forest University School of Law. Professor Davis teaches and writes about contracts and sports law. He recently co-authored "Sports Law and Regulation: Cases, Materials and Problems." He is also the co-author of "The Business of Sports Agents," which was published by the University of Pennsylvania Press. In addition, he has co-authored anthologies on sports law and on race and the law (both published by Carolina Academic Press) and numerous law review articles. He has presented papers and lectures at academic conferences and continuing legal education seminars. Professor Davis serves on the Review Board for the United States Anti-Doping Agency. He is also a member of the Board of Advisors for the National Sports Law Institute and the Sports Lawyers Association. He is a former chair of the Law and Sports Section of the Association of American Law Schools. Professor Davis is a member of the Contracts Drafting Committee of the National Conference of Bar Examiners. He has served on the Board of Governors of the North Carolina Bar Association and as chair of the Sports and Entertainment Law Section of the North Carolina Bar Association.

Professor Davis received his B.A. degree from Stanford in 1975 and his J.D. from the University of California at Berkeley in 1979. Professor Davis joined the Wake Forest faculty in 1998 and was elected Teacher of the Year by the 2005–2006 graduating class at Wake Forest University School of Law. Before then, he taught for nine years at Southern Methodist University School of Law, where he was the recipient of two teaching awards. Prior to teaching, Professor Davis practiced commercial litigation in Denver, Colorado, following a federal district court clerkship.

Tina Sloan Green is a professor emeritus in the College of Education at Temple University. During her 33 years at Temple University, she was co-principal investigator of Sisters in Sports Science, a program funded by the National Science Foundation. She was also director of the Temple University National Youth Sports Program. As head coach of Temple women's lacrosse team (1973–1992), she led her team to three national championships and 11 consecutive NCAA Final Four appearances. Professor Sloan Green has coauthored two books, *Black Women in Sport* and *Modern Women's Lacrosse* and has authored chapters in the books *Racism in College Athletics* and *Basketball Jones.* She was inducted into the Halls of Fame at both Temple and West Chester Universities as well as the Lacrosse Hall of Fame and the Women's Sport Foundation Hall of Fame. Professor Green competed on the U.S. Women's Lacrosse Team (1969–1973) and the U.S. Women's Field Hockey Squad (1966). Professor Sloan Green is also cofounder and president of the Black Women in Sport Foundation.

Linda Greene, a California native and a graduate of the University of California Berkeley Law School, is a professor at the University of Wisconsin Law School. She holds the Evjue-Bascom Chair and teaches constitutional and civil rights law and civil procedure. She has been a visiting professor at Harvard University Law School and Georgetown University Law School, as well as a distinguished visitor at other domestic and foreign law schools. She began her career as a lawyer at the NAACP Legal Defense Fund in New York. She was also counsel to the United States Senate Judiciary Committee from 1986–1989 (Antitrust, Courts, and Constitution subcommittees) where she advised on five Supreme Court nominees as well as numerous lower federal court judicial nominees. She has served as president of the Society of American Law Teachers and as chair of the American Association of Law Schools Section on Minority Groups, and she was founder and president of the Midwestern People of Color Legal Scholarship Conference. She is a political and legal analyst for television, radio, and print media.

Othlello Harris, Ph.D., is an associate professor and chair of the Department of Physical Education, Health, and Sport Studies at Miami University. His research interests include race and sport involvement, especially the extent to which sport enhances or impedes opportunities for social mobility for African Americans. His work has been published in *The Black Scholar, Sociology of Sport Journal, The Journal of Social and Behavioral Sciences, Journal of African American Males, Masculinities,* and *Sociological Focus.* In addition, he has authored chapters in numerous books.

C. Keith Harrison, Ph.D., is associate professor in the DeVos Sport Business Management Graduate Program at the University of Central Florida in the College of Business Administration. Dr. Harrison established the Paul Robeson Research Center for Academic and Athletic Prowess at the University of Michigan, Ann Arbor, in 1998, while on the faculty in sport management. Prior to joining UCF, he helped Arizona State University and the College of Education/Division of Educational Leadership and Policy Studies develop graduate classes with an emphasis on sport, culture, and higher education during his two years at the institution. Dr. Harrison has been the author and principal investigator for the Black Coaches Association (BCA) Hiring Report Card Study from 2003 to the present. In addition to his duties at the University of Central Florida and the BCA Hiring Report Card, Harrison is Scholar-in-Residence at Rush Philanthropic's Hip-Hop Summit Action Network (HSAN). This organization has supported and validated his research and writing about athletes facing stereotypes in terms of the "scholar baller" concept. Scholar Baller® is a social and cultural identity that affirms academic excellence through the salience of sport and entertainment to youth and young adults.

Louis Harrison, Jr., is an associate professor in the Department of Curriculum and Instruction at the University of Texas at Austin. He is a native of New Orleans and a graduate of the University of New Orleans, where he received his B.S. in 1979 and M.Ed. in 1987, both in physical education. He went on to complete his Ph.D. in kinesiology in 1997 at Louisiana State University. Dr. Harrison has focused his research on the influences of race-related self-schemata and African American racial identity on physical activity choices and performance. The purpose of this line of research is to investigate the factors that influence sport and physical activity participation, and identity developmental patterns of African Americans. Through his research he hopes to gain a deeper understanding of the racial labels ascribed to particular sports and physical activities, and how these labels affect participation, persistence, effort expended, and performance. Additionally, he wishes to investigate ways physical educators and coaches can precipitate changes in the development of self-schemata for sport and physical activities in an effort to erase these racial labels and broaden the perceived physical activity choices of all students.

Angela Hattery earned her B.A. in sociology and anthropology from Carleton College and her M.S. and Ph.D. in sociology from the University of Wisconsin—Madison. She joined the faculty at Wake Forest in 1998, where she teaches courses in Social Stratification and Inequality, Sociology of Gender, Contemporary Families, Self and Society (social psychology), and Methods. Her research has been focused in two main areas: the intersection of work and family (*Women, Work, and Family: Balancing and Weaving*, Sage, 2001) and intimate partner violence ("Violence in Intimate Partner Relationships," currently under review with Lynne Rienner). Her current work on IPV (with Professor Earl Smith) is framed by a race, class, and gender paradigm and is focused on the qualitative experiences of battering—for both the victim and the offender—in African American and Latino communities.

Billy J. Hawkins is an associate professor at the University of Georgia in the Department of Physical Education and Sport Studies. His teaching contributions are in the area of sociology of sport and cultural studies at the undergraduate and graduate level. His research focus is on racial issues in the context of sport and physical activity. This focus incorporates research in the following areas: the interworkings of race, religion, and sport; the representation of black male athletes in the mass media; examining the experiences of black student athletes at predominantly white NCAA Division I institutions; examining the use of midnight and evening basketball leagues to reduce criminal activity among young black males; and physical activity and body image among African American women. He received his Ph.D. from the University of Iowa in physical education and sport and cultural studies and an M.A. from the University of Wisconsin at LaCrosse. His book, *The New Plantation: The Internal Colonization of Black Student Athletes at Predominantly White NCAA Division I Institutions,* examines the experiences of black student athletes in intercollegiate athletics. He has also written several scholarly articles on black athletes and their intercollegiate athletic experiences, the media representation of black male and black male athletes, religion and sport, youth and sport, and physical activity and African American women.

Linda J. Kim is a graduate student at the University of California—Riverside. She earned a B.A. and an M.A. in sociology at the University of California—Los Angeles. Her research areas are gender, race, and class inequality; media; and sports.

Brianne Milan-Williams became interested in the topic of athletic retirement following the conclusion of her career as a collegiate student-athlete. Under the direction of Dr. Billy Hawkins at the University of Georgia, Brianne graduated with a master's of education in sport studies and concentrated her master's project on creating a questionnaire for former athletes. She currently resides in Colorado, where she is the head volleyball coach at a local high school and works as a guest service team leader for Target Corporation.

Fritz G. Polite is an assistant professor in the Sport Management Program at the University of Tennessee in Knoxville. Previously, he was an assistant professor and associate director of the Institute for Diversity & Ethics in Sport, DeVos Sport Business Management Program at the University of Central Florida (UCF). Prior to that, Dr. Polite was program director for The Florida State University's (FSU) Partnership for Enhancing Education Resources program, an after-school mentoring program funded by AT&T that provided tutoring, mentoring, academic support, and career counseling for "at-risk" youth. He earned his Ph.D. in sport administration from FSU; he received his master's of public administration degree from Troy State University and bachelor's degree in management from Simpson College. Sports have played prominently in Dr. Polite's career, including the following professional experience: New York Giants, National Football League—advising, evaluating, and testing (aptitude, psychological, and physical) of college athletes with potential for the annual NFL draft; general manager, Harlem Globetrotters; and sport program manager, Walt Disney World Sports. He has been a coach, player, and administrator at the professional level and has presented and published internationally in Finland, Canada, France, Germany, and Switzerland. His research focus, in the area of socio-cultural aspects of sport, includes hiring practices, diversity, and brand/vertical extension. He also has presented issues related to agents and university/high school student athletes.

George H. Sage is professor emeritus of Kinesiology and Sociology at the University of Northern Colorado. He has a B.A. in social science and physical education and an M.A. in secondary education from the University of Northern Colorado, and an Ed.D. in social foundations of physical education from UCLA. He is the author or editor of 15 books and over 100 scholarly articles and chapters in books. He is past president of the North American Society for the Sociology of Sport and of the National Association for Physical Education in Higher Education. He was the recipient of the Distinguished Scholar Award at the University of Northern Colorado and was selected for the Alliance Scholar Award by the American Alliance for Health, Physical Education, Recreation, and Dance.

Earl Smith, Ph.D., is professor of sociology and the Rubin Distinguished Professor of American Ethnic Studies at Wake Forest University, as well as the director of the American Ethnic Studies Program there. Previously, he was the chairperson (Comparative American Cultures) and professor of sociology at Washington State University in Pullman, Washington. Professor Smith has numerous publications (books, articles, and book chapters) in the area of professions, stratification, and urban sociology, has published research on university faculty, and has published extensively in the area of the sociology of sport. He is a member of the Society for the Study of Social Problems, Southern Sociological Society, Sociologists for Women and Society, and the American Sociological Association. Professor Smith has served as president of the North American Society for the Sociology of Sport.

Donald South is a retired professor of sociology at the University of South Alabama. He received his M.A. and Ph.D. from Louisiana State University. He has served on the university athletic-academic committee for 15 years. Dr. South has participated in baseball, basketball, and boxing. He has published extensively, contributing to books and authoring monographs. In addition, Dr. South has been active on editorial boards of sociological journals and has served as editor of *Sociological Spectrum*. He has also held offices in regional professional organizations.

Aaron B. Stills is a nationally known expert in the fields of multicultural counseling and cultural diversity training. Currently, he serves as the Senior Fellow for Graduate Academic Administration in the Graduate School, and associate professor of counseling psychology in the Department of Human Development and Psycho-educational Studies at Howard University. Since 1976, he has been the founder and chief executive officer (CEO) of the Center for Multicultural Management Systems, Inc. Dr. Stills is a licensed certified clinical mental health counselor and national certified counselor. Dr. Stills has presented numerous workshops, colloquiums, seminars, and keynote addresses on managing cultural diversity in the workplace, ethics training, stress management, behavioral intervention, and life skills career development. He has also served on and chaired several state and national boards and committees and published extensively in the area of cultural diversity and self-esteem issues relating to African American children. He is a frequent presenter at national conferences, including those of the American Psychological Association (APA), American Counseling Association (ACA), and the Association for Multicultural Counseling and Development (AMCD). He was the first president of the Association for Multicultural Counseling and Development.

Miguel Tabron is the unit director of the Washington Elementary Boys & Girls Club in Raleigh, NC. Prior to this role, he served as a community-based support counselor at Genesis Family Homes. In academia, Miguel served as a student member of NCAAPHERD and volunteered with the American Red Cross. Miguel is the president/founder of the Garvet Wilkerson Memorial Foundation, a local group founded in the memory of a childhood friend who was a victim of gun violence. As a graduate student, Miguel placed first at the Graduate School Research Symposium at Howard University. His educational background includes study at Johnson C. Smith University for a B.S., Hunter College City College of New York, and Howard University for an M.S.

Delano Tucker, formerly assistant to the dean of the College of Education at Wayne State University, is currently assistant professor in the Division of Health, Physical Education and Recreation and the Sports Administration Department. He earned an education administration degree (Ed.D.) from Wayne State University, an M.A. in educational psychology from Michigan State University, and a B.S. in psychology from Wayne State University. Dr. Tucker has served as athletic director and head coach at Livingstone College in North Carolina and as assistant football Coach at Wayne State University. During his time at the University of California—Davis, Dr. Tucker worked as academic advisor for Intercollegiate Athletics and Student Affairs and as assistant coach. He was a teacher and junior varsity football coach for the Detroit public schools and a teacher, assistant high school principal, and skills center coordinator for the East Lansing School District. In accordance with his extensive educational career, Dr. Tucker was the graduate assistant at Michigan State under Duffy Daugherty. He coached the offensive line at UC Davis, was the college coach of All-Pro player Ben Coates, and interned with the San Francisco 49ers and Detroit Lions.

Charlotte F. Westerhaus is vice president for diversity and inclusion at the National Collegiate Athletic Associaton (NCAA). Before taking the position at the NCAA, Westerhaus was the assistant to the president and director of equal opportunity and diversity at the University of Iowa. She was a member of the university's NCAA Certification Committee, the Student-Athlete Welfare Committee and worked with the Intercollegiate Athletics Department to create a clear, concise, and uniform code of conduct for University of Iowa student-athletes. Prior to her work at the University of Iowa, Westerhaus served as the director of Purdue University's affirmative action office and as the assistant to the chancellor for equity and diversity at the University of Wisconsin, Parkside. She has also worked as a student affairs professional at the University of California—Davis and Pomona College. In addition to her experience working with diversity and inclusion issues, Westerhaus was an attorney with Northwestern Mutual Life Insurance Company, Milwaukee, and an associate attorney with the Milwaukee law firm of Foley & Lardner where she practiced in civil litigation. According to Westerhaus, diversity and inclusion are concepts that have become an academic necessity, and her focus is to ensure that diversity and inclusion positively enhance the experience of all student-athletes.

David K. Wiggins is a professor and the director of the School of Recreation, Health, and Tourism at George Mason University. He received his A.B. and M.A. from San Diego State University and his Ph.D. from the University of Maryland. Dr. Wiggins' research has focused on the history of African American involvement in sport. Among his numerous publications are: *The Unlevel Playing Field: A Documentary History of the African American Experience in Sport* (with Patrick B. Miller); *Sport and the Color Line: Black Athletes and Race Relations in Twentieth-Century America* (with Patrick B. Miller); *Glory Bound: Black Athletes in a White America;* and *African Americans in Sport.*